Today's Bible
New Testament

by Ray Geide

Greek Text: Nestle27/UBS4

Breakthrough Version Publishing
Wichita, KS
breakthroughversion.com

TODAY'S BIBLE (TB)

The Today's Bible (TB) text may be quoted in any form (written, visual, electronic or audio), up to and inclusive of one hundred (100) verses without express written permission of the publisher, providing the verses do not amount to a complete book of the Bible nor do the verses quoted account for twenty-five percent (25%) or more of the total text of the work in which they are quoted.

When the TB is quoted in works that exercise the above fair use clause, the following notice of copyright must appear on the title or copyright page or opening screen of the work (whichever is appropriate):

TODAY'S BIBLE™, TB™ Copyright © 2026 by Ray Geide. Used by permission. All rights reserved worldwide. todaysbible.online

When quotations from the TB text are used in non-saleable media such as church bulletins, orders of service, posters, projections, or similar media, a complete copyright notice is not required, but the letters TB must appear at the end of each quotation, and the web address, todaysbible.online, must appear on the same page or presentation.

Permission requests for commercial use that exceed the above guidelines must be directed to, and approved in writing by, Breakthrough Version Publishing, 1725 Faulders Lane, Wichita, KS 67218.

Breakthrough Version Publishing
www.breakthroughversion.com

Legal Disclaimer - The publisher and the author make no representations or warranties with respect to the accuracy or completeness of the contents of this work and specifically disclaim all warranties, including without limitation warranties for a particular purpose. No warranty may be created or extended by sales or promotional materials. The advice and strategies contained herein may not be suitable for every situation.

ISBN-13: 978-0-9628012-8-0

© Copyright 2026 by Ray Geide All rights reserved. Published 2026

Table of Contents

Matthew	1
Mark	67
Luke	109
John	181
Acts	235
Romans	307
First Corinthians	337
Second Corinthians	365
Galatians	383
Ephesians	393
Philippians	403
Colossians	411
First Thessalonians	419
Second Thessalonians	425
First Timothy	429
Second Timothy	437
Titus	443
Philemon	447
Hebrews	449
James	471
First Peter	479
Second Peter	487
First John	493
Second John	501
Third John	503
Jude	505
Revelation	507

Translation Notes

Italics in the Bible text indicate words that have been added by the translator and are not in the Greek.

Brackets [ ] indicate variant Greek readings (words that not all of the Greek manuscripts have). Single brackets [ ] and double brackets [[ ]] correspond to the single and double brackets in Nestle27/USB4.

Brackets around words and phrases in Nestle27/USB4 are not shown, only brackets around sentences and passages.

Triple brackets [[[ ]]] mark passages omitted in Nestle27/USB4.

Matthew

1

1 *This is* a scroll of birth, *a genealogy* of Jesus, the Anointed King, a son of David, a son of Abraham.
2 Abraham fathered Isaac. Isaac fathered Jacob. Jacob fathered Judah and his brothers.
3 Judah fathered *twins*: Phares and Zerah, from Tamar *(his daughter-in-law)*. Phares fathered Hezron. Hezron fathered Aram.
4 Aram fathered Aminadab. Aminadab fathered Nahshon. Nahshon fathered Salmon.
5 Salmon fathered Boaz from Rahab. Boaz fathered Obed from Ruth. Obed fathered Jesse.
6 Jesse fathered David, the king. David fathered Solomon from the *widow* of Uriah.
7 Solomon fathered Rehoboam. Rehoboam fathered Abijah. Abijah fathered Asa.
8 Asa fathered Jehoshaphat. Jehoshaphat fathered Joram. Joram fathered Uzziah.
9 Uzziah fathered Jotham. Jotham fathered Ahaz. Ahaz fathered Hezekiah.
10 Hezekiah fathered Manasseh. Manasseh fathered Amos. Amos fathered Josiah.
11 Josiah fathered Jeconiah's *father* and his brothers before the resettlement in Babylon.
12 After the resettlement in Babylon, Jeconiah fathered Shealtiel. Shealtiel fathered Zerubbabel.
13 Zerubbabel fathered Abiud. Abiud fathered Eliakim. Eliakim fathered Azor.
14 Azor fathered Zadok. Zadok fathered Achim. Achim fathered Eliud.
15 Eliud fathered Eleazar. Eleazar fathered Matthan. Matthan fathered Jacob.
16 Jacob fathered Joseph, the husband of Mary. Jesus was born from her. He is the One that is called Anointed King.
17 So there are fourteen generations from Abraham until David. And there are fourteen generations from David until the resettlement in Babylon. And there are fourteen generations from the resettlement in Babylon until the Anointed King.

18 This is what the birth of Jesus, the Anointed King, was like when His mother Mary was promised to Joseph. Before they even came together, she was found to be pregnant by the Sacred Spirit.

19 Joseph (the man *promised to* her) was someone who did what is right. Since he didn't want to shame Mary publicly, he intended to dismiss her in a way that no one would notice.

20 When he contemplated these things, look, the Master's angel appeared to him in a dream. He said, "Joseph, son of David, you shouldn't be afraid to take Mary, the woman *promised to* you, along with you. You see, the baby in her was born from the Sacred Spirit.

21 She will deliver a son, and you will call His name Jesus *(which means Yahweh rescues)*. You see, He will rescue His ethnic group from their sins."

22 This whole thing happened so that what the Master stated through His preacher Isaiah might be achieved. *Isaiah* said,

23 "Look, the virgin will be pregnant and deliver a son. They will call His name Immanuel which is *Hebrew* and translated as 'God with us'" *(Isaiah 7:14)*.

24 When Joseph got up, he did what the Master's angel instructed him to do. He took along the woman *promised to* him.

25 He wasn't being intimate with her until she gave birth to a son. He called His name Jesus.

2

1 When Jesus was born in Bethlehem, Judea (in the days of Herod the king), look, gurus from the eastern regions showed up in Jerusalem.

2 They were asking, "Where is the Jewish people's king that was just born? You see, we saw His star in the east, and we came to bow down to Him."

3 When King Herod heard this, he was uneasy and all of Jerusalem *was uneasy* with him.

4 He gathered all of the head priests and the ethnic group's Old Testament transcribers together, and in a private meeting, he was inquiring where the Anointed King should be born.

5 "In Bethlehem, Judea," they said. You see, the preacher wrote about this:

6 "And you, Bethlehem, land of Judah, you are by no means the smallest among Judah's leaders. You see, a leader will come out of you, someone who will shepherd My ethnic group Israel" *(Micah 5:2)*.

7 At that time, Herod called for the gurus in a way that no one would notice. In a private meeting, he verified when they saw the shining star.
8 When he sent them to Bethlehem, he said, "After traveling there, question specifically about the young child. Whenever you find him, report it to me so that I also might go there and bow down to him."
9 The gurus listened to the king and traveled *to Bethlehem*. And, look, the star that they saw in the east was leading the way ahead of them until it came and stood up above where the young child was.
10 When they saw the star, they were terribly happy with great happiness.
11 And when they went into the house, they saw the young child with Mary, His mother. They got down and bowed to Him. Then they opened their stockpiles of supplies and offered up contributions to Him: gold, incense from the frankincense tree, and myrrh *(an expensive fragrant resin)*.
12 They were divinely instructed in a dream not to double back to Herod. So they took a back way through another road to their own country.
13 After the *gurus* took a back way out, look, the Master's angel appeared to Joseph in a dream. He said, "When you get up, escape into Egypt. Take the young child and His mother along, and stay there until I tell you. You see, Herod is going to look for the young child *because he wants* to destroy Him."
14 Joseph got up and took the young child and his mother along with him at night. They took a back way into Egypt.
15 He was there until Herod passed away so that what the Master had stated before through the preacher might be achieved: "Out of Egypt I called My Son" *(Hosea 11:1)*.
16 At that time, when Herod saw that the gurus disrespected him *(because they didn't do what he had told them to do)*, he was very angry. So he sent soldiers out to Bethlehem and the surrounding area to execute all the boys two years old and under. He chose those ages based on the time that he had verified with the gurus in his private meeting with them.
17 At that time, what God had stated before through Jeremiah, His preacher, happened. He said,
18 "A sound was heard in Ramah, much crying and mourning. Rachel is crying for her children. She doesn't want to be comforted because they are gone" *(Jeremiah 31:15)*.

19 After Herod passed away, look, the Master's angel appeared in a dream to Joseph in Egypt.
20 He said, "When you get up, take the young child and His mother and travel into the area of Israel. The people looking for the soul of the young child are dead."
21 After Joseph got up, he took the young child and His mother and went into the area of Israel.
22 When he heard that Archelaus was king of Judea in place of his father Herod, he was afraid to go away to there. After they were divinely instructed in a dream, they took a back way into certain parts of Galilee.
23 They ended up living in the city of Nazareth in order that what God had stated before through His preachers might be achieved: "He will be called a Nazarene."

3

1 In those days *when Jesus was living in Nazareth*, John the Submerger showed up in Judea's backcountry speaking publicly.
2 He was saying, "Change your ways. Heaven's monarchy has come near."
3 You see, this is what God stated through Isaiah, His preacher, when he said, "A voice is shouting in the backcountry, get the Master's road ready. Make His paths straight" *(Isaiah 40:3)*.
4 John wore *the same attire that Elijah and some old-time preachers wore*: attire made of camel's hair and a leather strap around his waist. His meals consisted of grasshoppers and wild honey.
5 At that time, people were traveling out to him from Jerusalem, from all around Judea, and from all around the rural area surrounding the Jordan River.
6 He was submerging them in the Jordan River as they admitted their sins out loud. *Submersion was a Jewish tradition that ritually cleaned the person being submerged.*
7 When he saw many of the Separatists and Sadducees coming out to his submersions, he told them, "You children of poisonous snakes, who put the warning in front of your face to escape the punishment that is going to come? *You don't see it, do you? So why are you here?*
8 Produce fruit that is deserving of the change *in you that God requires.*
9 Don't even think about saying among yourselves, 'Our father is Abraham. *God needs us to carry on Abraham's lineage.*' I tell you, God is able from these stones to raise up children for Abraham.

10 *God has already taken the ax out and* laid it facing the root of the trees. Every tree that doesn't produce nice fruit gets chopped down and thrown into the fire.

11 I certainly submerge you in water when you change your ways, but the One coming behind me is stronger than me. I am unfit to haul *His* sandals around. He will submerge you in the Sacred Spirit and fire, *the Sacred Spirit for those who trust Him, fire for those who don't*.

12 His shovel is in His hand. He will completely clear off His processing floor. He will gather His grain together into the grain bin, but the husks will be burned up with unextinguished fire."

13 Then Jesus showed up there. He had traveled from Galilee to John at the Jordan River *for one reason*, to be submerged by him.

14 John was flatly refusing and saying, "I need to be submerged by You. How are You coming to me?"

15 "Allow it for now," Jesus responded. "You see, this is the appropriate way for us to accomplish every bit of the right way." Then John allowed it.

16 After Jesus was submerged, as he stepped up out of the water, look, the sky opened to Him. He saw God's Spirit floating down as if it were a dove and coming over Him.

17 And look, a voice spoke from the sky. It said, "This is My loved Son. I am delighted with Him."

4

1 At that time, the Spirit led Jesus up into the backcountry to be harassed by the Accuser.

2 After not eating for forty days and forty nights, later, He was hungry.

3 The one who harasses people came up to Him and said, "If you are God's Son, demand that these stones become bread."

4 When Jesus responded, He said, "The Bible says, 'A person won't live on bread alone. But he will live on every statement traveling out of God's mouth' *(Deuteronomy 8:3)*."

5 Then the Accuser took Him along with him into the sacred city and stood Him on the winglet of the temple grounds.

6 "If you are God's Son, jump," he told Him. "You see, the Bible says, 'He will demand that His angels take care of You, and they will pick You up in their arms to keep You from ever stubbing Your foot on a stone' *(Psalm 91:11-12)*."

7 Jesus was declaring to him, "Again the Bible says, 'You will not try to harass the Master, your God' *(Deuteronomy 6:16)*."

8 The Accuser took Him along with Him again onto a very high mountain and showed Him all the world's monarchies and their magnificence.
9 "I will give you all these," he said, "if you will get down on the ground and bow down to me."
10 At that time, Jesus told him, "Make your way out of here, Opponent. The Bible says, 'You will bow down to the Master, your God, and minister to Him alone' *(Deuteronomy 6:13)*."
11 Then the Accuser left, and, look, angels came and were serving Jesus.
12 When Jesus heard that John had been taken into custody, He took a back way into Galilee
13 and left Nazareth behind. He went and lived in Capernaum. Capernaum was beside the Sea *of Galilee* on the border of Zebulon and Naphtali.
14 He did this so that what God stated through His preacher Isaiah might be achieved:
15 "Land of Zebulon and land of Naphtali, a road along the sea next to the Jordan River, the part of Galilee where non-Jews live,
16 the ethnic group *(the Jews)* who were sitting in darkness saw a great light. A light came up over the people sitting in a rural area and in death's shadow" *(Isaiah 9:1-2)*.
17 From then on, Jesus began speaking publicly and saying, "Change your ways. You see, heaven's monarchy has come near."
18 *One day* as He was walking around along the Sea of Galilee, He saw two brothers, Simon and Andrew. Simon is the one they call Peter. They were throwing a net into the sea. They were fishermen.
19 "Come follow Me," Jesus told them, "and I will make you fishermen of people."
20 Right away, the brothers left their nets and followed Him.
21 When He walked further down the shore, He saw two other brothers, James and John, in a boat with their father Zebedee. They were mending their nets. Jesus invited them *to follow Him*.
22 Right away, the brothers left their boat and their father and followed Him.
23 He was taking them all around Galilee. He was teaching in the synagogues, speaking publicly about the good news of God's monarchy, and healing every illness and frailty in the group.
24 *People started talking.* The talk went off into all of *the large area north of there,* Syria. People brought Jesus everyone who had something wrong with them: people who had various illnesses, people who were

restricted by excruciating pain, people who had lesser deities, people who were struck by the moon *(that is, people who had seizures)*, and people who were disabled. Jesus healed them.
25 Large crowds followed Him from Galilee, Decapolis, Greater Jerusalem, Judea, and the Jordan River area.

5

1 When He saw the crowds, He climbed up the mountain and sat down *like rabbis do when they teach their students*. His students came up to Him.
2 When He opened His mouth, He was teaching them.
3 He said, "A blessing for the people who see how *spiritually* poor they are is that they are a part of heaven's monarchy.
4 A blessing for the grieving people is that they will be comforted.
5 A blessing for the submissive people is that they will inherit the earth.
6 A blessing for the people hungering and thirsting for the right way is that they will eat until they are full.
7 A blessing for the kind forgiving people is that they will receive forgiving kindness.
8 A blessing for the people who keep their heart clean is that they will see God.
9 A blessing for the people creating peaceful solutions is that they will be called God's sons.
10 A blessing for the people who have been persecuted because they did what is right is that they are a part of heaven's monarchy.
11 When people criticize you, when people persecute you, when people lie and say every evil thing against you, *when they do these things* because you are Mine, you are blessed.
12 Be happy and excited because when you get to heaven, you will be paid well for those abuses. You see, the preachers that came before you were persecuted like that too.
13 You are the earth's salt. *You must have the flavor that I give.* What good is salt if it has no flavor? What will be salted with it? It isn't good for anything anymore except to be thrown outside so that people can trample on it.
14 You are the world's light. A city lying up on top of a mountain can't be hidden.
15 They don't put a burning lamp under the two gallon measuring basket either. They put it up high on a stand. There it shines for everyone in the house.

16 This is how your light must shine in front of people so that they might see your nice actions and praise the magnificence of your Father in the heavens.
17 You shouldn't assume that I came to tear the Law or the Preachers down. I didn't come to tear them down. No, I came so that what they say will happen might be achieved.
18 You see, amen, I tell you, as long as the sky and the earth are here, one small letter or even one hook of a letter will not in any way leave the Law until all the things written in it happen.
19 So whoever breaks even one of the Law's smallest demands and teaches the people to do the same thing, he will be called 'smallest' in heaven's monarchy. But whoever will do and teach the Law's demands will be called 'great' in heaven's monarchy.
20 You see, *the Old Testament transcribers know every little detail of the Old Testament because they copy it letter-by-letter. And the Separatists have many rules to ensure that they keep the Law. But* I tell you that unless your right way overflows to be more right than the right way of the Old Testament transcribers and Separatists, you won't in any way enter heaven's monarchy. *Here are some examples of how My right way completes and exceeds the Law.*
21 You have heard that *in the Law God* stated to the original people, 'You will not murder.' Because of this whoever murders will be eligible for sentencing in court.
22 But I tell you that everyone who is enraged at his brother will be eligible for sentencing in court. Whoever calls his brother 'Stupid!' will be eligible for sentencing in *the highest court*, the council. And whoever says, 'You fool!' will be eligible for sentencing in the fires of the Hinnom Valley.
23 So *maintain good relations with your brother.* If you are at the temple in Jerusalem offering up your contribution on the altar and there you remember that your brother has something against you,
24 *stop what you are doing,* leave your contribution there in front of the altar, and make your way back to that brother. First, settle the problem with him. Then go back and offer up your contribution.
25 You *also* must maintain good relations with anyone who is filing a complaint against you in court. Quickly agree to his demands all the way up to the time for you to stand before the judge. That way perhaps he won't turn you over to the judge, the judge won't turn you over to the underling, and you won't be thrown in jail.
26 Amen, I tell you, if you get thrown in jail, you won't in any way come out of there until you have paid back every last penny.

27 You heard that *in the Law God* stated, 'You won't cheat on your spouse.'
28 But I tell you that every husband who looks at a woman with the specific goal of desiring her has already cheated on his wife in his heart with that woman.
29 If your right eye is causing you to stumble, take it out, and throw it away. You see, it is to your advantage to destroy one of your body parts and prevent your whole body from being thrown into Hinnom Valley. *(The Hinnom Valley ran along the southwestern edge of Jerusalem. At one time children were burned to death there as sacrifices to idols. It is symbolic of the eternal lake of fire.)*
30 And if your right hand is causing you to stumble, chop it off, and throw it away. You see, it is to your advantage to destroy one of your body parts and prevent your whole body from going off into Hinnom Valley.
31 *You have been dismissing your wives and not divorcing them. In the Law, God* stated, "Whoever dismisses his wife must give her a divorce."
32 But I tell you that everyone who dismisses his wife *without divorcing her*, besides and outside of a matter of sexual sin, *is violating the 'you won't cheat on your spouse' demand because he* is making his wife cheat on him. And whoever marries a dismissed wife is also violating that demand.
33 Again you have heard that *in the Law God* stated to the original people, 'You will not lie when you make or take an oath, but you will pay back your oath to the Master.'
34 *When you guarantee something with an oath, you don't invoke the Master's name because you don't want to violate His name when you break that promise. So your guarantee invokes other things.* But I tell you not to guarantee at all. Don't invoke the sky because it is God's throne.
35 Don't invoke the earth because it is a footrest for His feet. And don't invoke Jerusalem because it is the city of the great King.
36 Don't invoke your head either when you guarantee something *because your head is controlled by God.* You aren't able to make one hair white or black. *God does that.*
37 Your answer must be yes or no. Anything more than that is from the evil one.
38 You heard that *in the Law God* stated, 'An eye for an eye and a tooth for a tooth.' *That means that if someone intentionally injures his neighbor's eye, that neighbor must injure the attacker's eye, and if someone*

intentionally breaks his neighbor's tooth, that neighbor must break the attacker's tooth.

39 But I tell you, don't stand in opposition to the evil person. If someone slaps you on the right cheek, turn your head and give him access to your other cheek.

40 If someone wants to sue you and take your shirt, allow him to take your coat too.

41 If *a Roman soldier* sequesters help from you for one mile, lead the way with him for two.

42 Give to the person who asks. If anyone wants to get an interest loan from you, don't turn him away.

43 You heard that *in the Law God* stated, 'You will love the person near you.' *Some rabbis have added to that,* 'And hate your enemy.'

44 But I tell you, love your enemies. Pray for the people persecuting you.

45 When you do this, you become sons of your Father in the heavens because He brings His sun up on evil people and on good people. He gives rain to both the people who do what is right and the people who do what is wrong.

46 You see, if you love the people who love you, what distinction does that earn you? Don't even the tax collectors do the same thing?

47 And if you say hello only to your brothers, how is that such a wonderful thing? Don't even the non-Jews *(the group of people that you consider to be sinful)* do the same thing?

48 *Go beyond that.* Become complete people. Do everything completely right, just as your Heavenly Father does everything completely right."

6 1 "When you are doing the things that are right, make sure that you aren't doing them in front of people with the specific goal of being seen by them. If you are doing that, *that is the only pay you will get.* Your Father in the heavens will definitely not pay you for doing them.

2 *For example,* when you make a charitable donation, don't blow a trumpet in front of you *so everyone will see you giving*. This is what the fakers do in the synagogues and in the streets so that people might elevate them to a place of magnificence. Amen, I tell you, they have all of their pay.

3 But as you make a charitable donation, *do it in a hidden way.* Your left hand must not know what your right hand is doing.

4 That will allow your charitable donation to be in a hidden world *that no one sees, no one except the Father*. The Father, who sees what goes on in the hidden world, will give back to you.

5 *Another example is prayer.* When you all pray, don't pray like the fakers. They are fond of praying standing in the synagogues and in the corners of the plazas so that people will see them. Amen, I tell you, they have all of their pay.

6 But when you pray, go into your storage room. After you close the door, pray to your Father in the hidden world, and your Father, who sees in the hidden world, will give back to you.

7 As you all pray, don't babble words like the non-Jews do. You see, they think that they'll be heard if they say many words.

8 Don't be like them. You see, your Father knows what you need before you ask Him.

9 So this is how you must pray: 'Our Father in heaven, Your name *and who You are* must be made sacred.

10 Your monarchy must come. What You want must happen. As *it must happen* in heaven, *it must* also *happen* on earth.

11 Give us the next day's bread today.

12 And forgive us for the times when we don't do what we ought to do. Forgive us in the same way that we forgive the people who don't do what we think they ought to do.

13 You won't carry us into trouble, but save us from the evil one.'

14 *Do you see what this prayer says about forgiveness?* If you forgive people of their infractions, your Heavenly Father will also forgive you.

15 But if you won't forgive people, your Father won't forgive you either.

16 *Something else that should be done privately is fasting.* When you go on a fast, don't become like the sad-faced fakers. You see, they make their *true* faces disappear. *Even though they aren't sad, they put on a sad face* so that people will know that they are fasting. Amen, I tell you, they have all of their pay.

17 But as you are fasting, dab perfume on your head, and wash your face.

18 That way people won't know that you are fasting, but your Father in the hidden world *will know*. And your Father, who sees in the hidden world, will give back to you.

19 Don't stockpile stockpiles of stuff for yourselves on the earth where a moth and a dinner make them disappear and where thieves break in and steal.

20 But stockpile stockpiles of stuff for yourselves in heaven where a moth or a dinner does not make them disappear and where thieves don't break in or steal.
21 You see, your heart will also be there where your stockpile is.
22 The eye is the lamp that brings light into your body. If your eye is dedicated *to its job of seeing*, your whole body will be lit up.
23 But if your eye is evil *and refuses to do its job correctly*, your whole body will be dark. If the light entering your body is darkness, how great that darkness is! *So be dedicated to looking at God and looking at what is good and right, or you will end up stumbling around in extreme darkness not knowing what is going on.*
24 No one can be a slave to two masters. You see, either he will hate the one *master* and love the other one, or he will keep the one *master* in front of him and ignore the other one. You can't be a slave to God and to wealth.
25 Because of this, I tell you, don't worry about your soul (what you will eat or drink) or your body (what you will put on). Isn't your soul more than the meal *it eats* and your body more than the attire *it puts on*?
26 Look at the birds in the sky. They don't plant seeds. They don't harvest crops. They don't gather *crops* into grain bins. Yet your Heavenly Father provides for them. Aren't you much more substantial than they?
27 Who from among you can add half a meter to your height by worrying?
28 And why do you worry about your attire? Carefully study how the wild flowers in the field grow. They don't labor. They don't make thread or fabric.
29 But I tell you that not even Solomon in all of his magnificence put clothes around himself like one of these.
30 If God decks out the grass of the field like this, that exists today and tomorrow is thrown into a fire pit, won't He do much more for you, you people who seldom trust Him?
31 So don't worry and say, 'What will we eat?', or 'What will we drink?', or 'What *clothes* will we put around ourselves?'
32 The non-Jews search for all these things. *Why do you? You have a Heavenly Father.* Your Heavenly Father knows absolutely everything that you need.
33 Look for God's monarchy first and His right way, and all of these things will be added to you.

34 You shouldn't worry about what will happen tomorrow. Tomorrow will worry about that. *It doesn't need your help.* It has enough problems *without you adding to them.*"

1 "Don't judge people so that people won't judge you.
2 You see, the judgment you judge others with is the judgment others will judge you with, and the amount of judging that you give is the amount you will receive.

7

3 Why do you see the wood chip in your brother's eye *(his tiny fault)*, but you refuse to take a close look at the log in your eye *(your huge fault)?*
4 Or how will you make this statement to your brother, 'Let me take the wood chip out of your eye,' when, look, there's a log in your eye?
5 Faker, first take the log out of your eye, and then you'll be able to clearly see the wood chip in your brother's eye so that you can take it out.
6 Don't give what is sacred to the dogs, and don't throw your pearls down in front of hogs. That way they won't trample on them with their feet, turn around, and rip you.
7 Ask, and it will be given to you. Look, and you will find. Knock, and *a door* will open to you.
8 You see, everyone asking receives. The person looking finds. And *a door* will open to the person knocking.
9 Or who from among you is a person who will give a stone to his son when he asks for bread?
10 Or *who is a father* who will give him a snake when he asks for a fish?
11 So if you, who are evil, know that you should give good presents to your children, how much more *will it be, that* your Father in heaven will give good things to those who ask Him?
12 *This is also how you should treat other people.* However many things that you may want people to do for you, do all that for them. You see, this is what the Law and the Preachers tell you to do.
13 Go in through the narrow gate because the wide gate and its spacious road lead off to ruin. Many are going in through it.
14 How narrow is the gate and road that winds its way through hard times as it leads people off to life! Few people are finding it.
15 Be cautious of the counterfeit preachers that are coming to you. They are wearing sheep costumes, but on the inside, they are vicious wolves.

16 You can correctly understand them by looking at their fruits, *what they produce. Grapes and figs are fruits*. You don't gather grape clusters from plants that have thorns, do you? And you don't pick figs from plants that have thistles, do you?
17 And so every good tree produces nice fruit. But every defective tree produces evil fruit.
18 A good tree can't produce evil fruit. And a defective tree can't produce nice fruit either.
19 Every tree that doesn't produce nice fruit is chopped down and thrown into a fire.
20 Clearly, by their fruits, you will definitely correctly understand them.
21 Not everyone who says to Me, 'Master, Master,' will enter heaven's monarchy. Only those who do what My Father in heaven wants will enter.
22 Many will make this statement to Me in that day, 'Master, Master, didn't we preach using Your name? Didn't we throw lesser deities out using Your name? Didn't we do many abilities using Your name?'
23 At that time, I will acknowledge to them, 'I never ever knew you. Get away from Me. You are the ones working on the crime.'
24 Everyone who listens to My messages and does them will be like the attentive man who built his house on bedrock.
25 When the rain poured, the rivers overflowed, and the wind blew, they pushed against that house, but it didn't fall. You see, its foundation had been laid on bedrock.
26 But everyone who listens to My messages and doesn't do them will be like a foolish man who built his house on sand.
27 When the rain poured, the rivers overflowed, and the wind blew, they pushed against that house, and it fell. Its fall was great."
28 When Jesus completely finished these messages, the crowds were impressed with His teaching.
29 You see, He was teaching them as someone with authority would (*as a king or a master would teach the people under him*). Their Old Testament transcribers didn't teach like that.

8

1 When He walked down from the mountain, large crowds followed Him.
2 And look, a man with a skin disease came and bowed down to Him. "Master," he said, "if you want, you can clear up my skin."

3 Jesus put out His hand and touched him. "I want to," He said. "Be cleared up." Right away his skin disease cleared up.
4 "Make sure that you don't tell anyone," Jesus told him, "but make your way back to the priest, show yourself to him, and offer the contribution stipulated by Moses. That will be a witness to them *of what happened to you.*"
5 When Jesus went into Capernaum, a lieutenant came up to Him begging.
6 "Master," he said, "my servant boy has been confined *to bed* in the house. He is disabled and being tortured dreadfully."
7 "I will come and heal him," said Jesus.
8 When the lieutenant responded, he was declaring, "Master, I am unfit for you to come in under the roof of my house. Just say a word, and my servant boy will be cured.
9 You see, I am a person under the authority *of the Roman Emperor.* I have soldiers under me. To this soldier, I say, 'Travel,' and he travels. To another, I say, 'Go,' and he goes. To my slave, I say, 'Do this,' and he does it. *I know that You also can say a word, and your unseen soldiers will cure my servant boy.*"
10 When Jesus heard this, He was amazed. He told the people following Him, "Amen, I tell you, I haven't found this much trust beside anyone in Israel.
11 I tell you that many will arrive *from outside of the Jewish nation,* from eastern regions and the western regions. They will recline with *the Jewish fathers* (Abraham, Isaac, and Jacob) in heaven's monarchy,
12 but *the Jews,* the sons of the monarchy, will be thrown out into the darkness that is outside and further away. There they will cry and grind their teeth *because they missed out on what was rightfully theirs.*"
13 Jesus told the lieutenant, "Make your way back home. It must happen as you trusted." In that hour, his servant boy was cured.
14 After Jesus went into Peter's house, He saw that Peter's mother-in-law had been confined *to bed* with a fever.
15 Jesus touched her hand and the fever left. She got up and started serving Him.
16 In the evening, they brought many people to Him, people who had lesser deities and people who had something wrong with them. He threw the spirits out with a word and healed all the others.
17 *He did this* in order that what God stated through Isaiah, the preacher, might be achieved, "He took our weaknesses and hauled the illnesses away" *(Isaiah 53:4).*

18 When Jesus saw the crowd surrounding Him, He gave the order to go off to the other side *of the Sea of Galilee*.
19 An Old Testament transcriber came up to Him and said, "Teacher, I will follow You wherever You go off to."
20 "Foxes have burrows to live in," Jesus told him, "and the birds of the sky have nests, but the Son of the Person doesn't even have a place to rest His head." *("The Son of the Person" is a generic term Jesus used of Himself. Ezekiel and Daniel were called "son of a person." "Son of a person" is also in Psalm 80:17.)*
21 A different one of His students said to Him, "Master, give me permission to first go off and bury my father *after he dies*."
22 But Jesus told him, "Follow Me, and leave the dead to bury their own dead."
23 He climbed on board the boat and His students followed Him.
24 As they were going to the other side, look, a large quake happened in the sea in such a way for the boat to be covered by the swells, but Jesus was sleeping.
25 They went and got Him up. "Master, rescue us," they said. "These swells are ruining us."
26 "Why are you cowards?" He asked them. "Why do you seldom trust?" Then He got up and told the winds and the sea to stop. They stopped, and it became very calm.
27 The people were amazed. "What kind of person is this," they were saying, "that even the winds and the sea obey Him?"
28 When they got to the other side, they came to the rural area of the Gadarenes. Two people who had lesser deities came out of the cemetery to meet Him. They were very fierce, so fierce that no one felt safe using the road that passed by there.
29 And look, they yelled, "Son of God, why are you interfering with us? Did you come here before the appointed time to torture us?"
30 A long way away from them, a large herd of hogs was grazing.
31 The lesser deities were begging Him, "If you throw us out, send us into the herd of hogs."
32 "Make your way out," said Jesus. When they went out, they went off into the hogs. And look, the entire herd rushed down the steep slope into the sea and died in the water.
33 The people grazing them escaped *from the stampede* and went off into the city. There they reported everything, even the things about the two with lesser deities.
34 And look, the entire city came out to meet with Jesus. *(They most likely were non-practicing Jews who made their living by raising hogs. Jews*

were not supposed to eat or even touch hogs.) After seeing Him, they begged Him to go somewhere else away from their borders.

9

1 He climbed on board the boat and crossed all the way back over. Then He went to His own city.
2 And look, people brought a disabled man to Him on a cot who had been confined *to bed*. When Jesus saw their trust, He said to the disabled man, "Be courageous, child. Your sins are forgiven."
3 And look, some of the Old Testament transcribers said to each other, "This Man is insulting God."
4 When Jesus saw what they were contemplating, He said, "Why are you contemplating evil in your hearts?
5 You see, which is easier to say, 'Your sins are forgiven,' or 'Get up and walk around?'
6 But so that you may see that the Son of the Person has authority on earth to forgive sins," at that time, He turned to the disabled man and said, "Get up, pick up your cot, and make your way back to your house."
7 The man got up and went off to his house.
8 When the crowds saw this, they were afraid and praised the magnificence of the God that gave this type of authority to people.
9 As Jesus passed by there, He saw a man sitting at the tax booth. His name was Matthew. "Follow Me," He told him. Matthew stood up and followed Him.
10 Later, it happened that He was chatting and feasting in Matthew's house. And look, many tax collectors and sinful people came and were chatting and feasting together with Jesus and His students.
11 When the Separatists saw it, they were asking His students, "Why is your teacher eating with the tax collectors and sinful people?"
12 When Jesus heard it, He said, "The people who are healthy and well don't need a doctor, but the people who have something wrong with them do.
13 As you travel home, learn what *the Bible means when it says*, 'I want forgiving kindness and not sacrifice' *(Hosea 6:6)*. You see, I didn't come to invite people who do what is right *to live for God*. I came to invite sinful people."
14 At that time, John's students came up to Him and asked, "Why do we and the Separatists often abstain from eating, but Your students don't?"

15 Jesus told them, "The 'sons of the bridal room' *(the people negotiating with the groom for the bride and helping her with the wedding)* can't be grieving as long as the groom is present, can they? *No, they are the bride's friends and are representing her to the groom. They must be happy.* But days will come when the groom is gone, then they will abstain from eating.

16 No one puts a patch of unprocessed cloth on a well-worn robe. You see, *if they do that*, the patch that fills in *the hole* lifts away from the robe and the tear becomes worse.

17 They don't put wine that is in the early stages of fermentation in worn-out leather bags either. If they were to do that, the leather bags definitely would rip open, the wine would spill out, and the leather bags would be ruined. No, they put wine that is in the early stages of fermentation in new leather bags. That way both the wine and the bag are preserved."

18 As He was speaking, look, one of the head people came forward and bowed down to Him, "My daughter passed away just now," he said, "but if You come and place Your hand on her, she will live."

19 Jesus got up. He and His students followed the man.

20 And look, a woman came up from behind and touched the fringe of His robe. This woman had been bleeding for twelve years.

21 She was saying to herself, "If only I could touch His robe, I will be rescued *from this bleeding*."

22 When Jesus turned and saw her, He said, "Daughter, be courageous, your trust has rescued you." From that hour, the woman was rescued *(her bleeding stopped).*

23 Jesus came into the head person's house and saw flute players and a crowd of people causing a disturbance *as they mourned for the girl.*

24 "Make room for us." Jesus said. "The girl has not died. She is sleeping." They laughed at Him.

25 When the crowd was thrown out, He went in the room where the girl was. He took hold of her hand, and she got up.

26 This news went out into all of that area.

27 As Jesus passed by there, two blind men started following Him. They were yelling, "Show forgiving kindness to us, Son of David." *(Son of David is a less specific term for Anointed King or Messiah.)*

28 After He went into a house, the blind men came up to Him. "Do you trust that I am able to do this?" Jesus asked. "Yes, Master," they said.

29 Then He touched their eyes. "It must happen to you aligned with your trust," He said.

30 Their eyes were opened. *They could see.* Jesus was stern with them, "Look. No one must know."
31 But after the *two* left, they thoroughly spread the news about Him in all of that area.
32 As they were going out, look, a person who couldn't speak and who had a lesser deity was brought to Him.
33 After the lesser deity was thrown out, the person who couldn't speak spoke. The crowds were amazed. They were saying, "Nothing like this has ever been shown in Israel."
34 But the Separatists were saying, "He is using the head of the lesser deities to throw the lesser deities out."
35 Jesus took His students around to all of the cities and villages. He was teaching in their synagogues, speaking publicly about the good news of the monarchy, and healing every illness and every frailty.
36 When He saw the crowds, He had sympathy concerning them because they had been irritated and tossed around. It was as if they were sheep that didn't have a shepherd.
37 At that time, He told His students, "There certainly is a big harvest, but there are *only* a few workers.
38 So plead with the master of the harvest so that he might put workers out into his harvest."

10

1 He called His twelve students together and gave them authority over spirits that are not clean. *This gave them the ability* to throw them out and to heal every illness and every frailty.
2 These are the names of the twelve missionaries: first, Simon (the one called Peter), Andrew (Peter's brother), James (Zebedee's son), and John (James' brother);
3 Philip and Bartholomew; Thomas and Matthew (the tax collector); James (Alpheus' son) and Thaddeus;
4 Simon (the Zealot) and Judas (the one from Kerioth, the one who also turned Him in).
5 Jesus sent these twelve out on missions *(this is why they were called missionaries). For this mission,* He gave these orders to them, "You won't walk down a road that goes to non-Jews, and you won't go off to even a city of Samaritans.
6 Instead, travel to the lost sheep of Israel's house *(the Jews who aren't on the right path).*
7 As you travel, speak publicly. Say, 'Heaven's monarchy has come near.'

8 Heal the weak. Bring the dead back to life. Clear up skin diseases. Throw lesser deities out. You received this for free, give it out for free. *Do not charge for your services.*
9 *You shouldn't take money with you.* Don't get gold, silver, or copper for your money belts.
10 Don't pack a tote bag for the road, or two shirts, or sandals, or a staff. You see, the worker deserves to be fed with a meal.
11 Whatever city or village you go into, question *people* about who in it deserves *to be blessed*. Stay there until you go out.
12 As you go into the house, say hello to everyone.
13 If the house is certainly deserving, stay there in peace. But if it isn't deserving, your peace must return to you *(in other words, you must leave without arguing, without fighting, and without getting upset--leave in peace).*
14 Whoever doesn't accept you or listen to your messages, as you go outside of the house or outside of that city, shake the dust off your feet.
15 Amen, I tell you, it will be more tolerable for the land of Sodom and Gomorrah on the day of sentencing than for that city.
16 Look, I am sending you out on this mission as sheep in the middle of wolves. Be attentive like snakes and unpolluted like doves.
17 Be cautious of people. You see, they will turn you into councils and whip you in their synagogues.
18 You will also be led before leaders and kings on account of Me for a witness to them and the non-Jews.
19 When they turn you in, don't worry about how or what you will speak. That will be given to you in the hour that you speak.
20 You won't be the ones speaking. Your Father's Spirit will be speaking in you.
21 A brother will turn a brother in to be put to death, and a father will turn a child in. Children will stand up against their parents and have them put to death.
22 You will be hated by all kinds of people because of My name. The person who persists to do what is right to the conclusion will be rescued.
23 When they pursue you in this city, escape to a different city. Amen, I tell you, you will not in any way finish the cities of Israel until the Son of the Person comes.
24 A student is not over his teacher, and a slave is not over his master either.

25 It is enough for a student to become like his teacher and a slave to become like his master. If they also called the homeowner Beelzebub *(the head of the lesser deities)*, how much more will they do the same thing to the people living in His house.
26 But don't be afraid of them. You see, everything that is covered up will be uncovered, and everything that is hidden will be known.
27 What I tell you in the dark, say in the light, and what you hear in the ear speak publicly on top of the houses.
28 Don't be afraid of the one who kills the body, but can't kill the soul. Instead be afraid of the One who can ruin both the soul and the body in Hinnom Valley.
29 Aren't two little sparrows sold for a few dollars? Yet one from them won't fall to the earth unaccompanied by your Father.
30 Even the hairs of your head have all been numbered.
31 So don't be afraid, you are more substantial than many little sparrows.
32 So everyone who will acknowledge being in Me in front of people, I will also acknowledge being in him in front of My Father in heaven.
33 But whoever denies Me in front of people, I also will deny him in front of My Father in heaven.
34 Don't assume that I came to put peace on the earth. I didn't come to put peace, but a dagger.
35 You see, I came to pit a son against his father, a daughter against her mother, and a bride against her mother-in-law.
36 A person's enemies will be the people in his own house.
37 Anyone who is fond of a father or mother more than he is fond of Me doesn't deserve Me. And anyone who is fond of a son or daughter more than he is fond of Me doesn't deserve Me.
38 A person who doesn't take up his cross *(or in other words, isn't ready to die for Me)*, and follow behind Me is not deserving of Me.
39 The person who finds his soul will lose it, but the person who loses his soul on account of Me will find it.
40 The person who accepts you accepts Me, and the person who accepts Me accepts the One who sent Me out on this mission.
41 The person who accepts a preacher simply because he is a preacher will receive a preacher's pay. And the person who accepts someone who does what is right simply because he is someone who does what is right will receive the pay of someone who does what is right.
42 And whoever gives one of these little ones a cup of cold drink simply because he is a student, amen, I tell you, he won't in any way lose his pay."

11

1 Jesus finished by specifically assigning *where each of* His twelve students *would go.* Then He happened to walk somewhere else so that He could teach and publicly speak in other cities.

2 John the Submerger was in prison. From there, he heard about what the Anointed King was doing. *It wasn't what he had expected.* So He sent his students to Him with this message:

3 "Are you the One coming, or should we expect a different person?"

4 Jesus answered John's students with these words, "After you travel back to John, report to him what you have heard and seen here.

5 Blind people see, crippled people are walking around, people with skin diseases are cleared up, hearing-impaired people hear, dead people get up, and good news is shared with poor people.

6 Also tell him that whoever does not stumble on Me is blessed."

7 As John's students traveled back, Jesus began to talk to the crowds about John, "What did you go out into the backcountry to watch, a stick disturbed by wind?

8 But what did you go out to see? Someone decked out in elegant clothes? Look, the people wearing the elegant clothes are in kings' houses.

9 But what did you go out to see? A preacher? Yes, I tell you, and much more than a preacher.

10 This is what has been written *in the Bible* about him, 'Look, I am sending My messenger out on a mission before Your face. He will construct Your road in front of You' *(Malachi 3:1).*

11 Amen, I tell you, a greater person than John the Submerger has not gotten up among all the people born to women. Yet the smaller person in heaven's monarchy is greater than him.

12 From the days of John the Submerger until now, people are forcing heaven's monarchy *down their road.* Forceful people are snatching it. *They are against God's new road.*

13 You see, all the Preachers and the Law preached until John. *That was the old system. But now a change has come.*

14 If you want to accept it, John is the Elijah that is going to come. *This is mentioned in the last two verses of the Old Testament (Malachi 4:5,6). There it says that Elijah is going to come before the Master's great and dreadful day and that He will bring in a change.*

15 The person who has ears must listen.

16 What will I liken this generation to? It is like when young children sit in the marketplaces and holler to different children.

17 'We played the flute for you,' they holler, 'and you didn't dance. We wailed, and you didn't beat your chests in grief.'
18 You see, when John came, he wasn't eating or drinking, and they said, 'He has a lesser deity.'
19 When the Son of the Person came, he was eating and drinking. But they said, 'Look, an excessive eater and a wine drinker, a friend of tax collectors and sinful people.' Insight is proven to be right by its actions. *Or in other words, what these people do gives insight into who they really are.*"
20 At that time, He began to criticize the cities that most of His abilities happened in because they didn't change their ways.
21 "What a tragedy it is to you, Chorazin! What a tragedy it is to you, Bethsaida! because if the abilities that happened in you had happened in Tyre and Sidon, they would have changed their ways a long time ago wearing sackcloth *(cloth that grieving people wear)* and throwing ashes on themselves *to express their grief.*
22 More importantly, I tell you, it will be more tolerable for Tyre and Sidon on the day of sentencing than for you.
23 And you, Capernaum, you won't be put up high, up to heaven, *as you think you will, just because I was often in your city*. You will be walked down to Hades *(the underworld of the dead)* because if the abilities that happened in you happened in Sodom, it would still be here today.
24 More importantly, I tell you, it will be more tolerable for the land of Sodom on the day of sentencing than for you."
25 Some time around then, Jesus responded and said, "Father, Master of heaven and earth, I admire the way You hid these things away from the scholars and scientists and uncovered them to infants.
26 Yes, Father, as You have seen, this has worked out quite well.
27 My Father turned everything over to Me. No one correctly understands the Son except the Father. And no one correctly understands the Father except the Son and whoever the Son intends to uncover the Father to.
28 Come to Me, everyone who labors and is loaded down. And I will get you to relax.
29 Strap yourself into My harness and learn from Me because I am submissive and lowly to the core. You will find relief for your souls.
30 You see, My harness is kind, and My load is light."

12

1 Some time around then, Jesus traveled through croplands on the Sabbaths. His students were hungry, so they began to pull off the heads of grain and eat them.

2 When the Separatists saw it, they told Him, "Look, your students are doing what they are not allowed to do on the Sabbath. *They are working. Work is not allowed on the Sabbath.*"
3 But Jesus told them, "Haven't you read what David did when he and the people with him were hungry?
4 *Haven't you read* how he went into God's house and they ate the display bread that he and the people with him were not allowed to eat? Only the priests were allowed to eat it. *Yet, the head priest gave it to them and they ate. Do you condemn David for doing that? No.*
5 Or haven't you read in the Law that on the Sabbaths the priests on the temple grounds profane the Sabbath, *they work on the Sabbath,* and they are innocent?
6 I tell you that something greater than the temple grounds is here.
7 But if you had known what *this part of the Bible* is, 'I want forgiving kindness and not sacrifice' *(Hosea 6:6),* you wouldn't have found the innocent guilty.
8 You see, there is a master over the Sabbath. It is the Son of the Person."
9 He walked somewhere else away from there and went into their synagogue.
10 And look, a man was there who had a deformed hand. They asked *Jesus about* him by saying, "*Tell us* if healing on the Sabbaths is allowed." *They were trying to get Him to say something* that they could use against Him.
11 "Who from among you will be a person who has one sheep," said Jesus, "and if this sheep should fall into a hole on the Sabbaths, will not grab it and get it up *out of the hole?*
12 So isn't a person much more substantial than a sheep? When it comes to things like this, you are allowed to do nice things on the Sabbaths."
13 Then He told the person with the deformed hand, "Put your hand out." He put it out, and it was established back healthy as the other hand.
14 After the Separatists left, they sought legal counsel against Him *that they could use* to ruin Him.
15 When Jesus knew it, He took a back way out of there. Large crowds followed Him. He healed everyone who needed healing
16 and shushed them so that they wouldn't show who He is.
17 This was so that what God stated through Isaiah, the preacher, might be accomplished:

18 "Look, My Servant Boy that I picked, My Loved *Servant Boy*. My soul is delighted with Him. I will put My Spirit on Him. He will decide *what is right and* report that to the nations.
19 He won't fight, He won't yell, no one will hear His voice in the plazas,
20 He won't break a crushed stick, and He won't extinguish a smoldering wick until He will throw out the judgment for victory.
21 Nations will anticipate good in His name" *(Isaiah 42:1-4)*.
22 Then they brought a man who had a lesser deity in him. He was blind and couldn't speak. Jesus healed him so that he could both speak and see.
23 All the crowds were astounded and saying, "This isn't the son of David, is it?"
24 When the Separatists heard this, they said, "This Person can't throw out lesser deities except with *the help of* Beelzebub, the head of the lesser deities."
25 When Jesus realized what they were contemplating, He told them, "Every monarchy that is divided and against itself becomes uninhabited, and every city or house that is divided and against itself will not be established.
26 If the Opponent throws the Opponent out, he is divided and disagrees with himself. How will his monarchy stand?
27 And if I throw the lesser deities out with Beelzebub's help, what about your sons? With whom do they throw them out? *Ask them. Their answers* will stand as judges over you.
28 But if I throw the lesser deities out with God's Spirit, clearly God's monarchy has already come to you.
29 How can anyone go into a strong person's house and take his stuff if he doesn't first tie him up? Then he can ransack his house. *I am able to throw out lesser deities because God's Spirit ties the Opponent up.*
30 The person who isn't with Me is against Me, and the person who doesn't gather with Me scatters My things.
31 Because of this, I tell you, every sin and insult will be forgiven to the people, but the insult of the Spirit won't be forgiven.
32 And whoever says something against the Son of the Person, it will be forgiven, but whoever speaks against the Sacred Spirit, it won't be forgiven, not in this span of time or the future *span of time*.
33 Either make the tree nice and its fruit nice, or make the tree defective and its fruit defective. You see, the tree is known by its fruit.
34 You children of poisonous snakes, how can you who are evil speak good? You see, from the excess of the heart, the mouth speaks.

35 A good person deals out good things from his stockpile of good, and an evil person deals out evil things from his stockpile of evil.
36 I tell you, on a day of judgment, the people will pay for every idle statement that they have spoken about His message.
37 You see, from your words, you will be made right, and from your words, you will be found guilty."
38 At that time, some of the Old Testament transcribers and Separatists responded to Him by saying, "Teacher, we want to see proof *that You are from God*."
39 But when Jesus responded, He said, "An evil and cheating generation searches for proof. No proof will be given to it except the proof of preacher Jonah.
40 You see, just as Jonah was in the large fish's belly for three days and three nights, so the Son of the Person will be in the heart of the earth for three days and three nights.
41 In the sentencing with this generation, Ninevite men will stand up and find it guilty because they changed their ways and did what Jonah yelled on their streets, and, look, a greater thing than Jonah is here.
42 In the sentencing with this generation, a queen from the south will get up and find it guilty because she came from the ends of the earth to hear Solomon's insight, and, look, a greater thing than Solomon is here.
43 When a spirit that isn't clean leaves a person, it passes through places that don't have water looking for relief, but doesn't find it.
44 At that time, it says, 'I will return back to the house that I left.' When it comes back, it finds a hangout that has been swept and decorated.
45 Then it travels, finds seven different spirits more evil than itself, and brings them along with it. When they go in, they live there, and it becomes *such that* the last *circumstances* of that person are worse than the first. This is how it will also be for this evil generation."
46 As He was still speaking to the crowds, look, His mother and brothers were standing outside looking for a way to speak to Him.
47 ["Look," someone told Him, "Your mother and Your brothers have been standing outside looking for a way to speak to You."]
48 "Who is My mother?" Jesus replied. "And who are My brothers?"
49 He put His hand out over His students and said, "Look, My mother and My brothers.
50 You see, whoever does what My Father in heaven wants, he is My brother, sister, and mother."

13

1 During that day, Jesus went out of the house and sat beside the Sea *of Galilee*.
2 Large crowds gathered to Him. So He climbed on board a boat and sat down. The crowd stood on the beach.
3 He told them many illustrations. He said, "Look, the person who plants crops went out to plant. *His method of planting was flinging handfuls of seeds on the ground throughout the whole field.*
4 As he flung out seeds, some fell along the road. When the birds came, they ate them.
5 Others fell on the rocky areas where there wasn't much soil. Right away plants sprang up from the rocks because they didn't have any depth of soil.
6 But when the sun came up and it got hot, they dried up and died because they didn't have roots.
7 Others fell where there were thorns. The thorns climbed up and choked them out.
8 Others fell on the nice soil. They grew up and produced fruit. Some produced a hundred fruit, some sixty, some thirty.
9 The person who has ears must listen."
10 His students came up to Him and asked, "Why are you telling them illustrations?"
11 "Because the privilege of knowing the secrets of heaven's monarchy has been given to you. It has not been given to those people," answered Jesus.
12 "You see, anyone who has, will get, and it will overflow, but anyone who does not have, even what he has will be taken away from him.
13 This is why I tell them illustrations, because as they see, they don't see, and as they hear, they don't hear or understand.
14 This fills up Isaiah's preaching that says, 'You will hear what you hear and not in any way understand, and as you look, you will look and not in any way see.
15 You see, the heart of this ethnic group *(the Jews)* became fat. *They were given much.* But they hardly heard with their ears. They shut their eyes so that they would never see with their eyes, hear with their ears, understand with their heart, and return back. Then I would have cured them' *(Isaiah 6:9-10)*.
16 But your eyes are blessed because they see, and your ears are blessed because they hear.
17 You see, amen, I tell you that many preachers and people who did what is right desired to see what you are looking at, but they didn't get

to. They desired to hear the things that you hear, but they didn't get to.

18 So you must listen to the illustration of the one who planted the crop.

19 *It shows different responses that people have to the monarchy's message.* With everyone who hears the monarchy's message and doesn't understand, the evil one comes and snatches up that seed that was planted in their heart. This is the seed that was flung along the road.

20 The seed that was flung on the rocky areas, this is the person who hears the message and right away happily receives it.

21 But it doesn't have any root in him. It is for the time being. When the message brings hard times or persecution, right away he stumbles.

22 The seed that was flung into the thorns, this is the person who hears the message *but it is surrounded by worry and wealth. The message has root and grows.* But worry *about the things that happen in this* span of time and wealth's fraud are also there. They come together and choke off the message. *The message is still in him, but* it is fruitless.

23 The seed that was flung on to the nice soil, this is the person who hears and understands the message *and who isn't overtaken by worry or wealth*. For sure, the message produces fruit and multiplies. In some it makes a hundred, in others sixty, and in others thirty."

24 He laid out another illustration for them, "Heaven's monarchy is like a person who planted high quality seed out in his field.

25 *One night* when people were sleeping, his enemy came, flung ryegrass seeds out in the middle of the field up on top of the wheat, and left.

26 When the stem budded and made its fruit, at that time, the ryegrass also appeared.

27 The slaves went to the property owner. 'Master,' they said, 'didn't you plant high quality seed in your field? So how does it have ryegrass?'

28 He was declaring to them, 'My enemy did this.' 'Do you want us to go off and gather up the ryegrass?' the slaves asked.

29 'No, don't,' he declares. 'I don't ever want any of the wheat to be uprooted at the same time when you gather up the ryegrass.

30 Leave both of them. Let them grow together until the harvest. At harvest time, I will make a statement to the harvesters to gather up the ryegrass first, tie it up into bundles with the specific goal of burning them, and then bring the wheat together into my grain bin.'"

31 He laid out another illustration for them, "Heaven's monarchy is like a kernel of mustard that a man took and planted in his field.

32 It not only was the littlest of all the seeds *that he had*, but when it grew, it was bigger than the vegetable plants. It became a tree so big that the birds of the sky came and nested in its branches."

33 He told them another illustration, "Heaven's monarchy is like yeast. A woman took it and hid it in three loads of dough until all of it was raised."

34 All these things that Jesus spoke to the crowds were in illustrations. He didn't speak anything other than illustrations.

35 He did this so that what God stated through the preacher might be achieved, "I will open my mouth in illustrations. I will utter things that have been hidden since the world was formed" *(Psalm 78:2)*.

36 At that time, He left the crowds and went into the house. His students came up to Him. "Explain the meaning of the illustration of the ryegrass in the field," they said.

37 Jesus answered by saying, "The person planting the high quality seed is the Son of the Person.

38 The field is the world. The high quality seeds are the sons of the monarchy, and the ryegrass seeds are the sons of the evil one.

39 The enemy who planted *the bad seed* is the Accuser. The harvest is the very conclusion of this span of time. The harvesters are angels.

40 So even as the ryegrass is gathered up and burned with fire, so will it be at the very conclusion of this span of time.

41 The Son of the Person will send His angels out on a mission to gather up from His monarchy all the obstacles and the people doing crime.

42 They will throw them into the furnace of fire. There they will cry and grind their teeth.

43 At that time, the people who did what is right will shine brightly like the sun in their Father's monarchy. The person who has ears must listen.

44 Heaven's monarchy is like a stockpile of treasure hidden in a field. When a man found it, he hid it. And because he was so happy, he made his way back home, sold everything that he had, and purchased that field.

45 Again heaven's monarchy is like a man, a wholesaler, looking for nice pearls.

46 When he found a very valuable pearl, he went off, put everything he had up for sale, and purchased it.

47 Again heaven's monarchy is like a net that was thrown into the sea and gathered all kinds of things together.

48 When it was full, they hauled it up on the beach, sat down, and went through what was in it. They gathered up the nice things into buckets, but threw out the defective things.
49 This is how it will be at the very conclusion of this span of time. The angels will go out and isolate the evil people out from the middle of the people who did what is right.
50 They will throw them into the furnace of fire. There they will cry and grind their teeth.
51 Do you understand all these things?" "Yes," they said.
52 "Because of this," Jesus said, "every Old Testament transcriber who becomes a student of heaven's monarchy is like a person, a homeowner, someone who goes through his stockpile of stuff and takes out new stuff and used stuff."
53 When Jesus finished these illustrations, He took off.
54 When He went into His hometown, He was teaching them in their synagogue. He made such an impression on them that they said, "Where does He get this insight and ability from?
55 Isn't this the son of the builder? Isn't His mother Mary, and His brothers James, Joseph, Simon, and Jude?
56 And aren't His sisters still with us? So where does this One get all these things from?"
57 They were stumbling on Him. "A preacher is only worthless," said Jesus, "in his hometown and in his house."
58 He didn't show many of His abilities there because they didn't trust Him.

14

1 Some time around then, Herod (the head of one of Palestine's four regions) heard the talk about Jesus.
2 "This is John the Submerger," he told his servant boys. "He has come back to life from the dead. That's why the abilities are active in Him."
3 You see, after Herod arrested John, he chained him up and put him away in jail because of Herodias. Herodias was his brother Philip's wife.
4 John had been telling him that he is not allowed to have her.
5 And as Herod wanted to kill him, he was afraid of what the crowd would do because they considered John to be a preacher.
6 When *one of the many* birthday celebrations for Herod happened, Herodias' daughter danced in the middle *of the room*, and Herod liked it.

7 So he acknowledged from there with an oath to give her whatever she asked for.
8 She was forced forward by her mother. "Give me," she declares, "here and now on a plate, John the Submerger's head."
9 This saddened the king, but because of the oath and the people chatting and feasting together with him, he gave the order for it to be done.
10 The order was sent to the jail, and John was beheaded.
11 His head was carried on a plate and given to the girl. She carried it to her mother.
12 His students went to the jail, took the corpse, and buried it. Then they went and reported it to Jesus.
13 When Jesus heard it, He took a back way from there to a boat and sailed to an uninhabited place to be by Himself. When the crowds heard that Jesus had left, they came out of the cities and followed Him on foot.
14 When He got out of the boat, there was a big crowd. When He saw them, He had sympathy for them and healed their sick.
15 In the evening, His students came up to Him and said, "This place is uninhabited, and it is already getting late. Dismiss the crowds so that they can go off into the villages and buy food for themselves."
16 "They don't need to go away," said Jesus. "Give them something to eat."
17 "We don't have anything here," His students said, "except five loaves of bread and two fish."
18 "Bring them here to Me," said Jesus.
19 He told the crowds to recline on the grass. He took the five loaves of bread and the two fish, looked up into the sky, and conferred a blessing on them. He split them and gave the pieces to His students. His students passed them out to the crowds.
20 Everyone ate until they were full. They picked up the pieces that were left over. There were twelve full baskets.
21 There were about five thousand men eating there, not counting the women and children.
22 Right away He urged His students to climb on board the boat and lead the way ahead of Him to the other side while He dismissed the crowds.
23 After dismissing the crowds, He climbed up into the mountain by Himself to pray. When evening came, He was there alone.
24 The boat was already several thousand feet away from land, and it was being tortured by the swells. You see, the wind was against them.

25 In the fourth guard shift of the night *(3 a.m. - 6 a.m.)*, He went to them walking around on the sea.
26 When His students saw Him walking around on the sea, they were uneasy. "It's a ghost," they yelled. They were afraid.
27 Right away Jesus spoke, "Be courageous. It's Me. Don't be afraid."
28 "Master, if it is You," Peter responded, "tell me to come to You on the water."
29 "Come," said Jesus. Peter stepped down out of the boat and walked around on the water to Jesus.
30 But when he saw the strong wind, he was afraid. He began to sink down. "Master," he yelled, "rescue me."
31 Right away Jesus put out His hand and latched on to him. "You seldom trust. Why did you doubt?"
32 They climbed up into the boat and the wind stopped blowing.
33 The people in the boat bowed down to Him. "You truly are God's son," they said.
34 After they crossed all the way over, they were in the land of Gennesaret.
35 When the men of that place recognized Him, they sent people out into all of the surrounding rural area. They brought Him all the people who had something wrong with them.
36 They were begging Jesus to just let them touch the fringe of His robe. As many as touched were completely restored.

15

1 At that time, the Separatists and Old Testament transcribers from Greater Jerusalem came up to Jesus.
2 "Why are your students violating the older men's tradition?" they asked. "You see, they aren't washing their hands whenever they eat bread."
3 When Jesus answered, He said, "And why do you violate God's demand with your tradition?
4 You see, God demanded, 'Value the father and the mother' *(Deuteronomy 5:16)*, and, 'The person who says bad things to a father or mother must pass away in death' *(Exodus 21:17)*.
5 But you say, 'Whoever tells the father or mother, "*the money* that I should have supported you with is a contribution to God,"
6 won't ever have to value his father.' You nullified God's message with your tradition.
7 Fakers, what Isaiah preached about you fits nicely. He said,
8 'This ethnic group values Me with their lips, but their heart keeps itself far away from Me.

9 Their worship of Me is futile, because the instructions that they teach are people's regulations, *not Mine*'" *(Isaiah 29:13)*.
10 Jesus called the crowd together and told them, "Hear, and understand.
11 What goes into the mouth doesn't contaminate a person, but what travels out of the mouth, this is what contaminates a person."
12 At that time, His students came up to Him and said, "Do you realize that the Separatists who heard what You said were offended?"
13 Jesus answered by saying, "Every plant that My Heavenly Father didn't plant will be uprooted.
14 Leave them alone. They are blind guides of blind people. If a blind person guides a blind person, both will fall into a hole."
15 When Peter responded, he said, "Explain the meaning of this illustration to us."
16 "Are you also still clueless?" said Jesus.
17 "Aren't you aware that everything traveling into the mouth, takes up room in the belly, and is thrown out into the sewer?
18 But the things traveling out of the mouth come out of the heart. Those things contaminate a person.
19 You see, evil ponderings, murders, times when someone cheats on a spouse, sexual sins, thefts, lies about what a person witnessed, and insults, all come from the heart.
20 They contaminate a person, but eating with hands that haven't been washed does not contaminate him."
21 Jesus went out from there and took a back way into parts of Tyre and Sidon.
22 And look, a Canaanite woman came out from the border area yelling, "Show forgiving kindness to me, Master, Son of David. My daughter has a lesser deity in a bad way."
23 But Jesus didn't respond with even a word to her. His students came up to Him. They were asking Him, saying, "Dismiss her because she keeps yelling behind us."
24 When He responded, He said, "I was only sent out to the lost sheep of Israel's house, *to the Jews who aren't on the right path*."
25 Then the woman came and bowed down to Him. "Master, help me," she said.
26 When Jesus replied, He said, "It is not nice to take bread away from the children and throw it to the puppies."
27 "Yes, Master, *you are right*," said the woman. "But even the puppies eat the crumbs that fall from their masters' table."

28 "O ma'am," responded Jesus, "your trust is great. It must happen as you want." Her daughter was cured within that hour.
29 After Jesus walked somewhere else away from there, He went along the Sea of Galilee. Then He climbed up a mountain and sat down.
30 Large crowds came up to Him. They had crippled people with them, blind people, physically wounded people, speech-impaired people, and many different ones. They tossed them at His feet, and He healed them.
31 The crowd was amazed seeing speech-impaired people speaking, physically wounded people well, crippled people walking around, and blind people seeing. They praised the magnificence of Israel's God.
32 Jesus called for His students and said, "I have sympathy for the crowd because they have stayed with me already for three days even though they don't have anything to eat. I don't want to dismiss them without food so that they won't ever have a hard time on the road *as they return home*."
33 "Where will we get enough bread to feed such a big crowd out here in this uninhabited place?" His students asked.
34 "How much bread do you have?" asked Jesus. "Seven loaves and a few small fish," they said.
35 He told the crowd to settle down on the ground.
36 Then He took the seven loaves of bread and the fish and was thankful. He split them and gave them to His students. His students passed them out to the crowds.
37 They all ate until they were full. Then they picked up the pieces that were left over. There were seven full large baskets.
38 Four thousand men had eaten, not counting the women and children.
39 He dismissed the crowds, climbed on board the boat, and went to Magdala's border.

16

1 The Separatists and Sadducees came up to Jesus to harass Him. They asked Him to show them proof from the sky *that He is from God*.
2 When He answered, He told them, "When evening comes, you say, 'Nice weather. You see, the sky is fiery.'
3 And in the morning, you say, 'It will storm today. You see, the sky is fiery, yet disappointing. *There are dark clouds.*' You certainly know when something is wrong with the sky's appearance, but *when you are surrounded by* the proofs of the times, you can't *see them*.

4 An evil and cheating generation searches for proof. No proof will be given to it except the proof of Jonah." He left them there and went away.
5 When they went to the other side *of the Sea of Galilee*, the students forgot to get *more* bread.
6 "See and be cautious of the Separatists and Sadducees' yeast," Jesus said.
7 They were pondering *this* among themselves. "It is because we didn't bring *enough* bread," they said.
8 When Jesus knew about it, He said, "Why are you pondering among yourselves, you people who seldom trust *God*, that you don't have *enough* bread?"
9 Aren't you aware yet *of what happened?* Don't you even remember the five loaves of bread among the five thousand and how many baskets you took up?
10 Don't you even remember the seven loaves of bread among the four thousand and how many large baskets you took up?
11 How aren't you aware that what I said was not about bread? Be cautious of the Separatists and Sadducees' yeast."
12 Then they understood that He didn't say to be cautious of the bread's yeast, but of the Separatists and Sadducees' teaching. *Yeast seems harmless, yet it spreads quickly to all of the dough and changes it. When the Separatists and Sadducees's teaching is bad, it is seldom seen as bad--it quickly spreads and causes ruin.*
13 When Jesus came into parts of Philip's Caesarea, He was asking His students, "Who do people say that the Son of the Person is?"
14 "Some, John the Submerger," they said, "others, Elijah; different ones, Jeremiah or one of the preachers."
15 "What about you?" Jesus asked. "Who do you say that I am?"
16 "You are the Anointed King," Simon Peter answered, "the Son of the living God."
17 "You are blessed, Simon, son of Jonah," Jesus responded, "because *a living physical being* (a physical body and blood) didn't uncover this to you. No, My Father in the heavens did.
18 I also will tell you that you are a rock. I will build My assembly on the rock *of your statement that I am the Anointed King, the Son of the living God*. The gates of Hades *(the underworld of the dead)* will not be strong against it.
19 I will give you the keys of heaven's monarchy. Whatever you lock up on the earth will be locked up in heaven, and whatever you unlock on the earth will be unlocked in heaven."

20 At that time, He warned the students not to tell anyone that He is the Anointed King.

21 From then on, Jesus began to show His students that He would have to go off to Jerusalem, suffer many injuries from the older men, head priests, and Old Testament transcribers, be killed, and be gotten up on the third day.

22 Peter took Him aside and began to tell Him to stop. "*God has* a remedy for You, Master," he said. "That will never happen to You."

23 Jesus turned and told Peter, "Make your way back behind Me, opponent. You are an obstacle to Me because you don't focus on God's things. You only focus on what people focus on."

24 Then Jesus told His students, "If anyone wants to come behind Me, he must flatly deny himself, pick up his cross *(or in other words, be ready to die for Me)*, and follow Me.

25 You see, whoever wants to rescue his soul will lose it, but whoever loses his soul on account of Me will find it.

26 You see, what benefit is it for a person to gain the whole world but sustain loss to his soul? Or what will a person give in exchange for his soul?

27 The Son of the Person is going to come in His Father's magnificence with His angels. At that time, He will give back to each person the kind of things that person repeatedly did during his life.

28 Amen, I tell you that some of the people standing here won't in anyway taste death until they see the Son of the Person coming in His monarchy."

17

1 After six days, Jesus took Peter, James, and John (James' brother) with Him up into a high mountain by themselves.
2 His appearance changed in front of them. His face shined as bright as the sun. His clothes became as white as light.
3 And, look, they saw Moses and Elijah speaking together with Him.
4 When Peter responded, he told Jesus, "Master, it's nice for us to be here. If you want, I'll make three tents here: one for You, one for Moses, and one for Elijah."
5 As he was still speaking, look, a lit-up cloud shined over them, and look, a voice spoke from the cloud, "This is My loved Son. I am delighted with Him. Listen to Him."
6 When the students heard the voice, they fell on their face and were terribly afraid.
7 Jesus came up to them and touched them. "Get up, and don't be afraid," He said.

8 When they looked up, they saw no one except Jesus alone.

9 As they walked down from the mountain, Jesus gave them a demand. He said, "You will tell no one what you have seen until the Son of the Person is gotten up from the dead."

10 *Since* the students *had just seen Elijah, they* asked, "So why are the Old Testament transcribers saying that Elijah must come first?"

11 "Elijah not only comes," Jesus answered, "and will reestablish everything, *as the Old Testament transcribers have been saying,*

12 but I tell you that Elijah already came and they didn't recognize him. They did as much as they wanted to do with him. This is also how the Son of the Person is going to be suffering under them."

13 At that time, the students understood that He was talking about John the Submerger.

14 When they came to the crowd, a man came up to Him. He kneeled and said,

15 "Master, show forgiving kindness to my son because he is struck by the moon *(that is, he has seizures)* and suffers in a bad way. You see, many times he falls into the fire or into the water.

16 I brought him to your students, and they weren't able to heal him."

17 "O untrusting and twisted generation," Jesus responded, "how long must I be with you? How long must I tolerate you? Bring him here to Me."

18 Jesus told the lesser deity to stop, and it came out. The boy was healed within that hour.

19 Then Jesus' students came to Him by themselves. "Why couldn't we throw it out?" they asked.

20 "Because you seldom trust," Jesus said. "You see, amen, I tell you, if you had a small amount of trust, as small as a kernel of mustard, you would state to this mountain, 'Walk from here to there,' and it would walk. Nothing would be impossible for you."

21 [[["But this kind doesn't travel out except in prayer and a time of fasting."]]] *Proper prayer and fasting aligns a person with what God wants to do and how. Then that person will do and trust what God has shown him.*

22 As they were huddled together in Galilee, Jesus said to them, "The Son of the Person is going to be taken into custody by the people.

23 They will kill Him, and He will be gotten up on the third day." This made them terribly sad.

24 After they came into Capernaum, the people who collect the double drachmas *(the temple tax)* came to Peter and said, "Isn't your teacher paying the double drachmas?"

25 "Yes," he said. When he came into the house, Jesus went up to him before he could say anything and said. "What do you think, Simon? From whom do the kings of the earth collect taxes and require an enrollment? From their sons or from others?"
26 "From others," said Peter. "So the sons are definitely free," declared Jesus.
27 "But so that we won't cause them to stumble, travel to the sea, throw in a hook, and keep the first fish that steps up *to attack the hook*. When you open its mouth, you will find a silver coin. Give that to them for Me and you."

18

1 In that hour, the students came to Jesus saying, "So who is greater in heaven's monarchy?"
2 He called for a young child and stood him up in the middle of them.
3 "Amen, I tell you, if you won't turn and become as young children," He said, "you won't in any way enter heaven's monarchy.
4 So the one who is greater in heaven's monarchy is anyone who will put himself down low, as low as this young child.
5 And whoever accepts one young child of this type based on My name accepts Me.
6 But whoever causes one of these little ones who trust in Me to stumble, it would've been to his advantage if instead a large millstone, the kind turned by a donkey, had been hung around his neck and he had been dropped in the deep part of the sea.
7 What a tragedy this world experiences from obstacles! You see, there is an obligation that obstacles come. But worse than that, what a tragedy it is to the person who is setting up the obstacle!
8 If your hand or your foot causes you to stumble, chop it off, and throw it away. Which is better, to go through life physically wounded or crippled, or to be thrown into the fire that spans all time having two hands and two feet?
9 If your eye causes you to stumble, take it out, and throw it away. Which is better, to go through life one-eyed, or to be thrown into the Hinnom Valley of fire having two eyes?
10 Look, no one should ignore one of these little ones. You see, I tell you that through every situation their angels in heaven see the face of My Father in heaven.
11 [[[You see, the Son of the Person came to rescue the lost *sheep*.]]]
12 What do you think? If it happened that a certain person had a hundred sheep and one sheep from them wandered off, wouldn't he

leave the ninety-nine in the mountains, travel off, and look for the one that wandered off?

13 And if he happened to find it, amen, I tell you that he would be happier about that than he would about the ninety-nine that have not wandered off.

14 In the same way, your Father in heaven doesn't want to see any of these little ones ruined.

15 If your brother does something sinful to you, make your way back to him and reprimand him. *Keep it* only between you and him. If he listens to you, you got your brother back.

16 But if he doesn't listen, take one or two people along with you *and talk to him about what he did.* That way every statement will be established by the mouth of two or three witnesses. *They can verify what is said and what his response is.*

17 If he disregards them, talk to the assembly. If he also disregards the assembly, *don't have any type of relationship with him.* He must be like a non-Jew and tax collector to you.

18 Amen, I tell you, whatever you all lock up on earth will be locked up in heaven, and whatever you unlock on earth will be unlocked in heaven.

19 Again, *concerning what I just said,* amen, I tell you that if two from among you on the earth harmoniously agree about every item of whatever they ask for, it will happen to them directly from My Father in heaven.

20 You see, where there are two or three that have been gathered together in My name, I am there in the middle of them."

21 At that time, Peter came up to Him and said, "Master, how many times will my brother do something sinful to me and I will forgive him? Seven times?"

22 "I don't say to you seven times," Jesus said. "I say seventy times, times seven.

23 Because of this, heaven's monarchy is like a person, a king, who wanted to settle his account with his slaves.

24 After he began to settle *with them,* one was brought to him who owed ten million dollars.

25 Since he couldn't pay it back, the master ordered that he, his wife, his children, and everything that he had be put up for sale so that he could be paid back.

26 The slave got down on his knees and was bowing to him. 'Be patient with me,' he begged, 'and I will give everything back to you.'

27 The master of that slave had sympathy. He dismissed him and forgave him of the debt.
28 But after that slave left, he found one of his fellow slaves who owed him five thousand dollars. He grabbed him and began choking him. 'Pay me back,' he said, 'if you owe me anything.'
29 His fellow slave got down on his knees and begged him, 'Be patient with me, and I will pay you back.'
30 He didn't want to. Instead, he went off and threw him in jail until he paid back what was owed.
31 When his fellow slaves saw what happened, they were terribly sad. They went to their master and explained to him everything that had happened.
32 At that time, his master called for him and said, 'Evil slave, I forgave every bit of what you owed me since you begged me to.
33 Wasn't it necessary for you to be kind and forgive your fellow slave the same way I was kind and forgave you?'
34 His master was enraged and turned him over to the torturers until he paid back every bit of what he owed.
35 My Heavenly Father will also do the same thing to each one of you if you don't forgive your brother from your heart."

19

1 When Jesus finished these messages, He took off out of Galilee and went to the borders of Judea on the other side of the Jordan River.
2 Large crowds followed Him, and He healed them there.
3 Separatists came up to Him to harass Him. "Tell us if a person is allowed to dismiss his wife for any type of accusation that he might have against her."
4 When Jesus responded, He said, "Didn't you read that the One who created them from the beginning made them male and female?
5 And, 'On account of this, a person will leave his father and mother, stick like glue to his wife, and the two will be one physical body?' *(Genesis 2:24)*
6 In such a way, they are no longer two, but one physical body. *God said this.* So what God strapped together, a person must not separate."
7 "So why did Moses demand to give a divorce decree and dismiss her?" they said.
8 "To address your hardhearted," He said, "*(hardheartedness that creates situations requiring divorce)*, Moses gave you permission to dismiss your wives *through divorce*, but from the beginning it wasn't like that.

9 *You dismiss your wives, but you don't give them a divorce.* I tell you that whoever dismisses his wife not based on sexual sin and marries someone else is cheating on the wife *that he dismissed."*
10 His students told Him, "If the man's accusation with the wife is like that, *if an accusation can't dismiss her,* it isn't to his advantage to marry."
11 "Not everyone would agree with that answer," said Jesus. "But it is for the people it has been given to. *There are people who are better off not getting married.*
12 You see, there are some who were castrated *when they came* out of *their* mother's belly, some who were castrated by someone else, and some who castrated themselves because of heaven's monarchy. The person who is able to live without marrying should do so."
13 At that time, young children were brought to Him so that He might place His hands on them and pray. But the students stopped them.
14 When Jesus saw it, He said, "Leave the young children alone, and don't keep them from coming to Me. You see, *children find it easy to trust.* Heaven's monarchy is made up of these types of children."
15 After He placed His hands on them, He traveled away from there.
16 And look, one person came to Him and said, "Teacher, what good thing should I do so that I might have life that spans all time?"
17 "Why do you ask Me about a good thing?" Jesus said. "There is One who is good. But if you want to enter the life that spans all time, keep the Demands."
18 "Which ones?" He asked. *"These six:"* Jesus said, "you won't murder, you won't cheat on your spouse, you won't steal, you won't lie when you're a witness,
19 value your father and mother, and you will love the person near you as yourself."
20 "I have observed all these," the young lad said. "What do I still lack?"
21 "If you want to be complete," Jesus declared, "make your way back home, sell your things, give to the poor (you will have a stockpile of treasure in heaven), and come, follow Me."
22 When the young lad heard this answer, He went away sad. You see, he owned many properties. *His properties kept him from following Jesus because they required His daily attention. The one thing he lacked was trust. He wouldn't trust the Teacher.*
23 Jesus told His students, "Amen, I tell you that it will be hard for a wealthy person as he goes into heaven's monarchy.

24 Again I tell you, it is easier for a camel to go through an eye of a needle than for a wealthy person to enter God's monarchy.
25 Upon hearing this, the students were terribly stunned. "So who can be rescued?" they asked.
26 Jesus looked at them and said, "With people this is impossible, but with God everything is possible."
27 At that time, Peter responded by saying, "Look, we left everything and followed You. So what will we get?"
28 "Amen, I tell you," Jesus said. "You, the ones who followed Me, in the rebirth when the Son of the Person will be seated on a throne of His magnificence, you will also sit on twelve thrones judging the twelve family lines of Israel.
29 And everyone, any who left houses, or brothers, or sisters, or a father, or a mother, or children, or fields on account of My Name will receive a hundred times that and inherit life that spans all time.
30 Many of the first will be last, and the last first."

20

1 "You see, heaven's monarchy is like a person, a property owner, someone who went out at the same time as the early morning guard shift *(6 a.m.)* to hire workers for his vineyard.
2 After he harmoniously agreed with the workers on a denarius for the day *(a coin equal to one day's wage)*, he sent them out into his vineyard.
3 Around 9 a.m., he went out to the marketplace and saw others that had stood around *all morning* with nothing to do.
4 'You also must make your way out into my vineyard,' he said, 'and I will pay you whatever is right.' But they left.
5 Again he went out around noon and 3 p.m. and did the same thing.
6 Around 5 p.m., he went out and found others who were just standing around. 'Why have you stood here the whole day with nothing to do?' he asked.
7 'Because no one has hired us,' they said. 'You also must make your way out into the vineyard,' he said.
8 When evening came, the vineyard's master told his administrator, 'Call the workers and pay them beginning with the last ones and proceeding to the first.'
9 When the workers who *started* around 5 p.m. came, they each received a denarius.
10 When the first workers came, they assumed that they would receive more, *but they didn't*. They also each received a denarius.

11 After they received it, they were grumbling against the property owner.
12 'These last workers only worked for one hour,' they said, 'and you have made them equal to us. We hauled the weight and heat of the day. *We worked all day. We worked when it was hot.*'
13 'Comrade,' the property owner replied to one of them, 'I didn't do anything wrong to you. Didn't you harmoniously agree with me to work all day for a denarius?
14 Take your pay and make your way back *home*. I want to give this last worker what I also gave you.
15 Am I not allowed to do what I want with my money? Or is your eye evil because I am good?'
16 This is how the last will be first and the first last."
17 As Jesus was walking up to Jerusalem, He brought the twelve students by themselves alongside of Him. On the road, He told them,
18 "Look, I am walking up to Jerusalem. The Son of the Person will be turned in to the head priests and Old Testament transcribers. They will find Him guilty and deserving of death.
19 They will give Him to the non-Jews so that the non-Jews can mock Him, whip Him, and nail Him to a cross. On the third day, He will be gotten up."
20 At that time, the mother of Zebedee's sons came to Him with her sons. She bowed down to Him and asked if He would do something for her.
21 "What do you want?" He asked. "Say that these two sons of mine," she said, "will be seated with You in Your monarchy, one on Your right side and one on Your left."
22 "You don't realize what you are asking for," Jesus answered. "Are you *two* able to drink the cup that I am going to be drinking?" "We are able," they said.
23 "You will certainly drink My cup," He said, "but this thing of being seated on my right and left is not Mine to give. No, those places are for the people made ready by My Father."
24 When the ten heard about this, they were frustrated about the two brothers.
25 Jesus called them together and said, "You realize that the head people of the nations act like masters over them and the great people put themselves in places of authority over them.
26 It won't be like that with you. Whoever wants to become great among you, he will be your server.
27 And whoever wants to be first among you, he will be your slave,

28 even as the Son of the Person didn't come to be served, but to serve and to give His soul as a payment for the release of many."
29 As they traveled out from *residential* Jericho, a big crowd followed Him.
30 And look, when two blind people sitting along the road heard that Jesus was passing by, they yelled and said, "Show us forgiving kindness, Master, Son of David."
31 The crowd shushed them so that they would be quiet. But they yelled louder. "Show us forgiving kindness, Master, Son of David."
32 Jesus stopped walking and hollered for them. "What do you want Me to do for you?" He said.
33 "Master," they said, "that our eyes would be opened."
34 Jesus had sympathy and touched their eyes. Right away they could see. They followed Him.

21

1 When they were near to Jerusalem, they came to Bethphage on the Mount of Olives *(a hill just east of Jerusalem)*. At that time, Jesus sent two students out on a mission.
2 "Travel into the village directly facing you," He told them. "Right away you will find a donkey that has been tied up. Her foal will be with her. After you release them, bring them to Me.
3 If anyone says anything to you, make this statement to them, 'The Master needs them.' Right away they will send them out."
4 This is so that what God stated through the preacher might be achieved:
5 "Tell the daughter of Zion, look, your king comes to you submissive and having climbed up on a donkey and on a foal, a son of a workhorse" *(Zechariah 9:9)*.
6 The students traveled and did just as Jesus dictated to them.
7 They brought the donkey and her foal and placed their robes on them. He sat up on top of them.
8 The biggest crowd spread out their own robes in the road. Others were chopping branches off the trees and spreading them out in the road.
9 The crowds leading the way ahead of Him and following Him were yelling *a chant*, "Hosanna! *O, rescue us,* Son of David! The One coming in the Master's Name has been conferred with blessings! Hosanna in the highest!"
10 When they came into Jerusalem, the entire city was disturbed. "Who is this?" they asked.

11 The crowds were saying, "This is the preacher Jesus, the One from Nazareth, Galilee."

12 Jesus went onto the temple grounds and threw out all the people who were buying and selling there. He turned over the currency exchangers' tables and the benches of the people selling the doves.

13 He told them, "The Bible says, 'My house will be called a house of prayer' *(Isaiah 56:7)*, but you are making it a cave of bandits."

14 On the temple grounds, blind and crippled people came to Him, and He healed them.

15 But when the head priests and the Old Testament transcribers saw the amazing things that He did and when they saw the boys yelling, "Hosanna to the Son of David!" on the temple grounds, they were frustrated.

16 "Do you hear what these boys are saying?" they asked Him. "Yes," said Jesus, "did you never even once read, 'From the mouth of infants, even nursing infants, You developed praise?'" *(Psalm 8:2)*.

17 He left them there and went outside of the city to Bethany. He slept outside in a courtyard there.

18 In the morning as He was taking His students up into the city, He was hungry.

19 He saw one fig tree up the road. When He went up to it, He found nothing except leaves. "No fruit will ever grow on you in our span of time," He said. At once the fig tree dried up.

20 The students who saw it were amazed. "How did the fig tree dry up at once?" they said.

21 "Amen, I tell you," answered Jesus, "if you have trust and don't consider it to be wrong, not only will you do what happened to the fig tree, but even if you say to this mountain, 'Be picked up and thrown into the sea,' it will happen.

22 And you will receive all things, as many as you trust and ask for in your prayer."

23 After He came onto the temple grounds, the head priests and the older men of the ethnic group came to Him as He was teaching. "With what kind of authority are you doing these things?" they asked. "And who gave you this authority?"

24 "I will also ask you one question," Jesus said. "If you answer it, I will state to you with what kind of authority I am doing these things.

25 John's submersion, where was it from, from heaven or from people?" They were pondering it among themselves. "If we say from heaven, He will state to us, 'So why didn't you trust him?'

26 But if we say from people, we are afraid of the crowd. You see, everyone considers John to be a preacher."
27 When they answered Jesus, they said, "We don't know." He also was declaring to them, "And I am not going to tell you with what kind of authority I am doing these things either."
28 "What do you think? A person had two children. He came to the first one and said, 'Child, make your way outside and work in the vineyard today.'
29 When the child responded, he said, 'I don't want to.' But later he regretted *his response* and left.
30 He came to the other child and said the same thing. When he responded, he said, 'I *am going*, master.' But he didn't leave.
31 Which son from the two did what the father wanted?" "The first," they said. "Amen, I tell you," Jesus said to them, "the tax collectors and prostitutes are leading the way into God's monarchy ahead of you.
32 You see, John came to you on the right road, and you didn't trust him. But the tax collectors and the prostitutes trusted him. When you saw *him bringing all these people back to God*, you still didn't regret *your response*, and *you didn't* later trust him.
33 Listen to another illustration. There was a property owner who planted a vineyard. He put a barrier wall around it, dug out a grape-smashing floor in it, and built a tower. Then he gave it out to farmers *who agreed to pay him a percentage of the harvest each year*, and he left the area.
34 When harvest time was near, he sent his slaves out to the farmers to collect his fruit.
35 The farmers took his slaves and beat one, killed another, and threw stones at the third one.
36 Again he sent out other slaves, *this time* more than the first. They did the same type of things to them.
37 Later he sent his son out on a mission to them. 'They will be embarrassed around my son,' he said.
38 But when the farmers saw the son, they started talking among themselves. 'This is the one who will inherit all of this,' they said. 'Come on, let's kill him. Then his inheritance will be ours.'
39 They grabbed him, threw him out of the vineyard, and killed him.
40 So when the master of the vineyard comes, what will he do to those farmers?"
41 "He will badly destroy those bad farmers," they answered, "and give the vineyard out to other farmers, farmers who will give him the fruits *(his percentage of the harvest)* when they are supposed to."

42 "Did you never even once read this *Old Testament* writing?" Jesus asked them. "'A stone that the builders rejected, this ended up being used for a corner's head *(a cornerstone, the primary stone of the whole building)*. This has happened directly from the Master, and it is amazing in our eyes' *(Psalm 118:22-23)*.
43 Because of this, I tell you that God's monarchy will be taken away from you and given to a nation producing the monarchy's fruits."
44 ["The person who falls on this stone will be smashed, and it will grind up whoever it falls on."]
45 The head priests and the Separatists heard His illustrations and knew that He was talking about them.
46 They were looking for a way to arrest Him, but they were afraid of the crowds since the crowds considered Jesus to be a preacher.

22

1 When Jesus responded, He again talked to them in illustrations.
2 "Heaven's monarchy is like a person, a king who hosted the wedding events for his son.
3 He sent his slaves out on a mission to tell the people who had been invited that it is time to come to the wedding events. No one wanted to come.
4 He sent other slaves out again with these instructions, 'Tell the people who have been invited, "look, my lunch is ready. I have killed my bulls and grain-fed steers. Everything is ready. Come to the wedding events."'
5 But they didn't care. Some went out to their own field. Others went off to their businesses.
6 The rest grabbed his slaves, injured them, and killed them.
7 The king was enraged. He sent his military forces out, and they destroyed those murderers and incinerated their city.
8 Then he said to his slaves, 'Not only is the wedding ready, but the people who had been invited were not deserving of the invitation.
9 So travel out to the intersections of the roads, and invite however many that you find to come to the wedding events.'
10 Those slaves went out onto the roads and gathered everyone that they found. Both evil and good people came. The wedding was full of people feasting and chatting.
11 But when the king came in to view the people feasting and chatting, he saw someone there who had not put on the wedding's attire.
12 'Comrade,' he said, 'how did you come in here and not wear the wedding's attire *that I provided for you?*' That person was quiet.

13 Then the king told the servers, 'Tie him up, feet and hands, and throw him out into the darkness that is outside and further away. There they will cry and grind their teeth.'
14 You see, many are invited, but few choose *to come*."
15 At that time, the Separatists traveled and received advice on how they might trap Him in His answers.
16 Then they sent their students out to Him with the Herod supporters. "Teacher," they said, "we realize that You are valid, You teach God's way in truth, and there is no bias in You toward anyone. You see, You don't look at people's labels.
17 So tell us, what do you think? Is giving Caesar an enrollment tax allowed or not?"
18 But Jesus knew their evil intentions. "Why are you harassing Me, fakers?" He said.
19 "Show Me the legal tender of the enrollment." They brought Him a denarius *(a coin equal to one day's wage)*.
20 "Whose image and inscription is this?" He asked.
21 "Caesar's," they said. "So give Caesar's things back to Caesar," He said, "and God's things back to God."
22 When they heard this, they were amazed. They left Him alone and went away.
23 During that day, Sadducees (who say there is no life after death) came to Him and asked,
24 "Teacher, Moses said that if anyone dies without children, his brother will also marry the wife and get a seed *(descendants)* up for his brother.
25 There were seven brothers who lived beside us. After the first brother got married, he passed away without having a seed *(without having any children)*. So his wife was left to his brother.
26 The second brother had a similar experience. And the third too. This happened to all seven of them. *They all passed away without giving her any children.*
27 Later the wife of all of them died.
28 So in the return back to life, whose wife will she be of the seven? You see, they all had her as their wife."
29 When Jesus answered, He said, "You are misled because you don't know the *Old Testament* writings or God's ability.
30 You see, in the return back to life, they don't marry and they don't plan to get married either. They are like the angels in heaven.
31 But about the return back to life of the dead, didn't you read what God stated to you?

32 'I am the God of Abraham,' He said, 'the God of Isaac, and the God of Jacob?' *(Exodus 3:6). He didn't say 'was'. He said 'am'. I am the God of Abraham, Isaac, and Jacob.* God is not a god of dead people. *Dead people don't have gods. They are dead.* He is a god of living people. *Abraham, Isaac, and Jacob were and are living in the afterworld."*
33 When the crowds heard this, they were impressed with His teaching.
34 When the Separatists heard that He quieted the Sadducees, they gathered together for the same thing, *to figure out how they could trap Him.*
35 One law expert from their law experts harassed Him by asking,
36 "Teacher, which demand is the great demand in the law?"
37 "You will love the Master, your God," He declared, "with your whole heart, with your whole soul, and with your whole mind.
38 This is the great and first demand.
39 The second is like it, 'You will love the person near you as yourself.'
40 The whole Law and the Preachers are hung on these two demands."
41 Since the Separatists were gathered together, Jesus asked them,
42 "What do you think? When it comes to the Anointed King, whose son is he?" They said, "David's."
43 He said to them, "So how does David in the Spirit call him Master? David said:
44 'The Master *(God)* said to my Master *(the Anointed King)*, "Sit down on My right side until I place Your enemies beneath Your feet?"' *(Psalm 110:1).*
45 So if David called Him master, how is He his son?"
46 No one was able to answer Him a word, and no one dared to ask Him anything else after that day either.

23

1 Then Jesus spoke to the crowds and to His students.
2 "The Old Testament transcribers and Separatists are seated on the legal bench of Moses.
3 So do and keep everything that they tell you, but do not do what they do. You see, they don't do what they tell you to do.
4 They detain heavy and hard-to-haul loads and place them on people's shoulders. But they don't want *to lift* their finger to *help* move them.
5 All of their actions are done with a specific goal--to be seen by people. You see, they enlarge their scripture boxes and make the fringes on their robes large.

6 They are fond of the front places in the feasts *(the place of honor)*, the front benches in the synagogues,
7 being greeted in the marketplaces, and being called Rabbi by people.
8 But you shouldn't be called Rabbi *(the Hebrew word for teacher)*. You see, there is One who is your teacher. You all are brothers.
9 And you shouldn't call any of you on the earth, Father. You see, there is One who is your Father, the Heavenly Father.
10 You shouldn't be called mentors either because there is One who is your mentor, the Anointed King.
11 The greater person among you will be your server.
12 Anyone who will put himself up high will be put down low, and anyone who will put himself down low will be put up high.
13 What a tragedy it is to you, Old Testament transcribers and Separatists, fakers, because you close up heaven's monarchy in front of people. You see, you don't go in, but you don't leave the people going in, alone so that they can go in either.
14 [[[What a tragedy it is to you, Old Testament transcribers and Separatists, fakers, because you eat up widows' houses even as you pray for a long time as a sham. Because of this, you will receive much more judgment.]]]
15 What a tragedy it is to you, Old Testament transcribers and Separatists, fakers, because you make your way around the sea and the dry land to make one convert, and when it happens, you make him two times more a son of Hinnom Valley than you.
16 What a tragedy it is to you, blind guides, those who say, 'Whoever invokes the temple to guarantee his promise, it is nothing, but whoever invokes the temple's gold to guarantee it is obligated.'
17 Foolish and blind people, you see, which is greater, the gold or the temple that made the gold sacred?
18 You also say, 'Whoever invokes the altar to guarantee his promise, it is nothing, but whoever invokes the contribution up on top of the altar to guarantee it is obligated.'
19 Blind people, you see, which is greater, the contribution or the altar that makes the contribution sacred?
20 So the person who invokes the altar to guarantee his promise, invokes the altar and everything up on top of it.
21 And the person who invokes the temple to guarantee his promise, invokes the temple and the One living in it, *God*.
22 And the person who invokes heaven to guarantee his promise, invokes God's throne and the One sitting up on top of it.

23 What a tragedy it is to you, Old Testament transcribers and Separatists, fakers, because you make sure to give a ten-percent offering from *the lesser plants in your garden* (sweet smelling mint, dill, and fennel) and leave out the heavier things of the law: justice, forgiving kindness, and trust. You must do these *heavier things* and not leave out those *lesser ones*.

24 You are blind guides who strain out the gnat, but swallow up the camel.

25 What a tragedy it is to you, Old Testament transcribers and Separatists, fakers, because you clean the outside of the cup and dish, but the inside is packed full of garbage from looting and a lack of restraint.

26 Blind Separatist, first clean the inside of the cup so that its outside might also become clean.

27 What a tragedy it is to you, Old Testament transcribers and Separatists, fakers, because you resemble gravesites that have been whitened with chalk, some that on the outside certainly appear beautiful, but on the inside are packed full of dead people's bones and all of what is not clean.

28 In this way, you also, on the outside, certainly make it appear to people that you do what is right, but on the inside you are full of faked behavior and crime.

29 What a tragedy it is to you, Old Testament transcribers and Separatists, fakers, because you build the gravesites of preachers, you decorate the burial vaults of the people who did what is right,

30 and you say, 'If we were living during the days of our fathers, we would not have had a part in *the killing* (the blood) of the preachers.'

31 In such a way, you are witnesses to yourselves that you are sons of the preacher's murderers.

32 *Like father, like son.* You also must do just as much as your fathers did.

33 Snakes, your parents were poisonous snakes and so are you, how will you escape away from the judgment of the Hinnom Valley?

34 Because of this, look, I am sending out preachers, insightful people, and transcribers to you. Some of them, you will kill and nail to crosses. Some, you will whip in your synagogues and pursue from city to city.

35 That way every drop of blood that has spilled out onto the earth from people who did what is right will also be on your hands, from the blood of Abel (who did what is right) to the blood of Zacharias (a son of Barachias, that you murdered between the temple and the altar).

36 Amen, I tell you, all these things will arrive on this generation.

37 Jerusalem, Jerusalem, the city that kills the preachers and throws stones at the people who have been sent out to it, how many times did I want to bring your children together in one place, the way that a hen brings her chicks together under her wings, and you didn't want it.
38 Look, your house is left to you uninhabited.
39 You see, I tell you, you all will not in any way see Me after this until you say, 'The One who comes in the Master's name has been conferred with blessings.'"

24

1 After Jesus left the temple grounds, as He was traveling away from it, His students came up to Him and showed Him its buildings.
2 Jesus responded by saying, "Do you see all these buildings? Amen, I tell you, a stone will not in any way be left on a stone here that hasn't been torn down *(this happened in 70 AD)*."
3 As He was sitting on the Mount of Olives, His students came up to Him by themselves and said, "Tell us when these things will happen. What is the indicator of Your arrival and the very conclusion of this span of time?
4 Jesus answered them by saying, "See that no one misleads you.
5 You see, many will come using My name. They will say, 'I am the Anointed King.' They will mislead many.
6 You will hear wars and much talk about wars. Look. Don't be alarmed. You see, this must happen, but it is not the conclusion yet.
7 A nation will rise up against a nation. A monarchy will rise up against a monarchy. There will be famines and earthquakes throughout some areas.
8 All these things are the beginning of labor pains.
9 At that time, they will turn you in to *give you* a hard time. They will kill you. You will be hated by all nations because of My name.
10 Then many will stumble. They will turn each other in and hate each other.
11 Many counterfeit preachers will rise up and mislead many.
12 Because crime will increase, the love of many will be cooled.
13 The person who persists to do what is right to the conclusion will be rescued.
14 This good news of the monarchy will be spoken publicly in the whole civilized world for a witness to all the nations, and then the conclusion will arrive.
15 The disgusting thing of the uninhabited time will stand in the sacred place. God stated this through the preacher Daniel. So when you see

that this has happened (the person reading *Daniel* must be aware of it),
16 at that time, the people in Judea must escape into the mountains.
17 The person on top of the house must not climb down into his house to get his things,
18 and the person working in the field must not return back to where his robe is and get it.
19 What a tragedy it will be for the pregnant women and the nursing women in those days!
20 Be praying so that your escape will not happen during a storm or on a Sabbath.
21 You see, at that time, there will be such great hard times *that they will be worse than any that* have ever happened since the beginning of the world until the present, yes, *worse than any* that will ever happen.
22 And if those days were not halted, no physical body would be rescued, but because of the people who have chosen God's way, those days will be halted.
23 At that time, if someone tells you, "Look, the Anointed King is here or there," don't trust it.
24 You see, counterfeit anointed kings and counterfeit preachers will rise and will show great proofs and incredible things in such a way to mislead, if possible, even the people who have chosen God's way.
25 Look, I have stated it to you beforehand.
26 So if they tell you, "Look, He's in the backcountry," don't go out there. Or if they say, "Look, He's in the storage rooms," don't trust it.
27 You see, the arrival of the Son of the Person will be even as the arrival of lightning as it goes out from eastern regions and shines to western regions.
28 Wherever the corpse is, there the raptors will be gathered together.
29 After the hard times of those days, right away the sun will darken, the moon won't give her glow, stars will fall out of the sky, and the sky's abilities will be disturbed.
30 Then the indicator of the Son of the Person will appear in the sky. And all the family lines of the earth will beat their chests in grief. They will see the Son of the Person coming on the clouds of the sky with ability and much magnificence.
31 With a great trumpet, He will send His angels out on a mission. They will bring the people who have chosen Him together in one place from the four winds *(the four compass directions)*, from the edges of heaven out to the *opposite* edges of it.

32 Learn an illustration from the fig tree: When its branch already becomes tender and it may sprout out leaves *at any time*, you know that summer is near.
33 In the same way, when you also see all these things happening, you know that it is near, at the door.
34 Amen, I tell you that a generation won't in any way pass by *from the beginning of all these things until the day He comes*.
35 The sky and the earth will pass, but My messages will not in any way pass.
36 But no one knows on which day and in which hour it will happen. Not even the angels in heaven or the Son *know*. Only the Father *knows*.
37 You see, the days of the Son of the Person's arrival will be even as Noah's days were.
38 In those days, in the days before the flood, they were eating and drinking, they were getting married and giving *their children* away in marriage, even up to the time when Noah went into the box *(the Ark)*.
39 Just as they didn't know *what was happening* until the flood came and took every single one of them away, this is also how it will be when the Son of the Person arrives.
40 At that time, two will be in the field; one will be taken along, and one will be left.
41 Two will be grinding flour on the millstone; one will be taken along, and one will be left.
42 So stay awake because you don't know on which day your Master is coming.
43 But you know that if the homeowner had known in which guard shift of the night that the thief would come, he would have stayed awake and not allowed his house to be broken into.
44 You also must be ready because the Son of the Person will come in an hour when you don't think He will.
45 So who is the reliable and attentive slave whom the master put in charge over his domestic servants to give the meal to them at the right time?
46 That slave is blessed when his master comes and finds him doing this.
47 Amen, I tell you that he will put him in charge over all his things.
48 But if the slave in that position is bad and says in his heart, 'My master is taking a long time,'
49 he might also begin to be hitting his fellow slaves; he may eat and drink with the drunks.

50 That slave's master will arrive on a day that he isn't expecting and in an hour that he doesn't know.
51 The master will cut him in two and put his part with the fakers. There they will cry and grind their teeth."

25

1 "At that time, heaven's monarchy will be like ten young ladies. After grabbing their torches, they went out to meet the groom *when he brings his new bride to his house from her parent's house.*
2 Five of them were foolish, and five were attentive.
3 You see, when the foolish young ladies grabbed their torches, they didn't take olive oil with them.
4 But the attentive young ladies took olive oil in flasks with their torches.
5 As the groom was taking a long time, they all nodded off and were sleeping.
6 In the middle of the night, someone yelled, 'Look, the groom, go out for a face-to-face meeting with him.'
7 At that time, all those young ladies got up and assembled their torches.
8 The foolish ones said to the attentive ones, 'Give us some olive oil. Our torches have gone out.'
9 'No,' the attentive young ladies answered, 'there won't ever in any way be enough for us and you. Instead travel to the people who sell *olive oil*, and buy some for yourselves.'
10 As they went off to buy olive oil, the groom came. The young ladies who were ready went in with him to the wedding events, and the door was closed.
11 Later the rest of the young ladies also came. 'Master, master, open *the door* to us,' they said.
12 The groom answered by saying, 'Amen, I tell you, I don't know you.'
13 So stay awake because you don't know the day or the hour.
14 You see, it is even like a wealthy person who went on a trip out of town. Before he left, he called his own slaves and gave all his things over to them.
15 To one he gave $5000. To another, he gave $2000, and to another, $1000. Each amount matched their own ability. Right away he left the area.
16 The slave with $5000 went out, worked with it, and gained another $5000.
17 The slave with $2000 in a similar way gained another $2000.

18 But the slave who received $1000 went off, dug a hole in the ground, and hid his master's silver.
19 After a long time, the master of those slaves came and settled his account with them.
20 The slave who received $5000 came forward and brought another $5000. 'Master,' he said, 'you turned $5000 over to me. Look, I gained another $5000.'
21 'Well done,' his master declared. 'You are a good and reliable slave. Since you were reliable with these few things of mine, I will put you in charge of many things. Come, be happy with your master.'
22 The slave who received $2000 also came forward. 'Master,' he said, 'you turned $2000 over to me. Look, I gained another $2000.'
23 'Well done,' his master declared. 'You are a good and reliable slave. Since you were reliable with these few things of mine, I will put you in charge of many things. Come, be happy with your master.'
24 The slave who had received $1000 also came forward. 'Master,' he said, 'I knew that you are a harsh man. You harvest where you didn't plant, and you gather things up from the places where you didn't disperse anything.
25 And because I was afraid, I went off and hid your $1000 in the ground. Look, here's your money.'
26 His master responded by saying, 'Evil and lazy slave, you realized that I harvest where I didn't plant and I gather things up from the places where I didn't disperse anything.
27 So you should have at least thrown my silver coins to the banker. That way when I came I could retrieve my money with interest.
28 Take the $1000 away from him, and give it to the slave with $10,000.
29 You see, everyone who has something will be given more, and it will overflow, but the person who has nothing, even what he has will be taken away from him.
30 And throw the inept slave out into the darkness that is outside and further away. There they will cry and grind their teeth.'
31 When the Son of the Person comes in His magnificence with all the angels, at that time, He will be seated on a throne of His magnificence.
32 And all the nations will be gathered together in front of Him. He will isolate them away from each other, like a shepherd isolates the sheep away from the goats.
33 He will certainly position the sheep to the right of Him, but the little goats to the left.

34 Then the King will state to the sheep to the right of Him, 'Come on, My Father has conferred blessings on you, inherit the monarchy that has been readied for you since the world was formed.
35 You see, I was hungry, and you gave Me something to eat. I was thirsty, and you gave Me a drink. I was a stranger, and you took Me home with you.
36 I was naked, and you threw a robe around Me. I was in frail health, and you kept an eye on Me. I was in jail, and you came to Me.
37 Then the people who did what is right will respond to Him, 'Master, when did we see You hungry and feed You, or thirsty and give You a drink?
38 When did we see You a stranger and take You home with us, or naked and put a robe around You?
39 When did we see You in frail health or in jail and come to You?'
40 The King will answer them by stating, 'Amen, I tell you, as much as you did to one of these smallest brothers of Mine, you did to Me.'
41 Then He will also state to the *goats* to the left of Him, 'Travel away from Me, you who have been cursed, to the fire that spans all time, the fire that has been readied for the Accuser and his angels.
42 You see, I was hungry, and you didn't give Me anything to eat. I was thirsty, and you didn't give Me a drink.
43 I was a stranger, and you didn't take Me home with you; naked, and you didn't throw a robe around Me; in frail health and in jail, and you didn't keep an eye on Me.'
44 Then they will also respond by saying, 'Master, when did we see You hungry, or thirsty, or a stranger, or naked, or in frail health, or in jail, and didn't serve You?'
45 Then He'll answer them, 'Amen, I tell you, as much as you didn't do for one of these smallest ones, you didn't do for Me either.'
46 These will go off into confinement that spans all time. But those who did what is right will go into life that spans all time."

26

1 When Jesus happened to finish all these messages, He told His students,
2 "You realize that after two days the Passover will happen and the Son of the Person will be turned in to be nailed to a cross."
3 At the time *that He was saying this*, the head priests and the ethnic group's older men were gathered together in the head priest Caiaphas's courtyard.
4 Together they advised to deceptively arrest Jesus and kill Him.

5 But they were saying, "Not at the festival so that a riot doesn't happen among the group."

6 *Later*, Jesus happened to be in Bethany in Simon's house, the one that had a skin disease.

7 A woman came with an alabaster jar of high-priced perfume. She spilled it down on Jesus' head as He was feasting and chatting.

8 When the students saw it, they were frustrated. "Why did she ruin this high-priced perfume?" they said.

9 "You see, it could have been put up for sale for a lot of money. That money could have been given to the poor."

10 When Jesus knew it, He said, "Why are you bothering the woman? You see, she has worked to do nice work for Me.

11 You will always have poor people with you, but you won't always have Me.

12 You see, when she put this perfume on My body, she did it with a specific goal--to prepare Me for burial.

13 Amen, I tell you, wherever this good news is spoken publicly in the whole world, what she did will also be spoken for a reminder of her."

14 At that time, one of the Twelve, the one called Judas from Kerioth, traveled to the head priests.

15 "How much do you want to give me," he said, "if I turn Him over to you?" The head priests stacked up thirty silver coins for him.

16 From then on, he looked for a good time to turn Him over to them.

17 The students went to Jesus concerning the first day of the Yeast-free Festival and said, "Where do You want us to get things ready for You to eat the Passover meal?"

18 "Make your way back into the city to [NAME REDACTED]," He said, "and tell him, 'The Teacher says, My time is near. I am doing the Passover at your place with My students.'"

19 The students did as Jesus dictated and they got the Passover meal ready.

20 When evening came, He was feasting and chatting with the Twelve.

21 As they ate, He said, "Amen, I tell you that one person from you will turn Me in."

22 They were terribly sad. They began to say to Him, each one, "It isn't me, is it, Master?"

23 When Jesus answered, He said, "The one who dipped *his bread* in the bowl with my hand will turn Me in.

24 The Son of the Person certainly will make His way back just as the Bible says, but what a tragedy it is to the person that turns Him in. It would have been better for him not to be born.
25 Judas (the one who would turn Him in) responded by saying, "It isn't me, is it, Rabbi?" "You said it," said Jesus.
26 As they were eating, Jesus took bread, conferred a blessing on it, and split it. He gave it to the students and said, "Take it. Eat it. This is My body."
27 He took a cup, was thankful, and gave it to them. "Everyone, drink from it," He said.
28 "You see, this is My blood that seals the deal. It is spilled out concerning many people for a forgiveness of sins.
29 I tell you, I won't in anyway drink juice from a grapevine from now on until that day when I drink it new with you in My Father's monarchy."
30 After they sang praise songs, they went out to the Mount of Olives.
31 At that time, Jesus said to them, "Tonight, all of you will stumble on Me. You see, the Bible says, 'I will strike the shepherd, and the sheep in His flock will disperse' *(Zechariah 13:7)*.
32 After I am gotten up, I will lead the way ahead of you into Galilee."
33 Peter responded by saying, "Even if all of them stumble on You, I will never ever stumble."
34 "Amen, I tell you," Jesus declared, "tonight before it is time for the rooster to crow, you will flatly deny Me three times."
35 "Even if I have to die with You," Peter said, "I will not in any way flatly deny You." All the students also said similar things.
36 At that time, Jesus went with them onto a parcel of land called Gethsemane. "Be seated here," He said to His students, "while I go off to there and pray."
37 He took Peter and the two sons of Zebedee along with Him. He began to be sad and heavyhearted.
38 At that time He told them, "My soul is overcome with sadness up to death. Stay here. Stay awake with Me."
39 He went on ahead a little, got down on His face, and prayed. "My Father," He said, "if it is possible, this cup must pass away from Me. But more importantly, it should not be as I want it. It should be as You want it."
40 He came to His students and found them sleeping. "Is this how it is?" He said to Peter. "Didn't you have enough strength to stay awake with Me for one hour?

41 Stay awake. Pray so that you won't get into trouble. The spirit certainly is eager, but the physical body is weak."
42 Again He went off a second time and prayed. "My Father," He said, "if this can't pass unless I drink it, what You want must happen."
43 When He came to His students again, He found them sleeping. You see, their eyes had been weighted down.
44 He left them again, went off, and prayed a third time. He again said the same words.
45 At that time, He came to the students and said, "Sleep for the rest of the time and relax." *After some time,* Jesus said, "Look, the time has come near. The Son of the Person will soon be turned over to sinful people's hands.
46 Get up. Let's lead the way. Look, the person turning Me in has come near."
47 As He was still speaking, look, Judas, one of the Twelve, came with a big crowd. The crowd had daggers and wooden clubs. They were sent to Him by the head priests and the ethnic group's older men.
48 Judas gave them *a way for him to* indicate *who it is*: "Whoever I am friendly with is Him. Take Him into custody."
49 Right away he came up to Jesus and was being very friendly to Him. "Happy to see You, Rabbi," he said.
50 "Comrade," Jesus said, "on to what you are here for." At that time, they came up, put their hands on Jesus, and took Him into custody.
51 And look, one of the ones with Jesus put out his hand, pulled out his dagger, struck the head priest's slave, and cut off his earlobe.
52 "Return your dagger back into its place," Jesus said. "You see, all who take a dagger will be ruined by a dagger.
53 Or do you think that I can't call My Father here and He will now stand up more than twelve legions *(Latin for regiments)* of angels here to protect Me?
54 But *if I did that,* how, then, would the *Old Testament* writings be completed, the ones that say it must happen like this?"
55 In that hour, Jesus said to the crowds, "Did you come out to apprehend Me with daggers and wooden clubs as if I were a bandit? Everyday I was seated on the temple grounds teaching. *How is it that* you didn't take Me into custody then?
56 But this whole thing has happened so that what the preachers' writings say, might be achieved." At that time, all the students left Him and escaped.

57 The *underlings* took Jesus into custody and led Him off to the head priest Caiaphas where the Old Testament transcribers and older men were gathered together.
58 Peter was following Him at a distance until they came to the head priest's courtyard. He went inside the courtyard and sat with the underlings to see the conclusion.
59 The head priests and the whole council were looking for a witness who would tell a lie about Jesus that they could use to put Him to death.
60 But they didn't find any among the many lying witnesses that came forward. Later, two witnesses came forward.
61 They said, "This Person was declaring, 'I can tear God's temple down and build it back up in three days.'"
62 The head priest stood up and said to Him, "Aren't You going to answer anything? What are these witnesses saying against you?"
63 But Jesus kept silent. "I am forcing you into an oath under the living God," the head priest said, "to tell us if you are the Anointed King, God's Son."
64 "You said it," Jesus said. "More importantly, I tell you, after this you will see the Son of the Person sitting at the right side of the Ability and coming on the clouds of the sky."
65 At that time, the head priest ripped his clothes apart *(to show how appalled he was by this)* and said, "He insulted God. What? Do we still need witnesses? Look. Now you heard His insult.
66 What do you think?" When they answered, they said, "He is eligible to be sentenced to death."
67 Then they spit in His face and slugged Him. The people slapped Him,
68 saying, "Preach to us, Anointed King. Tell us who struck You."
69 But Peter was sitting out in the courtyard. One servant girl came up to him and said, "You also were with Jesus, the Galilean."
70 He denied it in front of everyone. "I don't know what you are saying," he said.
71 When he went out into the gateway, another girl saw him. "This person was there with Jesus, the Nazarene," she said to the people.
72 Again he denied it, this time with an oath. "I don't know the person," he said.
73 After a little while, the people standing there came up to Peter and said, "You truly are one of them. You see, your speech makes it obvious."

74 At that time, he began to vow under the penalty of being doomed and to guarantee, "I don't know the person." Right away a rooster crowed.
75 Peter remembered the statement that Jesus had stated: "Before it is time for the rooster to crow, you will flatly deny Me three times." He went outside and cried bitterly.

27

1 When it became morning, all the head priests and the ethnic group's older men received counsel on how they would put Jesus to death.
2 After they tied Him up, they led Him off to *the Roman leader of that area,* Pilate, and turned Him over to him.
3 At that time, when Judas (the one who turned Him in) saw that He was found guilty, he regretted what he had done and returned the thirty silver coins to the head priests and older men.
4 "I sinned when I turned in blood that is not guilty," he said. But the head priests said, "What is that to us? *It's your problem.* You will see *to it.*"
5 He tossed the silver coins into the temple, took a back way, went off, and hung himself.
6 When the silver coins were given to the head priests, they said, "We aren't allowed to put this into the Corban *(the name of the offering boxes at the temple)* since it is a price of blood *(a payment for someone's life)*."
7 After receiving counsel, they purchased the clay worker's field with it for the burial of strangers.
8 This is why that field was called "Field of Blood." *It was still called that* until the day *that Matthew wrote this.*
9 Then what God stated through the preacher Jeremiah happened. He said, "And they took the thirty silver coins (the amount they had priced one of Israel's sons),
10 and they gave these for the clay worker's field aligned with what the Master dictated to me" *(Zechariah 11:12-13).*
11 *The soldiers* stood Jesus up in front of the Roman leader, and the leader asked Him, "Are You the Jewish people's king?" "You are saying it," declared Jesus.
12 The head priests and older men leveled many complaints against Him, but He answered nothing.
13 At that time, Pilate told Him, "Don't You hear how many things they are saying they witnessed against You?"
14 He didn't respond with even one statement. This really amazed the leader.

15 At each festival, the leader was accustomed to dismissing one prisoner, whoever the crowd wanted.
16 At that time, Barabbas was a well-known prisoner.
17 So since a crowd had gathered, Pilate told them, "Who do you want me to dismiss? Barabbas or Jesus, the One called Anointed King?"
18 You see, he realized that the Jewish leaders turned Him in because they were jealous of Him.
19 As he was seated at the judicial bench, his wife sent out *this message* to him: "Don't do anything to that Person who does what is right. You see, I suffered much today in a dream because of Him."
20 But the head priests and the older men persuaded the crowds to ask that Barabbas be released and Jesus be ruined.
21 When the leader responded, he said, "Which of the two do you want me to dismiss?" The crowds said, "Barabbas."
22 "So what should I do with Jesus," says Pilate, "the One who is called Anointed King?" Everyone says, "He must be nailed to a cross."
23 But the leader was saying, "What did He do that was bad?" They were yelling even louder, "He must be nailed to a cross."
24 When Pilate sees he is not helping the situation but instead a riot is starting, he ends up taking some water. He washed off his hands up in front of the crowd and said, "I am not guilty of this Man's blood. *It is your problem.* You will see *to it.*"
25 When the entire group responded, they said, "His blood is on us and on our children."
26 At that time, he dismissed Barabbas. But he thrashed Jesus with a whip and turned Him over *to the soldiers* so that they would nail Him to a cross.
27 Then the leader's soldiers took Jesus into the Roman palace and gathered the whole regiment together.
28 After they stripped Him, they put a red military cape around Him.
29 They wove an award wreath out of thorns and put it on His head. They put a stick in His right hand. Then they kneeled in front of Him and mocked Him. "Happy to meet You, King of the Jewish people," they said.
30 They spit on Him, took the stick, and were hitting Him on the head.
31 When they were done mocking Him, they stripped the military cape off of Him and put His clothes back on. Then they led Him out to be nailed to a cross.
32 As they came out, they found a Cyrenian man named Simon. They sequestered help from this man so that he might pick up His cross.

33 They went to a place called Golgotha which means "Place of a Skull."
34 They gave Him wine mixed with bile to drink. When He tasted it, He didn't want to drink it.
35 After they nailed Him to a cross, they divided up His clothes by throwing dice.
36 Then they sat down and were keeping guard of Him there.
37 They placed His accusation up above His head. *This was what* had been written, "This is Jesus, the Jewish people's king."
38 At that time, two bandits were also nailed to crosses, one to the right of Him and one to the left.
39 As people traveled by there, they were insulting Him and shaking their heads.
40 "The One who tears the temple down and builds it in three days," they were saying, "rescue Yourself if You are a son of God, and climb down off the cross."
41 The head priests were also mocking Him with the Old Testament transcribers and the older men in the same way.
42 "Others, He rescued," they were saying, "Himself, He can't rescue. Isn't He the King of Israel? He must climb down off the cross now, and we will trust Him.
43 He has been so sure about God. God must save Him now, if He wants Him. You see, He said, 'I am a son of a god.'"
44 The bandits, the ones nailed to crosses together with Him, were also criticizing Him in the same way.
45 At noon, it became dark over all the earth and stayed dark until 3 p.m.
46 Around 3 p.m. Jesus shouted loudly, "Eli, Eli, lema sabachthani?" That is *Aramaic for* "My God, My God, why did You abandon Me?"
47 When some of the people standing there heard it, they were saying, "This Person is hollering for Elijah."
48 Right away, one person from them ran, took a sponge, filled it with sour wine, put it around a stick, and gave Him a drink.
49 "Leave Him alone," everyone else said. "Let's see if Elijah comes to rescue Him."
50 Jesus let out a loud yell again and let the spirit go *(in other words, He died)*.
51 And, look, the temple's curtain tore in two from top to bottom, the earth shook, rocks tore apart,
52 burial vaults opened, and many sacred people's bodies that had fallen asleep got up.

53 (They didn't come out of the cemetery until after Jesus came back to life. At that time, they went into the sacred city and explicitly showed themselves to many.)
54 When the lieutenant and the soldiers with him (who were keeping guard of Jesus) saw the earthquake and what happened, they were terribly afraid. "This truly was a son of a god," they said.
55 Many women were there watching off at a distance. These were the ones that followed Jesus from Galilee and served Him,
56 Mary (the Magdalene), Mary (the mother of James and Joseph), and the mother of Zebedee's sons were among them.
57 In the evening, a wealthy man from Arimathaea named Joseph showed up. He was a student of Jesus.
58 He had gone to Pilate and asked for Jesus' body. At that time, Pilate had ordered *his soldiers* to give *the body* back to him.
59 Joseph took the body, wound a clean linen cloth around it,
60 and put it in his new burial vault that he had chiseled out of rock. He rolled a large stone over the doorway of the burial vault and left.
61 Mary (the Magdalene) and the other Mary were there sitting up in front of the gravesite.
62 The next day, the day that is after the *Festival's* preparation day, the head priests and the Separatists were gathered together facing Pilate.
63 "Master," they said, "we remembered that while that misleader was still alive, He said that He would be gotten up after three days.
64 So order *your soldiers* to secure the gravesite until the third day *is over*. That way His students won't ever go and steal His body, then tell the group that He was gotten up from the dead. If that happens, the last misleading scheme will be worse than the first."
65 "You have a Roman guard unit," Pilate declared. "Lead the way back there, and secure the gravesite however you think *it should be secured.*"
66 The head priests traveled over to the gravesite and secured it by putting a seal on the stone in the presence of the Roman guard unit.

28

1 The evening of the Sabbaths, as it was emerging into Day One *(which is Sunday)* after the Sabbaths, Mary (the Magdalene) and the other Mary went to watch the gravesite.
2 And look, there was a large earthquake. You see, after the Master's angel stepped down from heaven and went to the gravesite, he rolled the stone away and was sitting up on top of it.
3 He looked like lightning, and his attire was white as snow.

4 The soldiers who were keeping guard *of the tomb* shook with fear and became as dead people.

5 When the angel responded, he told the women, "You must not be afraid. You see, I realize that you are looking for Jesus, the One who has been nailed to a cross.

6 He isn't here. You see, God got Him up, just as Jesus said He would. Come. Look at the place where He was lying.

7 And travel quickly and tell His students that God got Him up from the dead and that, look, He is leading the way ahead of you into Galilee. You will see Him there. Look, I told you."

8 They quickly left the burial vault with fear and great happiness and ran to report it to His students.

9 And look, Jesus came to meet them. "Happy to see you," He said. The women came forward, took hold of His feet, and bowed down to Him.

10 "Don't be afraid," said Jesus. "Make your way back. Report to My brothers that I will go off into Galilee and they will see Me there."

11 As they were traveling off, look, some of the Roman guard unit went into the city and reported absolutely everything to the head priests.

12 The head priests gathered with the older men and received counsel *on what to do*. They decided to give an adequate amount of silver coins to the soldiers

13 and tell them, "Say that His students came at night and stole Him as you were sleeping.

14 If the leader hears this, we will persuade him and make it so that you have nothing to worry about."

15 The soldiers took the silver coins and did as they were told. This message *(that His students stole His body)* was thoroughly spread beside the Jewish people up to the day *that Matthew wrote this book*.

16 The eleven students traveled into Galilee to the mountain that Jesus previously arranged with them.

17 When they saw Him, they bowed down. But the people doubted *that it was really Jesus*.

18 Jesus went and spoke to them. "All authority in heaven and on earth was given to Me.

19 So after traveling, make students of all the nations. Submerge them in the name of the Father, the Son, and the Sacred Spirit,

20 and teach them to keep all the things that I demanded you. And look, I will be with you everyday until the very conclusion of the span of time.

Mark

1

1 Here is the beginning of the good news of Jesus, the Anointed King, God's Son.
2 The preacher Isaiah wrote about it. "Look, I am sending My messenger out on a mission before Your face. He will construct Your road" *(Malachi 3:1)*.
3 "A voice is shouting in the backcountry, 'Get the Master's road ready. Make His paths straight'" *(Isaiah 40:3)*.
4 John started submerging people in the backcountry. He was speaking in public about a change-of-ways submersion for forgiveness of sins. *Submersion was a Jewish tradition that ritually cleaned the person being submerged.*
5 All kinds of people from the rural area (Judea) and the Jerusalemites were traveling out to him. He was submerging them in the Jordan River after they admitted their sins out loud.
6 John put on *the same kind of clothes that Elijah and some old-time preachers wore:* clothes made of camel hair and a leather strap around his waist. He ate grasshoppers and wild honey.
7 When he was speaking publicly, he also was saying, "The One who is stronger than me is coming behind me. I am unfit to stoop and untie His sandals' straps.
8 I submerged you in water, but He will submerge you in the Sacred Spirit."
9 In those days, Jesus came from Nazareth, Galilee and was submerged by John in the Jordan *River.*
10 As He stepped up from the water, right away He saw the skies tore open. The Spirit came down to Him as a dove.
11 A voice came from the sky: "You are My loved Son. I am delighted with You."
12 Right away the Spirit threw Him out into the backcountry.
13 He was in the backcountry forty days being harassed by the Opponent. He was with wild animals, and angels were serving Him.
14 After John had been taken into custody, Jesus went into Galilee speaking publicly about God's good news.
15 "The appointed time has come," He said, "and God's monarchy has come near. Change your ways, and trust in the good news."

16 As He was passing along the Sea of Galilee, He saw Simon and Simon's brother (Andrew) throwing a net into the sea. You see, they were fishermen.
17 "Come on behind Me," Jesus told them, "and I will make you into fishermen of people."
18 Right away they left their nets and followed Him.
19 He walked on a little further and saw James (Zebedee's son) and James' brother (John) as they were in their boat mending the nets.
20 Right away He invited them. They left their father Zebedee in the boat with the hired workers and went off behind Him.
21 They traveled into Capernaum. Right away on the Sabbaths, He went into the synagogue and taught.
22 They were impressed with His teaching. You see, He was teaching them as someone with authority would *(as a king or a master would teach the people under him)*. This was not how the Old Testament transcribers taught.
23 Right away in their synagogue, there was a person who had a spirit that was not clean. The spirit yelled out.
24 It said, "Jesus, Nazarene, why are You interfering with us? Did You come to ruin us? I realize who You are, God's Sacred One."
25 Jesus stopped it, "Be quiet, and come out of him," He said.
26 The spirit that wasn't clean sent him into convulsions, hollered loudly, and came out of him.
27 Absolutely everyone was so perplexed that together they were posing questions to each other, "What is this new *way of* teaching *with authority?* He even gives orders to spirits that aren't clean and they obey Him."
28 Right away, talk about Him went out everywhere into the whole surrounding rural area of Galilee.
29 They left the synagogue and right away went into Simon and Andrew's house with James and John.
30 Simon's mother-in-law was lying down with a fever. Right away they told Jesus about her.
31 He went to her, took her hand, and got her up. Her fever left. She served them.
32 In the evening, after the sun set, they were bringing everyone to Him that had something wrong with them and the ones that had lesser deities.
33 The whole city had come together to one place facing the door.

34 He healed many people who had something wrong *with them, who had* various illnesses, and threw out many lesser deities. He wasn't allowing the lesser deities to speak because they knew Him.
35 In the morning while it was still very dark, He got up, left *the house*, went off to an uninhabited place, and was praying there.
36 Simon and the people with him hunted Him down.
37 When Simon found Him, he told Him, "Everyone is looking for You."
38 "Let's take some other way into the next towns," He said, "so that I may speak in public there too. You see, this is why I came out."
39 He went into their synagogues in all of Galilee speaking publicly and throwing out the lesser deities.
40 A man with a skin disease comes up to Him begging Him and kneeling. "If You want to, You are able to clear my skin up," he said.
41 Jesus had sympathy on him. He put out His hand, touched him, and told him, "I want to. Be cleared up."
42 Right away the skin disease went away from him, and he was cleared up.
43 After being stern with him, right away, Jesus threw him out.
44 "Look, don't tell anyone anything," He said. "But make your way back to the priest, show yourself to him, and for the clearing up of your skin disease go through *the eight day process* stipulated by Moses *in Leviticus 14*. That will be a witness to them *of what happened to you.*"
45 But when the man left, he began speaking in public often and thoroughly spreading the message *of what happened to him. He did this* so much that Jesus was no longer able to go into a city without hiding Himself. Instead He was outside in uninhabited places, and people were coming to Him from all directions.

2

1 After a few days, He went into Capernaum again. People heard that He was in a certain house,
2 and many gathered there. There were so many people that there wasn't room for even one more, not even around the door. He was speaking to them about the message.
3 Some people came bringing a disabled man to Him. Four of them carried him.
4 Since they couldn't get to Him because of the crowd, they removed the roof above where He was. After digging it out, they lowered the mattress *through the hole* with the disabled man lying down on it.
5 When Jesus saw their trust, He said to the disabled man, "Child, your sins are forgiven."

6 Some Old Testament transcribers were sitting there and pondering in their hearts:
7 "Why is this Person speaking like this? He is insulting God. *It is obvious that God crippled this man because of some terrible sins.* Who can forgive *those* sins? Only One, God."
8 When Jesus correctly understood with His spirit that this is what they were pondering, right away He told them, "Why are you pondering these things in your hearts?
9 Which is easier to say to the disabled man, 'Your sins are forgiven,' or, 'Get up, pick up your mattress, and walk around?'
10 But so that you may realize that the Son of the Person has authority to be forgiving sins on the earth...." He told the disabled man,
11 "I tell you, get up, pick up your mattress, and make your way back to your house."
12 Right away He got up, picked up his mattress, and went out in front of everyone. Everyone was astounded and praised the magnificence of God. "We have never ever seen anything like this," they said.
13 Jesus went out along the sea again. The entire crowd was coming to Him, and He was teaching them.
14 As He passed by the tax booth, He saw Levi (Alphaeus' son) sitting there. "Follow Me," He told him. Levi got up and followed Him.
15 After that, Jesus happened to be lounging in Levi's house. Many tax collectors and sinful people were feasting and chatting together with Jesus and His students. You see, there were many of them, and they were following Him.
16 When the Separatists' Old Testament transcribers saw that He was eating with sinful people and tax collectors, they were saying to His students, "He is eating with tax collectors and sinful people."
17 When Jesus heard it, He told them, "The people who are healthy and well don't need a doctor, but the people who have something wrong with them do. I didn't come to invite people who do what is right *to live for God*. I came to invite sinful people."
18 John's students and the Separatists' students were abstaining from eating. They came and said to Him, "Why do John's students and the Separatists' students abstain from eating, but Your students don't?"
19 Jesus told them, "The 'sons of the bridal room' *(the people negotiating with the groom for the bride and helping her with the wedding)* can't abstain from eating while the groom is with them, can they? *No, eating is a big part of the negotiation process and the wedding.* As long as the groom is there with them, they can't be abstaining from eating.

20 But days will come when the groom is gone, then they will be able to abstain from eating.

21 No one sews a patch of unprocessed cloth on a well-worn robe. *If they do that,* the *patch* that fills in *the hole* lifts away from it, the new from the well-worn, and the tear becomes worse.

22 And no one puts wine that is in the early stages of fermentation into worn-out leather bags. If they were to do that, the wine would rip the leather bags open, and the wine and the leather bags would be ruined. But they put wine that is in the early stages of fermentation into new leather bags."

23 He happened to be traveling along through the croplands on the Sabbaths. His students began pulling the heads of grain off the plants along the way.

24 "Look," the Separatists said to Him, "what they are doing *is work. Why are they working* on the Sabbaths? That is not allowed."

25 "Have you never even once read," He asked them, "what David and the people with him did when they had a need and were hungry?

26 *Haven't you read* how David went into God's house based on the head priest Abiathar's *approval*, ate the display bread (that no one is allowed to eat except the priests), and also gave it to the people with him? *Do you condemn David for doing that? No.*"

27 "God made the Sabbath for people," He told them. "He didn't make people for the Sabbath.

28 In this way, the Son of the Person is also the Sabbath's master." (*"The Son of the Person" is a generic term Jesus used of Himself. Ezekiel and Daniel were called "son of a person." "Son of a person" is also in Psalm 80:17.*)

3

1 He went into the synagogue again, and a man was there whose hand was shriveled up.

2 They were watching Him closely to see if He would heal him on the Sabbaths so that they might level a complaint against Him.

3 He told the man with the shriveled up hand, "Get up in the middle *of the room.*"

4 Then He turned to the people. "Which is allowed on the Sabbath?" He asked, "To do something good for this man or to do something bad? To rescue a soul or to kill?" But they were silent.

5 After He looked around at them with rage, He was saddened by the hardness of their hearts. "Put out your hand," He told the man. He put it out, and his hand was established back *to normal.*

6 Right away the Separatists and the Herod supporters left. They took counsel against Him on how they might ruin Him.

7 Jesus took a back way to the sea with His students. A very large number of people followed Him. They were from Galilee, Judea,

8 Greater Jerusalem, Idumaea, the other side of the Jordan *River*, and the area around Tyre and Sidon. Large amounts of people were hearing about all the things that He was doing. As they heard, they came to Him.

9 He told His students to have a small boat close by because of the crowd so that they wouldn't give Him a hard time.

10 You see, He healed so many that they were falling on Him. As many as had ailments were trying to touch Him.

11 And whenever the spirits that were not clean saw Him, they were falling toward Him and yelling, "You are the Son of God."

12 He was shushing many *spirits* in them so that they wouldn't show who He is.

13 He climbed up a mountain. *From there,* He called for people He was wanting, and they went off to Him.

14 From these, He made up a group of twelve that He also called missionaries so that they would be with Him and He could send them out on missions to speak publicly

15 and to have the authority to throw out lesser deities. The Twelve were

16 Simon (He gave him the name, Peter *or Rock*),

17 James (Zebedee's son), John (James' brother; He also gave these brothers the name, Boanerges, which is *Hebrew for* Sons of Thunder),

18 Andrew, Philip, Bartholomew, Matthew, Thomas, James (Alphaeus' son), Thaddeus, Simon (the Zealot),

19 and Judas from Kerioth (who also turned Him in). He went into a house,

20 and the crowd came together again in such a way for them not to be able to even eat bread.

21 When the people *who lived* beside Him heard about this, they went out to take Him into custody. You see, they were saying that He is deranged.

22 Old Testament transcribers walked down out of Greater Jerusalem to where He was. They were saying that He has Beelzebub in Him and that is how He throws lesser deities out since Beelzebub is the head of the lesser deities.

23 After calling for them, He was telling them in illustrations, "How is the Opponent able to be throwing the Opponent out?

24 If a monarchy is divided and disagrees with itself, that monarchy cannot be established.
25 And if a house is divided and disagrees with itself, that house won't be able to be established.
26 And if the Opponent stands up against himself and is divided, he can't stand. That would be the conclusion of him.
27 *So I am not throwing out lesser deities with Beelzebub. But I am throwing them out.* No one is able to go into a strong person's house *while he is there* and ransack his stuff unless he first ties him up. Then he can ransack his house.
28 Amen, I tell you that everything will be forgiven to the sons of people, the sins and the insults, however many things they might insult.
29 But whoever insults into the Sacred Spirit doesn't have forgiveness for the span of time. He is eligible for sentencing on sin that spans all time."
30 He said this because they were saying that He has a spirit that is not clean.
31 His mother and brothers came to where He was. As they stood outside, they sent someone out on a mission *to go in and* get Him.
32 Inside, a crowd was sitting around Him. They told Him, "Look, Your mother, brothers, and sisters are outside looking for You."
33 When He answered them, He said, "Who is My mother and brothers?"
34 After looking around at the people sitting in a circle around Him, He said, "Look, My mother and My brothers.
35 You see, whoever does what God wants is My brother, sister, and mother."

4

1 Again He began to teach beside the Sea *of Galilee*, and the biggest crowd gathered. He climbed on board a boat and sat in it so that He could sit and be in the sea. The whole crowd was on the land facing the sea.
2 He was teaching them many things in illustrations. In His teaching, He said,
3 "Listen. Look. The person who plants crops went out to plant. *His method of planting was flinging handfuls of seeds out on the ground throughout the whole field.*
4 As he was flinging seeds, *one* happened to fall along the road, and birds came and ate it.

5 Another *seed* fell on the rocky part where there wasn't much soil. Right away it sprang up because the soil didn't have any depth.
6 When the sun came up, it got hot, and because it didn't have roots, it dried up.
7 Another *seed* fell in thorns. The thorns climbed up, came together, and choked it out. It didn't give any fruit.
8 *There were* others. *This group* fell into nice soil and was giving fruit. It climbed up, grew, and was having fruit: one thirty, one sixty, and one a hundred."
9 He was also saying, "The person who has ears for listening must listen."
10 When He was alone *taking a break*, the people around Him together with the Twelve asked Him about the illustrations.
11 "The secret of God's monarchy," He told them, "has been given to you, but to those outside everything is in illustrations.
12 That way as they look, they can look and not see, and as they hear, they can hear and not understand. They'll never return back and be forgiven."
13 "Don't you know what this illustration shows?" He said. "How will you know all the illustrations?
14 *This illustration shows the different responses people have when they hear God's message.* The person who flings out *the seeds* flings out the message.
15 *When some people hear the message, they reject it.* These are the ones where the seed of the message falls along the road. When they hear it, right away, the Opponent comes and takes the message away that has been planted in them..
16 *When other people hear the message, they accept it for a while.* These are the ones that are flung on the rocky parts. When they hear the message, right away, they receive the message and are happy about it.
17 But the message doesn't have any root in them. It is for the time being. After that, when there are hard times or persecution, right away they stumble.
18 Others are like when the seeds are flung into the thorns. These hear the message,
19 but worry *about the things that happen in this* span of time, the fraud of wealth, and desires for the other things travel in. These come together and choke off the message. It becomes fruitless.

20 Others are like when the seeds are flung on the nice soil. They hear the message and warmly welcome it. They produce fruit: one thirty, one sixty, and one a hundred."

21 He was also telling them, "A lamp doesn't come into a room to be placed under the two gallon measuring basket or under the cot, does it? No, it comes into a room to be placed up high on a stand.

22 You see, something is not hidden if it can't ever be shown. Someone hides something away so that someday it might be shown.

23 If anyone has ears for listening, he must listen."

24 He was also telling them, "Watch what kind of things you listen to. The amount that you measure out will be measured to you and added to you.

25 You see, the person who has will get. And the person who doesn't have, even what he has will be taken away from him."

26 He was also saying, "God's monarchy is like this, like a person who threw a batch of seeds on the ground.

27 Day and night he slept and got up. The batch of seeds budded and grew taller. How? He doesn't know.

28 The earth automatically produces fruit: first a stem, after that a head of grain, then full grain in the head of grain.

29 But when the fruit turned up, right away he sent out the sickle *to harvest it* because the harvest had offered itself to him."

30 He was also saying, "How will we show what God's monarchy is like? Or in what illustration will we put it?

31 It is as a mustard kernel, that, when it is planted in the earth, it is littler than all *kinds of* seeds on the earth.

32 Yet whenever it is planted, it climbs up and becomes greater than all *kinds of* vegetables. It makes large branches so that the birds of the sky can nest under its shadow."

33 He was speaking the message to them with many of these types of illustrations, just what they were able to hear.

34 He wasn't speaking to them without an illustration. But He explained everything to His students when they were by themselves.

35 When evening came that day, He told them, "We will go across to the other side."

36 They left the crowd and took Him along in the boat since He was already in it. There were other boats with them.

37 A large blast of wind came. It was throwing the swells up into the boat in such a way for the boat to already be full of water.

38 He was in the back of the boat on the cushion sleeping. They got Him up and said, "Teacher, aren't you concerned that we are getting destroyed?"
39 When He was wide awake, He shushed the wind and told the sea, "Silence. Be quiet." The wind stopped blowing, and it became very calm.
40 "Why are you cowards?" He asked them. "Don't you have trust yet?"
41 They feared great fear. "So who is this?" they were saying to each other, "because even the wind and the sea obey Him?"

5

1 They went to the other side *(the eastern side)* of the Sea *of Galilee* to the rural area of the Gerasenes.
2 When He came out of the boat, right away a man who had a spirit that was not clean came to Him from the cemetery.
3 He was living in the cemetery. No one could chain him up anymore
4 because he had been locked up many times with foot shackles and chains, but he pulled the chains apart and crushed the foot shackles. No one was strong enough to tame him.
5 Through it all, night and day, he was yelling and cutting himself with stones in the graves and in the mountains.
6 When he had seen Jesus off at a distance, he ran and bowed down to Him.
7 He let out a loud yell and said, "What are You here for, Jesus, son of God, the Highest? I place you under an oath with God not to torture me."
8 You see, Jesus was telling it, "You, the spirit that is not clean, come out of the man."
9 He also was asking it, "What is your name?" "My name is Legion," it said, "because there are many of us. *(Legion is the Latin word for regiment.)*
10 And it was begging Him much to not send them outside of the rural area.
11 A large herd of hogs were there toward the mountain, grazing.
12 "Send us into the hogs," they begged Him, "so that we might go into them."
13 He gave them permission to go. When the spirits that were not clean came out, they went into the hogs, and the herd of about two thousand hogs rushed down the steep slope into the sea. There they drowned.

14 The people grazing them escaped *from the stampede* into the fields and the city. There they reported what had happened. The people from the fields and the city came to see it.
15 They are coming to Jesus and watching the man who has the lesser deities. The man who had the legion is sitting, clothed and sane. They were afraid.
16 Those who had seen what happened to the man and the hogs described it all to them.
17 They began to beg Him to leave their border area.
18 As He was climbing on board the boat, the man who had the lesser deities was begging Jesus to let him come along.
19 He didn't let him. Instead, He told him, "Make your way back to your people into your house, and report to them how much the Master has done for you and that He showed you forgiving kindness."
20 He went away and began speaking publicly in Decapolis about how much Jesus had done for him. Everyone was amazed.
21 After Jesus crossed all the way back over *the Sea of Galilee* in the boat, a big crowd gathered to hear Him. He again was beside the sea.
22 One of the synagogue's head rulers with the name Jairus came. When he saw Jesus, he got down on the ground facing His feet
23 and begged Him much. "My little daughter is dying," he said. "Please come and place Your hands on her so that she might be rescued and live."
24 Jesus went off with him. A big crowd was following Him and squeezing in on Him.
25 There was a woman who had been bleeding for twelve years.
26 She had suffered through many treatments from many doctors and spent everything she had, but she was not any better. Instead, she was getting worse.
27 When she heard about Jesus, she came up from behind in the crowd and touched His robe.
28 You see, she was telling herself, "If I just touch His robe, I will be rescued *from this bleeding*."
29 Right away the spring of her blood dried up, and she knew in her body that she had been cured from the ailment.
30 Right away Jesus recognized in Himself that *some type of* ability had gone out of Him. He turned around in the crowd. "Who touched My robe?" He said.
31 His students told Him, "You see how the crowd is squeezing in on You. How are You saying, 'Who touched Me?'"
32 He was looking around trying to see who did it.

33 But the woman, who had been afraid and was trembling, realized what had happened to her. She came, got down *on the ground* facing Him, and told Him the whole truth.
34 "Daughter, your trust has rescued you," Jesus told her. "Make your way back home in peace and be well from your ailment."
35 As He was still speaking, people from the head ruler's house came. "Your daughter died," they said. "Why irritate the teacher anymore?"
36 When Jesus overheard the message, He told the head ruler, "Don't be afraid. Just trust."
37 He only allowed Peter, James, and John (James' brother) to follow along with Him.
38 They went into the head ruler's house. He watched the disturbance caused by people crying and clanging things.
39 He went into the room and said, "Why are you causing a disturbance and crying? The young child isn't dead. She's sleeping."
40 They were laughing at Him. He threw everyone out. He took the father, the mother, and the *three* along with Him and traveled into where the young child was.
41 He took hold of the young child's hand and told her, "Talitha Cumi," which is *Aramaic* and translated as "Girl, I tell you, get up."
42 Right away the girl got up and started walking around. You see, she was twelve years old. They were immediately astounded with great astonishment.
43 He warned them much not to let anyone know about this and told them to give her something to eat.

6

1 He left there and went to His hometown. His students followed Him.
2 When the Sabbath came, He began to teach in the synagogue, and many listening were impressed. "Where does this Man get these things from?" they said. "What is the insight that has been given to this Man? What are these types of abilities that His hands do?
3 Isn't this the builder? Isn't He Mary's son? Isn't He the brother of James, Joses *(Joseph)*, Judah *(Jude)*, and Simon? Aren't His sisters living here with us?" They were stumbling on Him.
4 "A preacher is only worthless," Jesus told them, "in his hometown, among his relatives, and in his house."
5 He wasn't able to show even one of His abilities there, except that He placed His hands on a few sick people and healed them.

6 He was amazed at their lack of trust and was taking His students around to the circling villages, teaching.

7 He called for the Twelve and began to send them out on missions, two by two. He gave them authority over the spirits that are not clean.

8 He ordered them not to take anything for the road except a staff: no bread, no tote bag, no copper in their money belts *(that could be used as money)*.

9 "But put some shoes on and don't put on two shirts," He also told them.

10 "Whenever you go into a house, stay there until you leave that village.

11 If a place doesn't accept you or listen to you, as you travel out from there, shake off the dirt beneath your feet for a witness to them. *Don't tell them they are wrong. Don't argue with them. Just shake off the dirt. That is enough.*

12 They went out to the places where Jesus sent them and spoke publicly telling them to change their ways.

13 They threw many lesser deities out, dabbed olive oil on many sick people, and healed them.

14 King Herod heard about it. You see, *Jesus'* name became well known. "The John who submerges," he said, "has come back to life from the dead. That's why the abilities are active in Him."

15 But others were saying, "He is Elijah," and others, "He is a preacher who is like one of the preachers *in the Bible*."

16 After Herod listened to them, he was saying, "This is John that I beheaded. He has come back to life."

17 You see, Herod himself had sent someone out to arrest John and to lock him up in jail because of Herodias. Herod had married Herodias even though she was his brother Philip's wife.

18 John had been telling Herod, "You are not allowed to have your brother's wife."

19 Herodias was holding a grudge against John. She was wanting to kill him, but couldn't.

20 You see, Herod was cautious of John. He realized that John was a man who does what is right and is sacred. He was preserving him. When he listened to him, he wasn't sure what to think about many things, and so he was gladly listening to him.

21 *But Herodias hatched a special plan.* A well-timed day came during Herod's birthday celebrations. On that day, Herod threw a feast for his

greatest people, the commanding officers, and the most important people of Galilee.

22 Herodias' daughter went in and danced for them. Herod and those feasting and chatting together with him liked it. "Ask me for whatever you want," the king told the girl, "and I will give it to you."

23 He guaranteed it to her *by saying*, "I will give you whatever you ask for, up to half of my monarchy."

24 After she left, she asked her mother, "What will I ask for?" Her mother said, "The head of the John who submerges."

25 Right away, she went in a hurry to the king with her request. "I want you to immediately give me John the Submerger's head on a plate," she said.

26 The king was overcome with sadness, but because of the oaths and the people feasting and chatting there, he didn't want to disregard her request.

27 Right away the king sent a bodyguard out after giving him the order to bring his head. He went out and beheaded him in jail.

28 He brought his head on a plate and gave it to the girl, and the girl gave it to her mother.

29 When John's students heard what had happened, they went, took his corpse, and put it in a burial vault.

30 The missionaries returned *from their missions* and gathered around Jesus. They reported everything to Him, what they did and what they taught.

31 "Come on," He told them, "let's all go off by ourselves to an uninhabited place and relax for a little while." You see, there were so many people coming and making their way back *home* that they didn't even have a good time to eat.

32 They went off in the boat to an uninhabited place by themselves.

33 Many watched them make their way back and correctly understood where they were going. *People* from all of the cities ran there together on foot. They went on ahead of them.

34 Jesus came out of the boat and saw a big crowd. He had sympathy for them because they were like sheep without a shepherd. He began to teach them many things.

35 After it had already gotten late, His students came to Him. "This place is uninhabited," they were saying, "and it is already a late hour.

36 Dismiss the people so that they can go off into the circling fields and villages and buy themselves something to eat."

37 When Jesus answered, He told them, "You must give them something to eat." "We could go off," they told Him, "and buy two hundred denarii *($10,000)* worth of bread for them to eat."
38 "How many loaves of bread do you have?" Jesus said to them. "Make your way back. Look and see." When they knew, they said, "Five loaves and two fish."
39 He gave them the order for everyone to recline in social groups on the green grass.
40 They settled down in plots of hundreds and fifties.
41 He took the five loaves of bread and the two fish, looked up into the sky, and conferred a blessing on them. He split the bread up and was giving it to His students so that they could pass it out to everyone. He also divided the two fish out to everyone.
42 Everyone ate until they were full.
43 They picked up the bread pieces and fish, and it filled twelve baskets.
44 The number of men who ate the loaves of bread was five thousand.
45 Right away He urged his students to climb on board the boat and lead the way ahead to the other side, to Bethsaida, while He dismissed the crowd.
46 After He said good-bye to the crowd, He went off into the mountain to pray.
47 When evening came, the boat was in the middle of the sea, and He was alone on the land.
48 He saw them being tortured in rowing the boat forward (you see, the wind was blowing against them). In the fourth guard shift of the night *(3 - 6 a.m.)*, He came to them walking around on the sea. He was wanting to pass on by them.
49 But when they saw Him walking around on the sea, they thought it was a ghost, and they yelled out.
50 You see, everyone saw Him, and they were uneasy. But right away Jesus spoke with them. "Be courageous," He told them. "It's Me. Don't be afraid."
51 He climbed up to them into the boat, and the wind stopped blowing. They were very astounded *that Jesus could do something like that*.
52 You see, they didn't understand what the loaves of bread had shown, *that Jesus can do supernatural things*. Their hearts had become hard as stone.
53 When they had crossed all the way over and had come to the land, they sailed over to a town called Gennesaret and anchored there.

54 When they came out of the boat, right away people recognized Him.
55 They ran around that whole rural area and began to carry people who had something wrong with them on mattresses around to where they had heard that He is.
56 And wherever He was traveling into villages, into cities, or into fields, they were placing the people in frail health in the marketplaces and encouraging Him to let them just touch the fringe of His robe. However many touched Him were being rescued.

7

1 The Separatists and some of the Old Testament transcribers from Greater Jerusalem were gathered to Him.
2 They saw that some of His students ate bread with contaminated hands, that is with unwashed hands. (*Contaminated hands are hands that are no longer sacred because they have touched something that is not sacred.*)
3 You see, the Separatists and all the Jewish people don't eat unless they wash their hands *by scrubbing each hand* with a fist. This keeps a tradition that the older men *created to make their hands sacred*.
4 Also after coming from the marketplace, they don't eat unless they submerge themselves in water. There are many other things that they brought along to hold onto, *like* submerging cups, pots, copper items, and cots.
5 "Why don't Your students walk around aligned with the older men's tradition?" the Separatists and the Old Testament transcribers asked Him. "Why do they eat bread with contaminated hands?"
6 "What Isaiah preached fits you fakers nicely," He told them. "He wrote, 'This ethnic group values Me with their lips, but their heart keeps itself far away from Me.
7 Their worship of Me is futile because the instructions that they teach are people's regulations, *not Mine*' (Isaiah 29:13).
8 You leave God's demand and keep the people's tradition."
9 He also told them, "You conveniently disregard God's demand so that you can establish your tradition.
10 You see, Moses said, 'Value your father and mother' *(Exodus 20:12)* and 'The person who says bad things to a father or mother must pass away in death' *(Exodus 21:17).*
11 But you say that if a man tells his father or mother, '*The money* that I should have supported you with is a Corban, a contribution *to God*,'

12 he is allowed by you to no longer do anything for his father or mother.
13 In this way, you nullify God's message with your tradition that you give out. You are doing many things like this."
14 After He called for the crowd again, He was saying to them, "Listen to Me everyone, and understand.
15 There is nothing outside of a person traveling into him that can contaminate him, but the things traveling out from a person are what contaminates him."
16 [[["If anyone has ears for listening, he must listen."]]]
17 When He went into a house away from the crowd, his students were asking Him to explain the illustration.
18 "Are you also clueless like them?" He said to them. "Aren't you aware that everything on the outside traveling into a person can't contaminate him
19 because it is not traveling into his heart, but into his belly, and it travels out into the sewer? *Since food never travels into his heart,* all food is clean. *Food doesn't affect how sacred a person is.*
20 What contaminates a person is the thing that travels out from him.
21 You see, bad ponderings travel out from the inside, from the heart of people: sexual sins, thefts, murders,
22 times when someone cheats on a spouse, desires for more, evils, deception, indulgent activity, an evil eye, an insult, pride, and distraction.
23 All these evil things travel out from the inside and contaminate the person."
24 When He got up from there, He went off to Tyre's border area. When He went into a house, He didn't want anyone to know about it. But He was not able to go unnoticed.
25 Right away a woman heard about Him. Her little daughter had a spirit that was not clean. She came and got down at His feet.
26 The woman was Greek, *not Jewish*. She was born in Phoenicia, Syria. She was asking Him to throw the lesser deity out of her daughter.
27 "First, allow the children to eat until they are full," He was telling her. "You see, it isn't nice to take the children's bread and throw it to the puppies."
28 "Master," she answered, "even the puppies beneath the table are allowed to eat the crumbs that the young children drop."
29 "Because of this answer, make your way back," He told her. "The lesser deity has come out of your daughter."

30 When she went off to her house, she found that her child had been thrown on the cot and that the lesser deity had come out.

31 He again left Tyre's border area and went through Sidon to the Sea of Galilee up to the middle of Decapolis' border area.

32 They brought a hearing-impaired and tongue-tied man to Him and begged Him to place His hand on him.

33 After He took him off away from the crowd by Himself, He put his fingers into his ears, spit, and touched his tongue.

34 He looked up into the sky, groaned, and told him, "Ephphatha" (that is *Aramaic for,* "Open completely").

35 Right away his hearing opened up, his tongue's restraint was removed, and he was speaking correctly.

36 Jesus warned them not to tell anyone about it. But as much as He was warning them, the more they were speaking publicly.

37 They were even more impressed with this incredible thing. "He has done everything nicely," they were saying. "He makes both hearing-impaired people to hear, and nonspeaking people to speak."

8

1 In those days as there again was a big crowd and they didn't have anything to eat, Jesus called for His students and told them,

2 "I have sympathy for the crowd because they have already stayed here with Me for three days and they don't have anything to eat.

3 If I dismiss them to go home with nothing to eat, they will have a hard time on their way back, and some of them have arrived from a long way away."

4 His students responded to Him *by asking,* "Where will anyone be able to get enough bread here in this uninhabited place to feed these people?"

5 "How much bread do you have?" asked Jesus. They said, "Seven loaves."

6 He passed the order on to the crowd to settle down on the ground. Then He took the seven loaves of bread, and after He was thankful, He split them and was giving them to His students so that they could pass them out to the crowd.

7 They also had a few small fish. After He conferred a blessing on them, He told *His students* to also pass them out.

8 They ate until they were full. Then they picked up seven large baskets of leftover pieces.

9 There were about four thousand. After this, He dismissed them.

10 Right away, He climbed on board the boat with His students and went to parts of Dalmanutha *(an area on the western shore of the Sea of Galilee)*.

11 The Separatists came out and together began to pose questions to Him. They were harassing Him looking for a proof directly from Him *coming* out of the sky.

12 Groaning deeply to His spirit, He said, "Why is this generation searching for proof? Amen, I tell you, if proof will be given to this generation, *it won't accept it*."

13 He left them again, climbed back on board the boat, and went off to the other side.

14 They had forgotten to get *some more* loaves of bread. There was only one loaf left on the boat.

15 At this time, Jesus was warning them, saying, "Look. Watch out for the Separatists' yeast and Herod's yeast."

16 They started pondering toward each other that He said this because they had not brought *enough* loaves of bread.

17 When He knew it, He told them, "Why are you pondering that you don't have *enough* loaves of bread? Aren't you aware yet *of what happened?* Don't you even understand? Has your heart become hard as stone?

18 You have eyes. Don't you see? And you have ears. Don't you hear? And don't you remember?

19 When I split the five loaves of bread for the five thousand, how many full baskets of pieces did you pick up?" "Twelve," they said.

20 "When I split the seven for the four thousand, how many full large baskets of pieces did you pick up?" "Seven," they said.

21 He kept saying, "Don't you understand yet?"

22 As they were coming into Bethsaida, some people brought a blind man to Jesus and begged Him to touch him.

23 He latched on to the blind man's hand and took him outside of the village. He spit on his eyes, placed His hands on him, and was asking him, "Do you see anything?"

24 He looked up and was saying, "I see people walking around as trees."

25 After that, He placed His hands on his eyes again. He looked intensively at him and reestablished his vision. He was seeing absolutely all far away things clearly.

26 He sent him out to his house and said, "Don't go into the village."

27 Then Jesus and His students went out to the villages of Philip's Caesarea. On the road He was asking His students, "Who do the people say that I am?"
28 "John the Submerger, Elijah, or one of the preachers," they told Him.
29 "But you, who do you say that I am?" He was asking them. When Peter answered, he told Him, "You are the Anointed King."
30 He shushed them so that they wouldn't tell anyone about Him.
31 He began to teach them that it is necessary for the Son of the Person to suffer many things, to be rejected by the older men, the head priests, and the Old Testament transcribers, to be killed, and to get up after three days.
32 He was speaking the message with a clear public statement, so Peter took Him aside and began telling Him to stop it.
33 But Jesus turned around, looked at His students, and told Peter to stop it. "Make your way back behind Me, opponent," He said, "because you don't focus on God's things. You focus on people's things."
34 He called the crowd together with His students and told them, "If anyone wants to follow behind Me, he must flatly deny himself, pick up his cross *(or in other words, be ready to die for Me)*, and follow Me.
35 You see, whoever wants to rescue his soul will lose it, but whoever will lose his soul on account of Me and the good news will rescue it.
36 You see, what benefit is it to a person if he gains the whole world and sustains loss to his soul?
37 You see, what will a person give in exchange for his soul?
38 If anyone is ashamed of Me and My messages in this cheating and sinful generation, the Son of the Person will also be ashamed of him when He comes in His Father's magnificence with the sacred angels."

9

1 He was telling them, "Amen, I tell you that some people standing here will not in any way taste death until they see God's monarchy come in its ability."
2 Six days later, Jesus took Peter, James, and John along with Him and brought them up into a high mountain by themselves. His appearance changed there in front of them.
3 His clothes became very sparkling white, so *white* that no laundry on earth can whiten that *white*.
4 They saw Elijah together with Moses and they were speaking together with Jesus.
5 "Rabbi," responded Peter, "it is nice for us to be here. Let's make three tents: one for You, one for Moses, and one for Elijah."

6 You see, he didn't know how he should respond. They were frightened.
7 A bright cloud formed and shined over them. A voice came from the cloud, "This is My loved Son. Listen to Him."
8 All of a sudden when they looked around, they didn't see anyone with them anymore except Jesus.
9 As they walked down from the mountain, He warned them not to describe what they saw to anyone except when the Son of the Person has gotten up from the dead.
10 They grabbed on to the message and together posed questions to each other about what it meant for the Son of the Person to get up from the dead.
11 *Since they had just seen Elijah,* they also asked Jesus, "Why do the Old Testament transcribers say that it is necessary for Elijah to come first."
12 "Why?" declared Jesus, "because when Elijah certainly comes first, he reestablishes everything. And how is it that the Bible says that the Son of the Person will suffer many things and be treated as a nobody?
13 But I tell you that even Elijah has come, and they did to him as much as they wanted, just as the Bible says."
14 When they came to the students, they saw a big crowd around them. Old Testament transcribers together were posing questions to them.
15 Right away when the entire crowd saw Him, they were puzzled, and, running up, they were greeting Him.
16 "What were you together posing questions to them about?" He asked.
17 One man from the crowd answered Him, "Teacher, I brought my son to You. He has a nonspeaking spirit.
18 Wherever it takes him down, it rips him, he foams at the mouth, he grits his teeth, and he is shriveled up. I told Your students that they should throw it out, but they couldn't."
19 "O untrusting generation," Jesus responded, "how long do I have to be near you? How long do I have to tolerate you? Bring him to Me."
20 They brought him to Him, and when he saw Him, right away the spirit sent him into violent convulsions. He fell on the ground and was rolling around, foaming at the mouth.
21 "How much time *has it been* since this came to him?" asked Jesus. "From childhood," his father said.
22 "Many times it has also thrown him into fire and into water to ruin him. But if you are able to do something, have sympathy on us and help us."

23 "The thing is whether you are able," Jesus told him. "Everything is possible for the person who trusts."
24 Right away, the father cried out, "I trust. Help my untrust."
25 When Jesus saw that a crowd was quickly gathering around them, He stopped the spirit that was not clean by saying, "nonspeaking and hearing-impaired spirit, I order you, come out of him, and don't go back into him anymore."
26 After it yelled and sent him into many convulsions, it came out. It was as if he were dead, so much so that many were saying that he had died.
27 But Jesus took hold of his hand and got him up. He stood up.
28 When He and His students went into a house and they were by themselves, they were asking Him, "Why weren't we able to throw it out?"
29 "This kind can't go out in any way except in prayer," He told them.
30 When they left that place, they were traveling along through Galilee, and He didn't want anyone to know.
31 You see, He was teaching His students. He also told them, "The Son of the Person will be taken into custody by the people. They will kill him, and after He is dead for three days, He will be gotten up."
32 They were unaware of what that statement meant and were afraid to ask Him.
33 They went into Capernaum. When they were in the house, He was asking them, "What were you pondering on the road?"
34 But they kept silent. You see, on the road, they had discussions toward each other *about* who is greater.
35 He sat down and hollered for the Twelve. "If anyone wants to be first," He told them, "he will be last of all and servant of all."
36 He took a young child and stood him in the middle of them. Then He took him in His arms and told them,
37 "Whoever accepts one of these types of young children based on My name is accepting Me. Whoever is accepting Me, isn't accepting Me-- he is accepting the One who sent Me out on this mission."
38 "Teacher, we saw someone throwing lesser deities out in Your name," John declared, "and we were keeping him from doing it because he wasn't following us."
39 But Jesus said, "Don't keep him from doing it. You see, there is no one who will do an ability based on My name and will be able to quickly say bad things about Me.
40 The person who is not against us is over with us.

41 You see, whoever gives you a cup of water to drink in My name because you are the Anointed King's, amen, I tell you that he will not in any way lose his pay.

42 And whoever causes one of these little ones who trust in Me to stumble, it would have been better for him if instead a millstone (the kind turned by a donkey) had been put around his neck and he had been thrown into the sea.

43 If your hand causes you to stumble, chop it off. Which is better for you? To go into life physically wounded, or having two hands to go off into the Hinnom Valley, into the unextinguished fire? *(The Hinnom Valley ran along the southwestern edge of Jerusalem. At one time children were burned to death there as sacrifices to idols. It is symbolic of the eternal lake of fire.)*

44 [[[Where their maggot doesn't pass away and the fire isn't extinguished.]]]

45 And if your foot causes you to stumble, chop it off. Which is better for you? To go into life crippled, or having two feet to be thrown into the Hinnom Valley?

46 [[[Where their maggot doesn't pass away and the fire isn't extinguished.]]]

47 And if your eye causes you to stumble, throw it out. Which is better for you? To go into God's monarchy one-eyed, or having two eyes to be thrown into the Hinnom Valley?

48 Where their maggot doesn't pass away and the fire isn't extinguished.

49 You see, everyone will be salted with fire *(with problems). Your reaction to problems influences your flavor.*

50 The salt flavor is nice. But if the salt flavor has somehow become not salty, what will you season food with? You must have *My* flavor among yourselves, and you must be peaceful among each other.

10

1 When He got up from there, He went to Judea's border area and to the other side of the Jordan River. Crowds again traveled together to where He was, and as He was accustomed to doing, He again was teaching them.

2 Separatists came forward and were harassing Him by asking if a husband is allowed to dismiss a wife.

3 "What was Moses' demand to you?" responded Jesus.

4 "Moses gave us permission to write up a divorce decree and to dismiss," they said.

5 "He wrote you this demand for your hardheartedness," Jesus told them.
6 "But from the beginning of creation, He made them male and female.
7 On account of this, a person will leave his father and mother and stick like glue to his wife.
8 The two will be in one physical body. In such a way, they are no longer two, but one physical body.
9 So what God strapped together, a person must not separate."
10 Again in the house, His students were asking Him about this.
11 "Whoever dismisses his wife *without a divorce*," He told them, "and marries another is cheating on the wife *that he dismissed*.
12 And if she, after dismissing her husband *(without a divorce)*, marries another, she is cheating on her husband."
13 People were bringing young children to Him so that He might touch them, but the students stopped them.
14 When Jesus saw it, He was frustrated. "Leave the young children alone," He told them, "so that they can come to Me. Don't keep them from coming to Me. You see, *children find it easy to trust.* God's monarchy is made up of these types of children.
15 Amen, I tell you, whoever does not accept God's monarchy as a young child will not in any way go into it."
16 He took them in His arms and was conferring a blessing on each one by placing His hands on them.
17 As He was traveling out to a road, someone ran up to Him, kneeled, and was asking, "Good Teacher, what will I do so that I might inherit life that spans all time?"
18 "Why are you calling Me good?" said Jesus. "No one is good except One, God.
19 You know the Demands: You won't murder, you won't cheat on your spouse, you won't steal, you won't lie when you are a witness, you won't rob, you must value your father and mother."
20 "Teacher," he declared, "I have observed all of these from my youth."
21 Jesus looked at him and loved him. "You are lacking one thing," He told him. "Make your way back home, sell everything you have, give to the poor (and you will have a stockpile of treasure in heaven), and come, follow Me." *You see, the one thing he lacked was trust.*
22 But he was disappointed with the answer and went away sad. You see, he had many properties. *He couldn't follow Jesus because these properties required his daily attention.*

23 After Jesus looked around, He told His students, "How hard it will be for the people who have stacks of money as they go into God's monarchy!"
24 The students were perplexed at His words. "Children," Jesus again responded, "how hard it is to go into God's monarchy!
25 It is easier for a camel to go through the eye of a needle than for a wealthy man to go into God's monarchy."
26 This stunned them even more. "And who can be rescued?" they were saying to each other.
27 Jesus looked at them and said, "With people it is impossible, but not with God. You see, everything is possible with God."
28 Peter began to tell Him, "Look, we left everything and followed You."
29 "Amen, I tell you," declared Jesus, "There is not one person who left a house, brothers, sisters, a mother, a father, children, or fields on account of Me and on account of the good news
30 who will not now in this time receive a hundred times more (houses, brothers, sisters, mothers, children, and fields) with persecutions, and in the coming span of time, life that spans all time.
31 Many who are first will be last, and the last first."
32 They were on the road walking up to Jerusalem and Jesus was leading the way ahead of them. They were perplexed. *Jesus usually didn't walk in front by Himself.* Those who were following were afraid. When He brought the Twelve up alongside of Him again, He began telling them the things that were going to come together and happen to Him.
33 "Look, I am walking up to Jerusalem. The Son of the Person will be turned over to the head priests and the Old Testament transcribers. They will find Him guilty and deserving of death, and turn Him over to the non-Jews.
34 They will mock Him, spit on Him, whip Him, kill Him, and after three days, He will be gotten up."
35 James and John (the sons of Zebedee) traveled to Him, "Teacher," they said, "we want *You to do us a favor,* that You would do whatever we might request?"
36 "What do you want?" asked Jesus.
37 "Give us *two seats,*" they told Him, "one on the right *of Your throne* and one on the left *when You are king* in Your magnificence."
38 "You don't know what you are asking for," Jesus told them. "Can you drink the cup that I am drinking or be submerged in the submersion that I am submerged in?"

39 "Yes, we can," they told Him. But Jesus told them, "You will drink the cup that I drink, and you will be submerged in the submersion that I am submerged in,
40 but the seats to my right and left are not Mine to give. They are for the people that they have been prepared for."
41 When the other ten heard about this, they began to get frustrated about James and John.
42 Jesus called for them and told them, "You realize that the people who seem to be the head of the non-Jews act like masters over them and their powerful people put themselves in places of authority over them.
43 This is not how it is among you. Whoever wants to become great among you will be your servant.
44 And whoever wants to be first will be everyone's slave.
45 You see, the Son of the Person also didn't come to be served. He came to serve and to give His soul as a payment for the release of many."
46 They were going from *residential* Jericho *to municipal Jericho. They were about two miles apart.* As He, His students, and an adequate crowd traveled out from *residential* Jericho, Bartimaeus (a blind beggar), the son of Timaeus, was sitting alongside the road.
47 When he heard that it was Jesus, the Nazarene, he began to yell, "Son of David, Jesus, show me forgiving kindness." *(Son of David is a less specific term for Anointed King or Messiah.)*
48 Many were shushing him so that he would be quiet, but he was yelling even more, "Son of David, show me forgiving kindness."
49 Jesus stopped and said, "Holler for him." They hollered for the blind man. "Be courageous," they told him. "Get up. He is hollering for you."
50 He threw off his robe, stood up, and went to Jesus.
51 "What do you want Me to do?" responded Jesus. "Rabboni *(which means Great Rabbi)*, that I might see again," the blind man told Him.
52 "Make your way back," Jesus told him. "Your trust has rescued you." Right away he saw again and was following Him on the road.

11

1 When they are near to Jerusalem, near Bethphage and Bethany, headed toward the Mount of Olives *(a hill just east of Jerusalem)*, He sends two of His students out on a mission.
2 "Make your way back into the village directly facing you," He tells them, "and right away as you travel into it, you will find a foal *(a young*

donkey) that has been tied up. Not one person has sat on it yet. Untie it and bring it here.

3 If anyone asks, 'Why are you doing this?' say, 'The Master needs it. *He would like to use it* and right away to send it back here again.'"

4 They went off and found a foal that had been tied to a door outside on the road around the village. As they were untying it,

5 some of the people standing there asked them, "What are you doing untying the foal?"

6 The students told them just as Jesus had said, and they let them take it.

7 They led the foal to Jesus, they threw their robes on it, and He sat on it.

8 Many spread out their robes on the road. Others chopped down vegetation from the fields.

9 People were leading the way ahead of Him and people were following Him. They were yelling *a chant*, "Hosanna! *O, rescue us!* The One coming in the Master's name has been conferred with blessings!

10 Our father David's coming monarchy has been conferred with blessings! Hosanna in the highest!"

11 He went into Jerusalem onto the temple grounds. He looked around at everything, and since it was already evening, He went out to Bethany with the Twelve.

12 The next day when they left Bethany, He was hungry.

13 When He saw a fig tree off at a distance with leaves, He went up to it *wondering* if maybe He will find some figs on it. When He got there, He found nothing except leaves. You see, *fig trees produce figs before they get leaves, so this tree should have had figs even though* it was not the time for figs.

14 He responded by telling it, "No one will eat fruit from you anymore for the span of time." His students were listening.

15 They went into Jerusalem. When He went onto the temple grounds, He began to throw out the people buying and selling on the temple grounds. He turned over the currency exchange tables and the benches of the people selling doves.

16 He stayed there and would not let anyone carry a container through the temple grounds.

17 He started teaching them with these words, "Doesn't the Bible say, 'My house will be called a house of prayer for all the nations?' *(Isaiah 56:7)*. But you have made it a cave of bandits."

18 The head priests and the Old Testament transcribers heard *about this* and were looking for a way to ruin Him. You see, they were afraid of Him because the entire crowd was impressed with His teaching.
19 Each day when evening came, He was traveling out of the city.
20 As they were traveling along in the morning, they saw the fig tree. It had dried up from its roots.
21 When Peter was again reminded of the tree, he said, "Rabbi, look, the fig tree that you put a curse on has dried up."
22 Jesus responded by telling them, "You must have a trust of God."
23 "Amen, I tell you that whoever says to this mountain, 'You must get picked up and you must be thrown into the sea,' and in his heart does not consider it to be wrong, but trusts that what he speaks is happening, it will belong to him.
24 Because of this, I tell you, everything that you pray and ask for, trust that you received it, and it will belong to you.
25 Whenever you stand praying, if you have anything against anyone, you must forgive so that your Father in heaven also might forgive you of your infractions."
26 [[["But if you don't forgive, your Father in heaven won't forgive your infractions either."]]]
27 Again they came into Jerusalem. As He was walking around on the temple grounds, the head priests, the Old Testament transcribers, and the older men came to Him.
28 "With what kind of authority are You doing these things?" they were asking Him. "Or who gave You this authority so that You may do these things?"
29 "I will ask you one question," Jesus told them. "Answer that question, and I will state to you with what kind of authority I am doing these things.
30 John's submersion, was it from heaven or from people? Answer Me."
31 They expressed their concerns to themselves. "If we say 'from heaven', He will state, 'So why didn't you trust him?'
32 But *if* we say 'from people'"--they were afraid of the crowd. You see, absolutely everyone held that John really was a preacher.
33 "We don't know," they answered. "And I am not telling you with what kind of authority I am doing these things either," Jesus told them.

12

1 He began to speak to them in illustrations. "A person planted a vineyard, put a barrier wall around it, dug a trough beneath the grape-smashing floor, and built a tower.

He gave it out to farmers *who agreed to pay him a percentage of the harvest each year* and left the area.

2 At the right time, he sent a slave out on a mission to the farmers so that he might receive *his percentage* out of the vineyard's fruits directly from the farmers.

3 They took him, beat him, and sent him back empty.

4 Again he sent another slave out on a mission to them. They hit that slave in the head and belittled him.

5 He sent another out. They killed that one. There were many others: some they beat, others they killed.

6 He still had one, his son that he loved. He sent him out last to them, saying, 'They will be embarrassed around my son.'

7 But those farmers said to themselves, 'This is the inheritor. Come on. Let's kill him, and the inheritance will be ours.'

8 They took him, killed him, and threw his body out of the vineyard.

9 So what will the vineyard's master do? He will come, ruin the farmers, and give the vineyard to others.

10 Didn't you ever read this *Old Testament* writing? 'A stone that the builders rejected has ended up being used for a corner's head, *(a cornerstone, the primary stone of the whole building).*

11 This came directly from the Master, and it is amazing in our eyes' *(Psalm 118:22-23)*."

12 They were looking for a way to take Him into custody, and yet they were cautious of the crowd. You see, they knew that He told the illustration specifically for them. Then they left Him alone and went away.

13 But they were sending some of the Separatists and the Herod Supporters out to Him so that they might catch Him in the answers He gave them.

14 They came and told Him, "Teacher, we realize that You are valid and there is no bias in You toward anyone. You see, You don't look at people's labels, but You teach the way of God based on truth. Is it permitted to give an enrollment tax to Caesar or not?

15 Should we give or not give?" But Jesus realized that their behavior was fake. "Why are you harassing Me?" He told them. "Bring Me a denarius *(a coin equal to one day's wage)* so that I might see it."

16 They brought Him one. "Whose image and inscription is this?" He asked. "Caesar's," they said.

17 "Give Caesar's things back to Caesar and God's things back to God," Jesus told them. They were amazed.

18 Sadducees came to Him. The Sadducees say that there is no life after death. They were asking *Him a question.*
19 "Teacher," they said, "Moses wrote to us that if someone dies and leaves a wife behind without a child, that his brother should take the wife and bring up a seed *(descendants)* for his brother.
20 There were seven brothers. After the first took a wife, he died and didn't leave a seed *(he didn't have any children).*
21 The second took her and died without leaving a seed behind either. The same thing happened with the third.
22 The seven brothers didn't leave a seed *(descendants)*. Last of all, the wife also died.
23 In the return back to life when they come back to life, whose wife will she be? You see, all seven had her as a wife."
24 "Aren't you misled," declared Jesus, "because you don't know the *Old Testament* writings or God's ability?
25 You see, whenever they come back to life from the dead, they don't marry and they don't plan to get married either. They are like the angels in heaven.
26 But about the dead coming back to life, haven't you read in Moses' scroll, how God said to him at the bush, 'I am the God of Abraham, the God of Isaac, and the God of Jacob *(Exodus 3:6)?' He didn't say 'was'. He said 'am'. I am the God of Abraham, Isaac, and Jacob.*
27 God is not a god of dead people. *Dead people don't have gods. They are dead.* He is a god of living people. *Abraham, Isaac, and Jacob were and are living in the afterworld.* You are misled about many things."
28 One of the Old Testament transcribers came forward. He had listened to them together posing questions to Him and had seen that He answered them nicely. He asked Him, "Which is the first demand of all?"
29 Jesus answered, "First is, 'Listen, Israel, the Master, our God, is One Master,
30 and you will love the Master, your God, from your whole heart, from your whole soul, from your whole mind, and from your whole strength.'
31 Second is this, 'You will love the person near you as yourself.' There is no other demand greater than these."
32 "Teacher, You answered nicely based on truth," the Old Testament transcriber told Him, "because there is One, and there is not another other than Him.
33 And to love Him from the whole heart, from the whole understanding, and from the whole strength, and to love the person

nearby as oneself is even more than all the entirely burned offerings and sacrifices."

34 When Jesus saw that he answered thoughtfully, He told him, "You are not a long way away from God's monarchy." No one dared to ask Him anything anymore.

35 Jesus responded by saying this as He taught on the temple grounds: "How do the Old Testament transcribers say that the Anointed King is a son of David?

36 David himself said in the Sacred Spirit, 'The Master *(God)* said to my Master *(the Anointed King)*, Sit down on My right side until I place Your enemies beneath Your feet' *(Psalm 110:1)*.

37 David himself called Him Master. How is He his son?" The large crowd was gladly listening to Him.

38 In His teaching He was saying, "Look out for the Old Testament transcribers who want to walk around in long robes, who want people to greet them in the marketplace,

39 who want the front benches in the synagogues and the front reclining places in the feasts *(the place of honor)*,

40 who eat up widows' houses, and who pray long prayers for a sham. They will receive much more judgment."

41 When He was seated directly facing the treasury area, He was watching how the crowd threw copper coins into *the collection boxes in* the treasury area. Many wealthy people were throwing in much.

42 One poor widow came and threw in two tiny brass coins worth a penny.

43 He called for His students and told them, "Amen, I tell you that this poor widow threw more into the treasury area than anyone else.

44 You see, everyone threw in part of what they had left over, but she, even though she didn't make enough to live on, threw in everything, as much as she had, her whole life savings."

13

1 As He was traveling out of the temple grounds, one of His students told Him, "Teacher, look! What stones! And what buildings!"

2 "Do you see these large buildings?" Jesus told him. "Here a stone will not in any way be left on a stone that hasn't been torn down."

3 As He sat on the Mount of Olives directly facing the temple grounds, Peter, James, John, and Andrew were by themselves with Him. They were asking Him,

4 "Tell us. When will these things be? And what will indicate when everything is about to be completely finished?"

5 Jesus began by saying, "See that no one misleads you.

6 Many will come using My name and saying, 'I am Him.' They will mislead many.

7 When you hear wars and much talk about wars, do not be alarmed. This must happen, but it is not the conclusion yet.

8 You see, a nation will rise up against a nation and a monarchy against a monarchy. There will be earthquakes throughout some areas. There will be famines. These are the beginning of labor pains.

9 You all must look at yourselves. Some of your own people will turn you in to councils. You will be beaten in synagogues. You will stand before leaders and kings on account of Me for a witness to them.

10 First, it is necessary for the good news to be spoken publicly to all the nations.

11 Whenever they turn you in and take you away, don't worry beforehand about what you should speak, but speak whatever is given to you in that hour. You see, you are not the ones speaking, the Sacred Spirit is.

12 A brother will turn a brother in to be put to death; and a father, a child. Children will stand up against parents and put them to death.

13 You will be hated by everyone because of My name, but whoever persists to do what is right to the conclusion, this person will be rescued.

14 The disgusting thing of the uninhabited time will stand where it must not stand. The person reading *about this in Daniel* must be aware of it. When you see that this has happened, at that time the people in Judea must escape into the mountains.

15 The person on top of the house must not first climb down into the house or go in to take anything from his house.

16 The person in the field must not first return back to his stuff to take his robe. *Escape immediately.*

17 What a tragedy it will be for the pregnant women and the nursing women in those days.

18 Be praying so that your escape will not happen during a storm.

19 You see, those days will be hard times. That kind of *hard times* has not in anyway happened since the beginning of the creation that God created until now and will not in anyway happen *after that*.

20 If the Master didn't halt those days, no physical body would be rescued. But God halted those days because of the select people, *the people* who selected Him.

21 At that time, if someone tells you, 'Look, the Anointed King is here, look He's over there,' don't trust it.
22 You see, counterfeit anointed kings and counterfeit preachers will get up and give proofs and incredible things with a specific goal--to mislead away *from God*, if possible, the people who have chosen God.
23 You must look out *for these things*. I have stated it all to you beforehand.
24 In those days, after the hard times, the sun will darken, the moon won't give its glow,
25 stars will fall out of the sky, and heaven's abilities will be disturbed.
26 Then they will see the Son of the Person coming in clouds with much ability and magnificence.
27 Then He will send the angels out and bring the people who chose Him together in one place from the four winds *(the four compass directions)*, from the edge of the earth to the edge of heaven.
28 Learn this illustration from the fig tree. Whenever its branch already becomes tender and it sprouts the leaves out, you know that summer is near.
29 In this way also, whenever you see these things happening, know that it is near, at the door.
30 Amen, I tell you that a generation will not in any way pass by until all these things happen *(from their beginning until the day He comes)*.
31 The sky and the earth will pass, but My messages will not in any way pass.
32 No one except the Father knows the day or hour *of His coming*, not the angels in heaven, not the Son.
33 Look for *these things*! Don't go to sleep! You see, you don't know when the appointed time is.
34 *It is* like a man who left his house to go out of town. He gave his authority to his slaves. Each was to be responsible for his own work, and he gave a demand to the doorkeeper to stay awake.
35 In the same way, you also must stay awake. You see, you don't know when the house's master is coming: either evening, or middle of the night, or rooster-crowing time *(3-6 a.m.)*, or in the morning.
36 When he comes unexpectedly, he won't find you sleeping, will he?
37 What I say to you, I say to everyone, stay awake."

14

1 The Passover and the Yeast-free Festival was two days away. The head priests and the Old Testament transcribers

were looking for a way to kill Him once they took Him into custody using deception.

2 You see, they were saying, "Not at the festival so that there won't be a riot among the ethnic group."

3 As He was in Bethany lounging in the house of Simon (the man with a skin disease), a woman came with an alabaster jar of very expensive authentic Spikenard perfume. After she crushed the alabaster jar, she spilled it down on His head.

4 Some of them were frustrated at this. "Why would she ruin this perfume?" they said to each other.

5 "You see, this perfume could have been put up for sale for over three hundred denarii *($15,000)*, and that could have been given to the poor." They were stern with her.

6 "Leave her alone," said Jesus. "Why are you bothering her? She has worked to do nice work for Me.

7 You see, you always have the poor with you. Whenever you want, you can do something good for them. But you won't always have Me.

8 She did this because this is what she had. She brought it early to perfume My body for its embalming.

9 Amen, I tell you, wherever the good news is spoken publicly in the whole world, what she did will also be spoken for a reminder of her."

10 Judas (from Kerioth, one of the Twelve) went off to the head priests so that he might turn Him in to them.

11 When the head priests heard, they were happy and promised to give him silver. He was looking for a way to turn Him in.

12 For the first day of the Yeast-free Festival (when they sacrifice the Passover lamb), His students said to Him, "Where do You want us to go off to and get things ready for eating the Passover meal?"

13 He sent two of His students out. "Make your way back into the city," He told them, "and a person hauling a clay pitcher of water will meet you. Follow him.

14 Wherever he enters, tell the homeowner, 'The teacher says, "Where is My guest room? I need a place to eat the Passover meal with My students."'

15 He will show you a large room above the ground floor that has been set up and is ready. Get things ready for us there."

16 The students left, went into the city, and found just what He told them. They got the Passover meal ready.

17 When evening arrived, He came with the Twelve.

18 As they reclined and ate, Jesus said, "Amen, I tell you that one person from among you will turn Me in, the one eating with Me."

19 They began to be sad and to be saying to Him, one by one, "It isn't me, is it?"
20 "It is one of the Twelve," He told them, "the one dipping *bread* into the bowl with Me.
21 The Son of the Person certainly makes His way back just as the Bible says, but what a tragedy it is to that person through whom the Son of the Person is turned in. It would have been nice for that person if he had not been born."
22 As they were eating, He took bread, conferred a blessing on it, split it, and gave it to them. "Take it," He said. "This is My body."
23 When He took a cup, after being thankful, He gave it to them, and everyone drank from it.
24 "This is My blood of the deal," He told them, "the blood that is spilled out on behalf of many.
25 Amen, I tell you that I won't in any way drink juice from a grapevine anymore until that day, whenever I drink it new in God's monarchy."
26 After they sang praise songs, they went out to the Mount of Olives.
27 "All of you will stumble," Jesus told them, "because the Bible says, 'I will strike the shepherd, and the sheep will disperse' *(Zechariah 13:7)*.
28 But after I am gotten up, I will lead the way ahead of you into Galilee."
29 But Peter was declaring to Him, "Even if all of them stumble, I won't."
30 "Amen, I tell you," Jesus told him, "that you, today, on this night, before it is time for a rooster to even crow twice, you will flatly deny Me three times."
31 But Peter was insisting even more, "If I have to die together with You, I will not in any way flatly deny You." They all were also saying this.
32 They came into a parcel of land. Its name is Gethsemane *(Aramaic for oil press)*. "Be seated here while I pray," He told His students.
33 Then He took Peter, James, and John along with Him. He began to be puzzled and heavyhearted.
34 "My soul is overcome with sadness to death," He told them. "Stay here and stay awake."
35 After He went on ahead a little, He was getting down on the ground and praying that, if it is possible, the hour *(the events that were about to happen)* might go away.
36 This is what He was saying: "Daddy, the Father, all things are possible for You. Carry this cup off away from Me. But not what I want. What You want."

37 He came and found them sleeping. "Simon, are you sleeping?" He asked Peter. "Didn't you have enough strength to stay awake one hour?
38 Stay awake and pray so that you won't get into trouble. The spirit certainly is eager, but the physical body is weak."
39 He went off again and prayed the same words.
40 Again He came and found them sleeping. You see, their eyes were weighted down a lot, and they didn't know how to respond to Him.
41 When He came the third time, He told them, "Sleep for the rest of the time, and relax. He has it all." *Later, He said,* "The hour has come. Look, the Son of the Person is being turned over to sinful people's hands.
42 Get up. Let's lead the way. Look, the person turning Me in has come near."
43 Right away as He was still speaking, Judas, one of the Twelve, showed up. With him was a crowd carrying daggers and wooden clubs. They had come directly from the head priests, the Old Testament transcribers, and the older men.
44 Judas had given them a signal. "Whoever I am friendly with is Him," he told them. "Take Him into custody and lead Him away securely."
45 When he came, right away he went up to Jesus and said, "Rabbi." He was very friendly to Him.
46 They put their hands on Him and took Him into custody.
47 A certain student standing nearby, pulled out his dagger, struck the head priest's slave, and took off his earlobe.
48 "You came out to apprehend Me," responded Jesus, "with daggers and wooden clubs as if I were a bandit.
49 I was facing you on the temple grounds throughout the day teaching, and you didn't take Me into custody. But this is what the *Old Testament* writings said would happen."
50 All of His students left and ran away.
51 One of them was a certain young lad. He had been following Jesus having put only a linen cloth around himself over his naked body. They grabbed him.
52 But he left the linen cloth with them and escaped naked.
53 They led Jesus off to the head priest. All the head priests, older men, and Old Testament transcribers came together.
54 Peter followed Him off at a distance until He was inside, in the courtyard of the head priest. There Peter was sitting together with the underlings and warming himself facing the light.

55 The head priests and the whole council were looking for *something that* a witness *had seen Jesus do* which they could put Him to death for, but they weren't finding anything.
56 You see, many were lying about what they actually witnessed, and the witness accounts didn't match up.
57 Some stood up and were lying as they said,
58 "We heard Him say, 'I will tear this handmade temple down and in three days build another one made without hands.'"
59 But even their accounts about this didn't match up.
60 The head priest stood up in the middle and asked Jesus, "Are You not going to answer any of these? What are these people witnessing against You?"
61 But Jesus remained silent and did not answer. Again the head priest was asking Him and saying, "Are You the Anointed King, the Son of the One who has blessings conferred on Him?"
62 "I am," Jesus said, "and you will see the Son of the Person sitting on the right side of the Ability and coming in the clouds of the sky."
63 The head priest ripped his long undershirt apart *to show how appalled he was by this* and said, "What? Do we still need witnesses?
64 You heard the insult. What does it appear *to be* to you? What do you think?" They all found Him guilty and eligible to be sentenced to death.
65 Some began spitting on Him, blindfolding Him, slugging Him, and telling Him, "Preach." The underlings slapped Him as they took Him into custody.
66 As Peter was below in the courtyard, one of the head priest's servant girls came in.
67 When she saw Peter warming himself, she looked at him for a while. "You also were with the Nazarene, Jesus," she said.
68 But Peter denied it. "I don't know Him and I am not even aware of what you are saying either," he said. He went outside to the front yard, [and a rooster crowed].
69 When the servant girl saw him again, she began telling the people standing nearby, "This man is one of them."
70 But Peter denied it again. After a little while, the people standing nearby were telling Peter, "You truly are one of them. You see, you are even a Galilean."
71 But Peter began to vow and guarantee, "I haven't seen this person that you are talking about."
72 Right away a rooster crowed a second time, and Peter was reminded again of the statement that Jesus made to him, "Before it is time for a

rooster to crow twice, you will flatly deny Me three times." He put *his thoughts* on *Jesus' statement* and was crying.

15

1 Right away in the morning, the head priests took counsel with the older men, the Old Testament transcribers, and the whole council. Then they tied Jesus up, carried Him off, and turned Him over to *the Roman leader of that area,* Pilate.
2 "Are you the Jewish people's king?" Pilate asked Him. "You are saying it," Jesus answered.
3 The head priests were there leveling many complaints against Him.
4 Pilate was asking Jesus again, saying, "Aren't you answering anything? Look at how many complaints they are leveling against you."
5 But Jesus didn't answer anything anymore. This really amazed Pilate.
6 At each festival he dismissed one prisoner that they were asking *him to dismiss*.
7 There was a prisoner called Barabbas. He had been locked up with other disruptors who had committed murder in a disruption.
8 A crowd stepped up and began asking him to do just as he had always done.
9 Pilate answered them by saying, "Do you want me to dismiss the Jewish people's king?"
10 You see, he knew that the head priests had turned Him in because they were jealous of Him.
11 But the head priests shook up the crowd so that he would dismiss Barabbas instead.
12 Pilate responded again, "So what do you want me to do with the One that you say is the Jewish people's king?"
13 They yelled again, "Nail Him to a cross!"
14 "You see, what did He do that was bad?" asked Pilate. But they yelled even louder, "Nail Him to a cross!"
15 Pilate intended to do what was sufficient *to maintain order* with the crowd, so he dismissed Barabbas to them, but thrashed Jesus with a whip and turned Him over *to the soldiers* so that they would nail Him to a cross.
16 The soldiers led Him away inside the courtyard of the Roman palace. They called the whole regiment together.
17 They dressed Him in purple and put a thorny award wreath around His head that they had woven together.

18 They began greeting Him: "Happy to meet You, King of the Jewish people."
19 Then they were hitting Him on the head with a stick, spitting on Him, kneeling, and bowing down to Him.
20 After they mocked Him, they stripped the purple off Him and put His clothes back on. They led Him away to nail Him to a cross.
21 They sequestered help from someone passing by so that he might pick up His cross. It was Simon, a Cyrenian, the father of Alexander and Rufus. He was coming in from a field.
22 They brought Him to the place called Golgotha (which is *Aramaic* and translated as "Place of a Skull").
23 They were giving Him wine mixed with myrrh *(a painkiller)*, but He didn't take any.
24 They are nailing Him to a cross and dividing up His clothes by throwing dice on the clothes *to determine* who would take what.
25 It was 9 a.m. They nailed Him to the cross.
26 The inscription of His accusation that had been inscribed was "The Jewish people's king."
27 They are nailing two bandits to crosses together with Him, one to the right of Him and one to the left.
28 [[[What the *Old Testament* writing said would happen happened. It says, "And he was considered with criminals" *(Isaiah 53:12)*.]]]
29 The people traveling by were insulting Him, shaking their heads, and saying, "Ah, the One who tears the temple down and builds it in three days!
30 Rescue Yourself and climb down off the cross!"
31 Likewise, the head priests and the Old Testament transcribers were also mocking Him to each other. "Others, He rescued," they said, "Himself, He is not able to rescue.
32 The Anointed King, Israel's King, must climb down now off the cross so that we will see and trust." The bandits that had been nailed on crosses there with Him were also criticizing Him.
33 At noon it became dark over the whole earth and stayed dark until 3 p.m.
34 At 3 p.m., Jesus shouted loudly, "Eloi, Eloi, lema sabachthani." That is *Aramaic* and translated as "My God, My God, why did You abandon Me?"
35 When some of the people standing nearby heard it, they were saying, "Look, He is hollering for Elijah."

36 Someone ran and filled a sponge full of sour wine. He put it around a stick and gave Him a drink as he said "Leave Him alone, we will see if Elijah comes to take Him down."
37 Jesus let out a loud sound and breathed out His last breath.
38 The temple's curtain tore in two from top to bottom.
39 When the centurion *(Latin for lieutenant)* who had stood nearby facing Him, saw that He breathed out His last breath like this, he said, "This person truly was a son of a god."
40 Women were also there watching off at a distance. Mary (the Magdalene), Mary (the mother of little James and Joses), and Salome were among them.
41 They had been following Him and serving Him while He was in Galilee. Many other women who walked up to Jerusalem together with Him were also there.
42 Evening had already come. Since it was a preparation day (which is the pre-Sabbath day *that is spent preparing food and setting up for the next day, a day of rest, the first day of the Yeast-free Festival*),
43 Joseph (the one from Arimathaea) did a daring thing. He went in to Pilate and asked for Jesus' body. Joseph was a reputable advisor who himself also was awaiting God's monarchy.
44 Pilate was amazed that He would have already died. He called for the centurion and asked him if He had been dead for a while.
45 When he knew it from the centurion, he gave the corpse to Joseph for free.
46 He purchased linen cloth, took Him down, wrapped Him in the linen cloth, and placed Him in a burial vault that had been chiseled out of rock. He rolled a stone over the burial vault's door.
47 Mary (the Magdalene) and Mary (Joses' mother) were watching where He was put.

16

1 When the Sabbath had elapsed, Mary (the Magdalene), Mary (James' mother), and Salome purchased fragrant resins so that when they went to the burial vault, they could dab them on His body.
2 Very early in the morning of Day One *(which is Sunday)* after the Sabbaths, they went to the burial vault when the sun came up.
3 They were saying to themselves, "Who will roll the stone away from the burial vault's door for us?"
4 When they looked up, they saw that the stone had been rolled away. You see, it was terribly large.

5 They went into the burial vault and saw a young lad sitting on the right side. A long white robe had been put around him. They were puzzled.
6 "Don't be puzzled," he said. "You are looking for Jesus, the Nazarene, the One who was nailed to a cross. God got Him up. He's not here. Look, the place where they put Him.
7 But make your way back, tell His students and Peter, 'He is leading the way ahead of you into Galilee. There you will see Him, just as He told you.'"
8 They left and ran away from the burial vault. You see, they were overcome with trembling and astonishment. They didn't say anything to anyone. They were afraid.
9 [[After He came back to life in the morning on a first day *(Sunday)* after a Sabbath, He first appeared to Mary (the Magdalene). This is the Mary that He had thrown seven lesser deities out of.
10 She went and reported it to His people. They were still grieving and crying over Him.
11 When they heard that He is alive and that she had seen Him, they didn't trust.
12 After this, as two of them were out walking around, He was shown in a different form as they traveled to a field.
13 Those two went off and reported it to the rest of them. They didn't trust when they heard this either.
14 Later as they ate and chatted together, He was shown to the eleven. He criticized their distrust and hardheartedness because they didn't trust with those who had seen Him that had gotten up *from the dead*.
15 "When you travel into absolutely all of the world," He told them, "speak publicly about the good news to every created being.
16 The person who trusts and is submerged will be rescued, but the person who does not trust will be found guilty.
17 These proofs will follow alongside the people who trust in My name: They will throw lesser deities out, they will speak with new languages,
18 they will pick up snakes with their hands, and if they drink something deadly, it will not in any way hurt them. They will place their hands on people who are sick, and they will get well."
19 After Master Jesus spoke to them, He was taken up into the sky and was seated on the right side of God.
20 Those people went out and spoke publicly everywhere. The Master worked together with them and authenticated the message through the proofs following closely behind them.]] *It is possible that either the*

previous double bracketed passage (starting in verse 9), or the following double bracketed passage, or neither of these passages were in the original text. [[They briefly promoted all the orders that had been passed on to the people around Peter. Through them, after these things, Jesus himself also sent out from east to west the temple and immortal public speaking of the rescue that spans all time. Amen.]]

Luke

1

1 For sure it is true that many have attempted to again arrange a description of the events that have been well-established among us.

2 *This is* just how the eyewitnesses of these very events from the beginning turned them over to us after they also became underlings of the message.

3 I have followed alongside everything from the top. So it also seemed good to me to accurately write to you about these events in order, most powerful Theophilus.

4 *I have done this* so that you might correctly understand about the certainty of the messages that have echoed down to you.

5 In the days of Herod, king of Judea, there happened to be a certain priest named Zacharias. He was in the Abijah priest rotation. His wife's name was Elisabeth. She was a descendent of Aaron's daughters.

6 Both of them were doing what was right directly in front of God. They traveled without fault in all the Master's demands and right paths.

7 They didn't have any children due to the fact that Elisabeth was infertile and both of them were advanced in years.

8 He happened to be performing the priest duties in Jerusalem directly in front of God during his week of the priest rotation.

9 Aligned with the custom of the office of the priesthood, it was his turn to go into the Master's temple and burn incense.

10 As he went in at the hour of incense, there was a large group of Jewish people outside praying.

11 Inside he saw the Master's angel standing on the right side of the incense altar.

12 Zacharias was uneasy and fear fell on him.

13 "Don't be afraid, Zacharias," the angel told him, "because your plea has been heard. Your wife Elisabeth will give birth to a son for you, and you will call his name John.

14 It will be happiness and excitement for you. Many will be happy based on His birth.

15 You see, he will be great in the Master's sight. He shouldn't in any way drink wine or alcoholic beverages. He will be filled with the Sacred Spirit even while he is still in his mother's belly.

16 He will turn many of Israel's sons back to the Master, their God.

17 In God's sight, he will go on ahead in the spirit and ability of Elijah to turn fathers' hearts back to their children and unbelievers back to focus on what is right, to get ready an ethnic group that has been constructed for the Master."

18 Zacharias said to the angel, "How will I know that this is true? You see, I am an old man, and my wife is advanced in years."

19 "I am Gabriel," answered the angel. "I am the angel that stands nearby in God's sight. I was sent out on a mission to speak to you and to share this good news with you.

20 And look, you will be silent and not able to speak till the day that these things happen. *This is* for *the times* you didn't trust my words, words that will be accomplished at the appointed time."

21 The group was expecting Zacharias *to come out*. They were amazed that it was taking him such a long time in the temple.

22 When he came out, he couldn't speak. They correctly understood that he had seen something unusual in the temple. During the whole time, he was gesturing to them and grunting, unable to say any words.

23 As soon as the days of his public service in Jerusalem were finished; he went off to his house.

24 After these days, Elisabeth, his wife, conceived and hid herself from everyone for five months.

25 "Because this is what the Master has done for me," she said, "in days that He looked on me and took away the disdain people had for me *when they knew I was childless*."

26 During her sixth month, the angel Gabriel was sent out from God on a mission to a city of Galilee. Its name is Nazareth.

27 He was sent to a virgin that had been promised to a man whose name was Joseph. He was from the house of David *(or in other words, a descendant of David)*. The virgin's name was Mary.

28 The angel entered and told her, "Happy to meet you. You have been shown generosity. The Master is with you."

29 Mary was very upset by these words and was pondering what kind of greeting it was.

30 "Don't be afraid, Mary," the angel told her. "You see, you have found generosity that comes directly from God.

31 And look, you will conceive in your womb and give birth to a son. You will call His name Jesus.

32 This Jesus will be great and will be called Son of the Highest. The Master, God, will give Him the throne of David, His father.

33 He will be king over Jacob's house for the spans of time. There will be no conclusion to His monarchy."
34 Mary said to the angel, "How will this be since I don't know a man?"
35 "The Sacred Spirit will come on you," answered the angel, "and the ability of the Highest will shine on you. For this reason, the sacred Child being born also will be called Son of God.
36 Look, your relative Elisabeth has even conceived a son in her old age. She, the one called infertile, is in her sixth month
37 because no statement directly from God will be impossible."
38 "Look, here I am, the Master's slave," Mary said. "May *everything* happen to me aligned with your statement." Then the angel left.
39 Mary got up in the following days and traveled to the mountainous area in a hurry, into a city of Judah.
40 She went into Zacharias' house and greeted Elisabeth.
41 As Elisabeth listened to Mary's greeting, the baby jumped around in her belly and Elisabeth was filled with the Sacred Spirit.
42 She hollered loudly with a great yell and said, "Among women, a blessing has been conferred on you, and a blessing has been conferred on the fruit of your belly.
43 How is it that the mother of my Master would come to me?
44 You see, look, as the voice of your greeting came into my ears, the baby jumped around with excitement in my belly.
45 A blessing for the woman who trusted is that there will be a completion to the things that have been spoken to her directly from the Master."
46 "My soul makes the Master great," said Mary.
47 "And my spirit is excited about God, my Rescuer,
48 because He took a look at the lowliness of His slave. You see, look, from now on all generations will consider me to be blessed
49 because the One who is able *to do everything* did great things for me and His name is sacred.
50 His forgiving kindness is for generations and generations, to those who are cautious of Him.
51 He made power with His arm. He dispersed proud people with their heart's mind.
52 He took competent rulers down from thrones and put lowly people up high.
53 He filled hungry people up with good and sent wealthy people away empty.

54 He assisted His servant boy Israel to be remembered for forgiving kindness
55 for the span of time. This is exactly what He spoke to our fathers (to Abraham and his seed--*his descendants*)."
56 Mary stayed with her for about three months and then returned to her house.
57 For Elisabeth, her time to deliver the baby came and she gave birth to a son.
58 The houses around there and her relatives heard that the Master was showing her His forgiving kindness in a great way, and they were happy together with her.
59 It happened that on the eighth day, they came to circumcise the young child. They were in favor of naming him based on his father's name, Zacharias.
60 "Definitely not," his mother responded, "but he will be named John."
61 "None of your relatives are named with this name," they told her.
62 They were gesturing to his father about what he would want to name him.
63 He asked for a writing pad and wrote, "John is his name." Everyone was amazed.
64 At once his mouth and his tongue were opened. He was speaking, conferring a blessing on God.
65 Everyone living around them was in awe, and throughout the whole mountainous area of Judea, the people spoke in detail about all of these statements.
66 Everyone who heard wondered to themselves, "So what kind of young child will this be?" You see, it was obvious that the Master's hand was with him.
67 Zacharias, his father, was filled with the Sacred Spirit. He preached, saying,
68 "The Master, the God of Israel, has blessings conferred on Him because He kept an eye on His ethnic group and made the payment to release them.
69 He raised up a horn of rescue for us in the house of David, His servant boy.
70 This is just what He spoke through the mouth of His sacred preachers in a way that stands out in the span of time.
71 This horn will rescue us from our enemies and from the hand of all the people who hate us.

72 God is doing this to show forgiving kindness to our fathers and to remember His sacred deal,
73 an oath that He guaranteed to Abraham, our father.
74 He will save us from our enemies' hand so we may minister to Him fearlessly
75 in holiness and in the right way in His sight all our days.
76 And you, young child, will be called a preacher of the Highest. You see, you will travel immediately ahead of the Master to get His way ready,
77 by giving information to His ethnic group about their rescue in the forgiveness of their sins
78 because of our God's feelings of sympathy of forgiving kindness. In His feelings of sympathy, He will keep an eye on us rising from a high place
79 to shine on us (the people sitting in darkness and in death's shadow) and direct our feet down a road of peace."
80 The young child was growing and becoming strong in spirit. He was in the backcountry until the day that he was publicly shown to Israel.

2

1 In those days, a rule came directly from Caesar Augustus to register the whole civilized world.
2 This kind of registration first happened when Cyrenius was Syria's leader.
3 Everyone was traveling, each to his own city, to be registered.
4 Joseph also walked up out of Galilee from the city of Nazareth to Judea, to David's city, a certain city called Bethlehem (because he was from David's house and family tree).
5 He went together with Mary to be registered. She had been promised to him. She was in the later stages of pregnancy.
6 During the time that they were there, her days to deliver the baby came.
7 She delivered her firstborn son, wrapped Him in a strip of cloth, and reclined Him in a feed trough because there was no place for them in the guest room.
8 Shepherds were in the same rural area playing the flute in the field and standing guard over their flock through the guard shifts of the night.
9 The Master's angel stood over them and the Master's magnificence shined around them. They feared great fear.

10 "Don't be afraid," the angel told them. "You see, look, I am sharing good news of great happiness with you. It is good news for all of the ethnic group *(the Jews)*.

11 A rescuer was born to you today in David's city. He is the Anointed King, the Master.

12 This is the proof for you: You will find a baby wrapped in a strip of cloth and lying in a feed trough.

13 Unexpectedly, a large heavenly army appeared together with the angel. They were praising God and saying,

14 "God is magnificent among the highest things and on the earth! There is peace among people because God wants good for them!"

15 As soon as the angels went off into the sky, the shepherds were saying to each other, "For sure, we will go through to Bethlehem and see about this statement that they made since the Master let us know about it."

16 They went in a hurry. They looked for and found the baby lying in the feed trough with Mary and Joseph.

17 After seeing them, they let them know about the statement made to them about this young child.

18 Everyone who heard was amazed by the things the shepherds spoke about.

19 But Mary was preserving all these statements as she meditated on them in her heart.

20 The shepherds returned to their field elevating God to a place of magnificence and praising Him for everything that they heard and saw. It was just as the angel had said.

21 When eight days were finished, they circumcised Him and named Him Jesus. This is what the angel said to name Him before He had been conceived in her belly.

22 Moses' law *stipulates that after the birth of a son, the mother is ceremonially unclean until forty days have passed and a sacrifice has been made for her.* When the days of their cleansing were finished, they took Jesus up to Jerusalem to offer Him to the Master.

23 *This is* exactly what is written in the Master's law: "Every male that completely opens a womb *(or in other words, is a firstborn son)* will be called sacred to the Master" *(Exodus 13:2)*.

24 *They also went there* to give the sacrifice for Mary stated in the Master's law: "a pair of cooing doves or two baby doves" *(Leviticus 12:8)*.

25 Look, there was a man in Jerusalem named Simeon. He did what is right and was devout. He was awaiting a time when God would comfort Israel. The Sacred Spirit was on him.
26 He was divinely instructed by the Sacred Spirit that he would not see death *(in other words, he wouldn't die)* before he saw the Master's Anointed King.
27 The Spirit led him to go onto the temple grounds while the parents were also taking the young child Jesus onto the temple grounds. The parents were there to do what was required in the law for Him."
28 He accepted Him into *his* cradling arms, and conferred a blessing on God. He said,
29 "Now You are dismissing Your slave in peace, O God, my Owner, according to Your statement
30 because my eyes have seen the rescue that You are setting up,
31 that You have ready right in front of the face of all the ethnic groups,
32 a light for uncovering truth to non-Jews and for the magnificence of Your ethnic group, Israel."
33 His father and mother were amazed at the things spoken about Him.
34 Simeon conferred a blessing on them and said to Mary, His mother, "Look, this child lies here for the fall and return back to life of many in Israel and for proof that people will oppose
35 in order that the true ponderings in many hearts might be uncovered. *Because of their opposition,* a sword will go through your very soul."
36 Anna was a female preacher, Phanuel's daughter from Asher's family line. She was advanced in years. She lived with a husband for seven years when she was young.
37 She was an eighty-four year old widow. She was not staying away from the temple grounds. She was ministering there by going without food and making pleas to God, night and day.
38 In the same hour, she stood over them and was responding *to what Simeon had said.* She acknowledged that God *was in it.* She was speaking about Jesus to all of the people there who were awaiting God to provide some type of payment to release Jerusalem *from the Roman government.*
39 As soon as they had finished all the requirements of the Master's law, they returned back into Galilee to their city, Nazareth.
40 The young child was growing and becoming strong as He was filling up with insight. God was generous to Him.

41 Each year His parents were traveling to Jerusalem for the Passover Festival.
42 When He was twelve years old, they walked up to Jerusalem. They were observing the festival's custom along the way.
43 When the days of their stay were finished, during their return, Jesus, the boy, stayed behind in Jerusalem, and his parents didn't know it.
44 They assumed that He was among the group traveling together on the road. At the end of the first day's trip, they were looking all over for Him among their relatives and the people they knew.
45 When they didn't find Him, they returned to Jerusalem looking all over for Him.
46 After three days, they found Him on the temple grounds seated in the middle of the teachers. He was listening to them and asking them questions.
47 All the people who were gathered around and listening were astounded at His understanding and responses.
48 When His parents saw Him, they were impressed. "Child, why did You do this to us?" said His mother. "Look, Your father and I have been in agony looking for You."
49 "Why were you looking for Me?" He asked them. "Didn't you realize that I would have had to be among My Father's things?"
50 They didn't understand this statement.
51 He walked down with them, went into Nazareth, and was placing Himself under them. His mother was carefully keeping all the statements in her heart.
52 Jesus was advancing in insight, in age, and in generosity beside God and people.

3

1 It was the fifteenth year of Tiberius Caesar's leadership. Pontius Pilate was the leader of Judea. Herod was the head of one of Palestine's four regions (Galilee). Philip (his brother) was the head of another one of Palestine's four regions (the Ituraea and Trachonitis rural area). And Lysanias was the head of yet another one of Palestine's four regions (Abilene).
2 Annas and Caiaphas were the head priests. At this time, a statement of God came on John (Zacharias' son) in the backcountry.
3 So he went into the rural area surrounding the Jordan River speaking publicly about a change-of-ways submersion through which a person's sins could be forgiven. *It was a form of the Jewish tradition of submersion that ritually cleans the person being submerged.*

4 This was what had been written in a scroll of messages from Isaiah, the preacher, "A voice shouting in the backcountry, 'Get the Master's road ready. Make His paths straight.'
5 Every valley will be filled in, every mountain and hill will be put down low, the crooked things will be made into a straight road, and the rugged roads will be made into smooth roads.
6 Every physical body will see God's rescue process" *(Isaiah 40:3-5)*.
7 John was only speaking in rural areas, but soon crowds were traveling from the cities out to where he was so that they could be submerged by him. He was telling them, "You children of poisonous snakes, who put in front of your face the need to escape away from the punishment that is going to come? *You don't see it, do you? So why are you here?*
8 Produce some fruit of your change of ways. *Show us what you are doing that is* deserving of it. Don't begin to say among yourselves, 'Our father is Abraham. *God needs us to carry on Abraham's lineage.*' I tell you that God is able from these stones to raise up children for Abraham.
9 God has even already gotten the ax out and laid it facing the root of the trees. Every tree that does not produce nice fruit gets chopped down and thrown into a fire."
10 The crowds were asking him, "So what should we do?"
11 "The person who has two long undershirts must give one out to someone who doesn't have one," he answered. "And the person who has food must do likewise."
12 Some tax collectors had come to be submerged. They said to him, "Teacher, what should we do?"
13 "You must collect nothing more than what has been specifically assigned to you," John told them.
14 The ones serving in the military were asking, "And what about us? What should we do?" "You should not shake anyone violently," he told them. "Don't make false accusations. Be content with your wages."
15 As the ethnic group was expecting and everyone was pondering in their hearts that perhaps John is the Anointed King,
16 John responded by telling everyone, "I certainly submerge you in water, but the One stronger than me is coming. I am unfit to even untie His sandal strap. He will submerge you in the Sacred Spirit and fire *(the Sacred Spirit for those who trust Him, fire for those who don't)*.
17 His shovel is in His hand to completely clear the harvested crop off of His processing floor and to gather the grain together into His grain bin. The husks will be burned up with unextinguished fire."

18 So as he was encouraging them in many and different ways, he certainly was sharing good news with the ethnic group.
19 But since Herod (the head of one of Palestine's four regions) was being reprimanded by John about Herodias (his brother's wife) and about all the evil things that Herod had done,
20 he also added this thing on to all *his evil things*: He locked John up in jail.
21 Before that, during the time that absolutely all the ethnic group happened to be getting submerged by John, he also submerged Jesus. As Jesus was praying after His submersion, the sky opened,
22 and the Sacred Spirit floated down on Him in a bodily, visual image as a dove. A voice came from heaven, "You are My loved Son. I am delighted with You."
23 As Jesus was beginning, He was around thirty years old. He was a son (as it was assumed) of Joseph, who was Eli's son,
24 who was Matthat's son, who was Levi's son, who was Melchi's son, who was Janna's son, who was Joseph's son,
25 who was Mattathias' son, who was Amos' son, who was Nahum's son, who was Esli's son, who was Naggai's son,
26 who was Maath's son, who was Mattathias' son, who was Shimei's son, who was Joseph's son, who was Judah's son,
27 who was Joanan's son, who was Rhesa's son, who was Zerubbabel's son, who was Shealtiel's son, who was Neri's son,
28 who was Melchi's son, who was Addi's son, who was Kosam's son, who was Elmodam's son, who was Er's son,
29 who was Joshua's son, who was Eliezer's son, who was Jorim's son, who was Matthat's son, who was Levi's son,
30 who was Simeon's son, who was Judah's son, who was Joseph's son, who was Jonan's son, who was Eliakim's son,
31 who was Melea's son, who was Menan's son, who was Mattatha's son, who was Nathan's son, who was David's son,
32 who was Jesse's son, who was Obed's son, who was Boaz's son, who was Shelah's son, who was Nahshon's son,
33 who was Aminadab's son, who was Admin's son, who was Arni's son, who was Hezron's son, who was Phares' son, who was Judah's son,
34 who was Jacob's son, who was Isaac's son, who was Abraham's son, who was Terah's son, who was Nahor's son,
35 who was Serug's son, who was Reu's son, who was Peleg's son, who was Eber's son, who was Shelah's son,
36 who was Cainan's son, who was Arphaxad's son, who was Shem's son, who was Noah's son, who was Lamech's son,

37 who was Methushelah's son, who was Enoch's son, who was Jared's son, who was Mahalaleel's son, who was Cainan's son,
38 who was Enos' son, who was Seth's son, who was Adam's son, who was from God.

4

1 Jesus returned from the Jordan River full of the Sacred Spirit, and He was being led by the Spirit for forty days in the backcountry.
2 The Accuser was harassing Him. He didn't eat anything in those days, and when they were completely finished, He was hungry.
3 "If You are a son of God," the Accuser told Him, "tell this stone that it should become bread."
4 Jesus replied to him, "The Bible says, 'A person will not live on bread alone'" *(Deuteronomy 8:3)*.
5 He led Him up and showed Him all the monarchies of the civilized world in an instant of time.
6 "I will give You absolutely all this authority and their magnificence," the Accuser told Him, "because it has been turned over to me and to whomever I want to give it.
7 So if You bow down in my sight, it all will be Yours."
8 When Jesus responded, He told him, "The Bible says, 'You will bow down to the Master, your God, and only minister to Him'" *(Deuteronomy 6:13)*.
9 He led Him into Jerusalem, stood on the winglet of the temple grounds, and told Him, "If You are a son of God, jump off of here.
10 You see, the Bible says, 'He will demand that His angels guard you closely.
11 And they will pick you up in their arms so that you will never stub your foot on a stone'" *(Psalm 91:11-12)*.
12 When Jesus answered, He told him, "The Bible states, 'You will not try to harass the Master, your God'" *(Deuteronomy 6:16)*.
13 When the Accuser was completely finished with all of the harassment, he backed off from Him for a while.
14 Jesus returned to Galilee in the Spirit's ability, and news about Him went out throughout the whole surrounding rural area.
15 He was teaching in their synagogues, and everyone was elevating Him to a place of magnificence.
16 He went into Nazareth where He had been raised. Aligned with what He was accustomed to doing on the day of the Sabbaths, He went into the synagogue and stood up to read.

17 A scroll of the preacher Isaiah was given to Him. He unrolled it and found the place where it has been written:
18 "The Master's Spirit is on Me. Because of this, He anointed Me to share good news with the poor. He has sent Me out on a mission to speak publicly about forgiveness to incarcerated people and about sight restoration to blind people, to send shattered people out in forgiveness,
19 and to speak publicly about the Master's acceptance year" *(Isaiah 61:1-2). The acceptance year is a time when God accepts all who come to Him.*
20 He rolled up the scroll, gave it back to the underling, and sat down. All the eyes in the synagogue were staring at Him.
21 He began speaking to them, "Today, what this writing says will happen has been accomplished in your ears."
22 All were telling what they had seen Him do. They kept being amazed at the messages about God's generosity traveling out of His mouth. "Is this not a son of Joseph?" they were saying.
23 "By all means," He told them, "you will state this proverb to Me, 'Doctor, heal yourself *with the remedies that you prescribe to others*.' As many *miracles* as we heard about happening in Capernaum, do them here in your hometown too."
24 He also said, "Amen, I tell you that not even one preacher is accepted in his hometown.
25 But I tell you. It is true. There were many widows in Israel in Elijah's days when he closed the sky for three and a half years causing a large famine over the entire earth.
26 Elijah was not even sent in the direction of any of them, but into *a small foreign town* (Sarepta of the Sidonian) to a *foreign* woman, a widow.
27 And there were many people with a skin disease in Israel when Elisha was the preacher. Not even one of them was cleared up, but a Syrian (Naaman) was. *Why does God have to go to outsiders to find someone deserving of His blessing?*
28 Everyone in the synagogue was filled with anger when they heard these things.
29 They stood up, threw Him out of the city, and took Him up to an overhang of the mountain on which their city was built so that they could throw Him down the steep slope.
30 But He went through the middle of them and was traveling off.
31 He went down to Capernaum, a city of Galilee, and was teaching them on the Sabbaths.

32 They were impressed with His teaching because His message was with authority. *He was teaching like a king or master would.*
33 In the synagogue, there was a person who had a lesser deity's spirit, a spirit that was not clean. It yelled out with a loud voice,
34 "Ahhhh! Jesus, Nazarene, why are You interfering with us? Did you come to ruin us? I know who You are, God's Sacred One."
35 Jesus stopped him by saying, "Be quiet and come out of him." The lesser deity tossed him into the middle of the synagogue and came out without hurting him.
36 Everyone was perplexed. They were speaking together to each other, saying, "What is this answer *that He gave to the lesser deity?* He gives orders with authority and ability to spirits that are not clean and they come out."
37 Talk about Him was echoing around and traveling out into every place in the surrounding rural area.
38 He got up out of the synagogue and went into Simon's house. Simon's mother-in-law was restricted by a high fever. So they asked Him about her.
39 When He stood up above her, He told the fever to stop, and it left her. At once, she stood up and started serving them.
40 As the sun was setting, absolutely everyone brought Him as many people as they had who were in frail health with various illnesses. Jesus was placing His hands on each one of them and healing them.
41 Lesser deities were also coming out of many, yelling, "You are the Son of God." He was shushing them, not allowing them to speak because they knew that He was the Anointed King.
42 In the morning at the crack of dawn, He left and traveled into an uninhabited place. The crowds started looking for Him and went everywhere until they found Him. They were delaying Him so that He wouldn't travel somewhere else.
43 "I must share the good news of God's monarchy with different cities too," He told them, "because that's what I was sent out to do."
44 He was speaking publicly in the synagogues of Judea.

5

1 There was a time when the crowd was leaning on Jesus and listening to God's message. He happened to be standing beside Lake Gennesaret *(which is another name for the Sea of Galilee).*
2 He saw two boats sitting along the side of the lake. The fishermen had stepped out of them to rinse the nets.

3 He climbed on board one of the boats (Simon's) and asked him to take Him out a little bit away from the land. When he was seated, He was teaching the crowds from the boat.

4 When He was done speaking, He told Simon, "Take us out where it is deep and lower your nets for a catch."

5 "Boss, we have labored through the whole night," responded Simon, "and taken nothing. But based on Your statement, I will lower the nets."

6 When they did this, they captured a very large number of fish. Their nets were ripping apart.

7 They motioned to their teammates in a different boat so that they would come and bring them in together. They came and filled both boats so full that they were sinking down *into the water*.

8 After Simon Peter saw it, he got down at Jesus' knees and said, "Go out away from me because I am a sinful man, Master."

9 You see, he and the others with him were very perplexed about the catch of fish that together they had taken.

10 Likewise, James and John (Zebedee's sons) were also *very perplexed*. They were partners with Simon. "Don't be afraid," Jesus told Simon. "From now on, you will be catching people alive."

11 After they brought the boats up on land, they left everything and followed Him.

12 There was a time when He happened to be in one of the cities, and look, a man with a skin disease all over his body was there. When he saw Jesus, he got down on his face and pleaded with Him, "Master, if you want to, you can clear my skin up."

13 He put out His hand and touched him. "I want to," He said. "Be cleared up." Right away the skin disease went away from him.

14 Jesus ordered him not to tell anyone. "When you leave, show yourself to the priest," Jesus said, "and for the clearing up of your skin disease go through *the eight day process* just as it was stipulated by Moses *in Leviticus 14*. That will be a witness to them *of what happened to you*."

15 But the message about Jesus was going through there even more. Large crowds were coming together to listen to Him and to be healed from their frailties.

16 When He could, He was slipping away secretly to the uninhabited places and praying.

17 During one of those days, this is what happened. He was teaching, Separatists and law teachers were sitting there (they had come from

every village of Galilee and Judea, and from Jerusalem), and the Master's ability to cure was there.

18 And, look, outside some men were carrying a disabled man on a cot. They were looking for a way to carry him in and place him where Jesus could see him.

19 When they couldn't find a way to carry him in because of the crowd, they climbed up on top of the house and let him down with the bedding through the clay tiles into the middle of the room in front of Jesus.

20 When He saw their trust, He said, "Sir, your sins have been forgiven."

21 The Old Testament transcribers and Separatists began pondering this. They were saying, "Who is this? He is speaking insults *of God. It is obvious that God crippled this man for being a terrible sinner.* Who can forgive sins? Only God."

22 After Jesus correctly understood their ponderings, He responded by saying to them, "What are you pondering in your hearts?

23 Which is easier to say, 'Your sins have been forgiven,' or, 'Get up and walk around?'

24 But so that you may realize that the Son of the Person has authority on the earth to be forgiving sins...." He said to the disabled man, "I tell you, Get up and pick up your bedding. Travel to your house."

25 At once, he got up (they all watched him), picked up what he was lying down on, and went off to his house praising God's magnificence.

26 Absolutely everyone was astonished. They were praising God's magnificence and were filled with awe, "We saw unusual things today," they said.

27 After these things, as He left, He saw a tax collector (his name was Levi) sitting at the tax booth. "Follow Me," He told him.

28 He left everything there, got up, and started following Him.

29 Levi had a large reception for Jesus at his house. A big crowd of tax collectors and others were there lounging with them.

30 The Separatists and their Old Testament transcribers were whispering to His students: "Why are you eating and drinking with tax collectors and sinful people?"

31 Jesus responded by telling them, "Healthy people don't need a doctor, but the people who have something wrong with them do.

32 I have not come to invite people who do what is right to change their ways. I have come to invite sinful people to change their ways."

33 They said to Him, "John's students frequently abstain from eating and plead to God. Likewise, the Separatists' students also do this, but Yours eat and drink."

34 Jesus told them, "You can't make the 'sons of the bridal room' *(the people negotiating with the groom for the bride and helping her with the wedding)* abstain from eating while the groom is with them, can you? *No, eating is a big part of the negotiation process and the wedding.*"

35 But days will come when the groom is gone. Then they will be able to abstain from eating in those days."

36 He also was telling them an illustration, "No one puts a patch torn from a new robe on a worn-out robe. If that were done, both robes would definitely be ruined. The new robe would be torn, and the worn-out robe would have a patch on it that doesn't match.

37 And no one puts wine that is in the early stages of fermentation into worn-out leather bags. If that were done, the wine would definitely rip the leather bags, it would spill out, and the leather bags would be ruined.

38 But wine that is in the early stages of fermentation must be put into new leather bags.

39 And no one after drinking fermented wine wants wine that is in the early stages of fermentation. You see, they will say that the fermented wine is useful."

6

1 He happened to be traveling through croplands on a Sabbath. His students were pulling the heads of grain *off the plants*, rubbing them in their hands *to remove the husks*, and eating the grain.

2 "Why are you all doing what is not allowed on the Sabbaths?" asked some of the Separatists.

3 When Jesus answered them, He said, "Didn't you even read this thing that David did when he and those with him were hungry?

4 *Didn't you read* how he went into God's house, took the display bread, ate it, and gave it to the people with him? No one is allowed to eat the display bread except the priests. *Why don't you condemn David for what he did when he was hungry?*"

5 He was also telling them, "The Son of the Person is the Sabbath's Master." *("The Son of the Person" is a generic term Jesus used of Himself. Ezekiel and Daniel were called "son of a person." "Son of a person" is also in Psalm 80:17.)*

6 On a different Sabbath, He happened to go into the synagogue and teach. A man was there whose right hand was deformed.

7 The Old Testament transcribers and Separatists were watching Him closely to see if He would heal on the Sabbath. They were looking for a way to level a complaint against Him.
8 He realized their ponderings. He told the man who had the deformed hand, "Get up and stand in the middle." He got up and stood in the middle.
9 "I ask you," Jesus said to them, "when it comes to the Sabbath, which is allowed: to do good or to do bad, to rescue a soul or to ruin a soul?"
10 After He looked around at them all, He told him, "Put out your hand." He did, and his hand was established back to normal.
11 They were filled with insanity and were speaking in detail with each other about what they should do to Jesus.
12 On one of these days, He happened to go out into the mountain to pray. He continued through the night praying to God.
13 When day came, He hollered for His students. He selected twelve of them and gave them the name, missionaries. *He named them this because He was going to be sending them out on errands, on missions.*
14 They were Simon (that He also named Peter), Andrew (his brother), James, John, Philip, Bartholomew,
15 Matthew, Thomas, James (Alphaeus' son), Simon (the one called Zealot),
16 Judas (James's brother), and Judas from Kerioth (who became a traitor).
17 He walked down the mountain with them and stopped on a level area. A big crowd of His students and a very large number of the ethnic group were there from all of Judea, Jerusalem, and the sea coast of Tyre and Sidon. They came to listen to Him and to be cured of their illnesses.
18 He was healing people bothered by spirits that are not clean.
19 The entire crowd were looking for a way to touch Him because *the ability to heal* was coming out directly from Him and curing everyone.
20 He looked up at His students and said, "A blessing for you who are poor is that God's monarchy is yours.
21 A blessing for you who are hungry now is that you will be full. A blessing for you who are crying now is that you will laugh.
22 You are blessed when people hate you and when they isolate you, criticize you, and throw out your name as evil because of the Son of the Person.
23 Be happy in that day and skip *for joy*. You see, look, your pay is much in heaven. Their fathers were doing the same thing to the preachers.

24 More importantly, a tragedy to you wealthy people is that you have all of your comfort.

25 A tragedy to you who are filled up now is that you will be hungry. A tragedy to you who are laughing now is that you will grieve and cry.

26 What a tragedy it is when all the people talk nicely of you. You see, their fathers were doing the same thing to the counterfeit preachers.

27 But I tell you, you who are listening, love your enemies. Do nice things to the people who hate you.

28 Confer a blessing on the people who are hoping that something bad will happen to you. Pray for the people who are spiteful of you.

29 If someone hits you on the cheek, allow him to hit you on the other cheek too. If someone takes your robe, don't keep him from taking your long undershirt too.

30 When someone asks you for something, give it to him. When someone takes something that is yours, don't ask for it back.

31 Treat people in the same way *and* just as you also want them to treat you.

32 If you love the people who love you, what kind of generosity are you showing? You see, even sinful people love the people who love them.

33 And if you do good things for the people who do good things for you, what kind of generosity are you showing? Even sinful people do that.

34 If you give an interest loan to people you anticipate to receive from, what kind of generosity are you showing? Even sinful people give an interest loan to sinful people so that they will receive the things that are equal *to the full amount plus interest.*

35 More importantly, love your enemies, do good, and give an interest loan anticipating nothing back. Then your pay will be much, and you will be sons of the Highest because He is kind to the ungenerous and evil people.

36 Become compassionate just as your Father also is compassionate.

37 Don't judge, and you won't in any way be judged. Don't find people guilty, and you won't in any way be found guilty. Dismiss *people from what they should have done*, and you will be dismissed *from what you should have done.*

38 Give, and it will be given to you. They will give a nice amount that has been packed down and shaken together with even more spilling out over into your lap. You see, the amount that you measure out will be the amount measured back to you."

39 He also told them this illustration: "A blind person can't guide a blind person, can he? Won't both fall into a hole?

40 A student isn't above his teacher, but everyone trained by a teacher will be like his teacher.
41 Why do you see the wood chip in your brother's eye *(his tiny fault)*, but don't take a close look at the log in your own eye *(your huge fault)?*
42 How can you say to your brother, 'Brother, allow me to take out the wood chip in your eye,' when you yourself don't see the log in your eye? Faker, first take the log out of your eye, and then you'll see clearly to take out the wood chip in your brother's eye.
43 You see, a nice tree doesn't produce defective fruit, and a defective tree doesn't produce nice fruit.
44 Each tree is known by the fruit that it produces. *Figs and grapes are fruits.* People don't gather figs from thorn bushes. *Figs are on trees that don't have thorns.* They don't pick a cluster of grapes from a bush either. *Grapes are on vines.*
45 A good person brings out good things from his stockpile of good, and an evil person brings out evil things from his stockpile of evil. You see, his mouth speaks from the excess in his heart.
46 Why do you call Me, Master, Master, and don't do what I say?
47 Everyone who comes to Me, who listens to My messages, and who does them, I will put in front of your face who he is like.
48 He is like a person building a house, who excavated, went deep, and set a foundation on the bedrock. When a torrential rain came, the river crashed against that house and couldn't disturb it because it was nicely built.
49 But the person who listens and does not do, is like a person who built a house on the soil without a foundation. When the river crashed against it, right away it collapsed. The crash of that house became great.

7

1 Since He, for sure, filled up what the group heard with all His statements, He went into Capernaum.
2 A certain lieutenant's slave had something wrong with him and was going to pass away. The slave was important to him.
3 When the lieutenant heard about Jesus, he sent the Jewish people's older men out to Him asking Him to come and completely restore his slave.
4 When the *older men* showed up to *where* Jesus *was*, they were aggressively encouraging Him to go, saying that he deserves it.

5 "You see, he loves our nation," they told Him, "and he built the synagogue for us."
6 Jesus traveled to his house with them. As He already was not far away from the house, the lieutenant sent friends telling Him, "Master, don't be irritated. You see, I am unfit for you to come in under the roof of my house.
7 For this reason, I also didn't think that I deserved to come to You. But say the word, and my servant boy will have to be cured.
8 You see, even though I am a person arranged under the authority *of the Roman Emperor*, I have soldiers under me. I say, 'Travel,' to this one, and he travels. I say, 'Go,' to another, and he goes. To my slave, I say, 'Do this,' and he does it. *I know that you also can say a word and Your unseen soldiers will cure my slave.*"
9 When Jesus heard this, He was amazed. He turned to the crowd following Him and said, "I tell you, I haven't found this much trust even in Israel."
10 When the ones who were sent returned to the house, they found that the slave was well.
11 Sometime after this, He happened to travel into a city called Nain. His students and a big crowd were traveling together with Him.
12 As He came near the gate of the city, look, a dead *body* was being carried out to be buried. *The body was that of* an only biological son to his mother and she was a widow. An adequate crowd from the city was together with her.
13 When the Master saw her, He had sympathy for her and told her, "Don't cry."
14 He went up to the coffin and touched it. The people hauling it, stopped. "Young lad," He said, "I tell you, get up."
15 The dead boy sat up on his own and began speaking. Jesus gave him to his mother.
16 Fear took hold of everyone, and they were praising God's magnificence. They were saying, "A great preacher has risen among us," and, "God has kept an eye on His ethnic group."
17 These words about Him went out to all Judea and all the surrounding rural area.
18 John's students reported all these things to John.
19 John called for two certain students of his and sent them to the Master to question Him, "Are You the One coming, or should we expect another?"

20 When the *two* men showed up to where Jesus was, they said, "John the Submerger sent us out to ask You, 'Are You the One coming, or should we expect another?'"
21 In that hour, He healed many who had illnesses, ailments, and evil spirits. And as an act of generosity, He gave many blind people the ability to see.
22 When He answered them, He said, "Travel back, and report to John what you have seen and heard: Blind people see again, crippled people are walking around, people with a skin disease are cleared up, hearing-impaired people hear, dead people come back to life, and good news is shared with poor people.
23 Tell him that whoever doesn't stumble on Me is blessed."
24 When the messengers from John left, He began to talk to the crowds about John, "What did you go out into the backcountry to see? A stick disturbed by the wind?
25 But what did you go out to see? Someone decked out in elegant clothes? Look, the people who wear magnificent clothes and have lavish things are in kings' palaces.
26 But what did you go out to see? A preacher? Yes, I tell you, and much more than a preacher.
27 This is what Malachi wrote about, 'Look, I am sending My messenger out on a mission before Your face. He will construct Your road in front of You' *(Malachi 3:1)*.
28 I tell you, among people born to women, none is greater than John, but the smaller person in God's monarchy is greater than him.
29 All the ethnic group and tax collectors who listened to John showed that they considered God to be right when they were submerged with John's submersion.
30 But the Separatists and the law experts disregarded God's intention for them when they were not submerged by him.
31 So what will I liken the people in this generation to? What are they like?
32 They are like the young children sitting in the marketplace hollering to each other, 'We played the flute for you, and you didn't dance. We wailed, and you didn't cry.'
33 You see, John the Submerger has come without eating bread or drinking wine, and you say, 'He has a lesser deity.'
34 The Son of the Person has come eating and drinking, and you say, 'Look, an excessive eater and a wine drinker, a friend of tax collectors and sinful people.'

35 Insight is proven to be right by all her children. *The children of this insight show what the Separatists and law experts really are."*
36 One of the Separatists was asking Him to eat at his house. He went into the Separatist's house and reclined *on one of the couches around the table.*
37 And, look, there was a sinful woman in the city. When she correctly understood that He was lounging in the Separatist's house, she retrieved an alabaster jar of perfume
38 and stood behind Him next to His feet crying. She began to wet His feet with her tears and wipe them dry with the hair of her head. She was being very friendly to His feet and dabbing the perfume on them.
39 When the Separatist who invited Him saw it, he said to himself, "This Person, if He were a preacher, would know who and what kind of person this woman is that is touching Him, because she is sinful."
40 When Jesus responded, He told him, "Simon, I have something to say to you." "Teacher, say it," declared Simon.
41 "Two people owed money to a certain lender. One owed five hundred denarii *($25,000)*, the other, fifty *($2,500)*.
42 Since they didn't have any way to pay him back, in an act of generosity, he forgave both of them. So which of them will love him more?"
43 When Simon answered, he said, "I presume it would be the one to whom he forgave more." "You are correct," said Jesus.
44 He turned toward the woman and was declaring to Simon, "Do you see this woman? I came into your house. You didn't give Me water to wash My feet with, but she wet My feet with her tears and wiped them dry with her hair.
45 You didn't *greet Me and* give Me a friendly gesture, but she, from the moment that I came in, has not taken a break from being very friendly to My feet.
46 You didn't dab olive oil on My head, but she dabbed perfume on My feet.
47 *There is something that you can* thank for this, I tell you--Her many sins have been forgiven. That is why she is showing so much love. But the person who has been forgiven of little shows little love."
48 He told her, "Your sins have been forgiven."
49 The people feasting and chatting together with Him began to talk among themselves, "Who is this that even forgives sins?"
50 He told the woman, "Your trust has rescued you, travel into peace."

1 At that time, He also happened to be making His way in order through each city and village speaking publicly and sharing the good news of God's monarchy. The Twelve were together with Him.
2 Some women who had been healed from evil spirits and weaknesses were also with them: Mary (the one called "Magdalene" that seven lesser deities had come out of),
3 Joanna (a wife of Chuza, Herod's administrator), Susanna, and many different women. They were serving them with the things that they had.
4 As a big crowd was coming together and people were traveling on to Him from each city, He told an illustration:
5 "The person who plants crops went out to plant his batch of seeds. *His method of planting was flinging handfuls of seeds out on the ground throughout the whole field.* During this time, certainly there was a seed that fell along the road and was trampled on. The birds of the sky ate it.
6 A different seed fell down on the rock. After it sprouted, it dried up because it didn't have moisture.
7 A different seed fell in the middle of thorns. After they sprouted up together, the thorns choked it out.
8 A different seed fell into good soil. After it sprouted, it produced a hundred times more fruit." As He said these things, He was hollering, "The person who has ears for listening must listen."
9 His students were asking Him, "What is this illustration?"
10 "I have given you the opportunity to know the secrets of God's monarchy," He said, "but to the rest, I speak in illustrations so that they can't see as they see, and they can't understand as they hear.
11 *This illustration shows the different responses people have when they hear God's message.* The batch of seeds is God's message.
12 The ones along the road are the people who hear, but after that, the Accuser comes and takes the message out of their heart so that they won't trust and be rescued.
13 The ones on the rock are people who when they hear, they accept the message with happiness. These don't have root. They trust for a while until there is trouble, then they back off.
14 The seed that fell into the thorns, these are the people who hear while traveling under worries, wealth, and life's pleasures. These come together and choke them off. They obey the message, but not completely.

15 The seed in the nice soil, these are people who hear the message with a nice and good heart. They hold steady to it and their persistence produces fruit.

16 No one lights a lamp and then covers it up with some type of container or puts it beneath a cot. No, just the opposite, it is put *up high* on a stand so that the people traveling into the room may see the light.

17 You see, something is not hidden that won't end up being shown. And something isn't hidden away either that won't ever be known and be brought out to be shown.

18 So pay attention to how you hear. You see, whoever has, will get more, and whoever doesn't have, even what he seems to have will be taken away from him."

19 His mother and brothers showed up to where He was and weren't able to meet up with Him because of the crowd.

20 Someone reported to Him, "Your mother and brothers have been standing outside wanting to see You."

21 When He responded, He told them, "My mother and My brothers are these people, the ones listening to and doing God's message."

22 During one of those days, He and His students happened to climb on board a boat. "We will go across to the other side of the lake," He told them. So they set sail.

23 As they sailed, He fell asleep. A blast of wind stepped down across the lake. The boat was totally filling up with water, and they were in danger of sinking.

24 They went and woke Jesus up. "Boss, boss," they said, "we are being ruined." When He was wide awake, He shushed the wind and the wave of the water. They stopped, and it became calm.

25 "Where is your trust?" He told them. They were in awe and amazed. "So who is this?" they said to each other, "because He even gives orders to the winds and the water, and they obey Him."

26 They sailed down to the rural area of the Gerasenes which is on the opposite side from Galilee *(the eastern side)*.

27 When He came out on the land, a certain man who had lesser deities came to meet Him from the city. For quite a while, he hadn't worn any clothes or lived in a house. He stayed around the graves.

28 When he saw Jesus, he yelled out and fell toward Him. "Jesus, Son of the Highest God," he said with a loud voice, "why are You interfering with me? I plead with You to not torture me."

29 You see, He was ordering the spirit that was not clean to come out of the man. Many times it had seized him as he was being detained

with a chain and foot shackles. The lesser deity ripped the restraints apart and drove him into the backcountry.

30 "What is your name?" Jesus asked. "Legion," he said. *Legion is the Latin word for regiment. Its name was Legion* because many lesser deities had gone into him.

31 The lesser deities were begging Him so that He wouldn't give them the order to go off into the bottomless area.

32 There was a herd of an adequate amount of hogs grazing on the mountain. They begged Him so that He would give them permission to go into the hogs. He gave them permission.

33 The lesser deities came out from the man and went into the hogs. The herd rushed down the steep slope into the lake and were choked out.

34 When the people grazing them saw it, they escaped and reported it to the people in the city and in the fields.

35 Those people came out to see what had happened. When they came to where Jesus was, the person that the lesser deities came out of was sitting clothed and sane at the feet of Jesus. They were afraid.

36 Those who had seen what happened reported to them how the man with the lesser deities was rescued.

37 Absolutely all of the large number from the surrounding rural area of the Gerasenes asked Him to leave because they were restricted by great fear. He climbed on board a boat and returned *to where they had come from*.

38 The man that the lesser deities had come out of was pleading with Him to let him come along. But Jesus dismissed him and said,

39 "Return to your home, and describe to them all the things that God has done for you." He went off speaking publicly throughout the whole city about all the things that Jesus did for him.

40 When Jesus returned, the crowd gladly accepted Him. You see, they all were expecting Him.

41 And look, a man named Jairus came. He was head of the local synagogue. He got down at Jesus' feet and was begging Him to come into his house

42 because his only biological daughter, who was around twelve years old, was dying. As they made their way back to his house, the crowds were pushing and squeezing in on Him.

43 A woman was there who had been bleeding for twelve years. She had spent her whole life savings on doctors, *but none of their treatments worked*. She was not strong *enough* to be healed by any of them.

44 She came up to Jesus from behind and touched the fringe of His robe. At once her bleeding stopped.
45 "Who touched Me?" asked Jesus. Everyone denied touching Him. "Boss," Peter said, "the crowds are pushing and shoving You."
46 "Someone touched Me," Jesus said. "You see, I know that *healing* ability has gone out from Me."
47 When the woman saw that she didn't go unnoticed, she came trembling and got down facing Him. She reported in front of the entire group the reason why she touched Him and how that she was cured at once.
48 "Daughter," Jesus told her, "your trust has rescued you. Travel into peace."
49 As He was still speaking, someone came directly from the house of the head ruler of the local synagogue and said, "Your daughter has died. Don't irritate the Teacher anymore."
50 When Jesus heard it, He responded by telling him: "Don't be afraid. Just trust, and she will be rescued."
51 When He went into the house, He didn't allow anyone to go in with Him except Peter, John, James, and the girl's father and mother.
52 Everyone in the house was crying and beating their chests in grief for her. "Don't cry," Jesus said. "You see, she didn't die. She is sleeping."
53 They were laughing at Him because they had seen that she was dead.
54 He took hold of her hand and hollered, "Girl, get up."
55 Her spirit returned, she got up at once, and He specifically arranged for her to be given something to eat.
56 Her parents were astounded. Jesus ordered them not to tell anyone what had happened.

9

1 After calling the Twelve together, He gave them the ability to heal illnesses and authority over all the lesser deities.
2 He sent them out on a mission to speak publicly about God's monarchy and to cure the weak.
3 "Take nothing for the road," He told them. "Don't take a staff, a tote bag, bread, silver, or two long undershirts (only one apiece).
4 Stay there in whichever house you go into until you leave that city.
5 However many don't accept you, as you leave that city, knock the dust off your feet. That will be a witness against them."
6 They left and were going throughout the villages sharing good news and healing everywhere.

7 Herod, the head of one of Palestine's four regions, heard all the things that were happening. He was dumbfounded because some said that John had gotten up from the dead.
8 Others said that Elijah had appeared, and still others, that one of the original preachers had come back to life.
9 "I beheaded John," said Herod. "Who is this Person that I am hearing these kinds of things about?" He was looking for an opportunity to see Him.
10 When the missionaries returned, they described to Jesus all the things that they did. He took them along and slipped away secretly by Himself to a city called Bethsaida.
11 When the crowds knew about it, they followed Him. He was gladly accepting them and speaking to them about God's monarchy. He was curing the people who needed healing.
12 It was beginning to get late in the afternoon. The Twelve came up to Jesus and told Him, "Dismiss the crowd so that they can travel into the surrounding villages and fields, settle down for the night, and find some groceries because there is nothing here. This place is uninhabited."
13 "You must give them something to eat," He told them. "We don't have more than five loaves of bread and two fish here," they said, "unless we travel somewhere and buy food for this entire group."
14 You see, there were about five thousand men there. "Have them recline in reclining groups of about fifty each," He told His students.
15 This is what they did. Absolutely everyone reclined.
16 He took the five loaves of bread and the two fish, looked up into the sky, conferred a blessing on them, split them up, and was giving them to the students to pass out to the crowd.
17 They ate, and everyone was full. They picked up what was left over. There were twelve baskets of the pieces.
18 During a time that He was praying alone, the students happened to be together with Him. He asked them, "Who do the crowds say I am?"
19 "John the Submerger," they answered, "others Elijah, others that one of the original preachers came back to life."
20 "What about you?" Jesus asked. "Who do you say I am?" When Peter answered, he said, "God's Anointed King."
21 He shushed him and ordered them not to tell this to anyone.
22 "It is necessary for the Son of the Person to suffer many things," He told them, "to be rejected by the older men, the head priests, and the Old Testament transcribers, to be killed, and to be gotten up the third day."

23 He had been telling everyone, "If anyone wants to come behind Me, he must deny himself, daily pick up his cross *(or in other words, be ready to die for Me)*, and follow Me.
24 You see, whoever wants to rescue his soul will lose it, but whoever loses his soul on account of Me, this person will rescue it.
25 You see, what benefit is it to a person when he gains the whole world, but loses or sustains loss to himself?
26 You see, whoever is ashamed of Me and My messages, this person, the Son of the Person will be ashamed of when He comes in the magnificence of Him, the Father, and the sacred angels.
27 I tell you, truly some people standing here will not in any way taste death until they see God's monarchy."
28 It happened about eight days after these words. He took Peter, James, and John along and climbed up into the mountain to pray.
29 While He was praying, His face became visually different, and His clothes turned dazzling white.
30 And, look, two men were speaking together with Him: Moses and Elijah.
31 There was a glow of magnificence in the way they looked. They were talking about His exit that was going to be accomplished in Jerusalem.
32 Peter and the two with him had been weighted down with sleep. When they completely woke up, they saw His magnificence and the two men that had been standing together with Him.
33 During the *time* that the *two* happened to be completely separated away from *Jesus*, Peter told Him, "Boss, it is nice for us to be here. Let's make three tents, one for You, one for Moses, and one for Elijah." He didn't realize what he was saying.
34 As he said this, a cloud formed and shined over them. They were afraid as they entered the cloud.
35 A voice came from the cloud, saying, "This is My Son. I have selected Him. Listen to Him."
36 After the voice, Jesus was found to be alone. The three students kept quiet and didn't report anything to anyone in those days about what they had seen.
37 On the next day, after they came down from the mountain, a big crowd happened to meet together with Him.
38 And, look, a man from the crowd shouted, "Teacher, I am pleading with You, take a look at my son because he is my only biological son.

39 Look, a spirit takes him, he unexpectedly yells, it sends him into convulsions, foam comes out of his mouth, it wears him out, and he is crushed by the time it distances itself away from him.
40 I pleaded with Your students to throw it out, but they weren't able to."
41 When Jesus answered, He said, "O, untrusting and twisted generation, how long must I be near you and tolerate you? Bring your son here to Me."
42 As he was still coming, the lesser deity ripped him and sent him into violent convulsions. Jesus stopped the spirit that was not clean, cured the boy, and gave him back to his father.
43 Everyone was impressed with the greatness of God. Since everyone was amazed by all the things that He was doing, He told His students,
44 "You must put these words in your ears. You see, people are going to take the Son of the Person into custody."
45 The students were unaware of what this statement meant. It had been concealed from them so that they wouldn't comprehend it, and they were afraid to ask Him about it.
46 There was a pondering that came in among them: which of them would be the greatest.
47 When Jesus realized what they were pondering in their heart, He latched on to a young child and stood him beside Him.
48 "Whoever accepts this young child based on My name accepts Me," He told them, "and whoever accepts Me accepts the One who sent Me out. You see, the person who is littler among you all, this person is great."
49 "Boss," responded John, "we saw someone throwing out lesser deities in Your name, and we were keeping him from doing it because he isn't following with us."
50 "Don't keep him from doing it," Jesus told him. "You see, someone who is not against you is over with you."
51 In observance of the days of His being taken up *to heaven*, it happened that He also was determined to travel directly to Jerusalem.
52 He sent messengers out ahead of Him. The messengers traveled into a village of Samaritans to get things ready for Him.
53 They didn't accepted Him *or His request to spend the night there* because He appeared to be traveling into Jerusalem. *(This could have been due to their rivalry with Jerusalem or because they wanted Jesus to spend several days with them, not just one night.)*

54 When His students, James and John, saw it, they said, "Master, do you want us to tell fire to step down out of the sky and consume them?"
55 He turned around and shushed them.
56 They traveled to a different village.
57 As they traveled on the road, someone told Him, "I will follow You wherever You go off to."
58 "Foxes have burrows," Jesus told him, "and the birds of the sky have nests, but the Son of the Person doesn't even have a place to rest His head."
59 He told a different person, "Follow Me." But that person said, "Master, give me permission to first go off and bury my father *after he dies*."
60 "Leave the dead to bury their own dead," Jesus told him. "You must go and announce God's monarchy everywhere."
61 A different person also said, "I will follow you, Master, but first give me permission to go back home and spend a few days telling everyone good-bye."
62 But Jesus told him, "No one who is guiding a plow with his hands and looking back at where he left his stuff is suitable for God's monarchy."

10

1 After this, the Master showed everyone seventy different ones. He sent them out by twos on a mission to go ahead of Him into every city and every place where He was going to be going.
2 He was telling them, "There certainly is a big harvest, but there are *only* a few workers. So plead with the master of the harvest so that he might put workers out into his harvest.
3 Make your way out. Look, I am sending you out as lambs in the middle of wolves *(the vulnerable among the dangerous)*.
4 Don't haul a money bag, tote bag, or sandals around. Don't greet anyone along the way.
5 Whenever you go into a house, first say, "Peace to this house."
6 And if a son of peace is there, your peace will relax on it. But if *a son of peace is* definitely not there *(if they want to argue, fight, or get upset)*, your peace will double back on to you *(or in other words, quietly leave, leave in peace, just as you came)*.
7 Stay in the same house eating and drinking what they provide. You see, the worker deserves his pay. Do not go from house to house.

8 In whatever city you go to and they accept you, eat what they place in front of you,
9 heal the frail people in it, and tell them, "God's monarchy has come near over you."
10 But in whatever city you go to and they don't accept you, go out into its plaza and say,
11 'Even your city's dust that is stuck to our feet, we are wiping off against you. But the more important thing you should know is that God's monarchy has come near over you.'
12 I tell you that it will be more tolerable for Sodom in that day than it will be for that city.
13 What a tragedy it is to you, Chorazin! What a tragedy it is to you, Bethsaida! because if the abilities that happened among you happened in Tyre and Sidon, they would have changed their ways a long time ago wearing sackcloth *(the cloth that grieving people wear)* and sitting in ashes *to express their grief.*
14 More importantly, it will be more tolerable for Tyre and Sidon in the sentencing than for you.
15 And you, Capernaum, you will not be put up high, up to heaven, *as you think you will, just because I was often in your city*. You will be walked down to Hades *(the underworld of the dead).*
16 The person who listens to you listens to Me, and the person who disregards you disregards Me. The person who disregards Me disregards the One who sent Me out on a mission to this earth."
17 When the seventy returned, they were happy. "Master, even the lesser deities place themselves under us in Your name," they said.
18 "I was watching the Opponent fall from the sky as lightning," He told them.
19 "Look, I have given you the authority to trample up on top of snakes and scorpions and up on top of every ability of the enemy. Nothing will harm you in any way.
20 More importantly, don't be happy about this, that the spirits place themselves under you. Be happy that your names have been written in heaven."
21 In that same hour, He was excited in the Sacred Spirit and said, "I admire the way You, Father, Master of heaven and earth, hid these things from the scholars and scientists and uncovered them to infants. Yes, Father, as You have seen, this has worked out quite well.
22 My Father turned everything over to Me. No one knows who the Son is except the Father. And no one knows who the Father is except the Son and whoever the Son intends to uncover Him to."

23 He turned toward His students privately and said, "The eyes that see what you see are blessed.
24 You see, I tell you that many preachers and kings wanted to see what you are looking at and didn't. They wanted to hear what you hear and didn't."
25 And look, a certain law expert stood up, trying to harass Him. "Teacher," he said, "what is one thing that after I do it I will inherit life that spans all time?"
26 Jesus said to him, "What has been written in the law? How do you read it?"
27 When the law expert answered, he said, "You will love the Master, your God, from your whole heart, in your whole soul, in your whole strength, and in your whole mind, and the person near you as yourself."
28 "You answered correctly," He told him. "Do this and you will live."
29 But the law expert wanted to show that he was doing the right thing *because the people near him were good people. They were priests and Levites and he loved them. To flaunt this*, he asked Jesus, "And who is near me?"
30 When Jesus took it up, He said, "A certain person was walking down out of Jerusalem to Jericho. On his way there, bandits surrounded him, stripped him of everything, and put wounds on him, leaving him half dead.
31 By coincidence a certain priest was walking down to Jericho on that same road. When he saw him, he passed by on the other side.
32 Likewise, a Levite also happened to come to that place. After he went over and looked at him, he passed by on the other side.
33 But as a certain Samaritan was on a trip, when he went by him and saw him, he had sympathy for him.
34 He went over to him, poured olive oil and wine on his wounds, and bandaged them up. Then he loaded him onto his own animal, took him into an inn, and took care of him.
35 On the next day, he took out two denarii *(coins equal to one day's wage apiece)*, and gave them to the innkeeper. 'Take care of him,' he told him, 'and if you spend more than that on him, when I come back by here, I will pay you back.'
36 Which of these three do you think became near to the man who fell into the bandits?"
37 "The one who showed him forgiving kindness," he said. "Travel, and do the same thing," Jesus told him. *(The real question is not, 'Who is near me?' but, 'Will I become near to the people near me?')*

38 During the time that they were traveling, He went into a certain village. A certain woman was there named Martha. She invited Him to stay in her house.
39 *Martha* had a sister named Mary. Mary was seated beside the Master at His feet listening to His message.
40 Martha was being pulled *all* around with much serving. She stood over *Him* and said, "Master, aren't you concerned that my sister has left me back here to serve alone? So, talk to her so that she will get together with me and assist me."
41 "Martha, Martha," the Master answered, "you are worried and flustered about many things,
42 but there is one thing that's needed. You see, Mary selected the good part, something that won't be taken away from her."

11

1 During the time that He happened to be in a certain place praying, when He stopped, one of His students said to Him, "Master, teach us how to pray, just as John also taught his students."
2 "When you pray," He told them, "say, Father, Your name *and who You are* must be made sacred. Your monarchy must come.
3 You must give us the daily thing, our next day's bread.
4 And You must forgive us of our sins. You see, we ourselves also forgive everyone who owes us. And You won't carry us into trouble."
5 He also told them, "What if someone from among you will have a friend and he will travel to him in the middle of the night? He might tell him, 'Friend, loan me three loaves of bread
6 since, for sure, a friend of mine showed up at my house in the middle of his trip and I don't have any food to place in front of him.'
7 When that friend answers from inside, he could say, 'Don't bother me. I've already locked the door and my young children are with me in bed *asleep in my arms.* I can't get up and give you *some bread.'*
8 I tell you, even if the fact that he is his friend won't cause him to get up and give him some bread, the fact that he had the nerve to knock on his door in the middle of the night definitely will. He will give him as much as he needs.
9 I tell you, ask, and it will be given to you. Look, and you will find. Knock, and *a door* will be opened for you.
10 You see, everyone asking receives. The person looking finds. And *a door* will open to the person knocking.
11 Any father from among you, if your son asks for a fish, will you give him a snake instead?

12 Or if he asks for an egg, will you give him a scorpion?

13 So if you all, who are evil, know that you should be giving good presents to your children, how much more will the Father from heaven, give the Sacred Spirit to the people who ask Him?" *(The Sacred Spirit provides good presents.)*

14 He was throwing out a lesser deity from a man who couldn't speak. It happened that when the lesser deity came out, the speech-impaired man spoke. The crowds were amazed.

15 Some in the crowd said, "He throws the lesser deities out with the help of Beelzebub, the head of the lesser deities."

16 Different ones were harassing Him looking for a proof *to come* out of the sky directly from Him.

17 He, realizing their thoughts, told them, "Every monarchy that is divided and against itself becomes uninhabited, and a house against a house, falls.

18 If the Opponent also has been divided and against itself, how will his monarchy be established? *I am making this point* because you say that I am throwing the lesser deities out with the help of Beelzebub. *Look at what I am doing. Look at what I am teaching.* It is bitterly opposed to and against Beelzebub.

19 If I throw the lesser deities out with the help of Beelzebub, what about your sons? With whom do they throw them out? *Ask them. Their answers* will stand as judges of you.

20 But if I throw the lesser deities out with God's finger, clearly God's monarchy has already come to you.

21 When a fully armored strong person guards his courtyard, his things are safe.

22 But whenever someone stronger than the strong person comes up against him, he conquers him, takes his full body armor that gave him confidence, and passes out his spoils. *I am able to throw out lesser deities because I am using God's finger and it is stronger than the Opponent.*

23 The person who is not with Me is against Me, and the person who does not gather with Me scatters My things.

24 When a spirit that is not clean leaves a person, it passes through places that don't have water looking for relief. And not finding it, it says, 'I will return back into my house that I left.'

25 When it arrives, it finds that the house has been swept and decorated.

26 Then it travels, finds seven different spirits more evil than itself, and brings them along. When they go in, they live there, and it

becomes *such that* the last *circumstances* of that person are worse than the first."

27 During the time that He was saying these things, a certain woman from the crowd happened to raise her voice and say, "The belly that hauled You around and the breasts that nursed You are blessed."

28 He said, "So, of course, the people hearing and observing God's message are blessed."

29 As the crowds gathered more *people*, He began to be saying, "This generation is an evil generation. It is searching for proof *that God sent Me*. No proof will be given to it except the proof of Jonah.

30 You see, just as Jonah became proof to the Ninevites, so the Son of the Person will also be proof to this generation.

31 In the sentencing with the men of this generation, a queen from the south will get up and find them guilty because she came from the ends of the earth to hear Solomon's insight and, look, a greater thing than Solomon is here.

32 In the sentencing with this generation, Ninevite men will stand up and find it guilty because they changed their ways and did what Jonah yelled on their streets and, look, a greater thing than Jonah is here.

33 No one lights a lamp and puts it in a hidden place or under the two gallon measuring basket. No, it is put up high on a stand so that the people traveling into the room may see the light.

34 Light enters the body through the eye. Your eye is the body's lamp. When your eye is dedicated *to its job of seeing*, your whole body is lit up. But whenever it is evil *and refuses to do its job correctly*, your body is dark.

35 So look out for this: that the light in you is not darkness.

36 If your whole body is lit up, not having any dark spots, it will be lit up as when a lamp as bright as lightning lights things up for you."

37 During the time that He was speaking, a Separatist asked Him to have lunch at his house. When He went in, He settled down on one of the sofas.

38 When the Separatist saw this, he was amazed that He had not first submerged Himself in water before lunch. *Jews submerge themselves in water to make themselves ritually clean.*

39 The Master said to him, "Now you Separatists clean the outside of the cup and the plate, but your inside is still packed full of looting and evilness.

40 Aren't you distracted? When God made the outside of you, didn't He also make the inside? *Why aren't you concerned about your inside?*

41 A more important thing is to give the things inside of you as a charitable donation. *Let go of them.* Then, look, everything will be clean for you.

42 But what a tragedy it is to you, Separatists, because you make sure to give a ten-percent offering from the *lesser plants in your garden* (sweet smelling mint, rue leaves, and every vegetable) and pass by the heavier things: justice and the love of God. You must do these heavier things and not neglect those lesser ones.

43 What a tragedy it is to you, Separatists, because you love the front bench in the synagogue and people greeting you in the marketplace.

44 What a tragedy it is to you because you are like obscure burial vaults. The people walking around up on top of you do not realize that they are walking over a place of death."

45 One of the law experts responded by telling Him, "Teacher, what you are saying also injures us."

46 "And to you, the law experts," said Jesus, "what a tragedy it is because you load people down with heavy hard-to-haul loads and you yourselves don't even lightly touch those heavy loads with one of your fingers.

47 What a tragedy it is to you because you build the preachers' burial vaults, but your fathers killed them.

48 Clearly you are witnesses and agree that you think your fathers' actions were good because not only did your fathers kill them, but now you are building their burial vaults.

49 Because of this, God's insight also says, I will send preachers and missionaries out to them. They will kill and persecute some of them

50 so that the blood of all the preachers that has been spilled out *(by persecution)* since the world was formed will be intensively searched for from this generation,

51 from the blood of Abel to the blood of the Zacharias that was destroyed between the altar and God's house. Yes, I tell you, it will be intensively search for from this generation.

52 What a tragedy it is to you, the law experts, because you yourselves take away the key to the information. You didn't go in, and you keep the people from going in."

53 When He left that place, the Old Testament transcribers and Separatists began to hold a dreadful grudge against Him. They were getting Him to speak impromptu about more things,

54 lying in wait for him *wanting* to snag something out of His mouth *that they could use against Him.*

1 Meanwhile, when tens of thousands of the crowd were packing into one area so much that they were trampling on each other, He first began to tell His students, "You yourselves, be cautious of the Separatists' yeast. Their yeast is faked behavior. *(Yeast is unseen, yet it spreads quickly to all of the dough that it is in and changes it. The Separatists seem to be good, and their bad is unseen, but it quickly spreads and causes ruin.)*
2 There is nothing that has been covered up well that will not be uncovered, and nothing hidden that will not be known.
3 As many things as you said in the dark will be heard in the light, and what you spoke to someone's ear in a storage room will be spoken publicly on top of the houses.
4 I tell you, my friends, don't be afraid of those who kill the body and can't do anything more than that.
5 I will put in front of your face who you should fear. Fear the One who, after He kills, has authority to throw people into the Hinnom Valley. Yes, I tell you, this is the One to fear. *(The Hinnom Valley ran along the southwestern edge of Jerusalem. At one time children were burned to death there as sacrifices to idols. It is symbolic of the eternal lake of fire.)*
6 Aren't five little sparrows sold for a few dollars? Not one sparrow from them is forgotten in God's sight.
7 Even all the hairs of your head have been numbered. Don't be afraid. You are more substantial than many little sparrows.
8 I tell you, everyone who acknowledges being in Me in front of people, the Son of the Person will also acknowledge being in him in front of God's angels.
9 But the person who denies Me in the sight of people, I will flatly deny him in the sight of God's angels.
10 Everyone who states a word against the Son of the Person will be forgiven for that word, but the person who insults the Sacred Spirit will not be forgiven for it.
11 When they bring you in before the synagogues, the head rulers, and the authorities, do not worry how or what you might give for a defense or what you might say.
12 You see, the Sacred Spirit will teach you in the same hour what you must say."
13 Someone from the crowd said to Him, "Teacher, tell my brother to allocate some of the inheritance to me."
14 "Sir," Jesus told him, "who put Me in charge over you as a judge or distributor?"

15 And He told them, "Look, and guard yourselves from every desire for more, because during the time that someone is overflowing in wealth, he is not kept alive by all the things that he has."
16 He told an illustration to them: "A certain wealthy man's farmland was productive.
17 And He was pondering and saying to himself, 'What will I do because I don't have a place to gather my produce?'
18 'I will do this,' he said, 'I will take down my grain bins and build bigger. I will gather everything there, my grain and goods.
19 I will state to my soul, "Soul, you have many goods stored here for many years. Relax. Eat. Drink. Celebrate."'
20 But God told him, 'Aren't you distracted? Tonight they are asking to take your soul back from you. *You will die tonight.* Who will get the things that you prepared for yourself?'
21 This is how it is with the person who stockpiles stuff for himself and is not being wealthy to God."
22 "Because of this," He told His students, "I tell you, don't worry about the soul (what you will eat). And don't worry about the body (what you will put on) either.
23 You see, the soul is more than meals, and the body is more than the attire.
24 Take a close look at crows because they don't plant seeds or harvest, they don't have storage rooms or grain bins, yet God provides for them. How much more substantial are you than the birds?
25 Who from among you is able to add half a meter to your height by worrying?
26 So if you can't even do the least little thing like that, why are you worrying about everything else?
27 Take a close look at the wild flowers, how they grow. They don't labor. They don't make thread or fabric. But, I tell you, not even Solomon in all his magnificence put *clothes* around himself like one of these.
28 If God decks out the grass in a field like this, that exists today and tomorrow is thrown into a fire pit, will He not do much more for you, you people who seldom trust Him?
29 Don't be looking for something to eat or something to drink. And don't be anxious.
30 You see, the nations of the world are searching for all these, but your Father realizes that you need them.
31 More importantly, be looking for His monarchy, and these things will be added to you.

32 Don't be afraid, little flock, because it seemed like a good idea to your Father to give you His monarchy.
33 Sell your things and give *that money* as a charitable donation. Make money bags for yourself that do not wear out, a permanent stockpile in heaven, where a thief doesn't come near, and a moth doesn't devour it either.
34 You see, where your stockpile is, there your heart will also be.
35 Tuck your long undershirt up into your waist sash *(or in other words, get ready to work)*. Keep the lights on.
36 Be like people awaiting their master *to return* once he is released from the *late night* wedding events so that when he comes and knocks, right away they can open the door to him.
37 Those slaves that he found staying awake until he came are blessed. Amen, I tell you that he will tuck his long undershirt up into his waist sash *(or in other words, get ready to work)* and make them recline as he comes alongside and serves them.
38 And if he comes *late at night* in the second *guard shift--9 p.m. to midnight* or even *early into the next morning* in the third guard shift--*midnight to 3 a.m.* and finds them waiting for him, those slaves are blessed.
39 Know this, that if the homeowner had known what hour that the thief would come, he would have stayed awake and wouldn't have let his house be broken into.
40 You also must become people who are ready, because the Son of the Person comes at an hour that you don't think He will."
41 "Master," Peter said, "are you telling this illustration just to us or to everyone?"
42 "So who is the manager that the master trusts?" the Master said. "Who is the attentive one that he will put in charge over his attendants to give them portions of grain at the right time?
43 That slave is blessed when his master comes and finds him doing that.
44 Truly, I tell you, that he will put him in charge over all of his things.
45 But if that slave says in his heart, 'My master is taking a long time to come,' and begins to hit the servant boys and the servant girls, if he is eating, drinking, and getting drunk,
46 the master of that slave will arrive on a day that he is not expecting and in an hour he does not know. He will cut him in two and put his share of everything in the same place where the shares of the people who cannot be trusted are.

47 The slave who knows what his master wants and doesn't get it ready (or do anything pointed toward what he wanted) will be beaten many times.
48 But the slave who doesn't know *what his master wants* but does something deserving of wounds, will be beaten only a few times. They will look for a lot directly from everyone that they gave a lot to. And they will ask for much more from those that they invested a lot in.
49 I came to throw fire on the earth. And what do I want? If only it had already been started.
50 There is a submersion that I have to be submerged in. How I am constrained by it until it is finished!
51 Do you think that I showed up here to give peace in the earth? Definitely not, I tell you, but rather bitter division.
52 You see, from now on, there will be five that have been divided up in one house, three against two and two against three.
53 They will be divided up: a father against a son and a son against a father, a mother against her daughter and a daughter against her mother, a mother-in-law against her daughter-in-law and a daughter-in-law against her mother-in-law."
54 He also was saying to the crowds, "When you see clouds coming up over the western regions, right away you say, 'Severe weather is coming,' and that is what happens.
55 And when the wind blows from the south, you say, 'It will be a hot wind,' and it happens.
56 Fakers, you know to check the appearance of the earth and the sky, but how do you not know to check this appointed time?
57 Why don't you all also judge what is right on your own?
58 You see, since you are making your way back up to the head authority with your opponent in a court case, on the way, do all you can to settle the matter with your opponent so that the *head authority* won't ever drag you down to the judge, the judge turn you over to the bailiff, and the bailiff throw you into jail.
59 I tell you, you will not in any way get out of jail until you have paid back *every* last tiny brass coin."

13

1 Some people beside there were reporting to Him at the same time about certain Galileans whose blood Pilate mixed with their sacrifices *(or in other words, that Pilate killed while they were offering their sacrifices at the temple)*.

2 He responded by saying, "Do you think that these Galileans have suffered these things because they became more sinful than all the other Galileans?
3 Definitely not, I tell you, but if you don't change your ways, you will all be ruined in a similar way.
4 Or those eighteen that the tower in Siloam fell on and killed, do you think that they somehow ended up owing *God* more than all the *other* people living in Jerusalem?
5 Definitely not, I tell you, but if you don't change your ways, you will all be ruined in a similar way." *(Less than forty years after this, Roman soldiers brutally slaughtered all the Jews in Jerusalem.)*
6 He told this illustration, "A certain person had a fig tree that he had planted in his vineyard. He went looking for fruit on the fig tree, but he didn't find any.
7 'Look,' he told the vineyard worker, 'I have come looking for fruit in this fig tree for three years, and I have found none. So chop it down. Why keep it and prevent the ground from being used for something else?'
8 'Master,' responded the vineyard worker, 'leave it alone for this year too until after I excavate around it and put manure down.
9 Then if it produces fruit, that certainly *is good* for the future, but if not, you definitely will chop it down.'"
10 He was teaching in one of the synagogues on the Sabbaths.
11 And look, a woman was there who had had a spirit of frailty for eighteen years. She was stooping over and not able to stand all the way up straight.
12 When Jesus saw her, He hollered out to her, "Ma'am, you have been dismissed from your frailty."
13 He placed His hands on her, and at once she straightened up and started praising God's magnificence.
14 The synagogue's head ruler responded because he was frustrated with Jesus healing on the Sabbath. He told the crowd, "There are six days in which work must be done. So come and be healed during one of those days and not on the day of the Sabbath."
15 "Fakers," responded the Master, "doesn't each of you on the Sabbath untie his cow or donkey from the feed trough and lead it off *to where the water is* to give it a drink?
16 But this woman, who is a daughter of Abraham, whom the Opponent tied up for, look, eighteen years, isn't it necessary for her to be untied from this restraint on the day of the Sabbath?"

17 As He said these things, all the people who opposed Him were ashamed, and the entire crowd was happy for all the magnificent things that were happening through Him.

18 "What is God's monarchy like?" He was asking. "And what will I liken it to?

19 It is like a kernel of mustard that a man took and threw into his garden. It grew, turned into a tree, and the birds of the sky nested in its branches."

20 "What will I liken God's monarchy to?" He again said.

21 "It is like yeast that a woman took and hid in three loads of dough until it all was raised."

22 He was traveling along through cities and villages teaching and making a journey into Jerusalem.

23 Someone said to Him, "Master, tell us if it is true that only a few people are rescued." But Jesus said to them,

24 "Struggle to go in through the narrow door, because many, I tell you, will look for *an easy way* to go in and won't muster up the strength *to go in*.

25 But after the homeowner got up and closed the door, you all began to stand outside and knock on the door, saying, 'Master, open the door for us.' He will respond by stating to you, 'I don't know you *or* where you are from.'

26 At that time, you will begin to tell him, 'We ate and drank in your sight. You taught in our plazas.'

27 He will state to you, 'I don't know you *or* where you are from. Stay away from Me, all you workers of wrong.'

28 There you will cry and grind your teeth when you see *the Jewish fathers* (Abraham, Isaac, and Jacob) and all the Jewish preachers in God's monarchy, but you being thrown outside.

29 People will arrive *from outside of the Jewish nation,* from the eastern regions and the western regions, from the north and the south. They will recline in God's monarchy.

30 Look, the people who are last will be first, and the people who are first will be last."

31 In the same hour, some Separatists came to him and told Him, "Leave and travel away from here because Herod wants to kill You."

32 "Travel to Herod," Jesus told them, "and tell that fox, 'Look, I am throwing lesser deities out and finishing out curing people today and tomorrow. On the third day, I will be finished.

33 What is more important is that I must be traveling today, tomorrow, and the following day so that I can get to Jerusalem because it is unacceptable for a preacher to be ruined outside of Jerusalem.'
34 Jerusalem, Jerusalem, the city killing the preachers and throwing stones at those who have been sent out to her! How many times I wanted to bring your children together in one place, the way that a hen gathers her young chicks under her wings, and you did not want it.
35 Look, your house is left *in your hands*. I tell you, you all will in no way see Me again until *the time* arrives when you will say, 'The One conferred with blessings is coming in the Master's name.'"

14

1 He happened to go into the house of one of the head people of the Separatists on the Sabbath to eat bread. They were closely watching Him during the time that He was there.
2 And look, in front of Him was a certain person whose body was swollen.
3 Jesus responded by saying to the law experts and Separatists, "Is it permitted to heal on the Sabbath or not?"
4 They remained calm. He latched on to him, cured him, and dismissed him.
5 "If your son or cow falls into a well," He told them, "won't you pull him up right away even during the Sabbath?"
6 They couldn't *think of any way* to respond against Him.
7 He was giving the people who had been invited some advice as He was fixing His attention on how they were selecting the front reclining spots *(the place of honor)*. He told them,
8 "When someone invites you to wedding events, you shouldn't recline in the front reclining spot. What if perhaps someone more important than you has also been invited?
9 The one who invited both of you will come to you and state, 'Give your spot to this person.' Then with shame you will begin to move back to the last spot *in the back*.
10 But when you arrive at wedding events that you were invited to, settle down in the last spot *in the back* so that when the person who has invited you comes to you, he will state, 'Friend, move further up toward the front.' Then it will be magnificent for you, and all the people reclining together with you will see it.
11 Every person who puts himself up high will be put down low, and the person who puts himself down low will be put up high."

12 He also was saying to the person who had invited Him, "When you have a lunch or a feast, don't holler for your friends, brothers, relatives, or wealthy neighbors. That way it won't ever become a thing where they repay you in return by inviting you to one of their meals.
13 But whenever you have a reception, invite poor, badly wounded, crippled, and blind people.
14 You will be blessed because they don't have a way to repay you. You see, it will be repaid to you in the *next life* when the people who do what is right return back to life."
15 When someone who was feasting and chatting together with Him heard these things, he told Him, "Anyone who will eat bread in God's monarchy, *as we Jews will,* is blessed."
16 Jesus told him, "A certain person was having a large feast and invited many.
17 He sent his slave out an hour before the feast to tell the people who had been invited, 'Come, the meal is already ready.'
18 They all began, *starting* from one *consensus,* to come up with excuses. The first told him, 'I purchased a field, and I am obligated to go out and see it. I ask you to excuse me.'
19 A different one said, 'I purchased five pairs of cows and have to go check them. I ask you to excuse me.'
20 And a different one said, 'I *just* married a woman. That's why I can't come.'
21 When the slave showed up, he reported these things back to his master. At that time, the property owner was enraged and told his slave, 'Go out quickly into the plazas and streets of the city, and bring the poor, badly wounded, blind, and crippled in here.'
22 'Master,' said the slave, 'what you ordered has already happened and there are still empty places.'
23 The master said to the slave, 'Go out onto the roads and trails, and urge people to come in so that my house will be full.
24 You see, I tell you that none of those men who were invited will taste any of my feast.'"
25 Many crowds of people were traveling together with Him. He turned to them and said,
26 "If someone comes to Me and does not hate his own father, mother, wife, children, brothers, and sisters, and even yet his own soul, he is not able to be My student.
27 Anyone who does not haul his own cross *(or in other words, is not ready to die for Me),* and come behind Me is not able to be My student.

28 You see, who from among you that wants to build a tower, doesn't first sit down, count up how much it will cost, and make sure that he has enough money to complete the tower?
29 That way it will never be that after laying a foundation he can't finish off the tower and everyone watching begins to mock him
30 and say, 'This person began building and couldn't finish it off.'
31 Or what king traveling to meet up with a different king *for war* doesn't first sit down *with his advisors* and be advised if it is possible with his ten thousand soldiers to fight the one coming against him with twenty thousand?
32 If it isn't possible, as the other king is still far away, he will definitely send out a delegation of older men and ask him for his conditions of peace.
33 So in this same way, each one of you who does not say good-bye to all his things is not able to be My student.
34 Salt is nice, but if salt has no flavor, what will you season your food with?
35 *Without flavor, salt has no use.* It's not suitable for the ground or even for manure. It is just thrown out. The person who has ears for listening must listen."

15

1 All the tax collectors and sinful people were near to Him so that they could listen to Him.
2 And both the Separatists and the Old Testament transcribers were speaking in hushed tones among themselves, saying, "This Person accepts sinful people and eats together with them."
3 He told them this illustration,
4 "What person from among you who has a hundred sheep, if he loses one of them, does not leave the ninety-nine in the backcountry and set out looking for the lost sheep until he finds it?
5 When he finds it, he places it on his shoulders and is happy.
6 When he comes into his house, he calls his friends and neighbors together and tells them, 'Let's all be happy because I found the sheep that has been lost.'
7 I tell you that this is how in heaven they are happy over one sinful person who changes his ways rather than over ninety-nine that do what is right and don't need to change their ways.
8 Or what woman who has ten drachmas *(silver coins)*, if she loses one of them, does not light a lamp, sweep the house, and look carefully until she finds it?

9 When she finds it, she calls her friends and neighbors together and says, 'Let's all be happy because I found the drachma that I lost.'
10 This is how, I tell you, in the sight of God's angels there is happiness over one sinful person changing his ways."
11 He also said, "A certain person had two sons.
12 The younger one told his father, 'Father, give me the part of the assets being put away.' The father divvied out his life savings to them.
13 Not many days after that, the younger son gathered everything up, left the area, and went to a distant rural area. There he squandered his assets, living recklessly.
14 After he spent everything, there was a severe famine throughout that rural area, and he began to run out of food.
15 He traveled around looking for a job. One of the citizens of that rural area hired him and sent him into his fields to feed hogs.
16 *The food and pay were so scarce that* he was desiring to eat the *feed* (raw carob pods) that the hogs were eating until he was full. Yet no one was giving him any.
17 When he came to his senses, he was declaring, 'How many of my father's paid workers have more than enough bread, but I am being ruined here by a famine.
18 I will get up and travel to my father. I will state to him, "Father, what I did was sinful to heaven and in your sight.
19 I no longer deserve to be called your son. Treat me like one of your paid workers."'
20 He got up and went to his father. But as he was still a long way away, his father saw him and had sympathy. He ran out to him and threw his arms around his neck. He was very friendly to him.
21 'Father,' said the son, 'what I did was sinful to heaven and in your sight. I no longer deserve to be called your son.'
22 'Quick,' the father told his slaves, 'bring out the most important long robe, and put it on him. Give him a ring for his hand and sandals for his feet.
23 Bring the grain-fed calf, and kill it. After we eat, we will celebrate
24 because this son of mine was dead and now he has come back to life. He had been lost and now he has been found.' They began to celebrate.
25 His other son, the older one, was out in a field. On his way home, as he was near the house, he heard music and circle dancing.
26 He called for one of the servant boys and was inquiring what this could be.

27 'Your brother has arrived,' the boy told him, 'and your father killed the grain-fed calf because he received him back healthy.'
28 He was enraged and didn't want to go in. His father came out and was encouraging him to come in.
29 When he responded, he told his father, 'Look, for so many years, I have been a slave for you. I never even once neglected your demand. And you never once gave me even a goat so that I might celebrate with my friends.
30 But when your son came who ate up your life savings with prostitutes, you killed the grain-fed calf for him.'
31 'Child,' said the father, 'you are always with me, and all my things are yours.
32 We had to celebrate and be happy because this brother of yours was dead and now he lives, he had been lost and now he has been found.'"

16

1 He also was saying to the students, "There was a certain wealthy man who had a manager working for him. Someone had come to him and accused this manager of squandering the wealthy man's things.
2 He hollered for him. 'What is this I hear about you?' he said to him. 'Give the account back to me that you have been managing. You see, you can't be my manager anymore.'
3 The manager said to himself, 'What will I do because my master is taking the management away from me. I don't have the strength to plow and plant. I am ashamed to be asking people for money.
4 I know what I will do so that when I am dislodged from this management job people will accept me into their houses.'
5 He called for each person who owed something to his master. 'How much do you owe my master?' he asked the first person.
6 'Eight hundred gallons of olive oil,' he said. 'Here,' he told him, 'accept your documents, sit down quickly, and write four hundred.'
7 Following that, he said to a different person, 'You, how much do you owe?' 'A thousand bushels of grain,' he said. 'Here, accept your documents and write eight hundred,' he told him.
8 The master applauded the manager who did things the wrong way because he did *it* with a focus *on his future*. The sons of this span of time are more attentive to their own generation than the sons of the light are.
9 I tell you, make friends for yourselves using the wealth that is responsible for so much wrong so that when it ceases, they will accept you into the tents that span all time.

10 The person who can be trusted with the smallest thing can also be trusted with much, and the person who does the wrong thing with the smallest thing also does the wrong thing with much.

11 So if you eventually couldn't be trusted with the wealth that is wrong *to be fond of and to hoard*, who will trust you with the true wealth?

12 And if you eventually couldn't be trusted with the things belonging to others, who will give you your own things?

13 A domestic servant can't be a slave to two masters. You see, either he will hate the one *master* and love the other one, or he will keep the one *master* in front of him and ignore the other one. You can't be a slave to God and wealth."

14 The Separatists, who are fond of money, were listening to all these things and making fun of Him out loud.

15 "You are the ones who make yourselves right in the people's sight," Jesus told them, "but God knows your hearts. *He knows that you want to be the high thing that people value.* The high thing that people value is disgusting in God's sight.

16 The Law and the Preachers have been until the time of John. From then on, the good news *about God's monarchy being here* has been shared, and everyone is forcing their way into it.

17 It is easier for the sky and the earth to go away than for even one hook of a letter of the law to fall down.

18 Everyone who dismisses his wife *without divorcing her* and marries a different woman *is breaking one of the Ten Demands: He* is cheating on his wife. The man who marries someone who has been dismissed by her husband *(but not divorced)* is also breaking that demand.

19 A certain person was wealthy. He was dressing himself in purple and elegant linen having dazzling celebrations everyday.

20 A certain poor man named Lazarus who had become full of sores had been put facing the wealthy man's gateway.

21 He was desiring to eat from the things falling from the wealthy man's table until he was full, but the dogs were also coming *and eating*. They were licking on his sores.

22 The poor man happened to die and was carried by the angels off into Abraham's arms. The wealthy man also died and was buried.

23 In Hades *(the underworld of the dead)* he looked up, being in excruciating pain, and saw Abraham off at a distance with Lazarus in his arms.

24 'Father Abraham,' he hollered, 'show me forgiving kindness and send Lazarus to dip the edge of his finger in water and cool down my tongue because I am in agony in this blaze.
25 'Child,' said Abraham, 'remember that you received a full amount of good things in your life, and Lazarus likewise, a full amount of bad things. Now here he is comforted, but you are in agony.
26 And in all these regions between us and you, a large gap has been established in order that the people wanting to walk across from here to you are not able to. They may not cross all the way over from there to us either.'
27 'So I am asking you, Father,' he said, 'that you would send him into my father's house.
28 You see, I have five brothers. He can be a strong witness to them of this place so that they also won't come into this place of excruciating pain.'
29 'They have Moses and the Preachers,' said Abraham. 'They must listen to them.'
30 'They definitely won't, Father Abraham,' said the wealthy man, 'but if someone should travel to them from the dead, they will change their ways.'
31 'If they don't listen to Moses and the Preachers,' he told him, 'they won't be persuaded by someone coming back from the dead either.'"

17

1 "The expectation that obstacles won't come is unacceptable," Jesus told His students. "*They will come.* But worse than that, what a tragedy it is to the person who sets up an obstacle!
2 A fitting compensation for *such a person* would be if a stone from a mill were put around his neck and he were tossed into the sea. That would be better than him setting up an obstacle that might cause one of these little ones to stumble.
3 Pay attention to yourselves. If your brother sins, tell him to stop, and if he changes his ways, forgive him.
4 If seven times during the day he does something sinful to you, and seven times he returns to you and says, 'I am changing my ways,' you will forgive him."
5 "Add trust to us," the missionaries told the Master.
6 "If you have trust as small as a kernel of mustard," said the Master, "you would be saying to this black mulberry tree, 'Be uprooted and be planted in the sea,' and it would obey you. *Trust is about knowing what God wants and trusting Him to do it.*

7 Who from among you will state to a slave plowing his fields or shepherding his livestock when he comes in from the field, 'Go right away on up to your room and settle down?'
8 Will he not instead state to him, 'Get something ready for me. I'm going to eat dinner,' and, 'Tuck your long undershirt up into your waist sash *(or in other words, get ready to work)*, serve me while I eat and drink, and after I am done, you will eat and drink?'
9 He doesn't generously reward the slave because he did what he was specifically assigned to do, does he?
10 In this way, you also, when you do all the things that were specifically assigned to you, say, 'We are inept slaves. We have done what we were obligated to do.'"
11 During the time that He was traveling to Jerusalem, He also happened to be going through the middle of Samaria and Galilee.
12 As He went into a certain village, ten men with a skin disease met Him. They were standing far away.
13 They raised their voice and said, "Jesus, Boss, show us forgiving kindness."
14 When He saw them, He told them, "Travel back, and show yourselves to the priests." During the time that they were making their way back, their skin happened to clear up.
15 When one man from them saw that he was cured, he returned praising God's magnificence with a loud voice.
16 He got down at Jesus' feet with his face to the ground thanking Him. And he was a Samaritan.
17 When Jesus responded, He said, "Weren't there ten whose skin cleared up? But where are the nine?
18 Can no one be found who returned to give magnificence to God except this man from another ethnicity?"
19 "Get up," He told him, "and go home. Your trust has rescued you."
20 The Separatists asked Him when God's monarchy was coming. He answered them by saying, "God's monarchy isn't something that is observed visually.
21 And they won't state, 'Look, it is here,' or 'it is there,' either. You see, look, God's monarchy is inside of you."
22 "Days will come," He told the students, "when you will desire to see one of the days of the Son of the Person, and you won't see it.
23 And they will state to you, 'Look, He is there,' or 'Look, He is here.' You shouldn't go off *to there* or even pursue it.
24 You see, even as bright lightning shines from one end of the sky to the other, so will the Son of the Person be in His day.

25 But first, He must suffer many things and be rejected by this generation.
26 Just as it happened in Noah's days, so it will also be in the days of the Son of the Person.
27 They were eating, drinking, marrying, and planning to get married till the day that Noah went into the box *(the Ark)*. Then the flood came and ruined everyone.
28 Likewise, just as it happened in the days of Lot: They were eating, drinking, buying, selling, planting, and building.
29 But on the day that Lot left Sodom, it rained fire and sulfur out of heaven and ruined everyone.
30 It will be just like that on the day that the Son of the Person is uncovered.
31 In that day, if someone is on top of the house and his stuff is in the house, he must not climb down into his house and get his stuff, and if someone is in a field working, in the same way, he must not return back to where he left his stuff to get them.
32 Remember Lot's wife.
33 Whoever looks for a way to acquire his soul will lose it, but whoever loses it will help it survive.
34 I tell you on that night, there will be two laying on one cot; the one will be taken along, and the other will be left.
35 Two women will be grinding flour together; the one will be taken along, but the other will be left."
36 [[["Two will be in the field; the one will be taken along, and the other will be left."]]]
37 They responded by asking Him, "Where, Master?" "Where the body is," Jesus told them, "there the raptors also will come together to one place."

18

1 He was telling them an illustration with the specific goal of *showing how it is* necessary to always be praying and not to be getting discouraged.
2 He said, "There was a certain judge in a certain city who didn't fear God and wasn't embarrassed by people.
3 A widow in that city was coming to him, saying, 'Retaliate against my opponent for me in my court case.'
4 He was not wanting to for a long time, but in the end he said to himself, 'Even though I don't fear God and I am not embarrassed by people,

5 I will retaliate for this widow so that her coming here doesn't have a conclusion of giving me a black eye because always having her here is definitely annoying me.'"
6 The Master said, "You must listen to what the judge who did things the wrong way said.
7 *God does things the right way. God is good.* Won't He most definitely retaliate for the people who choose Him, the ones who are shouting to Him day and night? He is even patient with them.
8 I tell you that He will retaliate for them quickly. So a more important question is when the Son of the Person comes, will He find people on the earth who trust *Him?*"
9 He also told this illustration to some of them who had been confident of themselves that they were always right and who were treating everyone else as nobodies.
10 "Two people walked up to the temple grounds to pray: One was a Separatist and the other was a tax collector.
11 The Separatist stood up and was praying these things to himself, 'God, I thank You that I am not like everyone else: the vicious people, the people who are wrong, the people who cheat on their spouses, or even as this tax collector.
12 I go on a fast twice after the Sabbath. I give a ten-percent offering from everything that I get.'
13 The tax collector who had stood at a distance was not wanting to even look up to the sky, but was hitting his chest, saying, 'You must provide a remedy for me, God. I am a sinful person.'
14 I tell you, as this tax collector walked down to his house, God considered him to have done the right thing next to that *Separatist*, because everyone who puts himself up high will be put down low, but the one who puts himself down low will be put up high."
15 People were also bringing their babies to Him so that He would touch them. But when the students saw it, they were stopping them.
16 Jesus called for the babies. "Leave the young children alone so that they can come to Me," He said. "Don't keep them from coming. You see, *children find it easy to trust.* God's monarchy is made up of these types of young children.
17 Amen, I tell you, whoever does not accept God's monarchy as a young child will not in any way go into it."
18 A certain head person asked Him, "Good teacher, what is one thing that after I do it I will inherit life that spans all time?"
19 Jesus said to him, "Why are you calling Me good? No one is good except One, God.

20 You know the *Ten* Demands: You will not cheat on your spouse, you will not murder, you will not steal, you will not lie when you are a witness, value your father and mother."
21 "I have observed all these since I was young," said the head person.
22 When Jesus heard this, He told him, "One thing is still missing for you: Sell everything, as much as you have, pass it out to poor people (and you will have a stockpile of treasure in heaven), and come, follow Me." *The one thing he lacked was trust. He wouldn't trust the good Teacher.*
23 When he heard this, he became overcome with sadness. You see, he was terribly wealthy.
24 When Jesus saw that he became overcome with sadness, He said, "How hard it is for the people who have stacks of money as they travel into God's monarchy.
25 You see, it is easier for a camel to enter through the eye of a surgeon's needle than for a wealthy person to enter into God's monarchy."
26 Those who were listening said, "And who can be rescued?"
27 "The things that are impossible with people," said Jesus, "are possible with God."
28 "Look," Peter said, "we left our own things and followed You."
29 "Amen, I tell you," Jesus told them, "that there is not even one person who left a house, a wife, brothers, parents, or children on account of God's monarchy,
30 who won't receive back many times more in this time and life that spans all time in the coming span of time."
31 He took the Twelve alongside of Him and told them, "Look, we are walking up into Jerusalem and all the things that have been written by the preachers about the Son of the Person will be finished.
32 You see, He will be turned over to the non-Jews. And He will be mocked, injured, and spit at.
33 After whipping Him, they will kill Him, and on the third day, He will stand up."
34 They didn't understand any of these things. This statement was something that had been hidden from them, and they were not knowing the things it was saying.
35 During the time that He was coming near to *municipal* Jericho, a certain blind man happened to be sitting along the road asking for money.
36 When he heard a crowd traveling through there, he was inquiring what it was.

37 They reported to him that Jesus, the Nazarene, was passing by.
38 He shouted, "Jesus, Son of David, show forgiving kindness to me." *(Son of David is a less specific term for Anointed King or Messiah.)*
39 The people in the crowd leading the way ahead of Jesus were shushing him so that he would be quiet. But he started yelling much more, "Son of David, show forgiving kindness to me."
40 Jesus stopped and gave the order for him to be brought to Him. When he was near, Jesus asked him,
41 "What do you want me to do for you?" "Master," he said, "that I might see again."
42 "See again," Jesus told him. "Your trust has rescued you."
43 At once he saw again and started following Him praising God's magnificence. When the entire group saw it, they gave praise to God.

19

1 He entered and started going through *municipal* Jericho.
2 And look, there was a man named Zacchaeus. He was the head tax collector, and he was wealthy.
3 He was looking for a way to see which one was Jesus. He wasn't able to see Him in the crowd because he was short.
4 He ran up ahead and climbed up in a white mulberry tree so that he could see Him because He was going to be passing through there.
5 As Jesus came up to that place, He looked up and told him, "Zacchaeus, hurry up and climb down from there. You see, today I must stay in your house."
6 He hurried up and climbed down. He accepted Him into his house and was happy.
7 When everyone saw it, they were speaking in hushed tones among themselves, saying, "He went in and settled down with a sinful man."
8 Zacchaeus stood up and told the Master, "Look, Master, I am giving half of my things to the poor, and if I have made any kind of false accusation against anyone, I am giving it back quadruple."
9 "Today," said Jesus, "this house has been rescued. *I came into this sinful person's house on a rescue mission* due to the fact that he also is a son of Abraham.
10 You see, the Son of the Person came to look for and to rescue lost sheep."
11 As they listened, He added an illustration to what he had told them because of the fact that He was almost to Jerusalem and it seemed to them that God's monarchy was going to be spotted *by them* at once *as soon as they got there.*

12 So He said, "A certain person from a high-ranking family line traveled to a distant land to receive the title of king over his area and to return.
13 He called for ten of his slaves, gave them ten $20 silver coins, and told them, 'Invest these while I am gone.'
14 The citizens of his area hated him. After he left, they sent a delegation of older men out behind him on a mission to that distant land, saying, 'We don't want this person to be king over us.'
15 After he received the monarchy, he came back and happened to tell someone to holler for the slaves that he had given the silver to so that he might know what they earned through investing.
16 The first one showed up and said, 'Master, your $20 silver coin earned ten $20 silver coins.'
17 He told him, 'Well done, good slave. Because you have proven yourself to be reliable in the smallest thing, you must have authority over ten cities.'
18 The second slave came and said, 'Your $20 silver coin, Master, made five $20 silver coins.'
19 'And you,' he also told this slave, 'be over five cities.'
20 Another slave came and said, 'Master, look, here is your $20 silver coin that I have kept set aside in a towel.
21 You see, I was afraid of you because you are rough with people. You pick up what you did not put down and harvest what you did not plant.'
22 He told him, 'From your mouth, I will judge you, evil slave. You realized that I am rough with people, that I take what I did not put down and that I harvest what I did not plant.
23 So why didn't you give my silver to a bank so that when I came, I could withdraw it with interest?'
24 He told the people standing near him, 'Take the $20 silver coin away from him, and give it to my slave that has the ten $20 silver coins.'
25 'Master,' they told him, 'he already has ten $20 silver coins.'
26 He said, 'I tell you that everyone who has something will be given something, but the person who has nothing even what he has will be taken away.
27 More importantly, bring these enemies of mine here, the ones who didn't want me to be king over them, and slaughter them down here in front of me.'"
28 After He said these things, He was traveling up in front as He walked up to Jerusalem.

29 Since He happened to come near to Bethphage and Bethany and was headed toward the mountain that is called *the Mount* of Olives *(a hill just east of Jerusalem),* He sent two students out on a mission.
30 "Make your way back into the village directly facing us. As you travel into it, you will find a foal *(a young donkey)* that has been tied up. Not one person has ever been seated on it at any time. Untie it, and bring it here.
31 If someone asks you why you are untying it, this is what you will state, 'The Master needs it.'"
32 After the two who had been sent out went off, they found just what He told them.
33 As they were untying the foal, its masters said to them, "Why are you untying the foal?"
34 "The Master needs it," the two said.
35 They brought it to Jesus, tossed their robes on the foal, and loaded Jesus on it.
36 As He traveled along, they were spreading their robes out on the road underneath Him.
37 As He came near to where the road already started going down the Mount of Olives, absolutely all the large number of students were happy and began praising God with a loud voice about all the abilities that they saw.
38 "The King coming in the Master's name," they said, "has been conferred with blessings! Peace in heaven and magnificence in the highest!"
39 Some of the Separatists in the crowd told Him, "Teacher, stop Your students."
40 He responded by saying, "I tell you, if these people were to be silent, the stones would yell."
41 And since He was near, when He saw the city, He cried over it.
42 "O Jerusalem, if only on this day, you also knew the things that would bring you peace. But now it has been hidden from your eyes.
43 The days will arrive on you when your enemies will put up a blockade around you, completely surround you, and hold you in on all sides.
44 They will level you and your children in you down to the ground. They will not leave in you one stone on top of another *(this happened in 70 AD).* This will be for all the times that you didn't know the very thing that God had appointed to happen under your supervision."
45 When He went onto the temple grounds, He began throwing out the people who were selling.

46 He told them, "The Bible says, 'And My house will be a house of prayer' *(Isaiah 56:7)*, but you have made it a cave of bandits."
47 He was teaching daily lessons on the temple grounds, but the head priests, the Old Testament transcribers, and the most important men of the ethnic group were looking for a way to ruin Him.
48 Yet they weren't finding anything that they could do. You see, absolutely all of the group were listening and hanging on every word of His.

20

1 During one of those days as He was teaching the group on the temple grounds and sharing good news, the head priests and the Old Testament transcribers happened to stand over Him together with the older men.
2 "Tell us," they said, "what kind of authority are You doing these things with or who gave You this authority?"
3 When He answered, He told them, "I also will ask you a question, and you must answer it.
4 Was John's submersion from heaven or from people?"
5 They got together and considered it. They were saying to themselves, "If we say from heaven, He will state, 'Then why didn't you trust him?'
6 But if we say from people, absolutely all of the group will throw stones at us and take us down. You see, they are confident that John was a preacher."
7 They answered that they didn't know where it was from.
8 "I am not telling you with what kind of authority I do these things either," Jesus told them.
9 He began telling this illustration to the group, "A certain person planted a vineyard and gave it out to farmers. *The farmers agreed to pay him a certain percentage of the harvest each year.* He left the area for quite a while.
10 At harvest time, he sent a slave out on a mission to the farmers so they would give him *his percentage* out of the vineyard's fruit. But the farmers beat him and sent him back empty-handed.
11 He added another slave to send. Those farmers beat him, belittled him, and also sent him back empty-handed.
12 He added a third slave to send. They also wounded him and threw him out.
13 'What should I do?' said the vineyard's master. 'I will send my loved son. They will likely be embarrassed when he is there.'

14 But when the farmers saw him, they were pondering with each other and saying, 'This is the inheritor. Let's kill him so that we can have his inheritance.'

15 They threw him outside of the vineyard and killed him. So what will the vineyard's master do to them?

16 He will come and ruin these farmers. Then he will give the vineyard to other farmers." *When they heard this, they understood how this illustration showed that God would ruin the Jewish leaders and give His vineyard to others.* "That couldn't happen," they said.

17 Jesus looked at them and said, "So, what is this that has been written in the Bible? 'A stone that the builders rejected, this stone ended up being used for a corner's head, *a cornerstone, the primary stone of the whole building*' (Psalm 118:22)?

18 Everyone who falls on that stone will be smashed. It will grind up whoever it falls on."

19 In that same hour, the Old Testament transcribers and the head priests looked for an opportunity to put their hands on Him and were cautious of the group. You see, they knew that He told this illustration to them.

20 They watched Him closely and sent people out undercover to Him. They faked being people who do what is right. That way they could attack His message in such a way to turn Him over to the head Roman ruler and the leader's authority.

21 They asked Him *a question*. "Teacher," they said, "we realize that what You are saying and teaching is correct. You aren't fooled by anyone's appearance. You teach God's way based on truth.

22 Are we allowed to give a protection fee *(a Roman tax)* to Caesar or not?"

23 After taking a close look at their slyness, He told them,

24 "Show me a denarius *(a coin equal to one day's wage)*. Whose image and inscription does it have?" "Caesar's," they said.

25 "Well then," He told them, "give Caesar's things back to Caesar and God's things back to God,"

26 They couldn't *think of a way* to attack His statement directly in front of the group. His response amazed them. So they kept quiet.

27 When some of the Sadducees came forward (the ones who oppose life after death), they asked Him,

28 "Teacher, Moses wrote to us, 'If someone's brother who has a wife dies and this brother is childless, his brother should take the wife and bring up his brother's seed *(descendants)* from her.'

29 So there were seven brothers. After the first took a wife, he died childless.
30 The second took her and died.
31 The third took her and died. This happened to all seven brothers. They all took her and died without leaving any children behind.
32 Later the wife also died.
33 So in the return back to life when they come back to life, whose wife will she be? You see, all seven had her as a wife."
34 "The sons of this span of time," Jesus told them, "marry and plan to get married.
35 But the people who are considered as totally deserving to obtain that span of time and the return back to life from the dead don't marry and don't plan to get married either.
36 You see, they can't die anymore either. They are equal to angels. They are God's sons, sons of the return back to life.
37 Even Moses disclosed that the dead come back to life when he wrote about the bush. He said, 'the Master is the God of Abraham, the God of Isaac, and the God of Jacob.' *He didn't say "was". He said "is". The Master is the God of Abraham, Isaac, and Jacob.*
38 God is not a God of dead people. *Dead people don't have gods. They are dead.* He is a God of living people. *Abraham, Isaac, and Jacob were and are still living in the afterworld.* You see, from God's viewpoint, all are living."
39 Some of the Old Testament transcribers responded by saying, "Teacher, nicely said."
40 You see, they no longer dared to ask Him anything.
41 But He said to them, "How do they say that the Anointed King will be David's son?
42 You see, David himself says in a scroll of Psalms, 'The Master *(God)* said to my Master *(the Anointed King)*, Sit down at My right side
43 until I place Your enemies beneath Your feet so You can rest Your feet on them' *(Psalm 110:1)*.
44 David calls Him Master. So how is He his son?"
45 As the entire group was listening, He told His students,
46 "Be cautious of the Old Testament transcribers who want to walk around in long robes, who are fond of people greeting them in the marketplace, the front benches in the synagogues, and the front reclining places *(the places of honor)* in the feasts,
47 who eat up widows' houses, and who pray long prayers for a sham. These will receive much more judgment."

21

1 He looked up and saw wealthy people throwing their contributions into *the collection boxes in* the treasury area.

2 He also saw a certain needy widow throwing two tiny brass coins in.

3 "I tell you," He said, "that this poor widow truly threw in more than anyone else.

4 You see, all these people for their contributions threw in part of what they had left over, but she, even though she didn't make enough to live on, threw in everything that she had, her whole life savings."

5 Some were telling Him about the nice stones and donations that decorated the temple grounds.

6 "The days will come on these things that you see here," He said, "when not one stone will be left on a stone that hasn't been torn down *(this happened in 70 AD)*."

7 "Teacher, so when will these things be," they asked Him, "and what indicates when they are going to happen?"

8 Jesus said, "See that no one misleads you. You see, many will come using My name. They will say, 'I am Him,' and, 'The appointed time has come near.' Don't travel off after them.

9 When you hear wars and conflicts, don't panic. You see, these things must happen first, but the conclusion will not come right away."

10 Then He was saying to them, "A nation will rise up against a nation and a monarchy against a monarchy.

11 There will be both large earthquakes and throughout some areas, famines and diseases. There will be both fearful things and great indicators from the sky.

12 Before all these things, they will put their hands on you and persecute you. They will turn you in to the synagogues, throw you in jail, and take you before kings and leaders because of My name.

13 It will step out to you for a witness *(or in other words, it will give you a chance to tell about Me)*.

14 So resolve in your heart not to be concerned beforehand with how you will defend yourself.

15 You see, I will give you a mouth and insight that absolutely all your opponents won't be able to oppose or say anything against.

16 You will even be turned in by your parents, brothers, relatives, and friends. They will kill some of you.

17 You will be hated by everyone because of My name.

18 Not one of the hairs on your head will in any way be ruined.

19 In your persistence to do what is right, you will gain your souls.

20 When you see Jerusalem surrounded by army camps, at that time know that her time to be uninhabited has come near.
21 At that time, the people in Judea must escape into the mountains, the people in the middle of Jerusalem must get a long way away from her, and the people out in the rural areas must not go into her.
22 These are days of retaliation, the kind of retaliation that will accomplish all of what the Bible says.
23 What a tragedy it will be for the pregnant women and the nursing women in those days. You see, there will be a great shortage on the earth, and there will be rage against this ethnic group.
24 They will fall to the dagger's mouth and will be taken by force into all the nations. Non-Jews will trample Jerusalem till their appointed time is accomplished.
25 There will be indicators in the sun, moon, constellations, and on the earth. Nations will be distressed by the perplexity of an echo of the sea and surge.
26 People will stop breathing out of fear and expectation of the events coming on the civilized world. You see, heaven's abilities will be disturbed.
27 At that time, they will see the Son of the Person coming in a cloud with much ability and magnificence.
28 As these events begin to happen, stand up straight and raise your heads up because your paid release is near."
29 He told them an illustration, "Look at the fig tree and all the trees.
30 When they already thrust sprouts out, as you see this, you know all by yourselves that summer is already near.
31 In this way also, when you see these things happening, know that God's monarchy is near.
32 Amen, I tell you that a generation will not in any way pass by from the beginning of all these things until the day He comes.
33 The sky and the earth will pass, but My messages will not in any way pass.
34 Pay attention to yourselves so that your hearts won't ever be weighted down with a hangover, drunkenness, and worry about things in this life and so that that day won't stand over you when you aren't expecting it.
35 It will come like a trap. You see, it will come on all the people sitting on the face of all the earth.
36 Don't go to sleep. Plead every time that you should so that you may be strong enough to escape all these things that are going to happen and to be established in front of the Son of the Person."

37 During those days, He was on the temple grounds teaching. During the nights, He was leaving and sleeping outside in a courtyard at the mountain that is called *the Mount* of Olives.
38 The entire group was coming to Him on the temple grounds at daybreak to listen to Him.

22

1 The Yeast-free Festival, which is also called the Passover, was coming near.
2 And the head priests and Old Testament transcribers were looking at how they might execute Him. You see, they were cautious around the ethnic group.
3 The Opponent went into Judas, the one called "from Kerioth". He was one from the Twelve's number.
4 Judas went off and spoke with the head priests and captains together about how he could turn Him over to them.
5 They were happy and agreed to give him silver.
6 He entered into a verbal agreement with them and was looking for a good time to turn Him over to them when there wouldn't be a crowd *around Him*.
7 The day of the Yeast-free Festival came when the Passover lamb must be sacrificed.
8 Jesus sent Peter and John out on a mission. "Travel, and get the Passover meal ready for us," He said, "so that we might eat."
9 "Where do you want us to get things ready?" they asked Him.
10 "Look," Jesus told them, "when you go into the city, you will meet together with a person hauling a clay pitcher of water. Follow him into whichever house he travels into.
11 You will state to that house's homeowner, 'The Teacher says, "Where is the guest room that I may eat the Passover meal in with My students?"'
12 That person will show you a large room above the ground floor that has been set up. Get ready there."
13 They went off and found it just as He had stated to them, and they got the Passover meal ready.
14 When the hour came, He settled down together with the missionaries.
15 "I really desired to eat this Passover meal with you," He told them, "before My time to suffer.
16 You see, I tell you that I will not in any way eat it until whenever it will happen in God's monarchy."

17 When He accepted a cup, He was thankful and said, "Take this, and divide it up for yourselves.
18 You see, I tell you that I won't in any way drink juice from a grapevine from the present on until God's monarchy comes."
19 When He took bread, He was thankful, split it, and gave it to them. "This is My body that is given on your behalf," He said. "Do this to again remind yourself of Me."
20 He did the same thing with the cup after they ate dinner. "This cup is the new deal in My blood," He said. "This cup is spilled out on your behalf.
21 One more thing is, look, the person turning Me in, his hand is with Me on the table.
22 The Son of the Person certainly travels down the road that has been designated. But worse than that, what a tragedy it is to that person who turns Him in."
23 They began to together pose questions to each other about, so which one from among them it might be, who was going to be doing this kind of thing.
24 Also an argument ensued that they liked to have among themselves, the argument about which one of them seems to be greater.
25 "The nations' kings are masters over them," Jesus told them, "and they call those who have authority over them humanitarians.
26 You will not be like that, but the greater one among you must become as the younger one and the one leading as the one serving.
27 You see, who is greater, the one reclining or the one serving? Is it not the one reclining? But I am in the middle of you as the one serving is.
28 You are the ones who have stayed with Me through My troubles.
29 And I am making a deal with you for the monarchy (just as My father made a deal with Me)
30 so that you may eat and drink at My table in My monarchy. You will sit on thrones judging Israel's twelve family lines.
31 Simon, Simon, look, the Opponent made a request to shake you all up as grain is shaken in a sifter,
32 but I pleaded about you, Peter, that you wouldn't quit trusting. Once you return back, establish your brothers."
33 "Master," Peter told Him, "I am ready to travel with You even into jail and into death."
34 "I tell you, Peter," said Jesus, "a rooster will not crow today until you flatly deny three times to know Me."

35 "When I sent you all out on missions," He told them, "without a money bag, a tote bag, and sandals, did you lack anything?" "Nothing," said the students.
36 "But now the person who has a money bag," He told them, "must take it. The same thing is also true of a tote bag. And anyone who doesn't have them must sell his robe and buy a dagger.
37 You see, I tell you that this thing that has been written in the Bible must be finished in Me: the 'and He was considered to be with criminals' thing *(Isaiah 53:12)*. This thing about Me also has a conclusion."
38 "Master, look," said the students, "here are two daggers." "That is adequate," Jesus told them.
39 Aligned with the custom, He left and traveled to the Mount of Olives. His students also followed Him.
40 When they got to the place, He told them, "Pray so that you won't get into trouble."
41 He was pulled away from them about as far as a person can throw a stone. He placed His knees on the ground and was praying,
42 "Father, if You intend to, carry this cup off away from Me. More importantly, it shouldn't be what I want. What You want must happen.
43 [[They saw an angel from heaven invigorating Him.
44 He began to struggle and was praying more intensely. His perspiration became like clots of blood falling down on the ground.]]
45 When He got up from the prayer, He went to where the students were and found them asleep from the sadness.
46 "Why are you sleeping?" He asked. "Get up and pray so that you won't get into trouble."
47 As He was still speaking, look, a crowd, and the one called Judas (one of the Twelve) was going in front of them. He came near to Jesus to be friendly with Him.
48 "Judas, are you turning the Son of the Person in with a friendly gesture?" Jesus asked him.
49 When those around Him saw what was going to happen, they said, "Master, tell us if we will strike them with a dagger."
50 A certain one from them struck the head priest's slave and took off his right ear.
51 "Allow this for now," answered Jesus. He touched the earlobe and cured him.

52 Jesus told the people who showed up to arrest Him (the head priests, captains of the temple grounds, and older men), "Did you come out with daggers and wooden clubs as if I were a bandit?
53 Everyday as I was with you on the temple grounds, you didn't put your hands on Me. But this is your hour. This is the authority of the darkness."
54 After they apprehended Him, they led Him away and brought Him into the head priest's house. Peter was following at a distance.
55 When they lit a fire in the middle of the courtyard and were seated around it, Peter was sitting in the middle of them.
56 A certain servant girl saw him sitting near the light and stared at him. "This person was with Him too," she said.
57 But Peter denied it. "I don't know Him, ma'am," he said.
58 After a bit, another person saw him and was declaring, "You are one of them too." But Peter was declaring, "Sir, I am not."
59 After what seemed like one hour went by, someone else was strongly insisting, "It's true. This person was with Him too. You see, he also is a Galilean."
60 But Peter said, "Sir, I don't know what you are saying." At once, as he was still speaking, a rooster crowed.
61 The Master turned and looked at Peter. Then Peter quietly remembered the Master's statement, how He told him, "Before it is time for the rooster to crow today, you will flatly deny Me three times."
62 He went outside and cried bitterly.
63 The men holding Jesus were mocking Him and beating Him.
64 After they blindfolded Him, they were asking and saying, "Preach! Who struck You?"
65 They were insulting Him and saying many different things to Him.
66 As it became day, the board of the ethnic group's older men, the head priests, and the Old Testament transcribers gathered together in their meeting place. He was taken over to their council.
67 "If You are the Anointed King, tell us," they said. "If I tell you, you won't in any way trust Me," He told them.
68 "If I ask you a question, you won't in any way answer it.
69 But from the present on, the Son of the Person will be sitting at the right side of God's ability."
70 "So are You the Son of God?" everyone asked. "You are saying that I am," Jesus was declaring to them.
71 "What? Do we still need witnesses?" they asked. "You see, we ourselves heard it out of His mouth."

23

1 There was a large number of people in the council. Absolutely all of them got up and took Him before Pilate. 2 There they began to level complaints against Him. "We found this Man twisting our nation," they said. "He keeps people from giving protection fees *(a Roman tax)* to Caesar and says that He Himself is a king, the Anointed King."
3 Pilate asked Him, "Are You the Jewish people's king?" When Jesus answered him, He was declaring, "You are saying it."
4 Pilate told the head priests and the crowds, "I find no legal case against this person."
5 The people leveling complaints against Him were getting stronger. "He shakes up the ethnic group," they said. "He has been teaching throughout all of Judea. He even began out of Galilee and came all the way up to here."
6 When Pilate heard that, he asked if the Man is a Galilean.
7 When he correctly understood that He is from Herod's jurisdiction, he sent Him up to Herod, since he was also in Greater Jerusalem during these days.
8 When Herod saw Jesus, he was very happy. You see, for quite a while, he had wanted to see Him because he had heard a lot about Him. He was anticipating seeing Him show some type of miraculous proof.
9 He was asking Him an adequate amount of questions, but Jesus didn't answer him at all.
10 The head priests and Old Testament transcribers had been standing around methodically leveling complaints against Him.
11 Herod also together with his military forces treated Him as a nobody and mocked Him. They threw a dazzling outfit around Him and sent Him up to Pilate.
12 Both Herod and Pilate became friends on that same day. You see, previously they had a hostile relationship toward each other.
13 When Pilate called the head priests, the head people, and the group together,
14 he told them, "You brought this Man to me as someone who is turning the ethnic group against *Rome*, and look, when I investigated Him in your sight, I didn't find a legal case against Him in any of the complaints that you leveled against Him.
15 And Herod didn't either. You see, he sent Him up to us. And look, there is nothing that He has been doing that is deserving of death.
16 So after I administer some discipline, I will dismiss Him."
17 [[[He had an obligation to dismiss one prisoner to them at each festival.]]]

18 But they yelled out simultaneously, "Take this Man. Dismiss Barabbas to us"
19 (Barabbas had been thrown in jail because of a certain disruption in the city and because of murder).
20 Again Pilate hollered that he wanted to dismiss Jesus.
21 But they were hollering out, "Nail Him to a cross! Nail Him to a cross!"
22 Pilate said a third time, "You see, what bad thing did this Man do? I didn't find a legal case for death. So after I administer some discipline, I will dismiss Him."
23 But they were piling on with loud voices asking for Him to be nailed to a cross, and their voices were strong against him.
24 Pilate sentenced Jesus to what they were requesting.
25 He dismissed the one who had been thrown into jail because of a disruption and murder, the one they were asking for, and turned Jesus over to his soldiers so that they could do what the Jewish leaders wanted.
26 Since they led Him away, they latched on to someone *named* Simon, a Cyrenian, who was coming out of a field, and placed the cross on him to carry it behind Jesus.
27 A very large amount of the ethnic group and women were following Him. The women were beating their chests in grief and wailing for Him.
28 Jesus turned back toward the women and said, "Daughters of Jerusalem, don't cry for Me. More importantly, cry for yourselves and for your children
29 because, look, days are coming when they will state this as truth: 'The infertile women, the bellies that didn't give birth, and the breasts that didn't nurse are blessed.'
30 At that time, they will begin to say to the mountains, 'Fall on us,' and to the hills, 'Cover us up,'
31 because if they are doing these things to the wet wood, what will happen to the dry wood?"
32 Two different outlaws were also being taken out to be executed together with Him.
33 When they got to the place called Skull, they nailed Him and the outlaws there (one on the right, the other on the left) to crosses.
34 [["Father, forgive them," Jesus was saying. "You see, they don't realize what they are doing."]] As they divided up His clothes, they threw dice to see who would get His long undershirt.

35 The group had stood there watching. The head people were even making fun of Him out loud, saying, "He rescued others. He must rescue Himself if this is God's select Anointed King."
36 The soldiers also mocked Him. They went up to Him, offered Him sour wine,
37 and said, "If You are the Jewish people's king, rescue Yourself."
38 An inscription also was above Him: "This is the Jewish people's king."
39 One of the outlaws hanging there was insulting Him. "Are You not the Anointed King?" he said. "Rescue Yourself and us."
40 The other outlaw responded by shushing him and declaring, "Are you not afraid of God either? Because you have the same sentence. *You also are nailed to a cross,*
41 and we, certainly rightly so. You see, we are receiving what we deserve for the things that we constantly did. But this man constantly did nothing out of place."
42 He was telling Jesus, "Remember me when You come into Your monarchy."
43 "Amen, I tell you," Jesus told him, "today you will be with Me in paradise."
44 It already seemed like noon, *and the sun stopped shining*. It became dark over the whole earth until 3 p.m.
45 After the sun quit, the temple's curtain tore down the middle.
46 "Father," Jesus hollered with a loud voice, "I place My spirit directly in Your hands." When He said this, He breathed out *His last breath*.
47 When the lieutenant saw what happened, he was praising God's magnificence and saying, "This Man really was doing what is right."
48 All the crowds that came out together to watch this event, after watching what happened, were returning home hitting their chests.
49 All of the people He knew and the women who followed along with Him out of Galilee had stood off at a distance viewing these things.
50 And look, there was a man named Joseph, an advisor, who was also a good man and did what is right.
51 This man was on the council, but he had not voted in agreement with what they intended *to do* or any of the things they were repeatedly doing against Jesus. He was from Arimathaea, a Jewish city, and was awaiting God's monarchy.
52 This man went to Pilate and asked for Jesus' body.
53 He took it down off the cross, wound a linen cloth around it, and placed Him in a grave cut out of rock. No one had been laid in it yet.

54 It was a preparation day *(the day before a Sabbath that is spent preparing food and setting up for the next day, a day of rest)*. A sabbath, the first day of the Yeast-free Festival, was emerging.

55 Some of the women who had come together from Galilee followed behind Joseph. They saw the burial vault and how His body was placed in it.

56 They returned *to where they were staying* and prepared fragrant resins and perfumes for His body. They certainly calmed down on the Sabbath *(not wailing and beating their chests as it was customary to do after a death)*. This was aligned with the demand *about keeping the Sabbath holy*.

24

1 On Day One *(which is Sunday)* after the Sabbaths, long before daybreak, they went to the grave carrying the fragrant resins that they had prepared.

2 But they found that the stone had been rolled away from the burial vault's door.

3 When they went in, they didn't find the body of the Master, Jesus.

4 While they weren't sure what to think about this, look, two men happened to stand over them wearing bright clothes.

5 The women became afraid, even putting their faces down to the ground. The men asked them, "Why are you looking for a living person where dead people are?

6 He's not here, but God got Him up. Remember how He spoke about this to you as He was still in Galilee?

7 He said, 'It is necessary for the Son of the Person to be turned over into sinful people's hands, to be nailed to a cross, and to stand up on the third day.'"

8 They remembered His statements.

9 When they returned from the burial vault, they reported all these things to the eleven and all the rest.

10 They were Mary Magdalene, Joanna, Mary (James' mother), and the rest of the women that were together with them. They were telling these things to the missionaries.

11 These statements appeared in their sight *to be* as if *they were* nonsense. They were not trusting the women.

12 Peter got up and ran to the burial vault. When he got there, he stooped and peered in. He saw the linen strips alone. *No body was there.* He went off by himself, amazed at what happened.

13 And look, on the same day two of them were traveling to a village 7 1/2 miles away from Jerusalem. Its name is Emmaus.

14 They were chatting with each other about all these things that had come together and happened.
15 And while they were chatting and together posing questions, Jesus Himself happened to come near and was also traveling together with them.
16 Their eyes were kept from recognizing Him.
17 "What are these words that you are throwing back and forth to each other as you walk around?" He asked. They stopped sad-faced.
18 When the one named Cleopas answered, he said to Him, "Are you just a tourist in Jerusalem? Don't you know the things that happened there in the last several days?"
19 "What kind of things?" He asked. "The things about Jesus, the Nazarene," they told Him, "a man who became a capable preacher in His work and message directly in front of God and all the ethnic group,
20 and how the head priests and our head people turned Him over *to the Romans* for a death sentence and nailed Him to a cross.
21 We were anticipating that He is the One who is going to be paying for Israel's release. But definitely together with all these things, *God* is also bringing this third day since these things happened.
22 But also some of our women astounded us who went to the burial vault early in the morning.
23 When they didn't find His body, they came and said that they had also seen a sighting of angels, angels that said He is alive.
24 Some of the people who were together with us went off to the burial vault and found it just as the women had said, but they didn't see Him."
25 "O you people who are unobservant and slow to heartily trust everything that the preachers spoke," Jesus told them.
26 "Wasn't it necessary for the Anointed King to suffer these things and to enter His magnificence?"
27 Beginning with Moses and all the Preachers, He thoroughly interpreted to them the passages about Himself in all the *Old Testament* writings.
28 When they were near the village that they were traveling to, He pretended to be traveling farther.
29 "Stay with us," they urged Him, "because it is getting late in the afternoon and most of the day has already gone." He went in and stayed with them.
30 While He was reclining with them, He happened to take the bread, confer a blessing on it, split it, and give it to them.

31 Their eyes were completely opened, they recognized Him, and He disappeared.
32 "Was our heart not burning in us," they said to each other, "as He was speaking to us on the road, as He was completely opening the *Old Testament* writings to us?"
33 That same hour they got up and returned to Jerusalem. They found the eleven and those who had gathered together with them.
34 Those people told them that the Master really was gotten up and that Simon saw Him.
35 The two were recounting what happened on the road and how He was known to them in the splitting of the bread.
36 As they were speaking about these things, He stood in the middle of them and said to them, "Peace to you."
37 They panicked and became afraid. It seemed to them that they were seeing a spirit.
38 "Why have you been uneasy?" He asked. "Why do questions step up in your heart?
39 Look at My hands and My feet because it is Me, Jesus. Feel Me. Look at Me because a spirit doesn't have a physical body and bones just as you can see that I have."
40 When He said this, He showed them His hands and feet.
41 They were so happy and amazed that they still did not trust their *eyes*. "What do you have here to eat?" He asked.
42 They gave Him part of a cooked fish.
43 He took it and ate it in their sight.
44 "My very words that I spoke to you," He told them, "while I was together with you were, 'All the things that have been written about Me in the Law of Moses, the Preachers, and Psalms must happen.'"
45 At that time, He completely opened their way of thinking to understand the *Old Testament* writings.
46 "This is how the Old Testament has been written," He told them, "to show that the Anointed King would suffer, that He would come back to life from the dead the third day,
47 that a change of ways for forgiveness of sins would be spoken about publicly based on His name, and that this would head out from Jerusalem and go to all the nations.
48 You are witnesses of these things.
49 Look, I am sending My Father's promise out on you. You must be seated in the city until you put on ability from a high place."
50 He led them outside until they were close to Bethany, and when He raised up His hands, He conferred a blessing on them.

51 While He was conferring a blessing on them, He happened to stand further away from them and was carried up into the sky.
52 They bowed down to Him and returned to Jerusalem with great happiness.
53 Through every situation, they were going onto the temple grounds conferring blessings on God for what He had done.

John

1

1 The Message was at the beginning, the Message was pointed toward God, and the Message was God.
2 This Message was pointed toward God at the beginning.
3 Everything came to be through *the Message*, and without *the Message* not even one thing that has come to be came to be.
4 There was life in *the Message*, and the life was the people's light.
5 The light shines in the dark, and the dark doesn't take it down.
6 A man came on the scene who was sent out on a mission directly from God. His name was John.
7 This John came to be a witness. That way he might tell what he witnessed about the Light so that all might trust through him.
8 He was not the Light, but his purpose was to tell what he witnessed about the Light.
9 The true Light that lights things up for every person was coming into the world.
10 *The Message* was in the world, the world came to be through *the Message*, but the world didn't know *the Message*.
11 He went to His own home, and His own people didn't receive Him in.
12 But to as many as received Him, to the people trusting in His name, He gave the authority to become God's children.
13 *They do* not *become God's children* from *having the right* bloodlines, or from what a physical body wants, or from what a man wants either. No, they are born from God.
14 The Message became a physical body and camped among us. We viewed His magnificence, magnificence like that of an only biological child beside the Father, full of generosity and truth.
15 John told what he witnessed about Him. He even yelled it out: "I talked about this before," he said. "The One coming behind me has become in front of me because He was first over me."
16 This is true for all of us because we all received generosity upon generosity from His fullness.
17 Since the law was given through Moses, generosity and truth came through Jesus, the Anointed King.
18 No one has seen God at any time. Since that only biological God was in the Father's arms, He recounted *to us what He knows about Him.*

19 The Jewish people in Greater Jerusalem sent out priests and Levites to John to ask him, "Who are you?" This is the witness account that he gave.
20 He acknowledged what he had witnessed. He didn't deny it. He acknowledged it. "I am not the Anointed King."
21 "So who are you?" they asked. "Are you Elijah?" "I am not," he said. "Are you the Preacher *that Moses told about?*" "No," he answered.
22 So they asked him, "Who are you so that we may give an answer to the people who sent us? What do you say about yourself?"
23 He was declaring, "I am a voice shouting in the backcountry, 'Make the Master's road straight,' just as Isaiah, the preacher, said" *(Isaiah 40:3)*.
24 They had been sent out by the Separatists.
25 "So why do you submerge if you are not the Anointed King, or Elijah, or the Preacher?" they asked.
26 "I submerge in water," John answered. "He has stood in the middle of you all. You have not seen Him.
27 He is the One coming behind me. I don't deserve to even untie His sandal strap."
28 These things happened in Bethany, the Bethany next to the Jordan River where John was submerging people.
29 The next day, he saw Jesus coming toward him. "Look," he said, "God's Lamb that takes away the world's sin.
30 This is the One I talked about when I said, 'A Man is coming behind me who has become in front of me because He was first over me.'
31 And the thing is not that I had seen Him, but *I had seen* that God would show Him to Israel. This is why I came submerging in water."
32 John told what he witnessed. He said, "I have watched the Spirit float down from heaven as a dove and stay on Him.
33 And the thing is not that I had seen Him, but the One who sent me out here to submerge people in water, that One told me, 'If you ever see the Spirit floating down and staying on someone, this is the One who submerges people in the Sacred Spirit.'
34 I have seen and told what I witnessed: This is God's Son."
35 The next day, John and two of his students had again been standing around.
36 He looked at Jesus walking around and said, "Look, God's Lamb!"
37 The two students heard what he spoke and followed Jesus.
38 When Jesus turned around and saw them following Him, He asked them, "What are you looking for?" They said, "Rabbi, where are You

staying?" (Rabbi is *Hebrew*. It is translated as teacher and said instead of teacher.)

39 "Come, and you will see," He told them. So they went and saw where He was staying. They stayed there next to Him that day. It was the 4:00 hour.

40 Andrew (Simon Peter's brother) was one person from the two who heard directly from John and followed Him.

41 First, this Andrew found his own brother, Simon, and told him, "We have found the Messiah" (which is *Hebrew* and translated as Anointed King).

42 Andrew took him to Jesus. After Jesus looked at him, He said, "You are Simon, John's son. You will be called Cephas" (*Cephas is Aramaic and* is interpreted as Peter *or Rock*).

43 The next day Jesus wanted to go out into Galilee. He found Philip and told him, "Follow Me."

44 Philip was out of Bethsaida, the same city that Andrew and Peter were from.

45 Philip found Nathanael and told him, "We have found the One that Moses and the Preachers wrote about. He is Jesus, Joseph's son, the Joseph out of Nazareth."

46 "From Nazareth?" Nathanael said to him. "Can anything good be from Nazareth?" "Come and see," Philip told him.

47 Jesus saw Nathanael coming toward Him and talked about him, "Look, an Israeli that truly has no deception in him."

48 "Where do You know me from?" asked Nathanael. "Before Philip hollered to you, I saw you under the fig tree," answered Jesus.

49 "Rabbi," responded Nathanael, "You are God's Son. You are Israel's King."

50 Jesus responded and said, "Do you trust because I told you that I saw you underneath the fig tree? You will see greater things than these."

51 He also told him, "Amen, amen, I tell you, you will see heaven opened and God's angels stepping up into heaven and stepping down from heaven over the Son of the Person. (*"The Son of the Person" is a generic term Jesus used of Himself. Ezekiel and Daniel were called "son of a person." "Son of a person" is also in Psalm 80:17.*)

2

1 On the third day *after they left the Jordan River*, there was a wedding in Cana, Galilee, and Jesus's mother was there.
2 Jesus and His students were also invited to the wedding.

3 When they ran out of wine, Jesus' mother told Him, "They don't have wine."
4 Jesus told her, "Ma'am, what does this have to do with Me? My hour has not arrived yet."
5 His mother told the servants, "Do whatever He tells you."
6 Six stone water jars were lying there. They each had a capacity of 18 to 27 gallons. They were used to provide water for the Jewish cleansing rituals.
7 "Fill the water jars full of water," Jesus told them. They filled them full up to the top.
8 "Now ladle some out and carry it to the head waiter." They carried it to him.
9 The head waiter tasted the water that had become wine and didn't realize where it was from (but the servants who had ladled out the water realized where it was from). The head waiter hollered for the groom
10 and told him, "Every person puts the nice wine out first, and when they are drunk, the lesser wine. You have kept the nice wine until now."
11 Jesus performed this beginning proof in Cana, Galilee. He showed His magnificence, and His students trusted in Him.
12 After this, He, His mother, His brothers, and His students walked down to Capernaum and stayed there a few days.
13 The Passover of the Jewish people was near, and Jesus walked up to Jerusalem.
14 He found the people selling cattle, sheep, and doves, and the traders of small change sitting on the temple grounds.
15 After making a whip from ropes, He threw all of them off the temple grounds, even the sheep and the cattle. He spilled out the small change of the currency exchangers and overturned the tables.
16 "Take these things out of here," He said to the people selling doves. "Don't make My Father's house a house of merchandise."
17 His students remembered that the Bible says, "The passion of Your house will eat me up" *(Psalm 69:9)*.
18 The Jewish people answered and said, "What proof are You showing us that *allows you to* do these things?"
19 "Break down this temple, and in three days I will get it up," answered Jesus.
20 "This temple took forty-six years to build," said the Jewish people. "And you will get it up in three days?"
21 But that Jesus was talking about the temple of His body.

22 So when He was gotten up from the dead, His students remembered that He had been saying this, and they trusted in the *Old Testament* writing and in the words that Jesus said.
23 Since He was in Greater Jerusalem during the Passover, many at the festival trusted in His name *and who He is* as they watched the proofs that He was doing.
24 But Jesus was not trusting Himself to them because of the fact that He knew everyone.
25 He didn't need anyone to tell Him what they knew about a person. You see, He knew what was in the person.

3

1 There was a man from the Separatists named Nicodemus. He was one of the head Jewish people.
2 This Nicodemus came to Jesus at night and said to Him, "Rabbi, we realize that You have come from God as a teacher. You see, no one can be doing these proofs that You are doing unless God is with him."
3 "Amen, amen, I tell you," Jesus responded, "unless someone is born all over again, he cannot see God's monarchy."
4 Nicodemus said to him, "How can a person be born when he is an old man? He can't get into his mother's belly a second time and be born, can he?"
5 "Amen, amen, I tell you," Jesus answered, "unless someone is born from water *(a physical birth)* and spirit *(a spiritual birth)*, he can't go into God's monarchy.
6 The thing that has been born from the physical body is a physical body, and the thing that has been born from the Spirit is a spirit.
7 You shouldn't be amazed that I told you, you must be born all over again. *God and His monarchy are in the spiritual world. To be a part of the spiritual world, you must be born all over again, this time not from your mother's belly, but from the Spirit.*
8 The Spirit blows where it wants, and you hear its voice, but you don't know where it comes from and where it is making its way back to. This is how everyone is who has been born from the Spirit."
9 "How can these things happen like that?" responded Nicodemus.
10 "You are the teacher of Israel," Jesus answered, "and you don't know these things?
11 Amen, amen, I tell you that what we know, we speak, and what we have seen, we tell that we witnessed it, and you don't receive the account that we give.

12 If I told you these things using earthly metaphors and you don't trust, how will you trust if I tell you the heavenly things?
13 No one has stepped up into heaven, except the One who stepped down from heaven, the Son of the Person.
14 Just as Moses put the snake up high on a stick in the backcountry, so the Son of the Person must be put up high
15 so that everyone who trusts in Him may have life that spans all time.
16 You see, this is how God loved the world: He gave His only biological Son so that everyone trusting in Him wouldn't be ruined, but would have life that spans all time.
17 God didn't send His Son out into the world to judge the world. No, *He sent Him into the world* so that He might rescue the world through Him.
18 The person trusting in Him is not judged, but the person not trusting has already been judged because he hasn't trusted in the name of God's only biological Son.
19 This judgment is because light has come into the world and people loved the darkness rather than the light. You see, their actions were evil.
20 Everyone who repeatedly does useless things hates the light and does not come to the light because they don't want their actions to be reprimanded.
21 But the person who does the truth, *the things God says are true,* comes to the light so that it will show him what work that he has worked on is in God."
22 After this, Jesus and his students went into the Judaean area. There He was spending time with them and submerging people in the water.
23 John also was in Aenon near Salim submerging people because there was a lot of water there. People were showing up and being submerged.
24 You see, John hadn't yet been thrown in jail.
25 So John's students ended up questioning a Jewish man about cleansing. *Jews ritually cleanse themselves by submerging themselves in water. John's submersion came from that practice and now Jesus was also doing it.*
26 They came to John and told him, "Rabbi, the One who was with you on the other side of the Jordan River--you told what you witnessed about Him--look, He is submerging people and everyone is going to Him."

27 John responded by saying, "A person cannot receive even one thing unless it has been given to him from heaven.
28 You yourselves are my witnesses that I said I am not the Anointed King, but that I have been sent out on a mission in front of that one.
29 The groom has the bride. But the groom's friend, the one who stands and listens, is happy to hear the groom's voice. So this is my happiness. It is full.
30 That Person must grow, but I must be made less.
31 The One coming from above is up on top of everything. The one from the earth is from the earth and speaks from the earth. The One coming from heaven is up on top of everything.
32 What He has seen and heard, this is what He tells that He witnessed, and no one receives the account that He gives.
33 The person who received the witness account that He gives, put a seal on the fact that God is valid.
34 You see, the One that God sent out on a mission speaks God's statements. God doesn't give a limited amount of the Spirit to Him.
35 The Father loves the Son and has put everything into His hand.
36 The person trusting in the Son has life that spans all time, but the person not believing the Son won't see life, but God's punishment stays on him."

1 Jesus knew that the Separatists had heard He was making and submerging more students than John.
2 (And yet Jesus Himself was definitely not submerging people, but His students were.)
3 He left Judea and went off again into Galilee,
4 but He had to go through Samaria.
5 So He went to a city of Samaria called Sychar near the parcel of land that Jacob gave to his son Joseph.
6 Jacob's spring was there. Jesus had gotten tired from traveling on the road. So this is how it was that He was seated at the spring. It was around noon.
7 A woman from Samaria came to draw out water. "Give Me a drink," Jesus said to her.
8 You see, His students had gone off into the city to buy meals.
9 "How is it that you, who are Jewish," the Samaritan woman said, "is asking for a drink from me, a Samaritan woman?" You see, Jewish people don't associate with Samaritans.

10 "If you knew God's free handout," Jesus answered, "and who is saying to you, 'Give Me a drink,' you would ask Him, and He would give you living water."
11 "Master," the woman told Him, "You don't even have anything to get water out with, and the well is deep. So where are You getting the living water from?
12 You aren't greater than our father Jacob who gave us this well, are You? He, his sons, and his livestock drank from this well."
13 "Everyone who drinks from this water will be thirsty again," answered Jesus,
14 "but whoever drinks the water that I will give him won't in any way be thirsty for the span of time. But the water that I will give him will become a spring of water in him gushing out into life that spans all time."
15 "Master," said the woman, "give me this water so that I won't be thirsty or go through here to draw out *water*."
16 "Make your way back home," He told her. "Holler for your husband, and come here."
17 "I don't have a husband," answered the woman. "You are nice to say, 'I don't have a husband.'" Jesus told her.
18 "You see, you have had five husbands, and who you have now is not your husband. This that you have stated is valid."
19 "Master," said the woman, "I see that You are a preacher.
20 Our fathers bowed down to God in this mountain, and you all say that the place where everyone must bow down is in Greater Jerusalem."
21 "Trust Me, ma'am," Jesus told her, "because an hour is coming when you all won't bow down to the Father in this mountain or in Greater Jerusalem either.
22 You bow down to what you have not seen *in the Old Testament*. We bow down to what we have seen because the rescue plan is from the Jewish people.
23 But an hour is coming, and it is now, when the people who truly bow down to the Father will bow down in spirit and truth. You see, the Father is even looking for these types of people, people who are bowing down to Him.
24 God is a spirit, and the people bowing down to Him must be bowing down in spirit and truth."
25 "I realize that a messiah is coming," the woman told Him, "the One who is called Anointed King. When that messiah comes, He will announce absolutely everything to us."

26 "I, the One speaking to you, am Him," Jesus told her.
27 At this time, His students came and were amazed that He was speaking with a woman; however, no one said, "What are You looking for?" or "Why are You speaking with her?"
28 So the woman left her water jar and went off into the city. In the city, she was saying to the people,
29 "Come on. Look, there's a man out at the spring who told me all kinds of things that I did. This isn't the Anointed King, is it?"
30 They came out of the city and were coming toward Him.
31 In the meantime, the students were asking Him *to eat* by saying, "Rabbi, eat."
32 But Jesus told them, "I have a dinner to eat that you haven't seen."
33 So the students were saying to each other, "Someone didn't bring Him something to eat, did they?"
34 "My food is to do what the One who sent Me wants," Jesus told them, "and to complete His work.
35 Don't you say that there is yet a four-month waiting period and then the harvest comes? Look, I tell you, open your eyes, and view the rural areas because they are already white for harvest.
36 The person harvesting receives pay and gathers fruit for life that spans all time so that the person who planted the seed may be happy at the same time with the person who harvested it.
37 You see, the saying, 'One person plants and another harvests,' is true in this situation.
38 I sent you out on a mission to be harvesting what you haven't labored for. Others have labored, and you have come into their labor."
39 Many of the Samaritans from that city trusted in Him because of the woman's message as she told what she experienced--"He told me all kinds of things that I did."
40 So since the Samaritans came out to see Him, they were asking Him to stay beside them. *He did.* He stayed there for two days.
41 Many more trusted because of His message.
42 They also were telling the woman, "We no longer trust because of what you spoke about Him. You see, we ourselves have heard Him, and we realize that this is truly the world's rescuer."
43 After the two days, He went out from there into Galilee, *but not to Nazareth.*
44 You see, Jesus Himself told what He experienced, that a preacher doesn't have value in His own hometown.

45 So when He went into Galilee, the Galileans accepted Him because they had seen all the things that He did in Greater Jerusalem during the festival. You see, they also went to the festival.
46 So again He went to Cana, Galilee where He made the water wine. In Capernaum, there was a certain royal person whose son was in frail health.
47 This royal person heard that Jesus had arrived in Galilee from Judea. He went off to where He was and was asking Him to walk down to Capernaum and cure his son. You see, he was going to die.
48 "If you all don't see proofs and incredible things, you won't in any way trust," Jesus told him.
49 "Master, walk down to Capernaum before my young child dies," said the royal person.
50 "Travel back," Jesus told him. "Your son is alive." The man trusted the words that Jesus said to him, and traveled back.
51 When he was already walking down to Capernaum, his slaves met him and told him that his boy is alive.
52 So he inquired directly from them what hour of the day he got better. "His fever left yesterday in the first hour of the afternoon," they told him.
53 The father knew that it was in that hour that Jesus told him, "Your son is alive." He and his whole house trusted.
54 This was the second proof that Jesus performed as He went again from Judea into Galilee.

5

1 After these things, the Jewish people had a festival. Jesus walked up to Jerusalem.
2 In Greater Jerusalem, there is a swimming pool at the sheep *gate*. Its common name in Hebrew is Bethesda *(house of forgiving kindness)*. It has five columned shelters. *(The Greeks had previously made it an asclepion, a shine to the Greek god of healing, Asclepius)*
3 A large number of frail, blind, crippled, and deformed people were lying down in these shelters. [[[They were waiting for the water to shake.
4 You see, at certain times an angel was stepping down in the swimming pool and agitating the water. The first person who climbed in after the agitation of the water became well of whatever illness he had.]]]
5 There was a certain person there who had been in his frail condition for thirty-eight years.

6 Jesus saw this person lying down and knew that he already had been there a long time. "Do you want to become well?" Jesus asked him.
7 "Master," the frail man answered, "I don't have a person to throw me into the swimming pool when the water is agitated. But as I am going to the pool, someone else steps down into the pool before me."
8 "Get up," Jesus told him. "Pick up your mattress, and walk around."
9 Right away the man became well. He picked up his mattress and was walking around. But that day was a Sabbath.
10 So the Jewish people were telling the person who had been healed, "It is a Sabbath. You are not allowed to pick up your mattress on a Sabbath."
11 He responded to them by saying, "That Person who made me well told me, 'Pick up your mattress, and walk around.'"
12 "Who is the person who told you to pick up your mattress and walk around?" they asked him.
13 The one who was cured didn't know who it was. You see, Jesus had slipped off into the crowd that is in that place.
14 Later, Jesus found him on the temple grounds. "Look, you have become well," He told him. "Don't be sinning anymore so that something worse won't happen to you."
15 That person went off and announced to the Jewish people that Jesus is the One who made him well.
16 The Jewish people were pursuing Jesus because of this, because He was doing these things on a Sabbath.
17 Jesus responded to them, "My Father until now is working. I also am working."
18 So the Jewish people were looking to kill Him more because of this, because not only was He breaking the Sabbath, but He was also calling God His actual Father making Himself equal to God.
19 So Jesus responded by telling them, "Amen, amen, I tell you, the Son can't do anything on His own if it isn't something He sees the Father doing. You see, whatever that One does, the Son also does in a similar way.
20 The Father is fond of the Son and shows Him all kinds of things that He does. And He will show Him greater actions than these so that you may be amazed.
21 You see, even as the Father gets the dead up and gives them life, so also the Son gives life to whom He wants.
22 The Father doesn't even judge anyone, but He has given every judgment to the Son.

23 That way everyone may value the Son, just as they value the Father. The person who doesn't value the Son doesn't value the Father, the One who sent Him.
24 Amen, amen, I tell you that the person hearing My message and trusting the One who sent Me has life that spans all time and doesn't enter into judgment, but has stepped from death to life.
25 Amen, amen, I tell you that an hour is coming, and it is now, when the dead will listen to the Son of God's voice, and the ones who listen will live.
26 You see, even as the Father has life in Himself, so also did He give this to the Son: to be having life in Himself.
27 And He gave Him the authority to judge because He is the son of a person.
28 Don't be amazed at this because an hour is coming in which everyone in the cemetery will hear His voice.
29 And they will travel out: The ones who did the good things will stand up and travel to life, but the ones who constantly did the useless things will stand up and face judgment.
30 I can't do anything on My own. Just as I hear, I judge. And My judgment is right because I don't look for what I want. I look for what the One who sent Me wants.
31 If I am telling what I witness about Myself, My witness account is not valid.
32 There is someone else who is a witness about Me, and I have seen that His witness account about Me is valid.
33 You have sent people out on a mission to John to find out if he is the Anointed King, and he has told what he witnessed of the truth.
34 I don't receive the witness account that comes directly from a person *as solid proof of anything*, but I am saying these things so that you might be rescued.
35 That man was the burning and shining lamp. You wanted to be excited in his light for about an hour.
36 But I have the witness account that is greater than John's. You see, the actions that the Father has given Me to complete, the very actions that I do, they are a witness about Me. They show that the Father has sent Me out on a mission.
37 And the Father who sent Me, that Father has told what He witnessed about Me. You haven't heard His voice at any time or seen His visual image either.
38 And you don't have His message staying in you because you don't trust this One whom that One sent out on a mission.

39 Examine the *Old Testament* writings because in them it seems to you that you have life that spans all time. Those writings are the ones that tell what they witnessed about Me.
40 And you don't want to come to Me so that you may have life.
41 I don't receive magnificence directly from people.
42 But I have known you. And you don't have God's love in you.
43 I have come in My Father's name, and you don't receive Me. If someone else comes in his own name, you will receive that person.
44 How can you all trust magnificence that you receive directly from each other and not look for the magnificence that is directly from the only God?
45 Don't think that I will level a complaint against you to the Father. The one leveling a complaint against you is Moses, the one you all have anticipated good from.
46 You see, if you were trusting Moses, you would be trusting Me. That Moses wrote about Me.
47 But if you don't trust that Moses' documents, how will you trust My statements?"

6

1 After these things, Jesus went off to the other side of the Sea of Galilee *(which is also called the Sea* of Tiberias).
2 A big crowd was following Him because they were watching the proofs He was showing when He healed the people in frail health.
3 Jesus went up into the mountain and was sitting there with His students.
4 It would soon be the Passover, the Jewish people's festival.
5 So when Jesus looked up and saw that a big crowd was coming toward Him, He asked Philip, "Where can we buy bread so that these people can eat?"
6 But He was saying this to challenge him. You see, He knew what He was going to do.
7 "Ten thousand dollars worth of bread," answered Philip, "is not enough to give each of them a little bit."
8 One student from His students, Andrew (Simon Peter's brother), told Him,
9 "There's a little boy here who has five loaves of barley bread and two Opsarius *(a species of fish)*, but what good are these for so many people?"

10 "Have the people settle down on the ground," said Jesus. There was a lot of grass in that place. So the men (the number was about five thousand) settled down on the ground.

11 Jesus took the bread, gave thanks, and passed it out to the people reclining on the ground. He did the same thing with the Opsarius. *He did this* until they had as much as they wanted.

12 When they were full, He told His students, "Gather up the leftover pieces so that nothing is ruined."

13 So they gathered the pieces of the five loaves of barley bread that were leftover from the people who had eaten. They filled twelve baskets full.

14 When the people saw that He had shown a proof, they were saying, "This truly is the Preacher that Moses said would come into the world."

15 Jesus knew that they were going to come and take Him by force to make Him king, so He took a back way up into the mountain again alone.

16 When evening came, His students walked down to the sea.

17 They climbed on board a boat and left to go across the sea to Capernaum. It had already become dark, and Jesus had not yet come to them.

18 The sea was wide awake. A strong wind was blowing.

19 So having rowed the boat three or four miles, they saw Jesus walking around on the sea and coming close to the boat. They were afraid.

20 "It is Me," Jesus told them. "Don't be afraid."

21 They were wanting to get Him into the boat. And right away the boat came to the land they were making their way back to.

22 The next day the crowd that had been standing on the other side of the Sea *of Galilee* saw that there was no other small boat except for one and that Jesus did not get into the boat together with His students. His students had left alone.

23 Other small boats from Tiberias came near the place where they ate the bread after the Master gave thanks.

24 So when the crowd saw that Jesus and His students weren't there, they climbed into the small boats and went to Capernaum looking for Jesus.

25 When they found Him on the other side of the Sea *of Galilee*, they asked Him, "Rabbi, when did You get here?"

26 Jesus answered them by saying, "Amen, amen, I tell you, you all aren't looking for Me because you saw proofs *that I am from God*. No,

you are looking for Me because you ate some of the bread and were full.
27 Don't work for the dinner that gets destroyed. Work for the dinner that stays good for *life,* life that spans all time. The Son of the Person will give it to you. You see, God, the Father, put a seal on this Person."
28 "What should we do so that we may work on the things that God wants us to work on?" they asked Him.
29 "God's work is this," answered Jesus, "that you all should trust in the One that One sent out."
30 "So what proof are you showing so that we might see it and trust You?" they asked Him. "What is the work you are doing?
31 Moses made manna come down from heaven. Our fathers ate the manna that was in the backcountry, just as the Bible says, 'He gave them bread from heaven to eat' *(Psalm 78:24).*"
32 "Amen, amen, I tell you," Jesus told them, "Moses hasn't given you bread from heaven, but My Father is giving you the true bread from heaven.
33 You see, God's bread is the Bread stepping down from heaven and giving life to the world."
34 So they said to Him, "Master, always give us this bread."
35 "I am Life's Bread," Jesus told them. "Anyone who comes to Me won't in any way be hungry, and anyone who trusts in Me won't in any way be thirsty at any time.
36 But I say to you that you have even seen Me, and you don't trust.
37 Everything that the Father gives Me will arrive to where I am. And the person who comes to Me, I won't in any way throw out
38 because I haven't stepped down out of heaven so that I may do what I want. No, *I have stepped down out of heaven* so that I may do what the One who sent Me wants.
39 This is what the One who sent Me wants, that of everything that He has given Me, I wouldn't lose any, but that I will get it up during the last day.
40 You see, this is what My Father wants, that everyone watching the Son and trusting in Him may have life that spans all time, and that I will get him up during the last day."
41 So the Jewish people were grumbling about Him because He said, "I am the Bread that stepped down from heaven."
42 "Isn't this Jesus, Joseph's son?" they were saying. "We know His father and mother. How does He now say, 'I have stepped down from heaven?'"
43 "Don't grumble to each other," answered Jesus.

44 "No one is able to come to Me unless the Father, the One who sent Me, draws him. I will get him up during the last day.
45 It has been written in the Preachers, 'And all will be taught by God' (*Isaiah 54:13*). Everyone who has heard directly from the Father and learned comes to Me.
46 They come to Me because even though they have heard directly from the Father, they haven't seen Him. No one has seen the Father except the One who is directly from God. This One has seen the Father.
47 Amen, amen, I tell you, the person trusting has life that spans all time.
48 I am Life's Bread.
49 Your fathers ate manna in the backcountry and died.
50 This is the Bread that stepped down from heaven so that anyone might eat from Him and not die.
51 I am the Living Bread that stepped down from heaven. If anyone eats from this Bread, he will live for the span of time. But the bread is also My physical body that I will give on behalf of the life of the world."
52 So the Jewish people were arguing with each other. They were saying, "How can this Person give us His physical body to eat?"
53 Jesus told them, "Amen, amen, I tell you, if you don't eat the physical body of the Son of the Person and drink His blood, you don't have life in yourselves.
54 The person chewing My physical body and drinking My blood has life that spans all time, and I will get him up at the last day.
55 You see, My physical body is a valid dinner, and My blood is a valid drink.
56 The person chewing My physical body and drinking My blood stays in Me and I in him.
57 Just as the living Father sent Me out on a mission and I live because of the Father, that person chewing Me also will live because of Me.
58 This is the Bread that stepped down from heaven. Unlike how the fathers ate and died, the person chewing this Bread will live for the span of time."
59 He said these things as He was teaching in a synagogue in Capernaum.
60 So when many from among His students heard it, they said, "This message is harsh. Who is able to be listening to it?"
61 Realizing that His students were grumbling about this, Jesus asked them, "Are you stumbling on this?

62 So what if you watch the Son of the Person step up to where He was before?
63 The spirit is what gives life. The physical body is not a benefit in any way. The statements that I have spoken to you, they are spiritual statements and they are life.
64 But there are some from among you who don't trust." You see, from the beginning Jesus realized who were the ones not trusting and who was the one who would turn Him in.
65 He also was saying, "This is why I stated to you that no one is able to come to Me unless it has been given to him from the Father."
66 From this, many of His students went off to the *things they had left behind* and no longer walked around with Him.
67 "You don't also want to make your way back, do you?" Jesus asked the Twelve.
68 "Master," Simon Peter answered, "who will we go off to? You have statements of a life that spans all time.
69 And we have trusted and have known that You are God's Sacred One."
70 "Didn't I select you, the Twelve," responded Jesus, "and one of you is an accuser?"
71 He was talking about Judas (from Kerioth, Simon's son). You see, this man, one from the Twelve, was going to turn Him in.

7

1 After these things, Jesus walked around in Galilee. You see, He didn't want to walk around in Judea because the Jewish people were looking to kill Him.
2 The Jewish people's festival, the Tent-Setting-Up Festival, was near.
3 So His brothers told Him, "Walk somewhere else away from here, and make your way back into Judea so that Your students will also see the things that you are doing.
4 You see, no one does something in a hidden way and looks for it to be in a clear public statement. If You are going to do these things, do them where all the Jews are gathered, in Jerusalem. Show Yourself to the world."
5 You see, His brothers weren't trusting in Him either. *They didn't think He knew what He was doing.*
6 "The right time for Me isn't here yet," Jesus told them, "but the right time for you is always ready.
7 The world can't hate you, but it hates Me because I tell what I witness about it, that its actions are evil.

8 You all walk up to the festival. I am not walking up to this festival because the right time for Me hasn't come yet."
9 After He said these things, He stayed in Galilee.
10 Since His brothers walked up to the festival, at that time, He also walked up, not publicly, but as if it were in a hidden way.
11 So the Jewish people were looking for Him during the festival and were saying, "Where is that Man?"
12 There was much whispering about Him among the crowds. The people were certainly saying that He is a good man. But others were saying, "No, He isn't. He is misleading the crowd."
13 However, no one was speaking with a clear public statement about Him because they were afraid of the Jewish leaders.
14 When the festival was already halfway finished, Jesus walked up onto the temple grounds and was teaching.
15 So they were amazed. "How does this Man know documents?" they said. "He doesn't have any theological training."
16 "My teaching is not Mine," Jesus answered. "It is from the One who sent Me."
17 If anyone wants to do what He wants, he will know whether My teaching is from God or I am speaking on My own.
18 The person speaking out from himself looks for his own magnificence, but the person looking for the magnificence of the one who sent him, this person is valid, and there is no wrong in him.
19 Hasn't Moses given you the law? And not even one from among you does the law. Why are you looking to kill Me?"
20 "You have a lesser deity," the crowd responded. "Who is looking to kill You?"
21 Jesus answered by saying, "I did one thing, and everyone is amazed because of this.
22 Moses has given you circumcision (not that it is from Moses, but from the fathers), and during the Sabbath you circumcise a man.
23 If someone is circumcised during the Sabbath so that Moses' law won't be broken, why are you nasty to me because I made an entire person well during a Sabbath?
24 Don't judge according to the eyes, but judge the right judgment."
25 So some of the Jerusalemites were saying, "Isn't this who they are looking to kill?
26 And look, He is speaking with a clear public statement. They aren't saying anything to Him. Perhaps the head people truly know that this is the Anointed King.

27 But we have seen where this Man is from. Whenever the Anointed King comes, no one will know where He is from."
28 "You have both seen Me and seen where I am from," Jesus yelled as He was teaching on the temple grounds. "And I have not come on My own, but what you have not seen is the True One who sent Me.
29 I have seen Him because I am directly from Him, and that One sent Me out on a mission."
30 So they were looking to arrest Him. And yet no one put a hand on Him because His hour had not yet come.
31 Many from the crowd trusted in Him. They were saying, "When the Anointed King comes, He won't show more proofs than what this Man has shown, will He?"
32 The Separatists heard the crowd whispering these things about Him, and the head priests and the Separatists sent their underlings out to arrest Him.
33 "I am still with you for a short time," said Jesus. "And I am making My way back to the One who sent Me.
34 You will look for Me and won't find Me. You won't be able to go where I am."
35 So the Jewish people said to themselves, "Where is this Man going to be traveling to that we won't find Him? He's not going to be traveling to *the Jews* scattered throughout *distant* Greek-speaking countries and teaching the Greeks, is He?
36 What are these words that He said? 'You will look for Me and won't find Me. You won't be able to go where I am.'"
37 During the festival's last day (the big day), Jesus had been standing *watching the ceremonies*. "If anyone is thirsty," He yelled, "come to Me and drink.
38 The person trusting in Me, just as the *Old Testament* writing said, 'Rivers of living water will flow from his belly.'"
39 (He said this about the Spirit which those who trust in Him were going to be receiving. You see, the Spirit was not there yet because Jesus had not yet been elevated to His place of magnificence.)
40 So people from the crowd who listened to these messages were saying, "Truly this is the Preacher that Moses said would come."
41 Others were saying, "This is the Anointed King." But some were saying, "You see, the Anointed King does not come from Galilee, does He?
42 Didn't the *Old Testament* writing say that the Anointed King is from David's seed and comes out of Bethlehem (the village where David was *born*)?"

43 So there became a rift in the crowd because of Him.
44 Some from among them were wanting to arrest Him, but no one put their hands on Him.
45 The underlings returned to the head priests and Separatists. "Why didn't you bring Him here?" they asked them.
46 "No one ever spoke like this Man," answered the underlings.
47 "You haven't also been misled, have you?" responded the Separatists.
48 "None of the head people or Separatists have trusted in Him, have they?
49 But this crowd that doesn't know the law is cursed."
50 Nicodemus (the one who went to Jesus before) was one of them. He told them,
51 "Our law doesn't judge the person unless it first hears directly from him and knows what he does, does it?"
52 "You aren't also from Galilee, are you?" they answered. "Examine the *Old Testament* writings and you will see that a preacher does not come up from Galilee."
53 [[They each traveled to their houses.

8

1 Jesus traveled to the Mount of Olives *(a hill just east of Jerusalem)* and spent the night there.
2 At daybreak again, He showed up on the temple grounds, and the entire group was coming to Him. After He was seated, He was teaching them.
3 The Old Testament transcribers and the Separatists brought a woman who had been caught cheating on her husband. They stood her up in the middle
4 and told Him, "Teacher, this woman was caught in the very act of cheating on her husband.
5 In the law, Moses demanded us to attack these types of women with stones. So what do You say?"
6 They were saying this to harass Him so that they may have a complaint to level against Him. But Jesus stooped down and wrote in the soil with His finger.
7 Since *they stayed there and* kept asking, He stood up straight and told them, "Your first sinless person must throw a stone at her."
8 And again He stooped down and wrote in the soil.
9 After they heard this, they were leaving one by one beginning with the older ones. He was left there alone with the woman still standing in the middle.

10 Jesus stood up straight and asked, "Ma'am, where are they? Didn't anyone bring a charge against you?"
11 "No one, Master," she said. "I don't bring a charge against you either," said Jesus. "Go home, and from now on, don't sin anymore."]] *Beginning double brackets are in John 7:53.*
12 So again Jesus spoke to them. "I am the world's light. The person who follows Me won't in any way walk around in the dark, but He will have life's light."
13 So the Separatists told Him, "*When You say things like that,* You are telling what You witness about Yourself. Your witness account is not valid."
14 "Even if I should be telling what I witness about Myself," answered Jesus, "My witness account is valid because I realize where I came from and where I am making My way back to. But you don't know where I come from or where I am making My way back to.
15 You judge as the physical body judges, *unaware of the spiritual world.* I don't judge anyone.
16 Even if I judge, My judgment is true because I am not alone. The Father who sent Me stands with Me. It is I and the Father.
17 And in your law, it has been written, 'The witness account of two people is valid' *(Deuteronomy 17:6; 19:15).*
18 I am a witness about Myself, and He, the Father who sent Me, is a witness about Me."
19 "Where is Your Father?" they were asking Him. Jesus answered, "You don't know Me or My Father either. If you knew Me, you would also know My Father."
20 He spoke these statements in the treasury area as He taught on the temple grounds. No one arrested Him because His hour hadn't come yet.
21 So He again told them, "I am making My way back to where I came from, and you will look for Me and die in your sin. You can't go to where I am making My way back to."
22 So the Jewish people were saying, "He won't kill Himself, will He? Because He says, 'You can't go to where I am making My way back to.'"
23 He was also telling them, "You are from below. I am from above. You are from this world. I am not from this world.
24 This is why I told you, 'You will die in your sins.' You see, if you don't trust that 'I am', you will die in your sins."
25 *'I am' is a name of God, but it also was commonly used to say 'I am him'. Was Jesus saying that He is God? They didn't know.* So they were asking

Him, "You, who are you?" "Primarily, what I also am speaking to you," Jesus told them.
26 "There are many things for Me to speak and judge about you all, but I don't. The One who sent Me is valid and I am speaking these things that I heard directly from Him to the world."
27 They didn't know that He was telling them of the Father.
28 So Jesus told them, "When you put the Son of the Person up high *(as in 'up high on a cross')*, at that time, you will know that 'I am', and I do nothing on My own, but just as the Father taught Me, I am speaking these things.
29 The One who sent Me is with Me. He doesn't leave Me and make Me face things alone because I always do the things that He likes."
30 As He was speaking these things, many trusted in Him.
31 So Jesus was saying to the Jewish people who had trusted Him, "If you stay in My message, you truly are My students.
32 And you will know the truth, and the truth will set you free."
33 Some people responded, "We are Abraham's seed and haven't been slaves at any time to anyone. How are you saying, 'You will become free?'"
34 "Amen, amen, I tell you," answered Jesus, "that everyone committing a sin is a slave of that sin.
35 The slave doesn't stay in the Master's house for the entire span of time. *When his time of service is finished, he leaves.* But the son stays for the entire span of time.
36 So if the Son sets you free, you will really be free.
37 I realize that you are Abraham's seed, but you are looking to kill Me because there is no room in you for My message.
38 I am speaking what I have seen beside My Father, so you also are doing what you heard beside your father."
39 "Our father is Abraham," they responded. "If you were Abraham's children," Jesus told them, "you would be doing the kind of things that Abraham did.
40 But now you are looking to kill Me, a person who--I have spoken the truth to you that I heard directly from God. This is something Abraham didn't do.
41 You are doing the kind of things that your father did." "We weren't born as a result of sexual sin," they told Him. "We have one Father, God."
42 "If God were your Father," Jesus told them, "you would be loving Me. You see, I came out from God, and I have arrived. I didn't come on My own either. That One sent me out on a mission.

43 Why don't you know what I am speaking? Because you aren't able to hear My message.
44 You are from your father, the Accuser, and you want to do your father's desires. That accuser was a people-killer from the beginning and was not standing in the truth because truth is not in him. Whenever he speaks the lie, he speaks it on his own because he is a liar and its father.
45 But because I tell the truth, you don't trust Me.
46 Is there even one person from among you who reprimands Me for a sin? No. If I tell the truth, why don't you trust Me?
47 The person who is from God listens to God's statements. This is why you don't listen, because you aren't from God."
48 The Jewish people responded by telling Him, "Don't we put it nicely when we say that you are a Samaritan and you have a lesser deity?"
49 "I don't have a lesser deity," responded Jesus. "I value My Father, and you belittle Me.
50 I'm not looking for My own magnificence. My Father is the One looking for it, and He is judging.
51 Amen, amen, I tell you, if anyone keeps My message, he won't in any way see death for the span of time."
52 "Now we know that you have a lesser deity," the Jewish people told Him. "Abraham and the preachers died, and You are saying, 'If anyone keeps My message, he won't in any way taste death for the span of time.'
53 You are not greater than our father Abraham, someone who is dead, are You? The preachers also died. Who are You making Yourself out to be?"
54 "If I make Myself out to be magnificent," Jesus answered, "My magnificence is nothing. My Father is the One who elevates Me to a place of magnificence. You say that He is your God,
55 and yet you haven't known Him. But I have seen Him. If I even say that I haven't seen Him, I'll be like you, a liar, but I have seen Him, and I keep His message.
56 Your father Abraham was excited to see My day. He saw it and was happy."
57 "You aren't even fifty years old yet," the Jewish people told Him, "and You have seen Abraham?"
58 "Amen, amen, I tell you," Jesus told them, "before *it was time* for Abraham to come into existence, 'I am'."

59 *Now it was obvious that Jesus had used 'I am' to say that He is God,* so they got stones to throw at Him, but Jesus hid from them and left the temple grounds.

9

1 As He passed by, He saw a man who had been blind since birth.
2 "Rabbi," His students asked Him, "who sinned and caused this person to be born blind, this person or his parents?"
3 "This person didn't sin, and his parents *didn't sin* either," Jesus answered. "He was born blind so that God might show His work in him.
4 While it is day, we must work on the things that the One who sent Me wants us to work on. Night is coming when no one can work.
5 I am the world's light whenever I am in the world."
6 After He said this, He spat on the ground, made mud from the spit, and smeared it on his eyes.
7 "Make your way back," He told him, "and wash in Siloam's swimming pool." *Siloam is Hebrew and* is interpreted as 'having been sent out'. So he went off, washed, and came seeing.
8 So his neighbors and the people who had seen him begging before were saying, "Isn't this the one who sits and begs?"
9 Some were saying, "This is him." Others were saying, "No, but he looks like him." That man was saying, "I am him."
10 "So how were your eyes opened?" they were asking him.
11 "The Man, the One they call Jesus," he answered, "made mud, smeared it on my eyes, and told me, 'Make your way back into Siloam and wash.' So after I went off and washed, I could see."
12 "Where is that Man?" they asked him. "I don't know," he said.
13 They took the person who used to be blind to the Separatists.
14 It was a Sabbath when Jesus made the mud and opened his eyes.
15 So again the Separatists were also asking him how he could see. He told them, "He put mud on my eyes, I washed, and now I can see."
16 So some of the Separatists were saying, "This Man is not directly from God because He doesn't keep the Sabbath, *a day of rest.*" Others were saying, "How is a sinful person able to be doing these types of proofs?" And there was a rift among them.
17 So they asked the blind person again, "What do you say about Him because He opened your eyes?" "He is a preacher," he said.
18 So the Jewish leaders didn't believe this about him, that he had been blind and that it was only now that he could see, that is, until they hollered for his parents.

19 "Is this your son whom you say was born blind?" they asked them. "So how is it that now he can see?"
20 "We know that this is our son and that he was born blind," his parents answered.
21 "But how is it that he can now see? We don't know. Or who opened his eyes? We don't know. Ask him. He is of age. He will speak for himself."
22 His parents said this because they were afraid of the Jewish leaders. You see, the Jewish leaders had already come to the agreement that if anyone acknowledged Him as the Anointed King, he would be excommunicated from the synagogue.
23 Because of this, his parents said, "He is of age. Ask him."
24 So they hollered a second time for the man who had been blind and told him, "Give the magnificence to God, not to this Man. We know that this Man is sinful."
25 "Whether He is sinful or not, I don't know," that man responded, "but one thing I do know is that I, a blind person, now see."
26 "What did He do to you?" they asked him. "How did He open your eyes?"
27 "I already told you, and you didn't listen," he answered. "Why do you want to listen to it again? You aren't wanting to also become His students, are you?"
28 They put him down and said, "You are that Man's student, but we are Moses' students.
29 We know that God has spoken to Moses, but we don't even know where this Man is from."
30 The man responded and said to them, "You see, that is amazing. You don't know where He is from. He opened my eyes!
31 We know that God doesn't listen to sinful people, but if anyone is a God-worshipper and does what He wants, God listens to him.
32 Throughout the span of time, no one has ever heard of anyone opening the eyes of someone who has been born blind.
33 If this Man weren't directly from God, He wouldn't be able to do anything."
34 "You were born in sins, every part of you," they responded, "and you are teaching us?" They threw him out.
35 When Jesus heard that they threw him out, He found him and said, "Do you trust in the Son of the Person?"
36 That man answered by asking, "Who is He, Master, so that I might trust in Him?"

37 "You have both seen Him," Jesus told him, "and the One speaking with you is that One."
38 "I trust, Master," he was declaring, and he bowed down to Him.
39 "I came into this world *to prepare it* for judgment," said Jesus, "so that the people who don't see may see and the seeing people might become blind."
40 When some of the Separatists who were with Him heard these things, they said to Him, "We aren't also blind, are we?"
41 "If you were being *like* blind people," Jesus told them, "it might be that you were not having sin. But now you say, 'We see.' Your sin stays."

10

1 "Amen, amen, I tell you, the person who doesn't go through the door when he goes into the sheep's yard but climbs up some other way, that person is a thief and a bandit.
2 The one going in through the door is the sheep's shepherd.
3 The doorkeeper opens the door to this one, and the sheep listen to his voice. He hollers for his own sheep by name and leads them out.
4 Whenever he takes all of his own sheep out, he travels in front of them, and the sheep follow him because they know his voice.
5 They won't in any way follow another sheep's shepherd. They will run away from him because they don't know the voice of the other sheep's shepherds."
6 Jesus told them this analogy, but they didn't know what He was speaking to them about.
7 So again Jesus said, "Amen, amen, I tell you, I am the sheep's door.
8 All the people, as many as came before Me, were thieves and bandits, but the sheep didn't listen to them.
9 I am the door. If anyone comes in through Me, he will be rescued. And he will go in and out, and find pasture.
10 The thief only comes so that he might steal, kill, and ruin. I came so that they may have life and have much more.
11 I am the Nice Shepherd. The Nice Shepherd gives His soul for the sheep.
12 The hired worker isn't even a shepherd and doesn't have his own sheep. When he sees the wolf coming, he leaves the sheep and runs away. The wolf snatches some and scatters the rest.
13 He runs away because he is a hired worker and isn't concerned about the sheep.
14 I am the Nice Shepherd, I know My sheep, and My sheep know Me,

15 just as the Father knows Me and I know the Father. I give My soul for the sheep.
16 I also have other sheep that aren't from this yard. It is necessary for Me to lead those sheep too. They will listen to My voice and become one flock, one Shepherd.
17 The Father loves Me for giving my soul so that I might get it back again.
18 No one takes it away from Me. I give it on My own. I have the authority to give it, and I have the authority to get it back again. *There is a demand that gives me this authority.* I got this demand directly from My Father."
19 A rift again happened among the Jewish people because of these messages.
20 Many of them were saying, "He has a lesser deity. He's crazy. Why are you listening to Him?"
21 Others were saying, "These are not the statements of someone who has a lesser deity. A lesser deity is not able to open the eyes of blind people, is it?"
22 Then the initiations *(Hanukkah)* came. There was a storm in Greater Jerusalem,
23 and Jesus was walking around in Solomon's Columned Shelter on the temple grounds.
24 So the Jewish people surrounded Him. "How long will You keep our soul in suspense?" they were asking Him. "If You are the Anointed King, tell us with a clear public statement."
25 "I told you," Jesus answered them, "and you don't trust. The things that I do in My Father's name, these are witnesses about Me.
26 But you don't trust because you aren't from My sheep.
27 My sheep listen to My voice, I know them, and they follow Me.
28 And I give them life that spans all time, they won't in any way be ruined for the span of time, and no one will snatch them from My hand.
29 My Father who has given them to Me is greater than everyone, and no one can snatch them from the Father's hand.
30 I and the Father are one."
31 Again the Jewish people hauled up stones so that they might attack Him with them.
32 "I showed you many nice actions from the Father," responded Jesus. "For which of these are you attacking Me?"

33 "We aren't attacking You for a nice thing that You did," the Jewish people answered, "but for insulting God and because even though You are a human, You are making Yourself God."
34 "Hasn't it been written in your law, 'I said, You are gods?' *(Psalm 82:6),*" Jesus responded.
35 "If He called those people gods, the people God's message came to, and the *Old Testament* writing can't be undone,
36 how are you telling the One the Father made sacred and sent out into the world, 'You are insulting God,' because I said that I am a son of God?
37 If I am not doing My Father's actions, don't trust Me.
38 But if I am doing them, even if you don't trust Me, trust the actions so that you may come to know and keep on knowing that the Father is in Me and I am in the Father."
39 They were looking to arrest Him again, and He got away from them.
40 He went off again to the other side of the Jordan River to the place where John had been submerging the first time, and He stayed there.
41 Many went out to Him. "John certainly didn't show even one proof," they were saying, "but everything, as much as John said about this Man, is valid."
42 Many trusted in Him there.

11

1 There was a certain man who was in frail health. He was Lazarus out of Bethany. He was from the village that Mary and her sister Martha lived in.
2 Mary was the one who dabbed perfume on the Master and wiped His feet dry with her hair. Her brother Lazarus was in frail health.
3 So the sisters sent someone out to Jesus with this message: "Master, look, someone whom You are fond of is in frail health."
4 When Jesus heard it, He said, "This frail condition will not end in death. It is for God's magnificence so that God's Son might be elevated to a place of magnificence through it."
5 Jesus was loving Martha, her sister, and Lazarus.
6 So since He heard that Lazarus was in frail health, at that time He certainly stayed for two days in the place where He was.
7 Following that, He told the students, "We may lead the way into Judea again."

8 "Rabbi," said the students, "the Jewish people were just now looking to attack You with stones. Are You actually making Your way back there again?"
9 "Are there not twelve hours in the day?" answered Jesus. "If anyone walks around during the day, he doesn't trip because he sees this world's light.
10 But if anyone walks around at night, he trips because he doesn't have the light."
11 He said these things, and then He told them, "Our friend Lazarus has fallen asleep, but I am traveling there so that I might wake him up."
12 "Master," the students told Him, "if he has fallen asleep, he will be rescued, *and he will get better.*"
13 Jesus had made this statement about his death, but those students thought He was talking about dozing off and going to sleep.
14 So at that time, Jesus told them with a clear public statement, "Lazarus died,
15 and for your sake, I am happy that I wasn't there because now you might trust. But let's lead the way to him."
16 So Thomas (the one called Twin) told his fellow students, "Let's also lead the way so that we can die with Him."
17 When Jesus got there, He found out that he had already been in the burial vault for four days.
18 Bethany was close to Greater Jerusalem, less than 2 miles away.
19 Many of the Jewish people had come to Martha and Mary to comfort them concerning their brother.
20 Martha heard that Jesus was coming, so she went out to meet Him. But Mary was sitting in the house.
21 So Martha said to Jesus, "Master, if You were here, my brother wouldn't have died.
22 But I realize even now that whatever You ask God for, He will give it to You."
23 "Your brother will come back to life again," Jesus told her.
24 "I realize," said Martha, "that he will come back to life again in the return back to life in the last day."
25 "I am the Return Back to Life," Jesus told her, "and the Life. The person trusting in Me, even if he were dead, he will live.
26 And everyone living and trusting in Me will not in any way die for the span of time. Do you trust this?"
27 "Yes, Master," she answered. "I have trusted that You are the Anointed King, the Son of God, coming into the world."

28 After she said this, she left and went back *to her house*. She got her sister Mary's attention in a way that no one would notice and told her, "The Teacher is nearby and asking for you."
29 When that sister heard this, she got up quickly and went to Him.
30 Jesus hadn't yet come into the village but was still in the place where He was when Martha went to meet Him.
31 So when the Jewish people who were in the house with her and were comforting her saw that Mary quickly got up and left, they followed her thinking that she was making her way back to the burial vault so that she might cry there.
32 So as Mary came to where Jesus was, when she saw Him, she fell at His feet. "Master," she said, "if You were here, my brother wouldn't have died."
33 So Jesus was stern in His spirit and agitated Himself as He saw her and the Jewish people who came together with her crying.
34 "Where have you put him?" He said. "Master, come and see," they told Him.
35 Jesus teared up.
36 "Look how fond He was of him!" the Jewish people were saying.
37 But some of them said, "This Man opened blind eyes. Couldn't He also make it so that this man wouldn't die?"
38 So Jesus came to the burial vault being stern again inside Himself. The burial vault was a cave that had a stone leaning on *the entrance*.
39 "Take the stone away," said Jesus. Martha, the sister of the one who had passed away, said to Him, "Master, he already stinks. You see, he is a four-day-old corpse."
40 "Didn't I tell you that if you trust, you will see God's magnificence?" Jesus told her.
41 So they took the stone away. Jesus looked up and said, "Father, I thank You for listening to Me.
42 I know that You always listen to Me, but I said this because of the crowd standing around Me, so that they might trust that You sent Me out on a mission."
43 After He said these things, He loudly yelled, "Lazarus, come out here."
44 The man who had died came out. His feet and hands had been tied up with strips of cloth, and his eyes had a towel tied over them. "Release him," Jesus told them, "and let him make his way back home."
45 Many of the Jewish people who came with Mary and saw what He did trusted in Him.

46 But some of them went off to the Separatists and told them what Jesus did.
47 So the head priests and the Separatists gathered a council together. "What are we going to do?" they were saying, "because this Person is showing many proofs.
48 If we leave Him alone like we have, everyone will trust in Him, and the Romans will come and take both our place and nation away."
49 A certain one from among them, Caiaphas, who was the head priest that year, told them, "You don't know anything.
50 You also aren't considering that it is to your advantage that one person die on behalf of the ethnic group. Then the whole nation won't be ruined."
51 He didn't say this on his own, but being a head priest that year, he prophesied that Jesus was going to be dying on behalf of the nation.
52 But His death wasn't just on behalf of the nation. No, *it was* also so that He might gather God's dispersed children together into one nation.
53 So from that day on, they were advising that they should kill Him.
54 So Jesus was no longer walking around among the Jewish people with a clear public statement, but He went off from there into the rural area near the backcountry into a city called Ephraim. He stayed there with the students.
55 When the Jewish people's Passover was near, many walked up to Jerusalem from the rural area before the Passover so that they might consecrate themselves.
56 So as they stood on the temple grounds, they were looking for Jesus and saying to each other, "What? Do you think He won't come to the festival at all?"
57 The head priests and the Separatists had put out a demand that if anyone knows where He is, he should disclose *it to them* in order that they might arrest Him.

12

1 So six days before the Passover, Jesus went into Bethany where Lazarus was, the one that Jesus got up from the dead.
2 So they had a feast there for Jesus, and Martha was serving. Lazarus was one of the ones feasting and chatting together with Him.
3 Mary took twelve ounces of very valuable authentic Spikenard perfume, dabbed it on Jesus' feet, and wiped them dry with her hair. The house was filled with the smell of the perfume.

4 Judas (the one from Kerioth, one from His students, the one who is going to turn Him in) said,
5 "Why wasn't this perfume put up for sale for three hundred denarii ($15,000) and given to the poor?"
6 He didn't say this because he was concerned about the poor. No, he said it because he was a thief, and since he was hauling the money box, he was stealing what was being thrown into it.
7 "Leave her alone," said Jesus. "Let her keep it for the day of My embalming.
8 You see, the poor, you always have with you, but Me, you don't always have."
9 A big crowd from the Jewish people knew that Jesus was there. So they came not only because of Jesus but also so that they could see the Lazarus that He got up from the dead.
10 The head priests were advising that they should kill Lazarus too
11 because many of the Jewish people were making their way back and trusting in Jesus because of him.
12 On the next day, when the big crowd that had come to the festival heard that Jesus was coming to Jerusalem,
13 they took limbs from the palm trees and went out to meet Him. They were yelling *a chant*, "Hosanna! *O rescue us!* The One coming in the Master's name and Israel's king has been conferred with blessings!"
14 Jesus found a little donkey and was seated on it, just as it has been written in the Bible,
15 "Don't be afraid, daughter of Zion. Look, your king is coming sitting on a foal *(a young child)* of a donkey" *(Zechariah 9:9)*.
16 His students didn't know these things at first, but when Jesus was elevated to His place of magnificence, at that time they remembered that these things had been written about Him and that they did these things to Him.
17 So the crowd that was with Him when He hollered for Lazarus to come out of the burial vault and got him up from the dead was telling what they had witnessed.
18 A crowd also went to meet Him because of this, because they heard that He had shown this proof.
19 So the Separatists said to themselves, "Do you see that your tactics haven't helped in any way? Look, the world has gone off after Him."
20 There were some Greeks among the people walking up to Jerusalem. They were going there so that they could bow down *to God at the temple* during the festival.

21 These Greeks came up to Philip (the one out of Bethsaida, Galilee) and were asking Him, saying, "Master, we want to see Jesus."
22 Philip went and told Andrew. Andrew and Philip went and told Jesus.
23 But Jesus responded by saying, "The hour has come for the Son of the Person to be elevated to a place of magnificence.
24 Amen, amen, I tell you, if the kernel of wheat doesn't die after it falls into the ground, it stays there all alone. But if it dies, it has much fruit.
25 Anyone who is fond of his soul loses it, and anyone who hates his soul in this world will protect it for a life that spans all time.
26 If anyone serves Me, he must follow Me, and My servant will also be there where I am. If anyone serves Me, the Father will value him.
27 My soul has been uneasy now. And what should I say? Father, rescue Me from this hour? But this is why I came to this hour.
28 Father, elevate Your name to a place of magnificence." So a voice came from the sky, "I both elevated it and will elevate it again."
29 So the crowd that stood there and heard it were saying that it had thundered. Others were saying that an angel had spoken to Him.
30 "This voice didn't come because of Me, but because of you," responded Jesus.
31 "This world's judgment is now. The head of this world will be thrown out now.
32 And I, if I am put up high from the earth *on a cross*, I will draw everyone to Myself."
33 He was saying this to indicate what kind of death He was going to die.
34 "We heard from the law," the crowd responded, "that the Anointed King stays for the span of time. How are You saying that the Son of the Person must be put up high *on a cross?* Who is this Son of the Person?"
35 "The light is among you for a short amount of time yet," Jesus told them. "Walk around while you have the light so that darkness won't take you down. Anyone walking around in the dark doesn't see where he is making his way back to.
36 As you have the light, trust in the light so that you might become the light's sons." After Jesus spoke these things, He left and was hidden from them.
37 Although He had done so many proofs in front of them, they were not trusting in Him.

38 This was so that the message of the preacher Isaiah might happen, "Master, who trusted what they heard from us and to whom has the Master's arm been uncovered?" *(Isaiah 53:1)*.
39 This is why they weren't able to trust, because again Isaiah said,
40 *The truth* "has blinded their eyes and made their heart hard as stone so that they might not see with their eyes, be aware with their heart, turn, and I will cure them" *(Isaiah 6:10)*.
41 Isaiah said these things because he saw His magnificence and spoke about Him.
42 And yet, it is also true that even many of the head people trusted in Him, but because of the Separatists, they weren't acknowledging it. That way they wouldn't become excommunicated from the synagogue.
43 You see, they loved the magnificence that they could receive from the people rather than even God's magnificence.
44 Jesus yelled, "Anyone who trusts in Me doesn't trust in Me but in the One who sent Me.
45 And anyone who watches Me watches the One who sent Me.
46 I have come--a light into the world--so that everyone trusting in Me might not stay in the dark.
47 And if anyone listens to My statements and doesn't observe them, I don't judge Him. You see, I didn't come to judge the world. I came to rescue the world.
48 Anyone who disregards Me and doesn't receive My statements has My spoken message judging him. That will judge him in the last day
49 because I didn't speak on my own. No, the One who sent Me, the Father Himself, has given me a demand of what I will say and what I will speak.
50 And I realize that His demand is life that spans all time. So, the things that I am speaking, I am speaking just as the Father has stated them to Me."

13

1 Before the Passover Festival, after Jesus had seen that the hour had come for Him to step away from this world and go to the Father, He loved His own people in the world, and He loved them to the conclusion.
2 As the feast was happening, the Accuser had already put into Judas' heart (*the Judas* from Kerioth, Simon's son) to turn Jesus in.
3 Even though Jesus had seen that the Father had put everything in His hands, that He came out from God, and that He was making His way back to God,

4 He got up from the feast, put His robe to the side, and *did what the slave is supposed to do*. He took a linen towel, and tied it around His waist.
5 After that, He put water in the large bowl and began to wash the students' feet and wipe them dry with the linen towel that was tied around His waist.
6 So when He came to Simon Peter, Simon Peter said to Him, "Master, are You washing my feet?"
7 "You don't know what I am doing now," answered Jesus. "But you will know after I am done."
8 "You won't in any way wash my feet for the span of time," Simon Peter told Him. "If I won't wash you, you have no part in Me," answered Jesus.
9 "Master," Simon Peter told Him, "not just my feet, but also my hands and head."
10 "The person who has taken a bath only needs to wash his feet," Jesus told him. "You are clean, but not all of you."
11 You see, He knew the one who would turn Him in. Because of this, He said, "Not all of you are clean."
12 So after He washed their feet, picked up His robe, and settled down in His place again, He said to them, "Do you know what I have done to you?
13 When you holler at Me, you say 'Teacher' and 'Master', and you are nice to say that. You see, that is what I am.
14 So if I, the Master and the Teacher, washed your feet, you are obligated to also be washing each other's feet.
15 You see, I demonstrated this to you so that you may also do just as I did to you.
16 Amen, amen, I tell you, a slave is not greater than his master, and a missionary isn't greater than the one who sent him out either.
17 If you know these things, you are blessed if you do them.
18 I am not talking about all of you. I know who I selected, but *I selected him* so that the *Old Testament* writing might happen, 'The one chewing My bread raised up his heel against Me' *(Psalm 41:9)*.
19 From now on, I am telling you before it happens so that when it happens, you might trust that I am Him.
20 Amen, amen, I tell you, the person who receives whoever I sent receives Me. The person who receives Me receives the One who sent Me."

21 After Jesus said these things, He was uneasy in His spirit. And He told them what He had witnessed, "Amen, amen, I tell you that one from among you will turn Me in."
22 The students were looking at each other, not sure what to think about what He said.
23 One student from His students was reclining beside Jesus close to His chest (this was the student that Jesus kept loving).
24 So Simon Peter gestured to this student to inquire who it could be that He is talking about.
25 So when that student leaned back like that on Jesus' chest, he said to Him, "Master, who is it?"
26 "I will dip a piece *of bread in the sauce* for him and give it to him," Jesus answered. So after He dipped the piece, He took it and gave it to Judas (*the Judas* from Kerioth, Simon's son).
27 And after He gave him the piece *of bread*, at that time, the Opponent entered that student. So Jesus told him, "Do what you are doing faster."
28 None of the others reclining there knew why He said this to him.
29 You see, some thought that since Judas had the money box, that Jesus told him, "Buy what we need for the festival," or that he should give something to the poor.
30 So after that student took the piece of bread, right away, he left. It was night.
31 After he left, Jesus said, "It is time now for the Son of the Person to be elevated to a place of magnificence and for God to also be elevated to a place of magnificence in Him.
32 If God is elevated to a place of magnificence in Him, God will also elevate Him to a place of magnificence in Him, and right away He will elevate Him to a place of magnificence.
33 Little children, I will *only* be with you for yet a little while. You will look for Me, and just as I said to the Jewish people, I am also telling you now: 'You are not able to go to where I am making My way back to.'
34 I am giving you a new demand so that you may also love each other: Love each other just as I loved you.
35 In this way, everyone will know that you are students studying Me if you have love among each other."
36 "Master, where are you making your way back to?" asked Simon Peter. Jesus answered, "You can't follow Me now to where I am making My way back to, but you will follow later."

37 "Master, why can't I follow You now?" asked Peter. "I will give my soul for You."
38 "Will you give your soul for Me?" responded Jesus. "Amen, amen, I tell you, a rooster won't in any way crow until you flatly deny Me three times."

14

1 "Your heart must not be uneasy. You trust in God. Also trust in Me.
2 There are many places to stay in My Father's house. If I may not have told you before, *I am telling you now* that I am traveling there to get a place ready for you all.
3 And if I travel and get a place ready for you, I am coming again. And I will take you along with Me so that you may also be where I am.
4 You know the way to where I am making My way back to."
5 "Master, we don't know where You are making Your way back to," Thomas told Him. "How can we know the way?"
6 "I am the Way, the Truth, and the Life," Jesus told him. "No one goes to the Father except through Me.
7 If you have known Me, you will also know My Father. From now on, you know Him and have seen Him."
8 "Master, show us the Father," Philip told Him, "and it is enough."
9 "Have I spent so much time with you, Philip," Jesus told him, "and you haven't known Me? Anyone who has seen Me has seen the Father. How are you saying, 'Show us the Father'?
10 Don't you trust that I am in the Father, and the Father is in Me? The statements that I tell you, I don't speak them on My own. It is the Father who stays in Me. He is doing His work, *His actions*.
11 Trust Me because I am in the Father and the Father is in Me, but if you can't do that, trust Me because of the very actions that I do.
12 Amen, amen, I tell you, the person who trusts in Me, that person will also do the actions that I do, and he will do greater things than these because I am traveling to the Father.
13 Whatever you ask in My name *and on My behalf*, I will do so that the Father might be elevated to a place of magnificence in the Son.
14 If you ask Me for anything in My name *and on My behalf*, I will do it.
15 If you love Me, you will keep My demands.
16 I will ask the Father, and He will give you another Encourager so that He may be with you for the span of time.

17 He is the Spirit of Truth. The world can't receive Him because it does not see or know Him. You know Him because He stays beside you and will be in you.
18 I will not leave you *and make you* orphans. I am coming to you.
19 In a little while the world won't see Me anymore, but you will. You will live because I live.
20 In that day you will know that I am in My Father, you are in Me, and I in you.
21 The person who has My demands and keeps them is the one who loves Me. The one who loves Me will be loved by My Father, I will love him, and I will show Myself explicitly to him."
22 Judas (not the one from Kerioth) asked Him, "Master, what has happened that You are going to be showing Yourself explicitly to us and definitely not to the world?"
23 "If anyone loves Me," answered Jesus, "he will keep My message, My Father will love him, We will come to him, and We will make a place to stay beside him.
24 The person who doesn't love Me, doesn't keep My messages. And the message that you hear isn't Mine, but the Father's who sent Me.
25 I have spoken these things to you while I am staying beside you.
26 But that Encourager (the Sacred Spirit that the Father will send in My name *and on My behalf*) will teach you all kinds of things and will quietly remind you of everything that I said to you.
27 I am leaving peace with you. I am giving you My peace. I am not giving it to you as the world gives it. Your heart must not be uneasy, and it must not be cowardly either.
28 You heard Me say that I am making My way back *to the Father* and coming to you. If you were loving Me, you would be happy that I am traveling to the Father because the Father is greater than Me.
29 And now I have stated it to you before it happens so that when it happens you might trust.
30 I won't speak much to you anymore. You see, the head of the world is coming, and he has nothing in Me.
31 But *the things that are going to happen will happen* so that the world might know that I love the Father and I do what the Father demanded Me to do. Get up. Let's lead the way out of here."

15

1 "I am the True Vine, and My Father is the Farmer.
2 He takes off every vine branch in Me that doesn't have fruit, and He prunes every vine branch that does have fruit so that it can have more fruit.

3 You are already clean because of the message that I have spoken to you.
4 You must stay in Me and I in you. Just as the vine branch can't have fruit if it doesn't stay in the vine, so you also can't have fruit if you don't stay in Me.
5 I am the Vine. You are the vine branches. The one staying in Me and I in him has much fruit because without Me you can't do anything.
6 If anyone doesn't stay in Me, he is thrown out as a cut-off vine branch is. *A cut-off vine branch* shrivels up (they gather them together, they throw them in the fire), and it is burned.
7 If you stay in Me and My statements stay in you, you must ask for whatever you want, and it will happen to you.
8 This elevates My Father to a place of magnificence so that you may have much fruit and become students of Me.
9 I loved you just as the Father loved Me. Stay in My love.
10 If you keep My demands, you will stay in My love, just as I have kept My Father's demands and I stay in His love.
11 I have spoken these things to you so that My happiness may be in you and your happiness might be full.
12 This is My demand, that you should be loving each other, just as I loved you.
13 No one has a greater love than this, that someone would give his soul for his friends.
14 You are My friends if you do the things that I demand you to do.
15 I am no longer saying that you are slaves because a slave isn't aware of what his master is doing, but I have stated that you are My friends because I am letting you know about everything that I heard directly from My Father.
16 You didn't select Me. I selected you and placed you here so that you may make your way back, have fruit, and your fruit stay. That way the Father will give you whatever you ask Him for in My name *and on My behalf.*
17 I am demanding you to do these things so that you may love each other.
18 If the world hates you, you know that it has hated Me first over you.
19 If you were from the world, the world would be fond of its own thing. But because you aren't from the world, but I selected you from the world, the world hates you.

20 You must remember the message that I told you: 'A slave is not greater than his master.' If they pursued Me, your Master, they also will pursue you. And if they kept My message, they also will keep yours.
21 But the people who pursue you will do all these things to you because of My name *and who I am* and because they don't know the One who sent Me.
22 If I hadn't come and spoken to them, they wouldn't be harboring sin. But now the sham that they put up around their sin *to hide it* no longer *hides it*.
23 The person hating Me also hates My Father.
24 If I hadn't done what no other person has done among them, they wouldn't be harboring sin. But now they have even seen and hated both Me and My Father.
25 But this is so that the message that has been written in their law might happen, 'They hated Me for nothing' *(Psalm 35:19; 69:4)*.
26 I will send the Encourager directly from the Father to you. He is the Spirit of Truth that travels directly out from the Father. When He comes, He will be a witness about Me.
27 You also are witnesses because you have been with Me from the beginning."

16

1 "I have spoken these things to you all so that you won't stumble.
2 They will excommunicate you from the synagogue. An hour is coming when everyone who kills you will think that it is a way to offer up a sacrifice ritual to God.
3 They will do these things because they don't know the Father or Me.
4 But I have spoken these things to you so that when their hour comes, you may remember that I told you about them. I didn't tell you these things at the beginning because I was with you.
5 Now I am making My way back to the One who sent Me, and none of you are asking Me, 'Where are you making Your way back to?'
6 But because I have spoken these things to you, sadness has filled your heart.
7 I am telling you the truth. It is to your advantage that I go away. You see, if I don't go away, the Encourager won't come to you. If I travel away, I will send Him to you.
8 When that Encourager comes, He will reprimand the world concerning sin, concerning the right way, and concerning judgment.
9 He will certainly reprimand the world concerning sin because they don't trust in Me.

10 But He will also reprimand the world concerning the right way because I am making My way back to the Father and you won't see Me anymore. *I won't be here to show which way is the right way. The Encourager will do that.*
11 He will also reprimand the world concerning judgment because the head of this world has been judged.
12 I still have many things to say to you, but you aren't able to haul those things with you now.
13 When that Encourager, the Spirit of Truth, comes, He will guide you into every truth. You see, He won't speak on His own, but whatever He will hear He will speak, and as these things come, He will announce them to you.
14 That Encourager will elevate Me to a place of magnificence because He will receive from Me and announce it to you.
15 Everything the Father has is Mine. This is why I said that the Encourager receives from Me and will announce it to you.
16 A little bit and you won't see Me anymore, and again a little bit and you will look at Me."
17 So some among His students said to each other, "What is this that He is telling us, 'A little bit and you won't see Me, and again a little bit and you will look at Me,' and 'Because I am making My way back to the Father'?"
18 So they were saying, "What is He saying? What is this 'little bit' thing? We don't know what He is speaking about."
19 Jesus knew that they were wanting to ask Him about it. "Are you looking with each other," Jesus asked them, "for what I meant when I said, 'A little bit and you won't see Me, and again, a little bit and you will look at Me'?
20 Amen, amen, I tell you that you will cry and wail. The world will be happy. You will be sad. But your sadness will turn into happiness.
21 When a woman is delivering, she is sad because her hour *for labor and delivery* has come, *and it is hard*. But when the young child is born, she doesn't remember the hard part anymore because of the happiness she feels knowing that a human being has been born into the world.
22 So you also certainly have sadness now, but I will see you again. Then your heart will be happy, and no one will take your happiness away from you.
23 And in that day, you won't ask Me anything. Amen, amen, I tell you, if you ask the Father for anything, He will give it to you in My name *and on My behalf.*

24 Up until now you all haven't asked for anything in My name *and on My behalf*. You must ask and you will receive so that your happiness may be full.
25 I have been using analogies when I speak about these things. An hour is coming when I won't speak to you in analogies anymore, but I will report to you with a clear public statement about the Father.
26 In that day, you all will ask for things in My name *and on My behalf*. I'm not telling you that I'll ask the Father about it for you.
27 You see, the Father Himself is fond of you because you have been fond of Me and have trusted that I came directly from God.
28 I came directly from the Father and have come into the world. *I am making that transition once* again, *the other way*. I am leaving the world and traveling to the Father."
29 "Look, now you are speaking in a clear public statement," said His students. "You aren't using any analogies.
30 Now we realize that You have seen everything. You don't need anyone to ask You questions *because You already know what their questions are*. We trust that You came from God."
31 "Do you trust now?" responded Jesus.
32 "Look, an hour is coming, in fact, that hour is here, when you will be scattered. Each of you will go your own way and leave Me alone. And yet I am not alone because the Father is with Me.
33 I have spoken these things to you so that you may have peace in Me. In the world, you have hard times, but be courageous, I have conquered the world."

17

1 Jesus spoke these things and then looked up to the sky. "Father," He said, "the hour has come. Elevate Your Son to a place of magnificence so that the Son might elevate You to a place of magnificence,
2 just as You gave Him the authority of every physical body so that He might use everything that You have given Him to give them life that spans all time.
3 *This life that spans all time is* so that they may know You (the only true God) and the One that You sent out on a mission (Jesus, the Anointed King).
4 I elevated You to a place of magnificence on the earth as I completed the work that You gave Me to do.
5 And now, You, Father, elevate Me to a place of magnificence next to Yourself with the magnificence that I had next to You before the world existed.

6 I showed Your name *(who You are)* to the people that You gave Me from the world. They were Yours, You gave them to Me, and they have kept Your message.
7 Now they have known that everything You have given Me is directly from You
8 because the statements that You gave Me I have given to them. They received them, they truly knew that I came directly from You, and they trusted that You sent Me out on this mission.
9 My request concerns them. It doesn't concern the world. It concerns the ones that You have given Me because they are for You.
10 All My things are Yours and Your things are Mine. I have been elevated to a place of magnificence among Your people.
11 I won't be in the world anymore. They are in the world, and I am coming to You, Sacred Father. Keep them in Your name *(in who You are)*, the name that You have given to Me, so that they may be one, just as We *are one*.
12 When I was with them, I was keeping them in Your name *(in who You are)*, the name that You have given to Me. I guarded them, and not one of them was ruined except ruin's son so that the *Old Testament* writing might be accomplished.
13 Now I am coming to You. I am speaking these things in the world so that Your people may have My complete happiness in themselves.
14 I have given them Your message, and the world hated them because they aren't from the world, just as I'm not from the world.
15 I'm not asking You to take them from the world, but to keep them from the evil one.
16 They aren't from the world, just as I'm not from the world.
17 Make them sacred in the truth. Your message is truth.
18 Just as You sent Me out on a mission into the world, I also sent them out on a mission into the world.
19 And I make Myself sacred for them so that they themselves may also be made sacred in truth.
20 My request not only concerns these people, but also the people trusting in Me through their message
21 so that all may be one, just as You, Father, are in Me and I in You, so that they also may be in Us, so that the world may trust that You sent Me out on a mission.
22 And I have given them the magnificence that You have given Me so that they may be one, just as We are one.

23 I in them and You in Me so that they may be complete by being one, so that the world may know that You sent Me out on a mission and You loved them, just as You loved Me.
24 Father, what You have given Me is what I want for those people too, that they may be with Me where I am. That way they may see My magnificence that You have given to Me. You have given it to Me because You loved Me before the world was formed.
25 Father, You do what is right. Even though the world didn't know You, I knew You, and these people knew that You sent Me out on a mission.
26 I let them know Your name *and who You are*, and I will keep letting them know it so that the love that You loved Me with may be in them and I in them.

18

1 After Jesus said these things, He went out together with His students to the other side of the stormwater basin of the Kidron where there was a garden. He and His students went into *the garden*.
2 Judas (the one turning Him in) also knew the place because Jesus had gathered there with His students many times.
3 So Judas took the regiment and underlings from the head priests and Separatists and came there with lanterns, torches, and weapons.
4 Since Jesus knew everything that was going to happen to Him, He went out to meet them. "Who are you looking for?" He asked.
5 "Jesus, the Nazarene," they answered. "I am Him," He told them. Judas (the one turning Him in) had also stood with them.
6 So since He told them, "I am Him," they went off into the things behind them, and fell on the ground.
7 Again He asked them, "Who are you looking for?" "Jesus, the Nazarene," they said.
8 "I told you that I am Him," replied Jesus. "So if you are looking for Me, let these people make their way back."
9 He said this to accomplish the words that He had said *before*, 'I didn't ruin any of these that You have given to Me.'
10 Simon Peter pulled out the dagger that he had and struck the head priest's slave. He chopped off his right earlobe. The slave's name was Malchus.
11 "Put the dagger back into its sheath," said Jesus to Peter. "The Father has given Me this cup to drink. Shouldn't I at least drink it?"
12 The regiment, the commanding officer, and the Jewish leaders' underlings apprehended Jesus and tied Him up.

13 First, they took Him to Annas. You see, Annas was Caiaphas' father-in-law. *He had previously been the head priest and still had influence.* Caiaphas was that year's head priest.
14 It was Caiaphas who was strongly advising the Jewish people that it was to their advantage that one person die instead of the ethnic group.
15 Simon Peter and another student were following Jesus. That student was known to the head priest, and so he went into the head priest's courtyard together with Jesus.
16 Peter had been standing outside near the door. So the other student (the one known to the head priest) went out, talked to the doorkeeper, and brought Peter in.
17 So the doorkeeper, a servant girl, said to Peter, "You aren't also from the students of this Man, are you?" That Peter said, "I am not."
18 The slaves and the underlings had been standing there warming themselves around a bed of hot coals that they had made because it was cold. Peter also was standing with them warming himself.
19 So the head priest asked Jesus about His students and about His teaching.
20 "I have spoken with a clear public statement to the world," answered Jesus. "I always taught in a synagogue and on the temple grounds where all the Jewish people come together. I spoke nothing in a hidden way.
21 Why do you ask Me? Ask the people who have heard what I spoke to them. Look, these people here know what I said."
22 When He said this, one of the underlings who had been standing nearby slapped Jesus. "Are you answering the head priest like this?" he said.
23 "If I spoke something bad," answered Jesus, "tell what bad thing you witnessed. If I spoke nicely, why did you hit Me?"
24 So Annas had Him tied up and sent out to Caiaphas, the head priest.
25 Simon Peter had been standing and warming himself. So they asked him, "You aren't also from His students, are you?" That Peter denied it and said, "I am not."
26 One slave there from the head priest's slaves was related to the slave whose earlobe Peter chopped off. He said, "Didn't I see you in the garden with Him?"
27 So again Peter denied it. Right away a rooster crowed.
28 So they led Jesus out from Caiaphas into the Roman palace. It was morning, and they didn't go into the Roman palace so that they

wouldn't be desecrated by it. They wanted to eat the Passover *later that day, and they wouldn't have been able to if they had been desecrated.*
29 So Pilate came outside to them. "What criminal complaint are you bringing against this man?" he declared.
30 "If this man wasn't doing anything bad, we wouldn't have turned Him over to you," they answered.
31 "You must take Him and judge Him according to your law," Pilate told them. "We are not allowed to kill anyone," said the Jewish leaders to him.
32 (Jesus had indicated what kind of death He was going to die, *that He would die on a cross. That is a Roman punishment, not a Jewish one.* Jesus' words were accomplished *by the Jewish leaders when they turned Him over to the Roman leader to be killed.*)
33 Pilate went into the Roman palace again and hollered for Jesus. "Are You the Jewish people's king?" he asked Him.
34 "Are you asking this on your own, or did others tell you this about Me?" answered Jesus.
35 "I'm not Jewish, am I?" Pilate replied. "Your nation and the head priests turned You over to me. What did You do?"
36 "My monarchy isn't from this world," answered Jesus. "If My monarchy were from this world, My underlings would have been struggling to keep Me from being turned over to the Jewish people. But now, My monarchy isn't from here."
37 "So aren't You a king?" Pilate asked Him. "You are saying that I am a king," answered Jesus. "I have been born so that I might tell what I witnessed of the truth. I have come into the world for this. Everyone who is from the truth hears My voice."
38 "What is truth?" Pilate told Him. Once he said this, he went out again to the Jewish people. "I haven't found even one accusation that He can be charged with," he told them.
39 "But it is a policy with you that I should dismiss one prisoner to you during the Passover. So is it your intention that I would dismiss the Jewish people's king to you?"
40 So they yelled again and said, "Not this Man, but Barabbas." Barabbas was a bandit.

19

1 So at that time Pilate took Jesus and whipped Him.
2 After the soldiers wove an award wreath from thorns, they placed it on His head and threw a purple robe around Him.

3 They were coming to Him and saying, "Happy to meet You, King of the Jewish people." And they were slapping Him.
4 Pilate came outside again and told them, "Look, I am bringing Him outside to you so that you might know that I haven't found even one accusation to charge Him with."
5 So Jesus came outside wearing the thorny award wreath and the purple robe. Pilate told them, "Look, the Man."
6 When the head priests and underlings saw Him, they yelled, "Nail Him to a cross! Nail Him to a cross!" Pilate told them, "You must take Him and nail Him to a cross. You see, I haven't found an accusation to charge Him with."
7 "We have a law," responded the Jewish leaders, "and according to our law He ought to die because He made Himself a son of God."
8 When Pilate heard these words, he was more fearful.
9 He went into the Roman palace again. "Where are You from?" he asked Jesus. But Jesus didn't give him an answer.
10 "Are You not speaking to me?" Pilate said to Him. "Don't You realize that I have the authority to dismiss You and I have the authority to nail You to a cross?"
11 Jesus answered, "You don't have even one bit of authority against Me unless it had been given to you from above. Because of this, the one who turned Me over to you has a bigger sin."
12 From this time on, Pilate was looking for a way to dismiss Him, but the Jewish leaders yelled, "If you dismiss this Man, you aren't Caesar's friend. Everyone who makes himself a king is opposing Caesar."
13 So when Pilate heard these words, he took Jesus outside and sat at the judicial bench in a place called "Paved with Stone" (in Hebrew *it is called* Gabbatha).
14 It was the Passover's preparation day. It was around noon. He said to the Jewish people, "Look, your King."
15 Those people yelled, "Take Him away! Take Him away! Nail Him to a cross!" Pilate said, "Will I nail your King to a cross?" "We don't have a king except Caesar," answered the head priests.
16 So at that time, he turned Him over to the soldiers so that they could nail Him to a cross. They took Jesus along.
17 He was hauling His cross as He went out to the place called "Place of a Skull" (in Hebrew it is called Golgotha).
18 *This is* where they nailed Him to a cross with two others: one on one side and one on the other, but Jesus in the middle.
19 Pilate also wrote a placard and placed it on the cross: "Jesus, the Nazarene, the Jewish people's king."

20 Many of the Jewish people read this placard because the place where they nailed Jesus to a cross was near the city and it had been written in Hebrew, Latin, and Greek.
21 The Jewish people's head priests were telling Pilate, "Don't write, 'The Jewish people's king,' but 'That Man said, I am a king of the Jewish people'."
22 Pilate answered, "What I have written, I have written."
23 When the soldiers nailed Jesus to the cross, they took His clothes and divided them into four piles, one pile for each soldier. His long undershirt was left over. It didn't have any seams. It had been woven from the top throughout the whole piece.
24 "We shouldn't tear it up," they told each other. "We should throw dice to decide who will get it." This is what the *Old Testament* writing said would happen, "They divided up my clothes for themselves and threw dice on my garment" *(Psalm 22:18)*. The soldiers certainly did this.
25 His mother, His mother's sister, Mary (Clopas' wife), and Mary (the Magdalene) had stood beside Jesus' cross.
26 So when Jesus saw His mother and the student that He kept loving standing nearby, He said to His mother, "Ma'am, look, your son."
27 After that He told the student, "Look, your mother." And within that hour, the student took her to his own *place*.
28 After this, when Jesus had seen that all things had already been finished, He said, "I am thirsty," to complete the *Old Testament* writing in *Psalm 69:21*.
29 A container full of sour wine was lying there. So they put a sponge full of the sour wine around a hyssop stick and brought it up to His mouth.
30 After Jesus took the sour wine, He said, "It has been finished." He put His head down and gave up His spirit.
31 Since that day was a preparation day *(the day before a Sabbath that is spent preparing food and setting up for the next day, a day of rest)*, so that the bodies wouldn't stay on the cross during the Sabbath (you see, the day of that Sabbath was great), the Jewish leaders asked Pilate to break their legs and take them down.
32 So the soldiers went and certainly broke the legs of the first man and the other man that were nailed to the crosses together with Him.
33 But when they came up to Jesus, since they saw that He had already died, they didn't break His legs.
34 But one of the soldiers stabbed Him in the side with a spear, and right away blood and water came out.

35 The one who has seen it has told what he witnessed, and his witness account is true. That person knows that the things that he is saying are valid. He is saying them so that you also might trust.

36 You see, these things happened so that what the *Old Testament* writing says, might be accomplished: "None of his bones will be crushed" *(Exodus 12:46 and Psalm 34:20)*.

37 And again a different *Old Testament* writing says, "They will look at a person that they impaled" *(Zechariah 12:10)*.

38 After these things, Joseph from Arimathaea asked Pilate if he could take Jesus' body. Joseph was a student of Jesus, but he had stayed hidden because he was afraid of the Jewish leaders. Pilate gave him permission. Joseph went and took His body.

39 Nicodemus (the one who came to Jesus the first time at night) also came. He brought a mixture of about seventy-five pounds of myrrh *(an expensive fragrant resin)* and aloe *(another fragrant resin)*.

40 They took Jesus' body and bound it with linen strips with the fragrant resins. They followed the Jewish custom for preparing a corpse for burial.

41 There was a garden at the place where they nailed Him to a cross. In the garden, there was a new burial vault that no one had been placed in yet.

42 They put Jesus there because it was the Jewish people's preparation day and because the burial vault was near.

20

1 On Day One *(which is Sunday)* after the Sabbaths, Mary (the Magdalene) came to the burial vault in the morning while it was still dark and saw that the stone had been taken away from the burial vault's entrance.

2 So she ran off and went to Simon Peter and the other student whom Jesus kept being fond of. "They took the Master from the burial vault," she told them, "and we don't know where they put Him."

3 So Peter and the other student left and were going to the burial vault.

4 The two were both running. The other student ran ahead faster than Peter and came to the burial vault first.

5 When he stooped and peered in, he saw the linen strips lying there, and yet he didn't go in.

6 Simon Peter came following him. He went into the burial vault. He also saw the linen strips lying there.

7 The towel that was on His head wasn't lying with the linen strips. It was separate from them. It had been wound up into one place.

8 So at that time, the other student, the one who came first, also went into the burial vault. He looked and trusted. *He didn't know what had happened, but he trusted that whatever it was, it was something God had done.*
9 You see, they didn't yet realize that the *Old Testament* writing says He must come back to life from the dead.
10 So the students again went off to *where* they *were staying*.
11 But Mary had stood outside facing the burial vault crying. As she was crying, she stooped, peered into the burial vault,
12 and saw two angels in white sitting inside. One was toward the head and one was toward the feet of where Jesus' body had been lying.
13 Those angels said to her, "Ma'am, why are you crying?" "Because they took my Master away," she told them, "and I don't know where they put Him."
14 After she said these things, she turned to look behind her and saw Jesus who had been standing there. She didn't realize that it was Jesus.
15 "Ma'am, why are you crying?" asked Jesus. "Who are you looking for?" That Mary thought that He was the gardener and so she said to Him, "Master, if you hauled Him off, tell me where you put Him, and I will take Him away."
16 "Mary," Jesus said to her. When that Mary turned around, she said to Him in Hebrew, "Rabboni" *(which means Great Rabbi). Rabboni* is said in place of teacher.
17 "Don't touch Me," Jesus told her. "You see, I haven't stepped up to the Father yet. Travel off to My brothers, and tell them I am stepping up to My Father, your Father, My God, and your God."
18 Mary (the Magdalene) went and reported it to the students. "I have seen the Master," she said. She also told them the things that He had said to her.
19 In the evening of that day, Day One *(which is Sunday)* after the Sabbaths, the students had closed up the doors where they were because they were afraid of the Jewish leaders. Jesus went and stood in the middle of the room. "Peace to you," He told them.
20 After He said this, He showed His hands and side to them. The students were happy when they saw the Master.
21 "Peace to you," Jesus again told them. "Just as the Father has sent Me out on a mission, I am also sending you."
22 When He said this, He puffed on them. "Receive the Sacred Spirit," He said.

23 "If you forgive anyone's sins, they are forgiven to them. If you hold on to anyone's sins, they are held on to."
24 Thomas, one from the Twelve, the one called Twin, was not with them when Jesus came.
25 So the other students were telling him, "We have seen the Master." But Thomas told them, "Unless I see the shape of the spikes in His hands, put my finger into the shape of the spikes, and put my hand into His side, I won't in any way trust."
26 After eight days, His students were again inside with the doors closed. This time Thomas was with them. Jesus went, stood in the middle of the room, and said, "Peace to you."
27 After that He told Thomas, "Bring your finger here, and see My hands. And bring your hand and put it into My side. Don't become someone who won't trust, but become someone who trusts."
28 "My Master and My God," responded Thomas.
29 "You have trusted," Jesus told him, "because you have seen Me. The people who trust when they can't see are blessed."
30 There certainly are many other proofs that Jesus did in front of His students that haven't been written in this scroll.
31 These things have been written so that you might trust that Jesus is the Anointed King, the Son of God, and so that as you trust, you may have life in His name *(in who He is)*.

21

1 After these things, Jesus showed Himself again to His students on *the Sea of Galilee (which is also called* the Sea of Tiberias). This is how He showed Himself.
2 Simon Peter, Thomas (the one called Twin), Nathanael (the one from Cana, Galilee), Zebedee's sons, and two other students were together at the same place.
3 "I am making my way back to fishing," Simon Peter told them. "We're going with you too," they told him. They went out, climbed on board the boat, and caught nothing that night.
4 When it already had become morning, Jesus stood on the beach. However, the students didn't realize that it was Jesus.
5 So Jesus said to them, "Young children, you don't have anything for Me to eat with My bread, do you?" "No," they answered.
6 "Throw the net from the boat into the right sections," Jesus told them, "and you'll find some." So they threw it, and they captured such a large number of fish that they weren't having the strength to pull it *back into the boat.*

7 That student that Jesus kept loving told Peter, "It's the Master." When Simon Peter heard that it was the Master, he tied a jacket around himself (you see, he only had an undershirt on), and threw himself into the sea.
8 The other students came to shore in the small boat dragging the net of fish. You see, they weren't a long way away from land, only about 300 feet away.
9 As they stepped out onto the land, they saw a bed of hot coals laid out, an Opsarius *(a species of fish)* lying on them, and bread.
10 "Bring out the Opsarius that you just caught," Jesus told them.
11 So Simon Peter climbed up and pulled the net full of fish onto the land. There were one hundred fifty-three large fish in it. Even though there were so many, the net had not torn.
12 "Come on," Jesus told them. "Have breakfast." None of the students dared to question Him--"Who are You?"--because they knew it was the Master.
13 Jesus went, took the bread, and gave it to them. Then He did the same thing with the Opsarius.
14 This was already the third time that Jesus was shown to the students after He got up from the dead.
15 So when they ate breakfast, Jesus said to Simon Peter, "Simon, son of John, do you love Me more than these?" "Yes, Master," he told Him. "You have seen that I am fond of You." "Feed My lambs," He told him.
16 Again a second time He told him, "Simon, son of John, do you love Me?" "Yes, Master," he told Him. "You have seen that I am fond of You." "Shepherd My sheep," He told him.
17 The third time He told him, "Simon, son of John, are you fond of Me?" Peter was sad because the third time He said, "Are you fond of Me?" "Master, You have seen everything," he told Him. "You know that I am fond of You." "Feed My sheep," Jesus told him.
18 "Amen, amen, I tell you, when you were younger, you were putting your waist sash on by yourself and walking around where you wanted to. But when you have aged, you will put your hands out, and someone else will put your waist sash on for you and carry you where you don't want to go."
19 He said this to indicate what kind of death he would elevate God to a place of magnificence with. Then He told him, "Follow Me."
20 Peter turned around and saw the student following them that Jesus kept loving. He is the one who also leaned back on Jesus' chest at the feast and said, "Master, who is it? Who is turning You in?".

21 So when Peter saw this student, he said to Jesus, "Master, what about this one?"
22 Jesus told him, "If I want him to stay until I come, what is that to you? You must follow Me."
23 So this answer *that that student wouldn't ever die* went out to the brothers. Jesus didn't tell him that he wouldn't die, but "if I want him to stay until I come, what is that to you?"
24 This is the student who is writing these things and telling what he witnessed about them. We have seen that his witness account is valid.
25 There are also many other things that Jesus did. If each one were written out, I suppose that there wouldn't be enough room in the world for the scrolls.

Acts

1

1 I certainly made the first account *(the Good News according to Luke)*, O Theophilus. It is about all that Jesus began both to do and teach
2 till the day that He was taken up *to heaven. Here is the second account, the Acts of the Missionaries. Before Jesus was taken up* He gave demands to the missionaries that He had selected through the Sacred Spirit.
3 He also presented Himself to them alive after He had suffered *and died* with a lot of evidence. They saw Him for forty days. He told them many things about God's monarchy.
4 He brought them together for a meeting and passed the order on to them, "You are not to separate away from Greater Jerusalem. But stay around for the Father's promise that you heard about from Me.
5 John certainly submerged people in water, but you will be submerged in the Sacred Spirit not many days from now."
6 So when the people came together, they certainly were asking Him, "Master, are You going to reestablish the monarchy to Israel at this time?"
7 "It isn't yours to know times *(when things will happen)* or periods *(how long certain events will be)* that the Father put in His own authority," He told them.
8 "But you will receive the Sacred Spirit's ability when He comes on you, and you will be witnesses of Me both in Jerusalem and in all Judea and Samaria, and out to the last place on earth."
9 After He said these things, as they watched Him, He was raised up *into the air*, and a cloud took Him up away from their eyes *where they couldn't see Him anymore*.
10 They were staring into the sky as He traveled away. And look, two men in white outfits had been standing by them.
11 "Men, Galileans," they said, "why have you been standing here looking into the sky? This Jesus who was taken up away from you into the sky will come in this same way, the way that you watched Him travel into the sky."
12 At that time, they left the mountain that is named after an olive orchard, *the Mount of Olives,* and returned to Jerusalem. *The Mount of Olives* is near Jerusalem. It has a Sabbath's road *(most scholars think this*

refers to the distance that Jews are allowed to travel on a Sabbath, about 3/4 of a mile).

13 After they entered the city, they climbed up into the upstairs room where they were permanently staying. They were Peter, John, James, and Andrew; Philip and Thomas; Bartholomew and Matthew; James (Alpheus' son), Simon the Zealot, and Judas (James' son).

14 These all agreed that they would stay close to prayer. Women were there with them. Also Jesus' mother Mary and his brothers were there.

15 During these days, Peter stood up in the middle of the brothers. There was a crowd of names at the same place, about a hundred twenty.

16 "Men, brothers," he said, "what the Sacred Spirit already said in the *Old Testament* writing through David's mouth about Judas must happen. I am talking about the Judas that became a guide for those who apprehended Jesus.

17 He was one of us, one of the Twelve. He took his turn in doing his portion of this serving *that we did.*

18 (So *in an indirect way,* this Judas certainly got a parcel of land from his pay for doing the wrong thing. When he ended up on his stomach, his body broke open in the middle, and all his guts spilled out.

19 This is so well known to everyone living in Jerusalem that that parcel of land is called Aceldama in their own dialect which means "Land Parcel of Blood.")

20 You see, it has been written in a scroll of psalms, 'His hut must become uninhabited, no one must live in it' *(Psalm 69:25),* and 'A different person must take His position of supervision' *(Psalm 109:8).*

21 There are men here who have gone together with us all of the time that the Master Jesus came in and went out as our leader,

22 beginning when He was submerged by John until the day He was taken up from us to heaven. One of these men must become a witness together with us of His return back to life."

23 They had two men stand up: Joseph (the one called Barsabas, who also was called Justus) and Matthias.

24 After praying, they said, "You, Master, who knows everyone's heart, show everyone here which of these two You have selected

25 to take the place in this serving *that we do* and mission that Judas violated so that he could travel to his own place."

26 *They put stones in a bag, mixed them up, and dealt them out one by one to them.* The winning stone fell on Matthias, and he was counted as an additional member of the eleven missionaries.

2

1 During the observance of the Day of the Fiftieth, they all were at the same place at the same time.

2 Suddenly an echo came from the sky. It was driven even as a forceful breath. It filled the whole house that they were sitting in.

3 They saw tongues that looked like fire. They divided up and settled on each one of them.

4 They all were filled with the Sacred Spirit and began to speak in different languages. The Spirit was giving them the ability to verbalize each of these languages clearly.

5 Devout Jewish men from every nation under the sky were living in Jerusalem.

6 A large number of these devout men came together to see what this sound was. When they arrived, they were confused because each of them were hearing them speak in their own dialect.

7 They were astounded and amazed. "Look," they said, "aren't absolutely all of these who are speaking, Galileans?

8 How do we each hear in our own dialect, the dialect that we were born in?

9 We are Parthians *(from northeastern Iran)*, Medes *(from northwestern Iran)*, Elamites *(from southwestern Iran)*, the people living in Mesopotamia *(Iraq and parts of Syria, Turkey, and Iran)*, from Judea *(the southern part of the West Bank and parts of southern Israel)*, from Cappadocia *(central Turkey)*, from Pontus *(northeastern Turkey)*, from Western Turkey,

10 from Phrygia *(central part of western Turkey)*, from Pamphylia *(southern coast of Turkey)*, from Egypt, from the parts of Africa along Cyrene *(Libya)*, the Roman citizens making this their home, both Jewish people and converts,

11 Cretans *(from the island of Crete)*, and Arabians *(from Saudi Arabia)*. We are listening to them speak great things about God in our languages."

12 All were astounded and dumbfounded. They were asking each other, "What does *God* want this to be?"

13 Different ones made a joke out of it and said that they have had too much sweet wine.

14 But when Peter stood up with the eleven, he raised his voice and verbalized clearly to them, "Jewish men and all the people living in Jerusalem, you need to know this and you need to open your ears to my statements.

15 You see, these people aren't drunk as some of you have presumed. It is only 9 a.m.
16 This is what God has stated through His preacher Joel. Joel said,
17 'This is how it will be in the last days, says God, I will spill out from My Spirit on every physical body. Your sons and daughters will preach. Your young lads will see visions, and your older men will be inspired while they sleep with sleep inspirations.
18 I definitely will spill out from My Spirit on My male and female slaves in those days, and they will preach.
19 And I will put incredible things in the sky above and proofs on the earth below: blood, fire, and a smoky haze.
20 The sun will turn dark and the moon will turn blood red before the Master's great and gleaming day comes.
21 This is when everyone who called on the Master's name will be rescued' *(Joel 2:28-32)*.
22 Men, Israelis, hear these words: A man, Jesus the Nazarene, has been substantiated to you as being from God. God gave Him special abilities and did incredible things and proofs through Him in the middle of you all. You have seen it for yourselves.
23 *Even though* this *Jesus had resigned Himself* to the intention that had been designated *in the Bible* and to what God had already known *would be the* outcome, you fastened *Him to a cross* through the hand of criminals and executed Him.
24 God brought Him back to life after He released Him from the pains of death due to the fact that it was not possible for death to hold on to Him.
25 You see, David was speaking for Him when he said: 'I was seeing the Master right in front of me through every situation because He is on the right side of me so that nothing will disturb me.
26 My heart celebrated, and my tongue was excited because of this. Even my physical body will yet sleep in my tent based on anticipation
27 because you won't leave my soul down in Hades *(the underworld of the dead)*. You won't allow Your Holy One to see decay.
28 You made life's roads known to me. Your face will fill me up with celebration' *(Psalm 16:8-11)*.
29 Men, brothers, it is not disrespectful for me to talk with a clear public statement facing you about our head father David, that he both passed away and was buried. He did see decay. His grave is still here today.

30 So being a preacher and realizing that God had guaranteed to him with an oath that a fruit of his reproductive system *(his descendant)* would be seated on his throne,
31 David spoke about an event that he saw before it happened, the return back to life of the Anointed King. He saw that He was not left down in Hades *(the underworld of the dead)* and His physical body didn't see decay either.
32 God brought this Jesus back to life. We all are witnesses of it.
33 So when He was put up high, up to the right side of God, and received the promise of the Sacred Spirit, He spilled this out that you both see and hear directly from the Father.
34 You see, David did not step up into the heavens. He himself says, 'The Master *(the Father)* said to my Master *(the Anointed King)*, sit down on My right side
35 until I place Your enemies as Your feet's footrest' *(Psalm 110:1)*.
36 So everyone in Israel's house has to know with certainty that God made Jesus both Master and Anointed King, *this Jesus* that you nailed to a cross."
37 When they heard this, it stabbed each one in their heart, and they said to Peter and the rest of the missionaries, "Men, brothers, what should we do?"
38 "Change your ways," Peter declared to them. "And each of you must be submerged for the forgiveness of your sins based on the name of Jesus, the Anointed King, and you will receive the free handout of the Sacred Spirit.
39 You see, the promise of the Sacred Spirit is for you, for your children, and for everyone a long way away, however many that the Master, our God, will call forward."
40 Peter was a strong witness and was encouraging them with more *and* different messages. "You must be rescued out of this crooked generation," he said.
41 So the people who gladly accepted his message were certainly submerged, and about three thousand souls were added in that day.
42 They were staying close to the missionaries' teaching and to sharing in the splitting *and eating* of the bread and in the prayers.
43 Fear was coming over every soul. And many incredible things and proofs were happening through the missionaries.
44 All who were trusting were at the same place and absolutely all of the things that they had were being shared.

45 They were putting properties and possessions up for sale and dividing them up to all, to each and every one, whoever was having a need.
46 Each day they were unanimously staying close together on the temple grounds and splitting *and eating* bread in each house. They were receiving a share of the food in excitement and plainness of heart,
47 praising God and being generous to the whole group. At the same place, the Master was daily adding the people being rescued.

3

1 Peter and John were walking up to the temple grounds at the hour of prayer, 3 p.m.
2 There was a certain man who had been crippled *since he came* out of his mother's belly. Every day they were hauling him and placing him next to the door of the temple grounds, the one called Beautiful. That way he could ask the people traveling onto the temple grounds for a charitable donation.
3 When he saw that Peter and John were going to be entering the temple grounds, he was asking them for a charitable donation.
4 After Peter and John stared at him, Peter said, "Look at us."
5 He was fixing his attention on them expecting to receive something directly from them.
6 "I don't have silver and gold," Peter said, "but I'm giving you what I do have. In the name of Jesus, the Anointed King, the Nazarene, get up, and walk around."
7 Peter grabbed him by his right hand and got him up. At once, his feet and ankles strengthened.
8 He leaped up, stood, and started walking around. He went together with them onto the temple grounds, walking around, jumping, and praising God.
9 The entire group of people on the temple grounds saw him walking around and praising God.
10 They recognized him. They knew that he was the one who sat at the Beautiful Gate of the temple grounds asking for the charitable donation. They were totally perplexed and astonished at what had come together and happened to him.
11 While he was holding on to Peter and John, the entire group ran together to where they were at the columned shelter called Solomon's. They were puzzled.

12 When Peter saw what was happening, he replied to the group, "Men, Israelis, why are you amazed at this? Or why do you stare at us as if we have made him walk with our own ability or godliness?

13 The God of Abraham, the God of Isaac, the God of Jacob, and the God of our fathers, elevated His Servant Boy Jesus to a place of magnificence. You certainly turned Him in and denied Him right in front of Pilate's face when he decided to dismiss Him.

14 You denied the Sacred and Right One and asked Pilate to do you a favor and give you a man who was a murderer.

15 You killed Life's Head Leader, but God got Him up from the dead and we are witnesses of that.

16 Based on the trust of His name *and who He is*, His name strengthened this man that you see and recognize. Trust through Him gave him this wholeness up in front of you all.

17 And now, brothers, I realize that because you were not aware of what was going on, you repeatedly did exactly what your head people also did.

18 This is how God accomplished what He previously proclaimed through the mouth of all the preachers: that His Anointed King would suffer.

19 So change your ways, and return back for your sins to be erased. That way periods of rest and refreshment will come from the Master's face,

20 and He will send out the One who has previously been handed to you, the Anointed King Jesus.

21 It certainly is necessary for heaven to accept Him till the times when all the things that God spoke about are reestablished. God has spoken about this *reestablishment* through the mouth of His sacred preachers since the beginning of the span of time.

22 Moses certainly said, 'The Master, your God, will stand a preacher up for you from your brothers as me. You will listen to Him and to all the things that He speaks to you, whatever they might be.

23 It will be that each and every soul that does not listen to that preacher will be eradicated from the ethnic group' *(Deuteronomy 18:15).*

24 Even all the preachers consecutively from Samuel on, as many as spoke, also proclaimed these days.

25 You are the sons of the preachers and of the deal that God made with your fathers. He told Abraham, 'And in your seed, *your descendant,* all the earth's family trees will be conferred with blessings' *(Genesis 22:18).*

26 To you first, God stood His Servant Boy up and sent Him out on a mission conferring blessings on each of you when you turn away from your evils."

4 1 As they were speaking to the group, the priests, the captain of the temple grounds, and the Sadducees stood over them.
2 They were perturbed because they were teaching the group and proclaiming that the return back to life from the dead is in Jesus.
3 They put their hands on them and placed them in a holding cell for the next day. You see, it was already late afternoon.
4 Many of the people who heard their message trusted, and the number of the men became around five thousand.
5 On the next day, the head people, the older men, and their Old Testament transcribers happened to be gathered together in Jerusalem.
6 They were with Annas (the head priest), Caiaphas, John, Alexander, and all who were from the head priest's family.
7 They stood John and Peter up in the middle. They were inquiring of them, "In whose ability or in whose name did you do this?"
8 Then Peter, filled with the Sacred Spirit, told them, "Head people of the ethnic group and older men,
9 if we are being investigated today on a humane thing done for a frail person in which this man has been rescued from his condition,
10 be it known to all of you and to all of the ethnic group of Israel that in the name of Jesus, the Anointed King, the Nazarene, that you nailed to a cross, that God got up from the dead, in this name, this man has been standing here in your sight well.
11 This is the stone that you, the builders, treated as a nobody. He is the stone that ended up being used as a corner's head *(a cornerstone, the primary stone of the whole building)*.
12 And the rescue is in no one else. You see, there is no other name under the sky either, that has been given among people in which we must be rescued."
13 As they watched the clear public statement of Peter and John, and when they took down that they were uneducated and lower-class people, they were amazed and were recognizing them because they were together with Jesus.
14 And seeing the person who had been healed standing together with them, they had nothing to say in opposition to it.

15 After they gave the order for them to be taken off outside of the council, they were deliberating with each other.

16 "What should we do to these people," they said, "because, you see, everyone certainly knows that this miraculous proof happened through them. It is shown to everyone living in Jerusalem, and we can't deny it.

17 But so that it won't be circulated any further into the ethnic group, we will threaten them to no longer speak to any people about this name."

18 After calling them back in, they passed the order on to them not to ever verbalize or teach based on Jesus' name."

19 But when Peter and John responded, they told them, "Whether it is right in the sight of God to be listening to you rather than God, you must judge.

20 You see, we are not able to not speak about the things that we saw and heard?"

21 After they threatened them more, they dismissed them. They couldn't find a way to curtail them because of the group. Everyone was praising God's magnificence for what had happened.

22 You see, the man that had experienced this miraculous proof of the cure was more than forty years old. *He had been crippled that long and many people had known him for a long time.*

23 After they were dismissed, they went to their own people and reported everything to them that the head priests and the older men had said.

24 When the people heard it, they unanimously raised a voice to God and said, "Our Owner, You are the One who made the sky, the earth, the sea, and all the things in them.

25 Through the Sacred Spirit from the mouth of our father David, Your servant boy, You said, 'Why were non-Jews riled up, and why were ethnic groups concerned about empty things?

26 The kings of the earth stood by, and the head people were gathered together over the same thing: against the Master and against His Anointed King' *(Psalm 2:1-2)*.

27 You see, it is true. Both Herod and Pontius Pilate together with non-Jews and ethnic groups of Israel were gathered together in this city over Your Sacred Servant Boy Jesus that You anointed,

28 to do as many of the things that Your hand and Your intention already designated would happen.

29 And as to the things happening now, Master, look on their threats, and give Your slaves opportunities to speak Your message with every clear public statement
30 as You put out Your hand to cure, and proofs and incredible things happen through Your Sacred Servant Boy's name, Jesus."
31 And when they pleaded for these things, the place in which they had been gathered was disturbed, every single one of them were filled with the Sacred Spirit, and they were speaking God's message with a clear public statement.
32 The heart and soul of the large number of people who trusted were one. And not even one person was saying that any of the things he had were his own, but they shared absolutely everything that they had.
33 The missionaries with great ability were giving out what they witnessed of the Master Jesus' return back to life. Great generosity was on them all.
34 You see, no one among them was destitute either. You see, all that were property owners of parcels of land or houses, put them up for sale. They were bringing the money
35 and placing it at the missionaries' feet. It was being passed out to each person, to each and every one, whoever was having a need.
36 Joseph (the one that the missionaries also called Barnabas which is *Aramaic* and translated as 'son of encouragement') was one of them. He was a Levite and a Cyprian *(from the island of Cyprus)* by birth.
37 After he sold a field that he had. He brought the stack of money and placed it next to the missionaries' feet.

5

1 A certain man named Ananias together with his wife, Sapphira, sold property
2 and secretly kept a certain part of the money for himself. His wife was also aware of it. He brought a certain amount and placed it at the missionaries' feet.
3 But Peter said, "Ananias, how was the Opponent able to fill your heart with this idea of lying to the Sacred Spirit and secretly keeping part of the parcel of land's money?
4 As it remained, wasn't it remaining with you *(or in other words, while you owned it, wasn't it up to you what happened to it)*? And when it was put up for sale, it was under your authority. What is this thing that you placed in your heart? You didn't lie to people. You lied to God."
5 As Ananias heard these words, he fell down and stopped breathing. A great fear came on everyone listening.

6 The younger men got up, wrapped up his body, carried it out, and put it in a burial vault.
7 There happened to be an interval of about three hours, and his wife came in. She didn't know what had happened.
8 Peter replied to her, "Tell me if you gave the parcel of land away for this amount." "Yes," she said, "for that amount."
9 "How is it," Peter said to her, "that you harmoniously agreed to harass the Master's Spirit? Look, the feet of the people who buried your husband are at the door. And they will carry you out."
10 At once, she fell down next to his feet and stopped breathing. When the young lads came in, they found her dead. They carried her out and put her in the burial vault facing her husband.
11 A great fear came on the whole assembly and on all the people who heard these things.
12 Many proofs and incredible things were happening in the group through the missionaries' hands, and absolutely everyone was unanimous in Solomon's Columned Shelter.
13 None of the rest of the students dared to join the missionaries. Instead, the group was making them great.
14 More were trusting and being added to the Master, large numbers of both men and women.
15 They were even carrying the frail out into the plazas and placing them on cots and mattresses so that as Peter went by, his shadow might just fall on some of them.
16 Even the large number of cities around there were coming together to Jerusalem carrying people in frail health and people crowded by spirits that are not clean. Every single one was healed.
17 When the head priest and all the people together with him (the sect made up of the Sadducees) got up, they were full of hostile passion.
18 They put their hands on the missionaries and placed them in a public holding cell.
19 That night the Master's angel opened the jail's doors and led them out.
20 "Travel back to the temple grounds," he said. "Stand up and speak to the group. Tell them all the statements of this life."
21 After hearing this, they went onto the temple grounds just as the sun was about to come up and were teaching. When the head priest and the people together with him showed up to the council hall, they called the council and all the senate of Israel's sons together and sent *underlings* out to the prison to bring the missionaries there.

22 When the underlings showed up to the jail, they didn't find them there. They returned and reported it.
23 "We found that the prison had been securely locked up," they said, "and that the jailers were standing at the doors. But when we opened it up, we found no one inside."
24 Hearing these words, both the captain of the temple grounds and the head priests were dumbfounded about what happened.
25 But then someone showed up and reported to them, "Look, the men that you put in jail are on the temple grounds. They have been standing there and are teaching the group."
26 At that time, the captain went off together with the underlings and brought them back without force. You see, they were afraid of the group. They didn't want to be attacked with stones.
27 When they brought them in, they stood in the council. The head priest asked them,
28 "Didn't we give you an order not to be teaching on this name? Look, you have filled Jerusalem with your teaching, and you intend to bring this Person's blood onto us."
29 "We must be loyal to God rather than people," answered Peter and the missionaries.
30 "The God of our fathers got Jesus up, *the very Jesus* that you killed with your hands when you hung Him on a wooden cross.
31 God put this Head Leader and Rescuer up high, up to His right side. He did this to give Israel the opportunity to change its ways and have its sins forgiven.
32 We are witnesses of these statements and so is the Sacred Spirit that God gave to those being loyal to Him."
33 The people listening were being sawed in two. They were intending to execute them.
34 But someone in the council stood up. It was a Separatist named Gamaliel. He was a law teacher that all the ethnic group respected. He gave the order to take the missionaries outside for a bit.
35 Then he said to them, "Men, Israelis, pay attention to yourselves and to what you are going to repeatedly be doing to these people.
36 You see, before these days, Theudas stood up saying that he was somebody. A number of men, about four hundred, gravitated toward him. He was executed, and all who were being persuaded by him dissipated and became nothing.
37 After this, Judas, the Galilean, stood up in the days of the registration. He *convinced* a group to back off *and follow* behind him.

That one ruined himself, and all who were being persuaded by him dispersed.
38 And the things happening now, I tell you, back off from these people and leave them alone because if these people's intentions or this work is from people, it will be torn down.
39 But if it is from God, you won't be able to ever tear them down, and you will be found to be people who argue with God."
40 They were persuaded by him. They called for the missionaries to be brought back in. They beat them and gave them the order not to be speaking on the name of Jesus. Then they dismissed them.
41 So the missionaries certainly were happy when they traveled out from appearing before the council because they had been considered as totally deserving to be belittled for His name.
42 Every day on the temple grounds and in each house, they did not stop teaching and sharing the good news of the Anointed King Jesus.

6

1 In these days, as the students were increasing, the Greek-speaking students started grumbling about the Hebrew-speaking students because the Greek-speaking widows were being overlooked in the *assembly's* daily serving *of food.*
2 After the Twelve called for the large group of students, they said, "We do not like it that we have to leave God's message to serve tables.
3 Brothers, keep an eye on seven men from among you that you witnessed being full of the Spirit and insight. We will put them in charge of this need.
4 But we will stay close to prayer and serving the message."
5 All of the large group liked the answer. They selected Stephen (a man full of trust and the Sacred Spirit), Philip, Prochorus, Nicanor, Timon, Parmenas, and Nicolas (a convert from Antioch).
6 They had them stand in front of the missionaries. They prayed and placed their hands on them.
7 God's message was growing. The number of students in Jerusalem was increasing terribly *fast.* Even a large crowd of *Jewish* priests were obeying and trusting.
8 Stephen, full of generosity and ability, was doing incredible things and great proofs among the group.
9 *Jerusalem had many Jewish synagogues throughout the city. One* synagogue *was made up of and* named after *Jews who were* Libertines *(former slaves),* Cyrenians, Alexadrians, and the people out of Cilicia

(southeastern coastal area of Turkey) and Western Turkey. Some of them stood up against Stephen and together were posing questions to him.

10 They couldn't oppose the insight and the Spirit with which he was speaking.

11 Then they secretly brought in men who said, "We have listened to him speak insulting statements against Moses and God."

12 Together they shook up the group, the older men, and the Old Testament transcribers. They stood over him, seized him, and took him into the council.

13 They stood up lying witnesses that said, "This person doesn't stop speaking statements against this sacred place and the law.

14 You see, we have listened to him saying that this Jesus, the Nazarene, will tear this place down and change the customs that Moses turned over to us."

15 When all the people seated in the council stared at him, they saw that his face looked like the face of an angel.

7

1 "*Tell us,* if this is how these things are," said the head priest.

2 Stephen was declaring, "Men, brothers and fathers, listen. Our father Abraham saw the God of magnificence as he was in Mesopotamia before he lived in Haran.

3 And He said to him, 'Leave your land and your relatives, and come here into the land that I will show you.'

4 Then he left the land of the Chaldeans and lived in Haran. From there, after his father died, God relocated him to this land that you now live in.

5 He didn't give him an inheritance in it, not even one footstep. He promised to give it to him for a permanent possession and to his seed *(his descendants)* after him. At that time, he didn't have a child.

6 God spoke like this: that for four hundred years his seed *(his descendants)* would be a foreign resident in land belonging to others, and they would make *his seed* a slave and do bad to it.

7 God said, 'I will judge whatever nation they will be slaves to. And after these things, they will come out and minister to Me in this place.'

8 He offered him a *verbal* deal *and he accepted it through* circumcision. So he fathered Isaac, and he circumcised him on his eighth day. Isaac *did the same thing to* Jacob. And Jacob *did the same thing to his sons,* the twelve head fathers.

9 When the head fathers got mad at Joseph, they gave him away to Egypt, and God was with him.
10 He took him out of all his hard times and gave him generosity and insight directly in front of Pharaoh, the king of Egypt. He put him in charge as a leader over Egypt and over his whole house.
11 But a famine went through all of Egypt and Canaan. It was a very hard time. Our fathers couldn't find any feed for their cattle.
12 When Jacob heard that there was grain in Egypt, he sent our fathers off the first *time*.
13 During their second *trip to Egypt*, Joseph revealed himself to his brothers, and Joseph's family ended up being shown to Pharaoh.
14 Joseph sent his brothers out with supplies and wagons and summoned his father Jacob and all of the relatives. *There were seventy-five of them,* seventy-five souls.
15 Jacob walked down to Egypt, and he and our fathers passed away.
16 They transferred their corpses to Shechem *(which was back in the promised land)* and placed them in the grave that Abraham purchased with a certain amount of silver directly from Emmor's sons in Shechem.
17 As the time that God acknowledged to Abraham in His promise *(four hundred years)* was coming near, the ethnic group grew and increased in Egypt
18 till a different king stood up over Egypt who didn't know Joseph.
19 This king swindled our family and did a bad thing to our fathers when he made their babies be put out *in the river* so that they wouldn't survive.
20 In this period, Moses was born and he was a well-behaved *baby* to God. He was raised three months in his father's house.
21 When he was placed out *in the river*, Pharaoh's daughter took him up and raised him herself for a son.
22 Moses was disciplined in all of the insight *(the science and technology)* of the Egyptians. He was competent with words and with his actions.
23 As he accomplished the *first* forty-year period *of his life, the idea* stepped up in his heart to keep an eye on his brothers, the sons of Israel.
24 When he saw someone being hurt, he fended for him and retaliated against the Egyptian. He struck the Egyptian who was oppressing him.

25 He had been assuming that his brothers understood that God was going to rescue them through his hand, but the *brothers* didn't understand that.
26 And on the following day, he appeared as two of them were arguing. He was urging them together into peace. 'Men, you are brothers,' he said. 'Why are you hurting each other?'
27 The one who was hurting the *brother* near him pushed him away. 'Who put you in charge,' he said. 'Who made you a head person and referee over us?
28 Are you wanting to execute me the way you executed the Egyptian yesterday?'
29 Because of these words, Moses ran away and became a foreign resident in the land of Midian where he fathered two sons.
30 When he accomplished *another* forty years *of his life*, an angel appeared to him in the backcountry of Mount Sinai in a blaze of fire in a bush.
31 When Moses saw it, he was amazed at the sight. As he went up to it to take a close look, he heard the Master's voice.
32 'I am the God of your fathers, the God of Abraham, Isaac, and Jacob.' Moses started trembling inside and didn't dare take a close look.
33 'Take the sandals off your feet,' said the Master. 'You see, the place on which you have been standing is sacred ground.
34 I looked and saw how bad my ethnic group in Egypt is being treated. I heard their groans, and I am stepping down to take them out of Egypt. Now, come on, I will send you out on a mission to Egypt.'
35 This Moses, that they denied when they said, 'Who put you in charge? Who made you a head person and referee?', this *is the one that* God has sent out on a mission together with the hand of the angel that appeared to him at the bush. He sent him out to be both a head person and a provider of their release *from Egypt*.
36 This *is the one that* led them out after he performed incredible things and proofs in the land of Egypt, in the Red Sea, and in the backcountry for forty years.
37 This Moses is the one who said to Israel's sons, 'God will stand a preacher up for you from your brothers as me.'
38 This *Moses* is the one that came to be in the assembly in the backcountry with our fathers and with the angel who had spoken to him in the bush at Mount Sinai. There our fathers accepted live utterances to give to us.
39 Our fathers didn't want to become obedient to him. They pushed him away and turned back to Egypt in their hearts

40 when they said to Aaron, 'Make gods for us that will travel ahead of us. You see, we don't know what happened to this Moses who led us out from the land of Egypt.'
41 In those days, they made a calf, took a sacrifice up to the idol, and were celebrating in the actions of their hands *because their hands had made a god*.
42 God turned and gave them up to the army of stars in the sky *so they could worship the stars instead of Him*. They ministered to them. This is just what has been written in a scroll of the preachers, 'You didn't offer slaughtered animals and sacrifices up to Me forty years in the backcountry, house of Israel, did you?
43 You also took up the tent of Molech *(a god of the Amorites)* and the constellation of your god, Remphan *(an Egyptian god)*. You made copies of them and were bowing down to them. I will relocate you beyond Babylon' *(Amos 5:25-27)*.
44 In the backcountry, our fathers had the tent of the witness *(a visible witness and proof of God's tent in heaven)*. It was made just as the One who spoke to Moses specifically assigned for it to be made, aligned with the copy that he had seen.
45 With Joshua, they also brought it here. It was passed down in succession to our fathers in our permanent possession of the nations, *nations* that God pushed out away from our fathers' face until the days of David.
46 David found generosity in God's sight and asked if he could find a shelter for Jacob's God.
47 Solomon built Him a house.
48 But the Highest One doesn't live in handmade structures. This is just what the preacher said,
49 'The sky is a throne for Me. The earth is a footrest for My feet. What kind of house will you build Me? says the Master. Or what place is My resting place?
50 Didn't My hand make all these?' *(Isaiah 66:1)*.
51 Stiff-necked and uncircumcised in your hearts and ears, you always fall opposing the Sacred Spirit. You also do what your fathers did.
52 Which of the preachers did your fathers not persecute? They even killed the people who previously proclaimed the coming of the One who does what is right. And now you have become traitors and murderers of Him.
53 You are the ones who took the law into *a higher level by* arranging announcers *for it*. And you didn't observe it."

54 Hearing these things, their hearts were being sawed in two, and they were biting *the air* with their teeth at him.
55 He was full of the Sacred Spirit. He stared into the sky and saw God's magnificence and Jesus standing to the right of God.
56 "Look," he said, "I see the heavens completely opened and the Son of the Person standing to the right of God." (*"The Son of the Person" is a generic term Jesus used of Himself. Ezekiel and Daniel were called "son of a person." "Son of a person" is also in Psalm 80:17.*)
57 They yelled with a loud voice, held their ears, and unanimously rushed on him.
58 They threw him outside of the city and were throwing stones at him. The witnesses *to this event* put their robes away next to a young man's feet. His name was Saul.
59 They were throwing stones at Stephen who was calling on Jesus and saying, "Master, Jesus, accept my spirit."
60 He placed his knees on the ground and yelled with a loud voice, "Master, you shouldn't stack up this sin to them." After he said this, he fell asleep.

8

1 Saul was agreeing with the *others that Stephen's execution was a good thing*. On that day, there became a great persecution on the assembly in Greater Jerusalem. Everyone (other than the missionaries) was scattered throughout the rural areas of Judea and Samaria.
2 Together devout men retrieved Stephen's *body*. For a long while, many people beat their chests in grief over him.
3 Saul was wreaking havoc on the assembly. He was traveling into each house, dragging men and women out, and throwing them in jail.
4 So when they certainly were scattered out, they went through the rural areas sharing the good news of the message.
5 When Philip went down to the city of Samaria, he was speaking publicly to them about the Anointed King.
6 As the crowds heard about and saw the miraculous proofs that Philip was doing, they were unanimously paying attention to what he was saying.
7 You see, spirits that are not clean were shouting with a loud voice and coming out of many people. Many disabled and crippled people were being healed.
8 That city became very happy.

9 Previously, a certain man named Simon was using magic tricks in the city and astounding the nation of Samaria. He was telling everyone that he was some type of great person.
10 Everyone, from little to great, was paying attention to him and saying, "This is God's great ability."
11 They were paying attention to him because he had astounded them for an adequate amount of time with his magic tricks.
12 When they, both men and women, trusted Philip as he shared the good news about God's monarchy and the name of Jesus, the Anointed King, they were being submerged.
13 Even Simon himself trusted. After he was submerged, he was staying close to Philip and watching the proofs and great abilities that were happening. He was astounded.
14 When the missionaries in Greater Jerusalem heard that Samaria had accepted God's message, they sent Peter and John out on a mission to them.
15 They walked down to the city of Samaria and prayed about them so that they might receive the Sacred Spirit.
16 You see, He had not fallen on any of them yet. They had only been submerged in the name of the Master Jesus.
17 Then they were placing their hands on them, and they were receiving the Sacred Spirit.
18 When Simon saw that the Spirit was given through the missionaries laying their hands on them, he offered them stacks of money.
19 "Give me this authority too," he said, "so that whoever I place my hands on may receive the Sacred Spirit."
20 "May you and your silver be ruined together," Peter told him, "because you assumed that you could get God's free handout with stacks of money.
21 You don't have a part or a portion in these words that we have spoken. You see, your heart is not straight directly in front of God.
22 So change your ways from this badness of yours, and plead with the Master if maybe Your heart's viewpoint will be forgiven to you.
23 You see, the way I see things, you are in bitterness' bile and the wrong way's bondage."
24 "You must plead to the Master on my behalf," responded Simon, "so that none of what you have stated will come on me."
25 So the missionaries certainly were strong witnesses and spoke the Master's message. Then as they were returning to Jerusalem, they also were sharing good news with many Samaritan villages.

26 The Master's angel spoke to Philip and said, "Get up, and travel throughout the middle of the day on the road that steps down out of Jerusalem into Gaza. It is backcountry."
27 He got up and traveled. And look, a castrated Ethiopian man was there who was a competent ruler under Candace *(Candace was a title, like Pharaoh or Caesar, for queens in the capital city of Meroe)*, Queen of Ethiopians. He was over all of her royal treasury. He had gone to Jerusalem to bow down *to God*.
28 Now he was returning and sitting in his chariot. He was reading the preacher Isaiah.
29 The Spirit told Philip, "Go forward, and stay up close to this chariot."
30 When Philip ran up, he heard him reading the preacher Isaiah. "So do you definitely know," said Philip, "what you are reading?"
31 "You see, how would I be able to," he said, "if someone won't guide me?" He encouraged Philip to climb up and sit together with him.
32 The passage of the writing that he was reading was this: "As a sheep, He was led to the slaughter-house, and in the same way that a lamb is voiceless directly in front of the person shearing him, that is how He doesn't open His mouth.
33 In His lowliness, He was deprived of a fair trial. Who will describe His generation *(His middle age years)* because His life is taken away from the earth?" *(Isaiah 53:7-8)*.
34 The castrated man replied to Philip and said, "I plead with you, who is the preacher talking about? Is this about himself or about someone else?"
35 When Philip opened his mouth, he began with this *Old Testament* writing and shared with him the good news of Jesus.
36 As they were traveling down the road, they came upon some water. "Look, water," declared the castrated man. "What is keeping me from being submerged?"
37 [[["If you trust with your whole heart," said Philip, "it is allowed." "I trust that Jesus is God's son, the Anointed King," he replied.]]]
38 He gave the order to stop the chariot. Both Philip and the castrated man stepped down into the water, and he submerged him.
39 When they stepped up out of the water, the Master's Spirit snatched Philip. The castrated man didn't see him anymore. You see, he was traveling on his way, and he was happy.
40 Philip found himself in Azotus *(also called Ashdod, located on the Mediterranean coast halfway between Gaza and Tel Aviv)*. As he went through there, he was sharing good news with all the cities until he

came to Caesarea *(on the Mediterranean coast about 60 miles north of Azotus)*.

9

1 Still inhaling *the smell of* threat and murder for the Master's students, Saul went forward to the head priest 2 and asked for letters directly from him to the synagogues in Damascus *(a city in Syria) that would* authorize *him* to lock up and bring anyone from the Way *(followers of Jesus)*, including both men and women, if he found any, to Jerusalem.
3 As he was traveling and happened to be near Damascus, unexpectedly, a light beamed down all around him from the sky.
4 He fell on the ground and heard a voice saying to him, "Saul, Saul, why are you persecuting Me?"
5 "Who are You, Master?" he said. "I am Jesus who you are persecuting," said the Master. "[[[Isn't it harsh to you to be kicking against cattle prods?]]]
6 But get up, and go into the city. Someone will speak to you and tell you what you must do."
7 The men who were together with him on the trip had stood speechless. They certainly were hearing the voice, but they saw no one.
8 Saul got up off the ground. When he had opened his eyes, he wasn't seeing anything. They led him by the hand into Damascus.
9 For three days, he was not *able to* see. He didn't eat, and he didn't drink either.
10 There was a certain student *of Jesus* in Damascus named Ananias. In a vision, the Master said to him, "Ananias." Ananias said, "Look, I am here, Master."
11 The Master said, "Get up and travel on the street called Straight *(a main street in Damascus)*. Look in Jude's house for Saul by name. He is originally from Tarsus. You see, look, he is there praying.
12 In a vision, he saw a man named Ananias come in and place his hands on him so that he could see again."
13 "Master," responded Ananias, "I've heard from many people about this man and all the bad things he has done to Your sacred people in Jerusalem.
14 And here he has authority directly from the head priests to lock up all the people who call on Your Name."
15 But the Master told him, "Travel to him because I have selected him to be the kind of container that hauls My name before non-Jews, kings, and Israel's sons.

16 You see, I will put in front of his face all the things he must suffer on behalf of My name."
17 Ananias went off and entered that house. He placed his hands on him and said, "Saul, brother, the Master has sent me out to you. He is Jesus, the One who saw you on the road that you took here. He sent me here so that you might see again and be filled with the Sacred Spirit."
18 Right away, it was as if flakes had fallen off his eyes. He could see. He got up and was submerged.
19 After he took a meal, he was invigorated. He ended up being with the students in Damascus for some days.
20 Right away he was speaking publicly about Jesus in the synagogues. He was telling them that this Jesus is God's Son.
21 Everyone listening kept being astounded and saying. "Isn't this the one who damaged the people calling on this name in Jerusalem and who had come here to lock those people up and take them before the head priests in Jerusalem?"
22 Saul was becoming more competent and stirring up the Jewish people living in Damascus. He was making the conclusion that this Jesus is the Anointed King.
23 After an adequate amount of days had happened, the Jewish people together advised to execute him.
24 Their conspiracy was known to Saul. They were even closely watching the gates both day and night so that they could execute him.
25 His students took him at night and let him down through the wall by lowering him in a large basket.
26 When he showed up in Jerusalem, he was trying to join in with the students. Everyone was afraid of him. They weren't trusting *him when he told them* that he is also a student.
27 But Barnabas latched on to him and took him to the missionaries. He described to them how Saul saw the Master when he was on the road, that the Master spoke to him, and how in Damascus he made clear public statements in the name of Jesus.
28 He was with them traveling in and out *of many places* in Jerusalem. He was making clear public statements in the name of the Master.
29 He was both speaking to and together posing questions to the Greek-speaking Jews, but they were attempting to execute him.
30 When the brothers correctly understood this, they took him down to Caesarea *(a coastal city about 35 miles north of Tel Aviv)* and sent him off to Tarsus *(his hometown located in southern Turkey)*.

31 So the assembly certainly was experiencing peace throughout all of Judea, Galilee, and Samaria. The assembly was being built. As it was traveling in the fear of the Master and the encouragement of the Sacred Spirit, it was increasing.
32 As Peter was going through all kinds of places, he even happened to go down to the sacred people living in Lydda *(a town about 10 miles southeast of Tel Aviv)*.
33 There he found a certain person named Aeneas. He had been lying down on a mattress for eight years. He was disabled.
34 "Aeneas," Peter said to him, "Jesus, the Anointed King, is curing you. Stand up and spread your mattress out for yourself." Right away he stood up.
35 All the people living in Lydda and the plain of Sharon saw him. These are the ones that turned back to the Master.
36 There was a certain student in Joppa *(present day Jaffa in Tel Aviv)* named Tabitha (*Tabitha is Aramaic for gazelle.* Translated *into Greek, her name is* Dorcas). She was full of good actions and charitable donations that she was making *for others*.
37 In those days, she was in frail health and happened to die. They gave her body a bath and placed it in an upstairs room.
38 Since Lydda was near Joppa, when the students heard that Peter was in Lydda, they sent two men out to him to encourage him to come to Joppa. "You shouldn't hesitate to come on through to us," they told him.
39 Peter got up and went together with them. When he showed up, they led him up to the upstairs room. All the widows stood by him crying and showing all the long undershirts and clothes that Dorcas had been making when she was with them.
40 Peter threw everyone outside. He kneeled down on the floor and prayed. Then he turned around toward the body and said "Tabitha, get up." She opened her eyes. When she saw Peter, she sat up on her own.
41 He gave her his hand and got her up. He hollered for the sacred people and widows and presented her to them alive.
42 This became known throughout all of Joppa. Many trusted in the Master.
43 He happened to stay for an adequate amount of days with a certain Simon in Joppa, a leatherworker.

10

1 There was a certain man in Caesarea who was a lieutenant in the Italian regiment *(an elite unit)* of the Roman military. His name was Cornelius.

2 He was a godly man who also feared God together with everyone in his house. He made many charitable donations to the ethnic group and pleaded with God through everything.

3 Sometime around 3 p.m., he clearly saw God's angel in a vision. The angel entered *the room, came up* to him, and said, "Cornelius."

4 Cornelius stared at him and became afraid. "What is it, Master?" he said. "Your prayers and charitable donations stepped up for a reminder in front of God," he told him.

5 "Now send men to Joppa and send for a certain Simon, who is also called Peter.

6 This Simon is a guest staying with a certain Simon who is a leatherworker. His house is along the sea."

7 When the angel that was speaking to him left, Cornelius hollered for two of his domestic servants and a godly soldier that stayed close to him.

8 He recounted to them absolutely everything that had happened and sent them out on a mission to Joppa *(about 35 miles away)*.

9 The next day as those people were traveling on the road and were coming near to the city, Peter climbed up on top of the house to pray around noon.

10 He became very hungry and was wanting to taste the food. But while they were preparing it, he fell into a trance.

11 He watched the sky open up. A certain container stepped down. It looked like a large sheet being let down onto the earth by four corners.

12 All the four-legged animals and reptiles of the earth and winged birds of the sky were in it.

13 A voice came to him, "Get up, Peter. Kill and eat."

14 "No way, Master," said Peter, "because I have never even once eaten anything contaminated and not clean."

15 Again, a second time, a voice came to him, "You must not contaminate things that God cleaned."

16 This happened three times, and the container was taken directly up into the sky.

17 Since Peter was dumbfounded inside himself about what the vision that he saw might be, *he didn't see* the men that had been sent out by Cornelius. They had been asking around for Simon's house. Look, they stood at the gate.

18 They hollered and were inquiring if the Simon who is also called Peter was a guest there.
19 As Peter was intently contemplating about the vision, the Spirit told him, "Look, three men are looking for you.
20 But get up, climb down, and travel together with them. Don't consider anything to be wrong with this because I have sent them out."
21 Peter climbed down to the men. "Look," he said, "I am who you are looking for. Why are you here?"
22 "Lieutenant Cornelius," they said, "is a man who does what is right and fears God. The whole nation of the Jewish people has witnessed this. He was divinely instructed by a sacred angel to send for you *to come* into his house and to hear statements directly from you."
23 So he invited them in and provided a place for them to stay. On the next day, he got up and went out together with them. Some of the brothers from Joppa also went with him.
24 On the day after that, he came into Caesarea. Cornelius was expecting them. He had called his relatives and essential friends together.
25 Since they happened to meet together at the time that Peter went in, Cornelius got down *on the floor* at his feet and bowed down to him.
26 But Peter got him up. "Stand up," he said. "I myself also am a human being."
27 As he was chatting with him, he went in and found the many people who had come together.
28 "You are well aware," he was declaring to them, "how it is forbidden for a Jewish man to join in with or to be going up to someone from another family line. Yet God showed me not to say that anyone is contaminated or not clean.
29 For this reason, I also came without objecting when I was sent for. So I am inquiring, why did you send for me?"
30 "Four days ago, up to this hour," Cornelius was declaring, "I was praying the 3 p.m. prayer in my house. And look, a man in a dazzling outfit stood in my sight.
31 'Cornelius,' he declared, 'your prayer was heard and your charitable donations were remembered in God's sight.
32 So send men to Joppa and summon Simon who is also called Peter *to come to your house*. This Simon is a guest in a house of Simon who is a leatherworker. *His house* is along the sea.'

33 So I immediately sent my men to you, and you were nice enough to show up. So now we all are here in God's sight to hear all the things that the Master has instructed you to tell us."
34 When Peter opened his mouth, he said, "Since it is based on truth, I completely get that God is not someone who is swayed by appearances.
35 But the person in every nation who fears Him and works on what is right is accepted by Him.
36 God sent a message out to Israel's sons sharing the good news of peace through Jesus, the Anointed King. This Jesus is Master of all.
37 You realize that the statement of that message ended up throughout all of Judea after it headed out of Galilee with the submersion that John publicly spoke about.
38 Since God anointed the Jesus from Nazareth with the Sacred Spirit and ability, He went through many places doing humane things and curing all the people suppressed by the Accuser. God was with Him.
39 We are witnesses of all that He did, both in the Jewish people's rural area and in Jerusalem. They actually executed Him when they hung Him on a wooden cross.
40 God got this *Jesus* up on the third day and it became explicitly shown,
41 not to all the ethnic group, but to witnesses--to the people who had been handpicked beforehand by God--to us. We are the ones who ate and drank together with Him after He had come back to life from the dead.
42 And He passed the order on to us to speak publicly to the ethnic group and to be strong witnesses to the fact that this is the One that God designated to be the Judge of the living and the dead.
43 All the Preachers are witnesses to this one thing, that everyone who trusts in Him receives forgiveness of sins through His name."
44 As Peter was still speaking these statements, the Sacred Spirit fell on all the people who heard the message.
45 The trusting people from the circumcision *(the Jews)* were astounded (all the ones that came together with Peter) because the free handout of the Sacred Spirit also had been spilled out on the non-Jews.
46 You see, they were listening to them speak in languages and magnifying God. Then Peter replied,
47 "No one can keep the water from submerging these people who received the Sacred Spirit as we did, can he?"

48 He instructed them to be submerged in the name of Jesus, the Anointed King. Then they asked him to stay over for a few days.

1 The missionaries and the brothers throughout Judea heard that the non-Jews also accepted God's message.
2 When Peter walked up to Jerusalem, the people from the circumcision were considering him to be wrong.
3 "You went in to men who were not circumcised," they said, "and ate together with them."
4 But when Peter began, he laid everything out to them in order.
5 "I was in the city of Joppa praying," he said, "and I saw a vision as I was in a trance. A certain container stepped down from the sky, a large sheet being let down by four corners. It came until it got to me.
6 I stared at it and was taking a close look. I saw the earth's four-legged animals, the wild animals, the reptiles, and the winged birds of the sky.
7 I also heard a voice telling me, 'Get up, Peter. Kill and eat.'
8 'No way, Master,' I said, 'because never even once has anything contaminated or not clean come into my mouth.'
9 The voice responded the second time from the sky, 'You must not contaminate things that God cleaned.'
10 This happened three times, and absolutely everything was pulled up again into the sky.
11 And look, immediately three men stood at the house where I was. They had been sent out from Caesarea to me.
12 The Spirit told me to go together with them and not to consider anything to be wrong with it. They and these six brothers went together with me, and we went into the man's house.
13 He reported to us how he saw the angel in his house, how it stood up and said, 'Send men out to Joppa, and send for the Simon that is also called Peter.
14 He will speak statements to you that will rescue you and all your house.'
15 During the time that I was beginning to speak, the Sacred Spirit fell on them, just like it also fell on us in the beginning.
16 I remembered the Master's statement, how He used to say, 'John certainly submerged with water, but you will be submerged in the Sacred Spirit.'
17 So if God gave them the very same free handout as He also gave to us who trusted based on the Master Jesus, the Anointed King, who was I? Was I able to keep God from doing it?"

18 After hearing these things, they calmed down and praised God's magnificence. "Clearly God gave the change of ways into life," they said, "even to the non-Jews."

19 So not only did the people who were scattered out by the hard times that happened over Stephen go across as far as Phoenicia *(an area along the Mediterranean Sea in Israel, Syria, and Lebanon)*, Cyprus *(an island in the eastern Mediterranean Sea)*, and Antioch *(a major city located in Turkey, near the Syrian border, on the eastern bank of the Orontes River)* only speaking the message to Jewish people and no one else,

20 but when certain Cyprian *(from the island of Cyprus)* and Cyrenian *(from Cyrene, Libya)* men from among them went into Antioch, they were also speaking to the Greek-speaking people there and sharing the good news of the Master Jesus with them.

21 The Master's hand was with them. The large number who trusted turned back to the Master.

22 The message about them was heard in the ears of the assembly in Jerusalem, and they sent Barnabas off to go across as far as Antioch.

23 When he showed up and saw God's generosity, he was happy and was encouraging everyone to plan in their heart to still stay in the Master.

24 *Barnabas did all of this* because he was a good man and full of the Sacred Spirit and trust. An adequate crowd was added to the Master.

25 He went out to Tarsus *(83 miles away)* to look all over for Saul.

26 When he found him, he brought him to Antioch. They also happened to gather together in the assembly and teach an adequate crowd for a whole year. The students were first called Christians in Antioch.

27 During these days, preachers came down out of Jerusalem into Antioch.

28 When one from among them named Agabus stood up, he indicated through the Spirit that there was going to be a great famine throughout the whole civilized world. This happened when Claudius Caesar was emperor *(around 44-46 AD)*.

29 Since some of the students were well-off, each of them designated money to be sent to the brothers living in Judea for the serving *that they do* there.

30 They sent it out to the older men in Judea through the hand of Barnabas and Saul.

12

1 About that time, Herod, the king, put his hands on some of the people from the assembly to do bad things to them.
2 He executed James, the brother of John, with a dagger.
3 After seeing that it was something the Jewish people liked, he added to it by also apprehending Peter during one of the days of the Yeast-free Festival *(a week-long celebration that follows the Passover)*.
4 After arresting him, he put him in jail and turned him over to four squads of four soldiers to guard him. He intended to take him up to the ethnic group after the Passover.
5 So Peter certainly was being kept in the jail, but prayer was being offered up to God intensively by the assembly concerning him.
6 When Herod was going to bring him out, that night Peter was asleep between two soldiers. He had been chained to them with two chains. Jailers also were in front of the door keeping guard of the jail.
7 And look, the Master's angel stood over him, and a light shined in the cell. He struck Peter in the side and got him up. "Hurry up. Stand up," he said. His chains fell from his hands.
8 "Put your waist sash on," the angel told him, "and tie your sole pads on under your feet." He did so. "Throw your robe around yourself," he said, "and follow me."
9 When he left, he was following the angel. He didn't realize that what was happening through the angel was valid. It seemed like he was seeing a vision.
10 They went through the first and second jail and came up to the iron gate leading to the city. It automatically opened to them. They went out and went on ahead down one street. Right away the angel backed off away from him.
11 When Peter in himself came to, he said, "Now I truly realize that the Master sent out His angel and took me out of Herod's hand and every expectation of the Jewish people's group."
12 After he became aware *of what happened*, he went up to the house of Mary, the mother of the John who is also called Mark. An adequate amount of people had accumulated together there and were praying.
13 When he knocked at the door of the gateway, a servant girl named Rhoda came to the door to quietly listen.
14 When she recognized Peter's voice, out of the happiness, she didn't open the gate, but ran inside and reported that Peter had been standing in front of the gate.
15 "You are crazy," the people told her. She was strongly insisting that it is true. They were saying, "It is his angel."

16 Peter kept knocking. When they opened, they saw him and were astounded.
17 He motioned with his hand for them to be quiet and described to them how the Master brought him out of the jail. "Report these things to James and the brothers," he said. He left and traveled to a different place.
18 When it became day, there was more than a little agitation among the soldiers about, "So what happened to Peter?"
19 When Herod searched for him and didn't find him, he investigated the jailers and gave the order for them to be taken away. He went down out of Judea into Caesarea and was spending time there.
20 There was a heated argument between him and the people from Tyre and Sidon *(two cities located 55 and 70 miles north of Caesarea along the Mediterranean Sea)*. They unanimously were there about him. They persuaded Blastus, the person who was over the king's bedroom, to ask him for peace because their rural area received support from the royal treasury.
21 On an appointed day, Herod put on his royal outfit and was seated on the judicial bench. He was delivering a mob-inspiring speech to them.
22 The mob was hollering out, "A voice of a god and not of a person."
23 At once, the Master's angel struck him for the times that he did not give the magnificence to God. He became infested with maggots and stopped breathing.
24 God's message was growing and increasing.
25 After Barnabas and Saul accomplished the job of serving *the money* to Jerusalem, they returned *to Antioch*. They took the John who is also called Mark along together with them.

13

1 Preachers and teachers were throughout the assembly that was in Antioch: Barnabas, the Simon called Niger, Lucius (the Cyrenian), Manaen (a childhood companion of Herod, the head of one of Palestine's four regions), and Saul.
2 As they served the public for the Master and went without food, the Sacred Spirit said, "Isolate to Me, for sure, Barnabas and Saul for the work that I have called them to."
3 Then after they went without food, prayed, and placed their hands on them, they dismissed them.

4 So after they certainly were sent off by the Sacred Spirit, they went down to Seleucia *(a port city near Antioch)*, and from there they sailed off to Cyprus *(an island in the eastern Mediterranean Sea)*.
5 And when they ended up in Salamis *(a city on the east side of Cyprus)*, they were proclaiming God's message in the Jewish people's synagogues. They were also having John as an underling.
6 After they went through the whole island, they came to Paphos *(a city on the southwest side of Cyprus)*. There they found a certain Jewish man, a Magian guru, a counterfeit preacher named Son of Joshua.
7 He was together with the Roman Senate deputy, Sergius Paul, a man of understanding. This deputy called for Barnabas and Saul and searched to hear God's message.
8 But Elymas, the Magian guru (you see, this is what his *Arabic* name is translated as), was opposing them. He was looking to twist the Roman Senate deputy away from the trust.
9 Saul, the one who is also Paul, being filled with the Sacred Spirit, stared at him
10 and said, "O, You who are full of every deception and every mischievousness, you are the Accuser's son, the enemy of every right way. Will you not stop twisting the straight ways of the Master?
11 And now, look, the Master's hand is on you, and you will be blind, not seeing the sun till a certain time." And at once, blurriness and darkness fell on him. He went around looking for people to lead him by the hand.
12 Then when the Roman Senate deputy saw what had happened, he trusted and was impressed with the Master's teaching.
13 Paul and the people around him set sail from Paphos and went to Pamphylia's Perga *(a city on the southern coast of Turkey)*. John distanced himself away from them and returned to Jerusalem.
14 After they went through Perga, they showed up in Antioch, Pisidia *(in central Turkey)*. They went into the synagogue on the day of the Sabbaths and were seated.
15 After the reading of the Law and the Preachers, the synagogue's head rulers sent *someone* out to them who said, "Men, brothers, if there is some message of encouragement among you for the group, tell it."
16 Paul stood up and motioned with his hand. "Men, Israelis," he said, "and the people who fear God, listen.
17 The God of this ethnic group, Israel, selected our fathers and put the ethnic group up high in their foreign residency in the land of Egypt. With a high arm, He led them out of it.

18 He put up with them in the backcountry for about a forty-year period.
19 And after He took down seven nations in the land of Canaan, He portioned out their land for an inheritance.
20 *It had been* about four hundred fifty years *since God selected our fathers.* After these things, He gave judges until the time of Samuel, the preacher.
21 From there, they asked for a king and God gave them Saul (a son of Kish, a man from Benjamin's family line) for forty years.
22 After He dislodged him, He raised up David to be a king for them. He told them what He had seen in David. He said, 'I found David, Jesse's son, to be a man aligned with My heart, a man who will do all the things that I want.'
23 From the seed of this man, *from his descendants,* God brought a rescuer to Israel, Jesus, just as He had promised.
24 Before the appearance of Jesus' entrance, John spoke publicly about a change-of-ways submersion to all the ethnic group of Israel.
25 Since John was completing the race, he was saying, 'What do you suspect me to be? I am not that. But look, He is coming after me. I do not deserve to untie His feet's sandal.'
26 Men, brothers, sons of Abraham's family, and the people among you who fear God, the message of this rescue has been sent out to you.
27 You see, when the people living in Jerusalem and their head people were unaware of who this Man was and unaware of the voices of the Preachers that are read each and every Sabbath, they judged Him and accomplished what the voices say.
28 When they didn't find even one accusation deserving of death, they asked Pilate to execute Him.
29 Since they finished all the things that had been written about Him, they took Him down off the wooden cross and placed Him into a burial vault.
30 God got Him up from the dead.
31 The people who walked up together with Him out of Galilee into Jerusalem saw Him for several days. These are the ones who are now witnesses of Him to the ethnic group.
32 And we are sharing with you the good news of the promise that was given to the fathers:
33 that God has completely fulfilled this promise for their children, us, when He brought Jesus back to life, as it has also been written in the

second Psalm, 'You are My Son. I today have given birth to You' *(Psalm 2:7)*.

34 Because He brought Him back to life from the dead, He will not return to decay anymore. This is what He has stated, 'I will give you the holy things that David wrote about, things that can be trusted' *(Isaiah 55:3)*.

35 For this reason, also in a different psalm, He says, 'You will not give Your Holy One to see decay' *(Psalm 16:10)*.

36 You see, after working as an underling for his own generation doing what God intended for him to do, David certainly fell asleep, was placed *in a burial vault* facing his fathers, and saw decay.

37 But the One whom God got up did not see decay.

38 So be it known to you, men, brothers, that through this Man forgiveness of sins is proclaimed to you.

39 In the law of Moses, you were not able to be made right *by doing* everything in it. In this Man, everyone who trusts is made right.

40 So look out for *these things* so that you won't come up on what has been stated in the Preachers:

41 'You, the people who ignore God, look, be amazed, and disappear, because I am working a work in your days, a work that you will not in any way trust, even if someone describes it in detail to you' *(Habakkuk 1:5)*."

42 When they were outside, the people were encouraging them to speak these statements to them on the in-between Sabbath.

43 After the synagogue was released, many of the Jewish people and the worshipping converts followed Paul and Barnabas. These two were speaking to them and persuading them to still stay in God's generosity.

44 On the coming Sabbath, nearly all the city was gathered together to hear the Master's message.

45 When the Jewish people saw the crowds, they were filled with hostile passion and were opposing and insulting the statements spoken by Paul.

46 Paul and Barnabas made a clear public statement. "It was essential for God's message to be spoken to you first," they said. "Since, for sure, you are pushing it away and judging yourselves not deserving of the life that spans all time, look, *you have forced* us to turn to the non-Jews.

47 You see, this is how the Master has demanded it to be, 'I have placed you for a light of the non-Jews, the kind of light where you provide a rescue out to the last places of the earth' *(Isaiah 49:6)*."

48 As the non-Jews heard this, they were happy and praising the magnificence of the Master's message. And as many as had assigned themselves to life that spans all time trusted.
49 The Master's message was being carried through the whole rural area.
50 But the Jewish people incited the worshipping women (the reputable women) and the most important people of the city. They roused up persecution on Paul and Barnabas and threw them out of their borders.
51 They shook off the dust of their feet on them and went to Iconium *(a 95 mile walk from Antioch)*.
52 The students were being filled with happiness and the Sacred Spirit.

14

1 The same thing happened in Iconium. They went into the Jewish people's synagogue and spoke in such a way for a very large number of both Jewish people and Greeks to trust.
2 The Jewish people who didn't believe roused up the non-Jews against the brothers and did bad things to the non-Jews' souls.
3 So the missionaries certainly spent an adequate amount of time making clear public statements on the Master. The Master was a witness of the message of His generosity by allowing proofs and incredible things to happen through their hands.
4 The large number *of non-Jews* in the city were torn: some were together with the Jewish people and some were together with the missionaries.
5 Since there became a sudden impulse among both the non-Jews and the Jewish people together with their head people to injure and throw stones at them,
6 when they became aware of it, they escaped *(twenty miles away)* down to the cities of Lycaonia: Lystra, Derbe, and the surrounding rural area.
7 There they were sharing good news.
8 A certain man was sitting in Lystra. He wasn't able to use his feet. He was crippled *when he came* out of his mother's belly and had never walked even once.
9 This man listened to Paul speaking. When Paul stared at him and saw that he had the kind of trust needed to rescue him,
10 he said with a loud voice, "Stand up straight on your feet." He jumped up and was walking around.

11 When the crowds saw what Paul did, they raised their voice in Lycaonian and said, "The gods have become like people and stepped down to us."
12 They were calling Barnabas Zeus *(the king of the gods)* and Paul Hermes *(the god of public speaking)*, since, for sure, Paul was the one leading the message.
13 The priest of the Zeus that was in front of the city brought bulls and wreaths up to the gateway and was wanting to offer a sacrifice together with the crowds.
14 But when the missionaries, Barnabas and Paul, heard it, they ripped their robes apart and leaped out into the crowd yelling
15 and saying, "Men, why are you doing these things? We also are human beings who suffer in the same way that you do. We are sharing the good news with you to turn back from these futile gods to a living God who made the sky, the earth, the sea, and everything in them.
16 In the generations that have gone by, this living God allowed all the nations to travel their own ways.
17 And yet He didn't leave them without a witness of Him. He worked on good things. He gave you showers from the sky and seasons that produce fruit. He filled your hearts up with food and celebration."
18 Saying these things, with a lot of effort they quieted down the crowds so that they wouldn't offer sacrifices to them.
19 But Jewish people came up out of Antioch and Iconium. After they persuaded the crowds and attacked Paul with stones, they were dragging him outside of the city assuming that he had died.
20 When the students surrounded him, he got up and went into the city. On the next day, he left together with Barnabas and went to Derbe *(about 60 miles away)*.
21 After they both shared good news with that city and made an adequate amount of students, they returned to Lystra, Iconium, and Antioch *(in Pisidia)*.
22 *As they returned through these cities,* they further established the souls of the students, encouraging them to be staying in the trust and that "it is necessary for us to go through many hard times as we go into God monarchy."
23 After handpicking older men *to be provisional leaders* in each assembly, they prayed while going without food and placed them beside the Master that they had trusted in.
24 After going through Pisidia *(an area in south-central Turkey)*, they went to Pamphylia *(an area in southern Turkey)*.

25 They spoke the message in Perga and walked down to Attalia *(on the southern coast of Turkey)*.
26 From there, they sailed off to Antioch *(near the Syrian border)*. *This Antioch is* where they had been given over to God's generosity for the work that they had accomplished.
27 When they showed up and gathered the assembly together, they were announcing all of the things that God had done with them and that He had opened a door of trust to the non-Jews.
28 They were spending more than a small amount of time together with the students.

15

1 Some who came down out of Judea were teaching the brothers, "If you are not circumcised as Moses' custom dictates, you can"t be rescued."
2 After it caused a disruption and more than a small amount of questioning from Paul and Barnabas to them, they arranged for Paul, Barnabas, and some others from among them to walk up into Jerusalem to the missionaries and older men about this question.
3 So after being brought on their way by the assembly, they certainly were going through both Phoenicia and Samaria *on their 300 mile walk to Jerusalem* describing in detail the turnaround of the non-Jews. This created great happiness among all the brothers.
4 When they showed up in Jerusalem, they were accepted with a warm welcome from the assembly, the missionaries, and the older men. They announced all the things that God had done with them.
5 Some of the people from the Separatists' sect who had trusted stood up and said, "It is necessary to be circumcising them and to be passing the order on to them to keep Moses' law."
6 Both the missionaries and the older men were gathered together to see about this matter.
7 After there became much questioning, Peter stood up and told them, "Men, brothers, you are well aware that back in the beginning days among you, God selected through my mouth for the non-Jews to hear the message of the good news and to trust.
8 The Heart-Knower, God, told what He witnessed when He gave them the Sacred Spirit, just as He also gave us.
9 And He didn't consider anything to be different with the trust between us and them when He cleaned out their hearts.

10 So why are you now harassing God? Why are you putting a crossbeam on the student's neck that our fathers weren't strong enough to haul, and we weren't either?

11 But through the Master Jesus' generosity, we trust so that we can be rescued in the same way that those people also do."

12 All the large number of people kept quiet and were listening to Barnabas and Paul recounting how many proofs and incredible things God did among the non-Jews through them.

13 After they had kept quiet, James responded. "Men, brothers," he said, "listen to me.

14 Simon recounted just how God first kept an eye on taking a group out of the non-Jews for His name.

15 And the Preachers' messages harmoniously agree with this. This is just as it has been written in the Bible,

16 "'After these things I will return. I will rebuild David's fallen tent. I will rebuild the parts that they have dug up and removed. I will straighten it up.

17 That way the people who are left and all the non-Jews who call on My name will intensively search for the Master," says the Master doing these things,

18 things known throughout the span of time' *(Amos 9:11-12)*.

19 For this reason, I judge that the non-Jews who turn back to God should not be disturbed anymore.

20 But we should write them a letter telling them to keep themselves away from the contaminations of the idols, from sexual sin, from *animals that have been* choked *to death*, and from blood.

21 You see, since the beginning generations Moses has people in each city that speak publicly about Him in the synagogues. He is being read each and every Sabbath."

22 At that time, it seemed like a good idea to the missionaries and the older men together with the whole assembly that they select some men from among them and send them to Antioch together with Paul and Barnabas. They selected Judah (the one called Barsabas) and Silas. They were leaders among the brothers.

23 They wrote through their hand: "From: The missionaries and the older brothers. To: The brothers who are non-Jews throughout Antioch *and the area around Antioch:* Syria and Cilicia. Happy to meet you.

24 Since, for sure, we heard that some went out from us and agitated you with messages that plundered your souls, the kind of messages that we do not warn people with,

25 it seemed like a good idea to us (we became unanimous on this) that we select men and send them to you together with our loved brothers, Barnabas and Paul.
26 *Barnabas and Paul are* people who have given up their souls for the name of our Master Jesus, the Anointed King.
27 So we have sent Judah and Silas out on a mission to also report the same things through their message.
28 You see, it seemed like a good idea to the Sacred Spirit and to us not to be putting any more weight on you other than these crucial things:
29 to be keeping yourselves away from idol sacrifices, blood, *animals that have been* choked *to death*, and sexual sin. If you are carefully keeping yourselves from these things, you will constantly do well. Farewell."
30 So after they were dismissed, they certainly went down into Antioch. When they gathered the large number together, they gave the letter over to them.
31 After they read it, they were happy for the encouragement.
32 Both Judah and Silas were also preachers. Through their entire message, they encouraged and further established the brothers.
33 After they spent time there, they were dismissed with peace out from the brothers *to go back* to the people who sent them out on the mission.
34 [[[It seemed like a good idea to Silas to stay there.]]]
35 Paul and Barnabas were spending time in Antioch teaching and sharing the good news of the Master's message with many different people also.
36 After some days, Paul told Barnabas, "We, for sure, should return and keep an eye on the brothers in each and every city in which we proclaimed the Master's message and see how they are holding to it."
37 Barnabas was intending to also take the John who is called Mark along together with them.
38 Paul was thinking that the one who stayed away from them in Pamphylia and did not go together with them into the work, that this one didn't deserve to be taken along together with them.
39 It became such an annoyance to them that they separated apart from each other. Barnabas took Mark along and sailed out to Cyprus.
40 Paul said that Silas would also go with him and left after the brothers gave them over to the Master's generosity.
41 He was going through Syria and Cilicia *(the areas between Antioch and Derbe)* further establishing the assemblies.

16

1 He also made it to Derbe and Lystra. And, look, there was a certain student there named Timothy. His mother was a trusting Jewish woman, but his father was Greek.
2 The brothers in Lystra and Iconium were telling Paul what they had witnessed about him.
3 Paul wanted this student to go out together with him. He took him and circumcised him because of the Jewish people who were in those places. You see, absolutely everyone knew that his father was Greek.
4 As they were traveling through the cities, they were turning the rules over to them that the missionaries and older men in Jerusalem had decided they should observe.
5 So the assemblies certainly were becoming solid in the trust and overflowing in number daily.
6 They went through Phrygia and the Galatian rural area after they were kept by the Sacred Spirit from speaking the message in Western Turkey.
7 They went along Mysia *(an area in north-western Turkey along the Sea of Marmara)* and were trying to travel into Bithynia *(an area east of Mysia)*, but Jesus' Spirit did not allow them.
8 After they passed by Mysia, they walked down into Troas *(a coastal area west of Mysia)*.
9 Paul saw a vision through the night. A certain Macedonian man had been standing and encouraging him. "Step across into Macedonia and help us," he said.
10 Since he saw the vision, right away we looked to go out into Macedonia *(northern Greece)*. We made the conclusion that God had called us toward them to share good news with them.
11 After setting sail out of Troas, we sailed straight into the island of Samothrace. The following day we sailed into a young city *(Kavalla, Greece)*.
12 From there we went into Philippi. This is the Philippi that was the most important part of Macedonia and a *Roman* colony. We were spending some days in that city.
13 On the day of the Sabbaths, we went outside of the *city* gate along a river where we were assuming there would be prayer. We were seated and were speaking to the women who came together.
14 A certain woman named Lydia was listening. She was a seller of purple cloth from the city of Thyatira. She worshipped God. The Master completely opened her heart to pay attention to what was being spoken by Paul.

15 Since she and the people from her house were submerged, she begged us, "If you have judged me to be someone that the Master can trust, come into my house and stay there." And she compelled us.

16 One day as we were traveling to the prayer meeting, a certain servant girl who had a spirit, a Python (a clairvoyant spirit), happened to come to meet us. She was providing a lot of business for her masters using her psychic abilities.

17 She followed behind us and Paul. She was yelling, "These people are the highest God's slaves. They are proclaiming a way of rescue to you."

18 She was doing this for many days. Paul was perturbed. He turned around and told the spirit, "I pass the order on to you in the name of Jesus, the Anointed King, to come out from her." It came out the same hour.

19 When her masters saw that the anticipation of their business *(making money on her)* left, they latched on to Paul and Silas and pulled them into the marketplace to appear before the head people.

20 They brought them up to the captains and said, "These Jewish people are greatly agitating our city.

21 They proclaim customs that we are not allowed to warmly welcome or do since we are Roman citizens."

22 Together the crowd stood up against them. The captains ripped their robes *(to show how appalled they were)* and were giving orders to beat them with sticks.

23 After putting many wounds on them, they threw them into jail and passed the order on to the prison guard to keep them securely.

24 When he received this type of an order, he threw them into the inner jail and secured their feet in the wooden restraint.

25 Throughout the middle of the night, as Paul and Silas prayed, they were singing praise songs to God. The prisoners were listening to them intently.

26 Suddenly, a large earthquake happened in such a way for the foundations of the prison to be disturbed. At once, all the doors were opened, and everyone's restraints eased up.

27 The prison guard was jolted awake and saw that the jail's doors were open. He pulled out his dagger and was going to execute himself because he assumed that the prisoners had escaped.

28 Paul hollered with a loud voice, "You shouldn't be doing anything bad to yourself. You see, every single one of us is in here."

29 Once he asked for lights, he leaped in. He started trembling inside and fell toward Paul and Silas.

30 He brought them out and was declaring, "Masters, what must I do to be rescued?"
31 "Trust in the Master Jesus," they said, "and you will be rescued, you and everyone in your house."
32 They spoke the Master's message to him together with all the people in his house.
33 He took them along with him at that hour of the night and gave them a bath to clean off the wounds. He and all his people were submerged at once.
34 After he brought them up into the house, he placed a table of food beside them. He was excited, having trusted God with everyone in his house.
35 When it became day, the captains sent out the sergeants. "Dismiss those people," they said.
36 The prison guard reported the words to Paul, "The captains have sent out the sergeants to dismiss you. So go out now and travel in peace."
37 "After beating us publicly," Paul was declaring to them, "being Roman citizens, people that had not been found guilty, they threw us into jail. And now they are throwing us out in a way that no one would notice? You see, no, but they must come and bring us out themselves."
38 The sergeants reported these statements to the captains. They were afraid when they heard that they are Roman citizens.
39 They came and begged them. They brought them out and were asking them to go off away from the city.
40 After they left the jail, they went into Lydia's house. After seeing the brothers, they encouraged them and went out.

17

1 After making their way through Amphipolis and Apollonia *(two coastal cities on the 100 mile road between Philippi and Thessalonica)*, they went into Thessalonica *(a major city in northern Greece)* where there was a synagogue of the Jewish people.
2 Aligned with what Paul was accustomed to doing, he went in to them and over three Sabbaths had discussions with them out of the *Old Testament* writings.
3 He completely opened *the meaning of those writings* and placed *the conclusion* beside them that it was necessary for the Anointed King to suffer and to come back to life from the dead. And, "This is the Anointed King Jesus that I proclaim to you."

4 Some from among them were persuaded and joined Paul and Silas (both a very large number of the worshipping Greeks and not just a few of the most important women).
5 But when the Jewish people got mad, they took in some of the marketplace's evil men *(the bums)*. And after they drew a crowd, they were disturbing the city. They stood over Jason's house and were looking to bring Paul and Silas out into the mob.
6 When they didn't find them, they were dragging Jason and some brothers before the city leaders and shouting, "These people who upset the civilized world are here next to us too.
7 Jason has accepted them into his house. All these people are constantly doing things up against Caesar's rules. They say that there is a different king, Jesus."
8 They agitated the crowd and the city leaders who heard these things.
9 They took the adequate amount of money directly from Jason and the rest and dismissed them.
10 Right away the brothers sent both Paul and Silas off through the night to Berea *(a city 50 miles west of there)*. When they showed up there, they were already off into the Jewish people's synagogue.
11 These were a higher-ranking family line than the people in Thessalonica. They accepted the message with every bit of eagerness. Daily they were investigating the *Old Testament* writings to see whether this is how it has these things.
12 So certainly many from them trusted, both the Greek women (the reputable ones) and more than a few men.
13 Since the Jewish people out of Thessalonica knew that Paul was also proclaiming God's message in Berea, they went there too. They disturbed and agitated the crowds.
14 Then right away the brothers sent Paul off to travel down to the sea. Both Silas and Timothy stayed behind there in Berea.
15 The people who were put in charge of Paul took him to Athens *(a city about 300 miles south of Thessalonica and Berea)*. They received a demand for Silas and Timothy to come to him as quickly as possible. Then they left *Paul there and returned to Berea*.
16 As Paul was waiting for them in Athens, his spirit in him was annoyed as he watched how the city was entirely idolatrous.
17 So he certainly was having discussions in the synagogue with the Jewish people and the worshipping people and in the marketplace with the people who happened by each and every day.

18 Some of both the Epicureans *(students of the Greek philosopher Epicurus)* and Stoics (people fond of insight) were deliberating about him. Some were saying, "Whatever might this scrap-collector want to say?" But others were saying, "He seems to be a proclaimer of strange lesser deities," because he was sharing the good news of Jesus and the return back to life.

19 They latched on to him and led him onto Areopagus *(a prominent rock outcropping located northwest of the Acropolis. Areopagus means 'Hill of Mars.' Mars is the god of war.)*. They said, "Can we know what this new teaching is that you are speaking about?"

20 "You see, you are carrying some strange ideas into what we have heard. So we intend to know what you want to say about these things."

21 All Athenians and the foreigners who made *Athens* their home were having a good time of doing nothing more than talking about or hearing about something that is new.

22 When they stood Paul up in the middle of Areopagus, he was declaring, "Men, Athenians, in each and everything, I have watched how you are more zealous of lesser deities.

23 You see, as I was going through and observing the objects that you worship, I even found a platform inscribed with the words: 'To an unknown god.' So I am proclaiming this thing to you that you reverence even though you are unaware of what it is.

24 God, who made the world and everything in it, this God who is Master of heaven and earth, does not live in handmade temples.

25 He is not healed by human hands either *as your idols are*. He isn't pleading for anything. He is the One who gives life, breath, and all things to everything.

26 From one being, He made every nation of people to be living on all the face of the earth. He designated appointed times and set up the limits of their residence

27 so that they would be looking for God, if maybe they might definitely feel Him and find Him. He also definitely is not a long way away from each one of us.

28 You see, we live, move, and exist in Him. Even some of your poets have stated, 'You see, we are also His family.'

29 So since we are God's family, we have to assume that the divine is not like gold, silver, or stone. He is not a statue made by a person's skill and contemplation.

30 And so God certainly looks past the times people were not aware of Him and now gives the order to people everywhere for everyone to change their ways.
31 *This is* due to the fact that He has established a day when He is going to judge the civilized world in the right way. *He is going to judge them* in a Man that He designated when He provided Him as a way for all people to trust, when He brought Him back to life from the dead."
32 When they heard him mention a return back to life of dead people, some started joking about it, but the others said, "We will listen to you about this again."
33 This is how Paul went out from the middle of them.
34 Some men stuck like glue to him and trusted. Among them were also Dionysius (the Areopagite), a woman named Damaris, and different ones together with them.

18

1 After these things, he put some distance between him and Athens and went to Corinth *(a city in southern Greece about 50 miles west of Athens)*.
2 And when he found a certain Jewish man named Aquila and his wife Priscilla, he went to them. Aquila was a Pontican *(from Pontus, a region of northeastern Turkey on the southern coast of the Black Sea)* by birth. He recently had come out of Italy because Claudius had specifically arranged for all the Jewish people to be separated away from Rome.
3 And because they were in the same trade *as Paul*, he was staying beside them and working. You see, they were tentmakers by trade.
4 Each and every Sabbath, he was having discussions in the synagogue and persuading Jewish people and Greeks.
5 Since both Silas and Timothy had come down from Macedonia, Paul was committing himself to the message by being a strong witness to the Jewish people that Jesus is the Anointed King.
6 But they were placing themselves in opposition to it and insulting it. So Paul shook off his clothes and told them, "Your blood is on your head. I am clean of any guilt. From now on, I will travel to the non-Jews."
7 He walked somewhere else away from there. He went into the house of someone named Titus Justus. *Titus Justus* worshipped God. His house was up against the synagogue.
8 Crispus, the synagogue's head ruler, trusted the Master together with his whole house, and many of the Corinthians listening were trusting and being submerged.

9 The Master said to Paul at night through a vision, "Don't be afraid, but speak. You shouldn't be silent
10 because I am with you. No one will put his hand on you to do bad to you because a big group is with Me in this city."
11 He was seated a year and six months teaching God's message among them.
12 As Gallio was a Roman Senate deputy of Achaia *(the province that Corinth is in)*, the Jewish people unanimously stood up against Paul and took him before the judicial bench.
13 "This man motivates the people to be worshipping God contrary to the law," they told him.
14 As Paul was going to open his mouth, Gallio told the Jewish people, "Certainly if it were some wrong or evil mischief, O Jewish people, I would have to tolerate you and give you some type of answer,
15 but if it is questions about a message, names people use, and the law according to you, you will see to it yourselves. I do not intend to be a judge of these things."
16 He drove them away from the judicial bench.
17 Everyone latched on to Sosthenese, the synagogue's head ruler, and was hitting him in front of the judicial bench. None of these things were a concern to Gallio.
18 Paul still stayed yet an adequate amount of days. Then he said good-bye to the brothers and was sailing out into Syria. Priscilla and Aquila were together with him. He cut his hair in Cenchrea *(an eastern harbor of Corinth)*. You see, *this marked the completion of* a vow he had *previously* made. *The final step would be to offer a sacrifice at the temple in Jerusalem within 30 days.*
19 They made it to Ephesus *(a city in western Turkey)*. He left those *two (Priscilla and Aquila)* there, but went into the synagogue and had a discussion with the Jewish people.
20 They were asking him to stay over for a longer amount of time. He didn't nod.
21 But he said good-bye and, "I will double back to you again, as God wants." Then he set sail out of Ephesus.
22 He went down to Caesarea. He walked up *to Jerusalem* and said hello to the assembly. Then he walked down to Antioch.
23 After he did some time there, he went out again. He went in order through the Galatian rural area and Phrygia *(through the assemblies he had started in central Turkey)* and further established all the students.

24 A certain Jewish man named Apollos made it to Ephesus *(where Priscilla and Aquila were)*. He was an Alexandrian by birth and a man of words. He was competent in the *Old Testament* writings.
25 This was *someone* that the Master's way had echoed down to. Since he was passionate in the Spirit, he was speaking and teaching accurately about Jesus. He only was well acquainted with John's submersion. *(John's submersion taught that people must quit their sinful ways and be submerged to prepare the way for the Anointed King Jesus.)*
26 This man began to make clear public statements in the synagogue. After Priscilla and Aquila listened to him, they took him aside and more accurately laid out God's way to him.
27 Since he intended to go through into Achaia, the brothers wrote beforehand to the students in Corinth and urged them to gladly accept him. When he showed up there, he was a great help to the people who through God's generosity had trusted.
28 You see, he was methodically and thoroughly disproving the Jewish people by publicly showing through the *Old Testament* writings that Jesus is the Anointed King.

19

1 During the time that Apollos was in Corinth, Paul went through the upper parts *of western Turkey* and then down into Ephesus where he happened to find some students.
2 He told them, "Tell me if you received the Sacred Spirit after you trusted." "No," they told him, "we didn't even hear that the Sacred Spirit exists."
3 "So what were you submerged into?" he said. "Into John's submersion," they said.
4 "John submerged people when they changed their ways *and started living for God*," said Paul. "He told the ethnic group that *their submersion should be* into the One coming after him, that is, into Jesus, so that they might trust *in Him*."
5 When they heard this, they were submerged into the name of the Master Jesus.
6 Paul placed his hands on them, and the Sacred Spirit came on them. They were both speaking in languages and preaching.
7 There were about twelve men there.
8 For three months, he was going into the synagogue and making clear public statements. He was having discussions and persuading them about God's monarchy.
9 Some were hardening their hearts and not believing. Since they were saying bad things about the Way in the sight of the large number of

people, Paul backed off from them. He isolated the students and had daily discussions in Tyrannus' public hall.

10 This happened for two years in such a way that all the people living in Western Turkey, both Jewish people and Greeks, heard the Master's message.

11 Through Paul's hands, God was showing extraordinary abilities.

12 Towels or aprons were carried off from Paul's skin and put on the people who were in frail health. Their illnesses left and the evil spirits were traveling out of them.

13 Even some of the Jewish exorcists going around there attempted to name the name of the Master Jesus over the people who had the evil spirits. They said, "I place you under an oath with the Jesus whom Paul speaks about publicly."

14 There were seven sons of a certain Jewish head priest, Sceva, doing this.

15 When the evil spirit responded, it told them, "I certainly know Jesus, and I am well aware of Paul, but who are you?"

16 And the person that the evil spirit was in jumped on them and took control of all of them. He was so strong against them that they escaped from that house naked and wounded.

17 This became known to everyone (both Jewish people and Greeks) living in Ephesus, and fear fell on them all. The name of the Master Jesus was being made great.

18 Many of the people who had trusted were coming to admit out loud and announce the sins that they had repeatedly done.

19 There was an adequate amount of them who repeatedly did the things that work their way around *work (magic)*. They were bringing the scrolls *of these things* together and burning them up in the sight of everyone. They added up the prices of them and found it to be fifty thousand silver coins.

20 This is how the Master's message was powerfully growing and strong.

21 Since these things had been accomplished, Paul placed in his spirit to go through Macedonia and Achaia *(regions in Greece)* and travel to Jerusalem. He was saying, "After I am there, it is necessary for me to also see Rome."

22 After he sent out two of the people serving him (Timothy and Erastus) to Macedonia, he fixed his attention on Western Turkey *(Ephesus)* for a while.

23 Throughout that time, there was more than a little agitation about the Way.

24 You see, someone named Demetrius was a silversmith who made silver temples of Artemis *(a Greek goddess)*. He was providing more than a little work to the skilled workers.
25 He brought these skilled workers together with other workers of these types of things. He said, "Men, you are well aware that we make a fortune from this work.
26 And you see and hear that not only from Ephesus, but from nearly all of Western Turkey, this Paul persuades and dislodges an adequate crowd saying, 'No gods come into existence through *people's* hands.'
27 Not only is our part in this in danger of being reprimanded by everyone, but the temple grounds of the great goddess Artemis is going *to be in danger* of being considered to be nothing and her greatness that all of Western Turkey and the civilized world worship *is also in danger* of being taken down."
28 After listening and becoming full of anger, they were yelling, saying, "The Artemis of the Ephesian people is great."
29 The commotion filled the city. They seized Gaius and Aristarchus, Paul's Macedonian traveling companions, and unanimously rushed into the amphitheater.
30 (Paul was intending to go into the mob, but the students were not allowing him.
31 Even some of the head rulers of Western Turkey, who were his friends, were sending messages to him encouraging him not to go into the amphitheater.)
32 Others in the mob were certainly yelling something else. You see, the assembly had rushed together, and the majority did not realize why they had come together.
33 The Jewish people thrust Alexander forward and together the mob pulled him from the crowd. Alexander motioned with his hand wanting to give a defense to the mob.
34 When they correctly understood that he is Jewish, one voice rose up from everyone for about two hours, yelling, "The Artemis of the Ephesian people is great."
35 After the *town* transcriber brought the crowd under control, he declared, "Men, Ephesian people, you see, where is a person who does not know the temple servant of the great Artemis, the city of the Ephesian people, and the *statue here* that fell from Zeus.
36 So since no one objects to these things, it is necessary for you to control yourselves and not to repeatedly do anything obnoxious.
37 You see, you brought these men here, but they haven't pilfered any temples, and they haven't insulted our goddess either.

38 So certainly if Demetrius and the skilled workers who are together with him have a problem with someone, there are courts operating in the marketplace, and there are Roman Senate deputies. They must bring charges there against each other.
39 If you are searching for anything further to happen, it will be resolved in the lawful assembly.
40 You see, we are even in danger of being charged with a disruption for what happened today, since there is no *legal* answer that we will be able to give out to explain this illegal plot."
41 After he said these things, he dismissed the assembly.

20

1 After the disturbance stopped, Paul sent for the students and encouraged them. Then he said good-bye and went out to travel to Macedonia.
2 After he went through those parts and encouraged them with many messages, he came to Greece *(Achaia)*.
3 He did three months there. When the Jewish people came up with a conspiracy against him, as he was going to be setting sail for Troas on his way to Syria, he became of the opinion to return back through Macedonia.
4 He was being accompanied by Sopater (Pyrros' son, a Berean); Aristarchus and Secundus (Thessalonians); Gaius (a Derbaean) and Timothy; and Tychicus and Trophimus (Western Turks).
5 These people went on ahead and stayed in Troas *waiting* for us.
6 *We went to Philippi in Macedonia and* sailed out away from Philippi after the days of the Yeast-free Festival. It took us up to five days to come to them in Troas, where we spent seven days.
7 On Day One *(which is Sunday)* after the Sabbaths, as we had gathered together to split *and eat* bread, Paul was having discussions with them. And since he was going to be leaving the next day, he was prolonging the message up to the middle of the night.
8 There were an adequate amount of torches in the upstairs room where we were gathered together.
9 A certain young man named Eutychus was seated in the window. He was overcome by a deep sleep. As Paul was having discussions on more, when he was overcome from the sleep, he fell down from the third floor. When they went down and picked him up, he was dead.
10 Paul climbed down, got down on him, hugged him, and said, "Don't cause a disturbance. You see, his soul is in him."
11 He climbed up, split the bread, tasted it, and chatted for an adequate amount of time till the first light of day. This is how he left.

12 They took the boy home alive and were encouraged immeasurably.
13 We went on ahead on the boat. We set sail up to Assos *(a coastal city in northwestern Turkey 20 miles south of Troas)* since we were going to be picking up Paul there. You see, this is how he had specifically arranged it since he was going to be going on foot.
14 Since he was meeting up with us in Assos, we took him on the boat there and went to Mitylene *(a city on an island 30 miles south of Assos)*.
15 We sailed away from there. On the following day, we made it to outside of Chios. On a different day *(the third day)*, we pulled in alongside Samos. And on the day after that, we went to Miletus *(about 190 miles south from Mitylene)*.
16 You see, Paul had decided to sail past Ephesus so that it wouldn't happen that he would use up time in Western Turkey. He was hurrying so that, if it were possible, he would make it to Jerusalem for the Day of the Fiftieth.
17 From Miletus, he sent *a messenger* to Ephesus and summoned the older men of the assembly.
18 Since they showed up to him *before the boat left*, he told them, "You are well aware from the first day I walked up to Western Turkey, what I became all the time that I was with you.
19 I was a slave to the Master with every bit of lowly focus, tears, and the troubles that came together and happened to me in the Jewish people's conspiracies.
20 I backed off from none of the things that were advantageous for announcing to you and teaching you publicly and in each house.
21 I was a strong witness to both Jewish people and Greeks of how they must change their ways and trust in our Master Jesus.
22 And now, look, having been tied up by the Spirit, I am traveling to Jerusalem, not knowing what things will meet together with me there.
23 However, in each city the Sacred Spirit is a strong witness to me, saying that restraints and hard times remain for me.
24 But I don't make my soul valuable to myself in any way so that I may complete my race and the job of serving that I received directly from the Master Jesus, to be a strong witness of the good news of God's generosity.
25 And now, look, I realize that you will no longer see my face. I came through speaking publicly among you all about the monarchy.
26 Because of this, I am a witness to you on this day today that I am clean from the blood of everyone.

27 You see, I did not back off in any way from announcing every intention of God to you.
28 Pay attention to yourselves and to all the flock. The Sacred Spirit placed you among the flock to be supervisors who shepherd God's assembly that was acquired by His own blood.
29 I realize that after my departure heavy wolves will come in among you. They will not go easy on the flock.
30 Even from among you yourselves, men will stand up and speak things that have been twisted to pull the students away *and get them* to follow them.
31 For this reason, stay awake and remember that for a three-year period, night and day, I did not stop cautioning each one of you with tears.
32 Now I place you beside God and the message of His generosity. *That message* is able to build you and give you the inheritance that is among all the people who have been made sacred.
33 I desired no one's silver, or gold, or clothes.
34 You yourselves know that these hands worked like an underling for my needs and for the people who were with me.
35 I put everything in front of your face because laboring like this, it is necessary to be assisting the people who are weak and to be remembering the words of the Master Jesus that He Himself said, 'It is more blessed to give than to receive.'"
36 After he said these things, he placed his knees on the ground and prayed together with them all.
37 Then there was an adequate amount of crying from everyone. They were falling on Paul's neck and being very friendly to him.
38 They were especially in agony based on the words that he had stated, that they are no longer going to see his face. They were bringing him on his way to the boat.

21

1 Since the boat happened to set sail, we pulled away from them, sailed straight, and went to Cos. On the day after that we sailed to Rhodes, and from there to Patara *(a city on the southwestern coast of Turkey)*.
2 When we found a boat crossing all the way over to Phoenicia *(an area along the Mediterranean Sea in Israel, Syria, and Lebanon)*, we climbed on board and set sail.
3 When we spotted Cyprus and left it down to the left, we were sailing to Syria and went down to Tyre *(a coastal city in southern Lebanon)*. You see, the boat was unloading the cargo there.

4 We looked for and found the students. We stayed over there for seven days. Some were saying to Paul through the Spirit not to climb on board *the boat* to Jerusalem.

5 When we happened to fully use up the *seven* days, we left and were traveling together. They brought us on our way with their wives and children until we were outside of the city. We placed our knees on the beach and prayed.

6 We said good-bye to each other and climbed up into the boat. Those people returned to their own places.

7 We concluded the voyage out of Tyre and made it into Ptolemais *(a coastal city 25 miles south of Tyre)*. We greeted the brothers there and stayed for one day beside them.

8 On the next day, we left and went to Caesarea *(a coastal city 50 miles south of Ptolemais and 35 miles north of Tel Aviv)*. We went into the house of Philip (the sharer of good news who was from the Seven) and stayed beside him.

9 This Philip had four daughters (virgins) who preach.

10 As we stayed over for a few more days, a certain preacher named Agabus came down out of Judea.

11 He came to us, took Paul's sash off, tied up his own feet and hands, and said, "The Sacred Spirit says the things here: 'The Jewish people in Jerusalem will tie up the man like this whose sash this is and will turn him over to the hands of the non-Jews.'"

12 As we heard these things, both we and the people in that place were encouraging Paul not to walk up to Jerusalem.

13 "What are you doing, crying and pulverizing my heart?" responded Paul. "You see, I am ready, not only to be tied up, but also to die in Jerusalem on behalf of the Master Jesus' name."

14 Since he was not persuaded, we calmed down and said, "What the Master wants must happen."

15 After these days, we packed up and were walking up into Jerusalem.

16 Some of the students from Caesarea also went together with us. They took us to where we would be guests, the house of a certain Mnason, a Cyprian *(from the island of Cyprus)*, one of the original students.

17 When we came to be in Jerusalem, the brothers gladly accepted us with pleasure.

18 On the following day, Paul was going in together with us to visit James. All the older men also showed up.

19 After he said hello to them, he was recounting about each of the things that God did among the non-Jews through his serving.
20 The people listening were praising God's magnificence. And they said to him, "Brother, you are seeing how many tens of thousands there are among the Jewish people who have trusted, and they all have a passion for the law.
21 It echoed down to them that you teach a divorce from Moses to all the Jewish people throughout the nations and that you tell them not to circumcise their children or be walking around in the customs.
22 What then? They, by all means, will hear that you have come.
23 So do this thing that we say to you. There are four men with us who have a vow on themselves.
24 Take these men along with you, be consecrated together with them, pay to have their head shaved, and everyone will know that what echoed down to them is nothing, but you yourself also march in step with the law and observe it.
25 About the non-Jews that have trusted, we have already made a judgment on that and written a letter to them that they should guard themselves from the idol sacrifice, blood, the choked animal, and sexual sin."
26 Then Paul took the men along and was consecrated together with them on the next day. *On that day,* he entered onto the temple grounds and announced to everyone that he would fully observe the consecration days until the offering was offered on behalf of each one of them.
27 As the seven days were going to be completely finished, the Jewish people out of Western Turkey viewed him on the temple grounds. They began stirring up all the crowd, and they put their hands on him.
28 "Men, Israelis, help," they yelled. "This is the person teaching everyone everywhere against the ethnic group, the law, and this place. And he even still brought Greeks onto the temple grounds and has contaminated this sacred place."
29 You see, there were people who before had seen Trophimus (an Ephesian man) in the city together with Paul. They were assuming that Paul had brought him onto the temple grounds.
30 This moved the whole city. The group rushed together. They latched on to Paul and were pulling him outside of the temple grounds. Right away the temple ground's doors were closed.
31 As they were looking to kill him, news stepped up to the commanding officer of the regiment that all of Jerusalem is stirred up.

32 He immediately took soldiers and lieutenants and ran down on them. When the people saw the commanding officer and the soldiers, they stopped hitting Paul.
33 At that time, the commanding officer came near, latched on to him, and gave the order to lock him up with two chains. He was inquiring who he was and what he had done.
34 *Some people were hollering one thing.* Other people in the crowd were hollering out other things. Since he was not able to know for certain, because of the disturbance, he gave the order for him to be taken into the barracks.
35 When he came up to the stairs, things came together and it happened that he was being hauled by the soldiers because of the force of the crowd.
36 You see, a large number of the group was following, yelling, "Take him away."
37 As he was going to be taken into the barracks, Paul said to the commanding officer, "*Tell me* if I am allowed to say something to you." The commanding officer was declaring, "Do you know Greek?
38 So aren't you the Egyptian who upset and led the four thousand men of the Assassins out into the backcountry before these days?"
39 "I certainly am a Jewish person," Paul said, "originally from Tarsus of Cilicia, a citizen of a city that is not insignificant. I plead of you, give me permission to speak to the group."
40 After he gave permission, Paul stood on the stairs and motioned with his hand to the group. When there became a big hush, he hollered out in the Hebrew dialect, saying,

22

1 "Men, brothers and fathers, listen to my defense to you right now."
2 When they heard that he was hollering to them in the Hebrew dialect, they calmed down even more. He declared,
3 "I am a Jewish man who was born in Tarsus of Cilicia yet raised in this city at the feet of Gamaliel *(a highly respected law expert and teacher)*. I have been disciplined aligned with the strictness of the law handed down to us by our fathers. I am a person with passion for God, just as you all are today.
4 I persecuted this Way to the extent that I even killed some of them. I detained both men and women and threw them into jails.
5 Both the head priest and the entire older men's board are a witness of how I even accepted letters directly from them to the brothers so

that I could travel to Damascus, tie up the people there, and bring them to Jerusalem to keep them from ruining a valuable thing.

6 As I was traveling and happened to come near to Damascus, around the middle of the day, unexpectedly, an adequate amount of light beamed down all around me from the sky.

7 I fell to the ground and heard a voice saying to me, 'Saul, Saul, why are you persecuting Me?'

8 'Who are you, Master?' I replied. He told me, 'I am Jesus, the Nazarene that you are persecuting.'

9 The people together with me certainly viewed the light, but they did not hear the voice of the One speaking to me.

10 'What should I do, Master?' I asked. 'When you get up,' the Master told me, 'travel into Damascus, and there someone will speak to you about everything that has been arranged for you to do.'

11 Since the magnificence of the light made it so that I could not see, I went into Damascus led by the hand of the people together with me.

12 There was a certain devout man aligned with the law, Ananias. All the Jewish people living in Damascus are a witness *to how devout he is*.

13 He came to me and stood over me. 'Saul, brother,' he told me, 'see again.' That same hour I could see him.

14 He told me, 'The God of our fathers put these things in your hands in advance: to know what He wants, to see the One who does what is right, and to hear a voice from His mouth.

15 He has done this because you will be a witness for Him to all kinds of people of what you have seen and heard.

16 And now, what are you going to do? When you get up, be submerged and douse off your sins when you call on His name.'

17 I returned to Jerusalem, and as I was praying on the temple grounds, I happened to fall into a trance.

18 I saw Him telling me, 'Hurry up, and leave Jerusalem quickly because they will not warmly welcome what you say you witnessed about Me.'

19 And I said, 'Master, they are well aware that throughout the synagogues I was throwing the people who trusted in You in jail and beating them.

20 And when the blood of Stephen, Your witness, was being spilled out *at his execution*, I myself had even stood over him, both agreeing that it was good and guarding the robes of the ones executing him.'

21 He told me, 'Travel away, because I will send you off a long way away to non-Jews.'"

22 They were listening to him till he said these words. They raised up their voice. "Take this type of person away from the earth," they said. "You see, he was being too despicable to live."

23 They were yelling, tossing off their robes, and throwing dust into the air.

24 The commanding officer gave the order for him to be taken into the barracks and said that he would be interrogated with whips so that he could correctly understand the reason why they were hollering out at him like that.

25 When they stretched him out beforehand with the straps, Paul said to the lieutenant who was standing there, "If a person is a Roman citizen and not found guilty, are you allowed to order him to be whipped?"

26 When the lieutenant heard this, he went up to the commanding officer to report it. "What are you going to do?" he said. "You see, this person is a Roman citizen."

27 The commanding officer came up to Paul and said to him, "Tell me, are you a Roman citizen?" "Yes," Paul was declaring.

28 "I got this citizenship with a large amount of money," responded the commanding officer. "But I have actually been born *a Roman*," Paul was declaring.

29 So right away the soldiers who were going to be interrogating him backed off away from him. The commanding officer was also afraid when he correctly understood that he is a Roman citizen and that he had locked him up.

30 On the next day, intending to know for certain what the complaint was that the Jewish people had against him, he released him and gave the order for the head priests and all the council to come together. He led Paul down to them and stood among them.

23

1 After Paul stared at the council, he said, "Men, brothers, I have been a law-abiding citizen before God with every bit of a good conscience till this day."

2 Ananias, the head priest, ordered the people who had been standing by him to hit him in the mouth.

3 At that time, Paul said to him, "God is going to hit you, chalk-whitened wall. You actually sit judging me aligned with the law, and going contrary to the law you give an order for me to be hit."

4 The people who had been standing by him said, "Are you putting God's head priest down?"

5 "I didn't realize, brothers," Paul was declaring, "that he is the head priest. You see, the Bible says, 'You will not make a bad statement about the head person of your ethnic group.'"

6 When Paul knew that one part of the council is Sadducees, but the other part is Separatists, he was yelling in the council, "Men, brothers, I am a Separatist, a son of Separatists, I am being judged about anticipation and a return back to life of dead people."

7 After he said this, there became a disruption between the Separatists and Sadducees, and a large number of the council was torn.

8 You see, Sadducees certainly say that there is no return back to life, no angel, and no spirit, but Separatists acknowledge all of them.

9 They started to yell loudly. Some of the Separatists' Old Testament transcribers stood up and were arguing furiously. "We find nothing bad in this person," they said. "If a spirit or angel spoke to him...."

10 As the disruption became big, the commanding officer was afraid that Paul might be pulled apart by them, so he gave the order for the military unit to step down and snatch him from the middle of them and to take him into the barracks.

11 In the following night, the Master stood over him and said, "Be courageous. You see, as you were a strong witness about Me in Jerusalem, so it is necessary for you to also tell what you witnessed in Rome."

12 When it became day, the Jewish people came up with an illegal plot. They vowed under the penalty of dooming themselves not to eat (and not to drink either) until they killed Paul.

13 There were more than forty who made this vow together.

14 Some of them went forward to the head priests and the older men and said, "We vowed under the penalty of dooming ourselves with doom to not taste anything until we kill Paul."

15 So now you together with the council must explicitly show the commanding officer how he needs to bring him down to you since you are going to need to know more accurately what exactly about him is wrong. But we are ready to execute him before he comes near.

16 When Paul's *nephew* (the son of his sister) heard about the ambush, he showed up at the barracks, went inside, and reported it to Paul.

17 Paul called for one of the lieutenants and was declaring, "Take this young man off to the commanding officer. You see, he has something to report to him."

18 So he certainly took him with him and led him to the commanding officer. "The prisoner, Paul," he declared, "called for me and asked me

to bring this young lad to you because he has something to speak to you about."
19 The commanding officer latched on to his hand and went in the back privately. "What is it that you have to report to me?" he was inquiring.
20 "The Jewish people," he said, "agreed to ask you to bring Paul down to the council tomorrow as if it is going to be inquiring something more accurately about him.
21 So you shouldn't be persuaded by them. You see, more than forty men from them are lying in wait for him. They have vowed under the penalty of dooming themselves not to eat, and not to drink either, until they execute him. And they are ready now awaiting the promise from you to bring him down."
22 So the commanding officer dismissed the young lad after giving him this order: "Don't speak outside that you explicitly showed me these things."
23 He called for any two of the lieutenants and said, "Get two hundred soldiers ready to travel as far as Caesarea at 9 p.m. with seventy horsemen and two hundred lightly armed guards.
24 Animals are to stand by to load Paul on and keep him safe to Felix, the leader."
25 He wrote a letter having this format:
26 "From: Claudius Lysias. To: The most powerful leader, Felix. Happy to greet you.
27 After this man was apprehended by the Jewish people and they were going to execute him, I stood over *them* together with the military unit and took him out when I learned that he is a Roman citizen.
28 I intended to correctly understand the reason why they were charging him, so I took him down into their council.
29 I found that he was being charged concerning questions of their law, but it wasn't a charge of anything deserving of death or restraints.
30 When it was disclosed to me that there was a conspiracy against the man, I immediately sent him to you and also passed the order on to the complainants to talk to him in front of you."
31 So according to what had been specifically arranged with them, the soldiers certainly picked up Paul and took him through the night to Antipatris *(a town about 30 miles from Jerusalem and about halfway to Caesarea).*
32 On the next day they allowed the horsemen to go off *to Caesarea* together with him, and they returned to the barracks.

33 The horsemen went into Caesarea, handed over the letter to the leader, and presented Paul to him.
34 After he read the letter, he asked what kind of province he is from *(senatorial or imperial)*. He determined that he is out of Cilicia, *an imperial province*.
35 "I will hear you out," he was declaring, "whenever your complainants also show up." He gave the order for him to be guarded in Herod's Roman palace.

24

1 After five days, the head priest, Ananias, walked down with certain older men and a certain speaker, Tertullus, to explicitly show the leader their case against Paul.
2 After Paul was called, Tertullus began to lay out their complaint. "Since we obtain much peace through you," he said, "and reforms happen to this nation through your plan,
3 both in every way and everywhere, we gladly accept it with every bit of thankfulness, most powerful Felix.
4 But so that I may not interrupt you over more, I encourage you to listen to us briefly with your politeness.
5 You see, we found this man to be a disease. He incites disruptions with all the Jewish people throughout the civilized world. He is the most prominent leader of the sect of the Nazarenes.
6 He was even trying to profane the temple grounds. So we took him into custody [[[and wanted to judge him according to our law,
7 but Lysias, the commanding officer, came alongside us with much force and took him away out of our hands.
8 He ordered his complainants to come before you]]]. You will be able, after you yourself investigate, to correctly understand directly from him about all these complaints that we level against him."
9 The Jewish people also joined in the charge claiming that it is correct.
10 After the leader gestured for Paul to talk, he responded, "Being well aware that you have been a judge of this nation for many years, I cheerfully defend myself.
11 You are able to correctly know that it has not been more than twelve days from the day that I walked up into Jerusalem to bow down at the temple.
12 They didn't find me having a discussion with anyone on the temple grounds or generating tension in a crowd, in the synagogues, or throughout the city.

13 And they are not able to present proof to you either concerning the complaints that they right now level against me.
14 I acknowledge to you that I minister to the God handed down to us by our fathers according to the Way (what they call a sect). I trust all the things that are aligned with the Law and that have been written in the Preachers.
15 I anticipate a return back to life in the future of both people who do what is right and people who do what is wrong. These people themselves are also awaiting this same thing.
16 I also exert myself in having a conscience that is not in any way offensive toward God and the people.
17 When I showed up in Jerusalem, it had been more than a few years since I had been there. I came to make charitable donations to my nation and offerings to God.
18 This is how they found me. I had been consecrated on the temple grounds, not with a crowd, and not causing a disturbance. There are some Jewish people out of Western Turkey who should be here standing before you.
19 *They are the ones* who must be here before you leveling a complaint against me if they have anything against me.
20 Or these people themselves must say what they found wrong when I stood before the council.
21 Or it is about this one utterance that I yelled when I had stood among them, 'I am being judged before you today about a return back to life of the dead.'"
22 Felix knew more accurately about the Way. He put them off and said, "When Lysias, the commanding officer, walks down, I will know exactly what parts of your testimonies are wrong."
23 He specifically arranged with the lieutenant for Paul to be kept in a way that he could both have relief and none of his own people would be kept from working as an underling for him.
24 After some days, Felix together with his own wife, Drusilla (who is Jewish) showed up and sent for Paul. He listened to him tell about trust in the Anointed King Jesus.
25 They had discussions about the right way, self-restraint, and the judgment that is going to come. When Felix became afraid, he responded, "For the time being, travel out. After taking time with others, I will summon you,"
26 At the same time, he also was anticipating that Paul would give him stacks of money for his release. For this reason, he was sending for him more frequently and actually chatting with him.

27 After a two-year period had happened, Felix was replaced by his successor, Porcius Festus. Wanting to lay down something generous for the Jewish people, Felix left Paul locked up down there.

25

1 So Festus stepped *into his role* over the province *in Caesarea*. After three days he walked up to Jerusalem from Caesarea.
2 The head priests and the Jewish people's most important people explicitly showed him their case against Paul. They were encouraging him,
3 asking him for a favor against Paul, that he would send him to Jerusalem so that they could set up an ambush and execute him along the way.
4 So Festus certainly responded that Paul would be kept at Caesarea, but that he himself was going to be traveling out quickly.
5 "So when the capable people among you walk down together," he declared, "if there is anything out of place in the man, they must level a complaint against him."
6 After spending not more than eight or ten days among them, he walked down into Caesarea. The next day when he was seated on the judicial bench, he gave the order for Paul to be brought in.
7 The Jewish people had walked down out of Greater Jerusalem. When Paul showed up, they stood around him bringing many and heavy accusations against him that they couldn't substantiate.
8 Paul defended himself with, "I did not sin in any way against the Jewish people's law, or against the temple grounds, or against Caesar."
9 Festus wanted to lay down something generous for the Jewish people, so when he responded to Paul, he said, "Do you want to walk up into Jerusalem and be judged there before me concerning these things?"
10 "Having stood before the judicial bench of Caesar," said Paul, "I am where I need to be judged. I did nothing wrong to Jewish people as you also correctly understand more nicely now.
11 So if I certainly do what is wrong and *if* I have repeatedly done something deserving of death, I do not refuse to die, but if nothing exists of the things these people level against me, no one is able to give me to them as an act of generosity. I call on Caesar."
12 Festus spoke together with the counsel and then responded, "Caesar, you have called on. Up to Caesar, you will travel."

13 After some days had elapsed, Agrippa (the *young* king *of a small territory in Lebanon, Chalcis, and a son of the Herod that died in Acts 12*) and Bernice *(Agrippa's sister and partner)* made it to Caesarea and greeted Festus.
14 Since they were spending more days there, Festus laid out to the king the situation regarding Paul. "There is a certain man who has been left here as a prisoner by Felix," he said.
15 "When I came to be in Jerusalem, the head priests and the older men of the Jewish people explicitly showed me things about him and asked that *Lady* Justice be used against him.
16 I answered them that it is not a custom with Romans to give any person as an act of generosity before the defendant may even have the complainants right in front of his face and he may be given a chance to defend himself concerning the charge.
17 So after they came here together, I did not make even one delay. The next day when I was seated on the judicial bench, I gave the order for the man to be brought in.
18 When the complainants were stood up, they were not even bringing one accusation about him of evil things that I suspected.
19 They were having questions about Paul's own zeal for God and a certain Jesus who had died, that Paul was claiming to be living.
20 Since I wasn't sure what to think about their questioning of these things, I was asking if he intends to be traveling to Jerusalem and there to be judged concerning these things.
21 But when Paul called on being kept for the scrutiny of The Worshipped One, I gave the order for him to be kept until I will send him up to Caesar."
22 "I was intending to also listen to the person myself," Agrippa said to Festus. "Tomorrow, you will listen to him," Festus declared.
23 So on the next day, Agrippa and Bernice came with much fanfare and went into the hearing room together with both the commanding officers and the prominent men of the city. When Festus gave the order, Paul was brought in.
24 Festus declared, "King Agrippa and all the people who are together beside us, men, see this man. Absolutely all the large number of the Jewish people intervened with me both in Greater Jerusalem and here about him. They shouted that he must not be living anymore.
25 I took down that he had repeatedly done nothing deserving of death, but when this man himself called on The Worshipped One, I decided to send him.

26 I don't have anything certain to write to the master about him. For this reason, I brought him out before you all, and especially before you, King Agrippa, in order that I might have something to write of the investigation that happened.

27 You see, it seems irrational for me to send a prisoner and not indicate the accusations against him."

26

1 Agrippa was declaring to Paul, "Permission is given to you to talk about yourself." Then Paul put out his hand and was defending himself.

2 "King Agrippa, I have regarded myself blessed that I am going to be defending myself before you today concerning everything that I am charged with by Jewish people.

3 You are especially knowledgeable of all the things about Jewish people, both customs and questions. For this reason, I plead that you will listen to me patiently.

4 So certainly all the Jewish people realize that my way of life from my youth up, *my way of life* out from the beginning, happened in my nation and in Greater Jerusalem.

5 They know me from before, from the top, if they want to tell what they were a witness to: that I lived aligned with the strictest sect of our religion, a Separatist.

6 And now I have stood before them and been judged based on an anticipation of the promise made by God to our fathers.

7 Our twelve family lines minister in intensity night and day for this *anticipation* and they anticipate to make it *to a time when God will bring their dead bodies back to life*. It is about this same anticipation, King, that the Jewish people brought this charge against me.

8 What! Is it judged to be absurd beside you all if God gets dead people up?

9 So it certainly seemed necessary for me to repeatedly do many things on my own opposing the name of Jesus, the Nazarene.

10 I even did them in Greater Jerusalem. Also after receiving authority directly from the head priests, I locked many of the sacred people up in jails and threw down my pebble *as a vote against them* as they were being executed.

11 And to keep this valuable thing *(our religion)* from being ruined, I was urging them many times throughout all the synagogues to insult the name of Jesus. And becoming much more crazed, I was pursuing them even out into the cities outside of Jerusalem.

12 While doing this, as I was traveling to Damascus with the authority and permission of the head priests,
13 along the way in the middle of the day, King, I saw a light from the sky brighter than the sun. It was shining all around me and the people traveling together with me.
14 After we all fell down to the ground, I heard a voice saying to me in the Hebrew dialect, 'Saul, Saul, why are you persecuting Me? Isn't it hard for you to kick against cattle prods?'
15 'Who are you, Master?' I said. 'I am Jesus,' said the Master, 'that you persecute.
16 Get up and stand on your feet. You see, the reason I was seen by you was so that I could ordain you beforehand as an underling and a witness both of when you saw Me and when you will see Me.
17 As I take you out of the ethnic group and the non-Jews, I am sending you out on a mission to them
18 to open their eyes. That way they may turn back out of darkness into light and out of the Opponent's authority up to God, and they may receive forgiveness of sins and a portion among the people who have been made sacred by their trust in Me.'
19 From there, my response, King Agrippa, was not to become the type of person who doesn't believe the heavenly sighting that he saw.
20 No, I was reporting it first to the people in Damascus, then to Greater Jerusalem, to every rural area of Judea, and to the non-Jews. I was telling them to change their ways and turn back to God, to repeatedly do actions deserving of their change of ways.
21 Because of this, Jewish people apprehended me as I was on the temple grounds, and they were trying to kill me with their hands.
22 So having obtained the kind of assistance that comes from God til this day, I have stood as a witness to both little and great. I have said nothing outside of what both the preachers and Moses spoke was going to happen.
23 Whether or not the Anointed King is capable of suffering, whether or not He is the first of dead people to return back to life, *one thing is certain, both Moses and the preachers told that* He is going to be proclaiming light to both the ethnic group *(the Jews)* and to non-Jews."
24 As he was defending himself with these statements, Festus declared with a loud voice, "You are crazy, Paul. The many documents that you have read are turning you around into craziness."
25 "I am not crazy, most powerful Festus," declared Paul. "But I am clearly verbalizing statements of truth and proper focus.

26 You see, the king is well aware of these things. I also am speaking making clear public statements. I am persuaded that none of these things have gone unnoticed by him. This is not a thing that has repeatedly been done in a corner.
27 King Agrippa, do you trust the Preachers? I have seen that you do trust them."
28 "Are you persuading me with a few words so that you can make me a Christian?" Agrippa said to Paul.
29 "I wish to God both with a few words and with many words," said Paul, "not only you but also all these types of people listening to me today would become the kind of thing I also am, besides and outside of these restraints."
30 The king, the leader, Bernice, and the people sitting together with them got up.
31 They went in the back and were speaking to each other. *They were saying*, "This person is not repeatedly doing anything deserving of death or restraints."
32 Agrippa was declaring to Festus, "This person could have been dismissed if he had not called on Caesar."

27

1 Since it was decided that they would sail us off to Italy, they were turning both Paul and some different inmates over to a lieutenant named Julius. He was in The Worshipped One's *(Caesar's)* regiment.
2 After he climbed up on board an Adramyttium boat *(a boat made in Adramyttium, a city on the northwestern coast of Turkey)* that was going to be sailing to places along Western Turkey, we took off. A traveling companion of Paul, Aristarchus (a Thessalonian Macedonian), was together with us.
3 On a different day, we landed at Sidon *(70 miles north of Caesarea)*. Julius behaved benevolently to Paul and gave him permission to travel to his friends and obtain care.
4 From there, we set sail and sailed under Cyprus, *on the sheltered side*, because the wind was blowing against us.
5 After sailing across the deep part along Cilicia *(the southeastern coast of Turkey)* and Pamphylia *(the southern coast of Turkey)*, we went down to Myra, Lycia *(a city on the southern coast of Turkey)*.
6 There the lieutenant found an Alexandrian boat *(a boat made in Alexandria, a city in Egypt on the western edge of the Nile River Delta)* sailing to Italy and boarded us onto it.

7 We were sailing slowly for an adequate amount of days. After it took a lot of effort for us to come along Cnidus *(a city on the southwestern tip of Turkey)* and the wind was not permitting us to go any further, we sailed under Crete along Salmone *(the easternmost point of the island of Crete).*

8 And since it was taking a lot of effort for us to pass by it, we went to a certain place called Nice Harbors that was near Lasea City *(on the southern coast of Crete).*

9 An adequate amount of time had elapsed and the voyage was already hazardous because even the time of the Fast *(Yom Kippur, in September or October)* had already gone by. So Paul was suggesting

10 and telling them, "Men, I see that there is going to be injury and much loss in *the next part of our* voyage, not only loss of the load and the boat, but also of our souls."

11 But the lieutenant was being persuaded by the helmsman and the shipowner rather than by what Paul said.

12 The majority of them were set in their intention to set sail from there because the harbor was not suitable for spending the storm season in it. Their intention was to somehow be able to make it *to the other side of the island* to Phoenix and spend the storm season in a harbor of Crete facing *northeast and southeast which is downwind of* Lips *(the southwest wind)* and Choros *(the northwest wind).*

13 When the wind softly blew from the south, their plan seemed to have merit, so they took off and were passing by Crete closer than usual.

14 But not very long after that, a hurricane-like wind violently blew down from the *east-northeast. It was* called Euros *(the east wind)* Aquilo *(the northeast wind).*

15 It seized the boat, and the boat wasn't able to face into the wind. So we gave up, and the wind was carrying us off.

16 After running under a certain small island called Clauda *(which blocked some of the wind for a while)*, with a lot of effort, we were strong enough to pull up the dinghy and secure it to the boat.

17 After it was taken up, they were using things, *like ropes and chains,* to help tie up the underside of the boat. They were afraid of falling into the Syrtis *Major (the Gulf of Sidra located off the northern coast of Africa) and running aground on the vast constantly shifting beds of sand there.* So they lowered the gear on the mast, but they were still being driven along.

18 Since we were in a terrible storm, on the next day they were throwing things out.

19 And on the third day, they tossed the boat's furniture out with their own hands.

20 When both the sun and the constellations didn't shine for several days and it was obvious that this was more than a small storm bearing down on us, for the rest of the time, any anticipation of us being rescued was being taken away all around us.

21 When it had been a long time since anyone had eaten, Paul stood up in the middle of them and said, "It was certainly necessary for you who were loyal to me, O men, not to take off from Crete and gain this injury and loss.

22 And now I suggest that you cheer up. You see, there won't be even one casualty of a soul among you other than the boat.

23 An angel from the God that I belong to and that I minister to stood by me last night.

24 He said, 'Don't be afraid, Paul. It is necessary for you to stand up next to Caesar and, look, as an act of generosity, God has given you all the people sailing with you.'

25 For this reason, cheer up, men. You see, I trust God that this is how it will be: it will be aligned with the way that the angel has spoken to me.

26 But it is necessary for us to run ashore on a certain island."

27 On the fourteenth night of us being carried along *by the wind* in the Adriatic Sea, throughout the middle of the night the crewmen were suspecting that some land was approaching them.

28 When they measured the depth *of the water*, they found it to be twenty fathoms *(about 120 feet) deep. A fathom is the span of a man's outstretched arms.* After a *little* bit *of time* went by, they measured the depth again and found it to be fifteen fathoms *(about 90 feet) deep*.

29 They were afraid that we might run ashore somewhere along rugged terrain, so they put down four anchors from the back of the boat and were wishing for it to become day.

30 The crewmen were looking to escape from the boat. So they were lowering the dinghy into the sea acting as if they were going to be putting anchors out from the front of the boat.

31 "If these people don't stay in the boat," Paul said to the lieutenant and the soldiers, "you can't be rescued."

32 Then the soldiers chopped off the ropes of the dinghy and allowed it to fall off.

33 From then til day was about to come, Paul was encouraging absolutely everyone to take a share of the food, saying, "Today is the fourteenth day that we have expected this to end. You are thoroughly

finishing the day without eating any grain. You haven't taken in anything.

34 For this reason, I encourage you to take a meal with me. You see, this will strengthen you for your rescue. Not even one of you will lose a hair from your head."

35 After he said these things, he took bread and thanked God in the sight of everyone. He split it and began to eat.

36 Everyone cheered up and also took in a meal.

37 We were all the souls on the boat, two hundred seventy-six.

38 After they were stuffed from the meal, they were lightening the boat, throwing the grain out into the sea.

39 When it became day, they didn't recognize the land, but they were taking a close look at a certain bay that had a beach. They were advising that if they were able, they should push the boat out into it.

40 They released all the anchors around the boat and were allowing the anchors to remain in the sea. At the same time, after easing up on the bindings of the rudders and raising the foresail up to the blowing wind, they were holding it steady to the beach.

41 When they were swept into a place where two currents meet *forming a shallow sandbank*, they ran the ship aground. The front of the boat certainly got stuck and stayed there undisturbed, but the back of the boat was being broken up by the force of the swells.

42 It became the intention of the soldiers that they should kill the inmates so that no one would swim away and completely escape.

43 But the lieutenant intended to keep Paul safe, so he kept them from what they intended to do. He gave the order that those who could swim should jump off and be the first out on the land.

44 The rest should go, some on boards and others on some of the things from the boat. And this is how it happened that everyone ended up safe on the land.

28

1 Once we were safe, then we correctly understood that the island is called Melita *(present day Malta)*.

2 The natives *of the island* were providing us with extraordinary benevolence. You see, they lit a bonfire and took us all in because of the pouring rain that had been standing over *us* and because of the cold.

3 After Paul bunched a large number of dry sticks together and placed them on the bonfire, a poisonous snake came out of the heat and clamped down on his hand.

4 Since the natives saw the wild creature hanging from his hand, they were saying to each other, "Undoubtedly, this man is a murderer. Even after he is safe from the sea, *Lady* Justice didn't allow him to live."
5 Paul knocked the wild creature off into the fire and definitely didn't suffer anything bad.
6 They were expecting that he was going to swell up or to suddenly fall down dead. But during a long period of expecting and seeing nothing out of place happening to him, they switched and were saying that he is a god.
7 Among the properties around that place, there were parcels of land that belonged to the island's most important person. His name was Publius. He welcomed us in and courteously provided a place for us to stay for three days.
8 Publius' father was restricted by a fever and severe diarrhea and happened to be lying down. When Paul went in to him, prayed for him, and placed his hands on him, he cured him.
9 After this happened, the rest of the people in the island who also had weaknesses were coming to Paul and being healed.
10 The people also honored us with many valuables. And they placed things for our needs on the boat as we set sail.
11 We set sail after *being on the island for* three months. *We were* in a boat that had spent the storm season in the island. It was an Alexandrian boat marked on its side with the twin sons of Zeus.
12 We landed at Syracuse *(a city on the southeastern coast of Sicily, an island off the southern tip of Italy)* and stayed over for three days.
13 From there, we tacked *the boat,* and made it to Rhegium *(a city on the southern tip of Italy)*. After one day, a south wind came again, and we second-day people went to Puteoli *(200 miles up the Italian coast)*.
14 When we found brothers there, they encouraged us to stay over with them for seven days. This is how we went to Rome.
15 The brothers from there til Appii Forum and Three Shacks *(two towns on the Appian Way, a road going to Rome)* heard the news about us and came to meet us face-to-face. When Paul saw them, he thanked God and received courage.
16 When we went into Rome, Paul was given permission to stay by himself together with the soldier guarding him.
17 After three days, he happened to call together the Jewish people's most important ones. When they came together, *Paul sat before them chained to a Roman soldier.* He was saying to them, "Although I, men, brothers, did nothing against the ethnic group or our fathers' customs,

from Greater Jerusalem I was turned over as a prisoner to the hands of the Romans.
18 After some of them investigated me, they were intending to dismiss me because of the fact that there was not even one accusation of death in me.
19 But since the Jewish people were opposing it, I was urged to call on Caesar. I don't call on Caesar as a person who has some complaint to level against my nation.
20 So I called you here to see and speak to you because of this accusation. You see, I am lying around this chain for the thing that Israel is anticipating."
21 The people told him, "We have not accepted documents out of Judea about you. And none of the brothers who showed up have reported or spoken anything evil about you either.
22 But we think that the things you focus on deserve to be heard directly from you. You see, we certainly know that people everywhere oppose this sect."
23 He arranged a day with them. On that day, more people came to him in the guesthouse. From morning until late afternoon, he was laying it out to them. He was being a strong witness of God's monarchy and persuading them about Jesus out of both Moses' law and the Preachers.
24 Some of the people were being persuaded by what was being said, but the others were not trusting.
25 They were disagreeing with each other and were dismissing themselves after Paul said one statement: "The Sacred Spirit spoke nicely through Isaiah, the preacher, to our fathers.
26 He said, 'Travel to this ethnic group and say, "You will hear what you hear and not in any way understand, and you will look as you look and not in any way see.
27 You see, this ethnic group's heart became fat, they hardly heard with their ears, and they shut their eyes so that they might never see with the eyes, hear with the ears, understand with the heart, and return back, and I will cure them" *(Isaiah 6:9-10).*'
28 So it must be known to you that this rescue process of God is sent out to the non-Jews, and they will hear."
29 [[[And when he said these things, the Jewish people went away with much questioning back and forth among themselves.]]]
30 He stayed a whole two year period in his own rented house and was gladly accepting all the people traveling in to him.

31 Unhindered and with every clear public statement, he was speaking publicly about God's monarchy and teaching the lessons about the Master Jesus, the Anointed King.

Romans

1

1 From: Paul, a slave of the Anointed King Jesus, an invited missionary that has been isolated to God's good news.
2 *This good news* was previously promised through His preachers in the sacred *Old Testament* writings.
3 *It is* about His Son (the One who, regarding the physical body, came from David's seed,
4 the One who, regarding the Spirit of Sacredness, was designated God's son with ability from a return back to life of the dead), Jesus, the Anointed King, our Master.
5 Through Him, we received generosity and a mission to distribute the obedience of trust among all the nations on behalf of His name.
6 You are the ones among them who were also invited to belong to Jesus, the Anointed King.
7 To: All the people in Rome who are loved by God, invited, and sacred. Generosity and peace to you out from God, our Father, and our Master Jesus, the Anointed King.
8 First of all, I certainly thank my God through Jesus, the Anointed King, concerning you all because your trust is proclaimed in the whole world.
9 You see, God (the *God* that I minister to in my spirit in His Son's good news) is my witness how I constantly make a mention of you in my prayers.
10 I always plead in my prayers, if somehow, finally, I will be successful to come to you in a way that God wants.
11 You see, I yearn to see you so that I might give out some spiritual gift to you that will help establish you.
12 But this is so that through the trust in each of us (both your trust and my trust), we together might be encouraged.
13 I don't want you to be unaware, brothers, that many times I intended to come to you so that I might also have some fruit among you (just as I also have among the rest of the nations) and I was kept from it even till now.
14 I am indebted to everyone, to both Greeks and foreigners, to both insightful and unobservant people.
15 This is why I am eager to also share good news with you, the people in Rome.

16 You see, I am not ashamed of the good news. *The good news* is God's ability for rescue for every person who trusts, both the Jewish person first and the Greek.

17 You see, it uncovers God's right way from trust for trust. This is just what the Bible says, "The person who does what is right will live from trust" *(Habakkuk 2:4).*

18 *For the people who won't trust, God's right way brings punishment.* You see, God's punishment is uncovered from heaven on all godlessness and wrong of people, the ones holding down the truth in wrong.

19 *The reason why they are punished is* because what is known of God is shown in them--God showed it to them.

20 You see, as they perceive His invisible work (from the creation of the world to the things He does), they clearly see both His eternal ability and divinity. This makes them defenseless

21 because when they knew God, they didn't elevate God to a place of magnificence and they weren't thankful. But their ponderings were futile, and their clueless heart was made dark.

22 Claiming to be insightful people, they became foolish.

23 They changed the magnificence of the God that doesn't deteriorate into *an idol*, the likeness of an image of a deteriorating human, of winged birds, of four-legged animals, and of reptiles.

24 For this reason, God turned them over to the desires of their hearts, to what is not clean, to the belittling of their bodies among themselves.

25 These are the ones that exchanged God's truth for their lie. They worshiped and ministered to the thing that God created after passing up the God who created it, the One who has blessings conferred on Him for the spans of time. Amen.

26 Because of this, God turned them over to worthless lusts. You see, even their females exchanged the natural use of the male for what is contrary to nature.

27 And likewise, when the males also left the natural use of the female, they burned out in their craving for each other, males among males, working on and completing what is improper. They fully receive among themselves the payback that is necessary for their misleading lie.

28 And just as they did not approve of having a correct understanding of God, God turned them over to an unapproved way of thinking, to do the things that are too despicable.

29 They have been filled with all wrong, evilness, desire for more, badness (full of envy, murder, fighting, deception, and bad character), whisperers,
30 critical, God-detesting, injurers *of people*, proud, egoistic, inventors of bad things, unbelieving to parents,
31 clueless, not keeping agreements, hardhearted toward family, unkind, and unforgiving.
32 After correctly understanding the right path of God (that the people who repeatedly do these types of things are deserving of death), these are the ones that not only do these *wrong* things, but they also agree together with the people repeatedly doing them *and say* that *what they are doing* is good.

2

1 This is why you are defenseless, O person, every person who judges. You see, the thing that you judge to be wrong in the other person is the very thing that you yourself are guilty of. You, the person who judges, repeatedly do the same things.
2 We realize that God's judgment of the people who repeatedly do these types of things is based on the truth.
3 O person, the one who judges the people repeatedly doing these types of things and who also does them, are you considering that *it is a possibility that* you will escape out of God's judgment?
4 Or do you ignore the wealth of His kindness, tolerance, and patience, unaware that God's kindness leads you into a change of ways?
5 Your hardness and stubborn heart cause you to stockpile punishment for yourself until a day of punishment and a day when God's right judgment is uncovered.
6 In that day, what He gives out to each person will align with that person's actions:
7 to the people who persist to do good and look for magnificence, value, and the thing that doesn't deteriorate, He will certainly give back life that spans all time;
8 but to the people who are contentious about doing what is good and don't even believe the truth, but believe the wrong way, He will give back punishment and anger.
9 Hard times and difficulty are on every person's soul that is working on and completing what is bad (both the soul of a Jewish person first and of Greek).
10 But magnificence, value, and peace are for everyone who works on the good thing (both for a Jewish person first and for Greek).

11 You see, appearances don't matter beside God.

12 As many as sinned without the law will also be ruined without the law, and as many as sinned in the law will be judged through the law.

13 You see, it is not the hearers of the law that are right *standing* beside God. No, it is the doers of the law who will be made right.

14 When the non-Jews (who by nature don't have a law) do the law's things, these who don't have a law are a law to themselves.

15 They display the action of the law written in their hearts. *In their hearts,* their conscience concurs with *the law* as their reasonings interact between each other (leveling complaints against each other or even defending each other).

16 There will be a day when God judges the people's hidden actions aligned with my good news through the Anointed King Jesus.

17 If you have identified yourself as Jewish, you also relax based on the law, you brag about God,

18 you know what God wants, and you approve the substantial things being echoed down from the law.

19 And you have been confident that you yourself are a guide of blind people, a light for the people in darkness,

20 a discipliner of distracted people, a teacher of infants, someone who has the framework of knowledge and the truth in the law.

21 So, you who teach a different person, don't you teach yourself? You who speak publicly about not stealing, do you steal?

22 You who tell someone not to cheat on their spouse, do you cheat on your spouse? You who are disgusted with the idols, do you pilfer idol temples?

23 Do you who brag about the law belittle God through your violation of the law?

24 You see, the non-Jews insult God's name because of you, just as the Bible says *in Isaiah 52:5 and Ezekiel 36:22-23.*

25 Circumcision certainly is a benefit if you constantly obey the law, but if you are a violator of the law, your circumcision has become uncircumcision.

26 So if *the non-Jew,* the uncircumcision, observes the right paths of the law, won't his uncircumcision be considered as circumcision?

27 And the uncircumcision (which is how everyone is born) that finishes the law will judge you, the violator of the law (who has the law's document and circumcision).

28 You see, what is important is not that the person is Jewish visibly or that he is circumcised visibly, in the physical body.

29 But what is important is that a person is Jewish invisibly and that his heart is circumcised in spirit, not in some document. This person doesn't get high praise from people. His high praise is from God.

1 So what is the thing *that makes* the Jewish person much better *than the person who is not Jewish?* Or what is the benefit of the circumcision?
2 In every way, there is much. You see, first is certainly that they were trusted with God's utterances.
3 *God trusted them, but* you see, what if some of them did not trust Him? Their distrust won't make the trust of God useless, will it?
4 No, it could not happen. *When people disagree with God,* God is valid and every person is a liar. *This is* just as *David* wrote, "in order that You *(God)* might be made right in Your messages and *so that* You will conquer in what You decide" *(Psalm 51:4)*.
5 If we *insist on* standing our wrong way up together with God's right way, what will we be stating? God isn't wrong for bringing on the punishment, is He? (I am talking as a human might).
6 No, it could not happen. Or else how will God judge the world?
7 If my fabrication caused God's truth to overflow into His magnificence *(we're stating a hypothetical scenario here)*, why am I still even judged as a sinful person is?
8 And *would it* not be just like the insults people say about us? *Would it not be* just as some declare us to be saying: "We should do the bad things so that the good things might come?" The judgment that those people make is reasonable: *It is always wrong to do bad, even when it seems to accomplish something good.*
9 So what about the Jewish people? Are we Jewish people held in a better position? Not by any means. You see, we already accused everyone, both Jewish people and Greeks, to be under sin.
10 This is just what the Bible says: "There is not a person who does what is right, not even one."
11 "There is no one who understands. There is no one who is intensively searching for God."
12 "All slid away. They went bad at the same time. There is no one showing kindness. There isn't so much as one" *(Psalm 14:1-3; 53:1-3)*.
13 "Their throat is an open grave. They were deceiving people with their tongues" (Psalm 5:9). "The venom of cobras is under their lips" *(Psalm 140:3)*.
14 "Their mouth is packed full of cursing and bitterness" *(Psalm 10:7)*.
15 "Their feet spill out blood quickly.

16 Disaster and misery are on their roads,
17 and they didn't know a road of peace" *(Isaiah 59:7-8)*.
18 "There isn't a fear of God up in front of their eyes" *(Psalm 36:1)*.
19 We realize that as much as the law says, it speaks to the people in the law so that every mouth might be shut and the entire world might become legally liable to God
20 because doing what the law says won't make even one physical body right in His sight. You see, the law gives people a correct understanding of sin.
21 But right now, God's right way has been shown separate from the law. The Law and the Preachers witnessed it.
22 God's right way is through a trust of Jesus, the Anointed King. It is for all the people trusting. You see, there is no difference between Jew and non-Jew.
23 All *who trust* sinned and lack God's magnificence.
24 They are made right for free by His generosity through the paid release in the Anointed King Jesus.
25 God put the Anointed King in public view as a remedy (through the trust in His blood) for a display of God's right way. *This is* because of the way He passed by the sins that have already happened.
26 With God's tolerance, the display of His right way in the present time shows that He is right and He is the One who makes the person who trusts in Jesus right.
27 So where is the bragging? It was excluded. What kind of law excluded it? A law *that gets people to* do things? No, a law *that gets people to* trust.
28 You see, we consider a person with trust to be made right separate from the law's actions.
29 Or is He only the God of Jewish people? Is He not also the God of non-Jews? Yes, also of non-Jews
30 if it is true that God is one God. *Since God is the one and only God over everyone,* He will make circumcision right from trust and uncircumcision right through the same trust.
31 So do we make the law useless through this trust? No, it could not happen. On the contrary, we establish the law.

1 So what will we state that Abraham, our forefather, has found regarding the physical body?
2 You see, if Abraham was made right from things he did, he has something to brag about, but not to God.

3 You see, what does the *Old Testament* writing say? "But Abraham trusted God, and God considered him to be right *because of that*" *(Genesis 15:6).*
4 For the person working, the pay is not considered to be the result of generosity, it is considered to be what is owed to him.
5 But for the person who doesn't work but trusts the One who makes the person who is not godly right, God considers him to be right because of his trust.
6 This is exactly what David also says is the blessedness of the person that God considers to be right despite the things he does:
7 "People whose crimes are forgiven and whose sins are covered up are blessed.
8 A man who has a master that won't ever consider sin is blessed" *(Psalm 32:1,2).*
9 So is this blessedness on the circumcision only? Or is it not also on the uncircumcision? You see, we say that God considered Abraham to be right because of the trust.
10 So how was *it with Abraham when God* considered him to be right? Was he circumcised or uncircumcised? He was not circumcised. No, he was uncircumcised.
11 And he received circumcision as proof and a seal of the right way of his trust, trust that he had while he was uncircumcised. That way he could be a father of all the uncircumcised people who trust (so that they will be considered right because of trust too).
12 And he could be a father of circumcision (not the people who are circumcised only, but the ones who also march in step with the footsteps of the trust that our uncircumcised father Abraham took).
13 You see, the promise to Abraham or to his seed (the promise that he would inherit the world) is not through the law, but through the right way of trust."
14 If the inheritors are from the law, the trust has been meaningless and the promise has been rendered useless.
15 The law works on and completes punishment, but where there is no law, there is no violation either.
16 Because of this, the right way is gained from trusting so that it is the result of generosity. That way the promise will be firm to every seed, not to the seed that is only from the law, but to the seed that also is from Abraham's trust, the Abraham who is a father of us all.
17 This is just what the Bible says, "I have placed you as a father of many nations" *(Genesis 17:5). This was said to Abraham as he was* directly facing the One that he trusted, God, the One who gives life to

the dead and identifies the things that don't exist *yet* as if they do exist.

18 Beyond anticipation based on anticipation, Abraham trusted the promise that he would become a father of many nations. This matched up with what *God had stated after He told Abraham to look at the sky and see if he could count the stars. God* had stated: "This is how your seed will be" *(Genesis 15:5)*.

19 Even though he wasn't weak when it comes to trust, he took a close look at his own body. It already was as good as dead. He was almost a centenarian *(a hundred-year-old)*. And he took a close look at the deadness of Sarah's womb.

20 But he didn't consider God's promise to be wrong and so not trust. No, he became competent with the trust when he gave magnificence to God

21 and was well-established in the conviction that God is also able to do what He has promised.

22 For this reason, God considered him to be right.

23 The Bible doesn't only say it (that God considered him to be right) because of him,

24 but also because of us, the ones that God is going to consider to be right for trusting the One who got Jesus, our Master, up from the dead.

25 Jesus was turned in because of our infractions and was gotten up because of our verdict declaring that we did the right thing.

5

1 So since we have been made right from trust, we have peace with God through our Master Jesus, the Anointed King.

2 Through Him with the trust, we also have had the access into this generosity that we have been standing in, and we are optimistic based on an anticipation of God's magnificence.

3 Not only that, but we also are optimistic in the hard times realizing that the hard times work on and complete a persistence to do what is right,

4 the persistence to do what is right works on and completes a proven track record, and the proven track record works on and completes anticipation.

5 We are not shamed by the anticipation because God's love has been spilled out in our hearts through the Sacred Spirit that was given to us.

6 *His love is seen in the fact that* even though we were weak, the Anointed King still died at the appointed time on behalf of people who are not godly.

7 You see, it may be difficult, but some will die on behalf of a person who does what is right. And some will possibly even dare to die on behalf of a good person.

8 But God stands together with His own love for us, because the Anointed King died on our behalf while we were still sinful people.

9 So, it is much more certain now that since we were made right in His blood, we will be rescued out of the punishment through Him.

10 You see, if we, who were enemies, were restored to God through His Son's death, it is much more certain that after we are restored, we will be rescued in His life.

11 Not only that, but we also are optimistic in God through our Master Jesus, the Anointed King. It is through Him that we now have received the restored relationship.

12 Because of this, *we should be aware of how that relationship died.* Even as sin came into the world through one person and death came through the sin *(not just physical death but also death of the relationship with God),* so death also went through to everyone based on the fact that everyone sinned.

13 You see, sin was in the world before the law was given, but no one living then is found guilty of sinning since there was no law *telling them what is sin and what is not. There was only the story of Adam's violation.*

14 But death was still king during that time, from Adam up to Moses, even over the people who didn't sin in a similar way to Adam's violation. Adam is a type of the One that is going to come.

15 But the gift from the One is not like Adam's infraction even though in some ways it is. You see, if many died with the one person's infraction, it is much more certain that God's generosity and that One Person's free handout overflowed to the many from His generosity. That One Person is Jesus, the Anointed King.

16 And the free gift is not like what is through one person who sinned. You see, the judgment certainly goes from one person into a guilty verdict, but the gift goes from many infractions into the right path.

17 If death was king through the one person with his infraction, it is much more certain that the people receiving the overflow of the generosity and *the overflow* of the free handout of the right way will be kings in life through the One, Jesus, the Anointed King.

18 So clearly, as through one person's infraction, a guilty verdict is for all people, so also through one Person's right path, a verdict declaring that a person has done what is right is for all people, a verdict of life.
19 You see, even as one person's noncompliance caused many to be classified as sinful people, so also will the One's obedience cause many to be classified as people who do what is right.
20 The law quietly came in so that the infraction might increase. But where the sin increased, the generosity overflowed even more.
21 That way even as the sin was king in the death, so also might the generosity be king through the right way for life that spans all time through Jesus, the Anointed King, our Master.

6

1 So what will we state *when we realize that where sin increases, generosity overflows even more?* Should we stay over in the sin so that the generosity might increase?
2 No, it should not happen. How will we, the ones who died to the sin, still live in it?
3 Or are you not aware that as many of us as were submerged into the Anointed King Jesus, were submerged into His death?
4 So through the submersion, we were buried together with Him into death so that even as the Anointed King was gotten up from the dead through the Father's magnificence, so also we might walk around in newness of life.
5 You see, if we have become integrated into the likeness of His death, we also will be a part of the return back to life.
6 We know that our former person was nailed to a cross together with Him so that the body of sin might be rendered useless. *It is rendered useless* so that we won't be a slave to sin anymore.
7 You see, the one who died with the Anointed King has been made right. *He has been taken* out of sin.
8 If we died together with the Anointed King, we trust that we also will live together with Him.
9 We have seen that the Anointed King who was gotten up from the dead doesn't die anymore. Death isn't a master over Him anymore.
10 You see, when He died for sin, He died all at once, but as He lives, He is living for God.
11 This is how you also must consider yourselves to certainly be dead people for sin, but people living for God in the Anointed King Jesus.
12 So sin must not be a king in your dying body. Do not obey its desires.

13 Don't offer your body parts to sin either, to be weapons of the wrong way. But offer yourselves to God (as if you are living out of the dead) and your body parts to God to be weapons of the right way.
14 You see, sin won't be your master. You aren't under the law, you are under generosity.
15 So what *should we do?* Should we sin because we aren't under the law, but under generosity? No, it should not happen.
16 Haven't you seen that you are slaves to what you offer yourselves to be obedient slaves to, to what you obey, whether you are slaves of sin for death, or slaves of obedience for the right way?
17 Thank God that even though you were sin's slaves, from your heart you obeyed the type of teaching that you were handed over to.
18 After being set free out of sin, you were made slaves to the right way.
19 I am telling this human analogy because of your physical body's weakness. You see, in the same way that you offered your body parts to be slaves to what is not clean and to the crime for the crime, so also now offer your body parts to be slaves to the right way for sacredness.
20 When you were sin's slaves, you were free from the right way.
21 So what fruit were you having at that time? You are ashamed of those things now. You see, their conclusion is death.
22 But right now, you have been set free out of sin, but after being made slaves to God, you have your fruit for sacredness. The conclusion is life that spans all time.
23 You see, the wages of sin is death, but the gift of God is life that spans all time in the Anointed King Jesus, our Master.

7

1 Or are you not aware, brothers, (you see, I am speaking to people who know the law) that the law is a master over a person as long as he lives?
2 You see, the 'under-a-husband' woman *(a married woman)* has been tied to the living husband by the law. But if the husband dies, she becomes exempt from the law *that ties her to* the husband.
3 So clearly, as the husband is living, if she ends up with a different man, she will be called a cheating wife. But if the husband has died, she is free from the law, and she is not a cheating wife when she ends up with a different man.
4 In such a way, my brothers, the Anointed King's body also made you dead to the law so that you may end up with a different *man*, the *Man*

who was gotten up from the dead. That way we can produce fruit for God.

5 You see, when we were in the physical body, sins' hardships (the hardships through the law) were active in our body parts producing fruit for death.

6 But right now when we die in what was holding us down, we are rendered exempt from the law. That way we may be slaves in newness of spirit and not in the outdated nature of a document.

7 So what will we state? That the law is sin? It could not happen. No, I didn't know sin except through the law. You see, I hadn't even seen desire *for my neighbor's things*, except the law was saying, "You will not desire *your neighbor's house, his wife, his servants, his ox, and etc."* *(Exodus 20:17).*

8 But sin received an opportunity through the demand, and it worked on and completed all kinds of desire in me. You see, separate from a law, sin is dead.

9 In the past, I was living separate from a law, but when the demand came, sin came back to life. I died.

10 And I found that this demand that is for life is for death.

11 You see, when sin received an opportunity through the demand, it completely fooled me, and through this killed me.

12 In such a way, the law certainly is sacred, and the demand is sacred, right, and good.

13 So did the thing that is good for me become death? No, it could not happen. But the thing that is good for me denounced sin so that it might show that sin works on and completes death. That way sin might become even more sinful through the demand.

14 You see, we have seen that the law is spiritual, but I am physical. I have been put up for sale by sin.

15 I don't know what I work on and complete. *I want to do good. I hate sin.* I don't constantly do what I want to do. No, I do what I hate.

16 If I do what I don't want to do, I declare together with the law that the law is nice.

17 Right now, it isn't me who is working on and completing it anymore. No, it is sin that has a house in me.

18 You see, I have seen that good doesn't have a house in me, that is in my physical body. The *ability* to want the nice thing lies beside me, but not the *ability* to work on and complete it.

19 I don't do the good that I want, but the bad that I don't want, this I repeatedly do.

20 If I do what I don't want to do, it isn't me that is working on and completing it anymore. It is sin that has a house in me.
21 I clearly find the law with me wanting to do the nice thing is that the bad lies beside me.
22 You see, my inner person admires God's law,
23 but I see a different law in my body parts that is a soldier fighting against the law of my way of thinking and forcibly incarcerating me in sin's law, the law that is in my body parts.
24 I am a troubled person. What will save me from the body of this death?
25 Thank God through Jesus, the Anointed King, our Master. So clearly I myself am not only a slave to God's law with my way of thinking, but to sin's law with my physical body.

1 Clearly now the people in the Anointed King Jesus don't have even one guilty verdict against them.
2 You see, the law of the Spirit of Life in the Anointed King Jesus set you free out of the law of sin and death.
3 What the law found impossible to do because it was weak when dealing with the physical body, God did by sending His own Son in the likeness of sin's physical body and around sin. What He found to be guilty was sin in the physical body, *not the physical body itself*.
4 That way the right path of the law could be accomplished in us, the people who don't walk around aligned with the physical body, but aligned with the Spirit.
5 You see, the people who are aligned with the physical body focus on the physical body's things, but the people who are aligned with the Spirit focus on the Spirit's things.
6 The physical body focuses on death, but the Spirit focuses on life and peace.
7 Because of this, the physical body's focus is a hostile relationship to God. You see, it doesn't place itself under God's law, and it isn't able to either.
8 The people who are in the physical body aren't able to do anything that God would like.
9 You aren't in the physical body if it is true that God's Spirit has a house in you. You are in the Spirit. If anyone doesn't have the Anointed King's Spirit, this person is not His.
10 If the Anointed King is in you, the body certainly is dead because of sin *(because sin misses the target, it misses the right way)*, but the Spirit is alive because of the right way.

11 If the Spirit of the One who got Jesus up from the dead has a house in you, the One who got the Anointed King up from the dead will also give life to your dying bodies through His Spirit that has a house in you.
12 So, brothers, we clearly are not indebted to the physical body. We don't have to live aligned with the physical body.
13 You see, if you live aligned with the physical body, you are going to be dying, but if you make the things that the body repeatedly does, dead to the Spirit, you will live.
14 As many as are led by God's Spirit, these are God's sons.
15 You didn't receive a spirit of slavery again to be afraid. No, just the opposite, you received a spirit of adoption in which we cry out, "Daddy, the Father!"
16 The Spirit itself concurs with our spirit that we are God's children.
17 If we are children, we are also inheritors. Not only are we inheritors of God, but we are inheritors together with the Anointed King if it so happens that we suffer together with Him. That way we also will be made magnificent together with Him.
18 You see, I consider that the hardships of the present time are not deserving of the magnificence that is going to be uncovered in us.
19 The eager expectation of creation patiently waits for the uncovering of God's sons.
20 Creation was placed under uselessness, not voluntarily, but because of the One who placed it under it. He did this based on anticipation
21 because even the creation itself will be set free out of deterioration's slavery into the freedom of the magnificence of God's children.
22 You see, we realize that the entire creation groans together and together is in labor till the present.
23 Not only that, but we ourselves who have the first-part-offering of the Spirit, even we ourselves also groan within ourselves patiently waiting for an adoption, the paid release of our body.
24 You see, we were rescued with the anticipation *of good*, but anticipation that is seen is not anticipation. Does someone anticipate what he sees?
25 But if we anticipate what we don't see, we patiently wait with persistence.
26 Similarly, the Spirit also gets together with our weakness and assists it. You see, we don't realize what we should pray, we don't know what is aligned with what is necessary, but the Spirit itself intervenes on our behalf with unspeakable groans.

27 God, the One who examines the hearts, has seen what the Spirit's focus is because the Spirit intervenes aligned with God on behalf of sacred people.

28 We realize that all things work together for good to the people who love God, to the people who are invited aligned with a plan.

29 *The plan is* that the people He knew beforehand *(in that He knew they would be sinners)*, He also designated beforehand to be formed together into the image of His Son. That way His Son would be the firstborn among many brothers.

30 The people that He designated beforehand, these He also invited, and the people that He invited, these He also made right. The people that He made right, these He also elevated to a place of magnificence.

31 So what will we state *as we think* about these things? If God does these things on our behalf, who is against us?

32 He definitely didn't go easy on His own Son. He gave Him up on behalf of us all. How will He not also together with Him as an act of generosity give us everything?

33 Who will bring a charge against the people who choose God? God is the One making them right.

34 Who is the one finding them guilty? The Anointed King Jesus is the One who died, but more than that, who was gotten up, who also is at God's right side, and who also intervenes on our behalf.

35 Who will separate us away from the Anointed King's love? Will hard times, or difficulty, or persecution, or famine, or nakedness, or danger, or a dagger?

36 *We have suffered these things, but we still have the Anointed King's love. Our situation is* just as the Bible says, "On account of You, we are being put to death the whole day. We are considered as sheep that need to be slaughtered" *(Psalm 44:23)*.

37 But in all these things, we are more than conquerors through the One who loved us.

38 You see, I have been confident that *nothing*, not death, or life, or angels, or head rulers, or things that have stood here, or things that are going to be, or abilities,

39 or anything that is high, or anything that is deep, or any other created being will be able to separate us away from God's love in the Anointed King Jesus, our Master.

9

1 I am telling the truth in the Anointed King. I am not lying. My conscience concurs with me in the Sacred Spirit

2 that I have great sadness and a constant agony in my heart.
3 You see, I myself was wishing that I could be doomed away from the Anointed King in place of my brothers, my relatives as far as the physical body is concerned.
4 They are the ones who are Israelis. They have the adoption, the magnificence, the deals, the making of the law, the sacrifice ritual, and the promises.
5 The fathers are theirs. The Anointed King is from them as far as the physical body is concerned. The God that is over all things is theirs. He has blessings conferred on Him for the spans of time. Amen.
6 *Despite this, they are dooming themselves away from the Anointed King.* It is not such that God's message has failed. You see, Israel is not all these people from Israel.
7 And Abraham's seed is not all his children either. *Abraham had two sons: Isaac from his wife and Ishmael from his wife's maid.* But God told him, "You will call the descendants of Isaac your seed."
8 That is, these children of the physical body are not God's children. No, the children of the promise are considered to be the seed.
9 You see, this message is a message of promise: "At this time *next year*, I will come, and Sarah will have a son" *(Genesis 18:14)*.
10 Not only that, but Rebecca also *received a promise, and unlike Abraham, she* had only been in bed with one person, Isaac, our father.
11 (You see, *this promise was given when the children* were not yet born, when they had not repeatedly done anything good or useless. That way God's plan when it comes to selection may remain as not coming from actions that someone does, but from the One who does the inviting.)
12 It was stated to Rebecca, "*Two nations are in your womb. Two ethnic groups will be divided from your belly. One ethic group will have a higher position than the other.* And the greater *group* will be a slave to the lesser *group*" *(Genesis 25:23)*.
13 It is just as the Bible says, "I loved Jacob, but I hated Esau" *(Malachi 1:2, 3)*. God selected one grandchild of Abraham over the other to be the seed.
14 So what will we state? There isn't something wrong with what God did, is there?
15 You see, He tells Moses, "I will show forgiving kindness to whoever I show forgiving kindness to, and I will have compassion on whoever I have compassion on" *(Exodus 33:19)*.
16 So clearly *forgiving kindness* is not *a possession* of the one who wants it, and *it is not a possession* of the one who runs either. No, *it is a possession* of the One who shows forgiving kindness, God.

17 You see, the *Old Testament* writing says to Pharaoh, "I got you up out *there* for this very reason, in order that I might display My ability in you and in order that My name might be announced everywhere in all the earth" *(Exodus 9:16)*.
18 So clearly He shows forgiving kindness to who He wants to, and He hardens who He wants to.
19 So you will state to me, "So why does He still find fault? You see, has anyone been able to stand in opposition to what He intended to do?"
20 No, of course not, but who are you, O person, the one responding in opposition to God? Will the sculpture state to the one sculpting it, "Why did you make me like this?"
21 Or doesn't the clay worker have authority over the mud to make from the same batch a container that is valuable and one that is worthless?
22 What if God wanted to display His punishment and make known what He is capable *of doing?* And what if with much patience, He put up with containers of punishment that have been developed for ruin,
23 even so that He might make known the wealth of His magnificence on containers that He forgives, is kind to, and already prepared for magnificence?
24 And what if He also invited them, as He invited us, not only from among Jewish people, but also from among non-Jews?
25 This is what He also says in Hosea, "I will invite the child named 'Not My Ethnic Group' to be My ethnic group, and the child named 'Woman Who Hasn't Been Loved' to be a woman who has been loved" *(Hosea 2:23)*.
26 And, "It will be in the place where it was stated to them, 'You are "Not My Ethnic Group"' that there they will be invited to be sons of the living God" *(Hosea 1:10)*.
27 Isaiah cries out over Israel, "Though the number of Israel's sons is like the sand of the sea, only the part left over will be rescued" *(Isaiah 10:22)*.
28 You see, the Master will do a matter on the earth. He will completely finish it and completely cut it off.
29 And it will be just as Isaiah had stated before, "If the Master of Sabaoth *(Hebrew for army, the name of God's army)* didn't leave a seed down among us, we would have become as Sodom, and we would be like Gomorrah" *(Isaiah 1:9)*.
30 So what will we state? The non-Jews not pursuing the right way have completely gotten the right way, the right way from trust,

31 but Israel pursuing the law of the right way didn't already come into the law.

32 Why? Because they did not pursue it from trust, but they pursued it as if they could get it from their actions. They tripped on the stone of the trip hazard.

33 It is just as the Bible says, "Look, I place a stone of a trip hazard and rock of an obstacle in Zion. And the person trusting in it will not be shamed."

10

1 Brothers, certainly the good notion of my heart and my plea to God for them is that they would be rescued.

2 You see, I am a witness for them that they have a passion for God, but their passion is not aligned with a correct understanding.

3 They are unaware of God's right way. They are looking to establish their own right way. And so they haven't placed themselves under God's right way.

4 You see, the Anointed King is the conclusion of the law. He is the right way for everyone who trusts.

5 Moses writes about the right way from the law, "The person doing these things will live in them" *(Leviticus 18:5)*. *The right way from the law requires a person not just to do the demands of the law but to also live in them.*

6 But the right way from trust talks like this: "Don't say in your heart, 'Who will climb up into heaven?' (that is, to bring the Anointed King down),

7 or 'Who will climb down into the bottomless area?' (that is, to bring the Anointed King up from the dead)." *The right way from trust does not require a person to go to great heights (as high as heaven) to find it or to do great things (like bringing someone back from the dead) to earn it.*

8 But what does it say? "The statement is near you, in your mouth and in your heart." *What statement is near you? What statement is in your mouth and in your heart?* The statement of the trust that we speak about publicly.

9 If in your mouth you acknowledge Master Jesus and in your heart you trust that God got Him up from the dead, you will be rescued.

10 You see, with your heart, you trust Him for the right way. With your mouth, you acknowledge Him for rescue.

11 What the *Old Testament* writing says is for everyone: "The person who trusts in Him won't be shamed" *(Isaiah 28:16)*.

12 There is no difference between Jewish and Greek. The same Master is Master of everyone. He is wealthy to everyone who calls on Him.
13 "Everyone, whoever calls on the name of the Master will be rescued" *(Joel 2:32).*
14 So how do they call on a person that they don't trust? How would they trust a person that they haven't heard? How would they hear without anyone speaking publicly?
15 How would they speak publicly, if they weren't sent out? *It is a good thing to send people out to speak publicly just as the Bible says,* "How beautiful are the feet of the people sharing the good news of the good things" *(Isaiah 52:7).*
16 But not everyone obeys the good news. You see, Isaiah says, "Master, who trusted what was heard from us?" *(Isaiah 53:1).*
17 Clearly the trust is from what has been heard, but the thing that has been heard is through a statement of the Anointed King.
18 *You may say that Israel did not hear.* But I say, "Could it be that they didn't hear?" No, of course not. "Their sound went out into all the earth and their statements to the ends of the civilized world" *(Psalm 19:4).*
19 *And you may say that Israel did not know.* But I say, "Could it be that Israel didn't know?" First, *at the end of their law,* Moses *lays it all out to them and warns them. As part of the warning, he* says, "I will make you jealous over a nation that is not a nation. I will incite rage in you over a clueless nation" *(Deuteronomy 32:21).*
20 Then Isaiah dares to come out and say, "I was found among the people who were not looking for me. I became explicitly shown to the people who were not asking about me" *(Isaiah 65:1).*
21 *And in the next sentence,* he says to Israel, "All day long I extended my hands to an ethnic group that doesn't believe Me and that says things against Me" *(Isaiah 65:2).*

11

1 So I say, "God didn't push His ethnic group away, did He?" No, it could not happen. You see, I am also an Israeli from Abraham's seed of Benjamin's family line. *God didn't push me away.*
2 And He didn't push His ethnic group away either. He knew beforehand *what they would do. He was prepared for it.* Or don't you know what the *Old Testament* writing says in *the story about* Elijah? It is as if Elijah is intervening to God against Israel.
3 "Master, they killed your preachers. They dug up your altars and removed them. I am the only one left after *that,* and they are looking for my soul *so they can kill me*" *(1 Kings 19:10, 14).*

4 But what does the divine voice say to him? "I left seven thousand men behind for Myself. None of them have bent a knee down to Baal" *(1 Kings 19:18)*.
5 So this is how it also is now in the present time. A remaining few have become aligned with a selection of generosity.
6 If it is a selection of generosity, it is no longer from the actions a person does, or else the generosity becomes something that is no longer generosity.
7 So what happened? Israel hasn't obtain this thing that it is searching for, but the selection has. The rest have become hard as stone.
8 It is just as the Bible says, "God gave them a spirit of numbness, eyes that don't see" *(Isaiah 29:10)*, and ears that don't hear until this day today.
9 And David says, "Their table must become a trap for them, something that hunts them down, an obstacle, and a repayment to them.
10 Their eyes must be made dark so that they don't see. And through the whole ordeal, bend their back completely over with heavy loads" *(Psalm 69:22-23)*.
11 So I say, "Their slip won't cause them to fall, will it?" It could not happen. No, their infraction has brought the rescue to the non-Jews so that the Jewish people will become jealous.
12 If their infraction is the wealth of the world and their worsening is the wealth of the non-Jews, how much more would their fullness be?
13 I am talking to you non-Jews. So as much as I certainly am a missionary to non-Jews, I elevate the serving that I do to a place of magnificence.
14 *In doing so, I hope to* somehow make my physical kin jealous and rescue some from among them.
15 You see, if their casualty is the world's restored relationship, what will their readmission be if not life from the dead?
16 If the first part *of the batch that is given as an* offering to God is sacred, the *rest of the* batch also is. And if the root is sacred, the branches also are.
17 If some of the branches were split off, but you, being a wild olive tree, were grafted in among them and became a branch that shares the root and the fatness of the olive tree together with them,
18 don't brag about how much better you are than the natural branches. Even if you brag, you don't haul the root, the root hauls you.

19 So you will state, "Branches were split off so that I might be grafted in."
20 That was nice for you. They were split off because they did not trust, but you have stood because you trust. Don't be focused on high things, but be cautious.
21 You see, if God didn't go easy on the branches that are the natural branches, He won't somehow go easy on you either.
22 So look at God's kindness and fierceness. Not only is God fierce to the people who fell, but also God is kind to you if you stay over in His kindness. If not, you also will be chopped out.
23 If those branches don't stay over in their refusal to trust, they also will be grafted in. You see, God is able to graft them in again.
24 If you were chopped out of the wild olive tree that you were the natural *branches of and* contrary to nature, you were grafted into a cultivated olive tree, how much more will these, the natural *branches*, be grafted into their own olive tree?
25 I don't want you to be unaware, brothers, of this secret so that you won't be focused on yourselves. *This secret is* that a part of Israel has become stone hard til the fullness of the non-Jews comes in.
26 This is how all of Israel will be rescued. It is just what the Bible says, "The One who saves will arrive from Zion. He will turn godlessness away from Jacob.
27 This is also the deal with them that came directly from Me" *(Isaiah 59:20,21)*. "It is about a time when I will take away their sins" <I(Jeremiah 31:33,34). *(Both of these passages show that Israel will be brought back to God.)*
28 When it comes to the good news, they certainly are enemies because of you. But when it comes to the selection, they are loved because of the Father.
29 You see, God's gifts and invitation are things *the Father will* not regret.
30 It is just as when you didn't believe in God in the past, but now you have received forgiving kindness with these people's unbelief.
31 In the same way, these people don't believe now so that with your forgiving kindness they also might receive forgiving kindness.
32 You see, God closed everyone up into unbelief so that He might show forgiving kindness to everyone.
33 O the depth of God's wealth, insight, and knowledge! His judgments are so impossible to explore! His ways are so impossible to track!
34 You see, "Who knew the Master's way of thinking?" *(Isaiah 40:13)* or "Who became His counselor?" *(Isaiah 40:13)*

35 or "Who will He have to pay back because they gave to Him before *He gave to them?*" *(Job 41:11)*

36 All things are from Him, through Him, and for Him. He has the magnificence for the spans of time. Amen.

12

1 So through God's compassion, brothers, I encourage you to offer your bodies as a sacrifice that is living, sacred, well-liked by God, and your logical sacrifice ritual.

2 And don't be conformed to this span of time, but be transformed by renewing your way of thinking. That way you can prove what is the good, well-liked, and complete thing that God wants.

3 You see, through the generosity given to me, I say to everyone who is among you, "Do not focus above and beyond what is necessary to be focusing on. Focus on what is the proper focus for each person since God has allocated an amount of trust to each one.

4 This is exactly how *it is with our body.* In one body, we have many body parts, but all the body parts don't perform the same repetitive action.

5 In the same way, we, the many, are one body in the Anointed King, but the body is given to each one of us as body parts.

6 We each have specialized gifts according to the generosity given to us. If *someone's gift is* preaching, it is aligned with the portion of the trust *given to that person.*

7 If *someone's gift is* serving, it is in the serving *given to that person.* If the person is teaching, it is in the instruction *given to him.*

8 If the person is encouraging, it is in the encouragement *given to him.* The person giving *things* out *should do so* with dedication. The person presiding *over a group should do so* with care *for the people in that group.* The person showing forgiving kindness *should do so* in the providing of a remedy.

9 Love should not be faked. *As you love,* detest the evil thing, stick like glue to the good.

10 *As you love, when it comes* to brotherly kindness, treat each other like family and friends; *when it comes* to value, lead the way in front of each other;

11 *when it comes* to the care *of someone,* don't be lazy; *when it comes* to the Spirit, be passionate; *when it comes* to the Master, be a slave;

12 *when it comes* to the anticipation of good, be happy; *when it comes* to hard times, persist to do what is right; *when it comes* to prayer, stay close by;

13 *when it comes* to the needs of the sacred people, share with them, pursue being nice to strangers.
14 Confer blessings on the people pursuing *and persecuting* you. Confer a blessing on them. Don't hope that something bad will happen to them.
15 To be happy with the people who are happy and to cry with the people who are crying,
16 don't become the type of people who are focused on themselves. Focus on the same type of things for each other. Don't focus on the high things. But together let the lowly things lead you away *to do what is right.*
17 *If anyone does something bad to you,* don't give something bad back. Think of nice things *to do and do them* in the sight of all people.
18 If it is possible from you, be peaceful with all people.
19 Don't retaliate for yourselves, loved ones. Instead make room for God's punishment. You see, the Bible says, "'Retaliation is for Me. I will repay,' says the Master" *(Deuteronomy 32:35).*
20 But if your enemy is hungry, give him food. If he is thirsty, give him a drink. You see, as you do this, you will pile coals of fire on his head.
21 Don't be conquered by the bad, but conquer the bad in the good.

13

1 Every soul must place itself under the authorities that have a higher position. You see, no authority exists if it is not under God. The existing authorities exist having been arranged under God.
2 So then the person who places himself in opposition to the authority has stood in opposition to God's arrangement. The people who have stood in opposition will receive a judgment against themselves.
3 You see, the head people are not a threat to the good action, but to the bad. Do you want it so that you are not afraid of the person in authority? Do good, and you will have high praise from him.
4 He is God's servant to you. He is for good. But if you do something bad, be afraid. You see, he doesn't wear a dagger for no reason. He is God's servant. He retaliates against the person who repeatedly does what is bad by punishing him.
5 This is why you are obligated to place yourself under him, not only because of the punishment, but also because of the conscience.
6 You see, you also pay taxes because of the conscience. They are God's public servants staying close by for this very thing.

7 Give back the amounts owed to everyone: taxes to the *one you owe* taxes to, the fee to the *one you owe* the fee to, fear to the *one you owe* fear to, value to the *one you owe* value to.

8 Don't owe anyone anything except to be loving each other. You see, the one who loves the other person has accomplished what the law says to do.

9 The demands ("You will not cheat on your spouse, you will not murder, you will not steal, you will not be envious," and if there is any other demand) are summed up in this saying, "You will love the person near you as yourself."

10 Love does not work on anything bad to the person near you. So love is the fullness of the law.

11 And this is important when you realize the time. It is already the hour for you to get up from sleeping. You see, our rescue is closer now than when we trusted.

12 The night chopped a path forward. The day has come near. So let's put away the actions of darkness. Let's put on the weapons of the light.

13 Let's walk around reputably as people do during the day: not in wild parties and bouts of drunkenness, not in beds and indulgent activities, not in fights and hostile passion.

14 But put on the Master Jesus, the Anointed King, and don't make preparations for the physical body, for its desires.

14

1 Take a person in who is weak in trust without pondering the things you think are wrong with him.

2 There certainly is a person who trusts to eat all kinds of food, but the person who is weak eats vegetables.

3 The person who eats must not treat the person who doesn't eat as a nobody. The person who doesn't eat must not judge the person who does. You see, God has taken him in.

4 Who are you to judge someone else's domestic servant? He stands or falls for his own master, *not for you. His own master* will get him to stand *when he wants him to*. You see, the Master has the ability to get him to stand.

5 There certainly is a person who decides that one day *is more sacred* than another, but there also is a person who decides that every day *is the same*. Each one must be well-established in his own way of thinking.

6 The person who focuses on a *certain* day, focuses on it for the Master. And the person who eats, eats for the Master (you see, he thanks God

for his food). And the person who doesn't eat, it is for the Master that he doesn't eat (he also thanks God).

7 You see, not one of us lives by himself, and not one dies by himself.

8 If we live, we live with the Master, and if we die, we also die with the Master. So both if we live and if we die, we are the Master's.

9 The Anointed King died and lived for this very reason, so that He might be the Master of both dead people and people living.

10 Why do you judge your brother? Or also, why do you treat your brother as a nobody? You see, we will all stand up next to God's judicial bench.

11 The Bible says, "'*As sure as* I am living,' says the Master, 'every knee will bend down before Me, and every tongue will acknowledge God out loud'" *(Isaiah 45:23)*.

12 So clearly each one of us will give an answer concerning himself to God.

13 So we shouldn't judge each other anymore. But judge this instead, if what you do will place a trip hazard or an obstacle in the brother's way.

14 I have seen and have been confident in Master Jesus that nothing by itself is a thing that contaminates *someone's sacredness* except for the person who considers it to be something that contaminates. For that person it is something that contaminates.

15 You see, if *you know* your food makes your brother sad *and you eat it anyway*, you no longer walk around aligned with love. Don't ruin that brother with your food. That *brother is someone* the Anointed King died for.

16 So your good must not be an insult to him.

17 You see, God's monarchy isn't a dinner and drink. No, God's monarchy is the right way, peace, and happiness in the Sacred Spirit.

18 The person who is a slave to the Anointed King in these things is well-liked by God and the people approve of him.

19 So clearly we should pursue the things that are peaceful and the things that build each other.

20 Don't tear down God's work for the sake of food. All things certainly are clean, but it is bad if a person trips as he eats.

21 It is nice of you not to eat meat, drink wine, or do anything else that your brother trips on.

22 The trust that you have, you must have it by yourself in God's sight. If a person doesn't judge himself in what he approves, he is blessed.

23 If a person eats a certain thing that he has determined is wrong to eat, he is guilty because it is not from trust. Everything that is not from trust is sin.

15

1 We (the ones who are able) are obligated to be hauling the frailties of the ones who are not able and not to be doing what we ourselves would like.

2 Each of us must do what the person near us would like. *We must do it* for his good, to build him.

3 You see, even the Anointed King didn't do what He Himself would have liked, but just as the Bible says, "The criticisms of the people criticizing You *(God)* fell on Me *(the Anointed King)*" *(Psalms 69:9)*.

4 You see, as much as was previously written in the *Old Testament* writings was written for our instruction so that through them, through the persistence and encouragement in them, we may anticipate the good that will come.

5 May the God of persistence and encouragement give you the ability to be focusing on the same thing among each other aligned with the Anointed King Jesus.

6 That way you all unanimously with one mouth may praise the magnificence of the God and Father of our Master Jesus (the Anointed King).

7 For this reason, take each other in, just as the Anointed King also took you in for God's magnificence.

8 You see, I am saying that the Anointed King has become a servant of circumcision on behalf of God's truth to authenticate the promises of the fathers,

9 but *also to authenticate* the non-Jews on behalf of forgiving kindness to elevate God to a place of magnificence. This is just like what the Bible says, "Because of this, I will acknowledge You out loud among non-Jews and recite psalms to Your name" *(Psalm 18:49)*.

10 And again it says, "Non-Jews, celebrate with His ethnic group" *(Deuteronomy 32:43)*.

11 And again, "Praise the Master, all the non-Jews, and applaud Him, all the ethnic groups" *(Psalm 117:1)*.

12 And again Isaiah says, "He will be the root of Jesse and the One standing up to be heading non-Jews. Based on Him, non-Jews will anticipate good" *(Isaiah 11:10)*.

13 May the God of anticipation fill you with all happiness and peace during the time that you are trusting so that you may overflow with anticipation in the ability of the Sacred Spirit.

14 I, even I myself, have been confident concerning you, my brothers, that you yourselves are also full of goodness, that you have been filled up with all the information, and that you even are able to caution each other.

15 I wrote more daringly to you partly as a way of prompting you because of the generosity given to me by God.

16 *The generosity that God gave* me is to be the Anointed King Jesus' public servant for the non-Jews. I am a temple worker for God's good news so that the offering, the non-Jews, might become something that is well-received and has been made sacred in the Sacred Spirit.

17 So I have something to brag about when it comes to God's things in the Anointed King Jesus.

18 You see, I will not dare to speak about any of the things that the Anointed King didn't work on and complete through me. Through me, the Anointed King brought about the non-Jews' obedience in message and action.

19 He used the ability of proofs and incredible things and the ability of God's Spirit. In this way, I have filled up the areas from Jerusalem and circling up to Illyricum *(a region east of Italy)* with the Anointed King's good news.

20 But since I think it is important to share the good news where the Anointed King's name has not been mentioned, I only went to areas that hadn't heard. That way I would not build on someone else's foundation.

21 But this is just like what the Bible says, "People who haven't received the announcements about Him will see, and the people who haven't heard will understand" *(Isaiah 52:15)*.

22 For this reason, many things were also interrupting me from coming to see you.

23 But right now, I have no more place to go in these slopes and I have had an intense yearning to come to you for many years.

24 You see, whenever I travel to Spain, I am anticipating as I travel through there to see you and to be brought on my way through there by you if first, during part of that time, I might be filled up by you.

25 But right now I am traveling to Jerusalem to serve the sacred people there.

26 You see, it seemed like a good idea to Macedonia and Achaia *(regions in Greece)* to do a certain amount of sharing with the sacred people in Jerusalem that are poor.

27 You see, it seemed like a good idea to them, and rightly so, because they are indebted to them. If the sacred people in Jerusalem shared

their spiritual things with them, the non-Jews also are obligated to minister to them in the physical things.

28 So after I have finished this up and put a seal on this fruit to them, I will go off through you into Spain.

29 I realize that as I come to you, I will come full of the Anointed King's conferring of blessings.

30 I encourage you, brothers, through our Master Jesus, the Anointed King, and through the Spirit's love, to struggle together with me in the prayers on my behalf to God

31 that I might be saved from the people who don't believe in Judea and that my serving *of this money* in Jerusalem might become well-received by the sacred people.

32 That way when I come to you happy and doing what God wants, I might relax together with you.

33 May the God of peace be with you all. Amen.

16

1 I endorse Phoebe to you. She is our sister and a servant of the assembly in Cenchrea *(an eastern harbor of Corinth)*.

2 Warmly accept her in the Master in a manner deserving of the sacred people and stand by her in whatever item she may need from you. You see, she also became a sponsor of many and of myself.

3 Say hello to Prisca *(the formal name of Priscilla)* and Aquila, my co-workers in the Anointed King Jesus.

4 They have risked their own neck on behalf of my soul. Not only do I thank them, but also all the assemblies of the non-Jews thank them.

5 And say hello to the assembly throughout their house, to Epenetus, my loved one. He is the first-part-offering of Western Turkey for the Anointed King *(or in other words, the first one in Western Turkey to offer himself as an offering to the Anointed King)*.

6 Say hello to Mary, someone who labored in many ways for us.

7 Say hello to Andronicus and Junias, my relatives and people incarcerated together with me. They are well-known among the missionaries. They also came to be in the Anointed King before me.

8 Say hello to Amplias, my loved one in the Master.

9 Say hello to Urbanus, our co-worker in the Anointed King, and Stachys, my loved one.

10 Say hello to Apelles, the approved one in the Anointed King. Say hello to the people from Aristobulus.

11 Say hello to Herodion, my relative. Say hello to the people from Narcissus who are in the Master.

12 Say hello to Tryphena and Tryphosa, the women laboring in the Master. Say hello to Persis, the loved one. He labored in many ways for the Master.
13 Say hello to Rufus, the select one in the Master, and his mother and mine.
14 Say hello to Asyncritus, Phlegon, Hermes, Patrobas, Hermas, and the brothers together with them.
15 Say hello to Philologus and Julia, Nereus and his sister, Olympas, and all the sacred people together with them.
16 Say hello to each other with a sacred friendly gesture. All the assemblies of the Anointed King say hello to you.
17 I encourage you, brothers, to be keeping an eye out for the people who cause the factions and the obstacles contrary to the teaching that you learned. Slide away from them.
18 You see, these types of people are not slaves of our Master, the Anointed King. No, *they are slaves* of their own belly. Through their kind message and conferring of blessings, they completely fool the hearts of the people who are not bad.
19 You see, your obedience was spread to everyone, so I am happy about you. I want you to be insightful people in the good thing, but unpolluted by the bad thing.
20 The God of peace will crush the Opponent under your feet quickly. The generosity of our Master Jesus is with you.
21 Timothy (my co-worker) says hello to you, also Lucius, Jason, and Sosipater (my relatives).
22 I, Tertius, say hello to you. I am the one in the Master who wrote this letter *as Paul dictated it.*
23 Gaius (the host of me and the whole assembly) says hello to you. Erastus (the manager of the city) says hello to you, also Quartus (the brother).
24 [[[The generosity of our Master Jesus, the Anointed King, is with you all. Amen.]]]
25 [To the One who is able to establish you aligned with my good news and the public speeches of Jesus, the Anointed King, aligned with the uncovering of a secret that has been kept quiet to times that span all time,
26 yet is also now shown through the writings of the preachers, aligned with a directive for the obedience of trust, a directive of the God that spans all time, a directive that is made known to all the non-Jews;

27 to the only insightful God through Jesus, the Anointed King, *belongs* magnificence for the spans of time. Amen.]

First Corinthians

1

1 From: Paul (who was invited to be a missionary of the Anointed King Jesus because that's what God wanted) and Sosthenese (the brother).

2 To: God's assembly that is in Corinth *(a city in southern Greece)*, the people who have been made sacred in the Anointed King Jesus, the invited sacred people together with all the people in every place (theirs and ours) who call on the name of our Master Jesus, the Anointed King.

3 Generosity and peace to you out from God, our Father, and Master Jesus, the Anointed King.

4 I always thank my God about you based on God's generosity that was given to you in the Anointed King Jesus.

5 You became wealthy in Him in everything, in every message and all the information.

6 Even what the Anointed King witnessed was generously authenticated among you

7 in such a way for you not to be lacking in any gift, patiently waiting for the uncovering of our Master Jesus, the Anointed King.

8 He will also authenticate you until the conclusion. *You will be* people with no charges against you in the day of our Master Jesus, the Anointed King.

9 God can be trusted. Through Him, you were invited into the sharing of His Son Jesus, the Anointed King, our Master.

10 I encourage you, brothers, through the name of our Master Jesus, the Anointed King, that you should all say the same thing and that there shouldn't be rifts among you. You should be developed in the same way of thinking and in the same opinion.

11 You see, the people of Chloe made it obvious to me that there are fights among you, my brothers.

12 This is what I am saying. Each of you *chooses a side*. Some say, "I am on Paul's side;" others, "I am on Apollos' side;" others, "I am on the side of Cephas *(Aramaic for Peter)*;" still others, "I am on the Anointed King's side."

13 Has the Anointed King been divided? Paul wasn't nailed to a cross on your behalf, was he? Or were you submerged in the name of Paul?

14 I thank God that I submerged none of you except Crispus and Gaius.

15 That way no one will say that you were submerged in my name.

16 I also submerged the people living in Stephanas' house. Besides these, I don't think that I submerged anyone else.

17 You see, the Anointed King didn't send me out on a mission to submerge. No, He sent me out to share good news without an insightful message so that the Anointed King's cross might not be meaningless.

18 You see, the message of the cross certainly is foolishness to ruined people, but to us rescued people, it is God's ability.

19 The Bible says, "I will ruin the insight of the insightful people and invalidate the understanding of the understanding people" *(Isaiah 29:14)*.

20 Where is a scholar? Where is an Old Testament transcriber? Where is a philosopher of this span of time? Didn't God make the world's insight foolish?

21 You see, since, for sure, in God's insight, the world through its insight didn't know God, it seemed like a good idea to God to rescue the people who trust through the foolishness of public speaking.

22 Since, for sure, Jewish people actually ask for proofs *of God's ability* and Greeks look for insight,

23 we speak publicly about the Anointed King who has been nailed to a cross--not only an obstacle to Jewish people, but also foolishness to non-Jews.

24 But to the invited people (both Jewish and Greeks), to them, the Anointed King is God's ability and God's insight

25 because the foolishness of God is more insightful than *the insight of* people and the weakness of God is stronger than *the strength of* people.

26 You see, look at your invitation, brothers, because as far as the physical body is concerned, there aren't many insightful people, not many competent, and not many who are from a high-ranking family line.

27 But God selected the foolish things of the world so that He may shame the insightful people. And God selected the weak things of the world so that He may shame the strong things.

28 And God selected the things of the world that don't have a family, the things that have been treated as if they are nothing, and the things that don't exist, so that He might make the things that do exist useless.

29 That way every physical body will have nothing to brag about in God's sight.

30 It is from God that you all are in the Anointed King Jesus. He became insight from God to us and He also became the right way, sacredness, and the paid release for us.
31 That way just as the Bible says, "The person who brags must brag about the Master" *(Jeremiah 9:24-25)*.

2

1 And when I came to you, brothers, I didn't come aligned with the higher position that a message and insight have as I proclaimed God's secret to you.
2 You see, I decided that among you I would be as if I had seen nothing except Jesus, the Anointed King, and *the fact* that this Anointed King had been nailed to a cross.
3 And I became in a state of weakness, fear, and much trembling facing you.
4 My message and my public speaking were not in persuasive messages of insight, but in a show of the Spirit and ability
5 so that your trust wouldn't be in people's insight, but in God's ability.
6 We speak about insight among the people who are mature, but not the insight of this span of time or of the head people of this span of time. The head people are being rendered useless.
7 But we speak about God's insight in a secret that has been hidden away that God designated beforehand (before the spans of time) for our magnificence.
8 It is a secret that none of the head people of this span of time have known. You see, if they had known it, they wouldn't have nailed the Master of magnificence to a cross.
9 But just as the Bible says, "God has things ready for the people who love Him, things that an eye hasn't seen and an ear hasn't heard" *(Isaiah 64:4)*, and things that haven't stepped up in a person's heart.
10 God uncovered them to us through the Spirit. You see, the Spirit examines everything, even the depths of God.
11 You see, of *all* the people *in the world*, who has seen the things of the person if it isn't the person's spirit, the spirit in him? In this same way also, no one has known the things about God except God's Spirit.
12 It wasn't the spirit of the world that we received. No, it was the Spirit that is from God so that we can see the things that God gave us as an act of generosity.
13 We also don't speak about these things in messages that human insight taught us. No, *we speak* in messages that the Spirit taught us, comparing spiritual things with spiritual things.

14 A person focused on the psychological world doesn't accept the things of God's Spirit. You see, God's Spirit is foolishness to him. He isn't able to know the Spirit because the Spirit is investigated spiritually.
15 The person focused on the spiritual world investigates everything, but he himself is investigated by no one.
16 You see, who knew the Master's way of thinking? Who will pull Him together? *No one.* But we have the Anointed King's way of thinking.

3

1 And I, brothers, couldn't speak to you as I do to *people focused on the* spiritual *world*, but I spoke to you as I do to *people focused on the* physical *world*, as I do to infants in the Anointed King.
2 I gave you milk to drink, not food. You see, you couldn't eat food yet, but you still can't eat food now either.
3 You are still *focused on the* physical *world*. You see, where there is hostile passion and fighting among you, are you not *focused on the* physical *world?* Are you not walking around aligned with a human, not with God?
4 You see, when someone says, "I certainly am on Paul's side," but a different person, "I am on Apollos' side," what are you? Aren't you humans?
5 So what is Apollos? What is Paul? Servants. Through them, you trusted. Each has what the Master gave them.
6 I planted. Apollos watered. But God was growing it.
7 So then the one planting isn't anything, and the one watering isn't anything either, but *the one who is something is* the One growing it, God.
8 The person planting and the person watering are one. Each will receive his own pay according to his own labor.
9 You see, we are God's co-workers. You are God's farmland, God's building.
10 God's generosity gave me *the position and ability of an insightful general contractor.* As an insightful general contractor, I laid a foundation, but another contractor is building on it. Each person must watch how he builds on it.
11 You see, no one is able to lay another foundation contrary to the one lying there: Jesus, the Anointed King.
12 If someone builds gold, silver, valuable stones, wood, grass, and straw on the foundation,

13 each person's work will end up being shown. You see, the Day will make it obvious because fire uncovers it and the fire itself will prove what kind each person's work is.
14 If someone's work (what he built on the foundation) remains, he will receive pay.
15 If someone's work will be burned up, he will sustain loss. He himself will be rescued, but this is what it will be like: as if *he had gone* through a fire *and lost everything*.
16 Don't you realize that you all are God's temple and God's Spirit has a house in you?
17 If anyone worsens God's temple, God will worsen this person. You see, God's temple is sacred. This is what you are.
18 No one must completely fool himself. If anyone among you seems to be insightful in this span of time, he must become foolish so that he might become insightful.
19 You see, the insight of this world is foolishness beside God. The Bible says, "He is the One catching the insightful people in their slyness" *(Job 5:13)*,
20 and again, "The Master knows the ponderings of insightful people. He knows that their ponderings are futile" *(Psalm 94:11)*.
21 So then no one must brag about humans. You see, all things are on your side.
22 Whether Paul, or Apollos, or Cephas *(Aramaic for Peter)*, or the world, or life, or death, or things that have stood here, or things that are going to be, all are on your side.
23 You are on the Anointed King's side. The Anointed King is on God's side.

4

1 This is what a person must consider us to be: the Anointed King's underlings and managers of God's secrets.
2 Not only that, but *a quality* here that people look for among managers is that someone would be found who can be trusted.
3 It is the smallest thing to me that I might be investigated by you or by a human day *of judgment*. But I don't even investigate myself.
4 You see, I haven't been aware of anything *wrong that I have done*, but this hasn't made me right. The One who investigates me is the Master.
5 So then, until the Master comes, don't judge anything before the appointed time. He is also the One who will light up the hidden things

of the darkness and show the intentions of the hearts. And then, the high praise will come out from God to each person.

6 But I refashioned these things, brothers, into myself and Apollos because of you, so that you might learn that even with us *you should not elevate anyone* above what the Bible says *about people*. That way no one may be conceited when he is on one person's side and against the other.

7 You see, who considers that you might be wrong? What do you have that you didn't receive? If you also received it, why do you brag as someone who didn't receive it?

8 Have you already been stuffed? Were you already wealthy? Were you kings without us? If only you definitely even were kings so that we also might be kings together with you.

9 You see, it seems to me that God showed us, the missionaries, off last as people doomed to death because we became a spectacle to the world, both to angels and to people.

10 We are foolish because of the Anointed King, but in the Anointed King you all are focused. We are weak, but you are strong. You are magnificent, but we are worthless.

11 Till the present hour, we also are hungry, thirsty, naked, slugged, and homeless.

12 And we labor working with our own hands. As we are put down, we confer blessings. As we are persecuted, we tolerate it.

13 As people talk about us harshly, we encourage. As the world's grime, we became what is scrapped off of everything until now.

14 I am not writing these things to embarrass you, but since you are my loved children, I am cautioning you.

15 You see, though you may have ten thousand babysitters in the Anointed King, still you do not have many fathers. In the Anointed King Jesus through the good news, I gave birth to you.

16 So I encourage you, become imitators of me.

17 Because of this, I sent Timothy to you. He is my loved and reliable child in the Master. He will remind you again of my ways in the Anointed King Jesus, just as I teach everywhere in every assembly.

18 Some were conceited as if I would not come to you.

19 But I will come to you soon, if the Master wants me to, and I will know, not the message, but the ability of the people who have been conceited.

20 You see, God's monarchy is not in a message, but in ability.

21 What do you want? Should I come to you with a staff or with love and a spirit of submissiveness?

First Corinthians 5

1 People everywhere hear about the sexual sin among you. It is a type of sexual sin that isn't even among the non-Jews: someone having sex with his father's wife.
2 And you have been conceited and didn't instead grieve hoping that the man who repeatedly did this action would be taken out of the middle of you.
3 You see, even though I am away from you in the body, I am beside you in the spirit. This is how I certainly have already judged the man who worked on and completed this, as if I were beside him.
4 In the name of our Master Jesus, when you and my spirit are gathered together with the ability of our Master Jesus,
5 I will turn this type of man over to the Opponent to destroy his physical body so that his spirit might be rescued in the day of the Master.
6 Your optimism isn't nice. Don't you realize that a little yeast causes the whole batch of dough to rise?
7 Clean out the former yeast so that you may be a fresh batch of dough, just as you are *supposed to be* yeast-free. You see, even our Passover, the Anointed King, was sacrificed. *The Passover starts the Yeast-free Festival when all yeast must be thrown out and all bread must be yeast-free.*
8 So then we may observe the festival, not with former yeast, not with yeast of badness and evilness, but with yeast-free bread of genuineness and truth.
9 I wrote you in the letter and told you not to be interacting with people who commit sexual sin.
10 *I didn't mean that you* shouldn't *interact* at all with the people of this world who commit sexual sin, or who desire more and are vicious, or who are idol worshipers, or else you clearly would have to go out of the world.
11 I write you now and tell you that if anyone who is named a brother commits sexual sin, or desires more, or is an idol worshiper, or puts others down, or is an alcoholic, or is a vicious person, don't be interacting with him or eating together with this type of person.
12 You see, what authority do I have to judge the people outside? Don't you judge the people inside?
13 God will judge the people outside. Take the evil person out from among yourselves.

6

1 Do any of you who have something against a different brother dare to be judged before the people who do what is wrong and not before the sacred people?

2 Or don't you realize that the sacred people will judge the world? And if the world is judged among you, are you undeserving of the smallest courts?

3 Don't you realize that we will judge angels? *We should* definitely *be able to judge* this life's things, shouldn't we?

4 So if you certainly have courts for this life's things, seat these people as judges: the people who have been treated as nobodies in the assembly.

5 Much to your embarrassment, I say it like this: Isn't there even one insightful person among you who will be able to consider what is wrong up in the middle of his brother?

6 But a brother takes a brother to court, and this is how, by appearing before people who don't trust *God*.

7 So it certainly already is a defeat to you entirely because you have judgments against yourselves. Why not instead be wronged? Why not instead be robbed?

8 But you wrong and rob even this: brothers.

9 Or don't you realize that people who do what is wrong won't inherit God's monarchy? Don't be misled. It is not people who commit sexual sin, or idol worshippers, or cheating spouses, or elegant people, or homosexuals,

10 or thieves, or people who desire more, not alcoholics, not people who put others down, and not vicious people who will inherit God's monarchy.

11 And some of you were these things, but you doused yourselves off, but you were made sacred, but you were made right in the name of the Master Jesus, the Anointed King, and in the Spirit of our God.

12 For me, everything is allowed, but not everything is advantageous. For me, everything is allowed, but I won't be controlled by anything.

13 The foods *that we eat are* for the belly, and the belly is for the food, but God will make both this *belly* and these *foods* useless. The body is not for sexual sin. It is for the Master, and the Master is for the body.

14 God got the Master up, and He will also get us up out of here through His ability.

15 Don't you realize that your bodies are body parts of the Anointed King? So will I take the Anointed King's body parts and make them body parts of a woman who commits sexual sin? It should not happen.

16 Or don't you realize that the person sticking like glue to the woman who commits sexual sin is one body? You see, "The two," He declares, "will be in one physical body."

17 The person sticking like glue to the Master is one spirit.
18 Escape the sexual sin. Every sin that a person might ever do is outside of the body, but the person who commits sexual sin sins into his own body.
19 Or don't you realize that your body is a temple of the Sacred Spirit in you? Don't you realize that you got your body from God and you are not your own?
20 You see, you were purchased with something of value, the Anointed King's blood. Elevate God to a place of magnificence, for sure, in your body.

7

1 *Now let me address the questions* that you wrote about. It is nice for a person not to be touching a woman.
2 Because of the sexual sins, each man must have his own woman and each woman must have her own man.
3 The husband must give out what he is supposed to to the wife, but likewise also the wife *must give out what she is supposed to* to the husband.
4 The wife doesn't have authority over her own body, the husband does. Likewise, the husband also doesn't have authority over his own body, the wife does.
5 Don't rob each other *by not allowing the other person to be with you* unless you both have harmoniously agreed to separate for prayer and you have set a time to come back together. That way you can separately hang out to pray and be back together again at the agreed upon time. *You should do it like this* so that the Opponent won't take advantage of your lack of restraint.
6 I am saying this as a suggestion, not as a directive.
7 I want everyone to also be as I myself am. But each person has his own gift from God: the one certainly like this, but the other like that.
8 I tell the unmarried people and the widows: "It is nice for them if they also stay as I am.
9 But if they are not restraining themselves, they must marry." You see, it is better to marry than to be inflamed *with lust*.
10 I have an order to pass on to you people who have married (it is not from me, but from the Master): A wife is not to be separated away from a husband
11 (if she actually is separated, she must stay separated, not marrying anyone else, or be restored to her husband), and a husband is not to leave a wife.

12 To the rest, I say (I, not the Master), "If any brother has a wife that doesn't trust *in the Master* and she agrees that it is good to have a house with him, he must not be leaving her.
13 And if any wife has a husband that doesn't trust *in the Master* and this husband agrees it is good to have a house with her, she must not be leaving the husband."
14 You see, the husband that doesn't trust has been made sacred in the wife, and the wife that doesn't trust has been made sacred in the brother, or else clearly your children are not clean. Now they are sacred.
15 If the spouse who doesn't trust separates, let them be separated. The brother or the sister hasn't been made a slave in these types of situations. God has invited you in peace.
16 You see, how do you know, wife, whether you will rescue your husband? Or how do you know, husband, whether you will rescue your wife?
17 If not, this is how each person must walk around: as the Master allocated to him, as God has invited him *(or in other words, as he was when he became a Christian)*. And this is how I specifically arrange it in all the assemblies.
18 Was anyone invited having been circumcised? *Was he circumcised when he became a Christian?* He must not put a foreskin back on. Has anyone been invited in uncircumcision? He must not be circumcised.
19 Circumcision is nothing, and uncircumcision is nothing, but *what is something is* the keeping of God's demands.
20 Each person must stay in that invitation that he was invited in.
21 Were you a slave when you were invited? It must not be a concern to you. But if you can actually become free instead, do so.
22 You see, the slave who was invited in the Master is the Master's freed slave. Likewise, the free person who was invited is the Anointed King's slave.
23 You were purchased with something of value, *the Anointed King's blood*. Don't become people's slaves.
24 This is what each person must stay in *when he is* next to God, brothers: in what he was invited.
25 About the virgin women, I don't have a directive from the Master. I am giving an opinion as someone who has been shown forgiving kindness to be trusted by the Master.
26 So I assume this to be nice because of the shortage that has stood here. It is nice for a person to be a virgin.

27 Have you been tied to a wife? Don't look for a release. Have you been released from a wife? Don't look for a wife.
28 But even if you married, you didn't sin, and if the virgin married, she didn't sin. These types of people will have hard times in the physical body. I am making it easy for you.
29 I declare this, brothers, the appointed time has been wrapping up. That is why for the rest of the time, even the people who have wives should be like the people who don't.
30 And the people crying should be like people not crying. And the people who are happy should be like people who are not happy. And the people buying should be like people who don't ever have anything.
31 And the people using the world should be like people not overusing it. You see, this world is an entity that is passing on by.
32 I want you to be without worries. The unmarried man worries about the Master's things: how he might do what the Master would like.
33 But the man who is married worries about the world's things: how he might do what the wife would like.
34 This has divided him. And the unmarried woman and the virgin worries about the Master's things so that she may be sacred both in the body and in the spirit. But the woman who is married worries about the world's things: how she might do what the husband would like.
35 I say this for your own advantage, not so that I might throw a lasso on you, but toward the thing that is reputable and does a good job of attending beside the Master without distraction.
36 If anyone assumes that this is improper for his virgin daughter, if she is past the prime of her youth and so he ought to let it happen, he must do what she wants. He isn't sinning. They must marry.
37 But a person will do nicely who has stood stable in his heart, who is not obligated *to give her away because of a previously arranged marriage agreement* but has the authority to do what he wants and has decided in his own heart to do this *(to keep his own virgin daughter)*.
38 So then even the person who gives his own virgin away in marriage does nicely, and the person who doesn't give her away in marriage will do what is better.
39 A wife has been tied to her husband for as much time as he lives, but if the husband fell asleep, she is free to be married to whom she wants, only in the Master.
40 But she is more blessed if she stays like this, aligned with my opinion. I also seem to be having God's Spirit.

8

1 About the idol sacrifices, we realize that we all know *the truth about idols*. Knowing brings conceit, but love is constructive.
2 If anyone seems to have known anything, he doesn't yet know even what it is necessary to know.
3 But if anyone loves God, this person has been known by Him.
4 So concerning the dinner *where people eat what was* given to the idols, we realize that in this world an idol is nothing and that there is not even one god except the One God.
5 You see, even if it is true that there are things called gods, whether in heaven or on earth, even as, there are many gods and many masters *in people's lives*,
6 to us there is one God, the Father (everything is from Him and we are in Him), and there is one Master, Jesus, the Anointed King (everything is through Him and we are through Him).
7 But not everyone knows this. Until now, some still *follow* the idol's policy *when they eat* as if they are eating food that was given to an idol god, and their weak conscience is dirtied.
8 Food won't stand us up next to God. And we aren't lacking if we don't eat either, or overflowing if we do.
9 See to it that this authority of yours doesn't somehow end up making the weak trip.
10 You see, if anyone sees you, the one who knows *that idols are nothing*, lounging around in an idol temple, won't the conscience of the person who is weak *(the person who thinks idols are gods)* be built up to the *point where he starts* eating the idol sacrifices?
11 You see, the brother who is weak (the brother that the Anointed King died for) is ruined by what you know *to be true*.
12 In this way, as you do sinful things to the brothers and hit their weak conscience, you do sinful things to the Anointed King.
13 For this very reason, if food causes my brother to stumble, I won't in any way eat meat for the span of time so that I won't cause my brother to stumble.

9

1 Am I not free? Am I not a missionary? Have I not seen Jesus, our Master? Are you not my work in the Master?
2 If I am not a missionary to others, I definitely am to you. You see, *the fact that* you *are* in the Master is the seal of my mission.
3 My defense to the people investigating me is this.
4 Don't we have the right to eat and drink?

5 Don't we have the right to be bringing a sister, a wife, around with us, even as the rest of the missionaries, the Master's brothers, and Cephas *(Aramaic for Peter)* do?
6 Or is it only I and Barnabas who don't have the right to not work?
7 Who serves in the military at any time paying his own wages? Who plants a vineyard and doesn't eat its fruit? Or who shepherds a flock and doesn't eat from the milk of the flock?
8 I am not speaking about something *only* a person came up with, am I? Or doesn't the law also say these things?
9 You see, it has been written in Moses' law, "You won't muzzle cattle processing grain" *(Deuteronomy 25:4)*. God isn't concerned about cattle, is He?
10 Or does He say it undoubtedly because of us? You see, it was written because of us, because the person plowing ought to plow anticipating *that he will receive part of the harvest* and the person processing grain *ought to process the grain* also anticipating that he will receive part of the harvest.
11 If we planted spiritual things in you, is it a big deal if we will harvest your physical things?
12 If others take part in your authority, shouldn't we more? But we don't make use of this authority. No, we put up with all things so that we might not interrupt the good news of the Anointed King in any way.
13 Don't you realize that the people working with the temple things eat the *things* from the temple grounds? The ones attending to the altar receive an allotment of *the sacrifices offered on* the altar.
14 This is how the Master also specifically arranged for the people proclaiming the good news *(for example, when He sent out the Twelve and the seventy)* to live from the good news.
15 But I haven't made use of any of these things. I didn't write these things so that it might happen to me like this. You see, it would be nice for me instead to die, than...--no one will make my bragging meaningless.
16 You see, *the fact that* I share good news is not what I brag about. *I am obligated to share it and that* obligation is lying on me. What a tragedy it would be to me if I didn't share good news.
17 If I constantly do this voluntarily, I get pay, but if I am doing it involuntarily, it is because I have been trusted to be a manager *of the good news*.
18 So what is my pay? *My pay is* that as I share good news, I might make it available with no cost *to anyone*. I don't want to overuse my authority in the good news *by making money off it*.

19 You see, even though I am free from everyone, I make myself a slave to everyone so that I might gain more of them.
20 With the Jewish people, I became like a Jewish person so that I might gain Jewish people. With the people under the law, I became like a person under the law (even though I myself am not under the law) so that I might gain the people under the law.
21 With the criminals, I became like a criminal (not being a criminal to God, but a lawful obeyer of the Anointed King) so that I might gain the criminals.
22 With the weak, I became weak so that I might gain the weak. With all people, I have become all kinds of things so that I might undoubtedly rescue some.
23 I do all kinds of things because of the good news so that together with all these things I might become someone who shares good news.
24 Don't you realize that all the runners in a 200-yard-lap race certainly run, but one receives the prize? This is how you must run, so that you might receive the prize.
25 Everyone struggling *to prepare for a race* restrains himself from all kinds of things. So those people certainly do it to receive a deteriorating award wreath, but we, an award wreath that doesn't deteriorate.
26 Now then, this is how I run, not obscurely. This is how I box, not as if I am beating the air.
27 But I give my body a black eye and lead it like a slave. I do this so that I myself won't somehow become unapproved when speaking publicly to others.

10

1 You see, I don't want you to be unaware, brothers, that all our fathers were under the cloud, they all went through the sea,
2 they all were submerged into Moses in the cloud and in the sea,
3 they all ate the same spiritual food,
4 and they all drank the same spiritual drink. You see, they were drinking from a spiritual rock following them. The rock was the Anointed King.
5 Despite that, God wasn't delighted with the majority of them. You see, their dead bodies were scattered throughout the backcountry.
6 These things became examples for us so that we wouldn't be people who desire bad things just as those people desired bad things.

7 Don't become idol worshipers either, just as some of them became idol worshipers and, as the Bible says, "The group was seated to eat and to drink and got up to act like children" *(Exodus 32:6)*.

8 We shouldn't commit sexual sin either, just as some of them committed sexual sin and 23,000 fell in one day *(Numbers 25:1-9)*.

9 We shouldn't try to harass the Anointed King either, just as some of them harassed and were being ruined by the snakes *(Numbers 21:5-6)*.

10 Don't grumble either, exactly as some of them grumbled and were ruined by the Destroyer *(Numbers 16:41,49)*.

11 These things were coming together and happening to those people and creating examples. Each example was written down to correct us, the people that the conclusions of the spans of time have made it to.

12 So then the person who seems to have stood must see to it that he won't fall.

13 The only kind of trouble that has taken hold of you is human trouble. God can be trusted. He won't allow you to experience trouble above what you can handle. Together with the trouble, He will also give you a way out so that you can endure it.

14 For this very reason, my loved ones, run away from the idol worship.

15 I am talking to you as I do to focused people--judge what I declare.

16 The cup that confers blessing (*the cup* that we confer blessings on), doesn't it share the blood of the Anointed King? The bread that we split *and eat*, doesn't it share the body of the Anointed King?

17 Because we, the many, are one bread, one body. You see, we all take part in it *with pieces that are torn* from the one *loaf of* bread.

18 Look at Israel as far as the physical body is concerned. Aren't the people eating the sacrifices sharers of the altar?

19 So what am I declaring? That an idol sacrifice is anything? Or that an idol is anything?

20 No, *I am declaring* that what they sacrifice, they sacrifice to lesser deities, and not to God. I do not want you to become sharers with the lesser deities.

21 You can't be drinking the Master's cup and the lesser deities' cup. You can't be taking part in the Master's table and the lesser deities' table.

22 Or are we trying to make the Master jealous? We are not stronger than Him, are we?

23 Everything is allowed, but not everything is advantageous. Everything is allowed, but not everything is constructive.

24 No one must look for his own *preference*, but for the *preference* of the other person.

25 Eat everything sold in a meat market, investigating nothing, because of the conscience.

26 You see, the earth and its fullness are the Master's.

27 If any of the untrusting people invite you and you want to travel there, eat everything placed in front of you, investigating nothing, because of the conscience.

28 But if someone says to you, "This is a temple sacrifice," do not eat because of that person (the one who disclosed it) and the conscience.

29 I say conscience, definitely not your own conscience, but the other person's conscience. You see, why is it that my freedom is being judged by a different conscience?

30 If I am taking part in it in appreciation *of someone's generosity*, why are insults said about me over what I am thankful for?

31 So whether you eat, or drink, or do anything, do everything for God's magnificence.

32 Become people who are not offensive to both Jewish people and Greeks, and to God's assembly,

33 just as I also do all the things that all things would like. I am not looking for my own advantage. No, *I am looking for* the advantage of the many so that they might be rescued.

11

1 Become imitators of me, just as I also became an imitator of the Anointed King.

2 I applaud you because you have always remembered me and you hold steady to the traditions just as I gave them over to you.

3 I want you to realize that the head of every man is the Anointed King. The head of a wife is the husband. The head of the Anointed King is God.

4 Every man praying or preaching having his head *(the Anointed King)* down shames his head.

5 Every wife praying or preaching with her head *(her husband)* not completely covered shames her head. You see, it is one and the same as if she had all of her hair shaved off.

6 If a wife *(her private life)* is not completely covered, she also must cut her hair, but if it is shameful for a wife to cut her hair or to be shaved, *her private life* must be completely covered.

7 You see, a man certainly doesn't have to completely cover his head *(the Anointed King)* since he is an image and the magnificence of God, but the woman is the magnificence of a man.

8 A man is not *designed* from a woman, but a woman is *designed* from a man.

9 You see, also a man was not created because of the woman, but a woman *was created* because of the man.

10 Because of this, the woman has to have authority based on the head *(her husband)* because of the angels.

11 More importantly, in the Master, a woman is not separate from a man, and a man is not separate from a woman either.

12 You see, even as the woman is *designed* from the man, so also is the man through the woman. All things are from God.

13 Judge among yourselves. Is it appropriate for a woman to be praying to God completely uncovered?

14 Doesn't even nature itself teach you that certainly if a man grows his hair out, it is worthless to him?

15 But if a woman grows her hair out, it is magnificence for her because the long hair has been given to her for a cloak.

16 If anyone seems to be fond of quarreling, we don't have this type of policy, and the assemblies of God don't either.

17 As I pass this next order on to you, I don't applaud you because you are not coming together for the better thing, but for the worse thing.

18 You see, certainly first of all, I hear that there are rifts among you as you come together in an assembly, and I trust some part of it.

19 You see, it is even necessary that there be splinter groups among you so that it might become apparent who the approved people are among you.

20 So as you come together in the same place, it is not to eat a master feast.

21 You see, each person takes and eats his own feast before everyone arrives. When *it is time* to eat, one person is hungry and another is drunk.

22 Do you not in any way have houses to eat and drink in? Or do you ignore God's assembly and shame the people who don't have food? What should I say to you? Should I applaud you in this? I do not applaud you.

23 You see, I took in from the Master what I also turned in to you, that the Master Jesus took bread in the night that He was turned in.

24 And after He was thankful, He split it and said, "This is My body. It is for you. Do this to again remind yourselves of Me."

25 He also did a similar thing with the cup after they had eaten dinner. He said, "This cup is the new deal in My blood. Do this as often as you drink to again remind yourselves of Me."
26 You see, as often as you eat this bread and drink this cup, you proclaim the Master's death till He comes.
27 So then whoever eats the bread or drinks the cup of the Master in a manner undeserving of the Master will be eligible to be sentenced for the Master's body and blood.
28 A person must check himself, and this is how he must eat from the bread and drink from the cup.
29 You see, a person who eats and drinks and doesn't consider his body to be wrong, is eating and drinking a judgment to himself.
30 Because of this, many among you are frail and sick, and an adequate amount are asleep.
31 If we were considering ourselves to be wrong, we would not be judged.
32 But as we are being judged by the Master, we are being disciplined so that we might not be found guilty together with the world.
33 So then, my brothers, as you come together to eat, wait for each other.
34 If anyone is hungry, he must eat at home so that God won't judge you all when you come together. I will specifically arrange the rest of the things whenever I come.

12

1 About the spiritual things, brothers, I don't want you to be unaware *of them*.
2 You realize that when you were non-Jews, you were pointed toward the voiceless idols as often as you were being led. *Something* was leading you away *to them*.
3 For this reason, I am letting you know that no one speaking in God's Spirit says, "Jesus is doomed." And no one is able to say, "Jesus is the Master," except in the Sacred Spirit.
4 There are a variety of gifts, but the same Spirit.
5 There are a variety of serving roles and the same Master.
6 And there are a variety of actions, but it is the same God who is active in all the things that are in all things.
7 Each person is given the presentation of the Spirit toward the advantage *of all*.
8 You see, not only is a message of insight given to a person through the Spirit, but also a message of information is given to another person aligned with the same Spirit,

9 trust to another in the same Spirit, gifts of cures to a different person in the one Spirit,

10 actions of skills to a different person, preaching to a different one, discernments of spirits to a different one, families of languages to another one, and interpretation of languages to a different one.

11 The one and the same Spirit is active in all these divvying out to each his own gift just as He intends.

12 You see, exactly as the body is one and has many body parts, but all the body parts of the body, being many, are one body, so also is the Anointed King.

13 Also we all, whether Jewish people, or Greeks, or slaves, or free, were submerged into one body in one Spirit. And we all were given the drink of one Spirit.

14 You see, also the body is not one body part, but many.

15 If the foot were to say, "Because I am not a hand, I am not from the body," that wouldn't make it not from the body.

16 And if the ear were to say, "Because I am not an eye, I am not from the body," that wouldn't make it not from the body.

17 If the whole body were an eye, where would the sense of hearing be? If the whole were an ear, where would the sense of smell be?

18 But right now God placed each one of the body parts in the body just as He wanted.

19 If it were all one body part, where would the body be?

20 Now not only is it many body parts, but also one body.

21 The eye is not able to say to the hand, "I don't need you." Or again the head can't say to the feet, "I don't need you."

22 No, much more, the parts of the body that seem to be weaker are essential.

23 And we place much more value around these parts of the body that seem to us to be of lesser value, and our improper parts have a much better reputation.

24 Our reputable parts have no need. But God mixed the body together after giving much more value to the part that is lacking.

25 That way there may not be a rift in the body, but the body parts may have the same concern for each other.

26 If one body part suffers, all the body parts suffer together with it. And if a body part is elevated to a place of magnificence, all the body parts are happy together with it.

27 You all are a body of the Anointed King and body parts from a part *of it*.

28 God certainly placed body parts in the assembly: first, missionaries; second, preachers; third, teachers; following that, skills; following that, gifts of cures, assists, counselings, families of languages.
29 All are not missionaries, are they? All are not preachers, are they? All are not teachers, are they? All are not skilled, are they?
30 All don't have gifts of cures, do they? All don't speak with languages, do they? All don't translate, do they?
31 But be passionate about the bigger gifts, and yet I am showing you an even better way.

13

1 If I speak with the languages of the people and of the angels, but do not have love, I have become an echoing piece of copper or a clanging cymbal.
2 And if I have a sermon from God and have seen all the secrets and all the information, and if I have all the trust, even enough to dislodge mountains, but I don't have love, I am nothing.
3 And if I disperse all of my things, and if I turn in my body so that I might be burned, but I don't have love, it is of no benefit to me.
4 Love is patient. It is kind. Love does not get mad. Love does not brag. It is not conceited.
5 It is not improper. It does not look for its own things. It is not annoyed. It does not consider the bad thing.
6 It is not happy in the wrong way but is happy together with the truth.
7 It puts up with all things. It trusts all things. It anticipates good from all things. It persists to do what is right in all things.
8 Love never ever fails, but if there are sermons, they will be rendered useless, and if there are languages, they will stop, and if there is information, it will be rendered useless.
9 You see, what we know is from a part *of what can be known*, and what we preach is from a part *of what can be preached*.
10 But when the complete thing comes, the thing that is from a part *of it* will be rendered useless.
11 When I was an infant, I was speaking as an infant does, I was focusing on things as an infant focuses on them, and I was considering things as an infant considers them. Since I have become a man, I have made the infant things useless.
12 You see, now we see through a mirror, in a puzzle, but at that time, *we will see it* face to face. What I know now is from a part *of it*, but at

that time, I will correctly understand just as I was also correctly understood.

13 Right now trust, anticipation, and love remain, these three. But the greatest of these is love.

14

1 Pursue love. Be passionate about the spiritual things, but more importantly that you may preach.

2 You see, the person who speaks in a language *that no one else knows* doesn't speak to people, but to God. No one hears. He is speaking secrets to a spirit.

3 The person who preaches speaks about things that build, encourage, and comfort people.

4 The person speaking in a language *that no one else knows* builds himself, but the person preaching builds an assembly.

5 I want all of you to speak languages, but more than that that you may preach. The person preaching is greater than the person speaking with languages unless he translates so that the assembly might receive something that builds it.

6 Brothers, if I come to you now speaking languages, what benefit will it be to you if I don't speak either something God has uncovered, or information, or a sermon, or a teaching?

7 This is also true of soulless things that give off a sound. Whether it is a flute or a harp, if it doesn't make different notes, how will anyone know what is played on the flute or harp?

8 You see, if a trumpet also gives an obscure sound, who will prepare for war?

9 In this way, if you also don't give a clear message through your language, how will it be known what is spoken? You see, you will be people speaking into the air.

10 There are so many families of voices in the world (if they may all be obtained), and none are voiceless.

11 So if I don't recognize the ability of the voice *(what language it is speaking)*, I will be a foreigner to the person speaking, and the person speaking will be a foreigner to me.

12 Since you are passionate about spirits, you also must look to build the assembly like this so that you may overflow.

13 For this reason, the person speaking with a language must pray that he may translate.

14 You see, if I pray in a language *that no one else knows*, my spirit prays, but my way of thinking is fruitless. *No one benefits from my thoughts.*

15 So what will I do? I will pray with the spirit, but I also will pray with the way of thinking. I will recite psalms with the spirit, but I also will recite psalms with the way of thinking.

16 Or else if you confer a blessing on someone in spirit, how will the one *who has no education whatsoever (or as the Greek puts it,* who fills up the uneducated's place) state the amen based on your thankfulness, since, for sure, he doesn't realize what you are saying?

17 You see, it certainly is nice that you are thankful, but it doesn't build the other person.

18 I thank God. I speak with languages more than all of you.

19 But in an assembly I want to speak five words with my way of thinking so that I also might echo down other words, rather than ten thousand words in a language *no one else knows*.

20 Brothers, don't become young children in your focus. But in badness, act like infants. In your focus, become mature people.

21 It has been written in the law, "'I will speak to this ethnic group using different languages and using different people's lips, and they won't listen to Me in this way either,' says the Master" *(Isaiah 28:11-12)*.

22 So then, the languages are to prove *that what the Master said is true*. It is not for the people who trust. It is for the people who don't trust. But the sermon is not for the people who don't trust. It is for the people who trust.

23 So if the whole assembly were to come together to the same place and all the people were speaking in languages but uneducated people or people who don't trust were to come in, won't they state that you are crazy?

24 But if all the people are preaching, and a certain person who doesn't trust or a certain uneducated person comes in, he *feels as if he* is reprimanded by all the people, as if he is investigated by all the people.

25 The hidden things in his heart end up being shown, and in this way, he will get down on his face and bow to God, reporting that God is really among you.

26 So how is it with you, brothers? When you come together, each has a psalm, a teaching, something that was uncovered to him, a language, an interpretation. Everything must happen to build the assembly.

27 If someone speaks in a language, it must be by two, or at the most three, one at a time. And one must translate.

28 But if there is no interpreter, he must keep quiet in an assembly. He must speak to himself and to God.

29 Two or three preachers must speak and everyone else must consider whether it is right or wrong.
30 If something is uncovered to another person who is sitting, the first must keep quiet.
31 You see, you are all able to preach one by one so that all may learn and all may be encouraged.
32 And the preachers' spirits are under the preachers' control.
33 You see, God is not a God of conflict, but of peace. This is how He is in all the assemblies of the sacred people.
34 The wives must keep quiet in the assemblies. You see, they are not permitted to be speaking. No, they must be under their husbands' control, just as the law also says *(Genesis 3:16)*.
35 If they want to learn something, they must ask their own husbands at home. You see, it is shameful for a wife to be speaking in an assembly.
36 *You are doing things other assemblies are not doing. Why? Are you the first assembly?* Did God's message come out from you? Or *are you the only assembly?* Did *God's message* only make it to you?
37 If anyone seems to be a preacher or spiritual, he must correctly understand that the things I write to you are the Master's demand.
38 If anyone is unaware, God is aware of him.
39 So then, my brothers, be passionate about preaching, and don't keep people from speaking in languages.
40 Everything must happen reputably and aligned with an arrangement.

15

1 I am letting you know, brothers, about the good news that I shared with you. You also received it in. You also have stood in it.
2 You also are being rescued through it if you hold steady to a certain message (I myself shared the good news of it with you), unless you trusted for no reason.
3 You see, among the first messages that I turned over to you was what I also took in. It was that the Anointed King died on behalf of our sins aligned with the *Old Testament* writings,
4 that He was buried, that He has been gotten up on the third day aligned with the *Old Testament* writings,
5 and that He was seen by Cephas *(Aramaic for Peter)* and after that by the Twelve.

6 Following that, He was seen by over five hundred brothers all at once. The majority of them remain until now *(the time when this book was written)*, but some have fallen asleep.
7 Following that He was seen by James, after that by all the missionaries.
8 But last of all, he was also seen by me, *the one that was* to some extent just like the aborted fetus *(dead, undeveloped, wounded)*.
9 You see, I am the smallest of the missionaries. *Even though I am a missionary,* I am unfit to be called a missionary because I persecuted God's assembly.
10 But I am what I am with God's generosity. And His generosity for me wasn't something that became meaningless. No, I labored much more than they all. But *it was* not me, *it was* God's generosity together with me.
11 So whether it is I or those missionaries, this is how we speak publicly, and this is how you trusted.
12 If it is publicly spoken about the Anointed King that God has gotten Him up from the dead, how do some among you say that dead people do not return back to life?
13 If dead people don't return back to life, God hasn't gotten the Anointed King up either.
14 If God hasn't gotten the Anointed King up, clearly our public speaking is also meaningless, and your trust is meaningless.
15 We also are found to be lying witnesses of God because we told what we witnessed coming down from God--that He got the Anointed King up. But He didn't get Him up if it is clearly true that God doesn't get dead people up.
16 You see, if God doesn't get dead people up, God hasn't gotten the Anointed King up either.
17 If God hasn't gotten the Anointed King up, your trust is futile. You are still in your sins.
18 Also clearly the people who fell asleep in the Anointed King are lost.
19 If we who have anticipated good in the Anointed King are only in this life, we are more miserable than all people.
20 But right now *the fact is that* the Anointed King has been gotten up from the dead. He is a first-part-offering of the people who have fallen asleep. *As a first-part-offering, He is the first to come back to life, but the others will also come back to life later.*
21 You see, since, for sure, death is through a person, dead people returning back to life is also through a person.

22 Even as everyone in Adam dies, so also everyone in the Anointed King will be given life.
23 But each is in its own order: a first-part-offering (the Anointed King); following that, the Anointed King's people during His arrival;
24 after that, the conclusion when He turns the monarchy over to the God and Father when He will make every head ruler and every authority and ability useless.
25 You see, it is necessary for Him *(the Anointed King)* to be king till a time that He *(God)* will put all the enemies under His *(the Anointed King's)* feet.
26 The last enemy to be rendered useless is death.
27 You see, He placed all things under His feet. But whenever He said, "All things have been placed under Him," it is obvious that the One who placed all things under Him is excluded.
28 When all things are placed under Him, at that time the Son Himself will also be placed under the One who placed all things under Him so that God may be all in all.
29 If not, what will the people do who are submerged over with the dead. *As they are put under the water, they are identifying with the dead. But the whole point of the submersion is that they are brought back up out of the water. They are brought back to life.* If dead people aren't gotten up at all, why are they even submerged over with them?
30 Also why are we in danger every hour?
31 I die daily. *It is* as sure as the optimism that I have for you, brothers, in the Anointed King Jesus, our Master.
32 If I fought in person against wild animals in Ephesus, what benefit is that to me? If dead people aren't gotten up, "let's eat and drink because tomorrow we die."
33 Don't be misled; bad associations worsen useful morals.
34 Wake up from your drunkenness. *Wake up* to the right way, and don't sin. You see, some people are ignorant of God. I am speaking this about you and it is embarrassing.
35 But some will state, "How are the dead gotten up? *Their bodies deteriorate away after they die. They don't have bodies anymore.* What kind of body do they come back with?"
36 Distracted person, the seed that you plant is not given life, except it die.
37 And what you plant is not the body that it will become, but a naked kernel of wheat (if it may be obtained) or some of the rest of the seeds.

38 God gives it the body that He wanted, and He gives each of the seeds their own body.

39 Not every physical body is the same physical body, but certainly there is another physical body for people, another physical body for animals, another physical body for winged birds, and another one for fish.

40 There are heavenly bodies and earthly bodies, but certainly the magnificence of the heavenly is different, and the magnificence of the earthly is different.

41 The sun's magnificence is another thing, the moon's magnificence is another, and the stars' magnificence is another. You see, *one* star is more substantial than *another* star in magnificence.

42 This is also how the return back to life of the dead is planted in deterioration and is gotten up without any deterioration.

43 It is planted in worthlessness; it is gotten up in magnificence. It is planted in weakness; it is gotten up in ability.

44 It is planted *a psychological body* (a soul body); it gets up a spiritual body. If there is *a psychological body* (a soul body), there is also a spiritual body.

45 This is also what the Bible says, The first person, Adam, "came to be in a living soul" *(Genesis 2:7)*, the last Adam in a life-giving spirit.

46 But the spiritual body isn't first. No, the soul body is first, following that, the spiritual.

47 The first person is from the earth, a dirt person. The second person is from heaven.

48 The dirt people are also the same type of people as what the dirt person was. And the heavenly people are also the same type of people as what the heavenly person was.

49 And just as we wore the dirt person's image, we will also wear the heavenly person's image.

50 I declare this, brothers, that a physical body and blood is not able to inherit God's monarchy. And something that deteriorates doesn't inherit something that doesn't deteriorate either.

51 Look, I am telling you a secret: not all of us will sleep, but all of us will be changed

52 in a moment, in the twitch of an eye, in the last trumpet. You see, it will blow, the dead will be gotten up without any deterioration, and we will be changed.

53 It is necessary for this deteriorating body to put on something that doesn't deteriorate and for this dying body to put on deathlessness.

54 When this deteriorating body will put on something that doesn't deteriorate, and this dying body will put on deathlessness, at that time, the saying in the Bible will happen, "Death was swallowed up into victory.
55 Death, where is your victory? Death, where is your sting?" *(Isaiah 25:8; Hosea 13:14)*
56 The sting of death is sin. The ability of sin is the law.
57 Thank God, the One who gives us the victory through our Master Jesus, the Anointed King.
58 So then, my loved brothers, become stable people, unmovable, overflowing in the Master's work, always realizing that your labor in the Master is not meaningless.

16

1 About the collection of money for the sacred people, you must also do exactly what I specifically arranged with Galatia's assemblies.
2 On each Day One *(which is Sunday)* after a Sabbath, each of you must put aside and stockpile whatever he is successful in. That way whenever I come, there doesn't end up being a collection of money at that time.
3 When I show up, I will send whoever you approve through letters to carry off your generosity into Jerusalem.
4 If it deserves to also have me travel with it, they will travel together with me.
5 I will come to you whenever I go through Macedonia *(an area in Greece north of Corinth)*. You see, I am going through Macedonia.
6 After that is obtained, I will come to you. I will stay with you or even spend the storm season with you so that you might bring me on my way to wherever I travel.
7 You see, I don't want to see you *briefly* now while I am passing by there. I anticipate staying over with you for some time if the Master gives me permission to.
8 But I will stay over in Ephesus *(a city in Western Turkey)* until the Fiftieth Day Festival.
9 You see, a large and active door has opened to me, and many are lying in opposition to it.
10 If Timothy comes, see to it that he will end up not being afraid of you. You see, he works on the Master's work, as I also do.
11 So no one should treat him as a nobody, but bring him on his way in peace so that he might come to me. You see, I am waiting for him with the brothers.

12 About brother Apollos, I encouraged him many times to come to you with the brothers, and coming now was not what he wanted at all, but he will come when he has a good time to come.

13 Stay awake, stand in the trust, be a man, become strong.

14 Everything from you must happen in love.

15 You realize that Stephanas' house is a first-part-offering of Achaia *(the province in southern Greece that Corinth is in)*, and they assigned themselves to serving the sacred people. I encourage you, brothers,

16 to also place yourselves under these types of people and under everyone working together and laboring.

17 I am happy that Stephanas, Fortunatus, and Achaicus arrived because these *three* filled up your deficiency.

18 You see, they got my spirit and yours to relax. So you must recognize these types of people.

19 The assemblies of Western Turkey say hello to you. Aquila and Prisca *(the formal name of Priscilla)* together with the assembly throughout their house say hello many times to you in the Master.

20 All the brothers say hello to you. Say hello to each other with a sacred friendly gesture.

21 This is the greeting of Paul with my hand.

22 If anyone is not fond of the Master, he must be doomed. Maranatha *(Aramaic for "the Master is coming")*.

23 May the Master Jesus' generosity be with you.

24 My love is with all of you in the Anointed King Jesus.

Second Corinthians

1 From: Paul (a missionary of the Anointed King Jesus because that's what God wants) and Timothy (the brother). To: God's assembly that is in Corinth *(a city in southern Greece)* together with all the sacred people who are in all of Achaia *(the province that Corinth is in)*.

2 Generosity and peace to you out from God, our Father, and Master Jesus, the Anointed King.

3 The God and Father of our Master Jesus (the Anointed King) has blessings conferred on Him. He is the Father of compassion and the God of every encouragement.

4 He is the One encouraging us through all our hard times. *The purpose of His encouragement is* for us to be able to encourage people in all kinds of hard times through the encouragement that we ourselves are encouraged with by God.

5 Just as the hardships of the Anointed King overflow to us, so our encouragement also overflows through the Anointed King.

6 If we go through hard times, it is on behalf of your encouragement and rescue, and if we are encouraged, it is also on behalf of your encouragement. Your encouragement is active in your persistence to do what is right in the same hardships that we also suffer. And our anticipation for you is firm

7 because we realize that as you receive your share of the hardships, so you also receive your share of the encouragement.

8 You see, we don't want you to be unaware, brothers, about the hard times that happened to us in Western Turkey. We were weighted down *by them* even more than above our ability in such a way for us to be unable to find a way to even live.

9 But we ourselves have had the sentence of death on ourselves so that we won't be confident based on ourselves, but we will be confident based on the God who gets the dead up.

10 He saved us from such a great death, and He will save us in the future. In Him, we have anticipated that He also will still save

11 as you also work quietly together in your plea on our behalf so that the gift to us from many faces through many methods might be thankfulness for us.

12 You see, this is what we brag about, it is what our conscience witnesses, that we were busy in the world and much more toward you

with dedication and a genuineness of God. It was not in physical insight, but in God's generosity.

13 We are not writing you anything other than what you are reading or also correctly understanding. I am anticipating that you will correctly understand it until the conclusion,

14 just as you also correctly understood a part of us, because we are one of the things you brag about, exactly as you are also one of the things we brag about in the day of our Master Jesus.

15 And with this confidence, I was intending to come to you previously so that you might have generosity a second time,

16 to go across past you into Macedonia *(an area in Greece north of Corinth)*, to come again out of Macedonia to you, and to be brought by you on my way to Judea.

17 So as I was intending this *(to come to you)*, I clearly didn't behave with a flippant attitude, did I? Or the things that I advise myself on, do I advise myself aligned with a physical body so that the "yes, yes" directly from me may also be the "no, no?"

18 God can be trusted and so our message to you is not "yes and no."

19 You see, when we (I, Silas, and Timothy) spoke publicly about the Son of God, Jesus, the Anointed King, the One among you, it didn't become yes and no, but in Him, it became yes.

20 As many of God's promises as *there are*, in Him they are the "yes." For this reason, the "amen" to God is also through Him toward magnificence through us.

21 The God who authenticates us together with you for the Anointed King and who anointed us

22 is also the One who put a seal on us and gave the down payment of the Spirit in our hearts.

23 I call God on my soul as a witness *to this fact* that to make it easy on you I did not come into Corinth yet.

24 It wasn't that we are masters of your trust. No, we are co-workers of your happiness. You see, you have stood in the trust.

2

1 You see, I decided this for myself--not to come to you again in sadness.

2 If I make you sad, who is the one also celebrating with me if it isn't the one who is sad from me?

3 And I wrote this same thing so that when I come, the people who must be happy with me won't make me sad. I have been confident based on you all because you make me happy.

4 You see, I was shedding many tears when I wrote you. I was going through much hard times and my heart was in distress. I didn't write you so that you would be sad, but so that you would know the love that I have much more of for you.

5 If anyone has caused sadness, he has only caused me partial sadness so that I may not be a burden on you all.

6 This pressure that the majority of you put on this type of person is adequate.

7 In such a way, just the opposite, it is more important for you, as an act of generosity, to forgive and to encourage this type of man so that he might not somehow be swallowed up with much more sadness.

8 For this reason, I encourage you to make your love for him official.

9 You see, I also wrote for this reason, so that I might know what your proven track record is, if you are obedient in all things.

10 To anyone that you forgive anything as an act of generosity, I also forgive. You see, as an act of generosity, I have also forgiven what I have forgiven (whatever it may be) because of you, because we are in the presence of the Anointed King,

11 so that the Opponent might not take advantage of us. We aren't unaware of his patterns of thinking.

12 After I went to Troas for the good news of the Anointed King and a door had been opened to me in the Master,

13 I did not have relief to my spirit because I had not found Titus, my brother. But I said good-bye to them, and I went out to Macedonia.

14 Thank God *who is* the One always bringing us out in His victory parade in the Anointed King and showing the aroma of His information through us in every place.

15 *He shows His information's aroma through us* because we are the Anointed King's sweet fragrance to God among the people being rescued and among the people being ruined.

16 To the one, we are an aroma from death for death. To the other, we are an aroma from life for life. Who is even adequate to face these things?

17 You see, we are not as the many people who are dishonest with God's message. No, as people from genuineness--as people from God--we are speaking in the Anointed King directly facing God.

1 Are we beginning again to endorse ourselves? Or do we, unlike some, need endorsement letters to you or from you?

2 You are our letter that has been written in our hearts. It is known and read by all people.

3 It is shown that you are the Anointed King's letter that was served by us. *This is* not *a letter* that has been written in ink. No, *it is a letter that has been written* with the Spirit of the living God, not on stone slabs, but on slabs that are physical hearts.

4 This is the kind of confidence that we have through the Anointed King toward God.

5 It is not because we are adequate to consider something by ourselves as if it were from ourselves. No, our adequacy is from God.

6 *It is God* who also made us adequate to be servants of a new deal, not servants of a document, but servants of a spirit. You see, the document kills, but the Spirit gives life.

7 If the serving of the death (that has been imprinted in alphabetic characters in stones) became such a magnificent thing that the sons of Israel could not stare into Moses' face because of the magnificence of his face (the magnificence that is being rendered useless),

8 how will the serving of the Spirit not be more magnificent?

9 You see, if the serving of the guilty sentence has magnificence, the serving of the right way overflows much more with magnificence.

10 Even the thing that has been elevated to a place of magnificence has not been elevated to a place of magnificence in this aspect, on account of the superior magnificence of the Spirit.

11 You see, if the thing that is being rendered useless has gone through magnificence, the thing that remains is in even more magnificence.

12 So since we have this kind of anticipation, we use it with a very clear public statement.

13 *This is* not anything like Moses. He was putting a veil on his face with a specific goal--to keep the sons of Israel from staring at the conclusion of the thing that is being rendered useless.

14 But their patterns of thinking became hard as stone. You see, the same veil stays on the reading of the former deal til today. *The fact* that the Anointed King is rendering it useless is not unveiled to them.

15 But until today, whenever Moses is read, a veil lies on their hearts.

16 Whenever it turns back toward the Master, the veil will be taken away all around.

17 The Master is the Spirit. Where the Spirit of the Master is, there is freedom.

18 All of us who see the reflection of the Master's magnificence with an unveiled face are transformed into the same image from *one degree of magnificence* to another exactly as it is from the Master's Spirit.

1 Because of this, since it is our job to serve, just as we were shown forgiving kindness, we don't get discouraged.
2 But we denounced shame's hidden things. We didn't walk around in slyness or use God's message deceptively. No, with the presentation of the truth, we endorsed ourselves to people's every conscience in God's sight.
3 If our good news has actually been covered up, it has been covered up among the people being ruined.
4 The god of this span of time blinded the patterns of thinking of the untrusting people among them. That way the lighting of the good news of the Anointed King's magnificence (the One who is God's image) wouldn't radiate out.
5 You see, we don't speak publicly about ourselves. No, *we speak publicly* about Jesus, the Anointed King, the Master, and that we ourselves are your slaves because of Jesus.
6 God, the One who told the light to shine out from the darkness, the One who shined in our hearts, will shine toward lighting the information of God's magnificence in the presence of Jesus, the Anointed King.
7 This stockpile of treasure that we have is in ceramic containers so that the superior ability may be God's and not something from us.
8 We go through all kinds of hard times, but we are not restricted. We are unable to find our way, but we are able to find a way out.
9 We are persecuted, but not abandoned. We are thrown down, but not ruined.
10 We always carry Jesus' dying around in our body so that Jesus' life also might be shown in our body.
11 You see, even though we are living, we are always given over to death because of Jesus so that the life of Jesus might also be shown in our dying physical body.
12 In such a way, death is active in us, but life is active in you.
13 We have the same spirit of trust that is aligned with what the Bible says, "I trusted; this is why I spoke." We also trust; this is why we speak.
14 We realize that the One who got the Master Jesus up will also get us up together with Jesus and will stand by you together with you.
15 You see, all these things are because of you, so that when the generosity increases through more of these things, the thankfulness for God's magnificence might overflow.
16 For this reason, we don't get discouraged, but even if our outside person is devoured, still our inside is renewed day *in* and day *out*.

17 You see, the light weight of our hard times at this very instant works on and completes an even greater and greater weight of magnificence for us that spans all time.

18 We are not keeping an eye out for the things that are seen, but for the things that are not seen. The things that are seen are for the time being, but the things that are not seen span all time.

5

1 You see, we realize that if our earthly house of this tent *(our physical body)* is torn down, we have a building from God, a house made without hands in the heavens that spans all time *(an eternal body)*.

2 You see, we also groan in this tent, yearning to put our habitation from heaven on over it

3 if definitely after actually putting it on, we won't be found naked.

4 You see, we who are in the tent, also groan as we are weighted down. We don't want to strip it off. No, *we want* to put God's building on over it so that the dying might be swallowed up by the life.

5 God who worked on and completed us for this very thing gave us the down payment of the Spirit.

6 So we are always courageous, and we realize that while we are at home in the body, we are absent away from the Master.

7 You see, we walk around through trust, not through a visual image.

8 We are courageous, and it seems like a good idea to us instead to be absent from the body and to be at home facing the Master.

9 For this reason, we also think it is important, whether being at home or being absent, to be well-liked by Him.

10 You see, it is necessary for all of us to be shown in front of the Anointed King's judicial bench so that each might retrieve the kind of things that he repeatedly did through the body, whether good or useless.

11 So realizing that the Master is someone to fear, we are trying to persuade people. We have been shown to God, but I anticipate that we have also been shown in your consciences.

12 We are not endorsing ourselves again to you, but we are giving you an opportunity to brag for us. That way you may have it for the people who brag about appearance and not about the heart.

13 You see, if we were deranged, it was for God, and if we are sane, it is for you.

14 The Anointed King's love holds us together when we judge this way: that one died on behalf of all and so all clearly died.

15 And He died on behalf of all so that the people living may no longer live for themselves, but for the One who died on their behalf and was gotten up.
16 And so from now on, we have seen no one as far as a physical body is concerned. Even if we have known the Anointed King as far as a physical body is concerned, still, now we no longer know Him that way.
17 And so if anyone is in the Anointed King, he is a new creation, the beginning things are gone away. Look, they have become new.
18 All things are from God. *It is God* who restored us to Himself through the Anointed King and gave us the job of serving the restored relationship
19 since it is in the Anointed King that God is restoring the world to Himself (not considering their infractions as theirs). *God* also placed the message of the restored relationship in us.
20 So we are representatives on behalf of the Anointed King. Since God is encouraging *you* through us, we plead with you on behalf of the Anointed King, be restored to God.
21 He made the One who didn't know sin to be sin on our behalf so that we might become God's right way in Him.

6

1 As we work together, we also encourage you to accept God's generosity in a way that is not meaningless.
2 You see, He says, "I listened closely to you at an acceptable time, and I helped you during a day of rescue" *(Isaiah 49:8)*. Look! Now is a good acceptable time. Look! Now is a day of rescue.
3 We don't do anything that would give a trip risk in any way so that the serving that we do might not be blamed.
4 But we endorse ourselves in everything as God's servants: in much persistence to do what is right, in hard times, in shortages, in difficulties,
5 in wounds, in jails, in conflicts, in laboring, in sleepless nights, in going without food,
6 in consecration, in information, in patience, in kindness, in the Sacred Spirit, in love that is not faked,
7 in a message of truth, in God's ability through the right way's weapons, the right-handed *weapons (offensive)* and left-handed *weapons (defensive)*,
8 through magnificence and worthlessness, through harsh talk and good talk, as misleading and valid,

9 as being unaware and correctly understanding, as dying and, look, we live, as disciplined and not put to death,
10 as being sad but always being happy, as poor but making many wealthy, as having nothing and steadily having everything.
11 Our mouth has been open for you, Corinthians. We have widened our heart.
12 You are not restricted in us. You are restricted in your feelings of sympathy.
13 For the same payback (*I am talking* as I talk to children), you also must widen your hearts.
14 Don't become strapped to a crossbeam with a different type of animal, with people who don't trust. You see, what does the right way and crime have in common? Or what does light share with darkness?
15 What is the Anointed King's harmonious agreement toward Belial *(a name for Satan)*? Or what part does a person who trusts have with a person who doesn't trust?
16 What consensus vote *does* God's temple *make* with idols? You see, we are a temple of the living God, just as God said, "I will have a house in them and walk around among them" *(Leviticus 26:12)*, and, "I will be their God, and they will be My ethnic group" *(Ezekiel 37:27)*.
17 For this reason, "Come out from the middle of them, and isolate yourselves from them," says the Master. "Don't touch what is not clean, and I will accept you in."
18 And, "'I will *stand* in the place of a Father for you, and you will *stand* in the place of sons and daughters for Me,' says the Master, the All-Powerful One" *(2 Samuel 7:8, 14)*.

7

1 So having these promises, loved ones, let's clean ourselves off from every dirty spot of the physical body and spirit as we finish up sacredness in awe of God.
2 Make room in your heart for us. We didn't wrong anyone. We didn't worsen anyone. We didn't take advantage of anyone.
3 I am not talking toward a guilty sentence. You see, I have stated before, "You are in our hearts for one purpose, to die together and to be living together."
4 I have a very clear public statement toward you. I often brag for you. I have been filled with encouragement. I overflow even more with happiness from all our hard times.
5 You see, even after we came into Macedonia *(which is where I am writing this letter from)*, our physical body has not had even one bit of

relief. No, we are going through hard times in every way: on the outside--arguments; on the inside--fears.

6 But God, the One who encourages lowly people, encouraged us with Titus' arrival. *He just returned from visiting you.*

7 Not only did God encourage us with his arrival, but also with the encouragement from Titus that he received when he was encouraged by you. He announced your yearning to us, your mourning, your passion over me in such a way that I was even more happy.

8 Even though I made you sad with the letter, I do not regret it, even though I was regretting it. You see, I see that that letter made you sad (if it was even for an hour).

9 Now I am happy, not because you were saddened, but because when you were saddened, you changed your ways. You see, you were saddened aligned with God so that you would not sustain loss from us in anything.

10 The sadness that is aligned with God, works a change of ways for a rescue that no one regrets, but the sadness of the world works on and completes death.

11 You see, look at how much concern this same thing *(being saddened aligned with God)* worked on and completed with you, but also defense, but also outrage, but also fear, but also yearning, but also passion, but also retaliation. You endorsed yourselves to be consecrated to the matter in everything.

12 Clearly, even though I wrote you, I didn't write you on account of the person who did wrong, or on account of the person who was wronged. No, I wrote you on account of your concern for us so that your concern for us would be shown to you in God's sight.

13 We have been encouraged because of this. From our encouragement, we were even more happy based on Titus' happiness because his spirit had been relaxed by you all.

14 *His spirit had been relaxed by you* because if I have bragged any to him for you, I was not shamed by what he found when he was with you. But as everything that we spoke to you was true, so our bragging before Titus also became true.

15 And his feelings of sympathy for you are much more as he reminds himself again of the obedience of you all, how with fear and trembling you accepted him.

16 I am happy that in everything I am courageous among you.

8

1 We are letting you know about God's generosity, brothers, the generosity that has been given among the assemblies of Macedonia

2 because in a great proven track record of hard times, the overflow of their happiness and their deep down poverty overflowed into the wealth of their dedication.

3 I am a witness that according to their ability and beyond their ability, on their own,

4 with much begging, they pleaded that we *would accept their* generosity and *allow them to have a* share in serving the sacred people *with their money*.

5 Unlike what we anticipated, they first gave themselves to the Master and to us by doing what God wanted them to do.

6 This caused us to encourage Titus *to travel back to you* so that just as he had already begun *this when he was just with you*, so he might also finish up your part of this generosity.

7 But even as you overflow in everything (in trust, in message, in information, in every concern, and in the love in you from us), may you also overflow in this generosity.

8 I am not saying *this* aligned with a directive, but so that the realness of your love may be proved through your concern for different people.

9 You see, you know the generosity of our Master Jesus, the Anointed King, that He (being wealthy) became poor because of you. That way you, with that Anointed King's poverty, might become wealthy.

10 I am giving *my* opinion on this. You see, this is to your advantage. Since last year, you already began, not just the doing of it, but also the wanting of it.

11 But right now, finish up the doing of it too, in order that, exactly as you have the eagerness of the wanting of it, so also you might finish it up from what you have.

12 You see, if the eagerness is already there, what is well-received is *the gift that is* aligned with whatever a person has, not with what a person doesn't have.

13 It is not so that others get relief and you get hard times. No, it is to provide equality at the present time. Your excess is for their deficiency.

14 That way *in the future* their excess will also become for your deficiency in order that equality might happen.

15 *This is* just as the Bible says, "The one *who gathered* a large amount didn't get more *than two liters*, and the one *who gathered* a small amount didn't get less" *(Exodus 16:18)*.
16 Thank God that He put the same concern for you in Titus' heart
17 because he certainly accepted our encouragement, but being more concerned *than I expected*, he went out to you on his own.
18 Together with him, we sent the brother who receives high praise in the good news throughout all of the assemblies.
19 Not only that, but he also was handpicked by the assemblies to be our traveling companion together with this generosity that is served by us. *It is* toward the Master's magnificence and our eagerness.
20 As we are setting this up, no one should blame us in this abundance served by us.
21 You see, we are planning nice things, not only *things that are nice* in the Master's sight, but *things that are* also *nice* in people's sight.
22 Together with them, we sent our brother that we proved to be very concerned in many ways many times, but right now he is much more concerned about you with much confidence.
23 Whether it is something about Titus (my partner and a co-worker for you), or it is our brothers (missionaries of assemblies), the magnificence is the Anointed King's.
24 So you must display to the assemblies' face the display of your love and of our bragging to them for you.

1 You see, to me, writing you about serving the sacred people *with your money* certainly seems much more than I need to do.
2 I have seen your eagerness. I bragged about it for you to Macedonians, "Achaia has been prepared since last year." Your passion provoked the majority of them.
3 But I sent the brothers to you so that our bragging for you might not be empty *bragging* in this detail and so that you might be prepared just as I was saying.
4 What if somehow, when Macedonians came together with me, they actually found you unprepared? We (so that I may not say you) would be ashamed with this undertaking.
5 So I regarded it essential to encourage the brothers to go on ahead to you and develop your previously promised conferring of blessing before *I get there* so that it would be ready in this way: as a conferring of blessings from you and not as a desire for more *from me*.

6 Remember this: The one who is stingy as he plants, will also have a harvest that is stingy, and the one who is conferring a blessing as he plants, will also have a harvest that confers a blessing.

7 Each person must give just as he has chosen in his heart beforehand, not from sadness or from an obligation. You see, God loves a giver who wants to provide a remedy.

8 God has the ability to overflow every bit of generosity to you so that in everything always having every bit of contentment, you may overflow in every good action.

9 This is just what the Bible says, "He scattered it. He gave to the underprivileged. His right way stays for the span of time" *(Psalm 112:9)*.

10 The One who supplies more than a batch of seeds to the one who plants and bread for a dinner will supply and increase your batch of seeds. And He will grow the produce of your right way.

11 You will become wealthy in everything for every bit of dedication. This is something that works on and completes thankfulness to God through us

12 because the serving of this public service is not only furnishing the deficiencies of the sacred people, but it is also causing many thanks to overflow to God.

13 Through the proven track record of this serving *of money*, people praise God's magnificence based on *three things:* the compliance of your acknowledgment for the Anointed King's good news, your dedication to sharing with them and with everyone,

14 and their plea for you. They yearn for you because of God's superior generosity on you.

15 Thank God for His indescribable free handout.

10

1 I myself, Paul, encourage you through the Anointed King's submissiveness and politeness, I, who right in front of your face certainly am lowly among you, but who, when I am away from you, am courageous to you.

2 I am pleading with my confidence about the *fact that* when I am not beside you, I am courageous. With this *same confidence*, I am considering to dare confront some who consider us to be walking around as if we are aligned with a physical body.

3 You see, as we walk around in a physical body, but not aligned with a physical body, we are serving in the military.

4 The weapons of our military service are not physical, but with God they are able to take down forts.

5 We take down reasonings and every high thing that raises itself up against God's information. We forcibly incarcerate every pattern of thinking into the obedience of the Anointed King.
6 And we have ourselves ready to retaliate for every noncompliance when your obedience is accomplished.
7 Do you look at the things right in front of your face? If anyone has been confident of himself that he is the Anointed King's, he must consider this again about himself because just as he is the Anointed King's, so also are we.
8 You see, even if I bragged somewhat more concerning our authority that the Master gave to build you and not to take you down, I won't be ashamed.
9 That way it won't seem to you that my letters are frightening
10 because, "The letters certainly are heavy and strong," he declares, "but the presence of the body is weak and the message has been treated as if it is nothing."
11 This type of person must consider this, that such as we are with the message through letters being away from you, this is how we will also be in action as we are beside you.
12 You see, we don't dare to decide that we are among some who endorse themselves or *dare* to compare ourselves with them. But they, who measure themselves among themselves and compare themselves to themselves, don't understand.
13 We won't brag of the things that have no measurement, but *we will brag* aligned with the measurement of the territory that the God of measurement allocated to us to reach even out to you.
14 You see, it is not as if we are overextending ourselves and not reaching to you. We actually already came out to you with the good news of the Anointed King.
15 We aren't bragging of the things that have no measurement (in labors belonging to others), but we anticipate that your growing trust will become great in you throughout our territory to an overflow
16 to share good news to the places beyond you and not to brag about the places that are ready in someone else's territory.
17 The person who brags must brag in the Master.
18 You see, the person who is approved is not that person who endorses himself. No, it is *the person* that the Master endorses.

11

1 If only you would tolerate a little bit of a distraction from me, but you actually are tolerating me.

2 You see, I am passionate about you with God's passion. I arranged your marriage to one Man: for a consecrated virgin to stand up next to the Anointed King.

3 But as the snake completely fooled Eve with his slyness, I am afraid that somehow your patterns of thinking might get worse and turn away from your dedication and consecration to the Anointed King.

4 You see, certainly if the one who comes to you speaks publicly about another Jesus whom we did not speak publicly about, or you receive a different spirit that you did not receive or different good news that you did not accept, you tolerate it nicely.

5 You see, I consider nothing to have been inferior to the super missionaries.

6 Even if I am unskilled in *my delivery of* the message, still *I am* not *unskilled* with the facts, still we showed them to you in every way in all things.

7 Or did I commit a sin by putting myself down low so that you might be put up high? Because I shared God's good news with you for free?

8 I pilfered other assemblies when I took wages from them for serving you.

9 And when I was there facing you and I lacked something, I didn't freeload off anyone. You see, the brothers who came out of Macedonia furnished my deficiency. In everything, I kept and will keep myself weightless to you.

10 A truth in me that the Anointed King can attest to is that this bragging about the slopes of Achaia from me will not be shut up *(the recipients of this letter lived on the slopes of Achaia)*.

11 Why? Because I don't love you? God knows.

12 But what I do, I will also do so that I might chop off the opportunity of the people wanting an opportunity through their bragging to get people to find that they are also just like us.

13 You see, these types of people are counterfeit missionaries, deceptive workers, disguising themselves as the Anointed King's missionaries.

14 And this is not some amazing thing. You see, the Opponent disguises himself as an angel of light.

15 So it is not a great thing if his servants are also disguised as servants of the right way. Their conclusion will be aligned with their actions.

16 Again I say, "It should not seem to anyone that I am distracted." But even if it definitely does seem like I am distracted, accept me as a distracted person so that I might also brag about a little something.

17 What I am speaking, I am not speaking aligned with the Master. No, *I am speaking* as in a distraction in this undertaking of the bragging.
18 Since many brag aligned with the physical body, I also will brag.
19 You see, you gladly tolerate the distracted people, you who are focused.
20 You tolerate it if someone makes you a complete slave, if someone eats up your food, if someone takes your things, if someone raises up, if someone hits you in the face.
21 I say *these things* as if we are worthless because we have been weak. But in whatever some dare to be (I say this in my distraction), I also dare to be.
22 Are they Hebrew-speaking Jews? I also am. Are they Israelis? I also am. Are they Abraham's seed? I also am.
23 Are they the Anointed King's servants? I, who have the wrong focus, am speaking. I *have gone* beyond *that*: much more in hard labor, much more in jails, too often with wounds, many times in life-threatening situations.
24 Under Jewish people, five times I received forty *lashes* minus one.
25 Three times I was beaten with a stick. Once I was attacked with stones. Three times I was shipwrecked. I have done a night and a day in the deep sea.
26 Many times I have traveled on the road with the dangers of rivers, with the dangers of bandits, with the dangers from family, with the dangers from non-Jews, with the dangers in the city, with the dangers in the uninhabited place, with the dangers in the sea, with the dangers among counterfeit brothers,
27 with labor and difficulty, many times in sleepless nights, with famine and thirst, with many times of going without food, in cold and nakedness.
28 In addition to all these things and similar things is the daily tension on me for the care of all the assemblies.
29 Who is weak, and I am not weak? Who stumbles, and I am not inflamed?
30 If I must brag, I will brag about the things that are caused by my weakness.
31 (The God and Father of the Master Jesus, the *God and Father* who has blessings conferred on Him for the spans of time, knows that I am not lying.)
32 In Damascus, the governor under Aretas, the king, was watching over the city of Damascenes so that he could arrest me,

33 and I was lowered through a window in a rope basket through the wall and escaped from his hands.

12

1 Though it is necessary to be bragging, it certainly is not advantageous. I will come to sightings and things that the Master uncovers.
2 I know a person in the Anointed King (whether in a body, I don't know, or outside of the body, I don't know, God knows). This type of person was snatched up to the third heaven fourteen years ago.
3 And I know that this type of person (whether in a body or apart from the body, I don't know, God knows)
4 was snatched up into paradise and heard inexpressible statements that a person is not allowed to speak.
5 I will brag for this type of person, but I will not brag for me except in my weaknesses.
6 You see, though I might want to brag about my sightings and the things that the Master has uncovered to me, I won't be distracted. I will state the truth. I am going easy on the bragging so that someone won't consider me to be above what he sees in me or hears from me.
7 And this is why, with the superiority of the things the Master uncovered to me, so that I may not be raised too far up, a spike was given to me in my physical body, an opponent's announcer, so that it may slug me, so that I may not be raised too far up.
8 I begged the Master three times about this so that it might back off from me,
9 and He has stated to me, "My generosity is enough for you. You see, My ability is finished in weakness." So I will most gladly rather brag about my weaknesses so that the Anointed King's ability might be set up over me.
10 This is why I am delighted with weaknesses, with injuries, with shortages, with persecutions and difficulties on behalf of the Anointed King. You see, when I am weak, at that time I am able.
11 I have become distracted. You urged me. You see, you ought to endorse me. In nothing was I inferior to the super missionaries, even though I am nothing.
12 Certainly the missionary's proofs were worked on and completed in you in every bit of persistence with proofs, incredible things, and abilities.

13 You see, how is it that you were worse than the rest of the assemblies, except that I myself did not freeload off you? As an act of generosity, forgive me this wrong.

14 Look, I am ready to come to you this third time, and I will not freeload off you. You see, I don't look for your things. I look for you. Children aren't obligated to be stockpiling stuff for the parents. No, the parents *stockpile stuff* for the children.

15 I will most gladly spend and be completely spent on behalf of your souls. Though loving you much more, I am loved less.

16 It must be. I didn't press a heavy load down on you. But did I, being sly, take you with deception?

17 I didn't take advantage of you through any of the people that I sent out to you, did I?

18 I encouraged Titus to visit you, and I sent the brother out on a mission together with him. Titus didn't take advantage of you in any way, did he? Didn't we walk around in the same spirit, in the same footsteps?

19 Does it seem to you that we are spending all this time defending ourselves to you? We are speaking directly facing God in the Anointed King. Everything, loved ones, is on your behalf, to build you.

20 You see, I am afraid that somehow when I come to you I might not find you such as I want you to be and I might be found by you such as you don't want me to be. I am afraid that somehow there will be fighting, hostile passion, bursts of anger, contentions, bad comments, whispers, conceited attitudes, or conflicts.

21 I am afraid that when I come to you again, my God will put me down low before you and I will grieve for many of those who have previously sinned and did not change their ways in the area of what is not clean, sexual sin, and indulgent activity that they repeatedly did.

13

1 I am coming to you this third time. Every statement will be established based on the mouth of two and three witnesses.

2 To the people who have previously sinned and to all the rest, I have stated before as I did when I was beside you the second time, and I am telling you beforehand as I am away from you now that if I come into that situation again, I won't go easy on you.

3 Since you are looking for a proven track record of the Anointed King speaking in me, and since He is not weak to you but has ability among you, *I won't go easy on you.*

4 You see, He also was nailed to a cross from weakness, but He lives from God's ability. We also are weak in Him, but we will live together with Him for you from God's ability.

5 Challenge yourselves about whether or not you are in the trust. Prove yourselves. Or do you yourselves not correctly understand that Jesus, the Anointed King, is in you if you are not unapproved?

6 I anticipate that you will know that we are not unapproved.

7 Our wish to God is that you don't do anything bad. *We* don't *wish this* so that we might shine as approved people, but so that you may do the nice thing, and we, *compared to your nice thing,* may be like unapproved people.

8 You see, we are not capable of anything against the truth. We are over with the truth.

9 We are happy when we may be weak and you may be competent. We also wish for this: your full development.

10 Because of this, I am writing these things as I am away from you so that when I am beside you I might not behave severely aligned with the authority that the Master gave me to build you and not to take you down.

11 For the rest of the time, brothers, be happy. Be fully developed. Be encouraged. Focus on the same thing. Be peaceful, and the God of love and peace will be with you.

12 Say hello to each other with a sacred friendly gesture.

13 All the sacred people say hello to you.

14 May the generosity of the Master Jesus, the Anointed King, the love of God, and the sharing of the Sacred Spirit be with all of you.

Galatians

1

1 From: Paul (a missionary not *sent out* from people, and not *sent out* through a person either, but *sent out* through Jesus, the Anointed King, and through Father God, who got Him up from the dead).

2 *This is* also from all the brothers together with me. To: Galatia's assemblies (Galatia was an area in north central Turkey that included the cities of Pisidian Antioch, Iconium, Lystra, and Derbe).

3 Generosity and peace to you out from God, our Father, and Master Jesus, the Anointed King.

4 Jesus gave Himself for our sins in order that He might take us out of the evil span of time that has stood here in a way that is aligned with what our God and Father wants.

5 The magnificence for the spans of time of the spans of time *belongs* to our God. Amen.

6 I am amazed at how quickly you are transferring away from the One who generously invited you, the Anointed King, to a different good news.

7 It is not another good news. It is just that there are some people agitating you and wanting to alter the good news of the Anointed King.

8 But even if we or an angel from heaven should share good news with you contrary to what we shared with you, he must be doomed.

9 As we have stated before, I even now say again, "If anyone shares good news with you contrary to what you received in, he must be doomed."

10 You see, am I now persuading people or God? Or am I looking to do what people would like? If I were still doing what people like, I would not be the Anointed King's slave.

11 You see, I am letting you know, brothers, that the good news that I shared is not aligned with a person.

12 And I didn't receive it directly from a person either. And I wan't taught it either. But *I got it* through Jesus, the Anointed King, uncovering it *to me*.

13 You see, you heard of my behavior in the past in Judaism. I was pursuing God's assembly even more than others and damaging it.

14 I was progressing in Judaism above many my own age in my family. I had much more passion for the traditions passed down by my fathers.
15 But when it seemed like a good idea to the God who isolated me from my mother's belly and invited me through His generosity
16 to uncover His Son in me so that I may share the good news of Him among the non-Jews, I didn't consult with anyone right away, no one with a physical body and blood.
17 I didn't go up into Jerusalem to the *people who were* missionaries before me either. But I went off into Arabia and returned again into Damascus.
18 Following that, after three years, I went up into Jerusalem to visit Cephas *(Aramaic for Peter)*. And I stayed over with him for fifteen days.
19 But I didn't see a different one of the missionaries except James, the brother of the Master.
20 The things that I am writing to you, look, in the sight of God, I am not lying.
21 Following that, I went to the slopes of Syria and Cilicia (the southeastern coastal region of Turkey where Tarsus, Paul's birthplace, is).
22 Judea's assemblies in the Anointed King were unaware of my face.
23 They were only hearing, "The one pursuing us in the past is now sharing the good news of the trust that in the past he was damaging,"
24 and from me, they were praising God's magnificence.

2

1 Fourteen years following that, I walked up to Jerusalem again with Barnabas. We also took Titus along together with us.
2 I walked up there regarding what had been uncovered to me. And I laid out to them the good news that I speak about publicly among the non-Jews. But I *spoke* privately to the people who seem to be something *and showed them* how what I am running for and what I ran for is not meaningless. *I am running for our freedom in the Anointed King.*
3 But they did not urge Titus, the Greek, a non-Jew who was together with me, to be circumcised either.
4 We spoke to them privately because of the undetected counterfeit brothers. They are the ones that have quietly come in to spy out and plot against our freedom that we have in the Anointed King Jesus. *They do this* so that they will make us complete slaves.

5 We didn't give in to them or comply with them for even an hour so that the truth of the good news might stay through to you.
6 It is not substantial to me to be something from the people seeming to be something, whatever kind of people they were in the past. God does not receive a person based on his appearance. You see, the people seeming to be something imposed nothing on me.
7 But just the opposite, they saw that I had been trusted with the good news of the uncircumcision *(the non-Jews)*, just as Peter had been trusted with the good news of the circumcision *(the Jews)*.
8 You see, the One who was active with Peter for his mission to the circumcision, was also active with me for my mission to the non-Jews.
9 After knowing the generosity that God had shown to me, James, Cephas, and John (the ones seeming to be pillars) shook right hands with me and Barnabas *to confirm our* partnership. They agreed that we would go to the non-Jews and they would go to the circumcision.
10 They only asked that we would remember the poor. This very thing was something that I also made every effort to do.
11 But when Cephas came to Antioch, I stood in opposition to him right in front of his face because of what had been known against him.
12 You see, before certain people came out from James, he was eating together with the non-Jews. But when they came, he was backing off and isolating himself from the non-Jews because he was afraid of the people from the circumcision.
13 And the rest of the Jewish people also faked it together with him *and acted like they don't eat with the non-Jews*. Even Barnabas was led away together with their faked behavior.
14 But when I saw that they are not straight-footed toward the truth of the good news, I said to Cephas in front of everyone, "If you, being Jewish, are living like the non-Jews and definitely not like the Jews, how are you urging the non-Jews to become Jews?"
15 We are Jewish by birth. We are not sinful from non-Jews.
16 We realize that a person is not made right from doing what the law says if it is not through trusting Jesus, the Anointed King. And we trusted in the Anointed King Jesus so that we might be made right from our trust of the Anointed King and not from doing what the law says. No physical body will be made right from doing what the law says.
17 But if, as we were looking to be made right in the Anointed King, we ourselves were actually found to be sinful *because we ate with non-*

Jews, so what would the Anointed King be? A servant of sin? It could not happen.

18 You see, if I again build these things that I tore down, I myself stand together with a violator.

19 Through the law, I died to the law so that I might live for God.

20 I have been nailed to a cross together with the Anointed King. I no longer live, but the Anointed King lives in me. What I now live in a physical body, I live in trust of God's Son who loved me and turned Himself in on my behalf.

21 I don't disregard God's generosity. You see, if the right way is through the law, clearly the Anointed King died for nothing.

3

1 O unobservant Galatians, who tricked you? Right in front of your eyes, it was openly written to you that Jesus, the Anointed King, had been nailed to a cross.

2 I only want to learn this from you, did you receive the Spirit from doing what the law says or from what you heard about trust?

3 This is how you are unobservant. After beginning in the Spirit, now you are finishing yourselves up with the physical body.

4 Did you suffer so many things for no reason, if it definitely even is for no reason?

5 So the One who is supplying more than the Spirit to you and who is active with abilities among you, does He come from doing what the law says or from what you heard about trust?

6 Just as "Abraham trusted God, and it was considered to him for the right way" *(Genesis 15:6),*

7 clearly you must know that these people from trust are Abraham's sons.

8 When the *Old Testament* writing saw beforehand that God makes the non-Jews right from trust, it shared this good news with Abraham before it happened, "All the non-Jews will be conferred with blessings in you" *(Genesis 22:18).*

9 And so the people from trust are conferred with blessings together with the Abraham who trusted God.

10 You see, as many as are *trying to* do what the law says are under a curse. The Bible says, "Everyone is cursed who does not stay in *and do* all the things that have been written in the scroll of the law" *(Deuteronomy 27:26).*

11 It is obvious that not one person is made right beside God in the law because, "The person who does what is right will live from trust" *(Habakkuk 2:4)*.

12 The law is not from trust. No, the person who does the things written in the law will live in them *(Leviticus 18:5)*.

13 The Anointed King purchased us from the law's curse after becoming a curse on our behalf because the Bible says, "Everyone who hangs on a wooden pole is cursed" *(Deuteronomy 21:23)*.

14 That way Abraham's conferring of blessing would come to the non-Jews in the Anointed King Jesus so that we might receive the promise of the Spirit through the trust.

15 Brothers, I am saying that this is also true when it comes to a person. Once a deal from a person is made official, no one invalidates it or adds to it.

16 The promises were stated to Abraham and to his seed. He does not say, "and to the seeds," as if the promises would be based on many seeds, but as if they would be based on one seed, "and to your seed." That seed is the Anointed King.

17 What I am saying is this: The law (that happened 430 years after the deal) does not nullify the deal (that has been made official by God *long before the law appeared*). The law does not make the promise useless.

18 You see, if the inheritance is from the law, it is no longer from a promise. But it is through a promise that God, in an act of generosity, has given the inheritance to Abraham.

19 So why does the law exist? *The law exists* thanks to the violations. It was added till the seed would come: the Anointed King that had been promised. The law was specifically arranged through angels in the hand of a middleman, *Moses*.

20 The middleman is not a middleman of one. *He keeps the different parties separate.* But God is one. *He made the promise directly to Abraham.*

21 So is the law against the promises of God? It could not happen. You see, if a law that can give life was given, the right way really would have been from the law.

22 But the *Old Testament* writing closed everything up under sin so that the promise that comes from trusting Jesus, the Anointed King, might be given to the people trusting.

23 Before the time for the trust to come, the law was watching over us. We were being closed up into the trust that was going to be uncovered.

24 And so the law has become a babysitter of us for the Anointed King so that we might be made right from trust.
25 But after the trust comes, we are no longer under a babysitter.
26 You see, you are all God's sons through trust in the Anointed King Jesus.
27 As many of you as were submerged into the Anointed King have put the Anointed King on.
28 There is not Jewish or Greek. There is not slave or free. There is not male and female. You see, you all are one in the Anointed King Jesus.
29 If you are the Anointed King's, clearly you are Abraham's seed, inheritors aligned with a promise.

1 I am saying this: For as much time as the inheritor is an infant, he is nothing more substantial than a slave though he is master of them all.
2 But he is under administrators and managers till the time that has been predetermined by the father.
3 This is how we also, when we were infants, were made slaves by the world's conventional practices.
4 But when the time had fully come, God sent off His Son. His Son came from a woman and came under the law.
5 That way He could purchase the people under the law from the conventional practices so that we could fully receive the adoption.
6 And because you are sons, God sent off the Son's Spirit into our hearts yelling, "Daddy, the Father!"
7 And so you are no longer a slave, but a son. If you are a son, you are also an inheritor through God.
8 But at that time, when you certainly didn't know God, you were slaves to the things that by their very nature are not gods.
9 Now, after knowing God, rather, after being known by God, how are you turning back to the weak and poor conventional practices again and wanting to be slaves to them all over again?
10 You closely watch days, months, certain times, and years.
11 I am afraid when it comes to you that somehow I have labored for you for no reason.
12 Become like me because I also am like you, brothers. I plead with you. You didn't harm me in any way.
13 You realize that because of a weakness of the physical body I shared good news with you previously.

14 You *were* troubled by my physical body, but you didn't treat it as a bad thing. You didn't despise it. No, as if you were God's angel, you accepted me as if I were the Anointed King Jesus.
15 So where is your blessedness? You see, I am a witness to you that, if possible, you would have plucked out your eyes and given them to me.
16 And so, have I become your enemy because I am truthful with you?
17 They are not passionate about you in a nice way. But they want to exclude you from everything else so that you may be passionate about them.
18 It is nice to always be passionate in a nice way and not only during the time that I am close beside you.
19 My children, again I am in labor with you until the Anointed King is formed in you.
20 I was wanting to be close beside you now and change my voice because I am not sure what to think about you.
21 You who want to be under the law, tell me, don't you hear the law?
22 You see, the Bible says that Abraham had two sons: one from the servant girl and one from the free woman *(Genesis 16:3; 21:2)*.
23 But the son from the servant girl certainly has been born aligned with a physical body, and the son from the free woman has been born through a promise.
24 These things have another meaning. You see, these are two deals. One is certainly out of Mount Sinai. It gives birth to slavery. This is the one that is the servant girl, Hagar.
25 Hagar is Mount Sinai in Arabia. She is now marching in step together with Jerusalem. You see, she is a slave with her children.
26 The one from above is free Jerusalem. This is the one that is our mother.
27 You see, the Bible says, "Celebrate, infertile woman who doesn't give birth to children! Burst out and shout, the woman who hasn't been in labor, because the uninhabited *woman* has many children, more than the woman who has the husband" *(Isaiah 54:1)*.
28 You, brothers, are aligned with Isaac. You are children of promise.
29 But even as it was at that time, so it also is now. The one who was born aligned with a physical body was persecuting the one aligned with the Spirit.
30 But what does the *Old Testament* writing say? "Throw out the servant girl and her son. You see, the servant girl's son will not in any way inherit anything with the free woman's son" *(Genesis 21:10)*

31 For this reason, brothers, we are not the servant girl's children. We are the free woman's children.

5

1 The Anointed King set us free so that we can be free. So stand and don't be held in by a crossbeam of slavery again. 2 Look, I, Paul, tell you that if you all *think that you should* be circumcised, the Anointed King will in no way benefit you.
3 Again, I am a witness to every person being circumcised that he is obligated to do the whole law.
4 Any of you who *think that you* are made right in the law have pushed the Anointed King away and made it so that He is useless to you. You have fallen from God's generosity.
5 You see, we have the Spirit from trust. We patiently wait for the good that we anticipate from the right way.
6 In the Anointed King Jesus, circumcision doesn't have any strength and uncircumcision doesn't either. But *what has strength is* trust that is active through love.
7 You were running nicely. Who interrupted you to not be persuaded by the truth?
8 The persuasion *that you have* is not from the One who invited you.
9 A little yeast causes the whole batch to rise.
10 I have been persuaded that you will stay in the Master and not focus on anything else. The one agitating you will haul the judgment, whoever he may be.
11 I, brothers, if I am still speaking publicly *in favor of* circumcision, why am I still being persecuted? *If I am in favor of being a slave to the law,* I have clearly made *the freedom of* the cross that they stumble on useless.
12 If only the people upsetting you would also chop themselves off from you.
13 You see, you were invited based on freedom, brothers. Only *it is* not the freedom *that gives* the physical body an opportunity *to do whatever it wants*. No, *it is the freedom that allows* you to be slaves to each other through love.
14 The entire law has been accomplished in one message, in the *message that says*, "You will love the person near you as yourself."
15 If you bite and eat up each other, look out, you might be consumed by each other.
16 I say, "Walk around in the Spirit, and you will not in any way finish the physical body's desire."

17 You see, what the physical body desires is against the Spirit, and what the Spirit desires is against the physical body. These lie in opposition to each other so that you don't do whatever you may want to do.
18 If you are led by the Spirit, you are not under the law.
19 The kind of things the physical body does are apparent. These are the things that are sexual sin, anything that is not clean, indulgent activity,
20 idol worship, drug abuse, hostile relationships, fighting, hostile passion, bursts of anger, contentions, factions, splinter groups,
21 envies, bouts of drunkenness, wild parties, and things like these. I am telling you beforehand about these, just as I already said, that the people constantly doing these types of things will not inherit God's monarchy.
22 But the Spirit's fruit is love, happiness, peace, patience, kindness, goodness, trust,
23 submissiveness, and self-restraint. There is no law against these types of things.
24 The Anointed King Jesus' people have nailed the physical body to a cross together with the hardships and the desires.
25 If we live with the Spirit, we should also march in step with the Spirit.
26 Let's not end up having delusions of grandeur, hassling each other and envying each other.

1 Brothers, if a person is actually intercepted in a certain infraction, you, the spiritual ones, develop this type of person in a spirit of submissiveness. Keep an eye out for yourself, and you won't experience trouble.
2 Haul each other's heavy loads, and in this way, you will fully accomplish the law of the Anointed King.
3 You see, if someone who is nothing seems to think he is something, he is seducing himself.
4 Each person must check *and correct* his own work. Then he will be able to brag about what he himself alone has done and not what a different person has done.
5 You see, each person will haul his own load.
6 When the message echos down to someone. That person must share all kinds of good with the person who echoed it down to him.
7 Don't be misled. No one makes a fool of God. You see, whatever a person plants, this is what he will also harvest.

8 The person who plants into his own physical body will harvest deterioration from the physical body, but the person who plants into the Spirit will harvest life that spans all time from the Spirit.

9 We should not get discouraged as we do what is nice. You see, if we don't give up, when the time is right, we will harvest nice things from it.

10 So clearly, as we have time, let's work on what is good for everyone, but especially *what is good* for the people living in the house of trust.

11 Look at how big the letters are that I am writing to you with my hand.

12 All of these people who want to look good in the physical body urge you to be circumcised. It is only so that they won't be persecuted for the Anointed King's cross.

13 You see, the circumcised people themselves don't observe the law either, but they want you to be circumcised so that they might brag about your physical body.

14 May it never happen to me that I brag unless it is about the cross of our Master Jesus, the Anointed King. Through Him, to me, the world has been nailed to a cross, and to the world, I *have been nailed to a cross*.

15 You see, circumcision isn't anything, and uncircumcision *isn't anything* either, but *the thing that is something is* a new creation.

16 And peace is on as many as will march in step with this standard, and also forgiving kindness is on God's Israel.

17 For the rest of the time, no one must bother me. You see, I haul the branding scars of Jesus in my body.

18 May the generosity of our Master Jesus, the Anointed King, be with your spirit, brothers. Amen.

Ephesians

1

1 From: Paul, a missionary of the Anointed King Jesus because that's what God wants. To: The sacred people who are in Ephesus *(a city in Western Turkey)* and the people who trust in the Anointed King Jesus.

2 Generosity and peace to you out from God, our Father, and Master Jesus, the Anointed King.

3 The God who has blessings conferred on Him and the Father of our Master Jesus, the Anointed King, is the One who conferred blessings on us in every spiritual blessing in the heavenly regions in the Anointed King.

4 This is just how He selected us before the world was formed to be *in a special place*, in Him, *in the Anointed King,* so that we might be sacred and unblemished directly in His sight in love.

5 He designated us beforehand to be His adopted sons through Jesus, the Anointed King. *This is* aligned with the good notion of what He wants.

6 *It is* for high praise of the magnificence of His generosity. From it *(His generosity)*, He showed us generosity in the One that He has loved.

7 In Him, we have the paid release through His blood, the forgiveness of the infractions, aligned with the wealth of His generosity.

8 *His generosity* overflowed into us in every insight and focus.

9 This let us know the secret of what He wants aligned with His good notion that He put in Him beforehand.

10 For management of the fullness of the times, *He wants* to sum everything up in the Anointed King--*everything* in the heavens and *everything* on the earth.

11 In Him, we also were assigned an inheritance and were designated beforehand to be in Him. *This was* aligned with the purpose of the One who is active in all things aligned with the intention of what He wants.

12 *He wants* us who have anticipated good in the Anointed King beforehand to be for high praise of His magnificence.

13 In Him, after you also heard the message of the truth, the good news of your rescue, in Him, after you also trusted, you were sealed by the promise's Spirit, the Sacred Spirit.

14 The Sacred Spirit is a down payment of our inheritance that pays for the release of what He acquired for high praise of His magnificence.

15 Because of this, after also hearing of the trust of each of you in the Master Jesus and of your love for all of the sacred people,

16 I don't stop being thankful for you and making a mention of you in my prayers.

17 *I pray* that the God of our Master Jesus, the Anointed King, the Father of the magnificence, might give you a spirit of insight and a spirit that uncovers a correct understanding of Him.

18 *I pray* that the eyes of your heart will have things lit up for them so that you might see what is the anticipation of His invitation, what is the wealth of the magnificence of His inheritance in the sacred people,

19 and what is the superior magnitude of His ability for us who trust aligned with the influence of the power of His strength.

20 With His strength, He was active in the Anointed King when He got Him up from the dead and seated Him on His right side in the heavenly regions.

21 *There He is* over and above every head ruler, authority, ability, government, and every name that is named, not only in this span of time, but also in the span of time that is going to come.

22 He also placed all things under His feet and gave Him to the assembly as the head over everything.

23 The assembly is the thing that is His body. *It is* the fullness of the One who fills everything in everything.

2

1 *His body* even *includes* you who are dead with your infractions and sins.

2 In the past, you walked around in them aligned with this world's span of time aligned with the head of the air's authority (the spirit that is now active in the sons of unbelief).

3 All of us were messed up in the past among the sons of unbelief in the desires of our physical body doing the things that the physical body and the mind wants. We also were children of punishment by our very nature, even as the rest.

4 But God is wealthy in forgiving kindness. He loved us with His great love.

5 He brought us to life together with the Anointed King, even we who were dead with the infractions. You have been rescued by *God's* generosity.

6 And He got us up together and seated us together in the heavenly regions in the Anointed King Jesus.
7 That way in the upcoming spans of time He could display the superior wealth of His generosity in kindness that He showed to us in the Anointed King Jesus.
8 You see, with His generosity, you have been rescued by trusting. And this is not from anyone among you. It is God's contribution.
9 It is not from what you do. *It is from the One you trust.* That way no one can brag.
10 You see, we are what He made. We were created in the Anointed King Jesus to do the good actions that God had ready beforehand so that we might walk around in them.
11 For this reason, remember that in the past you were non-Jews in the physical body. You were called Uncircumcision by what is called Circumcision, circumcision that is handmade in the physical body.
12 At that time you were without the Anointed King. You had been alienated from the citizenship of Israel and were strangers to the deals of the promise. You had no anticipation of good. You were godless in the world.
13 But right now, in the Anointed King Jesus, you, the people who in the past were a long way away, became near in the blood of the Anointed King.
14 You see, He is our peace. He made both of them one and broke down the partition of the barrier wall.
15 With His physical body, He ended the hostile relationship after making the law of the demands in rules useless so that He might create the two into one new person in Him and make peace.
16 *He did this so that* He might completely restore both of them to God in one body through the cross and kill the hostile relationship with it.
17 He also came and shared the good news of peace to you (the people a long way away) and peace to the people near.
18 Through Him, we both have access to the Father in One Spirit.
19 So clearly you are no longer strangers and foreign residents. No, you are co-citizens of the sacred people and living in God's house.
20 You are built on the foundation of the missionaries and preachers. The primary corner *of God's house* is the Anointed King Jesus.
21 In Him, an entire building linked together grows into a sacred temple in the Master.
22 In Him, you also are built together into God's residence in the Spirit.

3

1 Thanks to this, I, Paul, am the prisoner of the Anointed King Jesus on behalf of you, the non-Jews.

2 *I don't know* if you definitely have heard of the responsibility that was given to me of managing God's generosity for you.

3 The secret was made known to me when God uncovered it. This is just as I wrote about previously in a few words.

4 You are able to be aware of my understanding in the secret of the Anointed King by reading it.

5 It was not made known to the sons of the people of different generations as it is now uncovered to His sacred missionaries and preachers in the Spirit.

6 *It was not known that* through the good news *the non-Jews were* to be inheritors together, a body together, and possessors together of the promise in the Anointed King Jesus.

7 I became a servant of this *good news* aligned with the free handout of God's generosity that was given to me aligned with the influence of His ability.

8 This generosity was given to me, the one who is smaller than the smallest of all sacred people, to share the good news with the non-Jews of the wealth of the Anointed King that is impossible to track

9 and to light up for everyone the responsibility of managing the secret that has been hid away from the spans of time in the God who created everything.

10 That way now, God's multifaceted insight might be made known to the head rulers and the authorities in the heavenly regions through the assembly.

11 *The assembly is* aligned with the purpose of the spans of time that He made in the Anointed King Jesus, our Master.

12 In Him, we have the clear public statement and access with confidence through the trust of Him.

13 For this reason, I am asking you not to get discouraged in the hard times that I experience on your behalf. It is, in fact, your magnificence.

14 Thanks to this, I bend my knees down to the Father

15 from whom every family tree in heaven and on earth is named.

16 That way He may give you the ability to become strong in the inner person through His Spirit aligned with the wealth of His magnificence in ability.

17 Once you have been rooted and have laid a foundation in love, the Anointed King is to live in your hearts through your trust

18 so that you might be strong enough to take down together with all the sacred people what is the width, length, height, and depth,
19 to know the Anointed King's love that is superior to knowledge so that you might be filled in all of God's fullness.
20 To the One who above everything is able to do even much more of what we ask for or are aware of aligned with the ability that is active in us,
21 to Him *belongs* the magnificence in the assembly and in the Anointed King Jesus for all the generations of the span of time of the spans of time. Amen.

1 So I, the prisoner in the Master, encourage you to walk around in a manner deserving of the invitation that you were invited with.
2 Walk around with every bit of lowly focus and submissiveness with patience, tolerating each other in love,
3 making every effort to keep the Spirit's oneness in the bond of peace:
4 one body and one spirit, just as you also were invited in one anticipation of your invitation,
5 one Master, one trust, one submersion,
6 one God and Father of everyone. He is on everyone, through everyone, and in everyone.
7 Generosity was given to each one of us aligned with the amount of the Anointed King's free handout.
8 For this reason, it says, "When He stepped up into a high position, He incarcerated the people who were incarcerated and gave presents to the people" *(Psalm 68:18)*.
9 How is it that He stepped up if He didn't also step down into the lower parts of the earth?
10 The One who Himself stepped down is also the One who stepped up over and above all of the heavens so that He might accomplish all things.
11 And He Himself gave not only the missionaries, but also the preachers, and the people who share the good news, and the shepherds and teachers.
12 *They work* toward the development of the sacred people for the work of serving, for building the Anointed King's body.
13 The goal *is that* we all might make it to the oneness of the trust and of the correct understanding of God's Son, to a complete man, to the measurement of the size of the Anointed King's fullness.

14 That way we will no longer be infants pushed back and forth and carried around by every wind of instruction, in the rigged game of the people, in slyness *pointed* toward the misleading lie's scheme.

15 But as we are truthful and loving, we will grow everything into the One who is the head, the Anointed King.

16 From Him, as the entire body is linked together and pulled together through every supply connection aligned with the amount of influence each one, each part, has, it makes the body grow and build itself in love.

17 So I say this (and I am a witness in the Master), "You shouldn't walk around anymore like the non-Jews also walk around." *They walk around* in the uselessness of their way of thinking.

18 They have been darkened in the mind. They have been alienated from God's life because of the lack of awareness that is in them because of the stone hardness of their heart.

19 In fact, they have stopped feeling anything. They give themselves over to indulgent activity. They work on everything that is not clean and desire more.

20 But this is not how you learned the Anointed King.

21 If you definitely heard Him and were taught in Him, just as truth is in Jesus,

22 you are to put away everything *that is* aligned with your prior behavior, your former person that is worsened because it is aligned with the fraud's desires.

23 But you are to rejuvenate the spirit of your way of thinking

24 and put on the new person that was created aligned with God in the right way and holiness of the truth.

25 For this reason, after putting away the lie, each of you must speak truth with the person near you because we are body parts of each other.

26 Be enraged, and don't sin. The sun must not go down on your fit of rage.

27 Don't give the Accuser a place *to stay* either.

28 The person stealing must not steal anymore. Instead he must labor, working what is good with his own hands so that he may have *something* to give out to the person who has a·need.

29 Don't let any defective message travel out from your mouth. But if something is good for building what is needed, *say it* so that it might give generosity to the people hearing it.

30 And don't make God's Sacred Spirit sad. *It is* in *the Spirit* that you were sealed for the day of the paid release.

31 Every bit of bitterness, anger, rage, yelling, and insult must be taken away from you together with all badness.
32 Become kind to each other, goodhearted, forgiving each other as an act of generosity, just as God also as an act of generosity forgave you in the Anointed King.

1 So become imitators of God as loved children,
2 and walk around in love, just as the Anointed King also loved us and turned Himself in on our behalf to be an offering and sacrifice to God for an aroma of a sweet fragrance.
3 Sexual sin and all of what is not clean or the desire for more must not be named among you either. This is just like what is appropriate for sacred people.
4 Also keep away from shameful behavior and foolish talk or a snide remark. These things don't meet God's high standards. But instead be thankful.
5 You see, realize this and know that every person who commits sexual sin, or who is not clean, or who desires more (which is what an idol worshiper does) does not have an inheritance in the Anointed King's and God's monarchy.
6 No one must fool you with empty words. You see, God's punishment comes on the sons of unbelief because of these things.
7 So don't become companions together with them.
8 You see, *in the dark, you can't see anything. In the light, you see everything.* You once were darkness, but now, in the Master, you are light. Walk around as children of light.
9 You see, the light's fruit is in all goodness, the right way, and truth.
10 *With your walk,* prove what is well-liked by the Master.
11 And don't share together in the fruitless actions of darkness. But instead even reprimand them.
12 You see, the things they end up hiding are shameful to even talk about.
13 All the things that are being reprimanded are being shown under the light. You see, everything shown is light.
14 For this reason, it says, "You who are sleeping, get up, come back to life from the dead, and the Anointed King will be a light over you."
15 So look specifically at how you walk around, not like people who don't have insight, but like insightful people
16 buying up the time *(or in other words, making good use of the time)* because the days are evil.

17 Because of this, don't become distracted, but understand what the Master wants.
18 And don't get drunk with wine in that drunkenness is reckless. But be filled in the Spirit
19 speaking to yourselves in psalms, praise songs, and spiritual songs, singing and reciting psalms in your heart to the Master,
20 always being thankful to your God and Father for everything in the name of *and on behalf of* our Master Jesus, the Anointed King,
21 and placing yourselves under each other out of respect for the Anointed King.
22 The Wives -- *Place yourselves* under your own husbands in the same way *that you place yourselves* under the Master
23 because a husband is the wife's head in the same way that the Anointed King is also the assembly's head. He is a rescuer of the body.
24 But as the assembly is placed under the Anointed King, so also the wives *are placed* under the husbands in everything.
25 The Husbands -- Love the wives just as the Anointed King also loved the assembly and turned Himself in on its behalf.
26 That way, He may make it sacred after cleaning it with the bath of the water in a statement
27 so that He might offer a magnificent bride to Himself--the assembly--not having a stain, or a wrinkle, or any of these types of things, but so that it may be sacred and unblemished.
28 This is how the husbands are also obligated to be loving their own wives, as their own bodies. The husband that loves his own wife loves himself.
29 You see, no one ever hates his own physical body, but he fully nurtures it and keeps it warm, just as the Anointed King also does with the assembly
30 because we are body parts of His body.
31 For this, "a person will leave his father and mother behind, stick like glue to his wife, and the two will be in one physical body" *(Genesis 2:24)*.
32 This secret is great. I am talking in reference to the Anointed King and the assembly.
33 More importantly, each and every one of you husbands also must love your own wife like this, as yourself, and the wife *must be loved* so that she may respect the husband.

6

1 The Children -- Obey your parents in the Master. You see, this is right.

2 Value your father and mother. This is, in fact, the first demand with a promise.

3 *The promise is* "so that it might become well with you and you will be on the earth for a long time."

4 And the Fathers -- Don't incite rage in your children, but fully nurture them in the Master's discipline and correction.

5 The Slaves -- Obey the masters (as far as the physical body is concerned) with fear and trembling. Dedicate your heart to them in the same way *that you dedicate your heart* to the Anointed King.

6 *When you dedicate your heart to them,* don't *do it* aligned with eye-slavery *(only obeying when the master is looking)* as if you are people pleasers, but as the Anointed King's slaves, doing what God wants from a soul.

7 Be slaves with a good attitude as if *you are having it* for the Master and not for people.

8 Realize that if each person does something good, this is what he will retrieve directly from the Master whether he is a slave or free.

9 And the Masters -- Do the same things to them. Ease up on the threat. Realize that the Master of both them and you is in the heavens and that appearances don't matter beside Him.

10 For the rest of the time, become competent in the Master and in the power of His strength.

11 Put on God's full body armor with the specific goal of being able to stand *when you are* facing the Accuser's schemes

12 because the wrestling match for us is not facing blood and a physical body, but facing the head rulers, facing the authorities, facing the global powers of this darkness, facing the spiritual elements of the evilness in the heavenly regions.

13 Because of this, take up God's full body armor so that you might be able to stand in opposition to them in the evil day, even after working on and completing absolutely everything needed to stand.

14 So stand after tying a sash around your waist in truth, after putting on the armored vest of the right way,

15 and after tying sole pads on under your feet in readiness of the good news of peace.

16 Take up the shield of trust in everything. With it, you will be able to extinguish all of the flaming objects that the evil one throws at you.

17 And accept the head protection of the rescue process and the dagger of the Spirit that is God's statement.

18 Every time that is the right time, pray in the spirit through every prayer and plea. And for the same thing, don't go to sleep at always staying close by and pleading concerning all the sacred people.

19 Do this on my behalf too so that when I open my mouth in a clear public statement, I might be given a message that will let people know about the secret of the good news

20 (I am an older man in chains on behalf of it) so that I might make clear public statements in it *(the good news)* in the way that it is necessary for me to speak.

21 Tychicus, the loved brother and reliable servant in the Master, will let you know about everything so that you also may realize the things regarding me, what I constantly do.

22 I sent Tychicus to you for this same reason, so that you might know the things about us and he might encourage your hearts.

23 Peace to the brothers and love with trust from Father God and the Master Jesus, the Anointed King.

24 *May* generosity be with all of the people who love our Master Jesus, the Anointed King, with *a love that* doesn't deteriorate.

Philippians

1

1 From: Paul and Timothy, slaves of the Anointed King Jesus. To: All of the sacred people in the Anointed King Jesus who are in Philippi together with the supervisors and servants. *(Philippi was a city in northern Greece where Lydia, the seller of purple, and the Philippian jailor lived.)*

2 Generosity and peace to you out from God, our Father, and Master Jesus, the Anointed King.

3 I am thankful to my God at every mention of you.

4 In every plea of mine for you all, I always make the plea with happiness

5 because you have shared in the good news from the first day till the present.

6 I have been confident of this very thing, that the One who began in on a good work in you will finish it up til the Anointed King Jesus' day.

7 It is right for me to be focusing on this about you because of the *fact* that I have you in the heart, both in my restraints and in the defense and authentication of the good news, since you are sharing the generosity together with me that God has given you.

8 You see, God is my witness how I yearn for you with the Anointed King Jesus' feelings of sympathy.

9 And I pray this, that your love may overflow yet more and more in having the correct understanding and all comprehension.

10 *The purpose of this is* for you to approve the substantial things so that you may be genuine and not offensive for the Anointed King's day

11 having been filled with the fruit of doing things the right way through Jesus, the Anointed King, for God's magnificence and high praise.

12 I intend for you to know, brothers, that the things against me have instead contributed to the progress of the good news

13 in such a way that my restraints became something that was shown to be in the Anointed King in the whole Roman palace and to all the rest.

14 And the majority of the brothers that are in the Master have been confident with my restraints and are much more daring to speak the message fearlessly.

15 Some also certainly speak publicly about the Anointed King because of envy and fighting, but some actually because they want *something* good *to come of it.*

16 The people from love certainly do it realizing that I am lying here for the defense of the good news.

17 But the people from contention proclaim the Anointed King in a disingenuous way supposing to raise hard times to my restraints.

18 You see, what is more important is that in every way, whether it is in a sham or in the truth, the Anointed King is proclaimed and I am happy in this, yes, and will be happy.

19 I realize that this will step out into a rescue for me through your plea and the supply of the Spirit of Jesus, the Anointed King.

20 This aligns with my eager expectation and anticipation that in nothing I will be ashamed, but in every clear public statement, as always and now, the Anointed King will be made great in my body, whether through life or through death.

21 You see, to me, the *opportunity* to be living is the Anointed King and the *opportunity* to die is gain.

22 But if the *opportunity is* to be living (in the physical body), to me, this is the fruit of work. And what will I choose? I am not making that known.

23 I am restricted by the two. I have the desire to be released and to be together with the Anointed King (you see, it is actually much better),

24 but because of you, it is more essential for me to stay over in the physical body.

25 I have been confident of this. I realize that I will stay and continue with you all for your progress and happiness of the trust.

26 That way your bragging about the Anointed King in me may overflow through my arrival to you again.

27 Only be law-abiding citizens in a manner deserving of the Anointed King's good news. That way whether I come and see you or I am away from you, I may hear these things about you: that you stand in one spirit, one soul, competing together as a team for the trust of the good news,

28 and you are not spooked by anything from the people who lie in opposition. In fact, to them, their lying in opposition is a display of ruin, but *it really is a display* of your rescue, and this *is a thing that will come* out from God.

29 The reason why *the good news* was given as an act of generosity to you on behalf of the Anointed King was not only so that you would trust in Him, but so that you would also suffer on His behalf.

30 You have the same struggle that you saw in me and now hear to be in me.

2

1 So if there is any encouragement in the Anointed King, if any comfort of love, if any sharing of the Spirit, if any feelings of sympathy and compassion,
2 fill up my happiness by focusing on the same thing. Be united souls having the same love, focusing together on the one thing,
3 nothing aligned with contention or delusions of grandeur, but with lowly focus regarding each other as having a higher position than yourselves.
4 Each of you should keep an eye out, not for your own things, but actually for the things of each of the others.
5 This is what you should focus on among you: what is also in the Anointed King Jesus.
6 He was in the form of God, but He didn't regard the *position of* being equal to God as *something that must be* tightly held on to.
7 No, He emptied Himself and took on the form of a slave when He became a being that is like people.
8 And after He found Himself to be in an entity as a person, He put Himself down low and became obedient up to death, a cross' death.
9 For this reason, God also put Him up high and in an act of generosity gave Him the name that is over every name.
10 That way every knee will bend down at the name of Jesus: every knee of heavenly beings, every knee of earthly beings, and every knee of underworld beings.
11 Every tongue will also admit out loud that the Master is Jesus, the Anointed King, for the magnificence of Father God.
12 And so, my loved ones, just as you always obeyed, not only in my presence, but now much more in my absence, work on and complete your own rescue with fear and trembling.
13 You see, God is the One who is active among you, both to want the good notion that He has and to be active for it.
14 Do everything without grumblings and ponderings
15 so that you might become faultless and unpolluted, God's unblemished children in the middle of a crooked and twisted generation. Shine among them as light sources in the world
16 as you fix your attention on the message of life. Then you will brag to me on the Anointed King's day that I didn't run or labor for a meaningless cause.

17 But if my blood is also poured out as an offering on the sacrifice and public service of your trust, I am happy. And I am happy together with you all.
18 You also must be happy in the same thing, and be happy together with me.
19 In Master Jesus, I anticipate sending Timothy to you soon so that I may also have a good soul when I know your circumstances.
20 You see, I have no one with an equal soul, someone who will really be concerned about your circumstances.
21 People all look for their own things, not the things of Jesus, the Anointed King.
22 You know his proven track record. He was a slave for the good news together with me, as a child with a father.
23 So I certainly anticipate sending this person immediately after I am able to look away from my circumstances.
24 I have been confident in the Master that I myself also will come soon.
25 I regard it as essential to send you Epaphroditus (my brother, co-worker, and fellow soldier, but your missionary and public servant of my need)
26 since, for sure, he was yearning for you all and heavyhearted because you heard that he was in frail health.
27 You see, he actually was in frail health, near to and beside death, but God showed forgiving kindness to him, not only to him, but also to me so that I would not have sadness on sadness.
28 So I more aggressively sent him so that when you see him again you might be happy and I may not be as sad.
29 So accept him in with every bit of happiness in the Master and hold these types of people as valued
30 because he was near up to the point of death because of the work of the Anointed King when he risked his soul so that he might fill up your deficiency, the public service to me.

3

1 For the rest of the time, my brothers, be happy in the Master. Writing the same things to you certainly is not lazy of me. *It is so that* you *will be* certain *of them.*
2 Look out for the dogs. Look out for the bad workers. Look out for the mutilators.
3 You see, we are the circumcision, the ones that minister in God's Spirit, that brag about the Anointed King Jesus, and that aren't confident in the physical body,

4 even though I *was* actually having confidence in the physical body. If anyone else seems to have been confident in the physical body, I have more.

5 *I was* circumcised *when I was* an eight-day-old baby. I am from Israel's family (the family line of Benjamin), and a Hebrew-speaking Jew from Hebrew-speaking Jews. Regarding the law, I was a Separatist.

6 Regarding passion, I persecuted the assembly. Regarding the right way in the law, I became faultless.

7 But the things that, in fact, were considered gains for me, these I have regarded as a loss because of the Anointed King.

8 So, yes, of course, I also regard all things to be a loss because of the higher position of the knowledge of the Anointed King Jesus, my Master. I sustained loss of all things because of Him, and I regard them to be garbage so that I might gain the Anointed King

9 and be found in Him, not having my right way from the law, but the right way that is through trust of the Anointed King, the right way from God based on trust.

10 This is so that I might know Him, the ability that His return back to life has, and the experience of sharing in His hardships as I am formed together into His death.

11 I want to be formed into His death if somehow I might make it to the *point of* standing up from the dead.

12 It is not that I already got it or already have become complete. But I pursue it if I might also completely get it. The Anointed King completely got me based on it.

13 Brothers, I don't consider myself to have completely gotten it, but one thing I do is I certainly forget the things behind and reach forward to the things in front.

14 I am aligned with a goal and pursue it for the prize of God's invitation above in the Anointed King Jesus.

15 So this is what we, as many of us as are mature, should focus on. And if you are focusing on something differently, God will uncover this to you too.

16 More importantly, we are to be marching in step with the same standard that we already came into.

17 Become imitators together of me, brothers. The people walking around like this are the ones you must keep an eye out for, just as you have us for an example.

18 You see, many walk around as enemies of the Anointed King's cross. I have talked about them many times, but now I am even talking crying.
19 Their conclusion is ruin. Their god is the belly and the magnificence in their shame. They are the ones focusing on the earthly things.
20 You see, our community is in the heavens. We also patiently wait for a rescuer from there, Master Jesus, the Anointed King.
21 He will refashion the body of our lowliness and form it together with the body of His magnificence aligned with the influence of the *fact* that He is capable and all things are placed under Him.

1 And so, my loved and yearned for brothers, my happiness and award wreath, this is how you must stand in the Master, loved ones.
2 I encourage Euodia and Syntyche to be focusing on the same thing in the Master.
3 Yes, I also ask you, my real brother who is strapped together with me, take them in together. They competed together as a team in the good news for me with both Clement and the rest of my co-workers. Their names are in the scroll of life.
4 Always be happy in the Master. Again I will state, "Be happy."
5 All people must know your polite *side*. The Master is near.
6 Don't worry about anything, but in everything let God know about your requests with the prayer and the plea with thankfulness.
7 And God's peace, that has a higher position than every way of thinking, will watch over your hearts and your patterns of thinking in the Anointed King Jesus.
8 For the rest of the time, brothers, as many things as are true, as many as are respectful, as many as are right, as many as are consecrated, as many as lead to friendship, as many as are good sounding, if there is any achievement and if there is any high praise, consider these things.
9 Constantly do these things that you learned, took in, heard, and realized in me, and the God of peace will be with you.
10 I was immensely happy in the Master because your focus on my needs for me finally flourished again. You actually were focusing on them before, but at that time, it wasn't the right time.
11 I am not saying that I don't have enough. You see, I learned to be content in the *situations* that I am in.
12 I realize both what it is like to be put down low and I realize what it is like to be overflowing. In every and in all *situations*, I have learned

the secret to be both full and hungry, to be both overflowing and lacking.

13 I have strength for everything in the One who gives me the ability that I need.

14 More importantly, you did nicely when you shared together in my hard times.

15 You also realize, Philippians, that in the beginning of the good news when I went out from Macedonia *(the region in northern Greece that Philippi is in)*, not even one assembly shared with me *by setting up* a giving and receiving account with me except you alone.

16 Even in Thessalonica, both once and twice, you sent money to me for my need.

17 It is not that I am searching for your present. No, I am searching for fruit increasing in your account.

18 I have all of everything, and I am overflowing. I have been filled up after accepting directly from Epaphroditus the *money* directly from you, an aroma of a sweet fragrance, an accepted sacrifice well-liked by God.

19 My God will fill up every need of yours aligned with His wealth in magnificence in the Anointed King Jesus.

20 The magnificence for the spans of time of the spans of time *belongs* to our God and Father. Amen.

21 Say hello to every sacred person in the Anointed King Jesus. The brothers together with me say hello to you.

22 All the sacred people say hello to you, but especially the people from Caesar's house.

23 May the generosity of the Master Jesus, the Anointed King, be with your spirit.

Colossians

1

1 From: Paul (a missionary of the Anointed King Jesus because that's what God wants) and Timothy (the brother).
2 To: The sacred and trusting brothers in the Anointed King in Colosse *(Colosse was a city in Turkey west of Galatia that Paul had not been to)*. Generosity and peace to you out from God, our Father.
3 We are always thankful to God, the Father of our Master Jesus, the Anointed King, as we pray concerning you
4 after we heard about your trust in the Anointed King Jesus and the love that you have for all the sacred people.
5 *We are also thankful* because of the anticipation of good that is set aside for you in the heavens. You heard about it before in the message of the truth of the good news.
6 As *the good news* is beside you, it is for you, just as it also is in all the world. It produces fruit and grows *in all the world,* just as it also *has produced fruit and grown* among you since the day that you heard and correctly understood God's generosity in truth.
7 It is just as you learned it from Epaphras, our loved fellow slave, who is a reliable servant of the Anointed King on your behalf.
8 He is the one who also made your love in the Spirit obvious to us.
9 Because of this, we also, since the day that we heard, don't stop praying for you and requesting that you might be filled up with the correct understanding of what He wants in every insight and spiritual understanding.
10 *That way you* may walk around in a manner deserving of the Master for every bit of what is liked in every good action. *This will allow you to* produce fruit and grow in the correct understanding of God,
11 to gain ability in every ability aligned with His magnificence's power for every bit of persistence to do what is right and for patience with happiness,
12 and to thank the Father who made you adequate for your part of the portion of the sacred people in the light.
13 He saved us from the authority of the darkness and dislodged us *out of it* into the monarchy of the Son of His love.
14 We have the paid release in Him, the forgiveness of sins.
15 He is an image of the invisible God. He is the firstborn of every created being

16 because all things in the heavens and on the earth were created in Him, the visible and the invisible, whether thrones, governments, head rulers, or authorities. All things have been created through Him and for Him.

17 He is before all things, and all things have been standing together in Him.

18 He is the head of the assembly's body. He is the beginning, the firstborn from the dead, so that He might become the One who is first in everything.

19 *God did it like this* because it seemed like a good idea for all the fullness to live in Him

20 and to completely restore all things to Him through Him, whether they are things on the earth or in the heavens. *This was* after God made peace through the blood of His cross through Him.

21 And in the past, with your evil actions, you had been alienated and were enemies to the mind, but right now He has completely restored you

22 in the body of His physical body through His death. *He did this* to offer you up, sacred, unblemished, and with no charges against you directly in His sight

23 if you definitely stay over in the trust. A foundation has been laid. It is stable and has not moved away from the good news' anticipation of good. You listened to it. It was spoken publicly among every created being under the sky. I, Paul, became a servant of it.

24 Now I am happy in the hardships that I suffered on your behalf. And it is my turn to fill up the deficiencies of the Anointed King's hard times in my physical body on behalf of His body, which is the assembly.

25 I became a servant of it *(the assembly)* aligned with the responsibility that God gave me of managing the accomplishment of God's message in you all.

26 This is the secret that has been hidden away from the spans of time and away from the generations, but right now it has been shown to His sacred people.

27 God wanted to let His sacred people know what the wealth is of the magnificence of this secret among the non-Jews. It is the Anointed King in you, the anticipation of magnificence.

28 We proclaim Him as we caution every person and teach every person in all insight so that we might offer up every person complete in the Anointed King.

29 I also labor for it as I struggle aligned with His influence that is active in me in ability.

2

1 You see, I want you to realize how great of a struggle I have over you, the people in Laodicea *(a city several miles west of Colossae)*, and as many as have not seen my face in the physical body.

2 *I struggle for the people who have not seen me* so that their hearts might be encouraged after being pulled together in love and into all the wealth of the full accomplishment of understanding into a correct understanding of God's secret, the Anointed King.

3 All the stockpiles of insight and information are hidden away in Him.

4 I say this so that no one may misguide you with a persuasive message.

5 You see, even if I am away from you in the physical body, still I am together with you in the Spirit. I am happy and I see the arrangement and the solidness of your trust for the Anointed King.

6 So walk around in the Anointed King Jesus, the Master, in the same way that you received Him in:

7 having been rooted, being built on top of that in Him, and being authenticated by trust, just as you were taught, overflowing in thankfulness.

8 See that no one will carry you off as stolen property through the philosophy and meaningless fraud aligned with people's tradition, aligned with the world's conventional practices, and not aligned with the Anointed King.

9 This is important because all the fullness of the Godhead lives in Him bodily,

10 and you are in Him. You have been filled up. He is the head of every head ruler and authority.

11 You also were circumcised in Him with a circumcision that is made without hands, in stripping away the physical body's body in the Anointed King's circumcision.

12 You were buried together with Him in your submersion. In it, you also were gotten up together with Him through the trust of the influence of the God who got Him up from the dead.

13 You were dead in the infractions and the uncircumcision of your physical body. He brought you to life together with Him when, as an act of generosity, He forgave us of all the infractions.

14 *He did this* after He erased the thing against us, a handwritten document that has the rules. It was a covert opponent to us. He also has taken it out from the middle of us after nailing it to the cross.

15 He stripped away the head rulers and the authorities and made an exhibit of them in a clear public statement when He brought them out in His victory parade in it.
16 So no one must judge you in a dinner and in drink, or in a detail of a festival, or a new moon, or Sabbaths.
17 These are a shadow of what is going to come, but the body *that casts the shadow is* the Anointed King's.
18 No one must disqualify you from receiving your prize. *That type of person* wants to have a lowly focus and a religion of the angels. He intrudes into things he has looked at. He is conceited for no reason by his physical body's way of thinking.
19 And he doesn't hold on to the Head. From *the Head*, the entire body grows God's growth as it is further supplied and pulled together through its connections and bonds.
20 If you died together with the Anointed King away from the world's conventional practices, why do you make up rules for yourselves as if you are living in the world?
21 *You make up rules, like,* "You should not touch it, you should not taste it, and you should not come into contact with it."
22 *These rules* are all for things that deteriorate as they are used up. They are aligned with people's regulations and instructions.
23 These are things that certainly are a message that has insight in invented religion, lowly focus, and not going easy on the body. *They are* not of any value toward filling up the physical body.

3

1 So if God got you up together with the Anointed King, look for the things above, where the Anointed King is sitting at the right side of God.
2 Focus on the things above, not the things on the earth.
3 You see, you died and your life has been hidden together with the Anointed King in God.
4 When the Anointed King (your life) is shown, at that time you also will be shown together with Him in magnificence.
5 So deaden the body parts on the earth: sexual sin, what is not clean, lust, bad desire, and the desire for more (this is what idol worship is).
6 God's punishment comes on the sons of unbelief because of these things.
7 You also walked around among them in the past when you were living among these things.
8 But right now you also must put away all these things: rage, anger, badness, insult, and the shameful word from your mouth.

9 Don't lie to each other because you stripped away the former person together with the things it repeatedly does
10 and put on the young person who is renewed to a correct understanding aligned with the image of the One who created the young person.
11 *This is* where there is not Greek and Jewish, circumcision and uncircumcision, foreigner, savage, slave, or free, but the Anointed King is all and in all.
12 So since you are God's sacred select people and you have been loved, put on compassion's feelings of sympathy, kindness, lowly focus, submissiveness, and patience.
13 Tolerate each other, and, as an act of generosity, forgive each other. If anyone has a complaint against someone, just as even the Master as an act of generosity forgave you, so you also must forgive.
14 Over all these things, put on the love that is a bond of your maturity.
15 And the Anointed King's peace must be the referee in your hearts. You were actually invited into *peace* in one body. Also become thankful.
16 The Anointed King's message must richly have a house in you in every insight. You must teach and caution yourselves with psalms, praise songs, and spiritual songs in generosity as you sing in your hearts to God.
17 And everything that you do, whatever it may be, whether in word or in action, do all things in the name *and on behalf* of the Master Jesus, and be thankful to Father God through Him.
18 The Women -- Place yourselves under the husbands since that has always met the high standards that are in the Master.
19 The Men -- Love the wives, and don't be bitter toward them.
20 The Children -- Obey the parents throughout all things. You see, this is well-liked in the Master.
21 The Fathers -- Don't provoke your children so that they won't feel dejected.
22 The Slaves -- Throughout all things, obey the masters as far as the physical body is concerned. Don't obey with eye-slavery *(only obeying when the master is looking)* as if you are people pleasers. No, *obey* with dedication of heart, fearing the Master.
23 Whatever you do, work from the soul as if it is for the Master and not for people.
24 Realize that you will fully receive the repayment of the inheritance from the Master. You are slaves to the Master, the Anointed King.

25 You see, the person who does wrong will retrieve what he did wrong in, and his appearance doesn't matter.

 1 The Masters -- Provide what is right and equal to the slaves, realizing that you also have a master in heaven.
2 Stay close to the prayer. Stay awake in the same with thankfulness.
3 At the same time, also pray about us so that God might open to us a door of the message, to speak the secret of the Anointed King (we also have been locked up because of this secret)
4 so that I might show it in the way that it is necessary for me to speak.
5 Walk around toward the people outside with insight, buying up the time *(or in other words, making good use of the time)*.
6 To realize how you must answer each one, your message must have always been seasoned with generosity salt.
7 Tychicus (the loved brother, reliable servant, and fellow slave in the Master) will let you know about all the things regarding me.
8 I sent him to you for this very purpose, so that you might know the things about us and he might encourage your hearts.
9 *I sent him* together with Onesimus (the reliable and loved brother who is from among you). They will let you know about everything here.
10 Aristarchus (the person incarcerated together with me) says hello to you, and Mark (the cousin of Barnabas--you received demands about him--if he comes to you, accept him)
11 and Joshua (the one who is called Justus). These people who are the only ones from the circumcision are my co-workers for God's monarchy. They are the ones that became a boost to me.
12 Epaphras (the Anointed King Jesus' slave from among you) says hello to you. He is always struggling over you in the prayers so that you, complete and having been filled, might be established in everything God wants.
13 You see, I am a witness for him that he has much anguish over you, the people in Laodicea *(a neighboring city to Colosse)*, and the people in Hierapolis *(a neighboring city to Laodicea)*.
14 Luke (the loved doctor) and Demas say hello to you.
15 Say hello to the brothers in Laodicea and to Nymphas and the assembly throughout her house.

16 And when this letter is read beside you, make sure that it is also read in the assembly of Laodiceans and that you also read the one from Laodicea.

17 And tell Archippus, "See to the job of serving that you received in the Master so that you may accomplish it."

18 This is the greeting of Paul with my hand. Remember my restraints. May generosity be with you.

First Thessalonians

1

1 From: Paul, Silas, and Timothy. To: The assembly of Thessalonians in Father God and Master Jesus, the Anointed King *(Thessalonica is a port city of Macedonia in Greece where Paul shared the good news for three weeks before being forced out by the Jews)*. Generosity and peace to you.

2 We are always thankful to God about all of you. We make mention of you on our prayers.

3 We constantly remember your work of trust, your labor of love, and your persistence to anticipate good from our Master Jesus, the Anointed King, in front of our God and Father.

4 We have seen that God has selected you, brothers, you who have been loved by God,

5 because our good news didn't come to you in message only, but also in ability, in the Sacred Spirit, and in a way that fully accomplished much. Just as *we have seen that God selected you, so* you have seen what kind of people we became among you because of you.

6 And you became imitators of us and the Master when in very hard times you accepted the message with happiness of the Sacred Spirit.

7 And so you became an example to everyone who trusts in Macedonia *(northern Greece)* and in Achaia *(southern Greece)*.

8 You see, the Master's message has reverberated out from you, not only in Macedonia and in Achaia, but in every place your trust toward God has gone out to. *It is* so *effective* that we don't need to speak anything.

9 They report about us. *They report* what kind of inroad we had to you and how you turned back to God from the idols to be slaves to the living and true God

10 and to stay and wait for His Son from the heavens, the Son that He got up from the dead, Jesus, the One saving us from the coming punishment.

2

1 You see, you yourselves, brothers, realize that our inroad to you has not become something that is meaningless.

2 No, after we previously suffered and were injured in Philippi (just as you know), we made clear public statements in our God to speak God's good news to you in a great struggle.

3 You see, our encouragement, *the encouragement that we give out,* is not from a misleading lie, or from what is not clean, or in deception.
4 But just as we have been approved by God to be trusted with the good news, so we speak, not as if we are doing what people would like, but as if *we are doing what* God *would like,* the One who approves our hearts.
5 You see, in the past, we didn't come with a message of flattery either, just as you know, or in a sham of a desire for more (God is a witness),
6 or looking for magnificence from people (not from you, not from others). As the Anointed King's missionaries, we could have been a heavy weight on you.
7 But we became infants in the middle of you, as when a nursing mother keeps her own children warm.
8 Being closely attached to you like this, it seemed like a good idea to us to not only give out God's good news to you, but also our own souls, because you became people that we love.
9 You see, brothers, you remember our labor and difficulty. As we worked night and day toward the *goal of* not being a burden on any of you, we spoke publicly to you about God's good news.
10 You and God are witnesses of how we became holy, right, and faultless to you who trust.
11 You have seen exactly how *we were with* each one of you. *We were* like a father with his own children. We encouraged you. We comforted you. And we were witnesses to you.
12 *We did this* so that you would walk around in a manner deserving of God, the One who invited you into His own monarchy and magnificence.
13 And because of this, we also are constantly thankful to God because when you took in a message of what you heard directly from us, a message of God, you accepted it, not as a message of people, but, just as it truly is, a message of God, who also is active in you, the ones who trust.
14 You see, you became imitators, brothers, of God's assemblies in Judea that are in the Anointed King Jesus. You actually suffered the same things under your own countrymen as they also *suffered* under the Jewish people.
15 *Those Jewish people* even killed the Master Jesus and the preachers. They chased us out. They do not do what God would like. And they oppose all people
16 as they keep us from speaking to the non-Jews (*We are speaking to the non-Jews* so that they might be rescued). They always fill up their

sins to the top. Their punishment for the conclusion already came on them.
17 But when we were made orphans by being away from you, brothers, for close to an hour's time, in presence, not in heart, we made much more of an effort with much desire to see your face
18 because we, certainly I, Paul, wanted to come to you both once and twice, and the Opponent interrupted us.
19 You see, what is our anticipation of good, or our happiness, or our bragging's award wreath? Is it not actually you in front of our Master Jesus during His arrival?
20 You are our magnificence and happiness.

3

1 For this reason, since I wasn't able to stand it anymore, it seemed like a good idea to us for me to be left down in Athens alone.
2 And I sent Timothy (our brother and a co-worker for God in the Anointed King's good news) for the purpose of establishing you and encouraging you on behalf of your trust.
3 *I did this* so that no one would be swayed in these hard times. You see, you yourselves have seen that we are placed here for this.
4 Even when we were facing you, we were telling you before it happened that we are going to be going through hard times, just as it also happened. And you have seen it.
5 And because of this, since I wasn't able to stand it anymore, I sent Timothy to you to know your trust. *I sent him* in case somehow the one who tries to cause trouble was trying to cause trouble with you and our labor might turn into something that is meaningless.
6 Just now, Timothy came to us from you and shared with us the good news of your trust, your love, and that you always mention good things about us as you yearn to see us, exactly as we also yearn to see you.
7 Because of this, brothers, we were encouraged from you in all our shortages and hard times by your trust
8 because now we live if you stand in the Master.
9 You see, what thanks can we repay to God concerning you over all the happiness that we are happy with in front of our God because of you?
10 We plead night and day even much more to see your face and to develop the deficiencies of your trust.
11 May our God and Father Himself and our Master Jesus direct our way to you.

12 May the Master cause you to increase and overflow in your love for each other and for everyone, exactly as we also increase and overflow in our love for you.
13 *This will* establish your hearts as faultless in sacredness in front of our God and Father during the arrival of our Master Jesus with all His sacred people. Amen.

1 *We told you* how you must walk around and do what God would like. *You received it in* directly from us. So for the rest of the time, brothers, we ask and encourage you in Master Jesus that just as you received it in and just as you walked around in it, you should overflow more.
2 You see, you have seen what the orders are that we gave to you through the Master Jesus.
3 This is what God wants--your sacredness. *He wants* you to keep yourselves away from sexual sin.
4 *He wants* each of you to know *that you need* to get your own container *(your body)* in sacredness and value,
5 not in lust of desire *(which is* exactly how the non-Jews who don't know God *live)*.
6 And *God wants each of you* not to step beyond and take advantage of his brother in the matter because the Master is a retaliator concerning all of these things. This is just as we also already told you and were a strong witness to.
7 You see, God didn't invite us based on *something* that is not clean. No, He invited us in sacredness.
8 So you see then, the person disregarding these things doesn't disregard a person but God, the One who also gives His Sacred Spirit to you.
9 But I don't need to write to you about brotherly kindness. You see, you yourselves are God-taught to love each other.
10 You actually do it to all the brothers in all of Macedonia, but we encourage you, brothers, to overflow more,
11 to think that it is important to remain calm, to constantly do your own things, and to work with your own hands. This is just how we passed the order on to you.
12 That way you may walk around reputably toward the people outside and have need of nothing.
13 We don't want you to be unaware, brothers, about the people who are asleep *(those who are dead)* so that you are not sad just as the rest *are sad* who actually have no anticipation of good.

14 You see, if we trust that Jesus died and came back to life, in the same way through Jesus, God will also bring together with Him the people who fell asleep *(who died)*.
15 This is what we are telling you in the Master's message, that we, the people living who are left around here for the Master's arrival, will not in any way precede the people who fell asleep
16 because the Master Himself when He gives the order (in the head angel's voice and in God's trumpet) will step down out of heaven, and the dead in the Anointed King will come back to life first.
17 Following that, we, the people living who are left around here, will be snatched up at the same time in clouds together with them for a face-to-face meeting of the Master in the air. And this is how we will always be together with the Master.
18 And so encourage each other with these words.

5

1 Brothers, I don't need to write you about the amounts of time and the appointed times.
2 You see, you yourselves accurately realize that the Master's day comes like this, as a thief in the night.
3 When they say peace and certainty, then unexpected destruction stands over them, even as labor pain stands over the pregnant woman. And they will not in any way escape from it.
4 But you, brothers, are not in darkness that the day might take you down as a thief *might*.
5 You see, *in the dark, you can't see anything. In the light, you see everything.* You all are sons of light and sons of day. We are not of night or of darkness.
6 So clearly let's not sleep as the rest do, but let's stay awake and be sober.
7 You see, the people who sleep, sleep at night, and the people who get drunk are drunk at night.
8 But we who are of the day should be sober and put on an armored vest of trust and love, and head protection--anticipation of rescue.
9 Let's do this because God didn't place us into punishment. No, He placed us into acquiring rescue through our Master Jesus, the Anointed King.
10 Our Master Jesus is the One who died for us so that whether we stay awake or whether we sleep, we might live at the same time together with Him.
11 For this reason, encourage and build each other, one on one, just as you also are doing.

12 We ask you, brothers, to realize who the people are that labor among you, that preside over you in the Master, and that caution you.
13 Regard them with love even much more because of their work. Be peaceful among yourselves.
14 We encourage you, brothers. Caution the defiant. Comfort the downhearted. Keep the weak in front of you. Be patient with everyone.
15 Look. No one should give bad back to anyone for bad, but always pursue the good thing both for each other and for all.
16 Always be happy.
17 Constantly pray.
18 In everything, be thankful. You see, this is what God wants for you in the Anointed King Jesus.
19 Don't extinguish the Spirit.
20 Don't treat the things that are said in a sermon as if they are nothing.
21 Check all things. Hold steady to the nice thing.
22 Keep yourselves away from every visual image of evil.
23 May the God of peace Himself make you sacred so that you can be entirely complete people. And may your entirely whole spirit, soul, and body be kept without any faults during the arrival of our Master Jesus, the Anointed King.
24 The One who invites you can be trusted. He will also do it.
25 Brothers, also pray about us.
26 Say hello to all the brothers with a sacred friendly gesture.
27 I place you under an oath in the Master to read this letter to all the brothers.
28 May the generosity of our Master Jesus, the Anointed King, be with you.

Second Thessalonians

1 From: Paul, Silas, and Timothy. To: The assembly of Thessalonians in our Father God and Master Jesus, the Anointed King. *(Thessalonica is a port city of Macedonia in Greece).*

2 Generosity and peace to you out from Father God and Master Jesus, the Anointed King.

3 We are obligated to always be thankful to God concerning you, brothers, just as you are deserving of it because your trust grows over and the love of each and every one of you is increasing for each other.

4 It is such that, in God's assemblies, we ourselves brag about you for your persistence to do what is right and your trust in all your persecutions and in the hard times that you tolerate.

5 God's right judgment is displayed in that you are considered totally deserving of God's monarchy for what you also suffer.

6 *God's right judgment is also displayed* if it so happens that God considers it right to repay hard times to the people who cause you hard times

7 and relief to you (the people going through hard times) with us in the uncovering of the Master Jesus from heaven with angels of His ability.

8 In the fire of a blaze, He will retaliate against the people who don't know God and the people who don't obey the good news of our Master Jesus.

9 In fact, they will pay the penalty *of their disobedience and face* justice: destruction that spans all time away from the face of the Master and away from the magnificence of His strength.

10 *This will happen* when He comes to be elevated to a place of magnificence among His sacred people and to amaze all the trusting people because in that day they trust the thing that we witnessed to you about.

11 We also always pray about you that our God might find that you are deserving of the invitation and might fill you with every good notion of goodness and work of trust in ability.

12 *We do this* in order that our Master Jesus' name *and who He is* might be made magnificent in you and you in Him aligned with the generosity of our God and Master Jesus, the Anointed King.

2

1 We ask you, brothers, regarding the arrival of our Master Jesus, the Anointed King, and our coming together in one place to Him
2 that you not be quickly disturbed away from your way of thinking or alarmed--not through a spirit, not through a message, not through a letter (even if it seems to be from us)--that the Master's day *has come and* has stood here.
3 No one should completely fool you in any way because *that day will not happen* if the divorce doesn't come first and if the person of the crime, ruin's son, isn't uncovered.
4 *Ruin's son* will lie in opposition to and be raised up over everything that is said to be a god or an object that people worship. It will be such that he will be seated in God's temple showing himself off that he is God.
5 Don't you remember that as I was still facing you I was telling you these things?
6 And now you realize what holds him down from being uncovered in his own time.
7 You see, crime's secret is already active. The thing holding him down now is only until it will end up out of the middle.
8 And then the criminal will be uncovered. The Master Jesus will execute him with the Spirit of His mouth and will make him useless when He shows up at His arrival.
9 *The criminal's arrival* is aligned with the Opponent's influence in every ability, in proofs, in incredible things of a lie,
10 and in every fraud of the wrong way. *It will happen* to the people who are ruined for the times that they did not accept the love of the truth that could rescue them.
11 And because of this, God sends them the influence of a misleading lie for *a reason,* so that they would trust in the lie.
12 That way all the people will be judged who didn't trust the truth but were delighted with the wrong way.
13 But we are obligated to always be thankful to God concerning you, brothers. You have been loved by the Master because God chose you to be a first-part-offering for rescue in sacredness of spirit and trust of truth.
14 He also invited you into this through our good news, into acquiring the magnificence of our Master Jesus, the Anointed King.
15 So clearly, brothers, stand and hold on to the traditions that you were taught, whether through a message or through our letter.

16 May our Master Jesus Himself, the Anointed King, and God, our Father, who loved us and gave encouragement that spans all time and good anticipation in generosity,
17 encourage your hearts and establish you in every good action and message.

3

1 For the rest of the time, brothers, pray about us that the Master's message may run and be elevated to a place of magnificence, just as it also *ran* toward you,
2 and that we might be saved from the people who are out of place and evil. You see, not everyone possesses the trust.
3 But the Master can be trusted. He will establish and guard you from the evil one.
4 We have been confident in the Master about you that you are doing and will do the orders that we pass on.
5 May the Master direct your hearts into God's love and into the Anointed King's persistence to do what is right.
6 In the name *and on behalf* of our Master Jesus, the Anointed King, we are passing the order on to you, brothers, that you should set yourselves up away from every brother that is walking around defiantly and that is not aligned with the tradition that they received directly from us.
7 You see, you yourselves realize how it is necessary to imitate us because we were not defiant among you.
8 We didn't eat bread directly from anyone for free either. No, with labor and difficulty night and day we worked toward the *goal of* not being a burden on any of you.
9 We didn't do this because we don't have the authority to not work. No, *we did it* so that we might give ourselves as an example to you for the *purpose* that you might imitate us.
10 You see, even when we were facing you, we were passing this order on to you, "If anyone does not want to work, he must not eat either."
11 We hear that there are some people walking around defiantly among you. They don't do any work except working their way around work.
12 We pass the order on to these types of people and encourage them in Master Jesus, the Anointed King, that they should work with calmness and eat their own bread.
13 You, brothers, should not get discouraged doing nice things.
14 If anyone does not obey our message through this letter, make an indication of the person and don't interact with him so that he might be embarrassed.

15 And don't regard him as an enemy, but caution him as a brother.
16 May the Master of peace Himself give you peace through everything in every way. The Master is with you all.
17 This is the greeting of Paul with my hand that is an indicator in every letter. This is how I write.
18 May the generosity of our Master Jesus, the Anointed King, be with all of you.

First Timothy

1 From: Paul, the Anointed King Jesus' missionary aligned with a directive from God, our Rescuer, and the Anointed King Jesus, our anticipation of good.

2 To: Timothy, a real child in trust. Generosity, forgiving kindness, and peace out from Father God and the Anointed King Jesus, our Master.

3 It is just like when I encouraged you to still stay in Ephesus *(a city in Western Turkey)* as I was traveling into Macedonia *(a northern region of Greece)* so that you might pass the order on to some not to be teaching a different doctrine

4 or to be paying attention to myths and endless genealogies. *Genealogies* are the things that give rise to searches rather than God's management in trust.

5 The conclusion of the order is love from a clean heart, from a good conscience, and from trust that is not faked.

6 Some missed the target on these and were turned from love to empty chatter.

7 They wanted to be law teachers even though they were not aware of the things that they say or the things that they rigorously authenticate.

8 We have seen that the law is nice if someone uses it according to the rules.

9 *We* have seen this: that the law is not lying here for the person who does what is right, but for criminals and unruly people, for godless and sinful people, for unholy and profane people, for father-beaters and mother-beaters, for murderers,

10 for people who commit sexual sin, for homosexuals, for human traffickers, for liars, for oath breakers, and if something else lies in opposition to the healthy instruction

11 aligned with the good news of the blessed God's magnificence that I was trusted with.

12 I am thankful to the One who gave me the ability that I need, the Anointed King Jesus, our Master, because He regarded me as someone who can be trusted when He put me into the job of serving.

13 Previously, I was an insulter, a pursuer, and an injurer. But I was shown forgiving kindness because I did *those things* when I was unaware *of who Jesus is and* during a time that I didn't trust Him.

14 Our Master's generosity greatly increased with the trust and love in the Anointed King Jesus.
15 This message can be trusted and deserves every bit of acceptance: The Anointed King Jesus came into the world to rescue sinful people and I am first among them.
16 But because of this, I was shown forgiving kindness so that the Anointed King Jesus might first display to me every bit of patience toward a prototype of the people who are going to be trusting in Him for life that spans all time.
17 Value and magnificence *belong* to the King of the spans of time, to the only undeteriorating invisible God for the spans of time of the spans of time. Amen.
18 I am placing this order beside you, child Timothy, aligned with the preachings leading the way ahead over you so that you may serve in the nice military service of these preachings.
19 Have trust and a good conscience. Some pushed these away and were shipwrecked around trust.
20 Hymenaeus and Alexander are *two* of them. I turned them over to the Opponent so that they might be disciplined to not insult.

2

1 So I encourage, first of all, that pleas, prayers, interventions, and thanks be made for all people,
2 for kings and all the people in a higher position so that we may lead our way through a quiet and calm life in every bit of godliness and respect.
3 This is nice and acceptable in the sight of our Rescuer, God.
4 He wants all people to be rescued and to come into a correct understanding of truth.
5 You see, there is one God. There is also one middleman between God and people, a person, the Anointed King Jesus.
6 *Jesus is* the One who gave Himself to pay for everyone's release. The witness of this is given when the times are right.
7 I was put into this as a public speaker and missionary. I am telling the truth. I am not lying. I am a teacher of non-Jews in trust and truth.
8 So it is my intention that men pray in every place raising up holy hands without rage and ponderings.
9 It is also my intention that women, in a similar way, decorate themselves in an orderly demeanor with modesty and proper focus, not in hair weaves and gold or pearls or very expensive clothes,

10 but in what is appropriate for women who promise to worship God through good actions.
11 A woman must remain calm as she is learning in total compliance.
12 I don't give a woman permission to be teaching or domineering over a man, but to remain calm.
13 You see, Adam was sculpted first, after that Eve.
14 And Adam was not fooled, but the woman, after being completely fooled, has ended up in violation of God.
15 But she will be rescued through the raising of children if they stay in trust, love, and sacredness with proper focus.

3

1 This message can be trusted: if anyone reaches out for a position of supervision *in God's house*, he desires nice work.
2 So it is necessary for the supervisor to be unattackable, one woman's husband, sober, properly focused, orderly, friendly to strangers, able to teach,
3 not beside wine, not a hitter, but polite, a non-arguer, and without greed.
4 He must preside over his own house nicely and have children in compliance with all respect.
5 If someone hasn't seen *to it* to preside over his own house, how will he take care of God's assembly?
6 He must not be a young convert so that when he gets blinded by smoke, he won't fall into the accuser's judgment.
7 It is also necessary that people from the outside have nice things to say about him so that he might not fall into a criticism and trap of the accuser.
8 Similarly, it is necessary for servants *in God's house* to be respectful, not a double-talker, not paying attention to a lot of wine, not pursuing shameful gain,
9 and having the secret of trust in a clean conscience.
10 These also must first be checked. After that, the ones having no charges against them must serve.
11 Similarly, it is necessary for women to be respectful, not accusers, sober, and reliable in all things.
12 Servants must be husbands of one woman, presiding over children and over their own houses nicely.
13 You see, the ones who serve nicely acquire a nice foothold for themselves and a very clear public statement in the trust that is in the Anointed King Jesus.

14 As I write these things to you, I am anticipating coming to you in a fast manner.
15 But if I am slow, *I am writing these things* so that you may realize how it is necessary to be busy in God's house. *God's house is* something that is the living God's assembly, a pillar and stabilizer of the truth.
16 And the secret of godliness is admittedly great: He was shown in a physical body, made right in the Spirit, seen by announcers, publicly spoken about among nations, trusted in the world, and taken up in magnificence.

4

1 The Spirit distinctly says that in later times some people will stay away from trust. They will pay attention to misleading spirits and instructions of lesser deities
2 in faked behavior of lying people whose own conscience has been scarred.
3 They keep people from marrying to keep themselves away from foods that God created. *God created these foods* so that the people who trust and have correctly understood the truth would receive them with thankfulness.
4 *This happens* because everything that God created is nice and nothing received with thankfulness is trash.
5 You see, it is made sacred through God's message and intervention.
6 As you put these things under the brothers, you will be a nice servant of the Anointed King Jesus nurtured in the messages of trust and the nice instruction that you have followed alongside of.
7 Refuse the profane and old wives' myths. Strenuously exercise yourself toward godliness.
8 You see, strenuous bodily exercise is beneficial for a few things, but godliness is beneficial for everything. It has a promise of life now and life that is going to be.
9 This message can be trusted and deserves every bit of acceptance.
10 You see, this is what we labor and are insulted for: because we have anticipated good based on the living God who is a rescuer of all kinds of people, especially people who trust.
11 Pass these orders on and teach them.
12 No one must ignore you because of your youth. But become an example of the people who trust, in message, in behavior, in love, in trust, and in consecration.
13 Pay attention to the reading, encouragement, and instruction until I come.

14 Don't stop being concerned about the gift in you that was given to you through preaching with the board of older men laying their hands on you.
15 Be concerned about these things. Be in these things so that your progress may be shown to everyone.
16 Fix your attention on yourself and on instruction. Stay over in them. You see, as you do this, you will rescue both yourself and the people listening to you.

5

1 You shouldn't pound on an older man, but encourage him as a father. Encourage younger men as brothers,
2 older women as mothers, and younger women as sisters in all consecration.
3 Value widows, the real widows.
4 If any widow has children or grandchildren. *Her children and grandchildren* must first learn to reverence their own house and to give reimbursements back to their predecessors *(or in other words, take care of their parents and grandparents)*. You see, this is acceptable in God's sight.
5 The real widow who has also been alone has anticipated good based on God and still stays in the pleas and the prayers night and day.
6 The widow living in luxury has died as she lives.
7 And pass these orders on so that they *(the widows and their children)* may be unattackable.
8 If anyone does not plan for his own, and especially for people living in his house, he has denied trust and is worse than someone who doesn't trust.
9 A widow not less than sixty years old having become one man's wife must be inducted *into the assembly's group of widows.*
10 People must have witnessed her in nice actions: if she nurtured children, if she accepted strangers, if she washed sacred people's feet, if she supported people going through hard times, if she followed closely behind every good action.
11 Refuse younger widows. You see, when they will be dominant against the Anointed King, they want to be marrying.
12 They have judgment against them because they disregarded their first trust.
13 At the same time, idle women also learn to go around to the houses. Not only are they idle, but they also are gossips and women who work their way around work. They speak about things that are not necessary.

14 So it is my intention that younger women marry, raise children, run the house, and not give the one who lies in opposition to them even one opportunity to use a put-down against them.
15 You see, some have already turned away behind the Opponent.
16 If any trusting *woman who is running a house* has widows, she must support them. The assembly must not be weighted down by them so that it might support the real widows.
17 The older men who have presided nicely must be thought of as deserving of double value, especially the ones laboring in the message and in instruction.
18 You see, the *Old Testament* writing says, "You will not muzzle a cow processing grain" *(Deuteronomy 25:4)*. Also, the worker is deserving of his pay.
19 Don't warmly welcome a criminal complaint against an older man, outside of except it is based on two or three witnesses.
20 Reprimand the people who sin in the sight of everyone so that the rest may also have fear.
21 I am a strong witness in the sight of God, the Anointed King Jesus, and the select angels that you should observe these things without prejudice, doing nothing aligned with bias.
22 Don't place hands on anyone quickly. Don't share in sins belonging to others. Keep yourself consecrated.
23 Don't be a water drinker anymore, but use a little wine because of your stomach and frequent weaknesses.
24 The sins of some people are evident. They lead the way ahead of them into judgment. But with some, they actually follow closely behind.
25 Similarly, nice actions are also evident, and the *nice actions* that have it otherwise *(that are not evident)* are not able to be hidden.

6

1 As many as are under a crossbeam (slaves) must regard their own owners to be deserving of all value so that God's name and instruction may not be insulted.
2 The slaves that have trusting owners must not ignore them just because they are brothers. No, instead, they must be slaves for them because they are trusting and loved owners assisting in their humane treatment. Teach and encourage these things.
3 If anyone teaches a different doctrine and does not come forward to messages that are healthy (the messages of our Master Jesus, the Anointed King) and to the instruction that is aligned with godliness,

4 he has been blinded by smoke and isn't aware of anything. But he is ill around questionings and arguments over words. Envy, fighting, insults, and evil suspicions come from these.

5 Societies of people who have been devoured by their way of thinking and robbed of the truth also come from these. They assume that godliness is a way to get gain.

6 Godliness with contentment is a way to get great gain.

7 You see, we carried nothing into the world *and it is obvious* that we are not able to carry anything out either.

8 We will be content with having food to nourish us and clothes to cover us.

9 But the people intending to be wealthy fall into trouble, a trap, and many unobserved and hurtful desires. In fact, these things sink people down into destruction and ruin.

10 You see, being fond of money is a root of all kinds of bad things. As some reached out for money, they were misled away from trust, and they stabbed themselves through with many agonies.

11 But you, O man of God, escape these things. Pursue the right way, godliness, trust, love, persistence to do what is right, and submissiveness of suffering.

12 Struggle in the nice struggle of trust. Latch on to life that spans all time. You were invited into this, and you acknowledged a nice acknowledgment of this in the sight of many witnesses.

13 I pass this order on to you in the sight of God (the One who gives life to all things) and the Anointed King Jesus (who told what He witnessed before Pontius Pilate in His nice acknowledgment):

14 you must keep the demand unspotted, unattackable up to the point when our Master Jesus, the Anointed King, shows up.

15 The blessed and only competent Ruler will show it *(the demand)* when the times are right. He is the King of the people who are kings and the Master of the people who are masters.

16 He is the only One who has deathlessness, who has a house in unapproachable light. No human sees Him and no *human* is capable of seeing Him either. Value and power that spans all time *belongs* to Him. Amen.

17 Pass the order on to the wealthy people in the present span of time not to be focusing on high things and not to have anticipated good based on the obscurity of wealth either. But *they are to anticipate good* based on God, the One who richly provides everything to us for our enjoyment.

18 The wealthy people must work on good things, be wealthy in nice actions, be benevolent, and be people who share.

19 The ones who do this stockpile a nice foundation for themselves in a safe place for what is going to come so that they might really latch on to life.

20 O Timothy, guard what is placed alongside of you. Turn from the profane meaningless voices and opposing positions of what is falsely named knowledge.

21 As some promise *knowledge*, they miss the target around trust. May generosity be with you.

Second Timothy

1 From: Paul, a missionary of the Anointed King Jesus because that's what God wants, a missionary aligned with a promise of life in the Anointed King Jesus.
2 To: Timothy, a loved child. Generosity, forgiving kindness, and peace out from Father God and the Anointed King Jesus, our Master.
3 I am thankful to the God that I minister to in a clean conscience out from my ancestors since I constantly mention you in my pleas night and day!
4 I remember your tears and I yearn to see you so that I might be full of happiness.
5 I received a quiet reminder of the trust in you, the kind of trust that is not faked. This is something that first had a house in your grandmother Lois and in your mother Eunice. I have been confident that it is also in you.
6 This is why I am reminding you again to be rekindling God's gift. It is in you from the time I laid hands on you.
7 You see, God did not give us a spirit of cowardice. No, *He gave us* a spirit of ability, of love, and of proper focus.
8 So you shouldn't be ashamed of what our Master witnessed, or of me (His prisoner), but suffer tough hardships together with me for the good news aligned with God's ability.
9 God is the One who rescued us and invited us with a sacred invitation. *This was* not aligned with our actions. No, *it was* aligned with His own purpose and the generosity that was given to us in the Anointed King Jesus before the times that span all time.
10 But now this rescue is shown through our Rescuer showing up, the Anointed King Jesus. Not only did He make death useless, but He also lit up life and non-deterioration through the good news.
11 I was placed into it *(the good news)* as a public speaker, a missionary, and a teacher.
12 This is also the reason why I suffer these things. But I am not ashamed. You see, I know whom I have trusted, and I have been confident that He is able to guard the thing placed alongside of me for that day.

13 Have a prototype of messages that are healthy (that you heard directly from me), *messages* in the trust and love that is in the Anointed King Jesus.
14 Guard the nice thing placed alongside of you through the Sacred Spirit that has a house in us.
15 You have seen this--that all the people in Western Turkey turned away from me. Phygellus and Hermogenes are *two* of them.
16 May the Master give forgiving kindness to Onesiphorus' house because he refreshed me many times and was not ashamed of my chain.
17 Yes, even when he ended up in Rome, he looked aggressively for me and found me.
18 May the Master give him the gift of finding forgiving kindness directly from a master in that day. You also know better *than me* how much he served in Ephesus *(a city in Western Turkey)*.

2

1 So, you, my child, become competent in the generosity that is in the Anointed King Jesus.
2 And place these things that you heard through many witnesses directly from me beside people who can be trusted, some who will be sufficiently capable to also teach different people.
3 Suffer tough hardships together with me as a nice soldier of the Anointed King Jesus.
4 No one serving in the military entangles himself in life's transactions so that he might do what the one who enlists the soldiers would like.
5 Also if someone competes, he is not crowned with an award wreath unless he competes according to the rules.
6 It is necessary for the laboring farmer to receive the first share of the fruits.
7 Be aware of what I am saying. You see, the Master will give you understanding in all kinds of things.
8 Remember that Jesus is the Anointed King. God got Him up from the dead. He is from David's seed. This is aligned with my good news.
9 I suffer tough hardships up to being locked up for my good news. *It is* as if I am an outlaw. But God's message has not been locked up.
10 Because of this, I persist in all things. *I persist* because of the select people. That way they also might obtain the rescue that is in the Anointed King Jesus with magnificence that spans all time.
11 This message can be trusted. You see, if we died together, we will also live together.

12 If we persist, we will also be kings together. If we will deny Him, that One will also deny us.
13 If we don't trust, that One remains as the One who can be trusted. You see, He is not able to deny Himself.
14 Quietly remember these things. Be a strong witness in God's sight not to be arguing about words over something that is not useful, over something that is a disaster for the people listening.
15 Make every effort to offer yourself up, approved to God, an unashamed worker, being straight with the message of the truth.
16 Stand clear of the profane meaningless voices. You see, they will progress on to a greater level of godlessness.
17 Their message will have a pasture like gangrene. Hymenaeus and Philetus are *two* of them.
18 They are the ones that missed the target concerning the truth. They say that the return back to life has already happened. They overturn the trust of some.
19 However, God's solid foundation has stood and has this seal: The Master knows the people who are His, and everyone who names the Master's name must stay away from the wrong way."
20 In a large house, there is not only gold and silver containers, but also wooden and ceramic *containers*. Some definitely have value, but some have no value.
21 So if anyone cleans himself off from these things, he will be a container that has value, that has been made sacred, that is very useful to the owner, and that has been readied for every good action.
22 Escape the more youthful desires. Pursue the right way, trust, love, and peace with the people who call on the Master from a clean heart.
23 Refuse the foolish and undisciplined questionings. Realize that they give birth to arguments.
24 The Master's slave must not be arguing, but he must be gentle to everyone, able to teach, and tolerant of bad things.
25 In submissiveness, he must discipline the people who oppose *God's* deal. That way perhaps God might give them a change of ways to a correct understanding of truth.
26 And *perhaps* the people who have been caught alive by the Accuser for what he wants might sober up again away from the Accuser's trap.

3

1 Know this, that in the last days, fierce times will stand here.

2 You see, the people will be fond of themselves, fond of money, egoistic, proud, insulting, not believing parents, not generous, not holy,
3 hardhearted toward family, refusing to enter into agreements, accusers, lacking restraint, mean, not fond of good,
4 traitors, obnoxious, and blinded by smoke. They will be fond of pleasure rather than *being* fond of God.
5 They will have a form of godliness but deny its ability. You also must turn away from these types of people.
6 You see, the people who sneak into houses and forcibly incarcerate wacky women who have been piled with sins are from these *people*. They are led by various desires.
7 They are always learning and never able to come to a correct understanding of truth.
8 These people stand in opposition to the truth in the same way that Jannes and Jambres stood in opposition to Moses. They have been entirely worsened by their way of thinking. They are not approved to be around trust.
9 But they will not progress on to more. You see, their insanity will be quite obvious to everyone as the insanity of those *people (Jannes and Jambres)* also became quite obvious.
10 You followed alongside my instruction, my leading, my purpose, my trust, my patience, my love, my persistence,
11 my persecutions, and my hardships (the kind of hardships that happened to me in Antioch, in Iconium, and in Lystra). I endured these persecutions, and the Master saved me from all of them.
12 All the people who also want to live godly in the Anointed King Jesus will be persecuted.
13 Evil people and impostors will progress on to something that is worse. They mislead and are being misled.
14 You must stay in the things that you have learned and have come to trust. Realize from whose side you learned them
15 and that from a baby you have seen the temple documents. The *temple documents* are able to provide you with insight into a rescue that is through trust in the Anointed King Jesus.
16 Every God-breathed writing is also beneficial toward instruction, toward a reprimand, toward rehabilitation, and toward discipline in the right way
17 so that the person of God may be developed by having been fully developed toward every good action.

1 I am a strong witness in the sight of God and the Anointed King Jesus to both Him showing up and His monarchy. He is the One who is going to judge people who are living and dead people.
2 Speak publicly about the message. Take a stand at easy times and at inconvenient times. Reprimand, shush, and encourage in every bit of patience and teaching.
3 You see, there will be a time when they will not tolerate healthy instruction, but they will pile up teachers for themselves that tickle what they hear. They will be aligned with their own desires.
4 And they certainly will turn what they hear away from the truth. They will turn them out based on myths.
5 You must be sober in all things. Suffer tough hardships. Do the work of someone who shares good news. Be well-established in your job of serving.
6 You see, my blood is already being poured out as an offering, and the time of my release has stood over me.
7 I have struggled in the nice struggle. I have finished the race. I have kept trusting.
8 For the rest of the time, the right way's award wreath is set aside for me. The Master is the judge who does what is right. He will give it *(the right way's award wreath)* back to me in that day, not only to me, but also to all the people who have loved Him showing up.
9 Make every effort to come to me soon.
10 You see, Demas abandoned me. He loved the present span of time. He traveled to Thessalonica *(a port city in northern Greece)*.. Crescens traveled to Galatia *(a region in north central Turkey)*. And Titus traveled to Dalmatia *(the coastal area across the Adriatic Sea from Italy)*.
11 Only Luke is with me. Pick up Mark on your way and bring him here with yourself. You see, he is very useful to me in serving.
12 I sent Tychicus out on a mission to Ephesus *(a city in Western Turkey)*.
13 As you come, bring the coat that I left behind beside Carpus in Troas *(a coastal city in northwestern Turkey)*. Also bring the scrolls, especially the sheep skins.
14 Alexander, the coppersmith, displayed many bad things to me. The Master will give back to him aligned with his actions.
15 You also must beware of him. You see, he stood very much in opposition to our messages.
16 In my first defense *in court*, no one showed up for me. Everyone abandoned me. I hope it isn't considered against them.

17 The Master stood by me and gave me the ability that I needed so that through me the public speaking might be well-established and all the non-Jews might hear. I was also saved from the lion's mouth.
18 The Master will save me out of every evil action and will rescue me for His heavenly monarchy. The magnificence for the spans of time of the spans of time *belongs* to Him. Amen.
19 Say hello to Prisca *(the formal name of Priscilla)*, Aquila, and the people in Onesiphorus' house.
20 Erastus stayed in Corinth *(a city in southern Greece)*, but I left Trophimus behind in Miletus *(a city on the western coast of Turkey)*. He is in frail health.
21 Make every effort to come before the storm season. Eubulus, Pudens, Linus, Claudia, and all the brothers say hello to you.
22 The Master is with your spirit. His generosity is with you all.

Titus

1

1 From: Paul, God's slave, but a missionary of Jesus, the Anointed King, aligned with the trust of God's select people and a correct understanding of the truth that is aligned with godliness.

2 *This is* based on an anticipation of life that spans all time. The God who does not lie promised it before the times that span all time.

3 He showed His message in public speaking when the times were right. I was trusted with it *(this public speaking)* from a directive of our Rescuer God.

4 To: Titus, a real child aligned with a shared trust. Generosity and peace out from Father God and the Anointed King Jesus, our Rescuer.

5 I left you behind in Crete *(the island in the Mediterranean Sea that Paul was on right before his shipwreck and to which he probably returned after his Roman imprisonment)* thanks to this one thing: so that you might set straight the things that were missing there and put older men in charge in each city as I specifically assigned you.

6 Consider an older man if he has no charges against him, is one woman's husband, and has trusting children who are not unruly or criminally accused of recklessness.

7 You see, *since you are putting the older men in charge, they must meet the requirements of a supervisor of God's house.* It is necessary for the supervisor to not have any charges against him as God's manager. He must not be pleasuring himself, not easily mad, not beside wine, not a hitter, and not pursuing shameful gain.

8 But *he should be* friendly to strangers, fond of good, properly focused, doing what is right, holy, and self-restrained.

9 He must keep in front of him the message that can be trusted *that is* aligned with the teaching. That way he may be able both to encourage with healthy instruction and to reprimand the people opposing it.

10 You see, many are also unruly meaningless talkers and seducers, especially the people from the circumcision *(the Jews)*.

11 It is necessary to put something over their mouths. They are the ones who, thanks to shameful gain, overturn whole houses and teach things that are unnecessary.

12 Someone from among them, their own preacher, said, "Cretans always are liars, bad, wild animals, and idle stomachs."

13 What this preacher witnessed is valid. This is the reason why you must reprimand them severely. That way they may be healthy in trust
14 and not pay attention to Judaean myths and demands of people who turn away from the truth.
15 All things are clean to clean people, but nothing is clean to desecrated and untrusting people. Both their way of thinking and conscience have been desecrated.
16 They acknowledge knowing God, but they deny Him with their actions. They are disgusting, unbelieving, and not approved to do any good action.

2

1 As for you, speak what is appropriate for healthy instruction.
2 Tell old men to be sober, respectful, properly focused, and healthy in trust, love, and persistence.
3 Similarly, tell old women to be temple-appropriate in conduct, not accusers, not having been made slaves to much wine, and teachers of nice things.
4 That way they may properly focus the young women to be fond of their husbands and fond of children.
5 Tell them to be properly focused, consecrated, housekeepers, good, and under their own husbands so that God's message won't be insulted.
6 Similarly, encourage the younger men to be properly focused.
7 Provide yourself as an example of nice actions in instruction concerning all kinds of things. Be an example of durability, respect,
8 and a healthy message with no known problems. That way the person from an opposing view will be embarrassed and have nothing useless to say about you.
9 Tell slaves to place themselves under their own owners in all things and to be well-liked, not opposing them,
10 not secretly keeping anything for themselves, but displaying every bit of good trust so that they may decorate the instruction of our Rescuer God in all things.
11 You see, God shines His rescuing generosity on all people.
12 His generosity disciplines us so that after we deny godlessness and the global desires, we might live properly focused, rightly, and godly in the present span of time
13 and await the blessed anticipation and showing up of the magnificence of the great God and our Rescuer Jesus, the Anointed King.

14 He gave Himself on our behalf so that He might pay the price to release us out of every crime and clean a special ethnic group for Himself with passion for nice actions.

15 Speak, encourage, and reprimand these things with every directive. No one must circumvent you.

3

1 Quietly remind them to be placing themselves under head rulers and authorities, to be loyal, to be ready for every good action,

2 to not insult anyone, to be non-arguers, to be polite, and to display all submissiveness to all people.

3 You see, in the past, we ourselves were also unobservant, unbelieving, misled, slaves to desires and various pleasures, leading our way through *life* in badness and envy, and detestable people who hate each other.

4 When our Rescuer God shined His kindness and benevolence on us,

5 He rescued us with a bath: the Sacred Spirit's rebirth and renewal. *This did* not *come* from our actions or the things that we did in the right way. No, it came down from His forgiving kindness.

6 He spilled it out richly on us through Jesus, the Anointed King, our Rescuer.

7 That way when we were made right by that One's generosity, we would become inheritors aligned with the anticipation of a life that spans all time.

8 This message can be trusted. And I intend for you to be rigorously authenticating it concerning these things so that the people who have trusted in God may be made to focus on presiding over nice actions. These are nice and beneficial for people.

9 But stand clear of foolish questionings, genealogies, fightings, and law arguments. You see, they are not beneficial. They are futile.

10 Refuse a person who divides people after he has received one *correction* and a second correction.

11 You have seen that this type of person has been turned inside out and sins finding himself guilty.

12 I will send Artemas to you or Tychicus. Whenever *that happens*, make every effort to come to me in Nicopolis *(a city in northwestern Greece)*. You see, I have decided to spend the storm season there.

13 Bring Zenas (the law expert) and Apollos aggressively on their way so that they won't miss anything.

14 Our people must also learn to be presiding over nice actions for the essential needs so that they may not be fruitless.

15 All the people with me say hello to you. Say hello to the people in trust that are fond of us. Generosity is with you all.

Philemon

1

1 From: Paul (a prisoner for the Anointed King Jesus) and Timothy (the brother). To: Philemon (the loved one and our co-worker),
2 Apphia (the sister), Archippus (our fellow soldier), and the assembly throughout your house.
3 Generosity to you and peace out from God, our Father, and Master Jesus, the Anointed King.
4 I am always thankful to my God as I make mention of you in my prayers,
5 and as I hear about your love and trust that you have toward the Master Jesus and for all the sacred people.
6 *I mention you in my prayers* in order that the sharing of your trust might become active in correctly understanding every good thing in us that is for the Anointed King.
7 You see, I had much happiness and encouragement over your love because the sacred people's feelings of sympathy have been relaxed through you, brother.
8 For this reason, in the Anointed King, I have *the opportunity to make a very clear public statement* in giving you an order that meets God's high standards.
9 Instead, because of love, I am encouraging you, I, this type of person who is as Paul is, an old man, but right now also a prisoner for the Anointed King Jesus.
10 *I want to* encourage you about my child whom I gave birth to in my restraints, Onesimus *(his name means profitable)*.
11 He was not useful to you in the past, but right now he is very useful both to you and to me.
12 I am sending him, his very self, up to you. This is my feelings of sympathy.
13 I was intending to steadily have him facing myself so that he may serve me on your behalf in the good news' restraints.
14 But I didn't want to do anything without your opinion. That way your good may be, as it were, not from an obligation, but from volunteering.
15 You see, he possibly was separated from you toward an hour because of this, so that you may have all of him that spans all time,

16 no longer as a slave, but above a slave, a loved brother, especially to me, but how much more to you, both in the physical body and in the Master.
17 So if you have me *classified as* a partner, take him in as me.
18 If he wronged you or owes you anything, put this on my account.
19 I, Paul, wrote it with my hand. I will pay *his penalty* in full. That way I may not tell you that you also additionally owe yourself to me.
20 Yes, brother, may I profit from you in the Master. Relax my feelings of sympathy in the Anointed King.
21 I wrote you because I have been confident of your obedience. I have seen that you will do even above what I say.
22 Also at the same time get a guesthouse ready for me. You see, I anticipate that through your prayers I will be given to you as an act of generosity.
23 Epaphras, the one incarcerated together with me in the Anointed King Jesus, says hello to you.
24 Mark, Aristarchus, Demas, and Luke, my co-workers, also say hello.
25 The generosity of the Master Jesus, the Anointed King, is with your spirit.

Hebrews

1

1 A long time ago, God spoke to the fathers in many parts and in many ways in the preachers.
2 Then at the last of these days, He spoke to us in a son, a son that He placed as an inheritor of all things. It was through Him that He also made the spans of time.
3 *This Son* radiates God's magnificence. He is an exact expression of what He is undertaking. And He carries all things with His ability's statement. After He cleaned out the sins, He was seated in the right side of the Majesty in high places.
4 He became so much better than the angels, so much so that He has inherited a more substantial name than they.
5 You see, to which of the angels did God ever say *(as He said in Psalms 2:7)*, "You are My Son, I have given birth to You today?" And again, to which of the angels did God ever say, "I will stand in the place of a father for Him, and He will stand in the place of a son for Me" *(2 Samuel 7:14)*.
6 When He again brings the Firstborn into the civilized world, He says, "And all God's angels must bow down to Him" *(Deuteronomy 32:43)*.
7 And pointing toward the angels, the Bible certainly says, "The One who makes His angels spirits and His public servants a blaze of fire" *(Psalm 104:4)*.
8 But pointing toward the Son, it says, "Your throne, God, is for the span of time of the span of time. And the staff of straightness is a staff of Your monarchy.
9 You loved the right way and hated crime. Because of this, God, Your God, anointed You with excitement's olive oil beside Your teammates" *(Psalm 45:6-7)*.
10 *Pointing toward the Son, it* also *says,* "You, Master, laid the earth's foundation from the very beginning, and the skies are works of Your hands.
11 They will be ruined. But You stay through everything, and they all will be worn out as a robe.
12 And You will fold them up as a robe, as if they were a cloak, and they will be changed. But You are the same, and your years will not cease" *(Psalm 102:25-27)*.

13 Which of the angels has He ever pointed toward and stated, "Sit down *at one of the* places to the right of Me until I place Your enemies as a footrest for Your feet?" *(Psalm 110:1)*.

14 Aren't they all spirits that serve the public being sent out on missions of service because of the people who are going to be inheriting a rescue?

2

1 Because of this, it is necessary for us to pay much more attention to the things *that people* heard so that we might not flow past them.

2 You see, if the message spoken through angels became firm and every violation and noncompliance of it received a reasonable payment that is earned,

3 how will we escape when we don't care for such a great thing as this rescue. This is the rescue that received its beginning through the Master speaking about it and was authenticated for us by the people who heard about it.

4 God corroborated it together with proofs, incredible things, various abilities, and the Sacred Spirit's distributions aligned with what He wants.

5 You see, He didn't place the future civilized world under angels, *the world* that we are speaking about.

6 But a certain person somewhere was a strong witness when he said, "What is a human being that You remind Yourself of him or a son of a human being that You keep an eye on him?

7 You made him somewhat less than angels. And You crowned him with an award wreath of magnificence and value.

8 You placed all things beneath his feet" *(Psalm 8:4-6)*. You see, when *this verse* placed all things under a human being, it left nothing unruly for him. But *we don't see that* now. We see that all things are not yet placed under Him.

9 We see Jesus as the One who has been made somewhat less than angels and who because of the hardship of His death has been crowned with an award wreath of magnificence and value. That way with God's generosity He might taste death for everyone.

10 You see, all things *exist* because of Him *(God)* and all things *exist* through Him. And so it was appropriate for Him, after bringing many sons into magnificence, to complete the Head Leader of their rescue through hardships.

11 Both the One who makes people sacred and the people who are made sacred, all of them are from One. This is the reason why He is not ashamed to be calling them brothers.

12 *He called them brothers in Psalm 22:22* when He said, "I will report Your name to My brothers. I will sing praise songs to You in the middle of their assembly."

13 And again *He is described in Isaiah 8:17*, "I will be the one who has been confident based on Him." And *then in the next verse, He* again *identifies Himself with His brothers*, "Look, I and the young children that God gave to Me" *(Isaiah 8:18)*.

14 So since the young children have shared a physical body and blood, He Himself also took part in the same things in a way that was near and beside them. That way He would make the one who has the power of death (that is, the Accuser) useless through His death

15 and relieve these people, as many as were eligible to be sentenced to the slavery of fearing death through every bit of living.

16 You see, maybe He does not latch on to angels, but He does latch on to a seed of Abraham.

17 From this, He ought to be like the brothers in all things so that He might become a kind, forgiving, and reliable head priest in the things that are pointing toward God. That way He can provide a remedy for the sins of the ethnic group.

18 You see, He is able to help the people experiencing trouble in what He has suffered when He Himself experienced trouble.

3

1 From this, sacred brothers (teammates of a heavenly invitation), take a close look at the Missionary and Head Priest of our acknowledgment, Jesus.

2 He is trusted by the One who made Him *the Head Priest* as Moses also was trusted in his whole house.

3 You see, *all the other head priests were inferior to Moses, but* this Head Priest has deserved more magnificence than Moses, inasmuch as the One who constructed the house has more value than the house.

4 Every house is constructed by someone, but the One who constructed all things is God.

5 And Moses certainly is trusted in His whole house as an attending servant. He was a witness of the things that would be spoken.

6 But the Anointed King is over His house as a son. We are His house if it is true that we steadily have the anticipation's clear public statement and optimism.

7 For this reason, it is just as the Sacred Spirit says, "Today, if you will listen to His voice,
8 you should not harden your hearts as your fathers did in their rebelliousness throughout their day of trouble in the backcountry.
9 There your fathers tried to cause trouble during an exam. And they saw My actions forty years.
10 For this reason, I was aggravated with this generation, and I said, 'They are always misled by their heart. They don't know My ways.'
11 It is as I guaranteed in My punishment, '*May My power and justice be unleashed upon Me and more* if they will come into My resting place'" *(Psalm 95:7-11).*
12 Brothers, see that there will never be an evil heart in any of you of not trusting when you stay away from the living God.
13 But encourage yourselves throughout each day till a time that is called the "Today," so that no one from among you might be hardened by sin's fraud.
14 You see, we have become teammates of the Anointed King if it is true that we steadily hold the beginning of our undertaking firm up to the conclusion.
15 This is why it says, "Today, if you will listen to His voice, you should not harden your hearts as your fathers did in their rebelliousness."
16 You see, who rebelled after they heard? But who? Not all the people who came out of Egypt through Moses.
17 Who was He aggravated with for forty years? Was it not with the people who sinned? The people whose carcasses fell in the backcountry?
18 To whom did He guarantee that they would not go into His resting place if it wasn't the people who did not believe?
19 And we see that they weren't able to go in because they didn't trust.

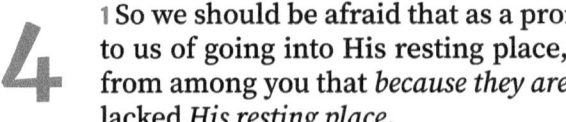

1 So we should be afraid that as a promise is left down here to us of going into His resting place, it may seem to some from among you that *because they are Jews* they haven't ever lacked *His resting place.*
2 You see, the good news has also been shared with us, exactly as it was also shared with those people who rebelled, but the message that was heard didn't benefit those people. They had not been mixed together with trust, *the trust* that people who hear a message *should have.*
3 We, the people who trust, come into the resting place. It is just as it has been stated, "As I guaranteed in My punishment, '...if they will come into My resting place'" *(Psalm 95:11). This shows that it is still*

possible for some people to come into His resting place even though *this rest is* from the work that happened back when the world was formed.

4 He has stated in a certain place about the seventh *day of creation* like this: "And God rested on the seventh day from all His work" *(Genesis 2:2).*

5 And in this *place in Psalms* again *as we just mentioned, it says,* "...if they will come into My resting place."

6 So since *the opportunity* is being left behind for some to go into His resting place, and the people that the good news was previously shared with did not go in because of unbelief,

7 again He later designated a certain day *to go into His resting place--* today. This was said in David's *psalm* such a long time *after the creation,* just as we have seen before: "Today, if you will listen to His voice, you should not harden your hearts."

8 You see, if Joshua gave them *(the Jews)* this rest *when he brought them into the Promised Land, David, a king over the Promised Land many centuries later,* would not be speaking about another day after these days.

9 Clearly a Sabbath-rest is left behind for God's ethnic group.

10 You see, the person who has come into His resting place has also himself rested from his work, even as God rested from His own work.

11 So let's make every effort to go into that resting place so that no one might fall by demonstrating the same unbelief.

12 You see, God's message is living and active. It is sharper above every double-edged dagger. It penetrates till it divides soul and spirit, and joints and marrows. It is able to judge a heart's contemplations and internal ways of thinking.

13 And creation is not unapparent in its sight. All things are naked and have been exposed to God's eyes. His message points toward Him and is for us.

14 So having a great head priest who has gone through the heavens, Jesus, the Son of God, we should hold on to the acknowledgment.

15 You see, we don't have a head priest who is not able to empathize with our weaknesses. *We have a head priest* who has experienced trouble in each and every way like we have, without sin.

16 So we may come with a clear public statement to the throne of generosity so that we might receive forgiving kindness and find generosity for well-timed help.

5

1 You see, every head priest is taken from people. He is put in charge of the things that are pointing toward God on behalf of people so that he may offer up both contributions and sacrifices on behalf of sins.

2 To a certain extent, he is able to be sympathizing with the people who are unaware and misled since he also has weakness lying around him.

3 And because of this, just as he is obligated to offer up contributions and sacrifices to cover sins that cover the ethnic group, he also *is obligated to offer up contributions and sacrifices* to cover himself.

4 And someone doesn't take this valued position on himself. No, he is invited by God, exactly as Aaron also was.

5 In this way also, the Anointed King did not elevate Himself to a place of magnificence to become the head priest. No, the One who spoke pointing toward Him *in Psalms, elevated Him to a place of magnificence when He said,* "You are My Son. I today have given birth to You" *(Psalm 2:7)*.

6 This is just like what He also said in a different *place,* "You are a priest for the span of time aligned with Melchizedek's arrangement" *(Psalm 110:4)*.

7 In the days of His physical body, He brought both pleas and petitions with a strong yell and tears pointing toward the One who was able to rescue Him from death. God listened to Him because of His devotion.

8 Even though He was a son, He learned obedience from what He suffered.

9 *His suffering* made Him a complete head priest. And when His head priesthood was complete, He became the cause of a rescue that spans all time for all the people obeying Him.

10 God publicly addressed Him as head priest aligned with Melchizedek's arrangement.

11 The message to us about this is big and its interpretation is hard to explain to you since you have become sluggish to what you hear.

12 You see, even though you ought to be teachers because of the *amount of* time *that you have been learning,* you again need us to teach you some primary elements of the beginning of God's utterances. And you have become people who need milk, not a solid meal.

13 You see, everyone who has a part in the milk is inexperienced with the right way's message. He is an infant.

14 A solid meal is for mature people, *people* who are in the habit of strenuously exercising their senses toward discerning both what is nice and what is bad.

6

1 For this reason, we should leave the message of the Anointed King's beginning and be carried up to His maturity. Don't again throw down a foundation of changing your ways away from your dead actions, of trust that is based on God,
2 of a teaching of submersions, of laying hands *on people*, of dead people returning back to life, and of judgment that spans all time.
3 And this is what we will do, *we will be carried up to His maturity*, if, in fact, God gives us permission.
4 You see, it is impossible for the people who were once lit up and who tasted some of the free heavenly handout, who became teammates of the Sacred Spirit,
5 who tasted God's nice statement and the abilities of the future span of time,
6 and who fell away, to make themselves new again by changing their ways. *Something can only be new once.* They are again nailing God's Son to a cross for themselves and making a public exhibit of Him.
7 You see, the ground that frequently drinks in the shower coming on it and that delivers feed suitable for those that it was also farmed for, receives a share of a conferring of blessings that come out from God.
8 But the ground that brings out thorns and thistles is unapproved and near a curse. Its conclusion comes in a burn.
9 But we have been confident of better things concerning you, loved ones, of things that include a rescue, even though we speak like this.
10 You see, God doesn't do what is wrong. He doesn't forget your work and the love that you displayed in His name. *He doesn't forget* that you served the sacred people and that you serve them.
11 We desire each of you to display the same concern pointing toward the full accomplishment of the anticipation of good till the conclusion.
12 That way you might not become sluggish, but you might become imitators of the people who inherit the promises through trust and patience.
13 You see, when God made His promise to Abraham, since He had no one greater to guarantee it with, He guaranteed it with Himself.
14 He said, "If it is true *that I most certainly am God*, as I confer blessings, I will confer blessings on you, and as I increase, I will increase you" *(Genesis 22:17)*.
15 And this is how Abraham obtained the promise after he was patient.

16 You see, people guarantee with the bigger thing and the oath for authentication is the end of every dispute for them.
17 Since God intends to do much more in this and show the inheritors of the promise the unchangeable attribute of His intention, He ratified it with an oath.
18 That way we may have strong encouragement through two unchangeable items, *a guarantee and an oath*. In these *two items, it is* impossible for God to lie. We are the ones who escaped down *the road* to take hold of the anticipation that is lying up ahead.
19 We have it *(this anticipation)* as an anchor of the soul. It is certain, firm, and goes into the inner *sacred room* of the temple's curtain.
20 *That is* where a scout, Jesus, went in on our behalf and became a head priest aligned with Melchizedek's arrangement for the span of time.

7

1 You see, this Melchizedek, king of Salem, priest of the highest God, is the one who met together with Abraham as he was returning from the slaying of the kings. He conferred blessings on Abraham.
2 Abraham also divided out ten percent of everything to him. First, his name, Melchizedek, certainly is interpreted as "king of the right way." But following that, he is also a king of Salem, that is a king of peace *(Salem is Hebrew for peace)*.
3 *The Old Testament doesn't mention his father, mother, genealogy, birth, or death. It is as if he is* fatherless, motherless, genealogyless, and doesn't have both a beginning of days or a conclusion of life. He has been made very much like God's Son. He stays a priest forever.
4 See how great this man was! Even Abraham, the head father, gave ten percent from the tops of the piles to him.
5 And certainly the people who are from Levi's sons who take the office of the priesthood have a demand handed down from the law to collect the ten-percent offering from the ethnic group (that is, from their brothers, even though they come out of Abraham's reproductive system *as the priests do*).
6 But Abraham gave a ten-percent offering to the one who is not genealogically traced from them, and he conferred blessings on the one who has the promises, Abraham.
7 One thing that is indisputable is that the better person confers blessings on the lesser person.
8 And here, people who certainly die collect the ten-percent offering, but there, what *the Old Testament* witnessed is that Melchizedek lives.

9 And since *there is* a point to be made, *here it is*: Even Levi (the one who collects ten percent) has given a ten-percent offering to Melchizedek through Abraham.

10 You see, he was still in his father's reproductive system, when Melchizedek met together with him.

11 So certainly if there was a completion through the setting up of the Levitical priesthood (you see, laws have been made for the ethnic group based on it), what further need would there be for a different priest to stand up *in Psalm 110:4*. And *what need would there be* to say that He is aligned with Melchizedek's arrangement and not with Aaron's arrangement? *Aaron's arrangement had already been set up by the law for over 500 years when Psalms was written.*

12 You see, since the priesthood has been transferred, there is also an obligation that the transfer of the law happens.

13 These things are said about someone who has been part of a different family line. No one from it *(this different family line)* has ever paid attention to the altar.

14 It is evident that our Master has come up from the family line of Judah. Moses didn't speak anything to this family line about priests.

15 And it is still much more than very obvious--if He is aligned with the likeness of Melchizedek, a different priest is standing up.

16 He hasn't become *a head priest that is* aligned with a law of a physical demand. No, *He has become a head priest that is* aligned with the ability of an indestructible life.

17 You see, the Old Testament is a witness to who He is: "You are a priest for the span of time aligned with Melchizedek's arrangement" *(Psalm 110:4)*.

18 Certainly when a demand leading the way becomes invalid, it is because of its weak and non-beneficial nature.

19 The law didn't complete anything, but what was brought in over it is a better anticipation of good. Through it, we are brought near to God.

20 And inasmuch as *it is not like the Mosaic priests*, it is not without an oath of guarantee.

21 You see, the people who have become priests certainly do so without an oath of guarantee. But the Anointed King has an oath of guarantee through the One who told Him, "The Master guaranteed and will not regret *it*, You are a priest for the span of time" *(Psalm 110:4)*.

22 Aligned with something so great, Jesus has become a security deposit of an even better deal.

23 There also certainly are more people who have become priests because of the fact that death keeps them from continuing on.

24 But because of the fact that Jesus stays for the span of time, He has the nontransferable priesthood.
25 From this place, He is also able to rescue to the maximum the people who come to God through Him since He is always living for the purpose of intervening on their behalf.
26 You see, this type of head priest was also appropriate for us. He is holy. He is not bad or desecrated. He is separated away from the sinful people. He even became higher than the heavens.
27 The head priests have a daily obligation to first carry up a sacrifice for their own sins and following that to carry up a sacrifice for the ethnic group's sins. *But He doesn't have that obligation.* You see, He did this when He carried Himself up all at once.
28 The law puts people who have a weakness in charge as head priests, but the message of the oath of guarantee that came after the law, puts the Son in charge for the span of time. It has been completed.

8

1 The main point on what is being said is that we have the type of head priest that is seated in the right side of the throne of the Majesty in the heavens.
2 He is a public servant of the sacred things and of the true tent that the Master, not a person, set up.
3 You see, every *Jewish* head priest is put in charge for the purpose of offering both contributions and sacrifices. From this, it is essential for this Head Priest to also have something that he might offer.
4 So certainly, if He *(Jesus)* were on earth, He would not even be a priest since there are *Jewish* priests that offer up the contributions that are aligned with the law.
5 In fact, they minister with a demonstration and shadow of the heavenly things. This is just as Moses had been divinely instructed as he was going to be finishing up the tent: "You see, look," He declared, "you will make everything according to the example shown to you in the mountain" *(Exodus 25:40).*
6 But right now, He has obtained a more substantial public service in that He is also *the* middleman of a better deal. This *better deal* is the thing that new laws have been made with based on better promises.
7 You see, if that first deal were faultless, no one would have looked for a place for a second deal.
8 *But that is what happened.* As He finds fault with them, He says, "'Look, days are coming,' says the Master, 'and I will completely finish a new deal for the house of Israel and the house of Judah.

9 It will not be aligned with the deal that I made with their fathers in a day when I latched on to their hand to lead them out of the land of Egypt. They didn't stay in My deal, and so I didn't care for them,' says the Master.

10 'This is the deal that I will make with the house of Israel after those days,' says the Master. 'As I give my laws, I will inscribe them into their mind and on their hearts. And I will be in the place of a God for them, and they will be in the place of an ethnic group for Me.

11 And they will not in any way teach. Each person *will not teach* other people in his city, and each person *will not teach* his brother. They will not say, 'You must know these things about the Master,' because everyone will see Me, from a little one up to their great one.

12 *Everyone will see Me* because I will be the remedy for their wrong ways. I will not in any way remember their sins anymore'" *(Jeremiah 31:31-34)*.

13 When He says "new" *(in verse 8)*, He has outdated the first deal. What is outdated and aging is near its disappearance.

9

1 So the first deal certainly also was having the right paths of a sacrifice ritual and the global sacred thing.

2 You see, a tent was constructed, and the first *room* had *three things*: the stand for lamps, the table, and the display of the loaves of bread. This is the room that is called the Sacred *Room*.

3 But after the second curtain *(which led into the second room)*, the tent is called Sacred *Room* of Sacred *Things*.

4 It had the gold incense altar and the deal's box that has been completely covered on all sides with gold. *The box* contained the slabs of the deal and a gold jar that had in it the manna and Aaron's staff that budded.

5 Cherubim of magnificence were over and above it. They threw a shadow on the remedy. There is not *enough time* now to talk about each part of these.

6 These have been constructed like this: through every situation the priests certainly enter into the first tent finishing up the sacrifice rituals,

7 but once a year the head priest enters into the second *tent inside the first tent* alone. He always has blood that he offers up on behalf of himself and the undiscovered actions of the ethnic group.

8 This is what the Sacred Spirit makes obvious: The way of the sacred things has not yet been shown as long as the first tent still has a standing.

9 This *first tent* is the thing that is an illustration for the time that has stood here. According to *this illustration,* when it comes to the conscience, both contributions and sacrifices are offered up that are not able to complete the person ministering to God with these.
10 These only lie on food, drink, and specialized submersions for right paths of a physical body up to the right time of reformation.
11 But the Anointed King showed up as a head priest of the good things that happened through the greater and more complete tent. *This tent* is not handmade, that is, it is not of this creation.
12 It was not through the blood of male goats and calves *that He went into it*. It was through His own blood that He went all at once into the sacred things after He found a release payment that spans all time.
13 You see, if the people who have been contaminated are sprinkled with the blood of male goats and bulls and with a young cow's ashes, *and if* that makes them sacred toward the physical body's cleaning,
14 how much more will the blood of the Anointed King (*the One* who offered Himself up unblemished through a spirit that spans all time) clean off our conscience from the dead actions that we do so that we may minister to the living God?
15 And because of this, He is *the* middleman of a new deal in order that a death might end up providing a paid release from the violations on the first deal *and in order that* the people who have been invited might receive the promise of the inheritance that spans all time.
16 You see, where *there is* a deal, *there is* an obligation to define *what will happen* when the person who makes the deal dies.
17 A deal is firm for dead people or else it never has strength when the person who made it is alive.
18 From this, the first deal has not been initiated without blood either.
19 You see, after Moses spoke every demand handed down from the law to all the ethnic group, he took the blood of the calves and the male goats with water, red wool, and hyssop and sprinkled both the very scroll and all the ethnic group.
20 He said, "This is the blood of the deal that God demanded of you."
21 In the same way, he sprinkled both the tent and all the containers for public service with the blood.
22 And according to the law, nearly everything is cleaned in blood, and forgiveness does not happen without a spilling out of blood.
23 So not only is there an obligation for the things that demonstrate what is in the heavens to be cleaned with these, but there is also an

obligation that the heavenly things themselves be cleaned with better sacrifices than these.

24 You see, the Anointed King didn't go into the handmade sacred things (a corresponding type of the true sacred things). No, *He went into heaven itself to now explicitly show Himself on our behalf before God's face.*

25 And He didn't go into heaven's sacred things so that he may offer Himself up many times either, even as the head priest goes into the sacred things yearly with blood belonging to others.

26 If that were the case, it would be necessary for Him to suffer many times since the world was formed, but right now, He has been shown once at the very conclusion of the spans of time to invalidate sin through His sacrifice.

27 And inasmuch as it is set aside for people to die once *and only once,* but after this, there is judgment,

28 in this way also, after the Anointed King was offered up once for the purpose of carrying up the sins of many, from a second arrival He will appear without sin for rescue to the people who patiently wait for Him.

10

1 You see, the law has a shadow of the good things that are going to come. It does not have the very image of the items. It is never ever able to complete the people coming to it each year with the same sacrifices that they offer up forever.

2 Or else wouldn't they stop being offered up because of the *fact* that the people ministering to God who have been cleaned once have no further conscience of sins?

3 But in these sacrifices, each year they are again reminded of sins.

4 You see, it is impossible for the blood of bulls and male goats to take away sins.

5 For this reason, as He is coming into the world, He says, "You didn't want a sacrifice and an offering, but You developed a body for Me.

6 You were not delighted by entirely burned offerings and offerings that cover sin.

7 At that time, I said, 'Look, this has been written about me in a roll of a scroll, I am arriving to do what You want, God'" *(Psalm 40:6-8).*

8 Further up *in this text,* it says, "You didn't want sacrifices, offerings, entirely burned offerings, and offerings that cover sin." And it says, "You were not delighted by them" either. These are offerings that are offered up according to the law.

9 Then He has stated, "Look, I am arriving to do what You want." He takes away the first so that the second might stand.
10 In *the scope of* what He wants, we are people who have been made sacred all at once through the offering of the body of Jesus, the Anointed King.
11 And every priest certainly has stood daily serving the public and offering up the same sacrifices many times. These are sacrifices that are never ever able to take away all the sins around us.
12 But this Man offered up one sacrifice on behalf of sins forever and was seated in the right side of God.
13 For the rest of the time, He is waiting until His enemies are placed as His feet's footrest.
14 You see, with one offering, He has completed forever the people who are made sacred.
15 The Sacred Spirit also is a witness to us *of this fact*. You see, this is after the Sacred Spirit has stated,
16 "'This is the deal that I will make facing them after those days,' says the Master. 'As I give My laws, I will inscribe them on their hearts and on their mind'" *(Jeremiah 31:33)*,
17 and, "I will not in any way be reminded of their sins and their crimes anymore" *(Jeremiah 31:34)*.
18 Where these are forgiven, an offering that covers sin is no longer needed.
19 Brothers, we have a clear public statement for the entrance of the sacred things in Jesus' blood.
20 He initiated this entrance for us. It is a recent and living way through the curtain, that is, through His physical body.
21 So since we have this type of entrance and we have a great priest over God's house,
22 we should come forward with a true heart in the full accomplishment of trust. Our hearts have been sprinkled with His blood to remove an evil conscience, and our body has been given a bath in clean water.
23 We should hold the acknowledgment of the anticipation of good steady without tilting. You see, the One who promised can be trusted.
24 And we should take a close look at each other for a stimulation of love and nice actions.
25 You shouldn't abandon the coming together of yourselves in one place, just as some are accustomed to doing. But you should encourage each other and so much more as you see the day coming near.

26 You see, if we are voluntarily sinning after the *point when we* receive the correct understanding of the truth, a sacrifice covering sins is no longer left behind for us.
27 But *what is left behind for us is* a certain fearful wait for judgment and a hostile passion of fire that is going to be eating up the covert opponents.
28 Anyone who disregards Moses' law dies without compassion based on two or three witnesses.
29 How much worse of an honor punishment does it seem to you the person will deserve who trampled on God's Son, who regarded the blood of the deal to be contaminated (the blood that he was made sacred in), and who maimed the Spirit of generosity?
30 You see, we know the One who said, "Retaliation is for Me. I will repay" *(Deuteronomy 32:35)*, and again *one verse later*, "The Master will judge His ethnic group" *(Deuteronomy 32:36)*.
31 It is a fearful thing to fall into a living God's hands.
32 But remind yourselves again of the previous days. After you were lit up in those days, you persisted to do what is right in a large competition of hardships.
33 *One thing that is* certainly *true* is this: You were made a public spectacle in both criticisms and hard times. But *something that is also true is* this: You became partners of the people who were always treated that way.
34 You see, you also empathized with the prisoners and happily awaited the looting of your things because you yourselves knew that you have a better and remaining possession.
35 So you shouldn't throw away your clear public statement. This is the thing that has a large payment that is earned.
36 You see, you need to be persistent so that after you do what God wants, you might retrieve the promise.
37 Yet in a very, very little while, "the One who is coming will arrive, and it will not take a long time" *(Habakkuk 2:3)*.
38 "The one from Me who does what is right will live from trust" *(Habakkuk 2:4)* and if he backs off, My soul is not delighted with him.
39 We are not *a part* of a backing off into ruin. No, *we are a part* of trust into acquiring the soul.

11

1 Trust is an undertaking of things that are anticipated. It is evidence of items that are not seen.
2 You see, people witnessed that the older men were in it, *in trust*.

3 With trust, we are aware that the spans of time have been developed by God's statement so that what we see has not come into existence from things that appear.

4 With trust, Abel offered up to God more of a sacrifice than Cain. It was witnessed that through it *(through trust)* he did what was right. God told what He witnessed based on his contributions. And after dying, Abel still speaks through it.

5 With trust, Enoch was transferred in a way for him not to see death. People were looking for him and not finding him because God transferred him. You see, before his transfer, people had witnessed that he was well-liked by God.

6 Without trust, it is impossible to be well-liked by God. You see, the person coming to God must trust that He exists and that He ends up paying out earnings to the people intensively searching for Him.

7 With trust, Noah was divinely instructed about the things that he hadn't yet seen, and he took it seriously. He constructed a box *(the Ark)* to rescue his house. Through it, he found the world guilty and became an inheritor of the right way that is aligned with trust.

8 With trust, a man called Abraham obeyed and went out to a place that he was going to receive for an inheritance. And he went out, not even aware of where he was going.

9 With trust, he was a foreign resident in the land that was promised *to him* as if the *land* was someone else's. He lived in tents with Isaac and Jacob, the inheritors together of the same promise.

10 You see, he was waiting for the city that had the foundations. That city's skilled worker and craftsman is God.

11 With trust, also Sarah, herself infertile, received the ability to form a seed, even beyond the proper age, since she regarded the One who promised it to be someone she could trust.

12 For this reason, even these descendants were born out of one *whose womb* had actually been dead. From her came the large number of descendants that are just as the sky's large number of constellations and as the countless sand along the shore of the sea.

13 These all died aligned with trust and did not receive the promises. But they saw them from far away, they greeted them, and they acknowledged that they are strangers and refugees on the earth.

14 You see, the people saying these types of things explicitly show that they are searching for a homeland.

15 And certainly if they were remembering that homeland that they walked out of and left, they would have had a time to double back.

16 But now they are reaching out for a better *homeland* that is a heavenly *homeland*. For this reason, God is not ashamed of them *when* they also call Him their God. You see, He got a city ready for them.
17 With trust, Abraham had offered Isaac up, even though he was troubled *by it*. And he was offering up his only biological son. *This was Abraham,* the one who welcomed the promises in.
18 God had spoken to him and said, "A seed in Isaac will be called yours."
19 He considered that God is able to get him up, even from the dead, and this is where he retrieved him from. And *he retrieved him* in an illustration *(of God's love).*
20 With trust, Isaac conferred blessings on Jacob and Esau that also was about things that were going to happen.
21 With trust, Jacob conferred blessings on each of Joseph's sons as he was dying and bowed down over the edge of his staff.
22 With trust, Joseph remembered about the exit of Israel's sons as he was passing away and gave them a demand about his bones.
23 With trust, after Moses was born, he was hidden for a three-month *period* by his parents because they saw that the young child was well-behaved and they didn't fear the king's ruling.
24 With trust, Moses, after he became great, denied *the privilege of* being called a son of Pharaoh's daughter.
25 He chose rather to be mistreated together with God's ethnic group than to have the enjoyment of sin for the time being.
26 He regarded the criticism of the Anointed King as greater wealth than Egypt's stockpiles. You see, he was looking off to the payment he would earn.
27 With trust, he left Egypt down below and wasn't afraid of the king's anger. You see, he was empowered by the invisible One as if he could see Him.
28 With trust, he has performed the Passover and the public spilling of its blood so that the one destroying the firstborn children would not come into contact with them.
29 With trust, they walked across the Red Sea as across dry land, land that swallowed the Egyptians up after they had trouble with it.
30 With trust, the walls of Jericho fell after being surrounded on seven *consecutive* days.
31 With trust, Rahab, the prostitute that accepted the spies with peace, was not ruined together with the people who didn't believe.

32 And what else may I say? You see, the time *will leave on me* describing about Gideon, Barak, Samson, Jephthah, and David, Samuel, and the preachers.
33 Through trust, they struggled against monarchies, worked for the right way, obtained promises, shut lions' mouths,
34 extinguished the ability of fire, escaped mouths of a dagger, gained ability out of weakness, became strong in war, and toppled army barracks belonging to others.
35 Women received their dead when their dead returned back to life. Other people were clubbed to death after they didn't accept the payment for their release so that they might obtain a better return back to life.
36 Different people had trouble from incidents of mockery and whips, but still others from restraints and jail.
37 They were attacked with stones. They were sawed *in half*. They died in murder with a dagger. They went around in sheepskins and in goat skins. They lacked things. They went through hard times. They were mistreated.
38 The world was not deserving of them. They wandered around on uninhabited places, mountains, caves, and the earth's openings.
39 And even though people witnessed that all these people did these things through trust, they did not retrieve the promise.
40 Beforehand God looked at something concerning us that was better--that they would not be completed without us.

12

1 So you see then, since we also have such a cloud cover of witnesses lying around us, we should put away all the extra weight and the sin that easily stands around us, and through persistence, we should run in the struggle that is lying up ahead of us.
2 We should look away to the Head Leader and Completer of the trust, Jesus. For the happiness lying up ahead of Him, He persisted to do what is right, He ignored a cross of shame, and He has been seated in the right side of God's throne.
3 You see, think about the One who has persisted to do what is right in this type of a dispute launched against Himself by the sinful people. That way you might not be exhausted in your souls and give up.
4 You haven't yet resisted up to *the point of losing* blood as you struggle in opposition to sin, have you?
5 And you have completely forgotten the encouragement *in the Bible*. It is the *encouragement* that has a discussion with you as sons, "My son,

don't consider the Master's discipline to be a small thing, and don't give up as you are being reprimanded by Him either" *(Proverbs 3:11).*

6 You see, the Master disciplines the one He loves. He whips every son that He warmly welcomes.

7 In discipline, you, as sons, persist to do what is right, and God is brought forward to you. You see, what son is there that a father does not discipline?

8 Everyone has become teammates of discipline. If you are without it, clearly you are illegitimate and not sons.

9 Add to that that we certainly had people discipline us (the fathers of our physical body), and we were embarrassed. Will we not much more place ourselves under the Father of the spirits and live?

10 You see, *the disciplining that our fathers were doing* certainly was aligned with what seemed good to them toward a few days, but *the disciplining that* the *Father does is* based on what is advantageous for receiving a share of His sacredness.

11 All discipline pointing toward what is beside you certainly doesn't seem to be a happy thing. No, *it seems to be* a sad thing. But later it gives back the right way's peaceful fruit to the ones who have been strenuously exercised by it.

12 For this reason, straighten up the hands that have been neglected and the knees that have been disabled.

13 And make straight tracks for your feet so that the crippled foot might not be turned outward, but instead it might be cured.

14 Pursue peace with everyone and pursue the sacredness that everyone must have to see the Master.

15 As you are supervising, *make sure* no one is lacking and moving away from God's generosity. *Make sure* no root of bitterness sprouts up so that it won't crowd in and many won't be desecrated by it.

16 And *make sure* there is no one who commits sexual sin or no profane person. Esau was *a profane person.* He gave away *something sacred,* his own firstborn rights, for one dinner.

17 You see, you must realize that even afterward, when he wanted to inherit the conferring of blessings, he was rejected. He did not find a place *where his father could* change his ways even though he intensively searched for it with tears.

18 You see, you haven't come to a mountain that can be felt, that has been burning with fire. *You haven't come* to overcast skies, to gloom, to a blowing storm,

19 to the echo of a trumpet, and to a voice making statements. After the people heard it *(God's voice)*, they refused to let it add another word.
20 They were not putting up with the terror they felt as they were being warned--even if a wild animal should come into contact with the mountain, stones will be thrown at it.
21 And this is how fearful the thing being revealed was: Moses said, "I am frightened and trembling inside."
22 But you have come to Mount Zion, to the city of the living God, to heavenly Jerusalem, to tens of thousands of angels,
23 to a mass rally, to an assembly of firstborn who have been registered in heavens, to the Judge of all people (God), to spirits of people who do what is right, who have been completed,
24 to Jesus, to the Middleman of a young deal, and to the blood of sprinkling that speaks something better than Abel.
25 See to it that you won't refuse the One speaking. You see, if those people that refused *Moses (the man* on earth who divinely instructs people), *if they* didn't escape, much more we *also will not escape* if we turn away the One who is out of the heavens.
26 His voice disturbed the earth at that time. But now He has promised, saying, "Yet, once more I will cause not only the earth to shake, but also the sky" *(Haggai 2:6)*.
27 The *phrase* "yet once more" *and the other statements that God made in Haggai 2:3-9* make it obvious that there is a transfer of the things that are disturbed (like, the things that have been made) so that the things that are not disturbed might stay.
28 For this reason, as we receive an undisturbed monarchy in, we may hold on to generosity. Through it, we may minister with devotedness and reverence in a way that is well-liked by God.
29 You see, our God also is a completely consuming fire.

13

1 The brotherly kindness must stay.
2 Don't forget to be nice to strangers. You see, by doing this, some provided angels with a place to stay and didn't notice it.
3 Remind yourselves of the prisoners (as if you have been locked up together with them) and the people who are mistreated (as if you yourselves are actually in their body).
4 Marriage is valuable in all situations, and its bed is not desecrated. You see, God will judge the people who commit sexual sin and cheating spouses.

5 The way to live is without greed. Be content with what you have beside you. You see, He has stated, "I will not in any way ease up from you, and I will not in any way abandon you either."
6 And so we are courageous, and we say, "The Master is a helper to me, and I will not fear what a person will do to me."
7 Remember your leaders. They are the ones who spoke God's message to you. As you observe the way out that their behavior *takes*, imitate their trust.
8 Jesus is the Anointed King. He is the same yesterday, today, and in the spans of time.
9 Don't be carried along by various and strange teachings. You see, it is nice for the heart to be authenticated with generosity, not with foods. The people walking around in foods were not benefited by them.
10 We have an altar that the people who minister at the tent don't have authority to eat from.
11 You see, the animals' blood that covers sin is carried into the sacred things by the head priest. The bodies of these are burned up outside of the camp.
12 For this reason, Jesus also suffered outside of the gate so that He might make the ethnic group sacred through His own blood.
13 Now then, let's go out to Him outside of the camp as we carry the criticism of Him.
14 You see, we don't have a city remaining here, but we are searching for the city that is going to come.
15 So we should carry up a sacrifice of praise through everything to God through Him. This sacrifice should be the fruit of lips that acknowledge His Name *and who He is*.
16 Don't forget to do good and to share. You see, these types of sacrifices are well-liked by God.
17 Believe your leaders, and surrender to them. You see, they don't go to sleep at night on behalf of your souls as leaders who will give back an answer. *Believe them and surrender to them* so that they may do this with happiness and without groaning. You see, this has no fitting compensation for you.
18 Pray about us. You see, we are persuaded that we have a nice conscience in all things wanting to be nicely busy.
19 But much more, I encourage you to do this so that I might be reestablished with you faster.

20 The God of peace brought the Great Shepherd of the sheep, our Master Jesus, up from the dead in the blood of a deal that spans all time.
21 May He develop you in every good thing for the purpose of doing what He wants as He does in us what is well-liked in His sight through Jesus, the Anointed King. The magnificence for the spans of time of the spans of time *belongs* to Him. Amen.
22 I am encouraging you, brothers. Tolerate the message of encouragement. You see, I wrote you a letter even through bits and pieces.
23 You know that our brother Timothy has been dismissed. If he comes faster, I will see you with him.
24 Say hello to all your leaders and to all the sacred people. The people out of Italy say hello to you.
25 May generosity be with you all.

James

1

1 From: James, a slave of God and of the Master Jesus, the Anointed King. To: the twelve family lines scattered throughout other countries. Happy to meet you.
2 Regard it total happiness, my brothers, when you fall into being surrounded by various troubles.
3 Know that the proving of your trust works on and completes persistence to do what is right.
4 The persistence must have a complete work so that you all may be complete and entirely whole, lacking in nothing.
5 If any of you lack insight, he must ask directly from the God who gives to everyone in a dedicated way and who does not criticize. If any of you asks for insight, it will be given to him.
6 He must ask in trust and consider nothing to be wrong. You see, the person who *asks in trust and* considers something to be wrong has depicted a wave of the sea blown by the wind and tossed around.
7 You see, that person must not suppose that he will receive anything directly from the Master.
8 A double-souled man is inconsistent in all his ways.
9 The lowly brother must be optimistic in his high position.
10 The wealthy person *must be optimistic* in his lowliness because he will pass by as a flower of grass.
11 You see, the sun came up together with the hot wind, it dried up the grass, its flower fell off, and the beauty of its appearance was ruined. This is also how the wealthy person will be snuffed out in his *money-making* journeys.
12 A man who persists to do what is right *when he is going through* trouble is blessed because when he becomes approved, he will receive life's award wreath. God promised it *(life's award wreath)* to the people who love Him.
13 Anyone who is experiencing trouble must not say, "The trouble that I am experiencing is coming out from God." You see, bad things don't trouble God. He does not try to cause trouble with anyone.
14 Each person experiences trouble as he, under his own desire, is drawn out and enticed.
15 After that, when the desire conceives, it delivers *a baby*, sin. But when the sin is finished out, it brings death out of the womb.
16 Don't be misled, my loved brothers.

17 Every good giving act and every completed free gift is from above. It steps down out of the Father of the lights. There is no change or shade of turning directly from Him.

18 He who intended *it to be this way* brought us out of the womb with a message of truth. *He did this* for the purpose of us being a certain first-part-offering of His created things.

19 Realize this, my loved brothers: Every person must be quick for the "to hear" *part*, slow for "to speak" *part*, slow for rage.

20 You see, a man's rage does not work on God's right way.

21 For this reason, after you put away all filthiness and overflow of badness, in submissiveness, accept the implanted message that is able to rescue your souls.

22 Become doers of the message and not just hearers, misguiding yourselves.

23 If anyone is a hearer of the message and not a doer, this person has depicted a man who takes a close look in a mirror at the face of his birth.

24 You see, he took a close look at himself, he has gone away, and right away he forgot what kind of *face* it was.

25 But the one who stooped and peered into the complete law of freedom and stayed with it, who did not become a hearer of forgetfulness, but a doer of action, this one will be blessed in the doing of it.

26 If anyone seems to be religious and is not bridling his tongue but is fooling his heart, this person's religion is futile.

27 Religion that is clean and not desecrated beside the God and Father is this, to keep an eye on orphans and widows in their hard times, to keep oneself unspotted away from the world.

2

1 My brothers, have the trust of our Master Jesus, the Anointed King, the Magnificence, in an environment where appearances don't matter.

2 You see, what if a man with a gold ring on his finger came into your synagogue in a dazzling outfit, but also a poor man in a filthy outfit came in?

3 You all may take a look at the person wearing the dazzling outfit, and say, "You sit here nicely," and you might say to the poor man, "You stand over there or sit down under my footrest?"

4 You didn't consider what is wrong among yourselves, and you became judges with evil ponderings.

5 Listen, my loved brothers, didn't God select the poor in the world to be wealthy in trust and to be inheritors of the monarchy that was promised to the people who love Him?
6 But you belittled the poor man. Don't the wealthy suppress you? And don't they themselves drag you into courts?
7 Don't they themselves insult the nice name that was called over you?
8 And yet if you finish the royal law handed down from the *Old Testament* writing, "You will love the person near you as yourself," you do nicely.
9 But if you are swayed by appearances, you are working on sin, and you are reprimanded by the law as violators.
10 You see, anyone who will keep the whole law but slip up in one point has become eligible to be sentenced for *breaking* all of it.
11 The *same* One who said, "You will not cheat on your spouse," also said, "You will not commit murder." If you don't cheat on your spouse, but you commit murder, you have become a violator of the law.
12 This is how you should speak and this is how you should do things-- as people who are going to be judged through *a different law,* a law that frees people.
13 You see, the judgment that has no forgiving kindness is for the person who didn't show forgiving kindness. Forgiving kindness brags about how much better it is than judgment.
14 What benefit is it, my brothers, if someone says that he has trust, but he doesn't have its actions? The trust is not able to rescue him, is it?
15 What if a brother or sister is naked and lacks that day's meal?
16 Some from among you might say to them, "Make your way back in peace. Be warm, and be full." But if you won't give them the body's needful things, what is the benefit of that?
17 This is also how trust is dead by itself if it doesn't have actions.
18 But someone will state that you have trust and I have actions. Show me your trust separate from the actions, and I will show you the trust from my actions.
19 You trust that there is one God. You do nicely. Even the lesser deities trust and shudder.
20 Do you want to know, O empty person, that trust separate from the actions is idle?
21 Wasn't Abraham, our father, made right from actions when he carried Isaac, his son, up onto the altar?

22 Do you see that his trust was working together with his actions, and from the actions the trust was completed?
23 And the *Old Testament* writing that says, "Abraham trusted God, and it was considered to him for the right way" *(Genesis 15:6),* was accomplished, and *in later writings,* he was called a friend of God *(Isaiah 41:8; 2 Chronicles 20:7).*
24 You *can* see that a person is made right from actions and not from trust only.
25 Likewise also, was not Rahab, the prostitute, made right from actions when she accepted the announcers under her roof and took them out a different way?
26 You see, even as the body is dead when it is separate from the spirit, so also trust is dead when it is separate from actions.

3

1 Don't become many teachers, my brothers. Realize that *if we do,* we will receive greater judgment.
2 You see, absolutely all of us slip up often. If anyone does not slip up in word, this person is a complete man. He is able to also bridle the whole body.
3 If we put bridles into horses' mouths so they are persuaded by us, we actually lead their whole body about.
4 Look also at the boats being such big boats as these. They are driven by harsh winds. The boat is led about by the smallest rudder to where the sudden impulse of the person steering intends.
5 This is also how the tongue is a little body part and brags about great things. Look, such a small fire starts such a large forest on fire.
6 And the tongue is a fire, the world of the wrong way. The tongue is classified among our body parts and stains the whole body, ignites the running wheel of birth, and is ignited by Hinnom Valley. (The Hinnom Valley ran along the southwestern edge of Jerusalem. At one time children were burned to death there as sacrifices to idols. It is symbolic of the eternal lake of fire.)
7 You see, the nature of a human tames and has tamed the nature of every *being,* of both wild animals and winged birds, of both reptiles and marine animals.
8 But no one is able to tame the tongue of humans. It is inconsistent, bad, full of lethal poison.
9 With it, we confer blessings on the Master and Father, and with it we put curses on the people who have become aligned with God's likeness.

10 From the same mouth comes a conferring of blessing and a curse. My brothers, these things do not need to be happening like this.
11 The spring doesn't emit sweet water and bitter water from the same opening, does it?
12 My brothers, a fig tree is not able to produce olives (or a vine, figs), is it? And salt water isn't able to produce sweet water either.
13 Who is insightful and intelligent among you? He must show his actions from his nice behavior in submissiveness of insight.
14 But if you have bitter hostile passion and contention in your heart, do not brag *about how much better you are* and lie against the truth.
15 This insight does not come down from above. No, it is earthly, psychological, like lesser deities.
16 You see, where hostile passion and contention are, there is conflict and every useless item.
17 But the insight from above certainly is first consecrated. Following that, it is peaceful, polite, easily persuaded, full of forgiving kindness and good fruits, not considering the wrong things, not faked.
18 The right way's fruit is seeded in peace for the ones who make peace.

4

1 Where are wars and arguments among you from? Aren't they from here? From your pursuits of pleasure that serve in the military of your body parts?
2 You desire and do not have. You murder, you get mad, and you aren't able to obtain. You argue and wage war. You don't have because of the *fact* that you aren't asking.
3 You ask and do not receive because you ask in a bad way. *You ask* so that you might spend it in your pursuits of pleasure.
4 *Aren't you married to God?* Cheating wives, don't you realize that the world's friendship has a hostile relationship with God? So whoever intends to be a friend of the world is classified as an enemy of God.
5 Or does it seem to you that the *Old Testament* writing meaninglessly says, "The spirit that lives in you yearns toward envy."
6 But He gives more generosity. For this reason, He says, "God places Himself in opposition to proud people, but gives generosity to lowly people."
7 So place yourselves under God. Stand in opposition to the Accuser, and he will escape away from you.
8 Come near to God, and He will come near to you. Clean your hands, sinful people, and consecrate your hearts, double-souled people.

9 Be troubled, grieve, and cry. Your laughter must be turned into grief and the happiness into dismay.
10 Put yourselves down low in the sight of the Master, and He will put you up high.
11 Don't speak badly about each other, brothers. The person speaking badly about a brother or judging his brother speaks badly about the law and judges the law. If you judge the law, you are not a doer of the law. No, you are a judge.
12 There is one Lawmaker and Judge. He is the One who is able to rescue and to ruin. Who are you to judge a person near you?
13 Now, bring *your attention here*, you who say, "Today or tomorrow we will travel to the city here, do things there a year, travel among them, and make money."
14 These are the people who are not even aware of what will happen tomorrow. What kind of life is your life? You see, you are a fog that appears for a little while and, following that, disappears.
15 In place of that, you should be saying, "If the Master wants it, we will also live and do this or that."
16 But now you brag about your egos. All of this type of bragging is evil.
17 So it is a sin when someone knows to do a nice thing and does not do it.

5

1 Now, bring *your attention here*, you wealthy people. Cry and howl over the miseries coming on you.
2 Your wealth has rotted, and your clothes have become moth-eaten.
3 Your gold and silver have become covered with tarnish. Their tarnish will be turned into a witness to you. They will eat your physical body as fire. You stockpiled wealth in the last days.
4 Look! The pay of the workers who brought in the crops of your rural areas, the *pay* that has been robbed by you, yells. And the shouts of the people who harvested have come into the ears of the Master of Sabaoth *(Hebrew for army, the name of God's army)*.
5 You had lavish things on the earth, and you lived in luxury. You nurtured your hearts on the day of slaughter.
6 The person who did what is right, you found him to be guilty. You murdered him. And he wasn't placing himself in opposition to you.
7 So be patient, brothers, until the Master's arrival. Look! The farmer waits for the valuable fruit of the earth. He is patient over it until it receives the early and late *showers*.

8 You also must be patient. Establish your hearts because the Master's arrival has come near.

9 Don't groan against each other, brothers, so that you might not be judged. Look! The judge has been standing in front of the doors.

10 Take a demonstration, brothers, of the hard suffering and patience of the preachers who spoke in the name of *and on behalf of* the Master.

11 Look! We consider the people who persisted to do what is right to be blessed. You heard of Job's persistence and saw the Master's conclusion--that the Master is very sympathetic and compassionate.

12 Before all things, my brothers, don't guarantee, not with the sky, or the earth, or any other oath, but your "yes" must be yes and your "no", no so that you might not fall under judgment.

13 Is anyone among you suffering tough hardships? He must pray. Is anyone cheered up? He must recite psalms.

14 Is anyone frail among you? He must call for the assembly's older men, and they must pray over him after dabbing olive oil on him in the name of *and on behalf of* the Master.

15 And the vow of trust will rescue the person who is exhausted, and the Master will get him up. If he has also committed sins, it will be forgiven him.

16 So admit the sins out loud to each other, and wish for good over each other in order that you might be cured. A plea that is active from a person who does what is right has much strength.

17 Elijah was a human who was suffering in the same way *that we do*. And he prayed a prayer for it not to rain, and it did not rain on the earth for three years and six months.

18 And again he prayed, and the sky gave a shower, and the earth budded its fruit.

19 My brothers, if anyone among you wanders off from the truth and someone returns him back,

20 he must know that the person who returned a sinful person back from his wandering way will rescue his soul from death and cover up a large number of sins.

First Peter

1 From: Peter, a missionary of Jesus, the Anointed King. To: Select refugees scattered throughout Pontus (northeastern Turkey), Galatia (north central Turkey), Cappadocia (central Turkey), Western Turkey, and Bithynia (northwestern Turkey),

2 *who are* aligned with what Father God knew beforehand in the Spirit's sacredness for obedience and a sprinkling of the blood of Jesus, the Anointed King. May generosity and peace increase to you.

3 The God (who has blessings conferred on Him) and Father of our Master Jesus, the Anointed King, is the One who gave us a rebirth aligned with His great forgiving kindness. *This rebirth is* for an anticipation of good that lives through the return back to life from the dead of Jesus, the Anointed King.

4 *It is* for an inheritance that has been kept in heavens for you, an inheritance that doesn't deteriorate, isn't desecrated, and isn't snuffed out.

5 *You are* the ones that God watches over in His ability through trust for a rescue that is ready to be uncovered in the last time.

6 You are excited about it for a little while now even if it is necessary for you to have been sad in various troubles.

7 That way the proving of your trust might be found for high praise, magnificence, and value in the uncovering of Jesus, the Anointed King. *The proving of your trust is* much more valuable than gold that is ruined but proven *to be gold* through fire.

8 You, who didn't see Him, love Him. You don't see Him now, but you trust in Him. You are excited with inexpressible and magnificent happiness.

9 You are retrieving the conclusion of your trust, a rescue of souls.

10 The preachers intensively searched and intensively examined about this rescue. They preached about generosity for you.

11 The Anointed King's Spirit witnessed to them beforehand about the hardships for the Anointed King and the magnificent things after these. They examined who it was for or which time His Spirit in them was making obvious.

12 It was uncovered to them that they were not serving these things to themselves, but to you. These things were announced to you now by the people who shared good news with you in the Sacred Spirit that

was sent out from heaven. Announcers desire to stoop and peer into these things.

13 For this reason, after you tie up the waists of your mind *(or in other words, after your mind is prepared to work)*, as you are completely sober, anticipate good. Base *this anticipation* on the generosity that is brought to you in the uncovering of Jesus, the Anointed King.

14 As children of obedience, don't conform to the prior desires that you had when you were not aware of anything.

15 But aligned with the Sacred One who invited you, you yourselves also must become sacred ones in every behavior

16 because it has been written *in the Bible*, "You will be sacred because I am sacred" *(Leviticus 11:44)*.

17 And if you call on the Father who is not swayed by appearances and judges each person according to his work, be cautious as you plow *your way through* the time of your foreign residency.

18 Realize that the price that released you from your futile behavior (the forefathers' traditional behavior) was not paid with deteriorating things, like silver or gold.

19 No, *it was paid* with valuable blood that is like the blood of an unblemished and unspotted lamb, the blood of the Anointed King.

20 He certainly had been known beforehand, before the world was formed, but He was shown at the last of the times because of you.

21 It is through Him that you are the people who trust in God. He *(God)* is the One who got Him *(the Anointed King)* up from the dead and gave Him magnificence in such a way for your trust and anticipation to be in God.

22 Since you have consecrated your souls to brotherly kindness in the obedience of the truth, *brotherly kindness* that is not faked, love each other intensively from a clean heart.

23 You are not reborn from a deteriorating reproduction process. No, *you are reborn from a* undeteriorating *reproduction process* through God's living and remaining message.

24 *This is* because every physical body is as grass, and all its magnificence is as a flower of grass. The grass dried up, and the flower fell off,

25 but the statement of the Master remains for the span of time. This is the statement of good news that was shared for you.

2

1 So when you put away all badness, every deception, faked behaviors, envies, and all bad comments,

2 as newborn babies, yearn for the message's deception-free milk so that in it you might grow into a rescue,
3 if you have tasted that the Master is kind.
4 As you come toward Him (a living stone that certainly has been rejected by people, but beside God, is select and valued),
5 you all (yourselves also as living stones) are built (as a spiritual house) into a sacred order of priests to carry up well-received spiritual sacrifices to God through Jesus, the Anointed King.
6 Because of this, there is a passage in an *Old Testament* writing: "Look, I put the primary cornerstone in Zion. It is select and valued. And the one who trusts based on it will not in any way be shamed" *(Isaiah 28:16)*.
7 So this is of value to you, the people trusting, but to the people who don't trust, a stone that was rejected by the builders, this stone ended up being used for a corner's head *(a cornerstone, the primary stone of the whole building)*.
8 It is also a stone of a trip hazard and rock of an obstacle. They trip on the message and don't believe what they actually were put into.
9 But you are a select family, a kingly order of priests, a sacred nation, an ethnic group that He acquired in order that you might promote the achievements of the One who invited you to come from darkness into His amazing light.
10 *You are* the people who were not an ethnic group in the past, but now are God's ethnic group. *You are* the people who had not received forgiving kindness, but who now receive forgiving kindness.
11 Loved ones, as foreign residents and refugees, I encourage you to be keeping yourselves away from the physical desires. These are the things that serve in the military against the soul.
12 The non-Jews speak badly about you, as if you are people who do bad things. Keep your behavior nice among them so that as they watch you in a day of supervision, from your nice actions, they might praise God's magnificence.
13 Place yourself under every human creature because of the Master, whether under a king as someone who has a higher position,
14 or under leaders as people sent by him to retaliate against people who do bad things and to highly praise people who do good things.
15 What God wants is like this: for people doing good to be muzzling the distracted people's ignorance.
16 As free people and not as *free people* who use their freedom to cover up their badness, but as *free people who are* slaves of God,
17 value all people, love the brotherhood, fear God, value the king.

18 The domestic servants must place themselves under their owners in all cautiousness, not only under the good and polite, but also under the crooked.
19 You see, generosity is this: if, because of a conscience of God, someone endures sadnesses as he suffers wrongfully.
20 What kind of recognition is there if you will persist to do what is right when you sin and are slugged *for sinning?* But if you will persist to do what is right when you do good and suffer *for doing good*, this is *the kind of* generosity *that is* beside God.
21 You see, you were invited into this because even the Anointed King suffered on your behalf. He left a master copy behind for you so that you might follow closely behind Him in His footsteps.
22 He didn't sin, and deception wasn't found in His mouth either.
23 As He was being put down, He was not responding with put-downs. As He was suffering, He was not threatening. He was giving in to the One who judges rightly.
24 He Himself carried our sins up in His body on the wooden cross so that we might live in the right way after getting away from the sins. His bruising cured you.
25 You see, you were as sheep wandering off, but now you are turned back to the Shepherd and Supervisor of your souls.

3

1 Likewise, the wives should be placing themselves under their own husbands so that even if any of them don't believe the message, they will be won through the wives' behavior unaccompanied by a message
2 when they watch your consecrated behavior in cautiousness.
3 Your makeup must not be on the outside, of an elaborate braiding of hair and decoration of gold, or of a dressing up in clothes.
4 No, it must be the hidden person of the heart in the *clothes* that do not deteriorate, *clothes* of the submissive and calm spirit that is very expensive in the sight of God.
5 You see, this is also how the sacred wives in the past who anticipated good in God were decorating themselves. They were placing themselves under their own husbands.
6 This is how Sarah obeyed Abraham and called him master. You, *wives*, become her children as you do good and aren't fearing any bit of panic.
7 The husbands likewise should be living in a house together with them aligned with knowledge, as with a weaker container, the woman *container*. You should dole out value to them as to people who

also inherit life's generosity together with you for the purpose that your prayers not be interrupted.

8 The conclusion is that everyone is agreeable, empathetic, brotherly, goodhearted, lowly focused,

9 not giving back bad for bad or put-down for put-down, but just the opposite, conferring blessings. This is what you were invited into so that you might inherit a conferring of blessings.

10 You see, the one who wants to love life and to see good days must stop his tongue away from bad and his lips from speaking deception.

11 He must slide away from bad and do good. He must look for peace and pursue it

12 because the Master's eyes are on people who do what is right and His ears are into their plea. The Master's face is on people who do bad things.

13 And who is the person who will do bad to you if you become people with passion for the good thing?

14 But you are blessed if you also suffer because of the right way. Don't fear the fear of them, and you shouldn't be uneasy either.

15 Make the Master (the Anointed King) sacred in your hearts. Always be ready to give a defense to everyone who asks you for an answer concerning the anticipation in you, but *be ready* with submissiveness and cautiousness.

16 Have a good conscience so that the people who are spiteful of your good behavior in the Anointed King might be ashamed in *the thing* that they speak badly about you.

17 You see, it is better to suffer for doing good (if what God wants should want it) than for doing bad

18 because the Anointed King also suffered once concerning sins--a Man who does what is right on behalf of people who do what is wrong--so that He might bring you to God. The Anointed King certainly has been put to death in the physical body, but was given life in a spirit.

19 After traveling in it, He also spoke publicly to the spirits in jail.

20 *He spoke to* people who did not believe in the past when God's patience was patiently waiting in the days of Noah as a box *(the Ark)* was being constructed. A few (that is, eight) souls were completely rescued in it through water.

21 A corresponding type of that also now rescues you: a submersion. *It is* not *a submersion* that puts away the filth of a physical body. No, *it is a submersion* that asks for God from a good conscience. It rescues you through the return back to life of Jesus, the Anointed King.

22 After traveling into heaven, He is in the right side of God, and angels, authorities, and abilities are placed under Him.

4 1 So since the Anointed King suffered in a physical body, you also must arm yourselves with the same internal way of thinking because the One who suffered in a physical body has stopped sin.

2 For your remaining time in a physical body, you should no longer live for people's desires, but for what God wants.

3 You see, enough time has passed by to have worked on and completed what the non-Jews intend to do. You have traveled in indulgent activities, desires, times with too much wine, wild parties, and drinking binges and forbidden idol worship.

4 They think it is strange that you don't run with the same reckless obsession together with them in what they are determined to do, and they insult you.

5 They will give an answer back to the One who is ready to judge living people and dead people.

6 You see, good news was also shared with dead people for this reason, so that they might certainly be judged aligned with people in a physical body but they may live aligned with God in a spirit.

7 The conclusion of everything has come near. So you all must be properly focused and sober in prayers.

8 Have intensive love among yourselves in front of everyone because love covers up a large number of sins.

9 Be friendly to the strangers among you unaccompanied by grumbling.

10 Just as each person received a gift, they must serve the same thing to themselves as nice managers of God's varied generosity.

11 If someone speaks, *he should speak as if it is* God's utterances. If someone serves, *he should serve as if it is* from the strength that God supplies. That way God may be elevated to a place of magnificence in all things through Jesus, the Anointed King. He has the magnificence and the power for the spans of time of the spans of time. Amen.

12 Loved ones, don't think that the burning among you that is becoming trouble for you is strange, as if there is a strange thing coming together and happening to you.

13 No, you are sharing in what is aligned with the hardships of the Anointed King. Be happy. That way you also might be happy and excited during the uncovering of His magnificence.

14 If people criticize you for the Anointed King's name, you are blessed because the spirit of magnificence and the Spirit of God relaxes on you.
15 You see, none of you must suffer as a murderer, or a thief, or a person who does bad things, or as a meddler.
16 But if someone suffers as a Christian, he must not be ashamed. He must elevate God to a place of magnificence in this name, *the Christian name,*
17 because it is time for the judgment to begin out from God's house. If it is out from us first, what will the conclusion be for the ones who don't believe the good news of God?
18 And if it takes a lot of effort to rescue the person who does what is right, where will the godless and sinful person appear?
19 In such a way, in the area of doing good, the people who suffer aligned with what God wants must also place their souls beside a Creator who can be trusted.

5

1 So I, the older colleague and witness of the hardships of the Anointed King, am encouraging the older people among you. I also am a partner of the future magnificence to be uncovered.
2 Shepherd and supervise God's flock among you, not because you are urged to, but voluntarily aligned with God, not for shameful gain either, but eagerly,
3 and not as people who act like masters over their portions either, but by becoming examples to the flock.
4 And when the Head Shepherd is shown, you will retrieve the unfading award wreath of magnificence.
5 Likewise, you younger people must place yourselves under the older people. You all must put on the lowly focus of a servant with each other because God places Himself in opposition to proud people but gives generosity to lowly people.
6 So put yourselves down low under God's powerful hand so that He might put you up high at the right time.
7 And toss your every worry on Him because He is concerned about you.
8 Stay sober. Stay awake. Your opponent in the court case, the Accuser, as a growling lion, is walking around looking for someone to swallow up.

9 You solid people must stand in opposition to him with trust because you have seen your brotherhood in the world finish up the same types of hardships.

10 But the God of all generosity (the One who invited you into His magnificence that spans all time in the Anointed King Jesus) will Himself (after you suffer a little) develop, establish, strengthen, and lay a foundation.

11 The power for the spans of time *belongs* to Him. Amen.

12 I wrote to you through Silas, the reliable brother (as I consider him to be). Through a few words, I am encouraging and corroborating this to be God's valid generosity in which you must stand.

13 The *woman* selected together with you in Babylon and Mark, my son, say hello to you.

14 Say hello to each other with a friendly gesture of love. Peace to you, all the people in the Anointed King.

Second Peter

1 From: Simon Peter, a slave and missionary of Jesus, the Anointed King. To: The people who took their turn with us in equally valuable trust in the right way of our God and Rescuer Jesus, the Anointed King.

2 May generosity and peace increase to you in a correct understanding of God and Jesus, our Master.

3 His divine ability has given us all kinds of things for free pointing toward life and godliness through the correct understanding of the One who invited us to His own magnificence and achievement.

4 Through *His magnificence and achievement*, the valuable and biggest promises have been given to us for free. That way, after escaping away from the deterioration in desire in the world, you might become sharers of the divine nature through these things.

5 For this very thing, also summon every effort you have and supply something else in your trust, the achievement--in the achievement, the information--

6 in the information, the self-restraint--in the self-restraint, the persistence to do what is right--in the persistence, the godliness--

7 in the godliness, the brotherly kindness--in the brotherly kindness, the love.

8 You see, as these things exist and increase in you, it puts you who are not idle or fruitless into the correct understanding of our Master Jesus, the Anointed King.

9 Whoever doesn't have these things beside him is blind. He is not able to see very well. He took no notice of the cleansing of his sins a long time ago.

10 For this reason, brothers, make more of an effort to make your invitation and selection firm. You see, as you do these, you will not ever in any way slip.

11 This is how the entrance into the monarchy of our Master and Rescuer Jesus, the Anointed King, that spans all time will be supplied to you more richly.

12 For this reason, I will always be about to quietly remind you about these things, even though you have seen them and have been established in the truth that is beside you.

13 I regard it to be right for as long as I am in this shelter to be waking you up with a quiet reminder.

14 I realize that the putting away of my shelter is soon, just as our Master Jesus, the Anointed King, also made obvious to me.
15 I will also make every effort to have you at each juncture after my exit to do *things* that remind you of these things.
16 You see, *it was* not after closely following myths that provide some type of insight *that* we let you know about the ability and arrival of our Master Jesus, the Anointed King. No, *it was* after we became eyewitnesses of the greatness of that One.
17 He received value and magnificence directly from Father God when such a great voice was carried to Him by the appropriately great magnificence, "This is My Son, My loved *Son*. I am delighted for Him."
18 We actually heard this voice that was carried from heaven as we were together with Him on the sacred mountain.
19 We also have something that is firmer *than a voice*: the preached message. You are doing nicely paying attention to it as a lamp shining in a dingy place until day should radiate through and the thing carrying light should come up in your hearts.
20 Know this first, that every preaching in the *Old Testament* writing does not come to be of its own explanation.
21 You see, in the past, a person did not carry preaching to what he wanted. No, as people were carried by a Sacred Spirit, they spoke out from God.

2 1 But counterfeit preachers also showed up among the ethnic group as there will also be counterfeit teachers among you. These are the ones who will quietly introduce sects of ruin. They even deny the Owner who purchased them. They bring quick ruin on themselves.
2 And many will closely follow their indulgent behaviors. Truth's road will be insulted because of them.
3 And in a desire for more, they will travel among you with manipulating messages. The judgment for them from a long time ago isn't idle, and their ruin isn't nodding off.
4 You see, if God did not go easy on angels that sinned but turned them over to cords of gloom when He put them in Tartarus *(the lowest part of hell)* to be kept for judgment,
5 and *if* He did not go easy on the original world (but guarded an eighth person, Noah, a public speaker for the right way) when He brought a flood onto a world of godless people,

6 and *if* He cremated the cities of Sodom and Gomorrah and found them guilty with a disaster (having set up a demonstration for future godless people),

7 and *if* He saved Lot who did what is right, who was oppressed by the noncompliant people's behavior in indulgent activity

8 (you see, as the one who did what is right lived among them from day to day, he was torturing a soul that was right with criminal actions by what was seen and heard),

9 *if the Master did these things like this,* He knows to save godly people from trouble, but to keep people who do what is wrong curtailed for a day of judgment.

10 *This is* especially *true* for the people traveling behind a physical body in a desire of desecration and ignoring government. They are self-pleasuring, daring people who do not tremble as they insult magnificent things.

11 *In a place* where angels (who are greater in strength and ability) don't bring an insulting judgment directly from the Master against them,

12 these counterfeit teachers (as natural irrational animals having been born for capture and decomposition) insult God in ways they are unaware of and will even be worsened in their deterioration.

13 They are wronged by the wrong way's pay. They regard the lavish things in a day to be pleasure. They are stains and blemishes. They are lavish in their frauds. They party together with you.

14 They have eyes that are full of cheating on spouses and that are addicted to sin. They entice unestablished souls. They have a heart that has been strenuously exercised with a desire for more. They are children of a curse.

15 They left the straight way behind and were misled after they closely followed the way of Balaam (the son of Beor) who loved the wrong way's pay.

16 But he had a reprimand of his own lawlessness--a voiceless workhorse that verbalized in a human's voice kept the preacher's wrong focus from going on.

17 These people are springs without water and mists driven by a blast of air. The gloom of the darkness has been kept for them.

18 You see, as they verbalize exaggerated statements of uselessness, they entice the people to indulgent activities in the physical body's desires. *They entice* the ones barely escaping away from the people who are messed up in a misleading lie.

19 They promise them freedom even though they themselves are slaves of deterioration. You see, this is what someone is made a slave to--what he has been defeated by.
20 If they escaped away from the world's desecrations by correctly understanding our Master and Rescuer Jesus, the Anointed King, but then they are entangled again in these desecrations and are defeated, the last desecrations have become worse for them than the first.
21 It was better for them not to have correctly understood the road of the right way, than, after correctly understanding it, to turn back from the sacred demand given over to them.
22 The valid analogy's picture has come together and happened to them: a dog that turned back to it's own vomit and a pig that bathed itself for a roll in the muck.

3

1 Loved ones, I am already writing this second letter to you. I am waking up your genuine mind in a quiet reminder in *this letter*
2 to remember the statements that have been previously stated by the sacred preachers and the demand of the Master and Rescuer from your missionaries.
3 Know this first, that on the last days, mockers will come in mockery traveling aligned with their own desires
4 and saying, "Where is the promise of His arrival? You see, since the fathers fell asleep, through *all this time* everything stays like this since the beginning of creation."
5 You see, this is unnoticed by them, and they want it to be unnoticed, that from a long time ago, there were skies and land. The land stood together from water and through water with God's message.
6 Through it, the world at that time was ruined when it was flooded with water.
7 Now the skies and the land have been stockpiled with the same message. They are kept for fire in a day of judgment and ruin of the godless people.
8 This one thing must not be unnoticed by you, loved ones--that one day beside the Master is as a thousand years, and a thousand years as one day.
9 The Master of the promise is not slow as some regard slowness, but He is patient for you, not intending that anyone be ruined, but that all would make room for a change of ways.

10 The Master's day will arrive as a thief. In that day, the skies will pass with a loud crash. As primary elements are on fire, they will be undone. Both the land and the actions in it will be found.

11 Since all these things are being undone like this, what kind of people must you be in sacred behaviors and expressions of godliness?

12 Expect and hurry the arrival of God's day. Flaming skies will be undone, and primary elements on fire are melted because of it.

13 But we expect new skies and new land where the right way lives according to His promise.

14 For this reason, loved ones, as you expect these things, make every effort to be found by Him in peace, unspotted and unblamed.

15 And regard the patience of our Master as a rescue, just as our loved brother Paul also wrote to you aligned with the insight given to him.

16 He speaks about these things in all *kinds of* letters. There are some hard-to-understand things in them. Unlearned and unestablished people pervert them as they also pervert the rest of the writings to their own ruin.

17 So you, loved ones, since you know these things beforehand, beware so that you aren't led away together with the misleading lie of the noncompliant and so that you don't fall from your own established position.

18 But grow in the generosity and information of our Master and Rescuer Jesus, the Anointed King. He has the magnificence both now and for a span of time's day. Amen.

First John

1

1 What was from the beginning, what we have heard, what we have seen with our eyes, what we viewed and our hands felt is about the message of life.
2 The life was actually shown. We have seen it. We are telling what we witnessed. And we are reporting to you about the life that spans all time. This was *the life* that was pointing toward the Father and was shown to us.
3 We are reporting what we have seen and heard to you too. That way you also may be in a sharing relationship with us, but our sharing relationship is also with the Father and with His Son Jesus, the Anointed King.
4 And we are writing these things so that our happiness may be filled up.
5 And this is the announcement that we have heard out from Him and are announcing to you: "God is light, and not even one bit of darkness is in Him." *(Light shows what exists, the way things are, the truth. Darkness hides it.)*
6 If we said that we are in a sharing relationship with Him and we walk around in the dark, we lie and do not do the truth.
7 But if we walk around in the light as He is in the light, we are in a sharing relationship with each other, and the blood of Jesus, His Son, cleans us off from every sin.
8 If we say that we don't have sin, we mislead ourselves and the truth is not in us.
9 If we acknowledge our sins, He can be trusted and He does what is right so that He will forgive us of the sins and clean us off from every wrong.
10 If we say that we haven't sinned, we make Him a liar and His message is not in us.

2

1 My little children, I am writing these things to you so that you might not sin. And if anyone sins, we have an encourager pointing toward the Father who does what is right, Jesus, the Anointed King.
2 And He is a remedy covering our sins. Not only *is He* covering ours, but *He is* also covering the whole world's.

3 And it is in this that we know that we have known Him, if we keep His demands.
4 The one who says, "I have known Him," and does not keep His demands is a liar. The truth is not in this.
5 But whoever keeps His message, in this, God's love has truly been completed. In this, we know that we are in Him.
6 The person who says that he is staying in Him is obligated to be walking around just as that One Himself also walked around.
7 Loved ones, it is not a new demand that I am writing to you. No, it is a former demand that you were having starting at the beginning. The former demand is the message that you heard.
8 Again I am writing a new demand to you. It is valid. It is in Him and in you because the darkness is passing on by and the true light is already shining.
9 The person who says that he is in the light and hates his brother is in the dark until now.
10 The person who loves his brother stays in the light, and there is no obstacle in him.
11 But the person hating his brother is in the dark, walks around in the dark, and does not realize where he is making his way back to because the dark blinds his eyes.
12 I am writing to you, little children, because you have been forgiven of your sins because of His name *and who He is*.
13 I am writing to you, fathers, because you have known the One who is from the beginning. I am writing to you, young lads, because you have conquered the evil one. I wrote to you, young children, because you have known the Father.
14 I wrote to you, fathers, because you have known the One who is from the beginning. I wrote to you, young lads, because you are strong, God's message stays in you, and you have conquered the evil one.
15 Don't love the world, and *don't love* the things in the world either. If anyone loves the world, the Father's love is not in him
16 because everything in the world (the desire of the physical body, the desire of the eyes, and the ego of life) is not from the Father. No, it is from the world.
17 And the world and its desire passes on by. But the person who does what God wants stays for the span of time.
18 Young children, it is the last hour. And just as you heard that the Anointed King's opponent is coming, and now many have become the Anointed King's opponents, from this we know that it is the last hour.

19 They went out from us, but they were not from us. You see, if they were from us, they would have stayed with us. But they went out so that it might be shown that all of them are not from us.
20 *This* also *shows that* you have an anointing out from the Sacred One, and you all have seen it.
21 I didn't write to you because you don't realize the truth, but because you realize it and that every lie is not from the truth.
22 Who is the liar if it isn't the one denying that Jesus is the Anointed King? This one is the Anointed King's opponent, the one who denies the Father and the Son.
23 Everyone who denies the Son does not have the Father either. The one who acknowledges the Son also has the Father.
24 You--what you heard from the beginning must stay in you. If what you heard from the beginning stays in you, you also will stay in the Son and in the Father.
25 And the promise that He promised us is this, life that spans all time.
26 I wrote these things to you about the people misleading you.
27 And you--the anointing that you received out from Him stays in you. You don't need someone to teach you. No, since His anointing teaches you about all things, since He is valid, since He is not a lie, you must stay in Him, just as He taught you.
28 And now, little children, stay in Him so that if He is shown, we might have a clear public statement and not be shamed away from Him during His arrival.
29 If you have seen that He does what is right, you know that everyone who is also doing things the right way has been born from Him.

3

1 Look at what kind of love the Father has given to us, that we might be called God's children (and we are). Because of this, the world does not know us, because it did not know Him.
2 Loved ones, now we are God's children, and it has not yet been shown what we will be. We realize that if it is shown, we will be like Him, that we will see Him just as He is.
3 And everyone who has this anticipation based on Him consecrates himself, just as that One is consecrated.
4 Everyone who is committing sin is also committing crime. Sin is crime.
5 And you realize that that One was shown so that He might take away the sins, and sin is not in Him.

6 Everyone who is staying in Him is not sinning. The one who is sinning has not seen Him or known Him.
7 Little children, no one must mislead you. The person who is doing things the right way is doing what is right, just as that One does what is right.
8 The person who is committing sin is from the Accuser because the Accuser sins from the beginning. It was for this that the Son of God was shown, so that He might undo the Accuser's actions.
9 Everyone who has been born from God is not committing sin because a seed of His stays in him. It is not able to be sinning because it has been born from God.
10 God's children and the Accuser's children are shown in this-- everyone who is not doing things the right way and who is not loving his brother is not from God.
11 This is the announcement that you heard from the beginning, that we should love each other.
12 Just don't be like Cain. He was from the evil one and slaughtered his brother. And thanks to what did he slaughter him? Because his actions were evil, and his brother's actions were right.
13 And don't be amazed, brothers, if the world hates you.
14 We realize that we have stepped from death into life because we love the brothers. The person who is not loving stays in death.
15 Everyone who is hating his brother is a people-killer, and you realize that every people-killer does not have life that spans all time staying in him.
16 We have known love in this: because that One gave His soul for us. We are also obligated to give our souls for the brothers.
17 Whoever has the world's livelihood, watches his brother have a need, and closes off his feelings of sympathy from him, how is the love of God staying in him?
18 Little children, we should not love with a word, and not with the tongue either. No, *we should love* in action and truth.
19 And we will know that we are from the truth and we will persuade our heart in front of Him in this:
20 because if our heart knows something against us, God is greater than our heart and knows all things.
21 Loved ones, if our heart doesn't know anything against us, we have a clear public statement facing God.
22 And whatever we request, we receive out from Him because we keep His demands and do the things that are liked in His sight.

23 And this is His demand, that we should trust in the name of His Son Jesus, the Anointed King, and love each other, just as He gave us a demand.
24 And the one who is keeping His demands stays in Him and He in him. And it is in this that we know He stays in us, from the Spirit that He gave us.

4

1 Loved ones, don't trust every spirit, but check the spirits as to whether a spirit is from God or not, because many counterfeit preachers have gone out into the world.
2 It is in this that you know God's spirit--every spirit that acknowledges Jesus as the Anointed King who has come in a physical body is from God.
3 And every spirit that doesn't acknowledge Jesus is not from God. This *refusal to acknowledge Jesus as the Anointed King* actually is the spirit of the opponent of the Anointed King that you have heard is coming and now is already in the world.
4 You are from God, little children, and you have conquered them because the One in you is greater than the one in the world.
5 They are from the world. Because of this, they speak from the world, and the world listens to them.
6 We are from God. The one who knows God listens to us. The one who isn't from God doesn't listen to us. It is from this that we know the Spirit of Truth and the spirit of the misleading lie.
7 Loved ones, let's love each other because love is from God and everyone who loves has been born from God and knows God.
8 The one who is not loving did not know God because God is love.
9 It was in this that God's love was shown among us because God has sent His only biological Son out on a mission into the world so that we might live through Him.
10 *The whole reason why* love is in this *is* not because we have loved God. No, *it is* because He loved us and sent His Son out as a remedy covering our sins.
11 Loved ones, if this is how God loved us, we also are obligated to be loving each other.
12 No one has viewed God at any time. If we love each other, God stays in us, and His love has been completed in us.
13 In this, we know that we stay in Him and He in us because He has given from His Spirit to us.
14 And we have viewed and are telling what we witnessed--that the Father has sent the Son out on a mission to be a rescuer of the world.

15 Whoever acknowledges that Jesus is the Son of God, God stays in him and he in God.
16 And we have known and have trusted the love that God has in us. God is love, and the one staying in love stays in God and God stays in him.
17 Love has been completed with us in this so that we may have a clear public statement during the day of judgment because just as that One is, *so* also are we in this world.
18 There is no fear in love. No, complete love throws the fear out because the fear has confinement. The person fearing has not been completed in love.
19 We love because He first loved us.
20 If anyone says, "I love God," and hates his brother, he is a liar. You see, the person who isn't loving his brother (that he has seen) is not able to be loving God (that he has not seen).
21 And we have this demand out from Him, that the person who is loving God should also love his brother.

5

1 Everyone who trusts that Jesus is the Anointed King has been born from God, and everyone who is loving the One who gave birth should also love the one that has been born from Him.
2 We know that we love God's children in this--when we love God and do His demands.
3 You see, this is God's love: that we should keep His demands. And His demands are not heavy
4 because everything that has been born from God conquers the world and this is the conquering element that conquered the world--our trust.
5 Who is the one conquering the world if it isn't the one who is trusting that Jesus is the Son of God?
6 This is the One who went through water *(submersion)* and blood *(martyrdom)*--Jesus, the Anointed King. He was not in the water only, but in the water and in the blood. And the Spirit tells what He witnessed because the Spirit is truth.
7 There are the three that are telling what they witness:
8 the Spirit, the water *(it witnessed God speak from heaven at Jesus' submersion)*, and the blood *(at the cross, it witnessed God make it dark for three hours, cause an earthquake, raise the dead, and more)*. And the three are for the one thing--*to be witnesses.*

9 If we receive people's witness account, God's witness account is greater because this is God's witness account that He has witnessed about His Son.

10 The person who is trusting in the Son of God has the witness account in himself. The person who is not trusting God has made Him a liar because he has not trusted in the witness account that God has witnessed about His Son.

11 And this is the witness account: that God gave us life that spans all time and this life is in His Son.

12 The one who has the Son has the life. The one who doesn't have the Son of God doesn't have the life.

13 I wrote these things to you who are trusting in the name of the Son of God *and in who He is* so that you may realize that you have life that spans all time.

14 And this is the clear public statement that we have facing Him that if we request anything aligned with what He wants, He listens to us.

15 And if we realize that He listens to us, whatever we request, we realize that we have the requests that we requested from Him.

16 If anyone has seen his brother sinning a sin not pointed toward death, he will request, and He will give life to him. This is for the people who are sinning a sin not pointed toward death. There is sin pointed toward death. I don't say that he should ask about that sin.

17 Everything that is wrong is sin, and there is sin not pointed toward death.

18 We realize that everyone who has been born from God is not sinning, but the One who was born from God keeps him, and the evil one does not touch him.

19 We realize that we are from God and the whole world lies in the evil.

20 We realize that the Son of God has arrived, He has given us a mind so that we may know the True One, and we are in the True One, in His Son Jesus, the Anointed King. This is the true God and life that spans all time.

21 Little children, guard yourselves away from the idols.

Second John

1 From: The older man. To: The select Kuria and her children. I, and not only I, but also all the people who have known the truth, love them in truth
2 because of the truth staying in us. It will be with us for the span of time.
3 Generosity, forgiving kindness, and peace directly from Father God and directly from Jesus, the Anointed King, the Son of the Father, will be with us in truth and love.
4 I was very happy to have found some of your children walking around in truth, just as we received a demand directly from the Father.
5 And now I am asking you, Kuria, that we should love each other. It is not as though I am writing a new demand to you. No, it is a demand that we had from the beginning.
6 And this is love--that we should walk around aligned with His demands. This demand is just as you heard from the beginning so that you may walk around in it
7 because many misleading people went out into the world. These people do not acknowledge that Jesus is the Anointed King coming in a physical body. This is the misleading one and the Anointed King's opponent.
8 Watch yourselves so that you won't ruin what we worked for, but *so that* you will fully receive full pay.
9 Everyone who leads the way ahead and does not stay in the Anointed King's teaching doesn't have God. The person who stays in the teaching, this person has both the Father and the Son.
10 If someone comes to you and doesn't bring this teaching, do not receive him into the house and don't tell him, "Happy to meet you."
11 You see, the person telling him, "Happy to meet you," shares in his evil actions.
12 Since I have many things for you, I did not intend to write through paper and ink, but I anticipate to come your way and speak face-to-face *("mouth-to-mouth" in Greek)* so that our happiness may be filled up.
13 The children of your sister, the select sister, say hello to you.

Third John

1 From: The older man. To: The loved Gaius that I love in truth.
2 Loved one, I wish you to be successful around all things and to be healthy, just as your soul is successful.
3 You see, I was very happy as brothers came and told what they witnessed about your truth, just as you walk around in truth.
4 I have no greater happiness than to hear that these children of mine are walking around in the truth.
5 Loved one, you are doing *work* that can be trusted, whatever you work on for the brothers, even this *that is for* strangers.
6 The brothers told what they witnessed of your love in the sight of the assembly. You will do nicely *for them* when you bring them on their way in a manner deserving of God.
7 You see, they went out on behalf of the name and took nothing away from the non-Jewish people.
8 So we are obligated to be taking these types of people up so that we may become co-workers to the truth.
9 I wrote something to the assembly, but the one who is fond of being first among them, Diotrephes, does not accept us.
10 Because of this, if I come, I will quietly remember his actions that he does--gossiping with evil words about us. And not content over these, he doesn't accept the brothers either. He also keeps the ones who intend on accepting them from doing so and throws them out of the assembly.
11 Loved one, do not imitate the bad. Imitate the good. The person who is doing good is from God. The person who is doing bad has not seen God.
12 Demetrius has been told what everyone and the truth itself witnessed. We also are telling what we witnessed, and you realize that our witness account is valid.
13 I had many things to write to you, but I don't want to be writing you through ink and a stick.
14 I am anticipating seeing you right away, and we will speak face-to-face *("mouth-to-mouth" in Greek)*. Peace to you. Your friends say hello to you. Say hello to our friends by name.

Jude

1

1 From: Jude (a slave of Jesus, the Anointed King, but a brother of James). To: The invited people who have been loved in Father God and have been kept by Jesus, the Anointed King.

2 May forgiving kindness, peace, and love increase to you.

3 Loved ones, as I was making every effort to write you about our shared rescue, I had an obligation to write you and encourage you to be strenuously struggling for the trust that was once turned over to the sacred people.

4 You see, some people sneaked in undetected. They previously had been written about a long time ago and put into this judgment--they are godless. They transfer our God's generosity into indulgent activity and deny the only Owner and our Master, Jesus, the Anointed King.

5 But I intend to quietly remind you (though you realize all these things) that the Master who once rescued the ethnic group from the land of Egypt, *did* the second thing--He ruined the people who did not trust.

6 And the angels that did not keep the beginning of themselves, but left their own habitation behind, He has kept in eternal restraints under gloom for the judgment of a great day.

7 It is like Sodom, Gomorrah, and the cities around them that were sexually promiscuous and went off after a different physical body *(the same way that these angels went off after something different)*. They are already laid out as an exhibit. They are held under the justice of fire that spans all time.

8 However, likewise also, these people, being inspired while they sleep, not only desecrate the physical body, but they disregard government, they insult magnificent things.

9 But when Michael, the head angel, considered the Accuser to be wrong and was having a discussion about the body of Moses, he didn't dare bring a judgment of insult on him. No, he said, "May the Master stop you."

10 But these people insult, not only as many of the things as they have not seen, but as many of the things as they are naturally (like the irrational animals) well acquainted with. They are worsened in these.

11 What a tragedy it is to them because they traveled the road of Cain, they were spilled out in the misleading lie of Balaam's pay, and they ruined themselves in Korah's dispute.

12 These are the ones in your love *events*, submerged boulders, partying together, fearlessly shepherding themselves. They are clouds without water being carried along by winds. They are leafless, fruitless trees that died twice, that were uprooted.

13 They are wild swells of the sea foaming out their own shames. They are stars, wanderers. To them, the gloom of the darkness has been kept for the span of time.

14 Enoch, the seventh from Adam, also preached to these. He said, "Look, the Master came in His sacred tens of thousands

15 to do judgment against all and to reprimand every soul about all the actions of their godlessness that were godless and about all of the harsh things that godless sinful people spoke against Him."

16 These are complaining grumblers traveling aligned with their own desires. Their mouths speak exaggerated statements as they are amazed at appearances (thanks to it being a benefit to them).

17 You, loved ones, remember the statements that have been stated before by the missionaries of our Master Jesus, the Anointed King,

18 because they were telling you that on the last time there will be mockers traveling aligned with their own desires of godlessness.

19 These are the ones who draw dividing lines, psychological people who don't have a spirit.

20 You, loved ones, as you build yourselves on your most sacred trust and pray in the Sacred Spirit,

21 keep yourselves in God's love as you accept the forgiving kindness of our Master Jesus, the Anointed King, for life that spans all time.

22 And there certainly are some that you must show forgiving kindness to even though they consider you to be wrong.

23 But there are others that you must rescue as you snatch them from fire, but still others that you must show forgiving kindness to in fear, hating even the long undershirt that has been stained from the physical body.

24 To the One who is able to guard you from slipping and to stand you directly in the sight of His magnificence as unblemished people in excitement,

25 to the only God, our Rescuer through Jesus, the Anointed King, our Master, to Him *belongs* magnificence, majesty, and power and authority, before the entire span of time, now, and for all the spans of time. Amen.

Revelation

1

1 The uncovering of Jesus, the Anointed King. God gave it to Him to show His slaves what things must happen quickly. He sent out and indicated it to His slave John through His angel.

2 John told what he witnessed of God's message and the witness account of Jesus, the Anointed King. He told as many things as he saw.

3 The person who reads and the people who hear the messages of this preaching and keep the things that have been written in it are blessed. You see, the appointed time is near.

4 From: John. To: The seven assemblies in Western Turkey. Generosity to you and peace out from the One who is, the One who was, and the One who is coming, out from the seven spirits that are in the sight of His throne,

5 and out from Jesus, the Anointed King (the Witness, the One who can be trusted, the Firstborn of the dead, and the Head of the kings of the earth). To the One who loves us and who released us from our sins in His blood

6 and made us a monarchy, priests to God and His Father, to Him *belongs* the magnificence and the power for the spans of time of the spans of time. Amen.

7 Look, He is coming with the clouds, and every eye will look at Him, even certain people who impaled Him. And all the family lines of the earth will beat their chests in grief over Him. Yes. Amen.

8 "I am the Alpha and the O" *(the first and last letters in the Greek alphabet)*, says the Master God. "*I am* the One who is, the One who was, and the One who is coming, the All-Powerful One."

9 I, John, am your brother and a sharer together with you in the hard times, monarchy, and persistence to do what is right in Jesus. I ended up on the island that is called Patmos because of God's message and the witness account of Jesus.

10 I entered a spiritual state in the master day and heard a loud voice behind me that sounded like it was from a trumpet.

11 It said, "Write what you see into a scroll and send it to the seven assemblies: to Ephesus, to Smyrna, to Pergamos, to Thyatira, to Sardis, to Philadelphia, and to Laodicea."

12 And I turned around to look at the voice. This was the voice that was speaking with me. And when I turned around, I saw seven gold stands for lamps.
13 And in the middle of the lampstands was someone like a son of a person. *("The Son of the Person" is a generic term Jesus used of Himself. Ezekiel and Daniel were called "son of a person." "Son of a person" is also in Psalm 80:17.)* He had put on a robe that went down to His ankles and a gold sash had been tied around Him toward His chest.
14 His head and hairs were white as wool (white as snow). His eyes were as a blaze of fire.
15 His feet were like fine copper, as *fine copper* that had been refined in a furnace. His voice was as the voice of many waters.
16 He had seven stars in His right hand. A sharp double-edged sword was traveling out from His mouth. And His eyes were as the sun shining in all its ability.
17 And when I saw Him, I fell toward His feet as a dead man. And He placed His right hand on me and said, "Don't be afraid. I am the First, the Last,
18 and the Living One. And I became dead, and, look, I am living for the spans of time of the spans of time. And I have the keys of Death and Hades *(the underworld of the dead)*.
19 So write what you saw, what is, and what is going to happen after these.
20 The secret of the seven stars that you saw on My right hand and the seven gold stands for lamps is that the seven stars are the announcers of the seven assemblies and the seven lampstands are the seven assemblies."

2

1 Write to the announcer of the assembly in Ephesus, "The One holding the seven stars in His right hand, the One walking around in the middle of the seven gold lampstands, says the things here:
2 'I have seen your actions, the labor, your persistence to do what is right, that you are not able to haul bad people around, and you tried to cause trouble with the people calling themselves missionaries (and they are not) and found them to be liars.
3 And you are persistent and hauled much because of My name *and who I am*. You haven't even gotten tired.
4 But I have something against you because you left your first love.

5 So remember where you have fallen from, change your ways, and do the first actions. But if not, I am coming to you, and I will move your lampstand from its place if you don't change your ways.
6 But you have this thing, that you hate the Nicolaitans' actions that I also hate.'
7 The person who has an ear must listen to what the Spirit says to the assemblies, 'I will give the person who conquers the right to eat from the wooden tree of life that is in God's paradise.'"
8 And write to the announcer of the assembly in Smyrna, "The First and the Last who became dead and lived, says the things here:
9 'I have seen your hard times, the poverty (but you are wealthy), and the insult from the people who say that they themselves are Jewish and they are not, but they are a synagogue of the Opponent.
10 Don't be afraid of any of the things that you are going to be suffering. Look, the Accuser is going to be throwing some from among you into jail so that you might experience trouble, and you will have hard times for ten days. Become someone who trusts till death, and I will give you the award wreath of life.'
11 The person who has an ear must listen to what the Spirit says to the assemblies, 'The person who conquers will not in any way receive harm from the second death.'"
12 And write to the announcer of the assembly in Pergamos, "The One who has the sharp double-edged sword says the things here:
13 'I have seen where you live--where the throne of the Opponent is. And you hold on to My name and did not deny your trust of Me, even in the days of Antipas, My reliable witness. He was killed beside you where the Opponent lives.
14 But I have a few things against you because you have people there who hold on to the teaching of Balaam, who was teaching Balak to throw an obstacle out in the sight of Israel's sons, to eat idol sacrifices and to commit sexual sin.
15 You even have people like this who likewise hold on to the teaching of the Nicolaitans.
16 So change your ways. But if not, I am coming to you quickly, and I will wage war with them with the sword of My mouth.'
17 The person who has an ear must listen to what the Spirit says to the assemblies, 'To the person who conquers, I will give him *some* of the manna that has been hidden. I will also give him a white pebble and a new name that has been written on the pebble that no one has seen except the one receiving it.'"

18 And write to the announcer of the assembly in Thyatira, "The Son of God who has His eyes as a blaze of fire and His feet like fine copper, says the things here:

19 'I have seen your actions, the love, the trust, the serving, your persistence to do what is right, and your actions. The last are more than the first.

20 But I have *something* against you because you leave the woman Jezebel alone, the one who calls herself a preacher. *You let her do whatever she wants.* And she teaches and misleads My slaves to commit sexual sin and to eat idol sacrifices.

21 I gave her time so that she might change her ways, and she doesn't want to change her ways from her sexual sin.

22 Look, I am throwing her onto a cot and the people cheating on their spouses with her into great hard times unless they will change their ways from her actions.

23 And I will kill her children with death and all the assemblies will know that I am the One who examines the kidneys *(inner thoughts)* and hearts *(intentions)*. And I will give to each of you according to your actions.

24 But I say to you, to the rest, the ones in Thyatira, as many as don't have this teaching, any who didn't know "the deep things of the Opponent" (as they say), I am not throwing another weight on you.

25 More importantly, hold on to what you have till whenever I might arrive.

26 And I will give the person who conquers and the person who keeps My actions till the conclusion authority over the nations,

27 and he will shepherd them with an iron staff in the same way that the clay containers are crushed, as I also have received directly from My Father.

28 And I will give him the morning star.

29 The person who has an ear must listen to what the Spirit says to the assemblies.'"

3

1 And write to the announcer of the assembly in Sardis, "The One who has God's seven spirits and the seven stars says the things here: 'I have seen your actions, that you have a name that you live and you are dead.

2 Become someone who stays awake, and establish the rest of the things that were going to die. You see, I haven't found that you have accomplished any actions in the sight of My God.

3 So remember how you have received and heard, keep guard, and change your ways. So if you don't stay awake, I will arrive as a thief, and you won't in any way know which hour I will arrive upon you.
4 But you have a few names in Sardis that didn't dirty their clothes. And they will walk around with Me in white because they are deserving.
5 The person who conquers like this will put white robes around himself. I won't in any way erase his name from the scroll of life. And I will acknowledge his name in the sight of My Father and in the sight of His angels.
6 The person who has an ear must listen to what the Spirit says to the assemblies.'"
7 And write to the announcer of the assembly in Philadelphia, "The sacred One, the true One, the One who has David's key, the One who opens and no one will close and who closes and no one opens, says the things here:
8 'I have seen your actions. Look, I have given a door in your sight that has been opened. No one is able to close it because you have little ability, you kept My message, and you did not deny My name.
9 Look, I may give you *some* from the Opponent's synagogue who say that they themselves are Jewish and they are not. But they are lying. Look, I will do *things with* them so that they will arrive and bow down in the sight of your feet. And they will know that I loved you.
10 Because you kept the message of My persistence to do what is right, I also will keep you from the hour of the trouble that is going to be coming on the whole civilized world to trouble the people living on the earth.
11 I am coming quickly. Hold on to what you have so that no one might take your award wreath.
12 The person who conquers, I will make him a pillar in the temple of My God, and he will not in any way go outside anymore. And I will write on him the name of My God, the name of My God's city (the New Jerusalem that steps down from the sky out from My God), and My new name.
13 The person who has an ear must listen to what the Spirit says to the assemblies.'"
14 And write to the announcer of the assembly in Laodicea, "The Amen, the reliable and true Witness, the Beginning of God's creation, says the things here:
15 'I have seen your actions, that you are not cold or boiling hot either. If only you were cold or boiling hot.

16 This is why I am going to vomit you out of my mouth, because you are lukewarm and not boiling hot or cold either,
17 because you say, 'I am wealthy, I have been wealthy, and I don't need anything.' But you have not seen that you are troubled, miserable, poor, blind, and naked.
18 I strongly advise you to buy gold directly from Me that has been refined from fire (so that you might be wealthy), white robes (so that you might throw them around yourself and the shame of your nakedness might not be shown), and collyrium *(medicated eye wash)* to anoint in your eyes (so that you might see).
19 However many people that I am fond of, I reprimand and discipline. So be passionate and change your ways.
20 Look, I have been standing at the door, and I am knocking. If anyone listens to My voice and opens the door, I will come in to him, eat dinner with him, and he with Me.
21 The person who conquers, I will give him the right to be seated with Me in My throne, as I also conquered and was seated with My Father in His throne.
22 The person who has an ear must listen to what the Spirit says to the assemblies.'"

4 1 After these things I looked, and look, there was a door that had been opened in the sky. The first voice that I heard speaking with me that sounded like it was from a trumpet said, "Step up here, and I will show you what must happen after these things."
2 Right away I entered a spiritual state, and look, a throne was situated in heaven and One was sitting on the throne.
3 The One sitting was like the sight of a jasper stone *(speckled red)* and a sardius *(vibrant reddish-orange)*. A halo that surrounded the throne was like the sight of an emerald stone *(vibrant green)*.
4 Twenty-four thrones were surrounding the throne, and twenty-four older men were sitting on the thrones. White robes had been thrown around *them*, and gold award wreaths were on their heads.
5 Lightnings, sounds, and thunders travel out from the throne. Seven torches of fire burn in the sight of the throne. They are God's seven spirits.
6 In the sight of the throne, there is something like a glassy sea that is like crystal. In the middle of the throne and circling the throne are four animals packed full of eyes, in front and behind.

7 The first animal is like a lion. The second animal is like a calf. The third animal has the face as a human. And the fourth animal is like a flying raptor.
8 The four animals, each one of them, have six wings apiece. The wings are packed full of eyes surrounding them and on the inside. They don't have relief day and night from saying, "Sacred, sacred, sacred Master God, the All-Powerful One, the One who was, the One who is, and the One who is coming."
9 When the animals will give magnificence, value, and thanks to the One who sits on the throne who lives for the spans of time of the spans of time,
10 the twenty-four older men will get down in the sight of the One who sits on the throne, bow to the One who lives for the spans of time of the spans of time, and throw their award wreaths in the sight of the throne. They will say,
11 "You, our Master and God, deserve to receive the magnificence, the value, and the ability because You created all things. They were existing and were created because that is what You wanted."

5

1 I saw a scroll on the right side of the One sitting on the throne. It had been written on the inside and on the back and had been sealed shut with seven seals.
2 I saw a strong angel speaking publicly in a loud voice, "Who deserves to open the scroll and break its seals?"
3 No one in heaven, on the earth, or beneath the earth was able to open the scroll or look at it.
4 I was crying a lot because not even one deserving person was found to open the scroll or look at it.
5 One *older man* from the older men says to me, "Don't cry. Look, the Lion from the family line of Judah, the Root of David, conquered to open the scroll and its seven seals."
6 And I saw in the middle of the throne and the four animals and in the middle of the older men, a lamb that had stood up. He was as a lamb that had been slaughtered. He had seven horns and seven eyes that are God's seven spirits that have been sent out on a mission into all the earth.
7 He went and has taken the scroll from the right side of the One sitting on the throne.
8 When He took the scroll, the four animals and the twenty-four older men got down in the sight of the Lamb. Each had a harp and gold bowls packed full of incense that are the prayers of the sacred people.

9 They sing a new song. They say, "You deserve to take the scroll and to open its seals because You were slaughtered and You purchased people for God in Your blood from every family line, language, ethnic group, and nation.
10 You made them a monarchy and priests to our God. They will be kings on the earth."
11 I looked and heard the voice of many angels circling the throne, circling the animals, and circling the older men. Their number was tens of thousands of tens of thousands and thousands of thousands.
12 They said with a loud voice, "The Lamb that has been slaughtered deserves to receive the ability, wealth, insight, strength, value, magnificence, and conferring of blessings."
13 I heard every created thing that is in heaven, on the earth, beneath the earth, on the sea, and all the things in them saying, "To the One sitting on the throne and to the Lamb *belong* the conferring of blessings, the value, the magnificence, and the power for the spans of time of the spans of time."
14 The four animals were saying, "Amen." And the older men got down and bowed.

6

1 I looked when the Lamb opened one *seal* from the seven seals. And I heard one *animal* from the four animals say as a voice of thunder, "Come."
2 And I looked, and, look, a white horse and the one sitting on it had a bow. An award wreath was given to him. He went out conquering and so that he might conquer.
3 When He opened the second seal, I heard the second animal say, "Come."
4 And another horse went out, a fiery horse. The one sitting on it was given the ability to take peace from the earth, even so that they will slaughter each other. And a large dagger was given to him.
5 When He opened the third seal, I heard the third animal say, "Come." And I looked, and, look, a black horse and the one sitting on it had a beam balance in his hand.
6 I heard what seemed like a voice in the middle of the four animals saying, "A quart of wheat for a denarius *(a coin equal to one day's wage)*, three quarts of barley for a denarius, and you should not harm the olive oil and the wine."
7 When He opened the fourth seal, I heard the voice of the fourth animal say, "Come."

8 And I looked, and, look, a green horse and the one sitting up on top of it. A name for him is Death. And Hades *(the underworld of the dead)* was following with him. Authority was given to them over the fourth part of the earth to kill with a sword, with famine, with death *(a plague)*, and by the wild animals of the earth.
9 When He opened the fifth seal, I saw souls beneath the altar. These were the souls of the people who had been slaughtered because of God's message and because of the witness account that they were having.
10 They yelled with a loud voice, saying, "Sacred and true Owner, how long are you not judging and retaliating against the people living on the earth for our blood?"
11 Each one of them was given a long white robe, and it was stated to them that they will relax for a short time yet until both their fellow slaves and their brothers (the ones that are going to be killed as they also had been) would be filled up.
12 I looked when He opened the sixth seal. A large earthquake happened. The sun became black as sackcloth made of goat hair. The whole moon became as blood.
13 The stars of the sky fell to the earth as a fig tree throws its unripe figs when it is shook by a strong wind.
14 The sky was separated apart as a scroll being folded up. And every mountain and island was moved from their places.
15 The kings of the earth, the greatest people, the commanding officers, the wealthy, the strong, and every slave and free person hid themselves in the caves and in the rocks of the mountains.
16 They say to the mountains and the rocks, "Fall on us, and hide us away from the face of the One sitting on the throne and away from the punishment of the Lamb
17 because the great day of Their punishment came and who is able to stand?"

7

1 After this, I saw four angels that had stood on the four corners of the earth holding on to the four *directional* winds of the earth so that wind wouldn't blow on the earth, on the sea, or on any tree.
2 And I saw another angel stepping up out of the rising of the sun having a seal of the living God. He yelled with a loud voice to the four angels that were given *the ability* to harm the earth and the sea.
3 He said, "You shouldn't harm the earth, the sea, or the trees till we will put a seal on the slaves of our God on their foreheads."

4 And I heard the number of the ones that had been sealed. *There were* 144,000 that had been sealed from every family line of Israel's sons.
5 From Judah's family line, 12,000 had been sealed. From Reuben's family line, 12,000; from Gad's family line, 12,000;
6 from Asher's family line, 12,000; from Naphtali's family line, 12,000; from Manasseh's family line, 12,000;
7 from Simeon's family line, 12,000; from Levi's family line, 12,000; from Issachar's family line, 12,000;
8 from Zebulon's family line, 12,000; from Joseph's family line, 12,000; from Benjamin's family line, 12,000 had been sealed.
9 After these things, I looked, and, look, there was a big crowd that no one was able to number. People from every nation, from family lines, ethnic groups, and languages had stood in the sight of the throne and in the sight of the Lamb. Long white robes had been thrown around them, and palm branches are in their hands.
10 And they are yelling with a loud voice, saying, "The rescue *belongs* to our God who sits on the throne and to the Lamb."
11 All the angels had stood circling the throne, circling the older men, and circling the four animals. They got down on their faces in the sight of the throne and bowed to God.
12 They were saying, "Amen. The conferring of blessing, the magnificence, the insight, the thanks, the value, the ability, and the strength *belong* to our God for the spans of time of the spans of time. Amen."
13 One *older man* from the older men responded and said to me, "Who are these people that the long white robes have been thrown around? And where did they come from?"
14 I have stated to him, "My master, you know." He said to me, "These are the people who come from the Great Hard Times. They rinsed their long robes and whitened them in the blood of the Lamb.
15 Because of this, they are in the sight of God's throne, and they minister to Him day and night in His temple. The One sitting on the throne will camp over them.
16 They won't be hungry or thirsty anymore, and the sun or any burning heat won't fall on them either
17 because the Lamb that is up in the middle of the throne will shepherd them and guide them onto springs of waters of life. And God will dab off every tear from their eyes."

8

1 When He opened the seventh seal, there became a hush in heaven as if it were half an hour.
2 And I saw the seven angels that had stood in the sight of God. Seven trumpets were given to them.
3 Another angel went and was stood on the altar. He had a gold incense burner. And much incense was given to him so that he will give it on the gold altar with the prayers of all the sacred people in the sight of the throne.
4 The smoke of the incense stepped up from the angel's hand with the prayers of the sacred people in the sight of God.
5 The angel has taken the incense burner. He filled it full of coals from the altar's fire and threw it to the earth. There became thunders, sounds, lightnings, and an earthquake.
6 The seven angels that had the seven trumpets got themselves ready to blow their trumpets.
7 The first one blew his trumpet, and there became hail and fire that had been mixed in blood. It was thrown to the earth. The third *part* of the earth was burned up. The third *part* of the trees were burned up. And all green grass was burned up.
8 The second angel blew his trumpet, and something like a large mountain burning with fire was thrown into the sea. The third *part* of the sea became blood.
9 The third *part* of the created things in the sea that had souls died. And the third *part* of the boats were devoured.
10 The third angel blew his trumpet, and a large star fell from the sky that burned as a torch. It fell on the third *part* of the rivers and on the springs of the waters.
11 The name of the star is called "The Absinthium." The third *part* of the waters turned into absinthium *(a very bitter herb)*. And many of the people died from the waters because they were bitter.
12 The fourth angel blew his trumpet, and the third *part* of the sun, the third *part* of the moon, and the third *part* of the stars was affected so that the third *part* of them would be made dark. And the day would not shine for the third *part* of it, and the night likewise.
13 I looked and heard one raptor flying in the middle of the sky. He said with a loud voice, "What a tragedy! What a tragedy! What a tragedy it will be for the people living on the earth because of the rest of the soundings of the three angels' trumpet that are going to be blowing."

9

1 The fifth angel blew his trumpet, and I saw a star that had fallen from the sky to the earth. The key of the shaft of the bottomless area was given to it.

2 It opened the shaft of the bottomless area, and smoke stepped up from the shaft as the smoke of a large furnace. The sun and the air were darkened from the smoke of the shaft.

3 Grasshoppers came out of the smoke to the earth, and they were given *the kind of* authority that scorpions have.

4 It was stated to them that they won't harm the grass of the earth, or any green thing, or any tree. *They would* just *harm* the people, any people who don't have God's seal on their foreheads.

5 They weren't given *the ability* to kill them. No, *they were given the ability* to torture them five months. The torture from them was as torture from a scorpion when it strikes a person.

6 In those days, the people will look for death and won't in any way find it. They will desire to die, and death escapes away from them.

7 The grasshoppers' likenesses were like horses that have been readied for war. On their heads were *things* as award wreaths, like gold. Their faces were as people's faces.

8 They had hair as women's hair. Their teeth were as lions'.

9 They had vests as iron vests. The sound of their wings was as the sound of chariots of many horses running to war.

10 They have tails like scorpions and stingers. And their authority to harm the people five months is in their tails.

11 They have a king over them, the angel of the bottomless area. A name for him in Hebrew is Abaddon *(Ruin)*, and he has a name in the Greek *language*, Apollyon *(Ruiner)*.

12 The one tragedy went away. Look, two tragedies are still coming after these.

13 The sixth angel blew his trumpet, and I heard one voice from the four horns of the gold altar in the sight of God.

14 It said to the sixth angel that had the trumpet, "Release the four angels that have been locked up on the great Euphrates river."

15 The four angels were released that have been readied for the hour, day, month, and year so that they may kill the third *part* of the people.

16 The number of the military forces of the horse unit was *two hundred million* (twenty thousand of ten thousands). I heard the number of them.

17 This is how I saw the horses in the sighting and the ones sitting on them. They have vests that are flaming, like a hyacinth *(a Greek god or*

a deep blue flower or mineral), and sulfurous *(a yellow combustible nonmetal element)*. The heads of the horses were as lions' heads. Fire, smoke, and sulfur travel out from their mouths.

18 The third *part* of the people were killed out of these three devastations: from the fire, the smoke, and the sulfur that traveled out from their mouths.

19 You see, the authority of the horses is in their mouth and in their tails. Their tails had heads like snakes, and they cause harm with them.

20 The rest of the people who were not killed in these devastations did not even change their ways from the works of their hands so that they won't bow down to the lesser deities and the gold, silver, brass, stone, and wooden idols that are not able to see, hear, or walk around.

21 And they did not change their ways from their murders, or from their drug use, or from their sexual sin, or from their thefts.

10

1 I saw another strong angel stepping down from the sky. A cloud has been thrown around him. The halo was on his head. His face was as the sun. His feet were as pillars of fire.

2 He had a little scroll in his hand that had been opened. He put his right foot on the sea, but the left on the land.

3 He yelled with a loud voice even as a lion roars. When he yelled, the seven thunders spoke their own voices.

4 When the seven thunders spoke, I was going to write. And I heard a voice from the sky say, "Put a seal on what the seven thunders spoke, and you will not write them."

5 The angel that I saw that had stood on the sea and on the land raised up his right hand to the sky.

6 He guaranteed with the One who lives for the spans of time of the spans of time (*the One* who created the sky and the things in it, the land and the things in it, and the sea and the things in it) that there will be no more time *left (no more delay)*.

7 But in the days of the sounding of the seventh angel, whenever he is going to be blowing the trumpet, God's secret was also finished. *It was* as the good news that He shared with His own slaves, the preachers.

8 The voice that I heard from the sky is speaking with me again and saying, "Make your way back, take the scroll that has been opened in the hand of the angel that has stood on the sea and on the land."

9 I went off to the angel and told him to give me the little scroll. He says to me, "Take, and eat it up. It will make your belly bitter, but in your mouth, it will be sweet as honey."
10 I took the little scroll from the hand of the angel and ate it up. It was sweet as honey in my mouth. And when I ate it, my belly became bitter.
11 They say to me, "It is necessary for you to preach again on many ethnic groups, nations, languages, and kings."

11

1 And a stick like a staff was given to me, saying, "Get up, and measure God's temple, the altar, and the people bowing down in it.
2 Put the temple's outer courtyard outside. You will not measure it because it was given to the non-Jews. And they will trample the sacred city forty-two months *(3 1/2 years)*.
3 I will give to My two witnesses, and they will preach 1260 days *(17 or 18 days less than 3 1/2 years)*. They have put sackcloth *(the cloth that grieving people wear)* around themselves.
4 These are the two olive trees and the two stands for lamps that have stood in the sight of the Master of the earth.
5 If anyone wants to harm them, fire travels out from their mouth and eats up their enemies. If anyone should want to harm them, this is how he must be killed.
6 These have the authority to close the sky so that a shower may not get the days of their preaching wet. And they have authority over the waters to turn them into blood and to strike the earth with every devastation as often as they might want.
7 When they finish their witness account, the wild animal that steps up from the bottomless area will make war with them, conquer them, and kill them.
8 And their corpse is on the plaza of the great city. This is the city that spiritually is called Sodom and Egypt where their Master was also nailed to a cross.
9 People from the ethnic groups, family lines, languages, and nations look at their corpse three and a half days. They are not allowing their corpses to be put into a grave.
10 The people living on the earth are happy based on them. They celebrate and will send contributions to each other because these two preachers tortured the people living on the earth.

11 After the three and a half days, a spirit of life from God came into them, and they stood on their feet. Great fear fell on the people watching them.
12 And they listened to a loud voice from the sky say to them, "Step up here," and they stepped up into the sky in the cloud. Their enemies watched them.
13 In that hour, a large earthquake happened, and the tenth *part* of the city fell. Seven thousand names of people were killed in the earthquake, and the rest became afraid and elevated the God of heaven to a place of magnificence.
14 The second tragedy went away. Look, the third tragedy is coming quickly.
15 The seventh angel blew his trumpet, and loud voices happened in heaven. They said, "The world's monarchy became our Master's and His Anointed King's. He will be king for the spans of time of the spans of time."
16 The twenty-four older men that sit on their thrones in the sight of God got down on their faces and bowed to God.
17 They said, "We are thankful to You, Master God, the All-Powerful One, the One who is, and the One who was, because You have taken Your great ability and were king.
18 The nations were enraged, and Your rage came. The time came for the dead to be judged, for You to give the pay to Your slaves (the preachers, the sacred people, and the people who fear Your name, the little and the great), and to devour the people who devour the earth."
19 And God's temple in heaven was opened. The box of His deal was seen in His temple. And there became lightnings, sounds, thunders, an earthquake, and large hail.

12

1 A great indicator was seen in heaven: a woman that has put the sun around herself, the moon beneath her feet, and an award wreath of twelve stars on her head.
2 She is pregnant and yells as she is in labor and is tortured to deliver.
3 And another indicator was seen in heaven. And look, there is a large fiery dragon that has seven heads and ten horns. There are seven crowns on his heads,
4 and his tail drags the third *part* of heaven's stars and threw them to the earth. The dragon has stood in the sight of the woman who is going to deliver so that whenever she delivers, he might eat up her child.

5 She delivered a male son who is going to be shepherding all the nations with an iron staff. And her child was snatched up to God and to His throne.

6 The woman escaped into the backcountry where she has a place there that has been readied by God so that they may nurture her there 1260 days *(which is 17 or 18 days short of 3 1/2 years)*.

7 A war happened in heaven: Michael and his angels were engaging in a war with the dragon. The dragon and his angels waged the war.

8 He did not have strength, and a place was not found for them in heaven anymore either.

9 The large dragon, the original snake, the one that is called Accuser and the Opponent, the one misleading the whole civilized world, was thrown out. He was thrown to the earth, and his angels were thrown out with him.

10 I heard a loud voice in heaven say, "Just now, the rescue, the ability, our God's monarchy, and His Anointed King's authority came because the complainant against our brothers was thrown out, the one who levels complaints against them in the sight of our God day and night.

11 They conquered him because of the blood of the Lamb and because of the message of their witness account. They did not love their soul till death.

12 Because of this, you heavens and the ones camping in them must celebrate. What a tragedy it is for the earth and the sea because the Accuser stepped down to you having great anger. He realizes that he has little time."

13 When the dragon saw that he was thrown to the earth, he pursued the woman. This is the woman that delivered the male.

14 The two wings of the great raptor were given to the woman so that she may fly into the backcountry, into her place where she is nurtured there for a time, times, and half a time away from a face of the snake.

15 The snake threw water from his mouth behind the woman as a river so that he might wash her away with the river.

16 The earth helped the woman. The earth opened its mouth and swallowed up the river that the dragon threw from his mouth.

17 The dragon was enraged over the woman and went off to make war with the rest of her seed, the people that keep God's demands and have Jesus' witness account.

13

1 He *(the dragon)* was stood on the sand of the sea. And I saw a wild animal stepping up from the sea that had ten horns

and seven heads. There were ten crowns on his horns and names of insult on his heads.

2 The wild animal that I saw was like a leopard. His feet were as a bear's and his mouth as a lion's mouth. The dragon gave him his ability, his throne, and great authority.

3 One *head* from his heads was as *a head* that had been slaughtered to death. The wound of his death was healed. And the whole earth was amazed behind the wild animal.

4 They bowed down to the dragon that gave the authority to the wild animal, and they bowed down to the wild animal. They said, "Who is like the wild animal? And who is able to wage war with him?"

5 A mouth was given to him that spoke great things and insults. Authority was given to him to do forty-two months *(3 1/2 years)*.

6 He opened his mouth in insults toward God to insult His name and His tent (the ones camping in heaven).

7 He was given *the ability* to make war with the sacred people and to conquer them. Authority was given to him over every family line, ethnic group, language, and nation.

8 Everyone living on the earth will bow down to him, everyone whose name has not been written in the scroll of life of the Lamb that has been slaughtered since the world was formed.

9 If anyone has an ear, he must listen.

10 If anyone *puts innocent people* into incarceration, he is making his way back into incarceration. If anyone kills *innocent people* with a dagger, he must be killed with a dagger. Here is the persistence to do what is right and the trust of the sacred people.

11 I saw another wild animal stepping up from the earth. He was having two horns like a lamb and speaking as a dragon.

12 He exercised every authority of the first wild animal in his sight. He made the earth and the people living in it to bow down to the first wild animal whose deadly wound was healed.

13 He did great proofs so that he may even make fire step down from the sky to the earth in the sight of the people.

14 He misleads the people living on the earth because of the proofs he was given *the ability* to do in the sight of the wild animal. He tells the people living on the earth to make an image to the wild animal that has the wound of the dagger and lived.

15 He was given *the ability* to give a spirit to the wild animal's image so that the wild animal's image would both speak and make it so that however many did not bow down to the wild animal's image would be killed.

16 He made all the little people, great people, wealthy people, poor people, free people, and slaves to give them a mark on their right hand or on their forehead.

17 He made it so that no one may be able to buy or sell except the person who has the mark (the wild animal's name or the number of his name).

18 Here is insight. The person who has a way of thinking must count the number of the wild animal. You see, it is the number of a person, and his number is 666.

14

1 I looked and, look, the Lamb has stood on Mount Zion and 144,000 are with Him that have His name and His Father's name written on their foreheads.

2 I heard a sound from heaven as a sound of many waters and as a sound of loud thunder. The sound that I heard was as harpists playing on their harps.

3 They sing what seems like a new song in the sight of the throne and in the sight of the four animals and the older men. No one was able to learn the song except the 144,000 that have been purchased out of the earth.

4 These are the ones that were not dirtied with women. You see, these are virgins that follow the Lamb wherever He may make His way back to. These were purchased out of the people. They are a first-part-offering to God and the Lamb.

5 Not one lie was found in their mouth. They are unblemished.

6 I saw another angel flying in the middle of the sky that had good news that spans all time so that he might share good news on the people sitting on the earth, on every nation, family line, language, and ethnic group.

7 And he said in a loud voice, "Fear God, give magnificence to Him because the hour of His judgment came. Bow down to the One who made the sky, the earth, sea, and springs of waters."

8 Another angel, a second one, followed. He said, "It fell. The great Babylon fell. It has given all the nations a drink from the wine of God's anger against her sexual sin."

9 Another angel, a third one, followed them. He said in a loud voice, "If anyone bows down to the wild animal and his image and receives a mark on his forehead or on his hand,

10 he also will drink from the wine of God's anger that has been poured undiluted in the cup of His punishment. And he will be tortured in fire and sulfur in the sight of sacred angels and in the sight of the Lamb.

11 The smoke of their torture steps up for spans of time of spans of time. The people who bow down to the wild animal and his image and whoever receives the mark of his name doesn't have relief day and night.

12 Here is the persistence to do what is right of the sacred people who keep the demands of God and the trust of Jesus."

13 I heard a voice from the sky say, "Write, 'The dead in the Master that die after right now are blessed.'" "Yes," says the Spirit, "that way they will relax from their labors. You see, their actions follow with them."

14 I looked and, look, there was a white cloud and someone like a son of a person was sitting on the cloud. He had a gold award wreath on His head and a sharp sickle in His hand.

15 Another angel came out of the temple. He yelled in a loud voice to the One sitting on the cloud, "Send Your sickle and harvest the earth because the hour to harvest came because the harvest of the earth is dried up."

16 The One sitting on the cloud threw His sickle on the earth, and the earth was harvested.

17 Another angel came out of the temple in heaven. He also had a sharp sickle.

18 Another angel that had authority over fire came out of the altar. He hollered with a loud voice to the one who had the sharp sickle and said, "Send your sharp sickle, and pick the grape bunches of the earth's vine because her clusters were ripe."

19 The angel threw his sickle into the earth, picked the earth's vine, and threw it into the large grape-smashing vat of God's anger.

20 The grape-smashing vat was trampled outside of the city, and blood came out of the vat up to the horses' bridles and it went out for 1600 track laps *(200 miles)*.

15

1 I saw another indicator in heaven, great and amazing--seven angels had seven devastations. *They are* the last *devastations* because God's anger was finished in them.

2 And I saw what seemed like a glassy sea that had been mixed with fire. The people who conquer out of the wild animal, out of his image, and out of the number of his name have stood on the glassy sea and have the harps of God.

3 They sing the song of Moses (God's slave) and the song of the Lamb. They say, "Your actions are great and amazing, Master, the All-Powerful God. Your ways are right and true, King of the nations.

4 Who would not in any way fear You, Master? And who will not in any way praise Your name's magnificence? Because only You are holy, because all the nations will arrive and will bow in Your sight, because Your right paths were shown."
5 After these things, I looked, and the temple of the tent in heaven that is a witness was opened.
6 The seven angels that have the seven devastations came out of the temple. They have put on clean dazzling linen and gold sashes have been tied around their chests.
7 One *animal* from the four animals gave the seven angels seven gold bowls packed full of the anger of the God who lives for the spans of time of the spans of time.
8 The temple was full of smoke from God's magnificence and from His ability. And no one was able to go into the temple till the seven angels' seven devastations were finished.

16

1 I listened to a loud voice from the temple say to the seven angels, "Make your way back and spill the seven bowls of God's anger out into the earth."
2 The first angel went off and spilled his bowl out into the earth. A bad and evil sore came on the people that had the mark of the wild animal and on the people that bow to his image.
3 The second angel spilled his bowl out into the sea, and it became blood, as the blood of a dead person. Every soul of life, the things in the sea, died.
4 The third angel spilled his bowl out into the rivers and springs of the waters, and it became blood.
5 I listened to the angel of the waters say, "You, the One who is and was, the Holy One, are right because You decided these things
6 because they spilled out the blood of sacred people and preachers, and You have given them blood to drink. They deserve it."
7 I listened to the altar say, "Yes, Master, the All-Powerful God, Your judgments are true and right."
8 The fourth angel spilled his bowl out on the sun, and it was given the ability to scorch the people in fire.
9 The people were scorched with a great burning heat, and they insulted the name of God who has the authority over these devastations. They did not change their ways to give magnificence to Him.

10 The fifth angel spilled his bowl out on the wild animal's throne, and his monarchy became dark. They were gnawing their tongues from the anguish.
11 They insulted the God of heaven from their anguishes and from their sores. They did not change their ways from their actions.
12 The sixth angel spilled his bowl out on the great river Euphrates, and its water dried up so that the way of the kings out from the rising of the sun might be readied.
13 I saw three spirits that were not clean come as frogs out of the dragon's mouth, out of the wild animal's mouth, and out of the counterfeit preacher's mouth.
14 You see, they are lesser deities' spirits that travel out doing proofs on the kings of the whole civilized world to gather them together for the war of the great day of the All-Powerful God.
15 "Look! I come as a thief. The person who stays awake is blessed and keeps his clothes so that he may not walk around naked and they see his indecency." *(A punishment to Roman soldiers who were caught sleeping while they were working was that they would be stripped naked.)*
16 He gathered them together into the place that in Hebrew is called Armageddon *(Hill of Rendezvous)*.
17 The seventh angel spilled his bowl out on the air, and a loud voice came out of the temple out from the throne. It said, "It has happened."
18 There became lightnings, sounds, and thunders. An earthquake became so large that such an earthquake has not happened since a person came into existence on the earth. This earthquake was so large.
19 The great city became *divided* into three parts, the cities of the nations fell, and the great Babylon was remembered in the sight of God to give her the cup of the wine of the anger of His punishment.
20 Every island escaped, and mountains were not found.
21 Large hail (around one hundred pounds) tumbled down from the sky on the people. And the people insulted God from the devastation of the hail because its devastation is terribly great.

17

1 One *angel* from the seven angels that have the seven bowls came and spoke with me. He said, "Come here. I will show you the judgment of the great prostitute sitting on many waters.

2 She is the one that the kings of the earth committed sexual sin with, and the people living on the earth got drunk from the wine of her sexual sin."
3 He carried me off into the backcountry in a spiritual state, and I saw a woman sitting on a red wild animal packed full of names of insult. It had seven heads and ten horns.
4 The woman has put purple and red around herself. She has embellished herself with gold, valuable stones, and pearls. She had a gold cup in her hand packed full of disgusting things and the things of her sexual sin that are not clean.
5 A name has been written on her forehead, "A Secret -- the Great Babylon, the Mother of the Prostitutes and of the Earth's Disgusting Things."
6 I saw the woman getting drunk from the blood of the sacred people and from the blood of the witnesses of Jesus. I was amazed, after seeing her, with great amazement.
7 The angel said to me, "Why were you amazed? I will state to you the secret of the woman and of the wild animal hauling her that has the seven heads and the ten horns.
8 The wild animal that you saw, was, is not, and is going to be stepping up from the bottomless area. He is making his way back into ruin. The people living on the earth, the people whose name has not been written on the scroll of life since the world was formed will be amazed as they see the wild animal that was, is not, and will be beside them.
9 Here is the way of thinking that has insight. The seven heads are seven mountains where the woman sits on them.
10 They are seven kings: the five fell, the one is, the other did not come yet. When he comes, it is necessary for him to stay a little while.
11 The wild animal that was and is not, even he is eighth. He is from the seven and makes his way back into ruin.
12 The ten horns that you saw are ten kings. These are the ones that did not receive a monarchy yet. But they receive authority as kings one hour with the wild animal.
13 These have one opinion. They give their ability and authority to the wild animal.
14 These will wage war with the Lamb, and the Lamb will conquer them because He is Master of masters and King of kings. The people with Him are invited, select, and trusting."
15 He says to me, "The waters that you saw where the prostitute sits are ethnic groups, crowds, nations, and languages.

16 The ten horns that you saw and the wild animal, these will hate the prostitute and will make her become uninhabited and naked. They will eat her physical body and burn her up in fire.
17 You see, God gave into their hearts to do His opinion, to do one opinion, and to give their monarchy to the wild animal till the messages of God will be finished.
18 The woman that you saw is the great city that has a monarchy over the kings of the earth."

18

1 After these things, I saw another angel stepping down from the sky having great authority. The earth was lit up from his magnificence.
2 He yelled in a strong voice and said, "It fell. The great Babylon fell. It became a residence of lesser deities, a guard station of every spirit that is not clean, a guard station of every bird that is not clean, and a guard station of every wild animal that is not clean and that has been hated
3 because all the nations have drunk from the wine of God's anger against her sexual sin, the kings of the earth committed sexual sin with her, and the wholesalers of the earth were wealthy from the ability of her dominance."
4 I heard another voice from the sky say, "Come out from her, My ethnic group, so that you won't share together in her sins and so that you won't receive devastations from her devastations
5 because her sins were pasted as high as the sky and God remembered the wrong things she did.
6 Give back to her even as she gave back, and double her double punishments aligned with her actions. Pour double to her in the cup that she poured.
7 As much as she elevated herself to a place of magnificence and was dominant, give her that much torture and grief, because in her heart she says, "I sit as a queen, I am not a widow, and I will not in any way see grief."
8 Because of this, her devastations will arrive in one day: death, grief, and famine. She will be burned up in fire because the Master God who judges her is strong.
9 The kings of the earth who committed sexual sin with her and were dominant will cry and beat their chests in grief over her when they see the smoke of her burning.

10 They have stood off at a distance because of the fear of her torture. They say, "What a tragedy! What a tragedy, the great city of Babylon, the strong city, because your judgment came in one hour!"
11 And the wholesalers of the earth cry and grieve over her because no one buys their cargo anymore:
12 cargo of gold, silver, valuable stone, pearls, elegant linen, purple, silk, and red dye; all citrus wood, every ivory container, every container from the most valuable wood, copper, iron, and marble;
13 cinnamon, amomum *(a fragrant plant from India)*, scents, perfume, incense, wine, olive oil, fine flour, grain, animals, sheep, things for horses, things for four-wheeled vehicles, things for bodies, and souls of people.
14 "The harvest season of your soul's desire went away from you, and all the extravagant and the dazzling things from you were ruined. You will not in any way find them anymore."
15 The wholesalers of these things who were wealthy from her will stand off at a distance because of the fear of her torture. They will cry and grieve.
16 They will say, "What a tragedy! What a tragedy it is for the great city that has thrown elegant linen fabric, both purple and red, around itself and has embellished itself in gold, valuable stone, and pearl
17 because in one hour so much wealth became uninhabited!" And every helmsman, everyone sailing over a place, crewmen, and as many as work the sea stood off at a distance.
18 They were yelling, looking at the smoke of her burning, and saying, "What city is like the great city?"
19 They threw dirt on their heads and were yelling, crying and grieving. They said, "What a tragedy! What a tragedy it is for the great city that made all the people that have boats in the sea wealthy from her great value because in one hour it became uninhabited!"
20 "Celebrate over her, heaven (also the sacred people, the missionaries, and the preachers), because God judged your judgment from her."
21 One strong angel picked up a stone as a large millstone and threw it into the sea. He said, "Like this, with violence, the great city of Babylon will be thrown and will not in any way be found anymore.
22 The sound of harpists, musicians, flute players, and trumpeters will not in any way be heard in you anymore. Every skilled worker of every trade will not in any way be found in you anymore. The sound of a millstone will not in any way be heard in you anymore.

23 The light of a lamp will not in any way shine in you anymore. And the sound of a bride and groom will not in any way be heard in you anymore. This will happen because your wholesalers were the greatest people of the earth because all the nations were misled in your drug use.
24 And the blood of preachers, sacred people, and all the people who have been slaughtered on the earth was found in her."

19

1 After these things, I heard what seemed like a loud sound of a big crowd in heaven saying, "Hallelujah *(which is Hebrew for "praise Yahweh")*! The rescue, the magnificence, and the ability is our God's
2 because His judgments are true and right because He judged the great prostitute. This is the one who was worsening the earth in her sexual sin. He retaliated for the blood of His slaves from her hand."
3 They have stated hallelujah a second time. Her smoke steps up for the spans of time of the spans of time.
4 The twenty-four older men and the four animals got down, bowed to God, the One sitting on the throne, and said, "Amen! Hallelujah!"
5 A voice came out from the throne that said, "All you His slaves and the ones who fear Him, the little and the great, give praise to our God."
6 I heard what seemed like the sound of a big crowd, the sound of many waters, and the sound of strong thunders, saying, "Hallelujah, because our Master, the All-Powerful God, was the king.
7 We should be happy and excited. We will give the magnificence to Him because the wedding of the Lamb came and His wife got herself ready.
8 She was given *the right* to throw clean, dazzling, elegant linen fabric around herself." You see, the elegant linen fabric is the right paths of the sacred people.
9 He says to me, "Write: 'The ones who have been invited to the feast of the Lamb's wedding are blessed.'" He also says to me, "These messages of God are true."
10 I got down in front of his feet to bow to him, and he says to me, "Look! No! I am a fellow slave of you and of your brothers who have the witness account that Jesus gave. Bow to God. You see, the witness account that Jesus gave is the spirit of preaching."
11 I saw that the sky had been opened. And look, there is a white horse and the One sitting on it is called Reliable and True. He judges and wages war in the right way.

12 His eyes are as a blaze of fire and many crowns are on His head. He has a name that has been written that no one knows except He Himself.
13 A robe has been thrown around Him that has been dipped in blood. His name has been called the Message of God.
14 The military forces in heaven were following Him on white horses. They have put on clean, white, elegant linen fabric.
15 A sharp sword travels out of His mouth so that He might strike the nations with it. He Himself will shepherd them with an iron staff, and He Himself tramples the grape-smashing vat of the wine of the anger of the All-Powerful God's punishment.
16 He has a name that has been written on His robe and on His thigh, "King of Kings and Master of Masters."
17 I saw one angel that had stood in the sun. He yelled in a loud voice and said to all the birds flying in the middle of the sky, "Come on, gather together for God's great feast
18 so that you can eat the physical bodies of kings, commanding officers, strong people, horses, the people sitting on them, and all kinds of people, both free and slave, both little and great."
19 I saw that the wild animal, the kings of the earth, and their military forces had been gathered together to make war with the One sitting on the horse and with His military unit.
20 The wild animal was captured and with him, the counterfeit preacher who did the proofs in his sight. With the *proofs*, he misled the people who received the mark of the wild animal and the people that bowed down to his image. The two were thrown still living into the lake of fire burning with sulfur.
21 The rest were killed with the sword coming out of the mouth of the One sitting on the horse. And all the birds were full from their physical bodies.

20

1 I saw an angel stepping down from the sky that had the bottomless area's key and a large chain on his hand.
2 He took hold of the dragon (the original snake who is an accuser and the Opponent) and chained him up a thousand years.
3 He threw him into the bottomless area, closed it, and put a seal up on top of it so that he would not mislead the nations anymore till the thousand years were finished. After these things, it is necessary for him to be released for a short time.

4 I saw thrones. They were seated on them, and judgment was given to them. I saw the souls of the people that had been executed with a double-headed axe because of the witness account that Jesus gave and because of God's message. And these people, the ones who did not bow down to the wild animal or his image and did not receive the mark on their forehead and on their hand, also lived. They were kings with the Anointed King a thousand years.
5 The rest of the dead did not live till the thousand years were finished. This is the first return back to life.
6 The person who has a part in the first return back to life is blessed and sacred. The second death doesn't have authority on these people, but they will be priests of God and of the Anointed King. They will be kings with Him for the thousand years.
7 When the thousand years are finished, the Opponent will be released from his jail.
8 He will go out to mislead the nations in the four corners of the earth, the Gog and Magog *(Gog is a leader and Magog is the area north of the Black Sea)*, to gather them together to the war. Their number is as the sand of the sea.
9 They walked up over the width of the earth and surrounded the camp of the sacred people and the city that had been loved. Fire stepped down from the sky and ate them up.
10 The Accuser that misled them was thrown into the lake of fire and sulfur where both the wild animal and the counterfeit preacher are. They will be tortured day and night for the spans of time of the spans of time.
11 I saw a great white throne and the One sitting on it. The earth and the sky escaped away from His face, and there was no place found for them.
12 I saw the dead, the great and the little, that had stood in the sight of the throne. Scrolls were opened, and another scroll was opened that is the scroll of life. The dead were judged from the things that had been written in the scrolls aligned with their actions.
13 The sea gave up the dead in it. And Death and Hades *(the underworld of the dead)* gave up the dead in them. They were judged, each aligned with their actions.
14 Death and Hades were thrown into the lake of fire. This lake of fire is the second death.
15 If anyone was found that had not been written in the scroll of life, he was thrown into the lake of fire.

21

1 I saw a new sky and a new earth. You see, the first sky and the first earth went away, and the sea does not exist anymore.

2 I saw the city, the sacred new Jerusalem, stepping down from the sky out from God. It had been readied as a bride that has been decorated for her husband.

3 I listened to a loud voice from the throne that said, "Look, God's tent is with the people, and He will camp with them. They will be His ethnic groups, and God Himself will be with them, their God.

4 He will dab off every tear from their eyes. Death will not exist anymore. Grief, screaming, and anguish will not exist anymore either because the first things went away."

5 The One sitting on the throne said, "Look, I am making all things new." And He says, "Write that these messages are reliable and true."

6 He said to me, "They have happened. I am the Alpha and the O *(the first and last letters in the Greek alphabet)*, the Beginning and the Conclusion. I will give water to the person who is thirsty. It will be for free from the spring of the water of life.

7 The person who conquers will inherit these things, and I will be a God to him, and he will be a son to Me.

8 But to the cowardly, to people who don't trust, to people who have been disgusting, to murderers, to people who commit sexual sin, to drug abusers, to idol worshipers, and to all the liars, their part is in the lake burning with fire and sulfur. This is the second death."

9 One *angel* from the seven angels that had the seven bowls packed full of the last seven devastations came and spoke with me. He said, "Come here. I will show you the bride, the wife of the Lamb."

10 He carried me off in a spiritual state on to a large and high mountain and showed me the city, the sacred Jerusalem, stepping down from the sky out from God.

11 It had God's magnificence which is its light source like a valuable stone, as a jasper stone *(speckled red)* that is crystal-clear.

12 It had a large and high wall that had twelve gateways. Twelve angels are on the gateways. And the names of the twelve family lines of Israel's sons have been inscribed on the gateways.

13 Three gateways are out from the east. Three gateways are out from the north. Three gateways are out from the south. And three gateways are out from the western regions.

14 The wall of the city has twelve foundations, and the twelve names of the Lamb's twelve missionaries are on them.

15 The one speaking with me had a gold measuring stick to measure the city, its gateways, and its wall.

16 The city lies with four corners. Its length is as much as also its width. He measured the city with the stick at 12,000 track laps *(1500 miles)*. Its length, width, and height are equal.

17 He measured its wall at 144 cubits *(approximately 216 feet)*. A cubit is the measurement from a person's *elbow to his fingertip*, which is the same as an angel's.

18 The composition of its wall is jasper *(speckled red)*. And the composition of the city is clean gold, like clean glass.

19 The foundations of the city's wall have been assembled with every valuable stone. The first foundation is jasper *(speckled red)*; the second, sapphire *(deep blue)*; the third, chalcedony *(milky translucent)*; the fourth, emerald *(vibrant green)*;

20 the fifth, sardonyx *(banded orange)*; the sixth, sardius *(vibrant reddish-orange)*; the seventh, chrysolite *(golden green)*; the eighth, beryl *(sea green)*; the ninth, topaz *(warm yellow)*; the tenth, chrysoprasus *(apple green)*; the eleventh, hyacinth *(deep blue)*; and the twelfth, amethyst *(purple sparkle)*.

21 The twelve gateways are twelve pearls. Each one of the gateways is from one pearl apiece. The plaza of the city is clean gold as transparent glass.

22 I didn't see a temple in it. You see, the Master, the All-Powerful God, and the Lamb is its temple.

23 The city has no need of the sun or the moon to shine in it. You see, God's magnificence lit it up, and its lamp is the Lamb.

24 The nations will walk around through its light. And the kings of the earth bring their magnificence into it.

25 Its gateways won't in any way be closed after a day. You see, there won't be night there.

26 They will bring the magnificence and the value of the nations into it.

27 And every contaminated thing, the person who does a disgusting thing, and a lie won't in any way go into it. Just the people who have been written in the Lamb's scroll of life will go into it.

22

1 He showed me a river of water of life, dazzling as crystal, traveling out of the throne of God and of the Lamb

2 in the middle of its plaza. On one side and on the other side of the river is a wooden tree of life producing twelve

fruits. It gives its fruit away aligned with each month. And the leaves of the wooden tree are for the healing of the nations.
3 All adverse doom will not exist anymore. The throne of God and of the Lamb will be in it. His slaves will minister to Him.
4 They will see His face, and His name will be on their foreheads.
5 Night will not exist anymore, and they have no need of a lamp's light and the sun's light because the Master God will light things up for them. They will be kings for the spans of time of the spans of time.
6 He said to me, "These messages are reliable and true. The Master, the God of the spirits of the preachers, sent His angel out on a mission to show His slaves things that must happen quickly."
7 "And look, I am coming quickly. The one who keeps the messages of the preaching of this scroll is blessed."
8 I, John, am the one hearing and seeing these things. When I heard and saw, I got down to bow in front of the feet of the angel that showed me these things.
9 And he says to me, "Look! No! I am a fellow slave of you, of your brothers (the preachers), and of the ones who keep the messages of this scroll. Bow down to God."
10 He also says to me, "You should not put a seal on the messages of the preaching of this scroll. You see, the appointed time is near.
11 The person doing wrong must still do wrong. The filthy person must still be filthy. The person who does what is right must still do things the right way. And the sacred person must still be made sacred."
12 "Look, I am coming quickly and My pay is with Me to give back to each person as his work is.
13 I am the Alpha and the O *(the first and last letters in the Greek alphabet). I am* the First and the Last, the Beginning and the Conclusion."
14 The people are blessed who rinse their long robes so that their authority will be over the wooden tree of life and they might go through the gateways into the city.
15 Outside are the dogs, the drug users, the people who commit sexual sin, the murderers, the idol worshipers, and everyone who is fond of and makes a lie.
16 "I, Jesus, sent My angel to be a witness to you of these things on the assemblies. I am the Root and the Family of David, the Dazzling Morning Star."
17 The Spirit and the bride say, "Come." The person who hears must say, "Come." The person who is thirsty must come. The person who wants water of life must take it for free.

18 I am a witness to everyone hearing the messages of the preaching of this scroll, "If anyone should add on to these things, God will add the devastations that have been written in this scroll on to him.

19 And if anyone should take away from the messages of the scroll of this preaching, God will take his part away from the wooden tree of life and out of the sacred city of the things that have been written in this scroll.

20 The One who is a witness to these things says, "Yes, I am coming quickly." Amen. Come, Master Jesus.

21 May the generosity of the Master Jesus be with everyone.

www.ingramcontent.com/pod-product-compliance
Lightning Source LLC
Chambersburg PA
CBHW071850290426
44110CB00013B/1086